California
WORKERS' RIGHTS

A MANUAL OF JOB RIGHTS, PROTECTIONS AND REMEDIES

FOURTH EDITION

By David A. Rosenfeld, Miles E. Locker and Nina G. Fendel

Based on previous editions by Joan Marie Braconi, Alan Nicholas Kopke, Mary Ruth Gross and Kirsten Snow Spalding

Center for Labor Research and Education

Institute for Research on Labor and Employment
University of California, Berkeley

California Workers' Rights: A Manual of Job Rights, Protections and Remedies

Fourth Edition

© 1986, 1995, 2001, 2010 by the Regents of the University of California

PUBLISHED BY:

Center for Labor Research and Education, UC Berkeley

Institute for Research on Labor and Employment

2521 Channing Way #5555

Berkeley, CA 94720-5555

http://laborcenter.berkeley.edu

ISBN: 978-0-937817-01-8

Library of Congress Control Number: 2010929726

PHOTO CREDITS:
Cover: Jupiterimages
Title page, pages 10, 17, 21, 38, 158, 166, 185, 189, 212, 228, 237 and 263: iStockphoto
Page 7: U.S. Air Force photo/James M. Bowman
Pages 29, 94 and 219: National Institutes of Health
Page 35, back cover (middle): U.S. Air Force photo/Staff Sgt. Desiree N. Palacious
Pages 45, 88 103, 125, 136, 162, 256, 274, 290, 299 and back cover (top): U.S. Census Bureau
Pages 50 and 283: Bill Branson
Page 56: U.S. Air Force photo/Margo Wright
Page 63: Bob Nichols, USDA Natural Resources Conservation Service
Page 68: U.S. Air Force photo/Lance Cheung
Page 72: Ernie Branson
Page 81: Ron Nichols, USDA Natural Resources Conservation Service
Page 108: U.S. Department of Agriculture
Page 120: U.S. Air Force photo/Staff Sgt. Lanie McNeal
Page 143: James Gathany, Centers for Disease Control and Prevention
Pages 150 and 205: U.S. Air Force photo/Tech. Sgt. Cohen A. Young
Page 155: John Crawford
Pages 178 and 197: Tim McCabe, USDA Natural Resources Conservation Service
Page 186: U.S. Air Force photo/Master Sgt. Jon Hanson
Page 211: FEMA/Mike Moore
Page 220: Jeff Vanuga, USDA Natural Resources Conservation Service
Page 223: National Institutes of Environmental Health Sciences/National Institutes of Health/Department of Health and Human Services
Page 226: U.S. Air Force photo/Steve Thurow
Page 235: U.S. Government Printing Office
Page 240: Service Employees International Union
Page 246: U.S. Air Force photo/Master Sgt. Jim Varhegyi
Page 269: Lynn Betts, USDA Natural Resources Conservation Service
Page 279 and back cover (bottom): FEMA/Jocelyn Augustino

Cover and text design by San Francisco Art Department

Index by James M. Diggins

Printed in the United States of America, by Consolidated Printers, Inc.

CONTENTS

PREFACE

This book is intended as a resource manual for workers and for the union representatives, leaders, organizers, lawyers, and others who represent workers. In addition, it will be useful to employers and human resources professionals, and aid them in complying with the law. It is written to present a basic overview of workers' rights, demystify the law, and give workers information that will empower them to speak up for their rights. The fourth edition of this book reflects substantial changes in content and organization, and provides updates regarding the many areas in which the law has shifted in recent years.

Citations to statutes and regulations are provided so that readers can begin to do the legal research necessary to answer their specific questions. Appendix A offers additional information on how to locate state and federal laws and regulations. Included are many agencies' websites that give details about the scope of the laws and the enforcement mechanisms. These are often invaluable sources of information. Appendix B provides access to government resources that will help readers pursue their claims and understand their rights. Appendix C offers a partial list of union organizations that could be of assistance to workers. Appendix D spells out many of the acronyms used in this book.

In some situations it will be possible to proceed without an attorney. While this book is not a substitute for legal advice, it will help workers to understand their rights and take constructive steps to protect them. Workers should be sure to consult their union or community law office for the most up-to-date changes or interpretations of the laws that apply to their particular circumstances. In more complex situations or those involving possible lawsuits, it is recommended that individuals seek legal advice. Be aware that the law changes frequently, and that changes taking place after this book went to press will not be reflected.

To report any errors or omissions in the book, or to provide other feedback, contact the Center for Labor Research and Education at the University of California, Berkeley.

Thanks to Joan Braconi, Alan Kopke, Mary Ruth Gross, and Kirsten Spalding, authors of the previous editions of *California Workers' Rights*. The authors of the fourth edition wish to thank the following people who made substantial contributions to this book: editors Jenifer MacGillvary, publications and production coordinator at the Labor Center at UC Berkeley, and Stefanie Kalmin, managing editor at the California Public Employee Relations Program, UC Berkeley; Ken Jacobs, chair of the Labor Center; and Janet Dawson, who handles external relations for the Labor Center, and who updated the appendices. Many attorneys gave generously of their time, advice, and expertise to make the fourth edition accurate and current. They include: Anne Yen, Vin Harrington, Stewart Weinberg, Barry Hinkle, and Linda Baldwin Jones of Weinberg, Roger and Rosenfeld; Amy Martin, general counsel, and Allyce Kimerling, staff attorney, Cal-OSHA; Juliann Sum, Labor Occupational Health Program, School of Public Health, UC Berkeley; Noreen Farrell, managing attorney, Equal Rights Advocates; Steve Siemers, formerly chief judge with the Workers' Compensation Appeals Board; and Raphael Shannon and Lori Nord of McCarthy, Johnson and Miller. Andrea Don provided invaluable assistance in legal research, drafting, and editing.

We hope that all users will find this edition valuable, and that it will enable workers and their representatives to use the California legal system to improve their workplaces and work lives.

David A. Rosenfeld, Attorney
Weinberg, Roger and Rosenfeld

Miles E. Locker, Attorney
Locker Folberg LLP

Nina G. Fendel, Attorney and Legal Educator
Weinberg, Roger and Rosenfeld, and Alliance for Labor Standards Education and Training

CHAPTER 1 **EXERCISING YOUR RIGHTS**

EXERCISING YOUR RIGHTS

I. LEARNING ABOUT WORKERS' RIGHTS

A. USING THIS BOOK

The body of law related to workers, employers, and the workplace in California is huge. This book focuses on selected areas: rights during the hiring process, investigations and police records, wages and hours, benefits, discrimination, health and safety, Workers' Compensation, union organizing, whistleblower protections, discharge and disciplinary actions, and personnel and medical files. To locate the section that addresses specific concerns, consult either the Table of Contents in the front of the book, the detailed list at the top of each chapter, or the Index. In the relevant chapter and section, there will be a description of rights, the laws and regulations that protect those rights, and the agencies responsible for enforcing particular rights. Many important exceptions to rights or coverage are noted. Sometimes the protections extend only to certain workers. Sometimes limits are imposed on how or when a worker can demand the protections. Some, but not all, of these exceptions are discussed in this book.

This book does not deal with special protections that California grants to certain limited groups of workers, such as the organizational protections given to farm workers or the many specific statutes protecting various groups of government workers. Very narrow laws or regulations that could not be covered in a book of this size affect almost every industry in California. To learn all of the protections that apply to specific types of workers, it may be necessary to do additional research or contact an organization or agency that concerns itself with these issues.

The many special protections given to minors (workers under age eighteen) by both state and federal law are not within the scope of this book. All the protections and rights covered here apply to minors as well as adults, but minors have many additional rights.

At the end of the book, appendices provide the names, addresses, phone numbers, and websites of state and federal enforcement agencies, central labor councils, and regional labor organizations.

B. OBTAINING INFORMATION FROM THE INTERNET

Armed with the information in relevant sections of this book, one can go to the Internet to obtain additional information. Many organizations, including unions, have websites. It is possible to locate the statutes, regulations, and decisions that apply to most situations by conducting Internet research.

Below are several of the most useful websites for researching workers' rights in California:

- California statutes: http://www.leginfo.ca.gov/calaw.html. This government-sponsored website provides links to all California laws. Most laws related to workers' rights are found in the Labor Code (laws governing wages, vacations, Workers' Compensation, and many aspects of working conditions), the Government Code (laws providing protections against discrimination and family leave rights), or the Unemployment Insurance Code (laws covering Unemployment Insurance and State Disability Insurance).
- California regulations: http://ccr.oal.ca.gov. The website covers administrative rules that implement state laws.
- California Department of Industrial Relations: http://www.dir.ca.gov. This government website contains links to many of the laws protecting workers in California.
- Industrial Welfare Commission: http://www.

dir.ca.gov/iwc. The website covers specific rules for particular industries and occupations.

Additional websites are also referenced in the chapters that follow.

C. OBTAINING INFORMATION FROM A LAW LIBRARY

Members of the public can go to a law library to examine (and copy) laws, regulations, court cases, books, legal encyclopedias, and articles on a wide variety of topics, including California employment rights. Every county maintains a public law library (usually in the courthouse). Most law schools maintain large law libraries. These libraries are often funded by the government and allow members of the general public to use their materials. Law librarians can be helpful in pointing people in the right direction. Lists of law libraries by county are available online at http://www.publiclawlibrary.org/find.html.

D. OBTAINING INFORMATION FROM ADMINISTRATIVE AGENCIES

California's administrative and governmental agencies have websites that are user-friendly and can provide valuable information on employment law issues. The websites of enforcement agencies often have guidelines that explain how to file claims or tips on how to interpret the laws. Generally, anyone without Internet access can visit the nearest office of the agency that enforces the rights in question and get help or guidance. An administrative agency's regulations are also available in law libraries. See Appendix B at the end of this book for addresses and websites of government agencies.

E. OBTAINING INDUSTRIAL WELFARE COMMISSION ORDERS

The state Industrial Welfare Commission establishes rules related to wages, hours, and working conditions in a variety of occupations, trades, and industries. They issue rules called IWC Orders that apply to specific types of jobs and industries. There are seventeen different IWC Orders. To find out which IWC Orders cover specific jobs, go to http://www.dir.ca.gov/IndexOfBusinessAnd

Occupations.pdf. Relevant IWC Orders should be posted in the workplace. They are also available at the offices of the California Labor Commissioner and online at http://www.management-advantage.com/products/IWCOrders.htm.

II. CONFRONTING THE EMPLOYER

A. THE IMPORTANCE OF GETTING HELP

It is usually best to avoid a one-on-one confrontation with the employer, particularly if workers are not covered by a collective bargaining agreement (union contract). If the employer makes an honest mistake in the computation of hours or any issue related to the rate of pay, in most instances it is appropriate to speak to the payroll or personnel office and work out the mistake informally. If, however, a violation of rights appears to be deliberate, it most likely is safest to let a third party confront the employer: a union steward, a staff member of the state labor commissioner's office, or a lawyer or other representative. A worker may ask to have another employee as a witness, but the employer can refuse to allow him to have that representative present.

Employees can gain protection in dealing with employers by taking action as a group. Group action is known as "concerted activity." One person's action is not considered concerted activity, but a group may be as few as two employees. A group of workers who take action, file a complaint, or take some other step to protect their wages, hours, or working conditions on their own behalf or on behalf of others are protected from retaliation by the National Labor Relations Act.

If many of the employees believe they need to take action to protect or improve working conditions, it is wise to contact a union. A union can help in several ways. It can deal directly and effectively with the enforcement agency on behalf of the workers. An experienced union representative can help gather all the relevant facts to present to the agency. And when the union is involved, the agency is more likely to conduct a timely and thorough investigation of the charges.

However, the most important way that a union can help is through a collective bargaining agreement. A collective bargaining agreement is a contract between the employer and the union, establishing wages, hours, and working conditions for the employees. Unions often can negotiate rights and protections more favorable than those provided by law, and employers are legally obligated to abide by those provisions. The collective bargaining agreement includes its own methods for enforcing the rights it contains. Generally, this is called a grievance procedure. The final step in a grievance procedure is frequently a process called arbitration, in which a neutral third party hears the case and makes a decision. Using a grievance procedure and arbitration is generally faster and less costly than filing a lawsuit in court. For information on the right to join and be represented by a union, see Chapter 9. For a list of labor councils, see Appendix C at the end of this book. The local labor council can refer workers to the union best suited to represent them.

B. PREPARING TO DOCUMENT THE CLAIM

To enforce workers' rights and prove a claim against an employer, it is helpful, but not essential, to have relevant documents. This takes preparation — the accumulation of work records throughout the period of employment. It may be difficult for a worker to gather the necessary evidence after she realizes her rights have been violated. Therefore, beginning with the application for employment, a worker should keep all records and documents related to that job, including:

- A calendar indicating the hours actually worked;
- All pay stubs;
- All documents and memos about benefits such as health and welfare, pension, vacation, sick leave, bonuses, severance pay, and insurance coverage of various kinds;
- All documents about work rules;
- A daily log of incidents (particularly if workers are involved in a union organizing campaign, have been visibly enforcing their rights, or are concerned about job issues), with notes about any conversations between the worker and supervisor or employer, particularly anything viewed as threatening or violating workers' rights;
- Copies of all receipts and vouchers for work-related expenses;
- Work-related credit card records.

The worker should store all of these logs, documents, and records at home; these records should not be left at work.

Despite the value of good record keeping, workers who lack documentation should not be afraid to pursue a claim. If workers do not have documents or records, the law allows agencies and courts to estimate damages based on the worker's testimony. Even if the worker did not keep records of overtime, missed lunches, or other details, he can still give an estimate. Courts will often accept those estimates, as long as they are reasonable and not contradicted by accurate employer records.

The worker should gather all the documents, facts, and witness information before contacting the enforcement agency that handles the problem. The names, home phone numbers, and addresses of possible witnesses should be made available. If possible, the worker should obtain written statements from potential witnesses. The worker should also attempt to find out how other employees have been treated in similar situations.

III. WHERE TO PURSUE THE CLAIM

A. UNION GRIEVANCE PROCEDURE

For those who are covered by a collective bargaining agreement (union contract), the grievance procedure often is the best choice for enforcing employment rights. (Union grievance procedures are not listed in the enforcement paragraphs of specific sections of this book because they are not available to all workers, only to those governed by union contracts.) Most contracts allow the union to grieve violations of the law, as well as other violations of the contract.

Some union agreements provide that any violation of federal or state law is subject to the grievance and arbitration procedures of the union contract. For example, the contract may provide: "The employer agrees to abide by all federal and state laws and regulations and all local ordinances." These provisions are helpful. Using the contractual grievance procedures (i.e., rather than the court system) saves everyone time and money.

B. COMPLAINTS TO THE LABOR COMMISSIONER

The state labor commissioner has the authority to enforce most of the labor laws of California, including the authority to investigate employee complaints and hold hearings on wage claims and related issues. In addition, some deputy labor commissioners are designated as "peace officers" and have the authority to arrest violators of the state labor laws.

1. Types of Claims Covered

Many of the rights and protections outlined in this book are enforced by the labor commissioner through administrative hearings held by government agencies and, in some cases, subsequent court actions. Among the claims that the labor commissioner can hear are:

- Failure to pay proper wages;
- Mechanics' liens (claims against owners of buildings or land to cover debts owed to workers who improved the property);
- Misrepresentation of conditions of employment;
- Unreturned bond money;

- Unreturned worker tools;
- Unauthorized deductions from the workers' paychecks;
- Vacation pay and severance pay violations;
- Lost wages resulting from certain unlawful discharges;
- Failure to provide meal or rest breaks; and
- Retaliation for asserting rights under the Labor Code.

As a matter of administrative policy, the labor commissioner usually will not handle complaints against government employers (except for health and safety complaints — see Chapter 7). Claims of state and local government employees may be handled by the Public Employment Relations Board (PERB) or a court. PERB is an administrative agency charged with administering and enforcing California's collective bargaining laws covering employees of California's public schools, colleges, and universities, employees of the State of California, employees of California local public agencies (cities, counties and special districts), trial court employees, and supervisory employees of the Los Angeles County Metropolitan Transportation Authority.

If the job is covered by a collective bargaining agreement with a binding arbitration clause, the labor commissioner generally will not hear wage claims that involve interpretation or application of the agreement. See Chapter 4 for more information on wage claims.

2. Filing a Simultaneous Federal Complaint

In addition to filing with the labor commissioner, workers can also file a federal claim for some wage and hour complaints, primarily overtime violations. If the labor commissioner is pursuing the claim, it may not be worth pursuing a federal claim as well, although federal law does provide more damages for some overtime violations.

The U.S. Department of Labor, Wage and Hour Division, will handle complaints even where there is a union contract or where the employer is a federal government agency. These claims generally involve failure to pay overtime or failure to meet the federal minimum wage.

C. COMPLAINTS TO OTHER ENFORCEMENT AGENCIES

A worker with a complaint should be persistent when dealing with enforcement agencies. If an intake worker (or other agency employee) says there is no case, the worker should not be discouraged. Workers at these agencies, especially intake workers, may not know all the important legal principles affecting a particular case. A complaint should be filed anyway, and the complainant should push to have it investigated. The complainant should check what the agency employee says against what is learned from research, the union, and lawyers.

> *A worker with a complaint should be persistent when dealing with enforcement agencies.*

A complainant should keep in mind that the enforcement agency will contact the employer when it investigates the case. Often, the employer will have a reason or excuse that sounds convincing. Workers filing complaints must be prepared to counter employers' explanations promptly. For example, suppose a worker was denied a promotion illegally. When the enforcement agency inquires, the employer explains that the worker was tardy six times in the past year. The worker needs to be ready with evidence showing that other employees who were late more than six times got the types of promotions that she was denied. Then the employer's explanation will be revealed as false, and the agency will protect the worker's rights. If the worker does not have a union to collect this sort of information, she and sympathetic coworkers have to do the job themselves.

Contact information for the principal enforcement agencies appear in Appendix B at the end of this book.

D. IN COURT

1. Small Claims Court Without an Attorney

Many sections of this book list "civil suit" as an enforcement mechanism. Filing a lawsuit to enforce rights nearly always requires a lawyer. However, those seeking a relatively small sum of money should consider going to small claims court. The limit in small claims court is $7,500. Neither side can be represented by a lawyer in small claims court, so money is saved. However, the worker will not have the expert advice of a lawyer to help win their case. (The State Bar of California website has a pamphlet on small claims court at http://www.calbar.ca.gov/state/calbar/calbar_generic.jsp?cid=10581&id=2175#1.) The local small claims court should have a legal adviser to assist with filing and preparing cases, and there is no charge for their services. To find out more, see http://www.alameda.courts.ca.gov/courts/divs/small/index.shtml.

Individuals going to small claims court should have copies of the laws and regulations relevant to the claim since it is likely the judge will have little experience with employment disputes. There are several widely available books with tips on how to win in small claims court. (A good resource is *Everybody's Guide to Small Claims Court*, by Ralph Warner, Nolo Press.)

2. Superior Court With an Attorney

Although this book is designed to help workers enforce their rights without having to hire an attorney, in some instances an attorney's assistance is necessary. Workers who are represented by a union may be able to get help from the union representative, or the union can make a referral to an attorney. Some unions have special programs in which their members get reduced rates from particular attorneys.

Workers who seek lawyers on their own should look for attorneys with expertise in labor and employment law. This is a specialized field, and it is important to find someone who knows the problem area thoroughly. A worker should not hesitate to ask two or three lawyers for their opinions. The worker should check with enforcement agencies and compare information received from various sources.

E. CRIMINAL PROSECUTIONS

In numerous instances, this book indicates that a complaint should be filed with the state attorney general or local district attorney. In most cases, this means that an employer who violates the law in question may be guilty of a criminal offense.

Only a public prosecutor can make the decision to bring criminal charges. Public prosecutors are generally the county district attorney, state attorney general, or United States attorney for the local area, depending on the law that is alleged to have been broken. Very few employment issues become criminal matters, and, given how busy most district attorneys are, attempts to initiate criminal complaints will be effective only in the most serious cases.

In almost every instance, it is best to discuss the situation with a lawyer before making a criminal complaint. It is especially important not to publicize possible criminal charges or threaten criminal action before exploring the likely consequences and results.

F. UNDER A CONTRACTUAL AGREEMENT TO ARBITRATE

Workers who are covered by a contractual agreement to arbitrate must submit many of their claims to arbitration (see the following section). The arbitration process is somewhat like a trial, but less formal, with fewer procedural steps, and faster. The case is decided by a neutral third party, who decides arbitration cases as a profession.

There are two kinds of contractual agreements to arbitrate. The first is a collective bargaining agreement that provides for binding arbitration. These agreements are negotiated between the union and the employer, so there are certain checks and balances that protect workers' rights. Workers who are represented by a union should discuss the problem with the union representatives before beginning an arbitration process.

The second type of agreement to arbitrate is one that applies to individual employees (not unions). Many employers are implementing arbitration procedures that are applicable to all employment claims except Workers' Compensation and claims under the National Labor Relations Act. The courts generally have upheld these agreements, where they meet the following standards:

- Remedies available under applicable laws must not be restricted by the agreement to arbitrate.
- The employee must not be required to pay for the arbitrator's services.
- It must be possible for the employee to gain access to information reasonably necessary to present the case.
- Both the employee and the employer must be mutually bound by the agreement to arbitrate.

To preserve their rights, workers should not sign any "waivers," "releases," or "settlements" offered by an employer during an exit interview (or at any other time) without advice from an attorney or their union. The employer cannot legally refuse to pay unpaid wages, pension contributions, vacation pay, or severance pay because the worker refuses to sign a release.

IV. SPECIAL RULES FOR WAGE AND HOUR CLAIMS UNDER UNION CONTRACTS

In general, the labor commissioner will not enforce wage claims for workers covered by a union contract that contains binding arbitration if the claim is based on the collective bargaining agreement, rather than on state law. Binding arbitration clauses in collective bargaining agreements provide for an arbitration process in which the decision is binding on the employer. In other words, the employer must comply with the decision, unless it is overturned by a court. For workers covered by union contracts with binding arbitration, it will be necessary to work through the union and use the grievance procedure. However, there are the following exceptions to this rule:

- The labor commissioner will enforce a wage claim if the claim is based on state law and it is possible to determine how much is owed without interpreting the collective bargaining agreement. The difference lies in whether one needs to decide what the collective bargaining agreement requires, or whether it is sufficient to simply consult it and the meaning is clear. For example, if the worker is paid late, the labor commissioner will enforce the penalty under Labor Code section 203 if all that is required is to consult the salary schedule under the collective bargaining agreement. However, if there is a dispute as to what the appropriate classification

is for the worker under the union contract, the labor commissioner will not enforce that claim.
- The labor commissioner will enforce claims about issues other than wages even for workers who have arbitration rights under union contracts if the claims are based on state law and do not involve interpretation of the collective bargaining agreement.
- The labor commissioner will enforce wage claims even for workers who have union contracts if the contract does not have a binding arbitration procedure, or if wages are specifically excluded from the arbitration process.
- The labor commissioner will enforce wage or other claims concerning loss of pay due to unsafe working conditions. See Chapter 7. Workers who have lost wages or jobs because of unsafe conditions can go to the labor commissioner (and in some circumstances to the U.S. Department of Labor), even though they have arbitration rights.
- The labor commissioner will enforce wage claims even though workers have arbitration rights if they earned the money working for a private contractor on construction of "public works." (Labor Code section 229.)

V. TYPES OF WORKERS NOT COVERED IN THIS BOOK

A. INDEPENDENT CONTRACTORS

Individuals working as "independent contractors" are not "employees" and therefore are not covered by this book. A growing number of workers are being told by unscrupulous employers that they are independent contractors when in fact they are still employees. Sometimes they are forced to sign statements or agreements stipulating that they are independent contractors when they are not. This kind of statement or agreement is illegal and invalid.

Employers inappropriately designate workers as independent contractors because they believe this benefits the company. The employer saves money because independent contractors are not covered by Workers' Compensation, Unemployment Insurance, State Disability Insurance, or Social Security. Independent contractors do not receive benefits such as vacation, sick leave, family leave, medical coverage, or retirement. Independent contractors are not covered by state or federal wage and hour protections. Employers do not pay payroll or other taxes for independent contractors. Unless a worker is truly an independent contractor, it is always to his disadvantage to work as one. There is a general presumption that workers are employees, not independent contractors.

1. Tests

There is no definitive legal description of an independent contractor. The various tests that are considered by California courts are set forth in the *Borello* case. (*S.G. Borello & Son v. Dept.of Industrial Relations* (1989) 48 Cal.3d 341.) A number of "tests" are applied. In separating bona fide independent contractors from employees, the key test concerns the right to control the work. (Labor Code sections 3353, 3357.) Does the employer have the right to control the methods and manner by which the work is carried out? Is the work supervised by the employer? If the employer has the right to control how the work is done, then the worker is almost certainly an employee, not an independent contractor.

The employer need not exercise the right of control. The fact that the employer has that right is sufficient, in most cases, to prove that the worker is an employee. The simplicity of the work itself may indicate that the employer does not need to exert much control but may still have the power to control. The amount of control exerted need not be extensive.

Under the *Borello* case, the most important question is whether the employer has control of how the work is done. If the answer does not settle the question of the worker's status, the courts will use a multi-factor test. The additional tests ask the following:

- Is the work being done by the worker separate and distinct from the primary business of the employer, or is it central to the business? This is an important factor.
- Who furnishes the tools or equipment?
- Who furnishes the place where the work happens?
- Is a special skill required to carry out the work?
- Does the individual hold a professional or contractor's license?
- Is the worker economically dependent on many businesses or just on a single business? Can the worker set prices charged to customers? If not, the worker is more likely to be an employee. Does the person providing the service have an opportunity to profit based on entrepreneurial skills?

Another set of tests, probably less determinative than those listed above, includes:

- How is the worker paid? Payment for a specific project, rather than by the hour, week, or month, leans heavily towards a finding of independent contractor. Does the employer have the right to discharge the person?
- How regular or permanent is the work?
- For how long is the individual employed?

No one test is determinative; one must look at the entire situation. The bias is in favor of finding that the worker is an employee, not an independent contractor, in order to carry out the purpose of remedial legislation.

Most workers who think they are independent contractors are not. They are actually employees, and all of the rights described in this book protect them. For more information, see the Department of Industrial Relations website at http://www.dir.ca.gov/dlse/faq_independentcontractor.htm.

2. Remedies

If the employer wrongly treats an employee as if she were an independent contractor, there are important legal consequences. Workers found to meet the qualifications of employees are entitled to Unemployment Insurance, State Disability Insurance, and Social Security benefits, even though the proper taxes were not paid. They are entitled to receive full Workers' Compensation benefits. (Labor Code section 3351.) The employer may end up paying back Social Security and federal and state income taxes. An employer who fails to deduct and pay these taxes can be made to pay the worker's share, along with interest and penalties, as well as the employer's share.

Workers who are being treated as independent contractors, but who think they actually may be employees, should keep accurate records. When it is time to act, workers should contact all the relevant enforcement agencies:

- File a Wage Claim with the Division of Labor Standards Enforcement. See general information at http://www.dir.ca.gov/dlse/faq_

independentcontractor.htm; see wage claim information at http://www.dir.ca.gov/dlse/HowToFileWageClaim.htm.

- File a claim with U.S. Internal Revenue Service. File form SS8 to request a determination regarding employee versus independent contractor status. The form is available at http://www.irs.gov/pub/irs-pdf/fss8.pdf. If the IRS agrees that the worker is an employee, she may file a special form with the Social Security Administration to correct the records. See http://www.irs.gov/newsroom/article/0,,id=176666,00.html.
- File a claim for Unemployment Insurance. See Chapter 5, section VIII., p. 148, for more information.

Situations involving improper classification of employees as independent contractors frequently involve wage and hour violations (for instance, failure to pay minimum wage or overtime, or to reimburse for business expenses). See Chapter 4 for more information on wage claims.

Each government agency applies a slightly different test and may be concerned with different problems (back wages, overtime and other rules, unpaid federal and state taxes, unpaid Social Security contributions, etc.). Some legal rights may last for a long time. When a worker retires or becomes disabled and needs to maximize Social Security payments, he may be able to go back many years to count time worked under a false independent contractor arrangement. Workers who are laid off or fired and need to draw Unemployment Insurance can base eligibility on time worked as a so-called independent contractor. If there is a union at the workplace, the worker should contact it to discuss this issue.

Changing status from independent contractor to employee can have tax implications. Workers who have not paid taxes on independent contractor income should seek legal advice before taking any of the steps outlined in this section.

Enforcement: File a complaint with the state labor commissioner, the Internal Revenue Service, the California Franchise Tax Board, the California Employment Development Department (which handles unemployment), the U.S. Social Security Administration, and the state Workers' Compensation Appeals Board. File a civil suit.

B. FEDERAL EMPLOYEES

Since this book focuses on California rights, and the state has no authority to control the federal government, federal workers are not included in most of the protections outlined. Although federal workers have not been listed specifically in the "exceptions" detailed for each right, it should be assumed that federal workers are not covered unless the text states otherwise.

> *In California, undocumented workers may pursue claims for wages that are earned.*

VI. UNDOCUMENTED WORKERS

California recognizes that undocumented workers may pursue claims for wages that are earned. (Labor Code section 1171.5.) If, for example, an undocumented worker did not receive overtime or did not receive her last paycheck, the labor commissioner is authorized to pursue that claim. The fact that a worker is undocumented may limit the remedies she is eligible to receive, particularly reinstatement where the immigration problems have not been resolved. (*Hoffman Plastic Compounds, Inc. v. NLRB* (2002) 535 U.S. 137.) Workers may be able to get orders of conditional reinstatement, which would require the employer to reinstate them once their immigration status has been worked out. California has adopted legislation permitting employees to pursue claims for unpaid wages in order to protect workers who are undocumented from exploitation. (Labor Code 1171.5.)

Undocumented workers are not entitled to all benefits. For example, they cannot collect Unemployment Insurance or State Disability Insurance. They can, however, collect Workers' Compensation benefits.

CHAPTER 2 **HIRING RIGHTS**

HIRING RIGHTS

I. SCOPE OF THE CHAPTER

Individuals have certain rights both when they apply for a job and after they are hired. This chapter describes the rights of job seekers in relation not only to prospective employers but also to employment agencies of various types. Generally, neither employment agencies nor employers are entitled to information about the applicant's personal life, such as his family situation, religious or political beliefs, nationality, ancestry, race, age, or financial status. They are not entitled to unlimited access to applicants' health records. Employers (and employment agencies) do have certain rights, however, to information that is relevant to the job the individual is applying for.

As an example, if someone applies for a job as a commercial driver, the employer is entitled to a copy of her driving record.

Employers cannot impose certain requirements as a condition of hiring, such as the obligation to invest in the employer's business. All information that a prospective employer gives a job applicant regarding a job must be accurate and truthful.

Job seekers have additional protections if they feel that they have been discriminated against because of membership in a protected class of people (for example, because of race, sex, or disability). See Chapter 6 for more information on discrimination at the time of hire or during employment.

II. RIGHTS BEFORE APPLYING FOR A JOB

Employment agencies, employment counseling services, and job listing services are regulated in terms of the fees they may charge and the information they must provide about their own services and about the worksites where they place applicants.

Employment agencies, employment counseling services, and job listing services must give job seekers a copy of their fee schedule before a counselor, agent, or employee of the agency or service interviews the job seeker. The contract between the agency and the job seeker must describe the specific services the job seeker will receive and the fee he will pay. The agency must give the job seeker the original contract before he is asked to pay a fee or deposit. It is illegal for the agency to tell job seekers falsehoods concerning the services that the agency will provide. The agency's job listing or contract must disclose the existence of any labor dispute the listing employer is having. Different rules may apply to different types of labor agencies or services.

A. REQUIREMENTS OF EMPLOYMENT AGENCIES

An employment agency is a service that, for a fee paid directly or indirectly by the job seeker, finds jobs for others or hires employees and sends them to work for its clients. (Civil Code section 1812.501.) No registration fee can be charged by an employment agency. (Civil Code section 1812.505(c).)

If a job seeker gets a job referral, the agency must give him a written copy of the referral. If a referral is made over the phone, the agency must mail two copies of the contract or receipt to the job seeker, with instructions that the job seeker sign them and return one copy to the agency. (Civil Code section 1812.504(d).) The agency cannot send an applicant to a job unless it has a request from an employer to refer prospective employees for a specified job. (Civil Code section 1812.507(a).) If there is a labor dispute at the place of employment, the contract must state this fact. (Civil Code section 1812.504(a)(8).)

If the individual does not accept a job, he is entitled to a refund of the fee paid. The refund must be made within forty-eight hours of the request for it. If the agency does not pay the person on time, he is owed twice the amount. (Civil Code section 1812.506(a).)

A temporary job is one in which the employee works for fewer than ninety days. (Civil Code section 1812.506(b).) The job fee for a temporary job cannot exceed one-ninetieth (1/90) of the job fee for permanent jobs, multiplied by each calendar day the job lasts. For example, if a person is employed for ten calendar days, the job fee paid the agency cannot exceed one-ninth of the fee for a permanent job (1/90 x 10 days = 10/90 = 1/9). (Civil Code section 1812.505(g).)

If an individual accepts a permanent job, but the job ends or she leaves the job for just cause within ninety days, then, upon request, the agency must reduce its fee to the fee for a temporary job. (Civil Code section 1812.505(f)(1).) If the agency takes more than ten working days after the request to pay the refund or to tell the individual in writing why it is denying a refund, then the individual is owed twice the refund amount. (Civil Code section 1812.506(c).) This reduction does not apply if the dismissal is for misconduct or the individual leaves the job without just cause, and the agency's fee schedules, contracts, and agreements specifically provide for further charge in such cases. (Civil Code section 1812.505(f)(2).) Just cause reasons for leaving the job include: because one cannot do the work; because of a strike or lockout; because one was given a different assignment, location, pay, or hours from those the agency described; or because one entered active military service. (Civil Code section 1812.506(b)(2).)

An employee cannot be charged any fee for a job working for the agency itself or for an employer that has a financial interest in the agency. (Civil Code section 1812.505(j)(2).) Job seekers cannot be charged any fee if the agency is furnishing help to the employer (for instance, screening applicants) or is deciding who gets the job. (Civil Code section 1812.505(j)(3).)

Enforcement: File a civil suit for triple damages and punitive damages, plus attorney's fees. Any violation is a misdemeanor. If the agency violates the law, the contract is void and the individual is owed a full refund of all money paid. These rights cannot be waived (even if the contract language says that the signer waives them). (Civil Code section 1812.523.)

Exceptions: These rules do not apply to the following: agencies that receives all their fees solely from employers; labor unions; certain nonprofit organizations; and schools that do not charge a fee for placement services. (Civil Code sections 1812.501 and 1812.502.)

B. REQUIREMENTS OF EMPLOYMENT COUNSELING SERVICES

An employment counseling service offers career counseling; vocational guidance; aptitude testing; career management, evaluation, or planning; executive consulting; personnel consulting; or the development of résumés and other promotional materials to prepare clients for employment. (Civil Code section 1812.501(b)(1).)

An employment counseling service cannot ask for a registration fee. It must provide a copy of its fee schedule before any interview and give the job seeker the original and one copy of the contract before he pays any fees or deposits. (Civil Code section 1812.512(a), (c).) The contract must describe the services to be received and the fees to be paid. (Civil Code section 1812.511(a).)

Individuals have the right to cancel the contract (by telegram or by delivery of written notice) within three business days after signing it. (Civil Code section 1812.511(a)(6).)

Enforcement: File a civil suit for triple damages and punitive damages, plus attorney's fees. Any violation is a misdemeanor. If the service violates the law, the contract is void, and the job seeker is owed a refund of all money paid. These rights cannot be waived (even if the contract language says that the signer is waiving them). (Civil Code section 1812.523.)

Exceptions: These rules do not apply to services that receive all its their fees solely from employers; certain vocational rehabilitation programs whose services are paid for by insurance benefits or someone other than the job seeker; services that provide only résumés and cover letters for a fee of $300 or less; public and private schools; or psychologists who do career counseling. (Civil Code sections 1812.501(b)(2), 1812.502.)

C. REQUIREMENTS OF JOB LISTING SERVICES

A job listing service matches job seekers with employers, provides lists of employers or openings, or prepares lists of job seekers for distribution to potential employers. (Civil Code section 1812.501(c).) Labor organizations and newspapers are not considered job listing services. A job listing service cannot list an opening without a job order from the employer. (Civil Code section 1812.519(c).) If there is a labor dispute at a listed place of employment, the listing must state that fact. (Civil Code section 1812.516(a)(8).)

Individuals have the right to cancel the contract with the service (by telegram or by delivering written notice) within three business days of signing it. (Civil Code section 1812.516(a)(6).)

Job seekers have the right to a full refund if they are not given information about three proper job openings (meaning a job lasting more than ninety days) through the service within seven business days after paying a fee or deposit. (Civil Code section 1812.518(a)(1).) This prevents the service from selling the same job for short periods of time to a series of applicants. If the job seeker does not obtain a job, or if the job lasts fewer than 90 days, she is entitled to a refund of all money paid, minus a $25 service charge. (Civil Code section 1812.518(b).) If the service does not provide a full refund within ten days of the request, it owes the job seeker a double refund. (Civil Code section 1812.518(c).)

Individuals cannot be charged any fee for taking a job working for the service itself or a subsidiary of the service. (Civil Code section 1812.517(e)(2).) Job applicants cannot be charged a fee if the service is furnishing help (for instance, screening all applicants) to an employer or person who has a financial interest in the job listing service. (Civil Code section 1812.517(e)(3).) If the service decides who gets the job, no fee is allowed. (Civil Code section 1812.517(e)(3).)

Enforcement: File a civil suit for triple damages and punitive damages, plus attorney's fees. Any violation is a misdemeanor. If the service violates the law, the contract is void, and the job seeker is owed all money paid. These rights cannot be waived (even if the contract language says that the signer waives them). (Civil Code section 1812.523.)

D. REQUIREMENTS OF NURSES' REGISTRIES

The rules outlined below apply exclusively to nurses' registries that refer nurses to private-duty nursing jobs (in which the nurse is a self-employed private contractor) paid by the patient. If the registry also refers any nurse to other types of positions (hospitals, medical offices, etc.) then the stricter employment agency rules apply. (Civil Code section 1812.524.)

A nurses' registry cannot ask for a registration fee. (Civil Code section 1812.530.) It can collect a fee only for an actual job assignment. (Civil Code section 1812.532.) It must provide a copy of its fee schedule before any interview. (Civil Code section 1812.527(a)(1).) It is not allowed to make any false statements to job seekers. (Civil Code section 1812.533.) It cannot split any fees with a physician, hospital, nurse, or patient. (Civil Code section 1812.531.) It must keep accurate records of all assignments. (Civil Code section 1812.529.)

Job seekers are entitled to a full refund of the fee paid for a job if they do not get that job, or are not paid for that job. If the registry does not provide the full refund within forty-eight hours of the request, the registry must pay twice the amount due. (Civil Code section 1812.532.)

Enforcement: File a civil suit for triple damages and punitive damages, plus attorney's fees. Any violation is a misdemeanor. If the registry violates the law, job seekers are entitled to a refund of all fees paid. These rights cannot be waived (even if language in the contract says that the signer waives the rights). (Civil Code section 1812.523.)

III. RIGHTS WHEN APPLYING FOR A JOB

A. RIGHT TO A COPY OF THE APPLICATION

When a job seeker is required to sign an application form (or any other form) in the process of obtaining a job, or while employed, she has a right to receive a copy of that form if she requests one. (Labor Code section 432.)

Enforcement: File a complaint with the state labor commissioner or local district attorney. Violation is a misdemeanor.

Exceptions: Railroad workers covered by the federal Railway Labor Act are not covered by this requirement (but can pursue their rights under federal law). (Labor Code section 434.)

B. QUESTIONS EMPLOYER MAY NOT ASK

Job seekers cannot be asked interview questions that would allow an employer to discriminate against them illegally (for example, based on gender, age, race, national origin, etc.) or because of their health or financial status. (Government Code section 12940(d); 2 California Code of Regulations section 7287.3.) See Chapter 6 for a full description of prohibited discrimination in hiring and employment. See also the Department of Fair Employment and Housing's pamphlet on pre-employment inquiries at http://www.dfeh.ca.gov/DFEH/Publications/PublicationDocs/DFEH-161.pdf.

1. Questions About Protected Characteristics

To ensure that employers, employment agencies, and apprenticeship or training programs do not reject job applicants for illegal reasons, limits are placed on the kinds of questions they may ask. Unlawful questions cannot be asked on written job applications, on questionnaires, or in personal or telephone interviews with the applicant or her references. If they are nevertheless asked, applicants can legally answer them falsely, incompletely, or incorrectly. If an applicant is denied a job because she refused to answer illegal questions, or because of how she answered them, there is a good chance that she can sue for the job or its equivalent (in addition to lost wages and benefits).

Special note on California state civil service: Laws governing state civil service contain similar prohibitions on discrimination. Enforcement is through complaints filed with the State Personnel Board. (Government Code sections 19700 et seq.)

a. Age

It is unlawful for employers to discriminate based on age against workers who are forty or older. A policy that does this is illegal even if it also discriminates against younger people. For example, a policy against hiring anyone "over thirty" or "over thirty-five" or who is retired is illegal because it affects those forty and over. (29 U.S. Code sections 623 and 631; Government Code sections

12926(b), 12940, 12941; 2 California Code of Regulations section 7295.2.)

- Job applicants generally cannot be asked their age or birth date when applying for a job. (Government Code section 12940(d); 2 California Code of Regulations sections 7295.5(a) and 7287.3(b).) However, the employer can ask for a person's age or birth date after hiring that individual.

- Applicants should not be asked for any information that would tend to identify them as more than forty years old. (Government Code section 12940(d); 2 California Code of Regulations section 7295.5.)

- Applicants cannot be asked their age in applying for an apprenticeship program. (29 Code of Federal Regulations section 1625.21; Government Code section 12940(c); 2 California Code of Regulations section 7295.2; Labor Code section 3077.5.)

- Applicants may be asked whether they are at least eighteen years old and whether they can show proof of age if they are hired (to ensure compliance with the child labor laws). Applicants who are younger than eighteen can be asked to submit a work permit after being hired. (Education Code section 49160.)

Enforcement: File a complaint with the state Department of Fair Employment and Housing (DFEH). See their website at http://www.dfeh.ca.gov/DFEH/Complaints/fileComplaint.aspx. File a charge with the federal Equal Employment Opportunity Commission. See their website at http://www.eeoc.gov/employees/charge.cfm. Be aware that in most cases, California anti-discrimination law is stronger than federal law, so it will make sense to file with the California DFEH, unless that agency does not have the power to deal with that kind of case (for example, cases involving federal agencies, military installations, etc.). File a civil suit.

Exceptions: Employers with fewer than five employees (under the FEHA) or fewer than twenty employees (under the Age Discrimination in Employment Act). (Government Code section 12926(d); 29 U.S. Code section 630(b).)

b. National Origin, Nationality, Ancestry, Race, and Color

It is unlawful to discriminate against a person because of his national origin, nationality, race, color, or ancestry. (Government Code sections 11135, 12921, 12940; 2 California Code of Regulations sections 7286.3 and 7289.5; 42 U.S. Code section 2000e-2; 29 Code of Federal Regulations sections 1606.1 et seq.; 41 Code of Federal Regulations sections 60-1.1, 60-50.1 et seq.) However, applicants may be asked if they are legally eligible to work in the United States. (8 U.S. Code sections 1324a and 1324b(a); 8 Code of Federal Regulations section 274a.2.)

- Applicants cannot be asked non-job-related questions about their birthplace or the birthplace of their parents, spouse, or other relatives.

- Applicants cannot be required to produce naturalization papers or papers related to a "green card" (which gives them permission to work legally in the U.S. before they are hired). The employer is allowed to say that these papers will be required *after* the applicant has been hired. The employer can ask whether the applicant will be able to submit verification of a right to work.

- Applicants cannot be asked non-job-related questions about what language they commonly use or speak. An employer may ask what languages the applicant speaks, reads, or writes, but not non-job-related questions about how the applicant learned the language.
- Applicants may be asked the name and address of a person to be contacted in an emergency, but cannot be asked whether that person is a relative or what nationality that person is. Minors (under eighteen), however, may be asked the name and address of their parent or guardian.
- Applicants cannot be asked or required to attach a photograph to a job application or questionnaire. The employer may say that after the applicant is hired, a photograph will be required.
- Applicants may not be asked any questions about their race or color.
- Applicants may not be asked the color (or complexion) of their skin, eyes, or hair.
- Applicants may not be asked non-job-related questions about their height or weight.

(Government Code section 12940; 2 California Code of Regulations sections 7286–7296; 42 U.S. Code sections 2000e et seq.; 29 Code of Federal Regulations sections 1606.1 et seq.; 41 Code of Federal Regulations sections 60-1.1–60-1.5, 60-50.1–60-50.5.)

"National origin" is interpreted broadly to cover physical, cultural, or linguistic characteristics of a particular national group. (29 Code of Federal Regulations section 1606.1.) The individual need not be born in the country of origin, as long as he is associated with it through ancestry or some other factor. (See *International Brotherhood of Teamsters v. United States* (1977) 431 U.S. 324, in which the employer discriminated against applicants with Spanish surnames.) However, distinctions may be lawfully made between equally qualified citizens and non-citizens in hiring. (*Espinoza v. Farah Manufacturing Co.* (1973) 414 U.S. 86; 8 U.S. Code section 1324b(a).)

Enforcement: File a complaint with the state Department of Fair Employment and Housing. See their website at http://www.dfeh.ca.gov/DFEH/Complaints/fileComplaint.aspx. File a charge with the federal Equal Employment Opportunity Commission if federal agencies are involved. See their website at http://www.eeoc.gov/employees/charge.cfm. File a civil suit.

Exceptions: Employers with fewer than five employees (under the FEHA) or fewer than fifteen employees (under Title VII). (Government Code section 12926(d); 42 U.S. Code section 2000e(b).) Government agencies may require their contractors and subcontractors to obtain information for security purposes that normally may not be asked. (Government Code section 12926.) Employers may be required to collect statistical data regarding race, sex, and national origin of applicants, but such data shall not be requested on the employment application form itself and must be kept separately from the personnel or applicant file. (2 California Code of Regulations section 7287.0.)

c. Immigration

No employer can discriminate in hiring or discharge because of citizenship or immigration status, as long as the applicant is legally entitled to work in this country. (Government Code section 12940; 2 California Code of Regulations section 7289.5(f); 8 U.S. Code sections 1324a and 1324b; 29 Code of Federal Regulations section 1606.5(a).) However, an employer may be allowed to prefer to hire an individual who is a U.S. citizen instead of an individual who is not if the two individuals are equally qualified. (8 U.S. Code section 1324b(a)(4).)

An I-9 form filled out by the employee and signed by the employer must be filed no later than three days after a new employee starts work. The employee must show the employer documents establishing her identity and right to work in the U.S., and the I-9 form must indicate which documents (for example, passport, green card, etc.) were examined. Employees can have someone assist them in filling out the form. The employer can copy the documents, but can use those copies only with the I-9 form and for no other purpose. (8 U.S. Code sections 1101, 1324a, 1324b.)

Enforcement: File a complaint with the Special Counsel for Immigration-Related Unfair Employment Practices for cases involving misuse of documents; or the California Department of Fair Employment and Housing or the EEOC for issues related to discrimination based on race or national origin.

Certain workers are not required to fill out I-9 forms:

- Employees hired before November 7, 1986;
- Domestic workers in private homes who are not employed on a regular basis;
- Certain minors under age sixteen.

d. Sex (Gender)

It is unlawful to discriminate because of sex, except for certain very limited situations (see section IV.A., p. 26, on bona fide occupational qualifications).

- Applicants generally cannot be asked their sex (gender) on an application form or pre-employment questionnaire. The employer may, however, compile this information for record-keeping purposes.
- Applicants cannot be asked how many children they have or care for.
- Applicants cannot be asked any questions about their family responsibilities (dependents, childcare, child support, or housework). (See the EEOC guidelines on discrimination against workers with caregiving responsibilities at http://www.eeoc.gov/policy/docs/caregiving.html.)
- Applicants cannot be asked questions about childbearing, fertility, pregnancies (past, present, or future), birth control, abortions, or sterilizations.
- When asked about prior work experience, applicants may include in their answer information about prior unpaid or volunteer work experience.

(Government Code section 12940; 2 California Code of Regulations sections 7290.6, 7290.9(b); 29 Code of Federal Regulations sections 1604.1 et seq.; 41 Code of Federal Regulations sections 60-20.1–60-20.6.)

Sexual stereotyping is a form of sex discrimination prohibited by Title VII and the FEHA. Employers cannot make assumptions about an applicant based on preconceived ideas based on the applicant's gender. They cannot insist or assume that an applicant conform to a sexual stereotype. (*Price Waterhouse v. Hopkins* (1989) 490 U.S. 228.)

Enforcement: File a complaint with the state Department of Fair Employment and Housing (see their website at http://www.dfeh.ca.gov/DFEH/Complaints/fileComplaint.aspx) or a charge with the federal Equal Employment Opportunity Commission (http://www.eeoc.gov/employees/charge.cfm). File a civil suit.

Exceptions: Employers with fewer than five employees (under the FEHA) or fewer than fifteen employees (under Title VII). (42 U.S. Code section 2000e(b), Government Code section 12926(d).) However, *all* employees are protected from sexual harassment. (Government Code section 12940(j)(4)(A).)

e. Sexual Orientation

Discrimination or different treatment in any aspect of employment or opportunity for employment based on actual or perceived sexual orientation is illegal in California. Job seekers or employees may not be asked questions about their sexual orientation. (Government Code section 12940(a).)

Enforcement: File a complaint with the state Department of Fair Employment and Housing (see their website at http://www.dfeh.ca.gov/DFEH/Complaints/fileComplaint.aspx). File a civil suit. Sexual orientation is not explicitly covered under Title VII, so complaints about discrimination based on sexual orientation should be filed under California law.

Exceptions: Employers with fewer than five employees are not covered under FEHA. (Government Code section 12926(d).) However, *all* employees are protected from harassment based on sexual orientation. (Government Code section 12940(j)(4)(A).) See Chapter 6 for more information on religious employers.

f. Marital Status

It is illegal to discriminate against job applicants or employees based on the fact that they are married, single, divorced, widowed, a single parent, a registered domestic partner, or living with a partner to whom they are not married. (Government Code sections 12920, 12921, 12940; 2 California Code of Regulations sections 7292.0, 7292.1.)

- Applicants generally cannot be asked to reveal their marital status. They may be asked if they have used another name or if any of their records (of work history or education) are listed under other names. (Government Code section 12940; 2 California Code of Regulations section 7292.4.)
- California regulations provide that employment decisions generally must not be based on whether an individual has a spouse employed by the employer. (2 California Code of Regulations section 7292.5(a).) Applicants can be asked if they have a spouse who presently works for the employer. (2 California Code of Regulations section 7292.4(c).) However, this information can be used only for the following purposes:
  ○ The employer can refuse to place one spouse

under the direct supervision of the other spouse, for legitimate business reasons (safety, supervision, morale, or security).

○ The employer can refuse to place both spouses in the same department for legitimate business reasons and only if the work involves potential conflicts of interest or other hazards that are greater for married couples than for other persons. (2 California Code of Regulations section 7292.5.)

• It is unlawful to discriminate against applicants for living with someone to whom they are not married, or for having children without being married. (*Chen v. County of Orange* (2002) 96 Cal.App.4th 926.)

Enforcement: File a complaint with the state Department of Fair Employment and Housing (http://www.dfeh.ca.gov/DFEH/Complaints/fileComplaint.aspx). File a civil suit. Discrimination based on marital status is not explicitly covered under Title VII, so complaints should be brought under California law.

Exceptions: Employers with fewer than five employees are exempt. (Government Code section 12926(d).)

> *Hiring standards must have a substantial relationship to the job to be performed.*

g. Pregnancy

It is illegal to discriminate against applicants or employees because they are pregnant or of child-bearing age. The prohibition on discrimination based on pregnancy also makes discrimination based on childbirth illegal. Employers may not ask questions about plans to have children, methods of birth control, or related topics. (Government Code sections 12926(p), 12940, 12945; 2 California Code of Regulations sections 7290.9(b)(3), 7291.0(c), 7291.5.)

h. Religion

It is, with only narrow exceptions, unlawful to discriminate on the basis of religion or lack of religious belief. (Government Code section 12940; 2 California Code of Regulations sections 7293.0 and 7293.1.) In general, applicants cannot be asked any of the following:

• If they have a religion;
• What religion they practice;
• What religious days or holidays they observe;
• If their religion prevents them from working weekends or holidays. The employer can state the regular days, hours, or shifts that are to be worked. When the job requires it, the employer may ask about availability for work on weekends or evenings. However, employers must explore reasonable means of accommodating religious observances, beliefs, and practices.

(Government Code section 12940; 2 California Code of Regulations section 7293.4; 29 Code of Federal Regulations section 1605.2; 41 Code of Federal Regulations section 60-50.3.)

An employer can legally inquire about religion only if the requirement is job-related (for example, a job as a member of the clergy or as head of a religious organization). See section IV.A., p. 26, on bona fide occupational qualifications. (Government Code section 12940(d); 2 California Code of Regulations section 7287.3(b)(1).)

Enforcement: File a complaint with the state Department of Fair Employment and Housing (http://www.dfeh.ca.gov/DFEH/Complaints/fileComplaint.aspx), or file a charge with the federal Equal Employment Opportunity Commission. (http://www.eeoc.gov/employees/charge.cfm). File a civil suit.

Exceptions: Employers with fewer than five employees (under FEHA) and under fifteen employees (under Title VII) are exempt. (Government Code section 12926(d); 42 U.S. Code section 2000e(b).) See Chapter 6 for more information on religious employers.

i. Disability

State and federal laws protect individuals with disabilities from discrimination during the hiring process as long as they are able to carry out the essential functions of the job (with or without reasonable accommodation). (Government Code section 12940.) For more information on disability discrimination, see Chapter 6. For more information on inquiries regarding medical records, see section VI., p. 32.

2. Questions About Bonding

An employer generally may not ask an applicant to provide a cash bond. (Labor Code section 402.) There are jobs, however, that require that an employee be bondable. It is the employer's duty to pay for the bond.

3. Questions About Arrest

Applicants cannot be asked if they have ever been arrested. Applicants can, however, be asked if they have been arrested and are currently out on bail or on their own recognizance (released without bail) pending trial. Applicants cannot be asked about certain offenses concerning marijuana (possession, sale, transport, being in the presence of use) that are more than two years old, or about participation in a diversion program. (Labor Code sections 432.7 and 432.8; 2 California Code of Regulations section 7287.4(d)(1).) The employer can ask whether the applicant has ever been *convicted* of a felony, or of a misdemeanor that resulted in imprisonment and that has not been expunged (wiped out) or sealed by the court or under a specific law.

There are several exceptions to the rules stated above for employers with a particular need to know about certain types of offenses. Applicants applying for positions with healthcare facilities where the job involves regular patient contact may be asked about arrests for sex offenses. (Labor Code section 432.7(f)(1); Health and Safety Code section 1250; Penal Code section 290.) If the job will involve access to drugs or medications, prospective employees may be asked about arrests for controlled substances. (Labor Code section 432.7(f)(2); Health and Safety Code section 11590.) School boards and private schools may receive reports from the Department of Justice regarding arrests or convictions for crimes involving sex, drugs, and serious or violent felonies, including arrests for which trial is pending, but not including arrests that resulted in acquittals or where charges were dropped. (Education Code sections 44237 and 45125; Penal Code sections 667.5 and 1192.7(c).) If applicants with these types of convictions can prove that they have been rehabilitated, they may still be eligible for employment and may not be denied employment solely because of the previous conviction. (Education Code section 44237(h), (i).)

4. Questions About Credit Rating

Questions about credit/finances are forbidden if they are not job-related. If the job involves the handling of large sums of money, the employer can probably request a credit check.

It is illegal to discriminate against an applicant based on the fact that the individual has filed for bankruptcy. (11 U.S. Code section 525.) Using an applicant's financial status as a factor in hiring decisions may have an illegal disparate impact. For example, discrimination against individuals with wage garnishments disproportionately affects minorities. (*Johnson v. Pike Corp. of America* (C.D. Cal. 1971) 332 F.Supp. 490.) A relationship also has been demonstrated between credit record and race and gender (minorities and single mothers tend to have lower credit ratings). Applicants generally cannot be asked questions about their current or past credit rating, assets, liabilities, debts, bankruptcies, or garnishments that do not relate to the job in question. They generally cannot be asked whether they own or rent their home.

If it is job-related, the employer may request a consumer report regarding an applicant (with the applicant's permission). However the report may not include information that the employer is not allowed to obtain in the pre-employment context (such as marital status, age, and residency). The employer must also follow the laws regarding credit reports. (Civil Code section 1786.20(c); 15 U.S. Code section 1681a(o)(5)(B); see also the DFEH pamphlet, "Employment Inquiries: What Can Employers Ask Applicants and Employees," at http://www.dfeh.ca.gov/DFEH/Publications/ PublicationDocs/DFEH-161.pdf.) For more information on disparate impact discrimination, see Chapter 6. For more information on the rights of applicants regarding credit reports, see Chapter 3.

5. Questions About Family Support Payments

An employer cannot refuse to hire an applicant because the applicant's wages have been assigned for child or family support. An employer who violates this law may be subject to a civil penalty of $500. (Family Code section 5290.)

6. Questions About Memberships, Associations, and Politics

Applicants cannot be required to list the organizations to which they belong. They can be asked to list job-related organizations but generally not labor organizations. Questions about whether they ever belonged to a union, how they feel about unions or strikes or whether they would support a union, or questions about their union beliefs or activities generally may be considered unlawful intimidation under the National Labor Relations Act. (29 U.S. Code section 157.) Applicants generally cannot be asked about political activities that are unrelated to the job description, or about the race, nationality, or sex of their friends.

7. Other Prohibited Questions

In addition to questions intended to draw out information regarding characteristics about which it is illegal to discriminate, other prohibited inquiries include:

- Have you ever been injured on the job?
- What prescription drugs do you take?
- How much sick leave did you use last year?
- Do you drink alcohol?

See Chapter 6 for more information on disability discrimination.

C. QUESTIONS PERMITTED OF COMMERCIAL DRIVERS

Applicants for jobs driving commercial vehicles (such as trucks or buses) may be required to list all commercial driving jobs (going back ten years) and the reasons for leaving past jobs. (Vehicle Code section 15230.)

Prospective employers will obtain copies of the applicant's current public record from the Department of Motor Vehicles. The public record contains information about accidents, license suspensions and revocations, and convictions for driving under the influence of drugs or alcohol. If the person is hired, the employer will participate in a "pull notice" system that provides the employer with the employee's current public driving record at six- or twelve-month intervals, depending on the size of the employer's firm. (Vehicle Code section 1808.1.)

D. QUESTIONS ABOUT MILITARY SERVICE

Employers may not discriminate against veterans, and, in California, may give them hiring preference. (38 U.S. Code sections 4301–4333; Military and Veterans Code section 394; Government Code section 12940(a)(4).)

Employers may inquire about relevant skills that an applicant acquired in military service. Other questions about military service, which are not job-related, may be considered discriminatory and should not be asked. (See the DFEH pamphlet, "Employment Inquires: What Can Employers Ask Applicants and Employees," at http://www.dfeh.ca.gov/DFEH/Publications/PublicationDocs/DFEH-161.pdf.)

IV. UNLAWFUL DISCRIMINATION DURING HIRING

Individuals have legal protections against discrimination in both the hiring and the promotion process. As discussed in section III.B., above, employers may not discriminate on the basis of the following protected characteristics: age, sex, race, color, sexual orientation, nationality, marital status, national origin, creed, ancestry, pregnancy, or physical or mental disability, medical condition, or religion. Hiring standards must have a substantial relationship to the job to be performed. There are several other grounds besides these on which employers may not discriminate. See Chapter 6 for a full description of prohibited employment discrimination, which laws apply to employers of various sizes, and applicable exemptions from coverage.

A. "BONA FIDE OCCUPATIONAL QUALIFICATIONS" OR "BUSINESS NECESSITY"

Two closely related defenses that an employer may use in defending himself in a lawsuit based on charges of discrimination are "bona fide occupational qualifications" and "business necessity."

An employer may intentionally discriminate in hiring based on a characteristic that it normally may not consider (for instance, national origin, gender, or religion) in certain limited circumstances in which the characteristic is a "bona fide occupational qualification" (BFOQ) necessary to the business operation. (42 U.S. Code section 2000e-2(e); Government Code section 12940.) Under Title VII, the BFOQ defense can apply only to hiring and employing decisions (not other terms and conditions of employment) and only to discrimination on the basis of religion, sex, and national origin. Race is specifically excluded and cannot be a BFOQ under Title VII. (42 U.S. Code section 2000e-2(e); *Knight v. Nassau County Civil Service Commission* (2d Cir. 1981) 649 F.2d 157.) Age may be a BFOQ under the Age Discrimination in Employment Act (ADEA). (29 U.S. Code section 623(f)(1).)

Under California law, the BFOQ defense can apply to discrimination on the basis of race, religion, color, national origin, ancestry, disability, medical condition, marital status, sex, age, and sexual orientation. (Government Code section 12940(a).)

The BFOQ exception is very narrow. In order to be a BFOQ, a qualification must relate to the "essence" or "central mission" of the employer's business. (*Auto Workers v. Johnson Controls, Inc.* (1991) 499 U.S. 187.) The employer has the burden of proving the characteristic is reasonably necessary to the normal operation of the business and that there is reasonable cause to believe that all or almost all of the people who are discriminated against would be unable to safely and efficiently perform the duties of the job. (2 California Code of Regulations section 7286.7(a).) For example, gender would be a BFOQ for an acting role that requires a specific gender for the purpose of authenticity. (29 Code of Federal Regulations section 1604.2(a)(2).)

If a hiring standard that appears to have a neutral basis (for instance, a strength test) results in a negative impact on a group with protected characteristics (for instance, the test has an impact on people of certain races or genders), the test may be allowed if the standard is job-related and consistent with "business necessity." (See Chapter 6 for a discussion of disparate impact discrimination.) A hiring standard that causes disparate impact discrimination (that is, that affects some groups with certain protected characteristics more than other groups) must be related to measuring an individual's ability to successfully perform the job in question in order to be justified by "business necessity." (*Griggs v. Duke Power Co.* (1971) 401 U.S. 424.) For example, tests that require individuals to lift heavy weights adversely impact women. However, firefighters may need to lift heavy objects, so a lifting requirement may be justified by business necessity. A hiring standard that is consistent with "business necessity" may still be illegal if a less discriminatory practice would accomplish the same purpose. (42 U.S. Code section 2000e-2(k)(1)(A)(ii).)

Under California law, the employer has the burden of proving that the hiring standard has an "overriding legitimate business purpose" and is necessary to the "safe and efficient operation of the business." The hiring standard may still be illegal if there is an alternative practice that would accomplish the business purpose with less of a discriminatory impact. (2 California Code of Regulations section 7286.7(b).)

The employer defense against disparate impact claims under the Age Discrimination in Employment Act (ADEA) is broader than the business necessity defense. The ADEA allows disparate impact age discrimination if the employment practice is based on "reasonable factors other than age." (29 U.S. Code section 623(f)(1).) Unlike the business necessity test, the "reasonable factors" test does not require an employer to use less discriminatory alternatives. (*Smith v. City of Jackson* (2005) 544 U.S. 228.)

B. DISCRIMINATION BASED ON CUSTOMER PREFERENCES

Individuals are protected against discrimination on the basis of discriminatory customer preference or request. It is against the law for a customer of an employer (or potential employer) to ask that individuals be denied employment, terminated, transferred, or otherwise discriminated against because of their age, sex, sexual orientation, race, color, religion, ancestry, national origin, physical or mental disability, medical condition, or because they have traveled to or lawfully conducted business in a foreign country (for example, Israel, Iraq, Cuba).

One exception to this rule is that if the characteristic is a "bona fide occupational qualification" (for instance, a female actress to play a female part), a customer request may be honored.

It is also illegal for the employer to discriminate against applicants in order to assist in a boycott of a foreign country (unless the U.S. government is boycotting that country), even if that boycott is supported by customers of the business. (Civil Code section 51.5; Business and Professions Code section 16721; 50 U.S. Code app. sections 2407 and 2410.)

Enforcement: File a complaint with the DFEH or EEOC. File a civil suit.

CHAPTER 2

C. DISCRIMINATION BASED ON SIGNIFICANT RISK OF INJURY OR DISEASE

If someone presents "a significant risk of substantial harm" to himself or others that cannot be eliminated by reasonable accommodation, an employer is permitted to deny this person a job. (42 U.S. Code sections 12113(b) and 12111(3).) The determination of this risk must be based on a reasonable medical judgment relying on *objective factual evidence* (not unsubstantiated fears) concerning the person's present ability to perform the essential functions of the job. Factors that should be considered are: how long the risk will exist; the nature and severity of the potential harm; the likelihood of the potential harm occurring; and how soon the potential harm may occur. (29 Code of Federal Regulations section 1630.2(r).) For example, a person who suffers from narcolepsy (frequent, uncontrollable episodes of falling asleep) could pose a significant risk of substantial harm in a job that requires driving. One court held that the diabetic condition of an employee who was responsible for monitoring chlorine processing in a chemical manufacturing plant posed a significant risk of substantial harm. Although the likelihood of a diabetic episode causing an accident was small, the severity and scale of the potential harm (lives lost due to chlorine gas exposure) supported a conclusion that the employee posed a significant risk of substantial harm. (*Hutton v. Elf Atochem North America, Inc.* (9th Cir. 2001) 273 F.3d 884.)

The basic principles to remember are:

- Individuals cannot be denied a job because of a slightly increased risk of harm.
- Individuals cannot be denied a job because of fears of a significant risk at some time in the future.
- Individuals cannot be denied a job because of fears of a significant risk that can be eliminated (or reduced to an acceptable level) by a reasonable accommodation.

These rules apply to hiring, promotion, job transfer, job bidding and assignment, reclassification, and other employment selection procedures.

People cannot be denied jobs because a pre-existing medical condition exposes them to a higher risk than others. Genetic or medical screening cannot be used to deny work. It is also unlawful for an employer to use statistical predictors to justify employment discrimination. The employer cannot use eye color, skin color, physical size, high blood pressure (hypertension), diabetes, sickle-cell trait, color blindness, hearing loss, chronic liver disease, lower-back problems, seizure disorder (epilepsy, abnormal EEG), obesity, use of tobacco, off-the-job use of alcohol, age, diet, exercise habits, reproductive status, childbearing plans, region of birth, or region of residence to deny a job. (Government Code sections 12926, 12940; 2 California Code of Regulations sections 7293.6, 7294.0, 7294.1; 42 U.S. Code sections 2000ff-1, 12112; 28 Code of Federal Regulations section 35.104.)

Enforcement: File a charge with the federal Equal Employment Opportunity Commission. File a complaint with the state Department of Fair Employment and Housing. File a complaint with the Office of Federal Contract Compliance Programs (for federal contractors). File a civil suit if the case is not resolved by such complaints.

D. DISCRIMINATION BASED ON BANKRUPTCY

Individuals cannot be discriminated against because they have filed for bankruptcy or participated in a wage-earner protection plan. This law applies to all employers and offers protection in all areas of employment: hiring, firing, discipline, and terms and conditions of work. People cannot be fired or refused a job, license, or permit for any bankruptcy-related reason.

People cannot be discriminated against because of any of the following:

- They filed bankruptcy;
- Their spouse filed bankruptcy;
- They or their spouse entered a wage-earner protection plan or is otherwise protected under the Bankruptcy Act;
- They were insolvent (broke, not paying bills, in debt) before they used the Bankruptcy Act; or
- They have not paid one or more debts (which were dealt with under the Bankruptcy Act). (11 U.S. Code section 525.)

Enforcement: File a civil suit.

E. DISCRIMINATION BASED ON AIDS SCREENING

No employer or potential employer may legally test the blood of applicants or employees for AIDS antibodies. (The AIDS antibodies test reveals exposure to the HIV virus.) No employer may ask applicants or employees to authorize an AIDS antibodies test. (Health and Safety Code section 120990.)

No one (except the individual herself) may tell an employer any results of an AIDS antibodies test she has taken. No employer may use any AIDS antibodies test results to determine whether to hire or fire.

No employer may ask whether applicants or employees have been given a diagnosis of AIDS, pre-AIDS, ARC (AIDS-related complex), or an AIDS-related condition, or whether they have been exposed to AIDS or have engaged in high-risk sexual or drug practices. (Health and Safety Code sections 120975–121125; Government Code section 12940.)

Enforcement: File a complaint with the DFEH or the EEOC. File a civil suit. (Health and Safety Code section 120980.)

V. REQUIREMENTS DURING HIRING

The law protects applicants from certain unfair requirements employers might otherwise demand before hire.

A. REQUIRING AN APPLICANT TO PAY FOR A FIDELITY BOND

A fidelity bond is an insurance contract that guarantees an employer reimbursement for a financial loss due to the dishonesty of an employee. Usually, bond amounts are $500 to $10,000. Many employers require that prospective employees be "bondable." Insurance companies generally refuse to bond employees who are ex-felons, have a history of drug or alcohol abuse, or have poor credit ratings. For options available if one is not bondable commercially, see below.

1. Employer's Obligation to Pay

If an employer requires a fidelity bond of current employees or as a condition of hiring, the employer is legally bound to pay for it. (Labor Code section 401.)

An employee of a savings and loan association may have to sign for a bond, but the employer must still pay the cost. (Financial Code sections 6200, 6203(b).)

Enforcement: File a claim with the state labor commissioner or a complaint with the local district attorney. File a civil suit. (Labor Code section 410.) An employer who violates this law may be subject to six months in jail or a $1,000 fine or both. (Labor Code section 408.)

Exceptions: An employer may sometimes accept a cash bond from the employee, in the limited situations in which this is allowed by law:

• The employee is entrusted with property of an equal value; or

• The employer regularly advances goods to be delivered or sold by the employee, the employer is regularly reimbursed, and the cash bond is limited to an amount that is enough to cover the value of the goods that have been advanced during the period before payment. (Labor Code section 402.)

2. Options When an Individual Is Refused a Bond

Despite ex-offender or credit status, a person may be eligible to be bonded under a special government program, the Federal Bonding Program (FBP). The program may provide a bond of up to $25,000 to any individual who is qualified for a job requiring bonding and has a firm job offer (or has the job), and who is not commercially bondable. For a person to be eligible, the job must offer steady full-time work; adequate working conditions and wages; and a reasonable expectation of permanence. (26 U.S. Code section 51; 42 U.S. Code section 13725.)

Either the job applicant or the prospective employer may apply for this program through the state Employment Development Department (EDD). If the local EDD is unfamiliar with the Federal Bonding Program, contact the U.S. Department of Labor, Employment and Training Administration, Federal Bonding Program. See the website at http://www.bonds4jobs.com for more information on this program.

Enforcement: Apply to the U.S. Department of Labor.

Exceptions: Self-employed workers are not eligible.

B. REQUIRING APPLICANTS OR EMPLOYEES TO INVEST IN THE BUSINESS

An employer cannot require applicants or employees to buy part of a business in order to get work or be considered for a job. They cannot be required to make an investment, make a loan, buy stock, or take part of their wages (or salary, commission, or compensation) in shares of the business. (Labor Code section 407.) This law applies to businesses, worker-owned cooperatives, and all other operations. Employers are even prohibited from advertising this sort of scheme.

Enforcement: File a claim with the state labor commissioner or a complaint with the local district attorney. An employer who violates this law is punishable by six months in jail, or a fine of $50 to $1,000, or both. (Labor Code sections 408, 410.)

C. REQUIRING APPLICANTS OR EMPLOYEES TO PATRONIZE THE BUSINESS

It is illegal for an employer to make applicants or employees shop at its store (or any other specific store), buy any particular brand of goods, or use a particular place of lodging, place of board, vehicle, or means of transportation. These prohibitions apply to anything of value, including food, services, tools, clothing, and office supplies, among other things. (Labor Code section 450.)

Enforcement: File a complaint with the local district attorney. An employer or employer's agent who violates this law is guilty of a misdemeanor. (Labor Code section 451.)

Exceptions: Employers are permitted to specify the style and brand of uniforms, but the employer must pay for them. Uniforms are defined as including "wearing apparel and accessories of distinctive design or color." (Labor Code section 452; Industrial Welfare Commission Orders, section 9 (section 8 for construction, mining, drilling and logging).)

D. REQUIRING APPLICANTS OR EMPLOYEES TO RESIDE WITHIN A PUBLIC EMPLOYER'S JURISDICTION

No city, county, or other local or regional public employer can impose a residence requirement on its employees or job applicants. They cannot be required to live in the city, county, or district. (California Constitution, art. 11, section 10(b).)

Enforcement: File a civil suit.

Exceptions: A public employer may require that an applicant or employee reside within a reasonable and specific distance of the place of employment (or other location). After one obtains a job, the public employer may require that the employee live no more than a specified commuting distance away, if this requirement is reasonably related to their duties. (California Constitution, art. 11, section 10(b).)

E. INDUCING JOB APPLICANTS AND EMPLOYEES TO MOVE BY MISREPRESENTING JOB CONDITIONS

Before changing a place of residence, even for a temporary job, employees and applicants have the right to be told the truth about job conditions. The employer, or anyone acting for the employer, must not misrepresent:

- Kind, character, or existence of the work;
- Length of time the job will last;
- Wages or benefits that will be paid;
- Sanitary or housing conditions of the work; or
- Existence or nonexistence of a strike, lockout, or labor dispute affecting the work.

This law prohibits employer misrepresentations, whether they are spoken, written, or appear in advertisements. Any employee or applicant move is protected, whether from one place to another within California, or from California to outside the state, or from outside the state to California. (Labor Code section 970.)

Enforcement: File a claim with the state labor commissioner or a complaint with the local district attorney. File a civil suit. An employer or employer's agent who violates this law is guilty of a misdemeanor punishable by six months in jail, or a fine of $50 to $1,000, or both, or may be sued in civil court and forced to pay double damages. (Labor Code sections 971 and 972.)

F. REQUIREMENTS REGARDING PHOTOGRAPHS

1. The Employer Must Pay for Any Required Photos

An employer cannot require applicants or employees to pay for any photo it requires. The employer must pay this cost. (Labor Code section 401.)

Enforcement: File a claim with the state labor commissioner or a complaint with the local district attorney. An employer who violates this law is guilty of a misdemeanor punishable by up to six months in jail, or a fine of $50 to $1,000, or both. (Labor Code section 408.)

2. Photos of Employees May Only Be Used With the Employee's Consent

In general, employers (or any other person or company) may not use a photograph of an employee or applicant in any advertising or solicitation without the person's consent. The employer cannot require that applicants or employees give that consent. This law also protects an individual's name, voice, signature, and likeness. (Civil Code section 3344.)

Enforcement: File a civil suit. An employer who violates this law is liable for damages of at least $750 (for loss of reputation, invasion of privacy, etc.). In addition, the employer may have to pay the person whose photo was used part of the profits from the use of the photo, plus damages, punitive damages, court costs, and attorney's fees. (Civil Code section 3344.)

Exceptions: News photos and pictures of very large groups are excluded from these provisions.

G. REQUIRING APPLICANTS TO TAKE LIE DETECTOR TESTS

California law prohibits non-governmental employers from requiring applicants or employees to take lie detector tests as a condition of employment. If an employer asks an employee or applicant to *voluntarily* take a lie detector test, that person must be advised in writing of their right to refuse to do so. (Labor Code section 432.2.) Federal law also prohibits requirements that applicants take lie detector tests as a condition of employment. (29 U.S. Code section 2002; 29 Code of Federal Regulation sections 801.1-801.4.) (Also, see Chapter 3, section II.C., p. 37.)

H. GROOMING, DRESS, AND APPEARANCE STANDARDS

Employers may set reasonable grooming and appearance standards, subject to some limitations. There must be some flexibility to allow for religious practices. (2 California Code of Regulations section 7293.3(c)(2).) Employers may differentiate appropriately between men and women, as long as it is not discriminatory (for instance, dress standards for one gender only) and unduly burdensome. (2 California Code of Regulations section 7291.1(f)(2).) However, an employer may not prohibit female employees only from wearing pants. (Government Code section 12947.5.) Obesity that is the result of a physiological condition and limits a major life activity is a disability within the meaning of the FEHA. Discrimination against people with such a condition is prohibited. (Government Code sections 12926(k) and 12926.1; *Cassista v. Community Foods, Inc.* (1993) 5 Cal.4th 1050.) Even if obesity is not the result of a physiological condition, it may be covered by the FEHA's provision that protects individuals regarded as having a physical condition that limits a major life activity. This area of the law is in flux and is still developing. For more information on California's regulations on grooming and dress requirements, see 2 California Code of Regulations sections 7287.6(c), 7291.1(f) (2), 7293.3(c)(2).

I. ENGLISH FLUENCY

Employers may assess English fluency when a lack of fluency would materially interfere with job performance. (29 Code of Federal Regulations section 1606.6(b)(1).) California law prohibits employers from requiring English fluency unless it is a bona fide occupational qualification. (Government Code section 12951.) Discrimination based on accent alone may be a form of prohibited discrimination based on national origin.

VI. RIGHTS REGARDING HEALTH INFORMATION DURING HIRING

Basic privacy rights prohibit overly intrusive questions from any employer. They also prohibit the dissemination of private information by any employer or healthcare provider or examiner. For a full description of privacy rights regarding health records, see Chapter 12. In general, an employer may require a medical exam only if an offer of employment has been made, and only if such exams are job-related, consistent with business necessity, and required of all employees in the job classification. (42 U.S. Code section 12112(d) (3); 29 Code of Federal Regulations section 1630.14(b); Government Code section 12940(e) (3).)

A. RIGHT TO AN UNBIASED MEDICAL EXAM

If an employer requires that applicants who have received a job offer take a medical or psychological examination when applying for a job, they have the right to a fair one. An employer may condition a job offer on an applicant's passing a medical or psychological examination only if all of the following rules are followed:

- No medical exam can be required until after the applicant has been chosen for the job in question. (Government Code Section 12940(e); 29 Code of Federal Regulations section 1630.14(b).)
- All employees entering similar positions must be subjected to the exam. It is illegal to require an exam of only those over age forty or only those with a record of disability. The exam standards must be no more stringent or difficult for those over forty or for those with a disability than for younger or nondisabled applicants. (2 California Code of Regulations sections 7294.0(d)(1), 7294.1; 29 Code of Federal Regulations sections 1630.10, 1630.14(b).)
- Exams, tests, and interviews must be made reasonably accessible to people with disabilities. For instance, exam rooms must be accessible to wheelchairs, and interpreters must be provided for the hearing-impaired. (2 California Code of Regulations section 7294.1(b)(3); 29 Code of Federal Regulations section 1630.11.)
- The exam results must be treated as confidential medical records. The results must be maintained separately from other employment and application records. (Civil Code sections 56.10 – 56.37; 2 California Code of Regulations section 7294.0(d)(3); 29 Code of Federal Regulations section 1630.14.)
- Any qualification standards based on medical or psychological exams must be geared to the specific duties of the prospective job. The employer must use different medical standards for jobs with different physical requirements. No test or exam of agility or strength can be used unless the strength or agility being tested is related to the actual work the employee will do on the job. The tests should be constructed so as not to discriminate against the disabled. For example, a standard test of strength may need to be altered to accommodate a wheelchair (if it is determined that a "reasonable accommodation"

would allow a person in a wheelchair to do the work). (2 California Code of Regulations section 7294.1.)

- Any qualification standards based on the exam must relate to *actual* and *essential* job functions, but not necessarily to all the related job functions listed in the job description. (2 California Code of Regulations sections 7293.8(g) and 7294.1; 42 U.S. Code section 12112(d)(4); 29 Code of Federal Regulations sections 1630.2(m), (n) and 1630.10.)
- Applicants must be given the right to contest any unfavorable exam results and to submit independent medical or psychological opinions to the employer before a final hiring decision is made. (2 California Code of Regulations section 7294.0(d)(2).)

Tests measuring physical abilities (strength or agility) are not considered medical tests. As long as they are reasonably related to the job and required of all applicants, they are generally allowable. (2 California Code of Regulations section 7294.1(b)(2).)

B. RIGHT TO LIMIT ACCESS TO MEDICAL RECORDS

The federal Health Insurance Portability and Accountability Act (HIPAA) strengthened the privacy rights of individuals regarding their medical records. The law sets limits on how health plans and healthcare providers may use individually identifiable information. Information may be shared for purposes of treatment with other healthcare providers, but may not be shared for purposes unrelated to medical treatment without the patient's consent (except for a few very narrow exceptions such as crime investigations, subpoenas, litigation against a healthcare provider by the patient, workers compensation cases, etc.). Release of medical information to prospective or current employers requires the written permission of the patient.

An individual who wishes to authorize release of medical information to an employer will generally be asked to sign a form authorizing release of such information. The individual may authorize release of only some types of information and not others. For instance, an individual might authorize release of information related to treatment of back problems (and restrictions on lifting), but not authorize release

of information for treatment of fertility problems. If there is no limitation on the signed authorization to release medical information, an employer may see all information relating to an individual's medical and psychological treatment. See websites on HIPAA at http://aspe.hhs.gov/admnsimp/final/pvcfact2.htm ("Protecting the Privacy of Patients' Health Information") and http://www.hhs.gov/ocr/privacy/hipaa/understanding/summary/privacysummary.pdf ("Summary of the HIPAA Privacy Rule") for more information on HIPAA.

California's laws also protect the confidentiality of medical records. See Chapter 12 for more information on both state and federal protections of medical record confidentiality.

C. RIGHT TO REFUSE TO SIGN A MEDICAL RELEASE

Laws protecting the confidentiality of medical information apply to all employers. Sometimes an employer attempts to get around these protections by asking individuals to sign an authorization for release of medical information when they apply for a job or after they are hired. It is illegal for an employer to retaliate in any way against someone who refuses to sign such a release. (Government Code sections 12940 and 19702; Civil Code section 56.20(b).) However, employers may take necessary action based on the lack of required information. For instance, if a school district does not get a medical clearance indicating the prospective employee does not have tuberculosis, the school district may refuse to put the person to work until the required information is provided. For information on revoking authorizations for release of medical information, see Chapter 12, section IV.A.2., p. 290.

D. DRUG TESTING

Tests for illegal drug use are generally not considered medical tests. (29 Code of Federal Regulations section 1630.16(c).) For more information on rights concerning medical information and drug testing, see Chapters 3 and 12.

INVESTIGATIONS AND POLICE RECORDS

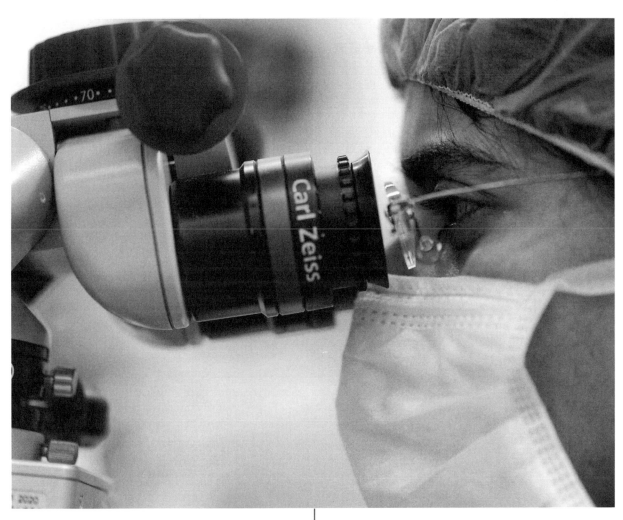

I. SCOPE OF THE CHAPTER

Employers often conduct investigations into a potential or current employee's background when deciding whether to hire the person or make other employment-related decisions. The law restricts both the kinds of information an employer may collect about an applicant or employee and how the employer may obtain and use that information. Generally, subject to certain legal restrictions discussed in this chapter, employers may collect only information which has a legitimate business purpose, that is, information related to an applicant's or employee's current or prospective job and his ability to perform it. Some information and some police records are not available to employers under any circumstances.

This chapter explains the kinds of information an employer may search for, gather, and use; the restrictions imposed on collection and use of that information; and job applicants' and employees' rights regarding information gathered about them.

For more information on personnel and health records, see Chapter 12; on privacy during hiring, see Chapter 2; and on discrimination issues, see Chapter 6.

II. EMPLOYER INVESTIGATIONS

A. RECORDS EMPLOYERS CANNOT OBTAIN

Neither an individual's present employer nor a possible future employer can obtain information about her from any of the following sources without the individual's consent:

- Insurance companies. (Insurance Code sections 791–791.26.)
- Public or private schools (student records). (Education Code section 49076; 20 U.S. Code section 1232d.)
- Junior colleges, colleges, or universities (student records). (Education Code sections 76240–76243.)
- Addiction treatment programs. (Health and Safety Code sections 123125(a), (b), 123135; Civil Code section 1798.24.)
- Providers of mental health services. (Civil Code section 56.10.)
- Any person or agency that has the results of an employee's or applicant's HIV antibody or HIV test. (Health and Safety Code section 120980.)

In addition, an employer cannot seek, possess, or use any information about the following:

- Arrests for which the individual was not convicted, for instance, when the case is dismissed, there is a verdict of not-guilty, or the district attorney informs the arresting agency that the case will be dropped. (Labor Code sections 432.7, 432.8.) Exception: If the individual is out of custody on bail or where bail is not required at the time the information is sought, employers may seek and obtain information about that arrest. (Labor Code section 432.7(a).)
- Marijuana convictions that occurred more than two years in the past. (Health and Safety Code section 11361.5.)
- Arrests that led to an individual's participation in a diversion program. (Labor Code section 432.7.)

Prohibited access to police records is discussed in detail later in this chapter

Enforcement: File a civil suit. In most cases, punitive damages and attorney's fees are available. (See discussion of specific types of records below.)

Exceptions: Protected information can be released if an applicant or employee provides a signed written authorization allowing his employer or someone else to gain access to that information. If the applicant signs a release as part of the hiring process, he is still entitled to protect his privacy later. To do so, the individual must send a letter to the agencies that have his personal information (for example, schools, insurance companies, credit agencies), stating that he is canceling any prior authorizations for release of those details. Once the agency receives this cancellation, it cannot release the individual's information to the employer.

B. EMPLOYEE PHOTOGRAPH OR FINGERPRINTS

Under California law, a prospective employer may require an applicant's photograph and fingerprints for the employer's own use. (Labor Code section 1051.) However, an employer cannot require an individual to be photographed or fingerprinted for the use of a third person (with certain exceptions listed below) if the photos or prints might be used in a way that could be harmful to the employee. For instance, an employer is prohibited in most circumstances from turning employee photographs or fingerprints over to other employers in order to prevent future employment, or to law enforcement agencies unless they are given out pursuant to a subpoena or court order. (Labor Code sections 1051, 1052.) Nor may an employer require an individual to be photographed or fingerprinted by any police department or other third party. The employer, not the applicant or employee, must pay the costs of photos and fingerprints. (Labor Code section 401.)

An employer cannot submit an applicant's or employee's fingerprints to local law enforcement officials in order to obtain criminal information (10 Opinions of the California Attorney General 19 (1947).), except in the situations listed later in this section.

Enforcement: File a complaint with the local district attorney. File a civil suit. An employer who gives an individual's photo to a third party for purposes that could be harmful to the employee, or who fails to take all reasonable steps to prevent a violation of these laws, is guilty of a misdemeanor. (Labor Code section 1052.)

In a civil suit against the employer, an applicant or employee may be awarded triple damages. (Labor Code section 1054.)

Exceptions: Certain employees are not covered by these protections:

- Workers in industries or professions that legally require federal or state licensing, such as the gaming industry or private patrol operators. (Business and Professions Code sections 19865, 7583.9.)
- Employees of banks and savings and loan companies. (Finance Code sections 550, 6525.)
- Anyone required to be fingerprinted by federal law (for example, securities brokers). (15 U.S. Code section 78q(f)(2).) (Labor Code section 1057.)
- Licensed childcare providers (including any adult who lives in a childcare facility or a home offering childcare). (Health and Safety Code sections 1596.871(a)–(c), (g)(c), (c)(1). 1596.603, 1597.54(c); 22 California Code of Regulations sections 101169(d)(13), 101170(b), (d).)
- Schoolteachers, employees in public recreation programs, and employees of entities doing business with school districts who have contact with students. (Education Code sections 44237, 10911.5, 44830, 44340, 45125.1.)

C. LIE DETECTOR TESTS

1. Right to Refuse to Take the Test

California law prohibits employers from requiring polygraph, lie detector, or similar tests as a condition of employment or continued employment. If an applicant or employee voluntarily submits to a lie detector test, the employer must, before the test begins, provide the individual with written notice about his rights, including the right to refuse to take the test. This law originally did not cover public employees, but the California Supreme Court struck down that exclusion. State and local public employees are now covered by the California law that prohibits employers from forcing employees to take lie detector or similar tests. (Labor Code section 432.2; *Long Beach City Employees Association v. City of Long Beach* (1986) 41 Cal.3d 937.) Additionally, California law prohibits polygraph testing of police officers and discipline of officers who refuse a test. (Public Safety Officers' Procedural Bill of Rights Act, Government Code section 3307.)

There is a similar federal law. (29 U.S. Code sections 2001–2009.) However, this law does not apply to federal, state, or local government employees. (29 U.S. Code section 2006(a).) It is unlawful under federal law for an employer to use, accept, refer to, or ask about the results of any lie detector test an applicant or employee has taken, without the employee's permission. An employer cannot dismiss, discipline, or discriminate against an individual for refusing to take a lie detector test. It is illegal for an employer to make even veiled threats or to punish an individual in any way for refusing to take the test or for exercising his rights under this law.

2. Restrictions if an Individual Consents to the Test

If an applicant or employee agrees voluntarily to take a lie detector test, his current or prospective employer must provide a written notice for the individual to read and sign. The notice must explain how the testing device works; how the testing results can be used; and the individual's rights under the law, including the right to refuse to take the test and not be punished for doing so, the right to stop the test at any time, and the right to be asked questions in a way that is not degrading or unnecessarily intrusive. (Labor Code section 432.2.) Before a polygraph test begins, the examiner must read the questions aloud to the test subject. It is illegal for the examiner to use any question that was not read to the test subject in advance. (29 U.S. Code section 2007(b)(2)(E).)

3. Potential Risks From Consenting to the Test

If, in spite of the law, an applicant or employee is asked to take a test, it is advisable for her to refuse, especially if she already has the job. There are serious risks involved in taking a polygraph test. If an employee agrees to the test and the machine operator decides that she is lying, the employer can fire the employee. Even if the individual is a job applicant, it is best not to take the test. It is illegal for an employer to suggest that only those who take the test will be hired. An employer who hires on that basis is guilty of a crime and may be sued. (Labor Code sections 432.2, 432.7(c), 433, 2698-2699.5; 29 U.S. Code section 2005(c).)

An applicant who chooses to take the test should pay careful attention to the questions asked. If asked illegal questions, the individual does not have to answer or take any action that may be against the law. (For a description of the kinds of questions a prospective employer cannot ask applicants, see Chapter 2.) Immediately after the test, the applicant should write down any improper questions to keep a record before they are forgotten.

Enforcement: File complaints with the U.S. Department of Labor, Wage and Hour Division; the Polygraph Examiners Board, California Department of Consumer Affairs; the labor commissioner or the local district attorney. A civil suit may also be filed in state court, based on violations of state law, but see Labor Code sections 2698-2699.5, which outline steps that must be taken prior to filing a lawsuit.

Exceptions: California law does not apply to federal employees. The federal Employee Polygraph Protection Act does not apply to federal, state, or local government employees. (29 U.S. Code section 2006(a).)

Under federal law, an employer can use a lie detector test in investigating an employment-related crime (for example, embezzlement or theft). Even so, at least forty-eight hours before the test, the employer must give the employee written notice that he is a suspect and must state when the test will be administered. Information that leads the employer to suspect that the employee was involved in the crime must be provable and reasonable (for instance, evidence in the case of a theft that the employee could have had access to the object stolen in the course of his job). (29 U.S. Code section 2006 (d).)

Under federal law, workers in certain industries are not protected from polygraph testing. Excluded workers are those in public safety and security-related work (for example, nuclear power or waste companies, public transportation, armored truck

services, security alarm companies) and drug manufacturers. (29 U.S. Code section 2006.)

Current legal protections regarding lie detector testing pertain only to mechanical devices that assess truth or falsehood by measuring physical responses. Some employers use paper-and-pencil tests to determine employee honesty (for example, requiring individuals to write responses to questionnaires or fill in the blanks). It is unclear whether the prohibition against use of "similar tests" in Labor Code section 432.2 will be interpreted to extend to such written honesty tests. An attorney should be consulted to determine the most up-to-date rulings on this subject if it arises.

D. VOICE STRESS ANALYSES AND VOICE PRINTS

A voice stress analysis or voice print uses a device that examines or records an individual's voice or voice patterns to determine whether he is telling the truth. No employer can use a voice stress analyzer on an individual without his permission. It is a crime to use this kind of device without the express written permission of the person analyzed. (Penal Code section 637.3.) Authorization must be obtained before any analysis is performed. It is also a crime for an employer to have, make, or use a voice print without an employee's express written authorization. The employer cannot require the employee to give permission for a voice stress analysis test or voice print. (Labor Code section 433.) In addition, an individual cannot be refused a job, fired, or disciplined for refusing to submit to these tests. (Labor Code section 432.2.)

Enforcement: File a complaint with the local district attorney. An employer who intentionally forces an individual to give permission for a voice print is guilty of a misdemeanor, punishable by a fine of up to $500. (Labor Code section 432.7(c).) A civil suit may also be filed. (Labor Code sections 432.7(c), 2699.3, 2699.5.)

Exceptions: This law does not apply to police officers in the course of their job duties or to federal, state, or local government agencies. (Labor Code section 432.2.) However, the California Supreme Court has extended the protections of Labor Code section 432.2 and Government Code section 3307 to other government employees. (*Long Beach City Employees Association v. City of Long Beach* (1986) 41 Cal.3d 937.)

E. SECRETLY RECORDED CONVERSATIONS

Under California law, it is illegal for an employer or any other person to record a confidential conversation without the consent of the person being recorded. (California Invasion of Privacy Act, Penal Code sections 630–637.3.) This is true even if the person doing the recording is taking part in the conversation. The law applies to face-to-face, as well as telephone, conversations. (Penal Code section 632a.)

To record a conversation without breaking the law, the recording party must announce the intention to record in advance of the conversation and obtain permission from all parties. It is customary, though not necessarily required, to include the request and agreement by the parties as part of the recording. This law applies to both employers and employees. If an individual wishes to record a conversation for his own purposes, he should include the other party's permission to do so as part of the recording.

See exceptions below related to the commission of a crime.

Federal law is less protective of privacy than state law. Generally, it will come into play in the employment context only for employees who work for the federal government. Federal law allows individuals to record their own conversations without notifying or obtaining consent from the other party, as long as the recording is not used to commit a crime (for example, blackmail). (18 U.S. Code section 2511(2)(d).)

Although an employee may want to record his employer or supervisor in order to prove a violation of law (for example, illegal discrimination), it is not worth the risk. The employee could lose his job for having done so without authorization.

A better strategy for the employee would be to speak with the other party only when accompanied by a reliable witness. Immediately after a suspect conversation, the employee and witness each should write down as many details as they can remember, especially direct quotes. The employee and witness should sign and date their own notes, and indicate the time the notes were written and transcribed (typed or rewritten more clearly), as well as the time the meeting took place and who was present. If the controversial conversation is by phone, the employee should take notes during the call and type or write them up clearly and immediately, before the details are forgotten. Even if the notes are not admissible in a legal proceeding, the information collected may help a lawyer assess whether to take the employee's case. It may also, in some situations, be useful to save the tapes on which voicemail messages are recorded.

Enforcement: File a complaint with the U.S. attorney general or local district attorney. File a civil suit. Under California law, an employee may be awarded damages, and the violator may be imprisoned in county jail or state prison for up to one year. (Penal Code section 631.)

Federal law also addresses the issue of liability for unauthorized eavesdropping or wiretapping. Federal penalties range from small to large fines and prescribe a range of terms of imprisonment. (47 U.S. Code section 605(e).) Violations may result in civil liability (through a lawsuit filed in federal court) or criminal complaint (filed through the U.S. attorney). The federal law on Wire and Electronic Communication Interception and Interception of Oral Communications establishes privacy rights with regard to actions of the government or communications service providers. (18 U.S. Code sections 2510 et seq.)

Exceptions: The California provisions do not apply to law enforcement agencies acting within their authority. (Penal Code section 633.) In California, an exception to the prohibition against recording conversations without permission also exists for a person participating in a conversation that she reasonably believes relates to the commission of any of the following crimes: extortion, kidnapping, bribery, or a felony involving violence against herself. In any of these cases, the person may record the conversation for the purpose of obtaining evidence. (Penal Code section 633.5.) Federal law enforcement officers are exempted from federal wiretapping statutes for certain purposes. (See 18 U.S. Code sections 2511 [permission to use wiretapping for purposes of foreign intelligence gathering], 2516 [procedure for requesting an order from the court allowing wiretapping for purposes of investigation], 2517 [permission for law enforcement officers to disclose information gleaned through wiretapping], 2518 [limitations on use of wire taps].)

F. EMAIL SURVEILLANCE

Employees should not assume that messages sent from computers or networks owned by their employers are private. The extent of privacy rights for emails sent from work or over employer networks varies, depending on a number of factors, including whether the employer has a policy notifying employees that their emails may be monitored. Most employers have adopted such policies in recent years. Although this area of the law is somewhat in flux, it is prudent to assume that the employer may see any message sent or received over the employer's email network. Federal laws specifically cover privacy rights regarding electronic and electronically stored messages, and limit the rights of Internet service providers and similar organizations to access the content of messages stored within or sent over their networks. However, their applicability to issues of employer access is not clear at this time. (18 U.S. Code sections 2510 et seq.)

> *Employees should not assume that messages sent from work computers are private.*

G. TEXT MESSAGES, TWITTER, AND BEYOND

The law is hard-pressed to keep up with the rapid expansion of new technologies, in terms of privacy rights. As of press time, the U.S. Supreme Court has agreed to hear a case involving the privacy rights of employees' text messages sent on pagers provided by an employer. (*City of Ontario v. Quon* (2009) 130 S.Ct 1011.) There is not yet any reported case involving Twitter. The principles, tests, and guidelines followed in other privacy cases will, most likely, be applied to future privacy rulings in these new forms of technology. Issues such as whether the employer is private or public, and whether the employee has a reasonable expectation of privacy, given the employer's technology policy, probably will be relevant factors. It is prudent, however, to assume that, in many situations, employers may get access to any messages sent or received on the employer's equipment or communication network.

H. VIDEO OR OTHER SURVEILLANCE IN CERTAIN WORK AREAS

No employer may use, or allow others to use, audio or video recording of an employee in a restroom, locker room, or room designated by the employer for changing clothes, unless such surveillance is authorized by a court order. (Labor Code section 435.) If an employer makes a recording in violation of this law, that recording may not be used by the employer for any purpose. This law applies to both public and private employees.

The prohibition against such surveillance also applies to employees wishing to video or record their employer or other employees. For more details, see the preceding section.

Enforcement: File a complaint with the local district attorney. File a civil suit. (Labor Code section 435.)

Exceptions: The law does not apply to employees of the federal government.

I. DRUG TESTING

1. General Considerations

Employers can require both job applicants and current employees to take drug tests. However, authority for such testing is limited by constitutional guidelines and restrictions. Generally, stricter limits apply to testing of current employees than apply to job applicants. (See discussion below.)

If an individual works in a job related to public safety (for example, a bus driver, commercial pilot, police officer, prison officer, or hazardous material handler), it is more likely that the employer will require periodic drug testing and that such testing will be legal. (See discussion below.) Under federal law, some employers are actually required to test employees for drug use. For example, the U.S. Department of Transportation requires drug testing of airline pilots and other transportation employees who hold jobs affecting public safety. The courts have upheld such testing against constitutional challenge. (See *Skinner v. Railway Labor Executives' Association* (1989) 489 U.S. 602; *National Treasury Employees Union v. Von Raab* (1989) 489 U.S. 656.) (For a list of U.S. Department of Transportation agencies that require drug testing and related details, see http://www.dot.gov/ost/dapc/oamanagers.html?inf.)

A public employer may not be able to require drug tests as a condition of a job offer if it cannot demonstrate a special need to screen for drugs. There must be a concrete danger in order for drug testing to be justified, absent specific cause for suspicion. Courts have looked at several considerations in determining whether it is permissible to require drug tests for job applicants. These include: (1) Is there a drug problem in the population with whom the applicant will be working? (2) Will the applicant be expected to confiscate or seize illegal drugs? (3) Will the applicant be involved in high-risk, safety-sensitive tasks? Tasks that have been held by the courts to be safety-sensitive include operation of airplanes, railroad cars, and heavy trucks; dealing with matters of national security; operating natural gas and liquefied gas pipelines; and transporting hazardous materials. In contrast, the position of a part-time library page was held by a court not to pose a substantial risk to public safety, and a requirement that a candidate for that job pass a pre-employment drug test was found not to be justified because a special need was not demonstrated. (*Lanier v. City of Woodburn* (9th Cir. 2008) 518 F.3d 1147.)

The California Drug-Free Workplace Act of 1990 (Government Code sections 8350–8357) requires entities performing services under a contract with a California state agency to certify that they will prohibit employee drug use. Similar requirements are imposed on federal contractors. (41 U.S. Code sections 701 et seq.) However, the existence of provisions authorizing an employer to demand a drug- and alcohol-free workplace is not to be interpreted as encouraging, prohibiting, or authorizing the use of drug testing or the making of employment decisions based on test results. (See 42 U.S. Code section 12114(d) [a related provision of the Americans With Disabilities Act].)

A recent court decision held that an employee could be fired for testing positive for marijuana, even though he had a prescription pursuant to California law and there was no showing of any adverse impact on his work performance. The employer successfully argued that its action was justified under federal law, which makes marijuana illegal, even with a doctor's prescription. (*Ross v. RagingWire Telecommunications, Inc.* (2008) 42 Cal.4th 920.)

2. Methods and Rules for Drug Testing

a. Methods

Drug testing can be done by analyzing an employee's urine, blood, hair, breath, saliva, or perspiration. Residue from past drug use may be found in hair as much as six months after the drug was last used.

b. Rules

i. For Job Applicants and New Hires

The California Supreme Court has held that applicants have less of a reasonable expectation of privacy than individuals who are already employed. (*Loder v. City of Glendale* (1997) 14 Cal.4th 846.) However, a recent federal court case has put that conclusion into question by failing to distinguish between the rights of job applicants and current employees, and finding that a prospective employer must have more than a generalized concern about drug use in society in order to justify testing job applicants when there is no particular reason for suspicion or concern about public safety issues at stake. (*Lanier v. City of Woodburn* (9th Cir. 2008) 518 F.3d 1147.) Both federal and California law are still somewhat unsettled as to whether the privacy expectations of job applicants are the same as those of current employees.

Based on California court cases, a pre-employment drug test requirement must meet three criteria to be valid. Under California's constitution:

- Applicants must be notified that drug testing will be part of the application process;
- The collection process must be minimally intrusive; and
- There must be procedural safeguards restricting access to the test results.
 (*Wilkinson v. Times Mirror Corp.* (1989) 215 Cal. App.3d 1034.)

In addition, under constitutional and statutory

prohibitions against discrimination, all job applicants must be treated similarly. (*Wilkinson v. Times Mirror Corp.* (1989) 215 Cal.App.3d 1034.) If an employer, for example, tested applicants of only one ethnic or racial group and not all applicants for similar positions, this practice would constitute illegal discrimination. (See Chapter 6 for a detailed discussion of prohibited discrimination in employment.)

If an employer requires an individual to sign an agreement to be tested as part of the application process, and the testing procedure and its use are lawful within the terms described above, the applicant may either submit to the test or decide not to apply for employment with that company or agency.

ii. For Current Employees

The California Supreme Court has held that requiring an individual to provide a urine sample intrudes on her reasonable expectation of privacy. (*Hill v. NCAA* (1994) 7 Cal.4th 1.) In addition, testing a urine sample has the potential to reveal a wide range of personal medical information that is outside the employer's area of legitimate interest. (*Hill v. NCAA* (1994) 7 Cal.4th 1.) Moreover, access to such information may be limited by other laws, such as those that protect against discrimination based on a disability.

For public employees or individuals subject to testing because of a governmentally imposed requirement, drug testing also affects employees' rights against unreasonable searches and seizures, protected by the Fourth Amendment to the U.S. Constitution. (*Loder v. City of Glendale* (1997) 14 Cal.4th 846.)

In the absence of a constitutionally valid law or regulation requiring drug testing in a particular job classification, there are two ways an employer can legally justify requiring a current employee to submit to a drug test. One is by demonstrating that (a) the employee's work is *safety-sensitive* in nature and (b) that the *employer's legitimate need* for testing *outweighs the employee's privacy interest*. The other is by demonstrating that (a) the employer has a particularized *reasonable suspicion of drug-related impairment* on the part of a specific employee, and (b), again, that the *employer's legitimate need* for the testing *outweighs the employee's privacy interests*.

If an employer demands that an employee submit to a drug test on the grounds that the employee's work is safety-sensitive in nature, and the employee subsequently challenges the demand and the matter results in a legal proceeding, two issues must be resolved. First, if there is a dispute regarding the nature of the employee's work (for example, what his specific job duties are), the issue is a factual one that must be decided by a jury. Once that determination is made, or if the parties do not dispute the nature of the employee's duties, then a court must decide whether the employee's job is safety-sensitive in nature. (*Luck v. Southern Pacific Transportation Co.* (1990) 218 Cal.App.3d 1.) If the job is safety-sensitive in nature, the constitutionality of the drug testing requirement is then determined by balancing the employer's asserted interest in conducting the test against the employee's constitutional privacy interest. An employee can rebut the employer's asserted need to conduct the test by demonstrating that less intrusive procedures (such as hand-eye coordination or alertness tests) could be used to satisfy the employer's legitimate interests.

If the employer requires a drug test based on a suspicion of drug-related impairment of a specific employee's job performance, then the employer's suspicion must be reasonably based on credible facts and the employer's interest in conducting the test must not be outweighed by the employee's privacy interests. (*Kraslawsky v. Upper Deck Co.* (1997) 56 Cal.App.4th 179.)

In *Hill v. NCAA* (1994) 7 Cal.4th 1, the California Supreme Court ruled that the right to privacy set forth in California Constitution, Article I, section 1, applies to both public and private employers. However, the court found that a closely monitored, random urinalysis drug test of college athletes, during which a nurse observed the athletes as they provided the required samples, did not violate their rights to privacy under California Constitution, Article 1, section 1. That decision relied heavily on the premise that athletes possess a reduced expectation of privacy in the locker room.

Employees, in contrast, possess a reasonable expectation that when they urinate they will not be visually observed by anyone. Thus, a blanket testing requirement for employees who do not occupy safety-sensitive positions has been ruled invalid if there is no particular reasonable cause for suspicion. The California Supreme Court has ruled that a suspicionless drug-testing prerequisite for employee *promotions* violated *public* employees' rights against unreasonable searches and seizures under the Fourth Amendment to the U.S. Constitution. (*Loder v. City of Glendale* (1997) 14 Cal.4th 846.) The California Supreme Court has not directly ruled on whether blanket suspicionless drug testing of *current* employees also violates the privacy protections in the California Constitution. However, a California appellate court (not the Supreme Court) has ruled that, under the privacy guarantees in California's state constitution, an employer must have a reasonable suspicion of drug-related impairment before it can require a current employee to undergo a drug test without impermissibly violating the employee's privacy rights. (*Kraslawsky v. Upper Deck Co.* (1997) 56 Cal.App.4th 179.) The law on this matter is in a state of flux at this time, both in California and on the federal level.

Even if an employer can legally justify requiring a drug test, the level of intrusiveness of the test remains constrained by employee privacy interests. Thus, an overly intrusive collection or analysis procedure may be constitutionally invalid even if the employer is entitled to require an employee to submit to some sort of drug screening procedure. For example, although a tester is permitted to take reasonable measures to ensure that the employee does not tamper with the test, some measures are too invasive and not permitted. For instance, the tester probably can require the employee to wear a hospital gown while being tested, can check that the sample is the right temperature, or can listen outside the stall while the employee provides a urine sample, but probably cannot watch as he does so.

The reasonableness of the employee's expectation of privacy is based on multiple factors, including the degree of the intrusion; the context, conduct, and circumstances surrounding the intrusion; the intruder's motives and objectives; the setting into which the intrusion is made; and the expectations of the individuals whose privacy is intruded upon (both their subjective expectations and the objective evidence of their expectations as revealed by their actions). (*Hill v. NCAA* (1994) 7 Cal.4th 1.)

Enforcement: File a civil lawsuit.

iii. *Effect of Laws Prohibiting Discrimination Based on Disability*

In California, employers with twenty-five or more employees must make reasonable efforts to accommodate any worker who is attending a drug or alcohol rehabilitation program and to safeguard the privacy of that employee. (Labor Code sections 1025, 1026.)

The federal Americans with Disabilities Act (ADA) excludes drug testing from the definition of "medical examination." (42 U.S. Code section 12114(d)(1).) ADA limitations on the use of medical tests generally do not apply to drug and alcohol testing. The act neither encourages nor discourages employer use of testing for illegal drugs — it is expressly neutral on the subject. (42 U.S. Code section 12114(d)(2).) Therefore, drug testing for illegal drugs is permitted under the act.

Prospective employers can inquire whether an applicant currently uses illegal drugs. (EEOC final enforcement guidance on pre-employment inquiries, at http://www.eeoc.gov/policy/docs/guidance-inquiries.html; 42 U.S. Code section 12114.) However, *addiction* is treated as a disability under the Americans with Disabilities Act once the individual is no longer using the illegal drug. Past addiction cannot lawfully be used as the basis for an employment decision, as long as the employee is no longer addicted to the illegal substance. (29 Code of Federal Regulations section 1630.3(b)(1), (2).)

If an applicant tests positive for illegal drugs, an employer is permitted to inquire regarding the individual's possible lawful use of the substance or other biomedical explanation for the result. (EEOC final enforcement guidance on pre-employment inquiries at http://www.eeoc.gov/policy/docs/guidance-inquiries.html.) This rule advances the ADA policy of protecting individuals who are using drugs for legitimate treatment of a disability as well as individuals who are regarded as being addicted to drugs but who are not currently using illegal drugs. Consistent with this policy, if an employee tests positive for methadone, the employer cannot terminate the employee for prior heroin addiction for which he is in rehabilitation, provided the employee is no longer using the illegal substance.

Under the ADA, during the prehiring process, prospective employers generally cannot inquire regarding use of medically prescribed drugs. (EEOC final enforcement guidance on pre-employment inquiries at http://www.eeoc.gov/policy/docs/guidance-inquiries.html.) If an employer's test for illegal drugs reveals an employee's use of prescribed medication, the employer must treat the discovered information as a confidential medical record. (29 Code of Federal Regulations section 1630.16(c).) For more on this issue, see Chapter 6.

Enforcement: File an EEOC charge or a civil lawsuit.

III. CONSUMER CREDIT REPORTS AND INVESTIGATIVE CONSUMER REPORTS

A. OVERVIEW

Employers are permitted to do consumer background checks on job applicants and employees. (Civil Code sections 1785.3(c)(2), 1785.11(a)(3)(B), 1786.12(d)(1); 15 U.S. Code sections 1681a(d)(1)(B), 1681b(a)(3)(B).) However, both state- and federal-level employee privacy protections limit employers' access to such information and place specific disclosure and prior consent requirements on employers who seek it. (Civil Code sections 1785–1786; 15 U.S. Code sections 1681 et seq.) Federal law establishes a basic standard for background checks, and California law builds on that standard.

A *consumer reporting agency* is any person who, for a fee or on a cooperative nonprofit basis, regularly collects or evaluates information about consumers for the purpose of providing consumer reports to third parties. (Civil Code sections 1785.3(d), 1786.2(d); 15 U.S. Code section 1681a(f).) There are two kinds of reports an employer may request from consumer reporting agencies regarding job applicants and employees: *consumer credit reports* and *investigative consumer reports*.

A *consumer credit report* is defined in California to include "any written, oral, or other communication of any information by a consumer credit reporting agency bearing on a consumer's credit worthiness, credit standing, or credit capacity, which is used… or collected…for the purpose of serving as a factor in establishing the consumer's eligibility for: (1) credit, or (2) employment purposes, or (3) home rental, or (4) other purposes authorized by law, including, in response to a court order, upon the written request of the consumer, for purposes of child or spousal support enforcement, licensing or other legitimate business purposes." (Civil Code sections 1785.3(c), 17.85.11; 15 U.S. Code section 1681a(d).)

Employment purposes means hiring, promotion, reassignment, or retention as an employee. (Civil Code section 1785.3(f).) Whether consumer credit reports can contain information regarding bankruptcies, civil lawsuits and judgments, unlawful detainer (tenant eviction) actions, tax liens, credit accounts placed in collections, and records of arrest and criminal prosecutions generally will depend on how old the action is and, in some instances, what the outcome was. (Civil Code section 1785.13(a); 15 U.S. Code section 1681c.)

An *investigative consumer report* is more detailed. In addition to the items included in a consumer credit report, it may include information regarding an individual's character, general reputation, personal characteristics, and "mode of living" obtained through interviews with people (for example, neighbors, friends, coworkers) (15 U.S. Code section 1681a(e).) or any other means. (Civil Code section 1786.2(c).) However, before a consumer reporting agency may disclose information gleaned from such interviews, either the information must be confirmed from an additional source with independent and direct knowledge of the information or the investigating agency must certify that the individual interviewed is the best possible source for such information. (Civil Code section 1786.18(d); 15 U.S. Code section 1681d(d)(4).)

The federal Fair Credit Reporting Act (FCRA) (15 U.S. Code sections 1681 et seq.) covers *all* reports by consumer reporting agencies, both credit reports and investigative consumer reports. However, investigative consumer reports are governed by stricter procedures and disclosure requirements than consumer credit reports.

B. RIGHTS OF CONSUMERS AND DUTIES OF REPORTING AGENCIES

Consumers have rights with regard to reports about them, and the reporting agencies have certain obligations to all consumers. Although these rights and duties apply generally to consumers and are not specifically labor law, employees should understand their rights since credit reports can be very important to employment.

1. Right to View File

A consumer has the right to see all the files and information that the consumer reporting agency collected about her, if the individual makes a written request. (Civil Code sections 1785.10(a), 1786.10(a); 15 U.S. Code section 1681g.) The sole exception is that an individual may be denied the names of people interviewed about her in the course of preparing an investigative consumer report. (Civil Code sections 1786.10(b), 1786.24(e); 15 U.S. Code section 1681g(a)(2).)

To view her files, the consumer must make a written request to the investigating agency at a reasonable time before she wishes to see the records. The agency must then allow the consumer to view her files during regular business hours or through reasonable means set by the agency. (Civil Code sections 1785.10, 1785.15, 1786.22; 15 U.S. Code section 1681h(b)(2).) In the case of investigative consumer reports, the consumer may require the agency to provide the information via certified mail upon written request accompanied by proper identification, or via summary over the telephone if requested by mail with proper identification. (Civil Code section 1786.22(b).) When the individual reviews the files, the agency must explain any coded information they contain. (Civil Code sections 1786.22(d), (e); 15 U.S. Code section 1681h(c).) The consumer also has the right to have one other person of her choice accompany her when viewing the files (for example, a union representative, attorney, friend, or relative). (Civil Code sections 1785.15(e), 1786.22(f); 15 U.S. Code section 1681h(d).)

The consumer is entitled to disclosure of the recipients of reports on the consumer provided by the agency. When an individual asks to see her credit reporting agency files, the law requires the agency to provide the following information. In the case of consumer credit reports:

- The name, address, and telephone number of every employer who has received a report on the individual in the past two years; and
- The name of every non-employer who has received a report on the individual in the past twelve months. (Civil Code section 1785.10(d); 15 U.S. Code section 1681g(a)(3).)

In the case of investigative consumer reports:

- The identity of every employer or insurer that has received a report within the previous three years and, upon request by the consumer, the

address and telephone number of the recipient; and
- The identity of any other party that received a report within the previous three years. (Civil Code section 1786.10(c).)

Whenever a consumer reporting agency provides an investigative consumer report to anyone other than the consumer, the agency must provide a copy of that report to the consumer upon request for at least two years after the date the report is provided to the person or entity that requested it. (Civil Code section 1786.11.)

As of January 1, 2010, the maximum an individual may be charged for a copy or summary of his file was $8. (Civil Code section 1785.17(a) (1); 15 U.S. Code section 1681j(f)(1)(A)(i).) Each year thereafter, increases to that fee may be authorized by the Federal Trade Commission. (15 U.S. Code section 1681j(f)(2).) The report must be given to a consumer without cost if the individual certifies in writing that she:

- Is unemployed and intends to apply for employment within the next sixty days;
- Is on public assistance;
- Believes that the agency's file contains inaccurate information because of fraud; or
- Has been denied employment, credit, insurance,

or rental housing because of the credit report within the past sixty days. (Civil Code sections 1785.17(b), 1786.26(b); 15 U.S. Code section 1681j(c).)

In addition, state and federal law require consumer reporting agencies to provide a consumer with a free copy of her investigative consumer report once each twelve-month period if the individual requests to see it. (Civil Code section 1786.26(c); 15 U.S. Code section 1681j(a).)

Credit reporting agencies must notify the individual, upon request, of his consumer credit score, the range of possible scores, all key factors that adversely affected the score (which cannot exceed four in number), the date the credit score was created, and the identity of the person or entity that created the score or possesses the files upon which the score was based. (Civil Code section 1785.15.1; 15 U.S. Code section 1681g(f).)

Enforcement: For both consumer credit reports and investigative consumer reports, file a civil suit for damages against the investigative reporting agency. (Civil Code sections 1785.31, 1786.50.)

2. Rights in Case of Identity Theft

Consumers who are the victims of identity theft have certain legal rights to obtain copies of their consumer credit reports, restrict access to their credit reports, and prevent placement of new, invalid information into their records, as follows.

a. Security Alert

If the consumer has a good-faith suspicion that he has been, or is about to become, a victim of identity theft, he may request a "fraud alert" or "security alert" from consumer reporting agencies that have a file on him. (Civil Code section 1785.11.1; 15 U.S. Code section 1681c-1(a)(1).) This alert must be placed within five days of the request and remain in place for at least ninety days unless the consumer requests to have it removed. The consumer may also request to have the alert renewed. (Civil Code sections 1785.11.1(e), (f).) The security alert notifies anyone who receives the credit report that the consumer's identity may have been used without consent to fraudulently obtain goods or services. (Civil Code section 1785.11.1(a).) Notice of the alert is to be sent to anyone receiving a copy of the consumer credit report. (Civil Code section 1785.11.1(b).) Anyone who receives the report must confirm the identity of the consumer before relying on the report. (Civil Code section 1785.11.1(g).)

An individual may obtain an identity theft report from the police or a DMV employee with peace officer status. A copy of this report may be submitted to credit reporting agencies to request additional protective measures.

When an identity theft report is submitted, the credit agency is required to provide the individual with up to twelve copies of his consumer credit report, at a rate of up to one copy a month for twelve months, free of charge. (Civil Code section 1785.15.3(b).)

Enforcement: File a civil lawsuit for reckless, willful, or intentional failure to place a security alert when requested. Damages may be awarded in an amount up to $2,500. (Civil Code section 1785.11.1(k).)

b. Block on Information Resulting From Identity Theft

If a consumer requests, the agency must block the reporting of information that resulted from an alleged identity theft. The consumer must submit proof of his identity as well as a copy of an identity theft report. He must identify information that resulted from an identity theft and submit a statement that the information is not related to any transaction he conducted. Within four business days of the request, the agency must block the reporting of the information. (15 U.S. Code section 1681c-2(a).)

c. Security Freeze

A consumer may also elect to have a "security freeze" placed on his account. The individual must request this in writing via certified mail. A security freeze prohibits a credit reporting agency from releasing the consumer's credit report or any information from it, other than that a freeze is in effect, without the express authorization of the consumer. (Civil Code section 1785.11.2(a).) The agency also is prohibited from changing the consumer's name, date of birth, Social Security Number, and address without sending written confirmation to the consumer within thirty days. (Civil Code section 1785.11.3(a).) If a consumer requests both a security alert and freeze on the account, the agency is required to provide the consumer, upon request, with a copy of the credit report at the end of the ninety-day period when the alert expires. (Civil Code section 1785.11.3(b).)

Upon written request by the consumer, the consumer reporting agency must place the freeze on the account within three business days and notify the consumer that the freeze is in effect within ten days of its placement on the account. (Civil Code section 1785.11.2(b), (c).) The consumer is provided a unique personal identification number or password, which is required for all requests for release of information from the individual's records. (Civil Code section 1785.11.2(c).)

When a freeze is in effect, a job applicant or employee whose credit records are subject to the freeze can authorize release of his credit report or information from it to a specified party or for a specified period of time. Thus, if an employer or prospective employer notifies the individual that it intends to seek a credit report for employment purposes, the applicant or employee must consent in writing to the employer (see discussion in section III.C.1., p. 51), and request that the consumer reporting agency remove the freeze for that employer.

When making a request to remove the freeze for a specific employer or other person or entity, the applicant or employee must provide:
• Proper identification;
• His identification number or password; and
• Accurate information regarding the party to whom the report is to be made available.
(Civil Code section 1785.11.2(d).)

Upon receipt of the proper information and request, the agency must provide the specified information to the employer within three business days. (Civil Code section 1785.11.2(e).)

If an individual applies for a job and does not request removal of the freeze for the prospective employer to access his credit records, the employer is authorized to treat the application as incomplete. (Civil Code section 1785.11.2(h).)

The freeze remains in effect indefinitely; it can only be removed or temporarily lifted upon request by the consumer, or if the freeze was procured based on a material misrepresentation of fact by the consumer. (Civil Code section 1785.11.2(g), (j).)

Consumer credit reporting agencies are permitted to charge a consumer $10 for each freeze, removal of the freeze, temporary lift of the freeze for a period of time, or temporary lift of the freeze for a specified party. (Civil Code section 1785.11.2(m).) The fees are not permitted

if the consumer is the victim of identity theft and submits a valid police report or DMV record alleging violation of Penal Code section 530.5 (identity theft).

Enforcement: File a civil lawsuit for unauthorized access to, or use of, information in a consumer's file. Damages are capped at $2,500 plus costs and attorney's fees. (Civil Code section 1785.19.) This is in addition to any other remedies provided by law. If other violations of a consumer's rights are alleged (such as the consumer agency's improper disclosure of credit information), damages for those violations would be in addition to damages for unlawful access to the consumer's information.

Exceptions: A freeze will not prevent access to an individual's credit information by an existing creditor; a state or local agency; a law enforcement agency; a trial court; a private collection agency acting pursuant to a court order, warrant, or subpoena; a child support agency acting under authority of state or federal law; the state Department of Health Care Services if investigating Medi-Cal fraud; the Franchise Tax Board if investigating or collecting delinquent taxes; an entity engaged in prescreening under the Fair Credit Reporting Act; or entities administering a credit monitoring service to which the consumer has subscribed. (Civil Code section 1785.11.2(k) (1-5).)

Despite a security freeze, a consumer reporting agency may disclose public record information obtained from an open public record to the extent otherwise permitted by law, though the agency may elect to apply a valid security freeze to the entire contents of a credit report. (Civil Code section 1785.11.2(n).)

For more information, see Chapter 12, section V., p. 299.

3. Right to Correct Inaccurate Information

It is illegal to provide a consumer credit reporting agency with information that the person knows is incomplete or inaccurate. As long as there is a dispute between the source of the information and the consumer regarding the completeness or accuracy of information on a specific transaction, the source must not provide the information to the agency without including a notice of the dispute. (Civil Code section 1785.25.)

Consumers have the right to correct inaccurate

CHAPTER 3

credit or investigation information about them contained in a reporting agency's files. To invoke this right, an individual must submit a written request to the agency with the inaccurate files. The request must explain the reason for the dispute, and include any information that supports the individual's version of the facts. Consumers who utilize this procedure should keep a copy of all correspondence sent or received.

Within thirty business days after receiving notice of the dispute, the agency must reinvestigate the facts and record the current status of the disputed information. The agency may end the reinvestigation if it determines that the dispute is frivolous or irrelevant. (Civil Code sections 1785.16, 1786.24; 15 U.S. Code section 1681i(a)(1), (3).)

If the agency decides to end the reinvestigation because the dispute is frivolous or irrelevant, it must notify the individual within five working days and provide an explanation of the reasons. Such a decision cannot be based simply on the fact that the agency's information differs from the consumer's version of the facts. (Civil Code sections 1785.16(b), (e), 1786.24(d), (h); 15 U.S. Code section 1681i(a)(3).)

If the agency conducts a reinvestigation because of an individual's complaint and finds either that the original version of the facts was wrong or that the information can no longer be verified, the agency must correct or delete the information in the file. Within five days of completing the reinvestigation, the agency must notify the consumer of the results in writing. The notice must include:

- A statement that the reinvestigation is completed;
- A copy of the report that is based on the consumer's revised file;
- A description of any changes in the report resulting from the reinvestigation;
- A description of any changes that the consumer asked for that were not made, and an explanation as to why;
- A notice of the consumer's right to request a description of the procedure used in the reinvestigation, right to add a statement of dispute to the file, and right to request that the agency notify past recipients of the report.

(Civil Code sections 1785.16(b), (d), 1786.24(e), (g); 15 U.S. Code section 1681i(a)(6).)

However, if the consumer's dispute was resolved by removing the disputed information from the credit report within three business days

of the agency's receipt of the request for removal, the notice requirements are simpler. A consumer credit agency need only provide written notice to the consumer that the information has been removed from the report within five business days. (Civil Code section 1785.16(j).) An investigative consumer reporting agency must provide the consumer with prompt notice of the deletion by telephone, written confirmation of the deletion, a copy of the investigative consumer report based on the revised file, and a statement of the consumer's right to request that the agency notify past recipients of the deletion. (Civil Code section 1786.24(m); 15 U.S. Code section 1681i(a)(8).)

If the agency refuses to investigate an individual's complaint, or if the individual is dissatisfied with the outcome of the reinvestigation, the individual has the right to insert a brief written statement in her file explaining the dispute and presenting her version of the facts. That statement must be included in any future reports. (Civil Code sections 1785.16(f), (g), 1786.24(i), (j); 15 U.S. Code section 1681i(b), (c).)

If information in the individual's file has been modified or deleted, or if the individual has submitted a statement of dispute, the individual should request that past recipients of reports be notified. Upon receiving such a request, the agency must send notification regarding the deletion or notation of disputed information to every employer who received a report within the preceding two years and to every non-employer who received one within the preceding six months. (Civil Code sections 1785.16(h), 1786.24(k); 15 U.S. Code section 1681i(d).)

The consumer has the right, after notification of the results of a reinvestigation, to request a description of the procedure used to determine the accuracy and completeness of the information, including the name, business address, and telephone number of the source of information contacted in connection with the reinvestigation. The agency must provide the description of the procedure within fifteen days after such a request. (Civil Code sections 1785.16(d), 1786.24(g); 15 U.S. Code section 1681i(a)(6), (7).) In the case of a consumer credit report, an individual may make a written request for correction from the source of the information that the consumer believes is inaccurate. If any reports are issued during this dispute, the consumer may require the agency to indicate on the reports those specific items. If the original source reporting the information finds the information to be inaccurate, the consumer may require the agency to delete or correct it. If, within ninety days, the consumer reporting agency does not receive any communication from the original source regarding the disputed information, the reporting agency must delete the information from its reports. In other words, the consumer's version wins by default. (Civil Code section 1785.30.) Consumers are advised to keep all correspondence and date-stamped envelopes to support their cases.

On its website, the Federal Trade Commission has a useful article on disputing errors in credit reports. Go to http://www.ftc.gov/bcp/edu/pubs/consumer/credit/cre21.shtm.

Enforcement and Exceptions: The section below covers enforcement and exceptions regarding the right to remove obsolete or prohibited information. The rules below apply equally to correcting inaccurate information, discussed above.

4. Right to Remove Obsolete or Prohibited Information

The law requires investigating agencies and credit agencies to remove obsolete information from consumer files. In addition, the law limits the kinds of information that agencies may include in their reports about an individual, even if that information is correct.

a. Credit Agency Files

No consumer credit reporting agency may include any of the following data in a consumer credit report:

- Bankruptcies more than ten years old;
- Lawsuits or legal judgments more than seven years old or complaints on which the statute of limitations (the legal period during which a party can still file suit) has expired. A local small claims court adviser or an attorney should be consulted to determine the applicable statute of limitations;
- Unlawful detainer (tenant eviction) actions unless the landlord won in court or the tenant (employee/applicant) signed a settlement agreement in which he consented to reporting the eviction;
- Paid tax liens more than seven years old;
- Uncollected debts more than seven years old;
- Conviction records more than seven years old;

- Any other negative information about the individual that is more than seven years old;
- Any medical information unless the individual has consented to the release of that information in writing.

(Civil Code section 1785.13; 15 U.S. Code sections 1681c(a), 1681b(g).)

Medical information must also be kept out of a consumer's file unless the consumer consents to its inclusion. (Civil Code section 1785.13(f).) For additional information on medical records, see Chapter 12.

A credit agency will include information on an individual's failure to pay overdue child or spousal support if the state Department of Social Services' automated system reports the failure to pay. If the information regarding failure to pay comes from any other source, the information must be verified by a federal, state, or local government agency before it can be included in an individual's credit report. (Civil Code section 1785.13(g); 15 U.S. Code section 1681s-1.)

b. Investigative Agency Files

No investigative consumer reporting agency can include any of the following data in investigative consumer reports:

- Bankruptcies more than ten years old;
- Lawsuits that were filed, and judgments that were paid, more than seven years prior to preparation of the report;
- Unpaid legal judgments more than ten years old;
- Unlawful detainer actions (tenant evictions) where the tenant (employee/applicant) prevailed or the matter was resolved by settlement agreement;
- Paid tax liens more than seven years old;
- Uncollected debts more than seven years old;
- Criminal arrest records, charging documents, and conviction records more than seven years after disposition, release, or parole; and records of arrest that did not result in a conviction (for additional information, see section VI., p. 58, on police records);
- Any other negative information about the individual that is more than seven years old; or
- Any medical information unless the consumer consents to the release of the report.

(Civil Code sections 1786.18, 1786.12(f); 15 U.S. Code section 1681b(g).)

Federal law is slightly more permissive. If the

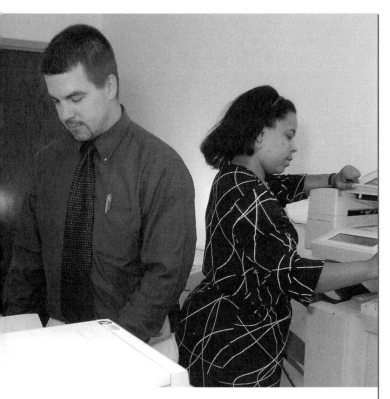

report is to be used in connection with a credit transaction or the underwriting of life insurance worth $150,000 or more, or with a job that pays $75,000 or more a year, an investigating agency may include information in its report regarding (1) bankruptcies more than ten years old; (2) lawsuits and records of arrest more than seven years old; (3) paid tax liens more than seven years old; (4) uncollected debts more than seven years old; and (5) any other negative information that is more than seven years old. (15 U.S. Code section 1681c(b).)

Any information collected from a source other than an official public record must have been confirmed through reasonable procedures from an additional source with independent knowledge of the information, or certified by the agency as having been obtained from the best possible source of the information. (Civil Code section 1785.18(b); 15 U.S. Code section 1681d(d)(4).)

See the previous section for a discussion on correcting inaccurate information. Consumers can also contact the Federal Trade Commission (FTC) to learn how to correct misinformation or delete obsolete information from their files. See Appendix B for FTC offices in California.

Enforcement: File a civil suit if a consumer suffers damages because of a report that contains false, seriously incomplete, or misleading information. Actual damages are recoverable for negligent violations. (Civil Code sections 1785.31, 1786.50; 15 U.S. Code section 1681o.) Actual and punitive damages are available if the violation was willful, and the consumer may also get injunctive relief (court orders) and attorney's fees. (Civil Code sections 1785.31, 1786.50; 15 U.S. Code section 1681n.)

A consumer who is injured by false information in a consumer credit report can also bring a lawsuit for defamation or invasion of privacy, but must prove that false information was furnished with malice or willful intent to injure him. (Civil Code section 1785.32.) To win damages in a lawsuit for defamation or invasion of privacy for injuries based on false information in an investigative consumer report (as opposed to a regular credit report), it is not necessary to show that the individual, informant, or investigative consumer reporting agency providing false information had malice or willful intent to cause injury. (Civil Code section 1786.50.) In the alternative, a lawsuit may be pursued in federal court under 15 U.S. Code sections 1681o and 1681n. However, pursuit of the federal lawsuit prevents pursuit of a lawsuit under the California Civil Code for similar types of actions. (Civil Code section 1786.52(a), (b).)

C. RIGHTS OF EMPLOYEES REGARDING REPORTS FOR EMPLOYMENT PURPOSES

In addition to the laws that protect consumers in general with regard to their credit reports, employees also have certain rights regarding the use of their credit reports for employment purposes. Employers may request consumer credit reports or investigative consumer reports regarding employees or applicants if the employer intends to use the information for permissible purposes (for example, employment purposes such as hiring, promotion, reassignment, or retention as an employee). (Civil Code sections 1785.11(a)(3)(B), 1785.14(a), 1786.12(d)(1); 15 U.S. Code section 1681b(a)(3)(B).) Investigative consumer reporting agencies are prohibited from providing an investigative consumer report unless they have a written agreement that the employer will only use the information for purposes permitted by law in Civil Code section 1786.12. (Civil Code section 1786.20(a); 15 U.S. Code section 1681b(f).)

Investigative consumer reporting agencies are prohibited from making an inquiry that would violate federal or state equal employment laws or regulations if made by the employer. (Civil Code section 1786.20(c); 15 U.S. Code section 1681a(o)(5)(B).)

1. Right to Notice

Certain steps must be taken before the reporting agency can release a consumer credit report or an investigative consumer report to an employer.

a. Consumer Credit Reports

Before the employer requests a consumer credit report, the employer must provide notice to the employee or job applicant of its intent to do so. (Civil Code section 1785.20.5.) The written notice must include the source of the report (for example, company or agency) and must contain a box that the applicant or employee can check to receive a copy of the report. If the individual checks the box, the employer must request a copy for him from the credit reporting agency. The applicant or employee must get his copy at no charge at the same time as the employer. (Civil Code section 1785.20.5(a).) The notice requirements pertaining to consumer credit reports apply only to individuals with mailing addresses in California. (Civil Code section 1785.6.)

California law does not require an applicant's or employee's consent before an employer or prospective employer obtains a copy of the individual's credit report. However, federal law imposes a prior-consent requirement. The Fair Credit Reporting Act (FCRA) requires that, before requesting a credit report, a prospective or current employer must notify an applicant or employee in writing that an investigation will be done and must receive the individual's written consent to the investigation prior to obtaining a copy of the report. (15 U.S. Code sections 1681a(o)(5)(A), 1681b(b)(2)(A)(ii).) The law provides that an employee's or applicant's credit status cannot be investigated for employment purposes without her consent. However, in practice, the right to refuse consent can be difficult to exercise. An employer may be able to require an employee to authorize the release of consumer reports as a condition of continued employment. A Federal Trade Commission advisory opinion letter expressed the view that the FCRA did not prohibit an employer

from taking an adverse action against an employee or applicant who refused to authorize the employer to obtain a consumer report. (Brinckerhoff-Fischel Letter, October 1, 1999, http://www.ftc.gov/os/statutes/fcra/fischel.shtm.) At least one court has held that an employer may fire an employee for refusing to give permission to obtain consumer reports for employment purposes. (*Kelchner v. Sycamore Manor Health Center* (M.D. Pa. 2004) 305 F.Supp.2d 429.)

Enforcement: In the case of a negligent violation, file a civil lawsuit to recover actual damages, court costs, and attorney's fees. (Civil Code section 1785.31; 15 U.S. Code section 1681o.) California law also provides for the recovery of lost wages and, if applicable, pain and suffering. (Civil Code section 1785.31.) In the case of a willful violation, both federal and California law provide stricter penalties. The U.S. Supreme Court recently held that a reckless disregard of a requirement of the FCRA qualifies as a willful violation. (*Safeco Insurance Co. of America v. Burr* (2007) 551 U.S. 47.) Under federal law, a consumer may file a civil lawsuit to recover (1) actual damages or damages of $100 to $1,000, or, in the case of a person (as opposed to a corporation) who obtains a consumer credit report under false pretenses or for an impermissible purpose, actual damages or $1,000, whichever is greater; (2) punitive damages; and (3) court costs and attorney's fees. (15 U.S. Code section 1681n.) Under California law, a consumer may file a civil lawsuit to recover actual damages, court costs, attorney's fees, lost wages, and, if applicable, pain and suffering, plus punitive damages of between $100 and $5,000, and an injunction (court order) to prevent or stop future violations of the consumer's rights. If a person (as opposed to a corporation) obtains a consumer credit report under false pretenses or for an impermissible purpose, the minimum damage award is set by law at $2,500. Class actions also may be brought. The party who brings the lawsuit (the plaintiff) and wins generally is entitled to an award of costs and attorney's fees. A plaintiff who obtains an injunction (court order) but obtains no award of damages is still entitled to attorney's fees. (Civil Code section 1785.31.)

b. Investigative Consumer Reports

For investigations regarding subjects *other than the employer's suspicion of wrongdoing* by the applicant or employee, the employer must notify the applicant or employee in writing before the investigative consumer report is procured. (Civil Code section 1786.16(a)(2)(B).) Federal law requires that the employee or applicant be notified within three days after the date that the report was first requested. (15 U.S. Code section 1681d(a)(1).) The notice must include the following information:

- The fact that there has been a request for an investigative consumer report;
- The name, address, and telephone number of the consumer reporting agency;
- The permissible purposes of the report;
- The fact that the report may include "information on the consumer's character, general reputation, personal characteristics, and mode of living"; and,
- The nature and scope of the investigation, along with a summary of Civil Code section 1786.22, which sets forth the consumer's right to inspect the files kept by the consumer reporting agency that supplies the investigative report. (Civil Code section 1786.16(a)(2)(B).)

Once the employee is provided such notice, the employer may obtain the report only if the employee gives his prior written consent. (Civil Code section 1786.16(a)(2)(C); 15 U.S. Code section 1681b(b)(2)(A)(ii).) However, the employer may be able to take an adverse employment action against an employee or applicant who refuses consent. See the previous section on consumer credit reports.

The employer also must provide the applicant with a box to check, either on the disclosure form (described above) or on a separate consent form, indicating that the employee wishes to receive a copy of the report. If the employee or applicant checks the box, the employer must forward to the employee, or contract with the consumer reporting agency to send the employee, a copy of the report within three business days of the date it was sent to the employer. (Civil Code section 1786.16(b)(1).)

Enforcement: Enforcement under federal law is the same for investigative consumer reports as for consumer credit reports. See the preceding section on enforcement. California law has different provisions for violations with regard to investigative consumer reports. A consumer may file a civil suit for actual damages or, except in the case of class actions, $10,000, whichever is greater; and for court costs and attorney's fees. If the violation was grossly negligent or willful, the consumer may recover punitive damages. (Civil Code section 1786.50.) A consumer may also seek damages for invasion of privacy or defamation. (Civil Code section 1786.52.)

Exceptions: None of the rules regarding notice, prior consent, or employee access to investigatory files apply to investigative consumer reports obtained by an employer as part of an investigation based on the employer's suspicion of misconduct by the employee. (Civil Code section 1786.16(c); 15 U.S. Code section 1681a(x).) Thus, employees may be prohibited from viewing such reports even if contained in their personnel files. For more information on personnel records, see Chapter 12.

c. Reports of Investigations Conducted Without Use of Consumer Reporting Agency

The employer may choose to perform an investigation on its own, without an outside investigative agency. Investigative reports regarding an individual's character, general reputation, personal characteristics, or mode of living, prepared for employment purposes, and based on public records without the use of an investigative consumer reporting agency are governed by different rules. (Civil Code section 1786.53.) "Public records" for purposes of such reports are "records documenting an arrest, indictment, conviction, civil judicial action, tax lien, or outstanding judgment." (Civil Code section 1786.53(a)(3).) Persons preparing such reports are required to provide to the employee or applicant a copy of the public records relied on within seven days *after* receipt of the information. (Civil Code section 1786.53(b)(1).)

The employer does not need to provide the employee or applicant with the same notice that is required for the use of reports from outside agencies. However, prospective employers who conduct such investigations are required to provide a box on the job application for the applicant to check if she wishes to waive the right to view the public records obtained by the employer. (Civil Code section 1786.53(b)(2).) If, without the use of an investigative reporting agency, an employer conducts an investigation based on a reasonable suspicion of wrongdoing by the employee, the employer can withhold disclosure of the public records until the investigation is complete. (Civil Code section 1786.53(b)(3).) Upon completion, the employer must provide the employee with a copy of the public records unless the employee waives her right to view them. (Civil Code section 1786.53(b)(3).)

Enforcement: Enforcement is the same as for violation of rights regarding investigative consumer reports. See the previous section.

2. Rights and Duties When a Negative Report Affects Employment Status

If the employer makes a negative employment decision (for example, refuses to hire an individual, or demotes, declines to promote, or fires an employee), then the employee has certain rights, as discussed in the following sections. The law prohibits employers from denying an applicant a job because of bankruptcy, a wage-earner protection plan, or debts discharged in bankruptcy. (11 U.S. Code section 525.) See Chapter 2.

a. Notice of Negative Outcome

Before any adverse employment action is taken based on a report, an employer must provide the employee with a copy of the report and a description of his rights. (15 U.S. Code section 1681b(b)(3).) After the adverse employment action is taken, an employer must promptly notify an applicant or employee in writing that he is denied a job, promotion, or transfer or is discharged based in whole or in part on information from a consumer credit report or investigative consumer report. The employer must tell the employee the name, address, and telephone number of the agency that did the investigation or credit check. (Civil Code sections 1785.20, 1785.20.5, 1786.40(a); 15 U.S. Code section 1681m(a).) The individual also must be notified in writing of his rights (such as the right to obtain a free copy of his credit report within sixty days from the agency identified by the employer, the right as a consumer to obtain a copy of his credit report from any other consumer credit reporting agency, and the right to dispute the accuracy or completeness of information contained in his credit report, as described in section III.B., p. 44). (Civil Code section 1785.20(a); 15 U.S. Code sections 1681b(b)(3), 1681m(a).)

There are fewer requirements for notice of negative outcome if the investigation concerns suspicion of misconduct or wrongdoing. (Civil Code section 1786.16(c); 15 U.S. Code section 1681a(x).) The federal Fair Credit Reporting Act requires disclosure of merely a summary of the report, not a copy of the report itself, and the employer need not disclose the sources used to prepare the report. (15 U.S. Code section 1681a(x)(2).)

b. Right to Inspect Investigation and Credit Records

In addition to an employee's right as a consumer to inspect files of consumer reporting agencies and investigative reporting agencies on the consumer, the employee also has certain rights to inspect personnel files of the employer on the employee. If an employer receives any reports, the employee or applicant has the right to inspect them at this workplace. Refusal to allow an individual to inspect those records is a misdemeanor punishable by a fine of at least $100 or up to thirty days in jail. (Labor Code sections 1198.5 (employee right to inspect personnel records) and 1199 (criminal sanctions for employer violations).) See Chapter 12 for more discussion on an employee's right to see his personnel file.

If an employer makes an adverse employment decision based on an investigative report prepared using public criminal history records but without the use of an investigative consumer agency, the public records relied on must be disclosed to the employee or applicant regardless of whether he waived the right to see them. (Civil Code section 1786.53(b)(4).)

Enforcement: File a civil suit for damages, punitive damages, and attorney's fees. (Civil Code sections 1785.31, 1786.50.) Alternatively, a civil suit for penalties and punitive damages may be brought under the Fair Credit Reporting Act. (15 U.S. Code sections 1681n, 1681o.) Pursuit of the federal lawsuit prevents pursuit of a lawsuit under the California Civil Code for similar types of actions. (Civil Code sections 1785.34, 1786.52.)

Exceptions: Certain investigations conducted solely by the employer's own staff may not be covered by the laws providing employees with the right to review employer personnel files on the employee. However, the employee does have the right to inspect reports from in-house investigations before that information is entered into his personnel file. (Civil Code section 1786.55; Labor Code section 1198.5.) Notwithstanding the foregoing, if an employer conducts its own investigation based on a reasonable suspicion of employee misconduct, relies on public criminal history records, and does not use a consumer investigative agency, the employer is permitted to withhold the public records relied on until the investigation is complete. (Civil Code section 1786.53(b)(3).) See Chapter 12 for more information on personnel files.

IV. RIGHT TO INSPECT AND CORRECT GOVERNMENT FILES

A. RIGHT TO INSPECT AND CORRECT STATE GOVERNMENT FILES

Individuals have the right under California law to see all state government files about themselves, whether or not they are state employees. (Civil Code section 1798.32.) This is important for a number of reasons related to employment. Incorrect information in government files may become a problem when applying for government jobs or private employment.

Upon request, every state agency must allow an individual to examine and copy all records kept about her. (Civil Code section 1798.34(a).) State agency files must be made available at a location near where the individual requesting to see them lives or must be mailed to her. (Civil Code section 1798.34(e).) An individual seeking to view her files also has the right to have a person of her choice help inspect the files. (Civil Code section 1798.34(b).) The state government agency that has the files must make them available within thirty days of the individual's request, unless the files are inactive ones kept in central storage, in which case the agency has sixty days to produce the files. (Civil Code sections 1798.34(a)–(b), 1798.66.)

All state files about an individual must, to the greatest extent possible, be accurate, relevant, timely, and complete. If any item in the files is inaccurate or incomplete, the individual may request in writing that the item be taken out of his file or corrected. The agency must respond within thirty business days after receipt of the request. (Civil Code sections 1798.35, 1798.36.) It is a good idea to keep a copy of all correspondence sent and received about one's government files. If the agency denies an individual's request to correct a file, the agency must give the reason for the denial and explain how to appeal the decision. (Civil Code section 1798.35(b).) If the individual appeals the refusal and the correction is still not made to the file, she may insert a statement into the file explaining her reasons for requesting the correction. (Civil Code section 1798.36.) That statement becomes a permanent part of the file. (Civil Code section 1798.37.)

State employees have the right to receive periodic performance appraisals or reports. A state employee has the right to receive a copy of such a report and to discuss it before it is placed in her file. (Government Code section 19992.2(a); 2 California Code of Regulations section 599.798.)

If a state employer intends to take negative employment action (for example, discipline, dismissal, demotion, or suspension against a state employee), the employer must first provide the employee with either personal or written notice containing all of the following:

- A statement of the nature of the adverse action;
- The effective date of the action;
- A statement of the reasons for the action in ordinary language;
- A statement advising the employee of her right to answer the notice orally or in writing; and
- A statement advising the employee of the time within which an appeal must be filed.

(Government Code sections 19570, 19574(a).)

The employee or her representative also has the right to review the evidence relied on and to interview all employees who might have information about the acts or omissions that form the basis for the employer's action. (Government Code section 19574.1(a).)

State employees also have the right to have letters of reprimand removed from their files and destroyed three years after the letters are issued. (Government Code section 19589.)

Exceptions: If the legal requirements previously outlined regarding state employee performance evaluation reports are in conflict with a collective bargaining agreement or memorandum of understanding ("MOU") negotiated between the state employer and a union representing a bargaining unit containing the state employee, the agreement or MOU prevails without further action by the Legislature. If the relevant MOU provision requires the expenditure of funds, it is not effective until the Legislature adopts the budget authorizing the expenditure. (Civil Code sections 19992.1-19992.4.)

Enforcement: A response to the notice of adverse action should be filed with the employer's governing board, and/or an appeal filed to the State Personnel Board (SPB); or use other procedures specified by the department or governing collective bargaining agreement or MOU. (For SPB procedures and forms, see http://www.spb.ca.gov/. See also Government Code sections 19570–19589. For an overview of laws governing public employees in California, see *California Public Sector Labor Relations*, edited by Kirsten L. Zerger, Peter A. Janiak, Janice E. Johnson, and William F. Kay, published by Matthew Bender; and the Pocket Guide Series published by California Public Employee Relations, which can be ordered at http://cper.berkeley.edu.)

B. RIGHT TO INSPECT AND COPY LOCAL GOVERNMENT FILES

The California Public Records Act and related provisions require local government agencies to allow individuals to inspect and copy files kept about them. (Government Code sections 6250–6259; Penal Code sections 13300–13305, 13320–13326.) If an individual works for a local government agency, he is also protected by the general personnel file access laws discussed in Chapter 12.

To access or obtain a copy of his local government files, an individual must submit a request to the agency that reasonably describes identifiable records. (Government Code section 6253.) The individual may inspect the records during office hours at the location of the agency's office or may request to have a copy of the records provided by mail. Reasonable fees may be charged for copying and transmitting the records. (Government Code section 6253.) The agency has a duty to assist the requesting party in properly formulating the records request and identifying the records sought. (Government Code section 6253.1.) It is a good idea to keep copies of any correspondence sent or received regarding a public records request. Within ten business days, the agency must either make the requested files available to the individual or notify him of the reasons it has declined to grant the request. (Government Code section 6253(c).) Under certain circumstances, the deadline for responding to a records request may be extended, upon notice to the requesting party.

Enforcement: File a civil court complaint against the local government agency for injunctive or declaratory relief to enforce the right to inspect and copy records. Plaintiffs who win their lawsuits are entitled to an award of court costs and attorney's fees. (Government Code sections 6258, 6259.)

Exceptions: Agencies do not have to reveal records concerning ongoing claims or lawsuits. Certain records regarding licensing, employment, or academic exams, and certain law enforcement records may also be excluded. Because a variety of exceptions apply to access to government files, parties interested in accessing local government files are advised to consult an attorney on this issue. (Government Code section 6276.)

C. UNION'S RIGHT TO INSPECT FILES ON EMPLOYEE'S BEHALF

A union generally can inspect the personnel file of an employee for the purpose of representing the employee. For more information on the union's right to inspect government files on behalf of employees, see Chapter 9.

V. RIGHT TO SEE AND CORRECT INSURANCE FILES

Individuals have the right to see and copy any records about them that are kept by an insurance company, broker, agent, or claim service. (Insurance Code section 791.08.) This right applies to work-related files, including disability, occupational illness or injury, sick leave, and Workers' Compensation, and to files kept by the agency, broker, or service that are not work-related.

To access these records, an individual must submit a written request. (Insurance Code section 791.08.) The insurer must respond to the request within thirty business days. (Insurance Code section 791.08(a).) If it is not convenient for the requesting party to inspect the files in person, she can request that copies be sent by mail. All the files must be provided in plain, easily understandable English; all codes used by the company must be translated into a form that a layperson can understand. (Insurance Code section 791.08(a) (2).) The response to a request for records must inform the requesting party of the nature and

substance of the recorded information, provide the name of anyone who has received a copy of the information within the past two years, and provide a summary of the procedures by which an individual may request correction, change, or deletion of recorded personal information. Medical information is to be provided either directly to the requesting party or to a medical professional she designates. Mental health records are to be provided to the requesting party only upon approval by the mental health professional who prepared them. (Insurance Code section 791.08(c).) (See further discussion at the end of this section.) The entity providing the information is permitted to charge a reasonable fee.

Individuals have the right to request that misinformation in their insurance files be corrected. (Insurance Code section 791.09.) When an individual inquires regarding information in his file, the company must tell him the procedure for making corrections. To correct misinformation in the file, the individual must send a written request detailing which information he would like to have amended, taken out, or corrected, and the reasons supporting the request. The company must respond to the request within thirty business days with notice either that it has corrected, changed, or removed the information as requested; or, that it has denied the request and its reasons for doing so. The company also must notify the requesting party that he has a right to file a statement of dispute regarding information that is not removed, amended, or corrected. (Insurance Code section 791.09(a).)

If the request for correction is granted, the company must notify the requesting party in writing, and must provide notice that a correction has been made to:

- Anyone the requesting individual identifies who may have received the inaccurate records within the previous two years;
- Any "insurance support organization" (which is defined to include any person or entity that prepares consumer credit reports or

investigative consumer reports [see Insurance Code section 791.02(l)(1)(A).]) if it has received the misinformation within the past seven years;

• Any insurance support organization that furnished the misinformation.

(Insurance Code section 791.09(b).)

If the company decides not to grant the request for correction, it must give the requesting party an explanation of its reasons and notify him of the right to submit a statement disputing the file information. (Insurance Code section 791.09(a).) If the individual continues to disagree and wants to explain why he disputes the contents of his file, he must be permitted to submit a brief statement setting forth what he believes is incorrect about the information and his reasons. (Insurance Code section 791.09(c).) This statement becomes a permanent part of the file. It must be provided to any future recipients of reports regarding the disputed information, as well as to the recipients who would have been notified if a correction had been made by the company, as discussed above. (Insurance Code section 791.09(d).) It is a good idea to keep this statement reasonable in length to make certain that it is read in its entirety by anyone who reviews the file in the future. As always, it is advisable to keep a copy of the statement and any responses received from the company.

Unless authorized by the employee, disability insurers are prohibited from releasing any information to an employer that would directly or indirectly indicate that an employee is receiving or has received services from a healthcare provider covered by the plan. This rule does not apply to Workers' Compensation insurers or to entities investigating allegations of insurance fraud. (Insurance Code section 791.27.)

It is a crime to knowingly and willfully obtain information about an individual under false pretenses from an insurance institution, agent, or insurance-support organization (such as a credit reporting agency or credit investigation agency). This crime is punishable by up to $10,000 in fines and up to a year in prison or both. (Insurance Code section 791.22.)

Enforcement: The insurance commissioner is empowered to investigate suspected violations of the rules governing disclosure of individuals' insurance records. If the insurance commissioner conducts such an investigation, it can order that any violation cease and desist. No matter how the commissioner rules, the insurance commissioner is required to notify the affected individual of the proceedings and their outcome. (Insurance Code sections 791.15, 791.16.) Upon a showing of good cause, the individual whose information is at issue can participate in proceedings against the company that allegedly violated the rules set forth in the law. (Insurance Code section 791.15(b).)

An individual who believes her rights regarding disclosure of her insurance records were violated and not remedied by the insurance commissioner can file a petition in court for review of the insurance commissioner's order or report. (Insurance Code section 791.18(a); Code of Civil Procedure section 1094.5.)

Regardless of whether or how the insurance commissioner rules regarding an alleged violation, an individual whose rights have been violated can file a civil court complaint for actual damages within two years of when the violation is, or should have been, discovered. (Insurance Code sections 791.18(c), 791.20(a), (b), (d).) The prevailing party is entitled to an award of court costs and attorney's fees. (Insurance Code section 791.20(c).) The statute prohibits suing for defamation or invasion of privacy unless it can be shown that the company furnished the information with malice or willful intent to injure the person. (Insurance Code section 791.21.)

If someone has willfully obtained insurance record information under false pretenses, the affected individual (the subject of the records) should contact the local district attorney's office.

Exceptions: As noted above, the insurance company does not have to release mental health records directly to the insured party. Instead, it may send the records to a medical professional named by that individual. The rationale is that reviewing one's own mental health records can be traumatic, and some people believe that doing so can interfere with proper treatment.

Mental health records are the only insurance records that the company can decide not to send directly to an insured party who requests them. (Health and Safety Code section 123115(b).) Individuals have the right to see all other information, including notes in the file stating what actions the insurer is taking regarding the insured's claims and its reasons for doing so.

VI. POLICE AND CRIMINAL INVESTIGATIONS AND RECORDS

A. LIMITS ON EMPLOYER'S ACCESS

Police records fall into several categories. Arrest records (sometimes called "rap sheets") contain, among other things, information on arrests which do not result in conviction. There are strong privacy protections regarding these records, since they may include information about arrests that resulted in acquittals or dropped charges, and other information that could be unfairly used against individuals. Some conviction records (indicating that a person was found guilty of a crime) may be accessed by employers or prospective employers, and others may be protected from disclosure in other situations. For a list of types of information that employers or prospective employers may not have access to, see section II.A., p. 36.

> ### There are strong privacy protections regarding "rap sheets."

Police records (involving information on all arrests) are generally confidential. It is a crime for an employer to obtain an applicant's or employee's police record or "rap sheet." (Labor Code section 432.7.) It is a crime for anyone to give an individual's arrest record to his employer (or prospective employer). It is a crime for an employer to possess such records. An employer cannot legally use an employee's or applicant's rap sheet to discipline or discharge, or refuse to hire or promote her. (Penal Code sections 11140–11143, 13302–13304.) Exceptions are made for certain employers. It is illegal for an employer to ask about the arrests and convictions listed above. The law applies to private sector and government employers, and covers both job applicants and current employees.

It is a crime for a police officer, law enforcement employee, or anyone else to disclose information with the intent to affect an individual's job status regarding an arrest or detention of, or other proceeding against, the individual that did not result in a conviction. (Labor Code section 432.7(g)(1).) Arrest information includes the fact that the individual was arrested or detained; the alleged offense for which she was arrested or detained; and the outcome of the arrest, detention, or charge that did not lead to a conviction. (Penal Code section 13125.)

No consumer investigative agency is permitted to report on convictions that are more than seven years old. (Civil Code section 1786.18(7).)

These rules apply to all information about arrests, whether from "rap sheets" or any other law enforcement source. (Penal Code sections 11105(b)(2), 11115, 11116.6, 11140–11143, 13151.1, 13152, 13301–13304; 11 California Code of Regulations sections 701, 720–724.)

If an employer nonetheless does ask a job applicant or employee questions or require answers about the kinds of arrests or detentions described above, the individual may be protected even if she responds with a lie. (Penal Code section 11116.5.) If an employer asks these questions and the individual replies truthfully, the answers cannot be used against her. (Labor Code section 432.7(a).)

Employers are forbidden to find out in any way about these arrests or convictions. An employer who nevertheless makes such discovery is prohibited from using that information against the applicant or employee. (Labor Code section 432.7(a).)

Enforcement: File a complaint with the state attorney general or local district attorney. File a civil suit. An employer who violates the law may be liable for actual damages or $200, whichever is greater, plus costs and attorney's fees. If the violation is intentional, the employer may be liable for triple damages, costs, and attorney's fees, and may be found criminally liable, with a penalty of six months in prison and a $500 fine. (Labor Code section 432.7(c).)

Exceptions: The Penal Code provides access to arrest records and other police and investigatory information to some government officials, including court personnel, the attorney general, district attorneys, police, probation officers, child support officials, tribal court personnel, public utilities whose workers will have access to individual residences, health department officials under certain circumstances, and those given specific access to information by particular laws. (Penal Code section 11105.)

B. DEFINITIONS OF LEGAL TERMS

For the purpose of this law, the following definitions apply:

- An arrest is a situation in which an individual was taken into custody by law enforcement personnel. (Penal Code section 834.) If the individual went to jail or the police station and was not allowed to leave, that was an arrest. An employer cannot ask any questions about arrests that did not lead to a conviction. However, this rule may not apply where there is a trial pending. (Labor Code section 432.7(a).)

- An arrest, detention, or proceeding that led to a conviction means an arrest in which the prosecutor filed formal charges against the individual and he pleaded either guilty or no contest (nolo contendere), or in which the charges resulted in a trial where a judge or jury found the individual guilty. An arrest not leading to conviction is one in which the defendant was found not guilty, the court dismissed charges, or the prosecutor dropped the charges. (Labor Code section 432.7(a).)

- A diversion program includes any program that an individual was referred to or participated in, whether before trial or after trial and conviction, and which results in the dismissal of charges. Diversion programs frequently require counseling, drug, or alcohol treatment; restitution to victims of the particular crime; or similar rehabilitative measures. An employer cannot ask about such a program or an arrest leading to participation in such a program, even if the individual participated following a trial and conviction. (Labor Code section 432.7(a).)

C. PROHIBITION AGAINST EMPLOYER'S ATTEMPT TO HAVE EMPLOYEE OR APPLICANT OBTAIN POLICE RECORD

As individuals, employees and job applicants have a right to see and copy their own police records. In most cases, however, it is unlawful for an employer to obtain police records about individuals. (Penal Code section 11125.) It is illegal for an employer to require an employee to take action to prove he does not have a police record, or to base hiring, firing, promotion, or transfer decisions even partly on an individual's obtaining his record. (Penal Code section 13326.)

Enforcement: File a complaint with the state attorney general or local district attorney. File a civil suit. An employer who violates the law may be liable for actual damages or $200, whichever is greater, plus costs and attorney's fees. If the violation is intentional, the employer may be liable for triple damages, costs, and attorney's fees, and may be found criminally liable, with a penalty of six months in prison and a $500 fine. (Labor Code section 432.7(c).)

D. RIGHTS WHEN ARRESTED

Although being arrested is traumatic and upsetting, it is important to remember that arrestees do have rights. If a person enters a guilty or no contest plea, thinking that he will avoid further cost and hassle, that person may be giving up important rights. He could be discharged from employment. Before pleading guilty or no contest to any charge, an individual who is arrested should discuss the issues with his lawyer.

E. RIGHTS REGARDING EXPUNGED RECORDS

Employers with five or more employees may not ask about convictions that have been legally sealed, expunged, eradicated, or dismissed. (2 California Code of Regulations section 7287.4(d)(1).)

Enforcement: File a complaint with the local district attorney. File a civil suit for actual damages, costs, and attorney's fees. An employer who violates the law intentionally is guilty of a misdemeanor. If the applicant or employee proves an intentional violation, she can be awarded attorney's fees plus triple damages. (Labor Code section 432.7(c).)

Exceptions: Most of these rules do not apply to job applicants or employees of criminal justice agencies. Railroad employees covered by the Railway Labor Act (45 U.S. Code sections 151–158.) are not covered by the Labor Code sections. However, the California Constitution and other statutes do protect people in these exempted categories. An attorney or union should be consulted about possible additional protections.

F. RIGHTS REGARDING EX-FELON OR PAROLE STATUS

It is in the interests of society that former offenders be able to earn a decent living. Therefore, the laws prohibit communicating ex-offender information for the purpose of depriving the former offender of work. These laws apply to ex-felons and to individuals who are on parole. (Penal Code sections 2947, 3058.)

This means that no one can inform a prospective employer of an individual's ex-felon status in an effort to keep him from being hired. No one can inform an individual's employer of that person's status in an effort to get that person fired or demoted. No one can inform someone else of the individual's status in the hope that the information will be passed on to an employer. Anyone who communicates any ex-felon information to an individual's employer with the intent of depriving him of work is in violation of the law. Intent may be inferred (assumed) from the person's actions. No one has the legal duty to contact an individual's employer and disclose the person's ex-felon status. Such an act is a crime.

The law applies to everyone, including people the ex-convict or parolee met in jail, police personnel, district attorneys, as well as court and probation personnel. The Department of Corrections may provide information concerning an individual's parole status to the police chief or sheriff where he resides while on parole, but not to an employer. Also, see section VI.C., p. 59.

Enforcement: File a complaint with the local district attorney. File a civil suit. Violation is a misdemeanor punishable by six months in jail or a $1,000 fine or both.

G. EMPLOYERS WITH ACCESS TO CERTAIN POLICE RECORDS

Special rules about an employer's access to police records apply to job applicants seeking positions in certain healthcare facilities; in agencies with supervisory or disciplinary power over minors; in community care facilities; in intermediate care facilities for the developmentally disabled; in public utilities; in government agencies; and in commercial banks, savings and loan associations, and credit unions. (Labor Code sections 432.7(b) et seq.)

Exceptions: Most of the rules outlined in this section do not apply to applicants for, or employees of, criminal justice agencies. (Labor Code section 432.7(e).) Applicants and employees covered by the Railway Labor Act are not covered by these Labor Code sections. (Labor Code section 434.)

1. Healthcare Facilities

If an employer is one of the following types of healthcare facilities, then individuals applying for specific positions (described below) may be asked about certain arrests. These facilities are: general acute-care hospitals, acute-care psychiatric hospitals, skilled-nursing hospitals, intermediate-care facilities, special hospitals for maternity or dentistry care, general acute-care and rehabilitation hospitals, and intermediate-care facilities for developmentally disabled individuals (whether the care is for rehabilitation or not). (Labor Code section 432.7(f); Health and Safety Code section 1250.)

a. Employees With Regular Access to Patients

If an individual applies for a position in which she will have regular access to patients, the employer can ask whether the applicant was ever arrested for one of the sex crimes listed in Penal Code section 290. The question is permitted even if the arrest did not result in a conviction. (The healthcare facility can also obtain police records about such arrests.) (Labor Code section 432.7(f)(1).)

b. Employees With Access to Drugs

If an individual applies for a position in which she will have access to medications, the employer can ask whether the applicant was ever arrested for one of the sex crimes listed in Penal Code section 290 or one of the drug crimes listed in Health and Safety Code section 11590. These questions are permitted even if the arrest did not result in a conviction. (Labor Code section 432.7(f)(1).) (The health facility can also obtain police records about such arrests.)

Healthcare facilities cannot ask applicants about any other kind of arrest that did not result in a conviction, regardless of the position for which the individual is applying, except about arrests for which the individual is out of custody on bail or on his own recognizance. (Labor Code section 432.7(a).)

Enforcement: File a complaint with the local district attorney. File a civil suit.

2. Agencies That Supervise or Discipline Minors

Human resource agencies, nonprofit corporations, and other organizations whose employees or volunteers have supervisory or disciplinary power over one or more children (under age eighteen) have the right, when an individual is applying for a position with such powers, to obtain the applicant's records of conviction, or of arrests pending adjudication, for offenses specified in Welfare and Institutions Code section 15660. These include sexual battery, sexual assault, sexual assault on a child, and elder abuse. (Penal Code section 11105.3(a), (f).) The state attorney general can also identify other employers whose employees or volunteers have this kind of power over minors and permit those employers to have access to convictions. (Penal Code section 11105.3(e).)

The state can legally send to these employers the records of a job applicant's convictions and commitments as a mentally disordered sex offender. The state must send the applicant a copy of the information it sends to the employer. (Penal Code section 11105.3(a).) The state cannot legally send any records of arrests that did not lead to conviction. See section VI.E., p. 59.

These employers are permitted to take applicants' fingerprints in order to conduct a criminal records check. (Penal Code section 11105.3(b).)

Enforcement: File a complaint with the state attorney general or local district attorney. File a civil suit.

3. Community Care and Daycare Facilities

Community care facilities are places that provide non-medical residential, day, or foster family care for mentally or physically disabled children or adults. Examples are daycare centers, foster homes, foster family agencies, and homes or treatment centers for the mentally or physically disabled. (Health and Safety Code section 1502.) The following are not considered community care facilities: residential care facilities for the elderly, healthcare facilities or clinics, juvenile placement facilities approved by the California Youth Authority or juvenile hall, child daycare facilities, religious facilities, school dormitories, homeless shelters, unsupervised group homes for addiction recovery, drug or alcohol abuse recovery or treatment facilities, homes of a relative caregiver, family homes, and various Native American facilities. (Health and Safety Code sections 1502.5, 1505.)

Most employees of community care facilities must submit their conviction records, fingerprints, and prior employment histories to their employers. Fingerprints are required prior to commencing employment. (Health and Safety Code section 1522(c).) The worker has to declare, under penalty of perjury, any criminal convictions. The law applies to all supervisory employees, all employees who reside in the facility, and all employees who provide client assistance in dressing, grooming, bathing, or personal hygiene, or who have frequent and routine contact with the clients. (Health and Safety Code section 1522(a), (b).)

4. Residential Eldercare Facilities

Separate rules apply to employees or applicants for employment with residential facilities for the elderly. (Health and Safety Code section 1502.5.)

If the worker has ever been convicted of a sex crime against a minor, child abuse, or a felony, the state requires termination of the employment. If the worker was convicted of another offense, either the worker must be terminated or the employer can seek an exemption. However, conviction of a minor traffic violation is not a ground for termination and does not require an exemption. (Health and Safety Code section 1569.17(c)(3).) The state Department of Social Services determines whether the worker can stay on the job until a decision is made about the exemption. (Health and Safety Code section 1569.17(c)(3).) The worker may appeal the decision by petitioning for a hearing under Health and Safety Code section 1569.58.

If an employer terminates an individual's employment or removes him from an eldercare facility based on notification of a criminal conviction, the individual can submit a request to the state Department of Social Services for an exemption from disqualification. (Health and Safety Code section 1569.17(c)(5).) The Department may issue an exemption if the individual's criminal history indicates she is of good character based on the age, seriousness, and frequency of the convictions. (Health and Safety Code section 1569.17(c)(4).) An exemption is permitted only if the Department has "substantial and convincing evidence" that the individual is of such good character as to justify granting the exemption. (Health and Safety Code section 1569(c)(4).)

However, individuals who have been convicted of any of the following crimes are not eligible to receive an exemption from the termination of employment (in other words, the employer cannot reinstate them):

- Assault with intent to commit a sexual act (Penal Code section 220);
- Sexual battery (Penal Code section 243.4);
- Rape with a foreign object (Penal Code section 264.1);
- Harm to or endangerment of a child (Penal Code section 273a);
- Cruel or inhuman corporal punishment (Penal Code section 273d);
- Lewd or lascivious act on a child (Penal Code section 288);
- Forcible sexual penetration (rape) (Penal code section 289);
- Sex crimes requiring registration as a sex offender (Penal Code section 290(a));
- Elder abuse (Penal Code section 368);
- Violent crimes against an individual that qualify as factors for enhancement of a sentence (resulting in a more severe sentence) in a future conviction (Penal Code section 667.5(c));
- Felony sexual exploitation by a physician, surgeon, psychotherapist, or alcohol or drug abuse counselor (Business and Professions Code section 729);
- Felony torture (Penal Code section 206);
- Felony carjacking (Penal Code section 215);
- Felony poisoning of food, pharmaceutical products, or water sources (Penal Code section 347(a));
- Felony brandishing of a firearm at a daycare or youth facility (Penal Code section 417(b)); or
- Felony arson (Penal Code section 451).

(Health and Safety Code section 1569.17(f)(1) (A), (B).)

If an individual's employment is terminated based on a record of criminal conviction, or the individual is denied an exemption and the decision is either affirmed on appeal under Health and Safety Code section 1569.58 or the individual does not appeal, she will not qualify for Unemployment Insurance. (Health and Safety Code section 1569.17(h).)

Enforcement: Appeal the termination or the decision to deny an exemption to the Community Care Licensing Division, California Department of Social Services (the agency that made the decision). (Health and Safety Code section 1569.58(c)(3), (4).) The procedures governing the hearing are set forth at Government Code sections 11500 et seq. If the appeal is unsuccessful, the department can reconsider its decision, upon its own motion or upon request by a party, within thirty days after the decision is mailed. (Government Code section 11521.) An employee may seek court review of the decision, but certain timelines apply, so the employee should not delay. (Government Code section 11523.) In addition, the employee may petition for reinstatement one year after the effective date of the decision affirming the termination or denial of exemption. (Health and Safety Code section 1569.58(h)(1)(B).)

Exceptions: The rules outlined above for residential eldercare facilities do not apply to employees who are not supervisors, are not residents of the facility, do not provide client assistance in grooming, or do not have frequent contact with the clients.

Fingerprints are not required of employees of most social rehabilitation facilities (residential facilities providing assistance, guidance, or counseling) unless they are supervisors or reside in the facility. But all employees of social rehabilitation facilities serving minors with alcohol- or drug-abuse problems must be fingerprinted.

5. Residential Facilities for the Developmentally Disabled

Agencies known as "intermediate care facilities/ developmentally disabled habilitative" provide twenty-four-hour care to, and help educate and train, developmentally disabled people. By law, this category of facilities includes only those with four to fifteen beds, no more than fifteen disabled clients, and medical certification that the clients do not need continuous skilled nursing care. (Health and Safety Code section 1250(e).)

Employees of these facilities must submit fingerprint cards within twenty days of being hired if they are either residents of the facility or "direct care staff." Direct care staff are all employees who are trained and experienced in the care of persons with developmental disabilities and who directly provide program and nursing services to

clients. Administrative and licensed personnel are considered direct care staff when they are providing program and nursing services directly to clients. (Health and Safety Code section 1265.5.)

When it receives the fingerprints, the state Department of Public Health checks the worker's conviction (not arrest) records. (Health and Safety Code section 1265.2.) If the employee has been convicted of a crime that is substantially related to his job duties, the department may require termination of the employment unless the Department of Public Health determines that the individual has been rehabilitated. (Health and Safety Code section 1265.2.)

Enforcement: Appeal the termination to the Licensing and Certification Division, state Department of Public Health (the agency that required the termination). If the appeal is unsuccessful, bring a civil suit. Be aware that the time limit for filing in court is short.

Exceptions: Workers who are not residents of the facility and not direct care staff are exempted from the fingerprint requirement.

6. Public Utilities

A public utility can receive certain police records about applicants for two types of jobs: those at nuclear power facilities and those that involve entry into private residences.

a. Jobs at Nuclear Power Stations

If an individual applies for a job that involves working on-site at a nuclear energy facility, the public utility employer can ask a local or state police agency for his police record. The police agency must give the applicant a copy of any information it gives to the utility. (Penal Code sections 11105(c) (1), 13300(c)(1).) The restrictions of Labor Code section 432.7 still apply: The police agency cannot lawfully send any information about arrests that did not lead to conviction (except arrests for which the individual is still awaiting trial), and the utility cannot consider non-conviction records.

Enforcement: File a complaint with the state attorney general or local district attorney. File a civil suit.

b. Jobs Involving Access to Residences

If an individual applies for, or already holds, a job that involves access to private residences, the public utility employer can request police records of the applicant's or employee's convictions (and arrests for which he is still awaiting trial). A local or state police agency that gives the utility these data must also give a copy to the applicant or employee. The utility must not disclose the information it receives. It must destroy all copies of this information not more than thirty days after the individual is granted or denied employment (or promotion or transfer). (If the applicant or employee is awaiting trial, the time limit for destruction of copies of this information is thirty days after the case is resolved.) (Penal Code sections 11105(c)(10), 13300(c)(9).)

The police agency cannot legally send any data about arrests that did not lead to conviction (except those for which the individual is still awaiting trial).

Enforcement: File a complaint with the state attorney general or local district attorney. File a civil suit. Violators are subject to six months in prison.

7. Government Agencies

Law enforcement agencies are permitted to ask job applicants about arrests and can obtain arrest and conviction records. (Labor Code section 432.7(e); Penal Code sections 11105(b)(1)–(7), (15), (c)(2), 13300(b)(1)–(7), (14), (c)(2).)

Other state and local agencies are in a different situation. They may receive and use conviction information only under certain circumstances. They can ask about or receive information about an arrest that did not lead to a conviction only if the individual is still awaiting trial on that arrest, and about drug or sex-crime arrests that did not result in a conviction only if the agency is one of the health facilities discussed in section IV.G., p. 60. The government agency has to specify in the legislation what kinds of convictions it is interested in and what will happen if an applicant has that kind of conviction.

There must be a reasonable connection between the type of conviction and the job sought. For example, the agency cannot lawfully refuse to hire a gardener because he was previously convicted of draft refusal. However, a public school district can legislate that its school bus drivers must not have been convicted of driving under the influence of intoxicants. The district has to pass a statute or ordinance specifying that it is permitted to seek records of any criminal convictions for driving under the influence of drugs or alcohol ("DUI"). After the law is passed, the district can ask driver applicants about such convictions and can obtain data about DUI convictions.

To obtain conviction records, the state or local agency's governing board must pass a statute, regulation, or ordinance that meets the following requirements:

- It must refer to specific criminal conduct. That is, it has to spell out the exact criminal law convictions on which it is seeking information.
- It must spell out the job requirements or exclusions that will be based on, or affected by, the specified convictions.
- The specified job duties, job requirements, or job exclusions must have a rational relationship to the specified convictions.

(Penal Code sections 11105(b)(10)–(11), 13300(b)(10)–(11).)

It is important to note that Labor Code section 432.7 still applies. The government cannot use any arrests that did not lead to conviction (arrests in which the case ended in a dismissal, a verdict of not-guilty, or communication by the district attorney to the arresting agency that the case will be dropped). State and local police agencies cannot send any information regarding such arrests. And

It is illegal to tell a prospective employer about someone's ex-felon status to keep that person from being hired.

the local and state government units cannot use any convictions except those that were spelled out in its statute or ordinance.

Enforcement: File a complaint with the state attorney general or local district attorney. File a civil suit.

8. Banking Institutions

Certain financial institutions may ask applicants and employees to allow their fingerprints to be taken so that it can check their theft-related conviction records. The following institutions are allowed to do this:

- Commercial banks (state or federal);
- Savings and loan associations (state or federal);
- Credit unions (state or federal).

These institutions can ask to obtain fingerprints and police records only if the individual is applying for employment and gives written consent. (Financial Code section 550.) If an individual refuses to give consent to the criminal background check, the employer may decide not to consider the person for the job.

The institution is forbidden to ask about arrests that did not lead to conviction, even if the applicant or employee gives written permission. All it can do is send the individual's fingerprints to a law enforcement agency, along with his written consent, and ask for information about convictions (or arrests for which the individual is still awaiting trial) for certain crimes.

The crimes include most property offenses: embezzlement, counterfeiting, burglary, bookmaking, robbery, forgery, computer fraud, credit card offenses, receiving stolen property, theft, obtaining funds by bad checks or false pretenses, and false financial statements. (Financial Code section 6525.)

The state cannot legally tell a financial institution about any arrests that did not lead to conviction.

Enforcement: File a complaint with the state attorney general or local district attorney. File a civil suit.

H. EFFECT OF CONVICTIONS ON JOBS THAT REQUIRE LICENSING OR CERTIFICATION

Many occupations require some form of state licensing or certification: school bus driver, security guard, teacher, and lawyer, among others. Criminal conviction records may affect employment as a result of the licensing process.

Often an employer will receive and process an individual's application for a license or certification. Some state government licensing agencies check police records. This process is controlled by various state and federal constitutional and statutory safeguards, but the licensing body is sometimes unaware of these provisions.

If a licensing agency refuses to license an individual, this may affect her job. Sometimes the agency tells the employer the reason for its refusal. If the reason is a criminal conviction that the licensing agency thinks is part of the individual's record, the individual has the following options:

- The individual may charge the agency or employer with violating the law if it did not have the right to check her police record. Individuals in this situation should consult their unions and lawyers. See the discussion of police records in section VI., p. 58.
- The individual may challenge the license refusal if the convictions on her record have nothing to do with the individual's ability to do the job. Again, consultation with a union and lawyer is advised.
- The individual may attempt to keep her job even though not licensed. The individual's union and lawyer should be consulted.

Enforcement: File a civil suit.

CHAPTER 3

WAGES AND HOURS

I. SCOPE OF THE CHAPTER

Wage and hour laws protect workers' rights to be fully paid for work performed. These laws, which are often called minimum labor standards, include the right to payment for all hours worked at no less than the minimum wage; the right to payment at an agreed rate equal to or higher than the minimum wage; the right to overtime pay for overtime work; the right to meal breaks and rest periods during the workday; the right to payment of all earned, unused vacation time when a job ends; and the right to be reimbursed for all necessary business expenses.

In addition, under these laws, employers are not allowed to make deductions from wages, except under very limited circumstances. These laws also establish deadlines for the payment of earned wages, both during employment and when a job ends.

There are exceptions to some of these laws, under which certain types of employees are classified as exempt from the coverage provided by the law. Many of the disputes in this area of law concern these exceptions. It is very common for employers to decide that an employee is not entitled to the protection of a wage and hour law when the employee actually is covered. Courts have usually decided that because these laws are designed to protect employees, exceptions to the law should be narrow.

Wage and hour requirements are found in both federal and state law, and sometimes in local ordinances. California law is more protective of workers than federal law. Employers must normally follow the law that provides the most protection to employees, so most of the discussion in this chapter will focus on workers' rights under state law.

Most rights discussed in this chapter can be enforced without an attorney by filing a complaint with the Office of the State Labor Commissioner (also known as the Division of Labor Standards Enforcement), which investigates and holds hearings on claims against employers for unpaid wages, penalties, or other compensation. Employees or groups of employees may also seek legal representation to file a lawsuit in court against an employer to recover amounts due. Amounts workers may recover include the wages that are owed, interest on the unpaid wages from the date such wages became due, penalties and other damages available under various laws, and, for cases that go to court, attorney's fees.

II. INDUSTRIAL WELFARE COMMISSION ORDERS AND EXEMPTIONS FROM THOSE ORDERS

A. DETERMINING WHICH WAGE ORDER APPLIES

Many of the rules governing wages and hours are established by California Industrial Welfare Commission (IWC) Orders. There are eighteen different wage orders. One order (IWC-MW) concerns the minimum wage and applies to the industries and occupations covered by the other wage orders. The other seventeen are more detailed orders covering specified industries and occupations.

If an employer is covered by a specific industry order, generally all of that employer's employees will come under that wage order, regardless of each employee's occupation. For example, IWC Order 1-2001 covers all employees whose employers are in the manufacturing industry. Large

numbers of employees are covered by IWC Order 5-2001, which covers all employees in the "public housekeeping" industry, including restaurants, and all other businesses that provide the public with food or lodging; IWC Order 7-2001, which covers retail stores and other businesses in the "mercantile industry"; and IWC Order 9-2001, which covers the transportation industry.

If an employer is not covered by a specific *industrywide* order, the employees of that employer are covered by the appropriate *occupational* order, such as IWC Order 4-2001, which covers a wide range of professional, technical, clerical, administrative, and mechanical occupations. Other occupational orders include IWC Order 14-2001, which covers agricultural employees; and IWC Order 16-2001, which covers on-site construction, drilling, logging, and mining workers.

Certain protections are found in all of the industry and occupational wage orders. Other protections are unique to specific orders. Likewise, certain exceptions are found in all wage orders, while other exceptions are found in one or more specific wage orders.

The Division of Labor Standards Enforcement (DLSE) pamphlet, "Which IWC Order," is helpful in determining which wage order applies. It is available at http://www.dir.ca.gov/dlse/WhichIWCOrderClassifications.PDF. All IWC orders are available at http://www.dir.ca.gov/iwc/wageorderindustries.htm.

B. EMPLOYEES WHO ARE COMPLETELY EXEMPT

An employee who is exempt from a wage order is not covered by its protections. IWC orders apply to all employees in California except for those types of employees who are specifically exempted. Some of these exemptions are total, so that no part of the IWC Order applies to the specified employees. Other exemptions are partial, so that the specified employees are exempt from only certain portions of the IWC Order.

The following categories of employees are totally exempt from the IWC orders: a parent, child, or spouse of the employer; a person under the age of eighteen employed as a babysitter for a minor child of the employer in the employer's home; persons participating in national service programs, such as AmeriCorps; persons employed by the federal government; and "outside salespersons" who spend more than half of their working time away from their employer's place of business selling goods or services. Salespersons who spend most of their working time at their employer's place of business, or delivering, installing, or repairing products for customers, do not fall under this exemption and are covered by the IWC wage orders. (*Ramirez v. Yosemite Water Co.* (1999) 20 Cal.4th 785.)

C. VOLUNTEERS AND INTERNS

Employees of non-profit humanitarian, public service, or religious organizations are covered by state wage and hour laws. However, bona fide volunteers for such organizations are generally not considered employees and are not covered by the IWC orders or the protections of the Labor Code. This exclusion for volunteers does not apply where the non-profit organization is operating a commercial enterprise (such as a restaurant or thrift store) that serves the public. Also, this exclusion does not extend to any private for-profit employers. Even when persons "volunteer" their services for a for-profit employer, those persons are covered by the IWC orders and the Labor Code.

Students working as interns may be exempt from California wage and hour requirements, if the internship is an essential part of an established course of an accredited school or institution approved to provide training for licensure or to qualify for a skilled vocation or profession. To be exempt, the student intern must not displace a regular employee, the internship must be supervised by a school or public agency, and the student must receive academic credit for the internship. If an intern is working for a for-profit private employer, the IWC requirements may apply if the employer benefits from the activities of the intern.

D. UNDOCUMENTED WORKERS

Undocumented workers are covered by the IWC wage orders and by all of the wage and hour provisions of the Labor Code. Regardless of the employee's immigration status, an employee is entitled to full payment of wages due for work performed. (Labor Code section 1171.5.)

E. THE "WHITE COLLAR" EXEMPTIONS

Persons employed in "executive, administrative or professional capacities" are exempt from most provisions in the IWC orders, including provisions governing overtime, recordkeeping (for example, on hours worked), and meal and rest periods. Employers often unlawfully misclassify employees as "exempt" managers, administrators, or professionals in order to avoid paying overtime. California law presumes that an employee is covered by wage and hour laws, and is therefore entitled to overtime. The burden rests with the employer to prove that an employee falls within an exempt category.

In order to be exempt as an executive, administrator, or professional, the employee must spend more than half of her working time performing duties that are considered exempt. The employee must be paid a monthly salary equal to at least twice the state minimum wage, based on a forty-hour week. Based on the state minimum wage of $8 an hour that went into effect on January 1, 2008, the required monthly salary must be more than $2,773.33 in order for an employee to be exempt from most wage protections as a "manager, administrator, or professional." This amount will increase whenever the minimum wage is raised. (The required minimum monthly salary was $2,340 from January 1, 2002, to December 31, 2006, and $2,600 from January 1 to December 31, 2007.) Employees paid by the hour for each hour worked, or by the day for each day worked, instead of receiving a set weekly or monthly salary, are not exempt from the IWC orders. They must be paid overtime compensation for all overtime hours worked. (Labor Code sections 515 and 1182.12.)

1. The "Salary Basis" Requirement

To be considered a salary, the compensation must be predetermined and paid regularly on a weekly or less frequent basis, and generally not be subject to reductions based on the changes in the quality or quantity of work performed. There are some exceptions to this requirement. Deductions in pay may be imposed for any full day in which the exempt employee is absent from work for personal reasons (for instance, unpaid sick leave or vacation time).

2. The "Primarily Engaged in Exempt Work" Requirement

Payment of the required salary is not itself enough to make an employee exempt from the requirements of the IWC orders. An employee will not be exempt from wage and hour protections unless, in addition to meeting the salary requirement, the employee spends more than half of his work time actually performing exempt work. This is called the "primarily engaged in" test. It applies to employees covered by the California laws and is more protective than federal law. Under the state test, the determination as to whether an employee is covered by, or exempt from, wage and hour laws is based on the *actual* activities performed by the employee, rather than on duties that may be listed on a job description. The state test does consider the "employer's realistic expectations and the realistic requirements of the job" as secondary factors, with less importance than the "first and foremost" factor — the amount of time the employee spends performing his various job tasks. (See, for example, IWC Order 4-2001 section 1.) (See subsections 4 through 7, below, for more information on specific activities that are considered to be exempt work.)

Employees who believe they may be misclassified as exempt should keep track of the amount of time spent performing their various work tasks during the course of a typical workweek, then compare the amount of time actually spent performing exempt tasks (for example, management tasks) and non-exempt tasks (for example, working on the sales floor). If the amount of time spent performing all of the exempt tasks does not exceed the amount of time spent performing all of the non-exempt tasks, the employee is entitled to overtime compensation for overtime hours worked.

3. The "Exercise of Discretion and Independent Judgment" Requirement

Administrative, executive, and professional exemptions are not applicable to any employee who does not "customarily and regularly exercise discretion and independent judgment." This means that the employee must have the authority to make independent choices, free from immediate supervision and direction, over matters of significance. To meet this test of the exemption, discretion and independent judgment must be exercised "normally and recurrently" in the day-to-day performance of the employee's job duties. An employee who merely applies his knowledge or skill in following required procedures is not considered to be exercising discretion and independent judgment. (Labor Code section 515(a).)

4. The "Executive" Exemption

The IWC orders set out additional requirements for the different categories of the "white collar" exemption. For example, the "executive" exemption will not apply unless the person manages the entire business for which he or she is employed, or manages a recognized department or subdivision of that business. Also, to qualify for this exemption, the employee must customarily and regularly supervise at least two full-time employees, or the equivalent number of part-time employees in the department the executive is managing.

Exempt executive work includes hiring, firing, or promoting employees; evaluating the work of employees; resolving employee grievances; directing and assigning work to employees; planning work for employees and determining the techniques, tools, and materials used in performing that work; and other work that is "directly and closely related to" these exempt tasks. A so-called "manager" who spends the majority of her work time doing the same work as her subordinates — such as providing service to customers, ringing up sales, getting merchandise from a storeroom, stocking shelves, keeping the premises clean, etc. — is not exempt. (IWC Orders section 1(A)(1); *Sav-On Drug Stores, Inc. v. Superior Court* (2004) 34 Cal.4th 319.)

5. The "Administrative" Exemption

"Administrative" work is defined as office or non-manual work of substantial importance that is directly related to the management policies or "general business operations" of the employer or the employer's customers. Administrative work is best understood as the business of running a business — for example, negotiating contracts for the business, or running the human resources department. Administrative work does not include sales or "production" work, that is, selling or producing the goods or services that the business produces or markets. (IWC Orders section 1(A)(2); *Eicher v. Advanced Business Integrators, Inc.* (2007) 151 Cal.App.4th 1363; *Bell v. Farmers Insurance Exchange* (2001) 87 Cal.App.4th 805.)

specified amount per hour for all hours worked in each workweek, or be paid a fixed salary not dependent on the number of hours worked. As of January 1, 2009, the hourly rate that must be paid (or exceeded) in order for an employee to be considered a "computer professional" and thereby exempt from most wage and hour laws is $37.94. The required annual rate is $79,500 per year, payable at not less than $6,587.50 per month. The compensation levels required for this exemption increase automatically every year on January 1, based on increases in the Consumer Price Index. The "computer professional" exemption is further limited to employees who spend most of their work time performing work that is intellectual and creative, and that requires the exercise of discretion and independent judgment, performing duties as a systems analyst or software or computer systems designer. This exemption does not apply to employees engaged in the operation of computers, or in manufacturing, repairing, or maintaining computer hardware, or in writing technical material such as product descriptions or set-up instructions, or in creating imagery for television or motion pictures. (Labor Code section 515.5.)

F. PUBLIC EMPLOYEES

Public employees are exempt from the IWC orders, except for provisions requiring payment of no less than the state minimum wage for all hours worked. State and local government and special district employees are covered by California minimum wage laws, but federal government employees are entirely exempt from the IWC orders. (IWC Orders section 1(B).)

G. TRUCK DRIVERS AND TAXI DRIVERS

Truck drivers and taxi drivers employed in the transportation industry are covered by IWC Order 9. However, drivers working for other industries (for example, drivers employed by department stores or grocery stores) are covered by the IWC order that regulates the specific industry in which the driver is employed.

Truck drivers whose hours of service are regulated by the U.S. Department of Transportation under the federal Motor Carrier Act, or by the California Highway Patrol under state law, are

6. The "Professional" Exemption

The "professional" exemption will not apply unless the employee is licensed or certified by the State of California as a lawyer, doctor, dentist, optometrist, architect, engineer, teacher, or accountant; or, the employee is primarily engaged in a so-called "learned or artistic profession." In order to be engaged in a "learned or artistic profession," an employee must be performing work that requires advanced knowledge that is generally acquired by a prolonged course of intellectual instruction and study (typically, through an advanced college degree in a specialized field of science or learning), or work that is original, creative, varied, and intellectual in character in a recognized field of artistic endeavor. Pharmacists and registered nurses are expressly excluded from the professional exemption. (IWC Orders section 1(A)(3); Labor Code sections 515(f) and 1186.)

7. The "Computer Professional" Exemption

As a result of recent changes in the law, certain computer software professionals may be exempt even if they are paid on an hourly, rather than a salary, basis. To fall under this exemption, the employee must be paid no less than a legally exempt from the overtime provisions of most of the IWC orders because they are subject to different hours-of-service requirements. Federal hours-of-service requirements apply to drivers of trucks that weigh between 10,000 and 26,000 pounds and are used to transport goods that have crossed or will cross state lines. (49 U.S. Code sections 31131 et seq.; 49 Code of Federal Regulations sections 395.1 et seq.) California law establishes specific hours-of-service requirements for drivers of trucks that have more than two axles or a manufacturer's gross vehicle weight rating of over 26,000 pounds. (Vehicle Code section 34500; 13 California Code of Regulations sections 1200 et seq.) With the exception of overtime provisions, these drivers are covered by all of the protections contained in the IWC orders, such as the right to payment of the minimum wage for all hours worked, the right to meal periods, etc. If the truck weighs less than 10,000 pounds and does not have more than two axles, hours of service are not regulated by state or federal transportation law, and the driver is entitled to overtime under all IWC orders except the one governing on-site construction, mining, and drilling (IWC Order 16). This exemption is found in section 3 of IWC Orders 1 through 15.

Taxi drivers are exempt from the overtime provisions of the applicable IWC order. However, taxi drivers are covered by all of the other IWC order protections. There is no exemption from overtime provisions for limousine drivers, or for airport or hotel shuttle drivers. (IWC Order 9-2001 section 3(M).)

H. THE COMMISSION SALES EXEMPTION

Employees who work in the retail sales industry, or for real estate brokers, insurance companies, banks, mortgage lenders, or other financial institutions, whose earnings exceed one-and-one-half times the minimum wage, and who earn at least half of their compensation from commissions, are exempt from overtime provisions under the applicable IWC orders. These compensation requirements must be met each workweek. The exemption cannot apply, and overtime must be paid, for any workweek in which the employee is not paid more than one-and-one-half times the minimum wage for every hour worked. In addition, the employee must spend at least half of her work time engaged in the sale of goods or services, and the "commissions" must be based on a percentage of the price of goods or services sold. Time spent producing, delivering, or installing the goods, making repairs, or otherwise providing the service that is sold, does not count as sales time. Compensation that is not tied to a percent of the price of the goods or services that are sold, such as a fixed-dollar-amount bonus for meeting specified sales goals, is not considered to be a "commission." (IWC Orders 4-2001 section 3(D); *Ramirez v. Yosemite Water Co.* (1999) 20 Cal.4th 785; *Keyes Motors, Inc. v. DLSE* (1987) 197 Cal.App.3d 557.)

I. PERSONAL ATTENDANTS

A "personal attendant" is defined as an employee who is employed to supervise, feed, or dress a child or person who needs supervision as a result of advanced age or physical or mental disability, where no more than 20 percent of the person's work time is spent performing other activities. If the employee spends more than 20 percent of his work time performing household cleaning chores, the employee will not be considered to be a "personal attendant," and will not be fall under the exemptions described below. (IWC Order 5-2001 sections 2(N), 3(E); IWC Order 15-2001 sections 1(B), 2(J).)

"Personal attendants" must be paid at least the minimum wage, but are exempt from overtime, meal and rest period requirements, and various other provisions of the applicable IWC order when they work in a private household and are employed by either a private householder or a third-party employer recognized in the healthcare industry.

Personal attendants employed by nonprofit employers operating nursing homes, or board and care or similar facilities, are covered by all IWC provisions except overtime.

J. EMPLOYEES COVERED BY COLLECTIVE BARGAINING AGREEMENTS

Employees who are covered by a collective bargaining agreement (a union contract) that provides "premium pay" (defined as any amount greater than the regular rate of pay) for all overtime hours worked and a regular hourly pay rate of not less than 30 percent more than the state minimum wage are exempt from state overtime requirements.

This exemption is limited to overtime; all other requirements of the wage orders apply to workers covered by a collective bargaining agreement. (Labor Code section 514.)

For these exempt employees, overtime hours are set by the collective bargaining agreement rather than state law. As a result, these employees may not be entitled to daily overtime for hours worked in excess of eight in one workday, as required under state law. However, the collective bargaining agreement itself may require daily overtime pay. Such a requirement in a collective bargaining agreement would be enforceable through the grievance procedure established by the agreement. Federal overtime law, however, has no exemption for collective bargaining agreements. These employees would still have the right to overtime compensation for hours worked in excess of forty in one workweek, as required under the Fair Labor Standards Act.

III. WAGES

Wages are defined as "all amounts for labor performed by employees of every description, whether the amount is fixed or ascertained by the standard of time, task, piece, commission basis, or other method of calculation." (Labor Code section 200.) The employer's obligation to pay wages for work performed is founded upon contract (an agreement, either written or oral, between the employer and the employee or the employee's bargaining representative), or law (Labor Code and IWC order provisions that set out various minimum labor standards that cannot be undercut, like the minimum wage, overtime, etc.), or both.

Once wages are earned, the employee is entitled to receive them in full, except for amounts deducted in accordance with the strict laws that prohibit deductions except for those that are expressly allowed under these laws (see section V., p. 92). Earned wages must be paid no later than the time required under the Labor Code for regular wage payments to currently employed workers, or for final wage payments at the end of employment (see section VII., p. 97). Once an employer agrees to pay a certain wage rate, the employer cannot then retroactively lower that rate for work already performed.

A. THE MINIMUM WAGE

Both California and the federal government set a minimum wage. The state minimum wage can never fall below the federal minimum wage. Over the past two decades, California's state minimum wage has almost always been greater than the federal minimum wage. Almost all California employees who are covered by the federal minimum wage are also covered by the state minimum wage. In that situation, the higher state rate applies. The state minimum wage covers both private and public employees, except for federal government employees. (Labor Code section 1182(b); IWC Orders sections 1(B) and 4.)

California's minimum wage has been $8 an hour since January 1, 2008, when it was increased from $7.50 an hour, the amount it had been set at throughout 2007. From January 1, 2002, to December 31, 2006, the state minimum wage was $6.75 an hour. (Labor Code sections 1182.12, 1197; IWC Minimum Wage Orders MW-2001, MW-2007; IWC Orders section 4.) To check the current minimum wage, go to http://www.dir.ca.gov/dlse/faq_minimumwage.htm. See section III.D., p. 78, for more information on cities that have living wage ordinances, which may be higher than minimum wage.

Any agreement to work for less than the minimum wage is unenforceable. If an employee files a lawsuit to recover unpaid minimum wages, the employee will be entitled to recover the unpaid minimum wages, interest on the unpaid wages, attorney's fees, and "liquidated damages," an additional amount equal to the unpaid minimum wages plus interest. (Labor Code sections 1194, 1194.2.)

California law allows for the payment of sub-minimum wages, or wages below the minimum wage, to the following categories of workers:

- *Learners.* During the first 160 hours of employment in an occupation in which the worker has no previous or related experience, a worker classified as a learner may be paid 85 percent of the state minimum wage rounded to the nearest nickel. This exception to the minimum wage is very narrowly applied. (IWC Orders section 4(A).) Just because a worker is in the first 160 hours of employment for a particular employer does not automatically make him a learner.

- *Workers with severe mental or physical disabilities.* The labor commissioner is authorized to issue special licenses authorizing the employment of disabled workers for less than the state minimum wage, and to issue licenses to employers to employ such workers. Any such licenses must be renewed annually. (Labor Code sections 1191 and 1191.5; IWC Orders section 6.)
- *Apprentices.* State minimum wage provisions do not apply to some registered apprentices enrolled in apprenticeship programs approved by the California Division of Apprenticeship Standards. (Labor Code section 1192; IWC Orders section 4(D).)

B. PAYMENT OF NO LESS THAN THE MINIMUM WAGE FOR ALL "HOURS WORKED"

The requirement to pay no less than the minimum wage for all hours worked applies regardless of how the employee is compensated. For employees who are not paid a fixed hourly wage, including employees paid by piece rate or commission, the minimum wage operates as a floor, below which their compensation cannot drop, regardless of low productivity or low sales totals. Compliance with the minimum wage is generally tested on a pay period basis.

California law is strict with regard to hourly paid employees. They must be paid no less than the state minimum wage for each and every separate hour, or part of every hour, worked. Even when the employer or the employment agreement designates certain time or work activities as "non-productive" or unpaid (such as travel time or time spent completing job-related paperwork), time spent engaged in those activities must be paid at no less than the minimum wage if the time constitutes "hours worked." (*Armenta v. Osmose, Inc.* (2005) 135 Cal.App.4th 314.)

Under state law, "hours worked" is defined as any time during which the employee is required to work, or is "suffered or permitted to work," or is subject to the control of the employer. An employee is "suffered or permitted to work" if the employer (or any of the employer's managers or supervisors) knows or reasonably should know that the employee is working. An employee is subject to the employer's control when the employee is required to be at a specified location at or during a specified period of time or to participate in a specified event. (*Morillion v. Royal Packing Co.* (2000) 22 Cal.4th 575.)

These requirements apply no matter where the work is performed, even when work is performed at the employee's home. If the employer knows or has reason to believe that the work is being performed, it must be counted as "hours worked." Even if an employer has a policy that prohibits overtime or "after hours" work without authorization, the employer must pay for any such time worked without authorization if the employer knew or reasonably should have known that work was then being performed. (29 Code of Federal Regulations sections 785.12–785.13.)

The employer is obligated to maintain accurate time records showing all hours worked. With regard to the time that work starts and ends each day, employers are usually permitted to "round off" the employee's time to the nearest five minutes, or tenth of an hour, or quarter hour. However, rounding is not permitted unless it operates in a neutral manner, under which the employee is as likely to "gain" time as he is to "lose" time, so that over a period of time, the employee is fully compensated for all hours worked. Rounding that operates in a manner that more often than not benefits the employer (like consistently "rounding down") will be disallowed. Rounding to more than the nearest quarter hour is not allowed. (Labor Code section 1174(d); IWC Orders section 7; 29 Code of Federal Regulations section 785.48.)

1. "On-Call" or "Stand-By" Time

a. Away From the Employer's Premises

Even though the employee is away from the employer's premises, an employee on-call or on stand-by status has to remain available to report to work upon demand. An employee may have a right to payment for on-call or stand-by time, depending first on whether the employer has agreed to pay for such time. Even if the employer has not agreed to pay for on-call time, the employee may have a right to payment as a matter of law, based on the degree to which the employee is subject to the employer's control, and the degree to which the employee is prevented from effectively using stand-by time for her own purposes. Factors considered include geographic restrictions, the required response time, the ability of the employee to refuse to respond to a call or to trade off the obligation to

CHAPTER 4

respond with other employees, and the frequency of calls. A requirement that the worker call in at specific times or carry a cell phone in case of emergency does not make the time compensable if the employee is generally free to engage in personal pursuits during this on-call time. (*Berry v. County of Sonoma* (9th Cir. 1994) 30 F.3d 1174.)

b. At the Employer's Premises

All time during which an employee is on-call or on stand-by status while restricted to the employer's premises, during which the employee is required to merely wait for some event to occur to which the employee is then required to respond, is considered "hours worked." (*Armour & Co. v. Wantock* (1944) 323 U.S. 126; *Skidmore v. Swift & Co.* (1944) 323 U.S. 134.) There is an exception to this for employees covered by IWC Order 5 who are required to reside on the premises (such as motel managers), as they may be required to remain on-call throughout the day and need only be paid for time actually carrying out their assigned duties. (IWC Order 5-2001 section 2(K); *Brewer v. Patel* (1993) 20 Cal.App.4th 1017.)

> *Undocumented workers are covered by the wage and hour provisions of the Labor Code.*

An employer can establish an hourly rate for on-call time that is lower than the hourly rate for normal on-duty time. However, if the on-call time constitutes "hours worked" under state law, the on-call time must be paid at or above the state minimum wage level. Whether or not the employee must be paid for on-call time, once the employee responds to a call or reports to work, she must be paid for such work time at the appropriate on-duty time hourly rate.

2. Payment for Travel Time

Time spent traveling at the employer's request or in connection with the performance of work is considered "hours worked," and is subject to payment of at least the minimum wage, unless it is considered "de minimus" (which means minimal time). An employee who performs work at two or more different worksites (for the same employer) during the workday must be compensated for time spent traveling between worksites. The employee must be paid for all time spent traveling from the first location at which he is required to report to any other location where work is performed, and must be paid for travel time returning from the final worksite to the location where he was required to report at the start of the workday. An employee who is required to travel out-of-town for business reasons must be paid for the time spent traveling out-of-town, except for time sleeping and for time spent in purely social activities not required by the job.

If the employee is paid an hourly rate in excess of the state minimum wage, travel time must be paid at that higher contractual rate. However, if the employer has previously established a travel rate that is lower than the hourly rate for normal on-duty time, travel time can be paid at this lower rate. However, travel time can never be paid at less than the minimum wage.

In general, employees are not required to be compensated for commute time during which the employee travels between home and the normal fixed worksite. But if the employer requires its employees to use employer-provided transportation and prohibits the employees from commuting using their own methods of transportation, this "compulsory travel time" is counted as compensable "hours worked." (*Morillion v. Royal Packing Co.* (2000) 22 Cal.4th 575.)

3. Time Spent Changing Into and Out of Required Uniforms and Other Preparatory or Concluding Tasks

Time spent by employees on the employer's premises, changing into and out of required uniforms, special clothing, or safety gear, is considered "hours worked" for which employees must be paid. Likewise, time spent waiting for such uniforms or gear to be distributed or collected, and time spent walking from the changing area to the work area, are considered "hours worked" under state law.

Time spent doing "preliminary" set-up work (for example, loading a truck with construction tools) and necessary tasks at the end of the day (for example, cleaning up or unloading a truck, or completing job-related paperwork) are also considered "hours worked" under state law.

State law is much more protective of workers than federal law with regard to time spent performing these sorts of tasks. (*Morillion v. Royal Packing Co.* (2000) 22 Cal.4th 575.)

4. Sleep Time

Under certain conditions, an employee is considered to be working even though some of her time is spent sleeping. Employees working shifts of fewer than twenty-four consecutive hours must be paid for all of those hours (except for off-duty meal periods, described at section IV.A., p. 90), including time during which the employee is permitted to sleep at the worksite. If the employee works a shift of twenty-four consecutive hours or longer, a regularly scheduled sleep period of up to eight hours may be uncompensated if the employer provides adequate sleeping facilities and if the employee receives at least five hours of uninterrupted sleep. If the employee does not receive at least five consecutive hours of uninterrupted sleep, she must be paid for the entire sleep period. Even if the employee receives five or more hours of uninterrupted sleep, the employee must be compensated for any time that the employee works during the scheduled sleep period. (*Aguilar v. Association for Retarded Citizens* (1991) 234 Cal.App.3d 21; 29 Code of Federal Regulations sections 785.20–785.22.)

There are two exceptions to these sleep time requirements:

- Employees covered by IWC Order 5 (public housekeeping) who are required to live on the premises (such as motel managers), and who are not employed in the healthcare industry, need to be compensated only for time actually spent performing assigned duties, so sleep time is not required to be paid regardless of the extent to which it is interrupted by work duties. (IWC Order 5-2001 section 2(K).)
- Live-in employees in private households are generally entitled to twelve consecutive hours free of duty during each workday, including

sleep time, and these employees need only be compensated for time actually spent working during these twelve off-duty hours, regardless of the extent to which the off-duty time is interrupted. (IWC Order 15-2001 section 3(A).)

5. Time Spent Attending Required Meetings or Training Programs

Time spent attending meetings or training programs is counted as "hours worked" unless all of the following apply:

- Attendance is voluntary. (Attendance is not voluntary if it is required or if the employee is led to believe that non-attendance could have a negative effect on his employment.)
- Attendance is outside regular work hours.
- The meeting or training program is not directly related to the employee's job.
- The employee does not perform any productive work while attending the meeting or training program.

(29 Code of Federal Regulations sections 785.27–785.31.)

6. Time Spent Resolving Grievances With the Employer

For workers not covered by a collective bargaining agreement, time spent resolving grievances with the employer, during a time when the employee is required to be at work, counts as working hours for which the employee must be paid. For workers covered by a collective bargaining agreement, the agreement or the practice of the parties will determine whether the time is compensable. (29 Code of Federal Regulations section 785.42.)

7. Time Spent Attending Civic or Charitable Functions

Time spent working for civic or charitable purposes at the employer's request, or under the employer's direction and control, or while the employee is required to be at the employer's premises, constitutes hours worked, regardless of whether this work is performed outside the employee's normal work hours. But time spent voluntarily, outside normal work hours, engaged in such functions does not constitute hours worked. (29 Code of Federal Regulations section 785.44.)

C. FORM OF PAYMENT OF MINIMUM WAGE

IWC Order MW prohibits employers from applying any non-wage forms of payment as a credit or offset against the minimum wage. In California, an employer cannot reduce an employee's wages by the amount of tips received by that worker. Nor can an employer use the value of an employer-provided benefit, such as health insurance, as a credit against the minimum wage. However, a credit can be taken against the minimum wage where an employer provides an employee with meals or lodging, and there is a prior voluntary written agreement between that employer and employee, or the employee's union, authorizing the credit for meals or lodging actually provided. But this credit for meals and lodging cannot exceed the amounts permitted under the IWC orders. Under the orders, as of January 1, 2008, the meal credit cannot exceed $2.90 for breakfast, $3.97 for lunch, and $5.34 for dinner; the lodging credit cannot exceed $31.06 a week for a shared room, $37.63 for a room not shared, $451.89 a month for an apartment unless a couple is employed, in which case the employer can only credit a total of $668.46 a month from both employees together. Deductions cannot be made for meals not received or lodging not used.

If, as a condition of employment, the employee is required to reside at the worksite or in any property owned or controlled by the employer, that employee, regardless of how much he is paid, cannot be charged rent in excess of the amounts allowed by the IWC as credits against the minimum wage. (See, for example, IWC Order 4-2001 section 10.)

Exception: An employer may charge a resident apartment manager up to two-thirds of the fair market rental value of the apartment supplied to the manager, if no credit for the apartment is used to meet the employer's minimum wage obligation to the manager, and provided that this arrangement is set out in a voluntary written agreement. (Labor Code section 1182.8.)

The ability of an employer to take credit against payment over the minimum wage level depends on the terms of the particular employment agreement or collective bargaining agreement and requires the employee's consent in most instances. See section V., p. 92, for more information on other lawful and unlawful deductions.

D. LIVING WAGE ORDINANCES — REQUIRED PAYMENTS ABOVE THE STATE MINIMUM WAGE

Some California cities and counties have adopted local ordinances, which require the payment of a "living wage" or local minimum wage above the state minimum, for work covered by the local ordinance.

San Francisco adopted an ordinance that took effect in February 2004, which set a minimum wage of $8.50 an hour for all work performed within the geographic boundaries of San Francisco. This ordinance provides for automatic annual increases in the city's minimum wage tied to changes in the Consumer Price Index. Effective January 1, 2009, the San Francisco minimum wage increased to $9.79 per hour.

Other local ordinances have more limited application, covering only those employers with service contracts under which they receive payments from a public entity, employers that lease land from a public entity, or employers that receive public subsidies. Counties that have adopted these sorts of ordinances include Los Angeles, Marin, and Ventura. Cities that have adopted these sorts of ordinances include Los Angeles, Oakland, San Jose, Sacramento, Pasadena, Berkeley, Ventura, Oxnard, Santa Barbara, West Hollywood, Santa Monica, Irvine, Santa Cruz, Watsonville, Hayward, San Fernando, Sebastopol, Sonoma, Fairfax, and San Francisco (which provides for a higher rate than the city's general minimum wage ordinance).

In many cases, violations of these local ordinances may be investigated and prosecuted by the local enforcement agency established for that purpose. Alternatively, violations can be prosecuted directly by the affected employees through the filing of a lawsuit. At present, the state labor commissioner will not enforce local living wage ordinances.

E. PREVAILING WAGES ON PUBLIC WORKS PROJECTS

State law requires payment of no less than the applicable "prevailing wage," which is a special kind of minimum wage, for all work performed by privately employed workers in the performance of a public works contract. Public works include construction, alteration, demolition, installation, and repair work that is paid in whole or part out of state or local funds. The prevailing wage is an hourly wage rate plus an amount for benefits. If the employer does not provide benefits, the amount for benefits established by the prevailing wage determination must be paid to the worker. The prevailing wage rate is based on the type of craft and the local area where the work is performed. Prevailing wage determinations are typically issued twice a year by the California Department of Industrial Relations. Information about prevailing wages can be obtained from the Department of Industrial Relations at http://www.dir.ca.gov/DLSR/PWD/index.htm.

Non-union employers sometimes unlawfully pay less than the required prevailing wage to their employees working on public works projects. Typical schemes to pay less than the required prevailing wage include falsely claiming that the work performed consisted of lower paying unskilled trades work rather than higher paid skilled trades work, "shaving hours" (under-reporting hours worked), and unlawfully requiring employees to "kick back" a portion of their wages to the employer. In kickback situations, the employer first issues paychecks that appear to be full payment of the required prevailing wage. The workers sign these checks, then pay money back to the employer in an attempt to disguise the kickback.

Contractors and subcontractors performing work on a prevailing wage job are required to keep accurate payroll records, which must to be made available for inspection and copying at the contractor's principal office, at the office of the public entity that awarded the contract, and at the local office of the Division of Labor Standards Enforcement. (Labor Code section 1776.) It is a criminal violation for an employer to falsely produce payroll records that contain inaccurate information about the work performed, hours worked, or wages paid, or to take any portion of an employee's prevailing wages. Information about these kinds of violations can be reported to the county district attorney for the filing of criminal charges. (Labor Code sections 1777, 1778.) Employees concerned about their own liability in a situation involving kickbacks (for instance, a bookkeeper forced by an employer to falsify records) should consult an attorney. See Chapter 11 for more information.

The Division of Labor Standards Enforcement (DLSE) recently issued a Public Works Manual that is a useful source of information about prevailing wage laws and DLSE enforcement policies. It is available online at http://www.dir.ca.gov/dlse/PWManualCombined.pdf.

The Public Works Compliance Network provides another helpful computer-based resource, available through an annual subscription, at http://publicworkscompliance.com.

Enforcement: Complaints about prevailing wage underpayments can be filed with the Office of the Labor Commissioner's Public Works Unit. Information on how to file such a complaint is available at http://www.dir.ca.gov/dlse/HowToFilePWComplaint.htm. The labor commissioner may investigate the complaint, and when wages are owed, may issue a Civil Wage and Penalty Assessment against the contractor and/or sub-contractor to collect unpaid wages and penalties. Alternatively, the employees can file a lawsuit against the contractor and/or sub-contractor to recover the wages and other amounts owed. (Labor Code sections 1720–1815; *Road Sprinkler Fitters Local Union No. 669 v. G & G Fire Sprinklers, Inc.* (2002) 102 Cal.App.4th 765.)

F. RIGHT TO FULL PAYMENT OF PROMISED WAGES

When an employer agrees or promises to pay a certain wage, and the employee then performs work, there is a binding, enforceable contract. It is illegal for the employer to actually pay less than the agreed upon rate. (Labor Code sections 221–223.)

An agreement between an employer and an individual employee for wages above the minimum wage may be changed at any time, so long as the original agreement was not for a specified period of time (in which case the wage rate may not be changed during that period). The new rate cannot apply to work already performed. By continuing to work for the employer following notification of a change in the wage rate, the employee is assumed to have accepted the new wage rate. (*DiGiacinto v. Ameriko-Omserv Corp.* (1997) 59 Cal.App.4th 629.)

In the non-union workplace, employees can enforce a promise to pay wages higher than the minimum wage by filing a wage claim with the labor commissioner, or by filing a lawsuit in state court. Workers covered by union collective bargaining agreements must enforce their union contract claims through the union grievance procedure. However, unionized employees can use the labor commissioner or the state courts to enforce claims that are based on state law, and that do not require interpretation of a union contract, like claims for payment of minimum wages for hours worked for which the employee received less than the minimum wage, claims for reimbursement of business expenses, or penalties for late payment of final wages. (*Livadas v. Bradshaw* (1994) 512 U.S. 107.)

G. MISREPRESENTATIONS OF PAY PROHIBITED

It is illegal for an employer, or for anyone acting on behalf of an employer, to knowingly make a false statement about wages, benefits, or the availability of work, in any advertisement or offer of employment. A person harmed by this kind of false statement can file a lawsuit for twice the actual damages suffered as a result of the misrepresentation. Also, the local district attorney can file criminal misdemeanor charges against the person who made the false statement. (Labor Code sections 970–972.)

H. RIGHT TO EQUAL PAY FOR EQUAL WORK

Under state and federal equal pay acts, an employer is not allowed to pay an employee less than other workers simply on account of the employee's sex. However, the employer can pay a wage differential based on seniority, merit, quantity or quality of work, bona fide differences in job tasks, or any other lawful factor other than the employee's sex.

Enforcement: File a complaint with the federal Equal Employment Opportunity Commission or the state Division of Labor Standards Enforcement; or file a civil suit. A civil suit to recover wages could result in double back pay with interest, plus attorney's fees, but it must be filed within two years after the incident occurs, unless the violation was willful. In the case of willful violations (done on purpose), the deadline is extended to three years. (Labor Code section 1197.5.)

An employee may proceed with an equal pay claim under both state and federal law. If the employee recovers amounts due in both the state and federal claims, the lesser amount recovered must be returned to the employer.

(Labor Code sections 98.7, 1197.5, 1199.5; Government Code section 12940; 2 California Code of Regulations section 7291.1; 29 U.S. Code section 206(d); 42 U.S. Code section 2000e-2; 29 Code of Federal Regulations sections 1620.1 et seq.)

I. TIPS AND SERVICE CHARGES

Any tip left by a customer is the sole property of the employee or employees to whom it was paid, given, or left, whether paid in cash or on a credit card. For tips paid by credit card, the employer must pay the employees the full amount of the designated tip no later than the next regular payday following the date the customer authorized the credit card payment. It is also illegal for an employer to deduct, collect, or take any portion of an employee's tips (including the cost of processing tips made by credit card). The employer cannot credit any part of a tip against an employee's wages. No matter how much an employee makes in tips, in California employees are still entitled to full payment of the minimum wage (or the contractually agreed upon wage rate, if higher than the minimum wage), and any applicable overtime payments.

An employer may require involuntary tip pooling or sharing among employees who provide service to customers. Under a mandatory tip pooling arrangement, all or part of the total tips are grouped together and then distributed to employees under a formula created by the employer. There have been many court cases on whether certain categories of employees who do not provide "direct table service" (such as cooks and dishwashers) may be included in the distribution of shared tips. Some court decisions indicate that shared tips must be limited to those employees who provide "direct table service." Other decisions hold that shared tips may be distributed to any employee in the "chain of service," including employees who may never interact with any customer (for instance, cooks).

It is never legal for supervisors, managers, or owners to take any part of the tips given to or left

for non-supervisory employees. However, shift supervisors who spend the overwhelming amount of their work time serving customers may share in the pooled tips placed by customers into tip jars when the tips were left for all employees who provided service to the customers.

Service charges are different than tips. Service charges are mandatory fees imposed by the employer on customers. Employers are generally permitted to keep all or part of a service fee, or to distribute all or part of the fee to any group of employees, including supervisors and managers. However, if the employer misleads customers into believing that these service charges are tips when in fact the money does not get distributed to any employees who provide service to customers, the employer may be required to pay them to the appropriate employees as tips.

(Labor Code sections 350–356; *Chau v. Starbucks Corp.* (2009) 174 Cal.App.4th 688; *Etheridge v. Reins International California, Inc.* (2009) 172 Cal.App.4th 908; *Jameson v. Five Feet Restaurant* (2003) 107 Cal.App.4th 138; *Leighton v. Old Heidelberg, Ltd.* (1990) 219 Cal.App.3d 1062.)

J. COMMISSION WAGES

Commissions are wages that are based on a percentage of the price of goods or services sold. Commissions are usually earned by selling goods or services.

Certain types of wages, though frequently labeled "commissions" by employers, are not bona fide commissions under California law, and an employee must be paid overtime rates for excess hours unless more than half the employee's compensation consists of bona fide commissions. Payments that are not bona fide commissions include the following:

* Wages paid to employees for making a product or for providing a service (rather than for selling the product or service), regardless of whether those wages are determined by the number of products made or services performed or by a percentage of the price of the products made or services provided;
* Wages that are based on the number of customers who agree to purchase goods or services, or on the number of products or services sold, rather than on the price of those products or services;
* Wages that are based on a percentage of the employer's profits.

(*Harris v. Investor's Business Daily, Inc.* (2006) 138 Cal.App.4th 28; *Keyes Motors, Inc. v. DLSE* (1988) 197 Cal.App.3d 557.)

Bona fide commissions are generally calculated on the basis of the sales of an individual employee. However, an employer may pay a group of employees under a "pooled commission" arrangement, where each employee is paid a percentage of the pooled commissions, provided that each participating employee is primarily engaged in sales work.

The agreement between the employer and the employee will determine how commissions should be calculated and when the commission is considered earned. The agreement may provide that the commission is earned at the time of the sale, or when the goods are received, or when the customer's payment is received, or when some other event takes place. Once the commission is earned and can be calculated, it must be paid within the time set under the Labor Code for the payment of wages to current or separated employees.

Deductions can also be made for returned goods,

but only from the specific employee who sold the returned goods. No deduction can be taken where the employer cannot identify the salesperson of the returned goods. An employer cannot make deductions from an employee's commissions for cash shortages, merchandise shortages, breakage, or other business losses, even if the shortage or loss was caused by the employee's negligence. Employees are entitled to recover all amounts that were unlawfully deducted or forfeited. (*Hudgins v. Neiman Marcus Group, Inc.* (1995) 34 Cal.App.4th 1109.)

Many commission agreements provide for the payment of a guaranteed base wage for the employee. This base wage is paid to the employee each pay period, even if the employee does not earn enough in commission to cover it. In those instances, the employee "draws" against his future commissions enough funds to reach the guaranteed base wage. His future commissions will be discounted by the amount of the draw, at a date specified in the commission agreement. Under these arrangements, the employee essentially receives an advance on his salary, which is made up by future commissions that are in excess of the guaranteed base wage. (*Agnew v. Cameron* (1967) 247 Cal.App.2d 619.)

K. COMMISSION PAYMENTS FOLLOWING SEPARATION FROM EMPLOYMENT

Commissions earned prior to the end of employment cannot be taken away. Like any other final wages, they are due and must be paid immediately upon discharge or layoff, or within seventy-two hours of a voluntary quit. The employer cannot delay payment, regardless of how long currently employed workers must wait for payment of their commissions.

The employee will generally be entitled to commissions on sales that closed following the end of employment if that employee was responsible for the sale, even if other persons later completed the sale. If the contract specifies that commissions are not earned until the sale is "closed" or until the employee performs certain post-sale duties, and the salesperson's employment ended after making the sale, but without completing all of the requirements for earning the commission, recovery will generally depend on the provisions of the employment agreement.

L. BONUSES

1. General Rules Regarding Bonuses

A bonus is money promised to an employee in addition to the salary, commissions, piece rates, or hourly wages that are the employee's usual compensation. Bonuses are a form of wages. Bonuses generally receive the same protections as other wages. Bonuses based on a definite promise made by the employer must be included in calculating the regular rate of pay for computing overtime pay. Discretionary bonuses (additional payments made at the sole choice or discretion of the employer and not based on any prior contract, promise, or agreement) and "special occasion bonuses" (gifts not computed on the basis of hours worked, production, or efficiency) do not get included in the regular rate of pay for purposes of figuring out the rate of overtime pay. (29 Code of Federal Regulations sections 778.208–778.212.)

The promise of a bonus is enforceable as a contract. If there was a definite promise to pay a bonus, once the employee begins performance of the work, the employer is obligated to pay the bonus as long as the conditions of the promise to pay the bonus (for instance, satisfactory performance, meeting a particular sales goal, etc.) have been met. (*Chinn v. China National Aviation Corp.* (1955) 138 Cal.App.2d 98.)

2. Bonus Payment Issues Following Separation From Employment

The right to payment of a bonus after the end of employment will generally depend on the terms of the promise to pay the bonus. If the employer requires employment throughout a specified period (or on the day of payment) in order to qualify for a bonus, an employee who voluntarily quits before the completion of that qualifying period (or prior to the day of payment) will generally not be entitled to any payment of the bonus. However, an employee who is discharged before the end of the qualifying period (or prior to the day of payment) may be entitled to a pro-rata (or full) share of the promised bonus, if the discharge did not result from employee misconduct or poor work performance. Entitlement to the bonus will depend on the terms of the promise to pay it. (*Lucian v. All States Trucking Co.* (1981) 116 Cal. App.3d 972; *Neisendorf v. Levi Strauss & Co.* (2006) 143 Cal.App.4th 509.)

3. Criteria Used to Calculate Bonus

It is unlawful for an employer to directly impose deductions against earned bonuses for costs that under the law must be shouldered by the employer, such as cash and merchandise shortages resulting from employee negligence or factors beyond the employees' control, Workers' Compensation expenses, and third-party personal injury claims made against the employer. However, an employer that gives employees bonuses on the basis of the employer's profits (a profit-sharing plan) may include the costs listed above in determining how much profits the employer has made. (*Prachasaisoradej v. Ralphs Grocery Co.* (2007) 42 Cal.4th 217.)

M. OVERTIME PAY

1. Basic Overtime Requirements Under State Law

a. General Provisions

Employees are entitled to overtime pay at no less than one-and-one-half times the employee's regular rate of pay for all hours worked in excess of eight in one workday or forty in one workweek, or for the first eight hours on the seventh consecutive day of work in any one workweek. Employees are entitled to double the regular rate of pay for all hours worked in excess of twelve in one day, or in excess of eight on the seventh consecutive day of work within a workweek. (Labor Code section 510; IWC Orders 1-2001–13-2001, 15-2001, 16-2001 section 3.)

b. Exceptions From Basic State Overtime Requirements

i. *Complete Exemptions*

See sections II.B., p. 69, through II.I., p. 73, for a discussion of the various categories of employees who are completely exempt from (not covered by) state overtime requirements, and for the requirements for each exemption. Basic state overtime requirements apply unless the employee meets all of the requirements for an exemption. Some categories of employees who are exempt from state overtime requirements may still be covered by the overtime provisions of the federal Fair Labor Standards Act. Public employees who work for the state, or for political subdivisions of the state (including counties and cities), or for the University of California, or for local special districts, are exempt from state overtime laws, but are protected by federal overtime law.

Federal law is less protective than state law. Under federal law, there is no requirement to pay overtime rates for hours worked in excess of eight in a day. However, federal law, like state law, requires payment of overtime rates of one-and-one-half times the employee's regular rate of pay for all hours worked in excess of forty in a workweek. (29 U.S. Code section 207(a); 29 Code of Federal Regulations section 553.3.)

ii. *Less-Protective Requirements*

Certain categories of employees, though not covered by the basic overtime requirements, are covered by less-protective state law requirements:

- Agricultural Employees Covered by IWC Order 14. These employees are not entitled to overtime compensation unless they work more than ten hours in a day, or seven days in a row in a workweek. However, overtime is not required for the seventh day if the employee did not work more than thirty hours during the week and did not work more than six hours on any one workday. If the employee worked over thirty hours in the preceding week or more than six hours on any single day in the preceding week, overtime pay is required. Overtime compensation must be paid at not less than one-and-one-half times the employee's regular rate of pay for all hours worked in excess of ten hours in one workday, and for the first eight hours of the seventh consecutive day of work in a workweek. Double time (twice the regular amount of pay) is required for all hours worked in excess of eight hours on the seventh consecutive day of employment. Farm workers are exempt from the overtime provisions of the Fair Labor Standards Act so there is no federal requirement for overtime compensation for hours worked over forty hours in a workweek. (Note: There are two other IWC orders that apply to certain agricultural workers: IWC Order 8-2001 (Industries Handling Products After Harvest) and IWC Order 13-2001 (Industries Preparing Agricultural Products for Market, on the Farm), which contain the more-protective provisions of the basic state overtime law.)
- Live-In Employees in Private Households Covered by IWC Order 15. Live-in employees

who are not exempt from overtime under the personal attendant exemption (described at section II.I., p. 73) must be given twelve hours in a row off-duty each day. But if the employee is required or permitted to work during this scheduled off-duty time, the employee must be paid at one-and-one-half times the employee's regular rate of pay for all such hours worked. Also, such employees cannot be required to work more than five days in any one workweek without a day off of twenty-four consecutive hours except in an emergency. If the employee works more than five days in a workweek, the employee must be paid at one-and-one-half times the employee's regular rate of pay for all hours worked up to nine hours in a day on the sixth and seventh workdays in the workweek, and at double the employee's regular rate of pay for all hours worked over nine hours on the sixth and seventh workdays of the workweek.

2. Alternative Workweek Schedules

There is an exception to the basic state daily overtime requirements for employees working under a properly adopted "alternative workweek schedule." An alternative workweek schedule is defined as any regularly scheduled workweek in which an employee is required to work more than eight hours in a workday. If properly adopted, the alternative workweek schedule may provide for up to ten hours of work per day within a forty-hour workweek without the payment of overtime. In the healthcare industry, the schedule may provide for up to twelve hours of work per day within a forty-hour workweek without the payment of overtime.

Under a properly adopted alternative workweek schedule, employees are entitled to overtime compensation at the rate of one-and-one-half times the regular rate of pay for all hours worked in a day in excess of the regularly scheduled day's hours, and for all hours in excess of forty in a workweek. Payment of double the regular rate of pay must be paid for all hours in excess of twelve in any workday and for all hours in excess of eight hours worked on any day in which the employee is not regularly scheduled for work.

Employers are prohibited from reducing an employee's regular rate of pay as the result of the adoption, repeal, or discontinuance of an alternative workweek schedule.

To establish an alternative workweek schedule,

the employer must conduct a secret ballot election under very strict procedures, which are difficult to comply with. (Labor Code section 511; IWC Orders section 3.)

3. Collective Bargaining Agreement Exemption

There is an exception to state daily overtime rules for employees who are covered by a collective bargaining agreement that provides "premium pay" (any amount greater than regular pay) for all overtime hours worked (as defined by the collective bargaining agreement) and that establishes a regular hourly rate of pay of at least 30 percent more than the state minimum wage. Premium pay is defined as any amount greater than the regular rate of pay. Overtime hours are defined by the collective bargaining agreement. If these conditions are met, the collective bargaining agreement, not the state overtime laws, will apply. There is no collective bargaining exemption under federal law. Under federal overtime law, overtime at the rate of one-and-one-half times the regular rate must be paid for all hours worked in excess of forty in a workweek, regardless of the collective bargaining agreement.

4. Determining the Regular Rate of Pay

Overtime. compensation is based on the employee's "regular rate of pay." Therefore, it is essential to properly calculate the regular rate of pay. Generally, all amounts paid by an employer for work performed by an employee are counted in determining the regular rate of pay. Any hourly pay, and all amounts earned as salary, commissions, or piece rate wages are counted. Bonuses based on a pre-established formula are also included in regular rate calculations, as is the value of any goods or services (such as meals or lodging) that are provided as part of the employee's compensation.

However, the following types of payments are not counted in calculating the regular rate of pay:
- Amounts received as discretionary gifts;
- Holiday, vacation, and sick pay;
- Reimbursements for mileage and other business expenses;
- Extra compensation for hours worked over eight in a day or forty in a week;
- Rates of pay higher than the normal rate ("premium pay") for work performed on

weekends, holidays, or regular days off, if the amount paid is at least one-and-one-half times the regular rate of pay;

- Premium pay (including extra amounts received for overtime) for work performed outside the employee's normal work hours in a workday, if the amount paid is at least one-and-one-half times the regular rate of pay;
- Payments to a trust fund under a bona fide ERISA plan (which follows the government's rules for such plans) for pension benefits, or health, accident, or life insurance when the payment cannot be reclaimed by the employer;
- Payments made pursuant to a bona fide profit-sharing plan where payments to employees are made without regard to hours of work, production, or efficiency;
- Stock options.
(29 U.S. Code section 207(e).)

Whether the employee is paid on an hourly, salary, commission, or piece-rate basis, the regular rate of pay is always expressed as an hourly rate. The regular rate is determined on a week-to-week basis.

> *In California, an employer cannot reduce an employee's wages by the amount of tips received.*

Under federal law, the regular rate for an employee paid on an hourly, piece-rate, or commission basis is determined by taking all of their earnings for the workweek, and dividing that amount by the total number of hours worked during the workweek.

A different method is used, under California law, for calculating the regular rate for salaried employees. All amounts paid as salary are divided by not more than forty hours for the week to determine the regular rate for a salaried employee.

There are also differences between methods of calculating the rate of overtime pay, depending on

whether the employee receives a salary or is non-salaried (for example, paid by the hour, by the piece, or on commission). For employees who are entitled to overtime pay, the salary covers regular hours, not overtime hours. Unless they are exempt from overtime pay requirements (see section II.B. through I., pp. 69-73, for more information on who is exempt), they are owed the full applicable overtime rate (either one-and-one-half times or double the regular rate, as described above) for overtime hours. However, workers who are paid for all of their work hours on an hourly, piece-rate, or commission basis are considered to have already been paid their straight-time wages for all such hours, including overtime hours worked. Therefore, in computing overtime compensation owed these non-salaried workers, the employee is entitled to an extra one-half of the regular rate of compensation for all overtime hours in situations where overtime must be paid at one-and-one-half times the regular rate. They are entitled to an additional amount equal to the regular rate for all overtime hours that must be paid at twice the regular rate.

N. MAKEUP WORK TIME OR COMPENSATORY TIME OFF INSTEAD OF OVERTIME PAY

1. Makeup Work Time

The law permits an employer to allow an employee to take time off during a workweek, and to make up that time by working extra hours in any other day(s) during that workweek, without paying daily overtime for the makeup hours, if all of the following conditions are met:

- The employee provides the employer with a signed, written request to take time off and work makeup time.
- The employee working makeup time does not work more than eleven hours total (regular hours plus makeup time) in any workday.
- The request was initiated by the employee for the employee's benefit; employers are prohibited from requiring or encouraging employees to request makeup time instead of overtime pay.
- The makeup time is worked in the same workweek in which the employee took the time off.

The employer is not required to approve an

employee's request for makeup time. If makeup time is requested and approved, the employer must still pay daily overtime for all hours worked in excess of eleven in any workday, and for all hours worked in excess of forty in the workweek. (Labor Code section 513.)

2. Compensatory Time Off — Private Sector Employees

Although state law appears to permit compensatory time off (CTO) instead of overtime pay under certain circumstances, federal law does not permit private sector employers to substitute CTO for required overtime pay. For private sector employees, federal law requires payment of overtime for all hours worked over forty in any workweek, regardless of any state law permitting CTO instead of overtime pay. But federal law does not provide for daily overtime, so CTO may be allowed instead of daily overtime pay (where the employee does not work more than forty hours in a workweek), under certain conditions:

- Before working overtime, the employee voluntarily asked in writing to be granted CTO instead of overtime pay, or the employee is working under a collective bargaining agreement that allows CTO instead of overtime pay.

- The employee has not accrued more than 240 hours of CTO. Once an employee has a balance of 240 accrued hours of CTO, the employee must receive overtime pay for any additional overtime work.

- The employee is regularly scheduled to work at least forty hours in a workweek. Employees regularly scheduled to work fewer than forty hours a week cannot be provided with CTO instead of overtime pay.

- The employee is covered by one of the following IWC Orders: IWC Order 2-2001 (personal service industry), IWC Order 4-2001 (professional, technical, clerical, mechanical, and similar occupations), IWC Order 6-2001 (laundry, linen supply, dry cleaning, and dyeing industries), IWC Order 7-2001 (mercantile industry), IWC Order 9-2001 (transportation industry), IWC Order 10-2001 (amusement and recreation industry), IWC Order 11-2001 (broadcasting industry), IWC Order 12-2001 (motion picture industry), IWC Order 15-2001 (household occupations), or IWC Order 16-2001 (certain on-site occupations in construction,

drilling, logging, and mining industries). Employers are prohibited from providing CTO instead of overtime pay to workers covered by IWC Order 1-2001 (manufacturing industry), IWC Order 3-2001 (canning, freezing, and preserving industry), IWC Order 5-2001 (public housekeeping industry, which includes restaurants and hotels), IWC Order 8-2001 (industries handling agricultural products after harvest), IWC Order 13-2001 (industries preparing agricultural products for market on the farm), or IWC Order 14-2001 (agricultural occupations).

CTO must be provided at the applicable overtime rate. This means that the employee is entitled to one and one-half hours of CTO for each overtime hour worked during the eighth to twelfth work hours of any work day, and two hours of CTO for each overtime hour worked beyond the twelfth hour of work of any work day.

Upon the request of an employee, the employer must pay overtime compensation instead of CTO for any CTO that has carried over at least two pay periods. Upon termination of employment, all accrued CTO must be paid out to the worker at the worker's final regular rate of pay or at the worker's average regular rate covering the final three years of employment, whichever is higher. The employer must keep accurate records reflecting all CTO earned and used. (Labor Code section 204.3.)

3. Compensatory Time Off — Public Sector Employees

State and local government employees are not covered by state overtime or CTO requirements. However, they are covered by federal law, under which they have the right to be paid at least time-and-a-half for hours worked in excess of forty a week. There is no daily overtime under federal law. Public employees may receive CTO (at the rate of time-and-a-half) instead of overtime pay under the following conditions:

- If employees are represented, the public employer must have an agreement with their labor organization before the compensatory or "comp" time option can be allowed.

- If employees are not represented, the employer must secure individual agreements with any employees who wish to use the comp time option, before the work is performed. However, if the employer had a regular practice before

April 15, 1986, of allowing the accumulation of comp time, no individual agreement is necessary for those employees who were hired before that date.

- Employees may not accrue more than a maximum amount of accumulated comp time. The maximum allowed for safety, emergency, and seasonal employees is 480 hours. For all other employees, the maximum is 240 hours. Additional overtime worked must be paid at the applicable overtime rate. For employees who were hired before April 15, 1986, these caps only apply to work performed after that date.
- An employee who has accumulated comp time must be allowed to take the time off within a reasonable period after making the request, as long as the request does not unduly disrupt the operation.
- If the employee works on another day to make up for comp time taken earlier, the employee shall be compensated at the regular rate of pay.
- Upon termination of employment, the employee must be paid for all unused, accrued comp time, at either the employee's final regular rate of pay, or at the average regular rate of pay received during the employee's final three years of employment, whichever is higher. (29 U.S. Code section 207(o).)

O. PAY FOR THE SEVENTH WORKDAY OF THE WEEK

When an employee works seven days in a row during a workweek, the employer must pay the employee premium pay for all hours worked during that seventh day at the rate of one-and-one-half times the employee's regular rate of pay for all time worked during the first eight hours, and double the regular rate of pay for all hours worked over eight hours in a day. (Labor Code section 510; IWC Orders section 3(A).)

Normally, an employer cannot require an employee to work more than six days out of seven. However, if the nature of the work reasonably requires the employee to work seven or more consecutive days (for example, utility workers after a bad storm or earthquake), the employer can "bank" the weekly day off and provide the worker with the monthly equivalent of one day off for each seven days worked (for example, by giving workers four days off following twenty-four consecutive

days worked). This restriction on consecutive days worked does not apply to "any cases of emergency," or to work performed in the protection of life or property from loss or destruction, or to any person employed in an agricultural occupation under IWC Order 14, or to any common carrier engaged in the movement of trains. Also, this restriction does not apply to any employee for any workweek in which the employee worked fewer than thirty hours and during which the employee did not work more than six hours in any single workday. (Labor Code sections 551–556.)

P. SPLIT-SHIFT PAY

A "split shift" is defined as an unpaid interruption in the workday, established by the employer, other than a bona fide meal or rest period. An employee who works a split shift is entitled to a "split-shift premium" of one hour of pay at the minimum wage (currently $8 an hour), in addition to the required minimum wage for all hours worked that workday. Amounts paid over the minimum wage for hours worked during the workday may be used as a credit against an employer's obligation to pay the split-shift premium. (IWC Orders sections 2 and 4.)

Exceptions: The following employees are not entitled to split-shift premiums:

- Employees who live at their places of employment (IWC Orders section 4);
- Employees covered by IWC Order 16-2001 (on-site construction, logging, drilling, and mining employees), as that IWC order does not provide for such premiums.

Q. REPORTING-TIME PAY

If an employee reports to work for a regularly scheduled shift, and is given less than half the usual or scheduled hours of work (or is furnished no work at all), the employee must be paid at his regular rate of pay for at least half of those usual or regularly scheduled hours, with a minimum of at least two hours pay, and a maximum of four hours pay.

If an employee is required to report to work a second time in one workday (for example, reporting for the second part of a split shift, or reporting for overtime work after an unpaid break other than a required meal period of not longer than one hour), the employee must be paid for at least two hours of work for reporting for work a second time.

If an employee is required to report to work for an unspecified or unscheduled number of hours, but is not assigned to work, the employee must be paid for at least two hours for reporting to work.

The employer is not liable for reporting-time pay if the lack of work is the result of "an act of God" or some unexpected cause entirely beyond the employer's control, such as a power failure, a civil emergency, earthquake, or bad weather. However, if work is interrupted due to a failure of the employer's equipment, the employer will generally be held responsible for the interruption, and will therefore be liable for reporting-time pay. (IWC Orders section 5.)

R. VACATION PAY

Employers are not required by California or federal law to provide employees with paid vacation. However, if an employer agrees to provide paid vacation, then vacation pay is regulated by state law. State law protects vacation pay in the ways described below.

1. Pro-Rata Vacation

Vacation time is considered a form of deferred wages for work performed, that "vests" (that is, becomes the legal property of the employee) as it is earned, and is earned as work is performed, on a pro-rata basis. In other words, if an employer policy provides for three weeks vacation a year, an employee who has worked for half a year has earned one-and-one-half weeks of vacation time. The employee's accrued vacation time increases with each day of work performed. Employers are generally allowed to establish vacation plans under which vacation is not earned for some specified period of time at the beginning of employment. However an employer is not allowed to establish such a plan as a "subterfuge" to evade the general requirement of "pro-rata" vacation. See http://www.dir.ca.gov/dlse/faq_vacation.htm for more information on this topic.

2. No Forfeiture of Accrued Vacation Time

Once earned, vacation time cannot be forfeited by the employer. This means that "use it or lose it" policies are illegal. Earned vacation time "lost" as a result of such a policy will be restored by the labor commissioner or the courts. However, employers are allowed to establish reasonable limits or caps on accrued vacation time. Once the employee's earned vacation reaches the cap, no further vacation may be earned until the employee takes vacation time, thereby reducing the amount accrued to a level below the cap. It is doubtful whether an employer could enforce a cap if the employee is denied permission to actually take time off work. A cap can be established by the employer at the beginning of the employment or any time thereafter. However, if at the time a cap is established the employee is already above or near the cap, the new policy cannot take effect for that employee without first giving her a reasonable chance to use enough vacation time to get below the cap in accrued vacation.

3. Payment of Unused Accrued Vacation Time at Separation of Employment

All unused accrued vacation time, no matter how long ago it was earned, must be paid out to the employee along with the employee's final wages, upon separation of employment. Separation of employment includes discharge, layoff (other than very short-term furloughs with a definite recall date), completion of a fixed work assignment for which the employee was hired, voluntary quit, or any other termination of employment. The accrued vacation must be paid to the employee at the final rate of pay. (Labor Code section 227.3; *Suastez v. Plastic Dress-Up Co.* (1982) 31 Cal.3d 774; *Boothby v. Atlas Mechanical, Inc.* (1992) 6 Cal.App.4th 1595; *Church v. Jamison* (2006) 143 Cal.App.4th 1568; *Owen v. Macy's, Inc.* (2009) 175 Cal.App.4th 462.)

4. Exceptions

a. Employees Covered by Collective Bargaining Agreements

Different requirements concerning vacation wages that are expressly contained in a collective bargaining agreement will preempt these state law requirements. (Labor Code section 227.3.)

b. Employees Covered by Voluntary Employees' Beneficiary Association (VEBA) Plans

Employees whose vacation wages are paid out of the assets of a third-party ERISA vacation trust fund, rather than out of the employer's general assets, may not be governed by state law. Instead, their entitlement to payout of accrued vacation upon separation of employment may depend on the terms and conditions of the vacation plan.

S. PAY FOR TIME SPENT PERFORMING CIVIC DUTIES

Various state laws require employers to pay employees for time spent performing the civic duties described below.

1. Voting

If an employee does not have sufficient time outside of normal working hours to vote in a statewide election, the employee may take off enough time (up to two hours) to vote, without loss of pay. The employer may not discipline the employee for taking this time to vote, and must pay the employee for this voting time. This paid time for voting must be taken at either the end or the beginning of the work shift, unless the employer agrees to allow the time to be taken during the shift. If the employee knows at least three working days before the election that time off will be needed to vote, the employee must give the employer at least two working days' notice in order to be paid for the time off. These requirements apply to both public and private employees. (Elections Code sections 14000–14002.)

2. Serving on a Jury

All employers are prohibited from retaliating against an employee for serving on a jury if the employee gives the employer reasonable notice that she been called to jury duty. Unless otherwise provided by a collective bargaining agreement, employers must allow employees to use any available vacation, personal leave, or compensatory time off to cover lost wages for time spent serving on a jury. If a collective bargaining agreement does not require the employer to allow employees to use available leave during jury duty, private employers are not required to pay any wages to employees for time spent serving on a jury. Many public employers, including school districts and community college districts, are required to pay employees for time spent on jury duty. (Labor Code section 230; Education Code sections 44037, 87036; Government Code section 1230.)

3. Testifying as a Witness Pursuant to Subpoena

All employers are prohibited from retaliating against employees for taking time off to appear in court to comply with a subpoena or other court order requiring attendance as a witness. Private employers are not required to pay employees for time spent testifying, unless it is the employer that is requiring the employee to testify, in which case the time is compensable as "hours worked." Public employers, including the state, local governments, school districts, and special districts, must pay an employee's regular wages for time spent testifying under subpoena, less any witness fees paid by the party that issued the subpoena, unless the employee is a party (a plaintiff or defendant) in the proceeding, or the employee is testifying as an expert witness. (Government Code sections 1230, 1230.1.)

IV. MEAL PERIODS AND REST BREAKS

A. MEAL PERIODS

As a general rule, employees are entitled to one "off-duty" meal period, consisting of at least thirty minutes, for each five hours worked. The employee must be relieved of all duty during the thirty-minute meal period. An employee who works more than ten hours in a day is therefore entitled to a second meal period. Off-duty meal periods can be unpaid. (Labor Code section 512; IWC Orders section 11.)

As of this book's press time, there is a case pending before the California Supreme Court, *Brinker Restaurant Corp. v. Superior Court*, which will decide the issue of exactly what an employer must do to meet its obligation to provide employees with meal periods in accordance with the provisions of the applicable IWC order. Current court decisions confirm that employers must "relieve their employees of all duty" during an off-duty meal period, and that it is unlawful for an employer to require an employee to perform any work during a required meal period, or to prevent, discourage, or dissuade an employee from taking a required meal period. Beyond that, it is unsettled whether an employer violates the law by failing to take reasonable steps to prohibit its employees from working during a required off-duty meal period, or by otherwise permitting employees to work during such meal period.

The *Brinker* case will also decide what employers must do to comply with the meal period timing requirement. For many decades, the labor commissioner and the IWC interpreted the language of the wage orders that "no employer shall employ a person for a work period of more than five hours without a meal period" to mean that the required meal period must occur at or near the middle of a workday, so that no more than five hours elapse between the start of work and the start of the meal period, and so that no more than five hours elapse between the end of the meal period and the end of a workday in which only one meal period is required. In accordance with this timing requirement, a meal period must commence sometime between the third hour and the fifth hour of an eight-hour work day. Some employers dispute this timing requirement. Instead, they argue that the meal period can be "made available" anytime during the workday. The final decision in this case will determine employers' obligations with regard to meal periods.

Under the IWC orders, there are very limited circumstances under which meal periods can be waived (not taken) by mutual consent of the employer and the employee. A waiver can occur only if a work shift of not more than six hours will complete the day's work; or if the total hours worked for the day do not exceed twelve hours and the first meal period was taken, the second meal period can be waived by agreement between the employer and the employee.

Also, if "the nature of the work" prevents the employee from being relieved of all duty during an off-duty meal period, the employee can agree to an "on-duty" paid meal period. Such an agreement must be in writing, and must specify that the employee may cancel the agreement at any time in writing. The fact that it may increase an employer's cost of doing business to provide an off-duty meal period is not sufficient to meet the "nature of the work" requirement for an on-duty meal period, and the employer is expected to make reasonable efforts to ensure that the employee can be relieved of all duty during required meal breaks. See http://www.dir.ca.gov/dlse/opinions/2002-09-04.pdf.

If an employee has any work duties during the meal period, or if the employee is restricted to the work premises during the meal period, the meal period is considered to be "hours worked," and the employee must be paid for that time. Employees must be allowed to leave the worksite during an off-duty, unpaid meal period. (*Bono Enterprises v. Bradshaw* (1995) 32 Cal.App.4th 968.)

Exceptions:
- Agricultural employees under IWC Order 14-2001. Employers are not required to ensure that farm workers are not performing any work during required meal periods. Instead, such employers need only authorize and permit these workers to take off-duty meal periods. There is no violation if the farm worker is advised of the right to take the off-duty meal period and then freely chooses, voluntarily and without pressure, not to take a meal break.
- Healthcare employees under IWC Orders 4-2001 or 5-2001. These employees may be required to stay on the employer's premises

during an off-duty meal period, as long as the employer has suitable facilities for eating. The meal period can be unpaid, provided it is not interrupted by a return to work before it is over.

- Wholesale baking industry employees. These employees are exempt from meal period requirements if they are covered by a collective bargaining agreement that provides for five seven-hour days, with overtime at one-and-one-half times the regular rate of pay for all work over seven hours per day, and a rest period of at least ten minutes for every two hours worked. (Labor Code section 512(c).)
- Employees in the broadcasting and motion picture industries under IWC Orders 11-2001 or 12-2001. These employees are exempt from the meal period requirements specified in the Labor Code and IWC orders if they are covered by a collective bargaining agreement that provides for meal periods, and that includes a monetary remedy for any instance in which the employer violates the meal period policy outlined in the collective bargaining agreement. (Labor Code section 512(d).)
- Employees in the manufacturing industry. These employees are excluded from state meal break requirements if they are covered by collective bargaining agreements and agree to a meal period starting no later than the sixth hour of work. (IWC Order 1-2001 section 11(A).)

An employer who violates meal period requirements must pay each affected employee one additional hour of pay at the employee's regular rate of pay for each day that the policy was violated. This extra hour of pay constitutes "wages." An employee filing a claim with the labor commissioner for payment for missed meal breaks can go back three years from the date the claim is filed to recover the amounts owed. The employee can also seek penalties under Labor Code section 203 if the employee was not paid wages for missed meal breaks upon separation from employment. (Labor Code section 226.7(b); *Murphy v. Kenneth Cole Productions, Inc.* (2007) 40 Cal.4th 1094.)

B. REST PERIODS

Employees who work more than three-and-a-half hours in a day are entitled to one paid rest period. Employees who work more than six hours in a day are entitled to two paid rest periods.

Employees who work more than ten hours in a day are entitled to three paid rest periods, with an additional paid rest period for each additional four hours worked in a day. It is unlawful for an employer to require an employee to work during any required rest period.

> *Rest periods must be paid at the employee's regular rate of pay.*

The rest period must be paid at the employee's regular rate of pay. Each rest period must be at least ten minutes long. Most employers of employees who work in indoor facilities are required to provide their employees with an area for resting, separate from toilet rooms. Time required to walk to or from the rest area does not count as part of the ten-minute rest period.

As far as is practical, each rest period must be given as close as possible to the middle of the "work period." In a typical eight-hour day, the first rest period should be provided to the employees near the midpoint between the start of the day's work and the start of the meal break. The second rest period should be provided to the employees near the midpoint between the end of the meal break and the end of the day's work.

An employer who violates rest period requirements must pay each affected employee one additional hour of pay at the employee's regular rate of pay for each day that the policy was violated.

This extra hour of pay is considered to be "wages." An employee filing a claim with the labor commissioner for payment for missed rest breaks can go back three years from the date the claim is filed to recover the amounts owed. The employee can also seek penalties under Labor Code section 203 if the employee was not paid wages for missed rest breaks upon separation from employment. (Labor Code section 226.7; IWC Orders section 12.)

V. WAGE DEDUCTIONS

A. UNLAWFUL DEDUCTIONS AND REQUIRED PAYMENTS

An employer may not lawfully deduct money from an employee's wages, except:

- When, under federal or state law, the employer is required or authorized to deduct or withhold wages for the purpose set out in such law;
- When a deduction is expressly authorized in writing by an employee to cover medical or other insurance premiums, or other permissible deductions "not amounting to a rebate" from required wages; or
- When deductions to cover bona fide health and welfare or pension plan contributions are expressly authorized by a collective bargaining agreement or employment contract. (Labor Code sections 221–224.)

Employees can recover amounts that were unlawfully deducted from their wages, or amounts that they were unlawfully required to pay to employers, by filing a claim with the labor commissioner, or by filing a lawsuit. The types of deductions from wages described below are unlawful.

1. Deductions to Repay Loans Made by the Employer

Employers are not allowed to collect debts owed by employees by deducting or withholding the amounts owed from wages. An employer and employee can enter into a voluntary agreement for payment of a debt, or the employer can file a lawsuit against the employee for recovery of amounts owed. But the employer cannot use its position as an employer to take "self-help" deductions from wages to recover debts owed.

2. Deductions to Recover Wage Overpayments

Wage overpayments resulting from an employer's error cannot be recovered by involuntary paycheck deductions. (*CSEA v. State of California* (1988) 198 Cal.App.3d 374.) (This sort of erroneous overpayment situation is different from a lawful pre-existing agreement between an employer and employee for advances against wages not yet earned; see section III.J., p. 81.) The

employer must go through the process known as wage garnishment to collect the alleged erroneous overpayment. See section V.B.1., p. 94, for more information.

3. Deductions or Required Payments for Loss, Breakage, or Shortage

Employers are strictly forbidden from making any deductions from an employee's wages, or from requiring any reimbursement from an employee, for cash shortage, breakage or damage, or loss of equipment, unless the employer can prove that the cash shortage, breakage, damage, or loss was caused by the employee's dishonesty, theft, deliberate property destruction or other willful act, or gross negligence. There can be no deductions from wages or required reimbursement when the loss, shortage, damage, or breakage was caused by an employee's "simple negligence." And, of course, there can be no deductions or required reimbursement when the loss, shortage, damage, or breakage was caused by factors outside the particular employee's control, or when the cause is unknown. (IWC Wage Orders section 8; *Kerr's Catering Service v. Dept. of Industrial Relations* (1962) 57 Cal.2d 319; *Hudgins v. Neiman Marcus Group, Inc.* (1995) 34 Cal.App.4th 1109.)

Accidents, damages, or losses resulting from inattention or mere carelessness or failure to exercise ordinary and reasonable care do not rise to the level of "gross negligence." (*People v. Thompson* (2000) 79 Cal.App.4th 40.) Some examples of unlawful deductions include deductions for cash register shortages, for inadvertently charging a customer less than the correct price, for damage to an automobile caused by carelessness in getting out of a parking space, or for the cost of meals served to customers who skip out of a restaurant without paying their bills.

4. Deductions for Employee's Failure to Return Employer-Provided Tools or Uniforms

It is unlawful for an employer to deduct any amount from an employee's final paycheck to cover the cost of required uniforms, tools, or equipment provided by the employer but not returned, unless there is prior written permission from the employee allowing such a deduction. No deduction can be made for normal wear and tear to tools, equipment, uniforms, or similar items.

An employer can lawfully require an employee to post a cash bond to insure the return of property, but only by following the detailed procedures set out at Labor Code sections 400–410, which are described below (see section V.B.3., p. 94). (IWC Orders 1-2001–15-2001 section 9.)

Exception: Employers of employees covered by IWC Order 16 (on-site construction, drilling, logging, and mining) are forbidden from making any such deduction from an employee's paycheck, even if the employee authorized the deduction. (IWC Order 16-2001 sections 7–8.)

5. Fines and Penalties

Employers are absolutely forbidden from imposing "fines" against employees. Monetary penalties are illegal, whether the fines go to the employer, a supervisor, a fellow worker, a charity, the coffee fund, or even a fund that may be repaid at some point to the fined employee. (Labor Code sections 221, 222, 223.)

6. Fees for Medical or Physical Examinations

Employers are prohibited from withholding or deducting from wages, or requiring any employee or prospective employee or job applicant to pay any fee, for any pre-employment medical or physical examination required as a condition of employment. Employers are also prohibited from withholding or deducting from wages, or requiring any employee to pay any fee, for a medical or physical examination required by federal, state, or local law or regulation. Employers must cover these expenses. (Labor Code section 222.5.)

7. Kickbacks

It is illegal for an employer or supervisor to require, collect, or receive a "kickback" of any amount from an employee's wages. A kickback occurs when an employer or supervisor takes back a portion of the worker's wages, in exchange for letting the worker keep the job. An employer cannot require an employee to purchase any part of the business, or make any investment in the business. It is also illegal for an employer to charge any fee to an employee for cashing a paycheck. (Labor Code sections 221, 407.)

8. Forced Patronage of Employer or Third Party

It is unlawful for an employer to force an employee or applicant for employment to patronize the employer or any third party, in the purchase of anything of value. For example, a clothing store cannot require its employees to purchase clothes sold by that store, even if those clothes are sold at an employee discount. It is also unlawful for an employer to require a job applicant to pay a fee to obtain a job application, or to pay a fee for processing a job application. (Labor Code section 450.)

9. Deductions for Workers' Compensation Costs

It is unlawful for an employer to take any deduction from an employee's wages or to receive from an employee any contribution to cover the cost of Workers' Compensation benefits. (Labor Code section 3751.)

B. LAWFUL DEDUCTIONS AND REQUIRED PAYMENTS

Examples of lawful paycheck deductions include:
- State and federal income tax withholdings;
- Social Security and/or State Disability Insurance (SDI) contributions;
- Court-ordered wage garnishments or wage "assignments" for child support, family support, or other legitimate obligations;
- Tax liens for unpaid federal or state taxes;
- Voluntary deductions, authorized in writing by the employee, for contributions to charities, purchases of U.S. bonds, or deposits in banks and credit unions;
- Deductions made pursuant to a collective bargaining agreement for union dues or assessments;
- Deductions authorized in writing by the employee or by a collective bargaining agreement for contributions to retirement plans, insurance plans, or hospital or medical plans, for the benefit of the employee.

The types of allowable deductions or employee payments described below are governed by strict requirements that provide various protections to employees.

1. Garnishments

A garnishment, also called an earnings withholding order, is a withholding of wages based on a court order following a court proceeding for payment of a debt. Garnishments may also be imposed for the collection of unpaid federal or state taxes, or for child or spousal support payments. Employee consent to a deduction is not required for deductions based on wage garnishments.

An employee is entitled to notice of any garnishment. Generally, no more than 25 percent of the employee's earnings can be withheld. However, this 25 percent limit does not apply where the employee's wages are withheld due to a court order for child or spousal support, a court order for the collection of past due child or spousal support, a federal or state tax debt, or a federal bankruptcy court order.

It may be possible to reduce the amount taken from wages by proving to the court that the garnishment is creating a hardship to the employee and the employee's family, and that unless the garnishment is reduced, the employee will be unable to support his dependents. This reduction is not available if the garnishment is for past due child or spousal support. To request a reduction, the employee must file a Claim for Exemption form and a Financial Statement form. Information on how to complete and serve these

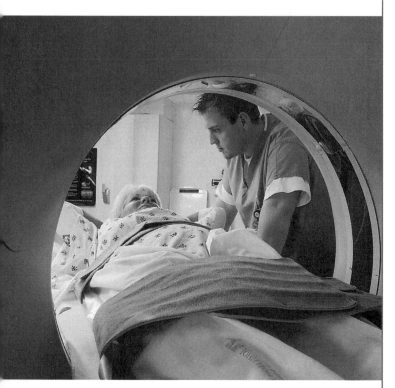

forms is available online at http://www.courtinfo. ca.gov/cgi-bin/forms.cgi. (Code of Civil Procedure sections 706.010–706.109.)

2. Wage Assignments

A wage assignment is a voluntary authorization by an employee directing his employer to pay part of the employee's wages to some other person, agency, or business. To be valid, an assignment must be in writing, must state the amount to be assigned and the person or entity to whom payment should be made, and it must be signed by the employee and notarized. Also, if the employee is married, the written consent of the employee's spouse must be attached to the assignment. If the employee is unmarried, the assignment must state that fact. No more than 50 percent of an employee's wages can be withheld and transmitted based on any assignment.

No more than one assignment can be in effect at any one time for the same transaction or series of transactions. An assignment cannot go into effect while an earnings withholding order (a court ordered garnishment for the benefit of a creditor, or for child or spousal support) is already in effect. An existing assignment terminates once the employer is served with an earnings withholding (garnishment) order. An assignment of wages can be withdrawn at any time by the employee who made the assignment by providing written notice of the revocation to the employer.

If money is taken out of a worker's paycheck for any other reason without a court order or pursuant to a collective bargaining agreement, the rules outlined above governing assignments apply. If the rules governing assignments are applicable, and were not strictly followed, the employee can recover all of the money that was illegally deducted from his wages. (Labor Code sections 224 and 300.)

3. Cash Bonds

An employer can require an employee to pay a reasonable deposit for uniforms, tools, equipment, merchandise, and other property provided by the employer to the employee. This deposit is known as a "cash bond." It cannot exceed the value of the items provided by the employer to the employee.

The cash bond must be held in trust. It cannot be commingled (mixed) with the employer's assets. The bond must be accompanied by a written agreement between the employer and employee setting out the conditions under which the bond is given. Cash bonds (plus any accrued interest) must be returned to the employee immediately upon the employee's return of the property that was provided by the employer, or the employee's fulfillment of the agreement, subject to any deduction necessary to settle the account between the employer and employee. Any amount that is retained by the employer cannot exceed the value of the unreturned property, which, due to normal wear and tear, may be less than the value of the property when it was first provided to the employee. (Labor Code sections 400–410.)

VI. REIMBURSEMENT OF EXPENSES

Employers must reimburse employees for losses and reasonable expenses incurred in the performance of the employee's job duties. This law is intended to prevent employers from passing their operating expenses on to their employees (Labor Code section 2802). Also, the IWC wage orders contain provisions specifically directed at expenses for tools, equipment, and uniforms.

A. NECESSARY EXPENSES

Employers must "indemnify" (reimburse) employees for all necessary expenditures and losses incurred in the performance of their job duties. With respect to expenses, the key is whether the expenditure was reasonable under the circumstances. For example, an employee who is required to stay overnight on an out-of-town business trip will be entitled to reimbursement of *reasonable* costs for travel and lodging, rather than for *actual* expenses if those expenses were unreasonable (for instance, staying at a five-star hotel). An employer can set a limit on reimbursement amounts for various categories of expenses, provided this cap is reasonable and was made known to the employee before the expenses were incurred. (Labor Code sections 2802, 2804.)

B. VEHICLE EXPENSES

If an employer requires or allows an employee to use a personal vehicle for business travel, the employer must reimburse the employee fully for costs incurred. There is no mileage reimbursement rate set by law, though as a practical matter an employer can use the Internal Revenue Service (IRS) mileage rate, which is presumed to cover the costs of vehicle usage. The IRS mileage rate changes every year. The current rate can be found by doing an Internet search for "IRS mileage rate." Alternatively, an employer can reimburse employees for mileage by paying a lump sum periodically, but this sum must be sufficient to fully reimburse the employee for vehicle use.

If the employer provides the employee with a company vehicle for business travel, the employer must reimburse the employee for actual expenses incurred in fueling, maintaining, servicing, and repairing the vehicle. (Labor Code sections 2802, 2804; *Gattuso v. Harte-Hanks Shoppers, Inc.* (2007) 42 Cal.4th 554.)

C. FORM OF REIMBURSEMENT

An employer can reimburse any employee for business expenses through either separate reimbursement payments that are clearly distinct from the employee's paycheck, or through an increase in the employee's base wages in the form of a higher salary or commission rate than would otherwise be paid to the employee if the employee were not incurring any business expenses. However, if the employer reimburses expenses through increased wage payments, the employer must make this known to the employees in advance, and must clearly identify the portion of the payment that is the expense reimbursement. Separate business expense reimbursement payments are not taxed. However, increased wages subject the employee to increased tax liability. For that reason, an employer that uses the increased wage method of reimbursing expenses must ensure that the amount paid for such reimbursements will be sufficient to also reimburse the employee for the increased tax liability. (*Gattuso v. Harte-Hanks Shoppers, Inc.* (2007) 42 Cal.4th 554.)

D. REIMBURSEMENT FOR LOSSES

Any losses incurred in the discharge of an employee's duties must be reimbursed by the employer. For example, if the employee's personal work tools are stolen at the jobsite during non-work hours, where it is impractical for the employee to carry the tools back and forth from home to the jobsite, the employer is required to reimburse the employee for the cost of the tools. (*Machinists Automotive Trades Dist. Lodge v. Utility Trailers Sales Co.* (1983) 141 Cal.App.3d 80.)

E. REIMBURSEMENT FOR LEGAL EXPENSES

If an employee is sued by a third party for conduct in the course and scope of employment, the employer must reimburse the employee for attorney's fees and costs related to defending the lawsuit. If the employee loses the lawsuit, the employer must reimburse the employee for the amount of the judgment. Indemnification (the legal term for covering costs) is required as long as the employee was acting within the scope of her employment, regardless of whether the employee wins or loses the lawsuit, or whether the employee is found to have done nothing wrong or is found to have been negligent in some aspect of her job. Indemnification is not required if the employee was sued for, and was found to have engaged in, certain types of willful misconduct, such as serious sexual harassment, that fall outside the course and scope of employment, even if the conduct occurred during work hours on the employer's premises. (*Farmers Insurance Group v. County of Santa Clara* (1995) 11 Cal.4th 992; *Jacobus v. Krambo Corp.* (2000) 78 Cal.App.4th 1096.) However, if the conduct falls short of extremely wrongful, the employer will generally be required to pay for the employee's legal expenses.

Usually, when an employee is sued in connection with work-related conduct, the employer is also sued. The employer may provide the employee with representation by the same attorney who is representing the employer. Because the legal interests of the employee may differ from those of the employer, it is often advisable for the employee to consult and possibly hire an independent attorney to ensure there is no conflict of interest. In certain cases, where the legal interests of the employer and the employee are not the same, and the conduct on which the suit is based was within the scope of the job, the employer will be obligated to cover the cost of independent counsel. (*Grissom v. Vons Companies* (1991) 1 Cal.App.4th 52.)

F. COSTS OF TOOLS AND EQUIPMENT

The IWC orders provide that when tools or equipment are required by the employer or are necessary to perform the job, they must be provided and maintained by the employer. There are two exceptions to this requirement, for all workers except construction workers:

- Employees whose wages are at least two times the minimum wage may be required to provide and maintain hand tools and equipment customarily required by their trade or craft. The IWC has explained that the term "hand tools and equipment" is limited to hand (as opposed to power) tools and personal equipment, such as tool belts or tool boxes, that are needed by employees to secure these hand tools.
- Employers do not have to provide tools to registered apprentices.

The employer must furnish tools and equipment that are necessary for safety under Cal-OSHA, the health and safety law. For example, if heavy-duty insulated gloves are required to safely perform a certain kind of electrical work, the employer must provide those gloves. (Labor Code sections 6401, 6403; 8 California Code of Regulations sections 3380–3411, 3556; IWC Orders 1-2001–15-2001 section 9, IWC Order 16-2001 section 8; IWC Statement as to the Basis for 2001 Wage Orders.)

G. COSTS OF UNIFORMS AND PROTECTIVE APPAREL

When an employer requires uniforms to be worn as a condition of employment, it must provide and maintain them. Uniforms are defined as "wearing apparel or accessories of distinctive design or color." Clothing that is specific to an employer, such as a particular color combination, constitutes a uniform. An employee can recover the cost of a required uniform in a claim for unpaid wages. (*Dept. of Industrial Relations v. UI Video Stores, Inc.* (1997) 55 Cal.App.4th 1084.)

Maintenance of the uniform includes dry cleaning, ironing, or separate laundering, where such special maintenance is necessary. If the uniform becomes worn or torn due to normal use and must be replaced or repaired, the employer must pay for the replacement or repair. (IWC Orders 1-2001–15-2001 section 9, IWC Order 16-2001 section 8.)

Exception: Government employees may be required to pay for required uniforms and uniform maintenance. (*In re. Work Uniform Cases* (2005) 133 Cal.App.4th 328.)

VII. PAYCHECK REGULATIONS

A. TIMING OF REGULAR PAYCHECKS

Every employer must post a "payday notice," where it can be seen by employees, stating the days, time, and place of regular wage payments. Regular wage payments must be made on these regular paydays. (Labor Code sections 204(a), 207.)

For most employees, these regular paydays must be scheduled twice a month. Work performed between the first and fifteenth of the month that is not overtime work must be paid between the sixteenth and twenty-sixth of the same month. Work performed between the sixteenth and the last day of the month that is not overtime work must be paid between the first and the tenth of the following month. Overtime work must be paid no later than payday for the next regular pay period following the performance of the work. (Labor Code section 204(a), (b).)

Employees of farm labor contractors must be paid on a weekly basis, and they must be paid for all work performed up to and including the fourth day before the weekly payday. (Labor Code section 205.) All other farm workers (except for those who receive meals and lodging from their employer) must be paid no less than twice a month. All work performed between the first and fifteenth days of the month must be paid between the sixteenth and twenty-second of that month. All work performed between the sixteenth and the last day of the month must be paid between the first and seventh day of the following month. (Labor Code section 205.5.)

Employees who are paid weekly (other than employees of farm labor contractors) must be paid no more than seven calendar days following the close of the pay period during which the work was performed. (Labor Code section 204b.)

Certain employees need only be paid once a month. Employees who may be paid monthly include:

- Farm workers and household domestic workers who receive meals and lodging from their

employers. Their monthly pay must include all wages earned during the month up to the regular payday. (Labor Code section 205.)

- Salespersons employed by motor vehicle dealers, with respect to their commission wages. However, all wages earned other than commissions must be paid to these salespersons at least twice a month. (Labor Code section 204.1.)

- Salaried administrative, executive or professional employees who are exempt from overtime. If paid monthly, they must be paid on or before the twenty-sixth day of the month for that month's salary, including the unearned portion between the date of payment and the last day of the month. (Labor Code section 204(a).)

Exceptions: These provisions do not cover public employees. (Labor Code section 220.) Employees covered by a collective bargaining agreement are not subject to many of the above payday timing laws if the agreement provides for different pay arrangements. (Labor Code sections 204(c) and 204.1.)

B. TIMING OF FINAL PAYCHECKS

1. Employees Who Are Fired or Laid Off

If an employee is discharged, all earned and unpaid wages are due and payable immediately. An employee who is laid off and not given a specified recall date within the same pay period is considered to have been discharged and is entitled to immediate payment. Employees hired for a specific assignment or for a specified period of time are considered to have been discharged upon conclusion of the assignment or expiration of the period for which they were hired. These final payments must be made at the place of discharge, or, if authorized by the employee, by direct deposit to the employee's bank account. (Labor Code sections 201, 208, 213(d); *Smith v. Superior Court (L'Oreal USA, Inc.)* (2006) 39 Cal.4th 77.)

2. Employees Who Quit

If an employee quits and provides the employer with at least seventy-two hours prior notice, all earned and unpaid wages are due at the end of the last day of employment. If the employee quits without providing seventy-two hours notice, these wages are due within seventy-two hours of the last

CHAPTER 4

day of employment. Payment must be made at the employer's office in the county where the work was performed, or, if authorized by the employee, by mail to the mailing address designated by the employee or by direct deposit to the employee's bank account. (Labor Code sections 202, 208, 213(d).)

These laws governing the timely payment of wages upon separation of employment cover both non-union and unionized workers. There is no exception to these laws for workers covered by collective bargaining agreements. (*Livadas v. Bradshaw* (1994) 512 U.S. 107.)

3. Exceptions to General Rules Governing Timing of Final Paychecks

Some limited exceptions exist to the requirements outlined above.

- Laid-off seasonal employees in the canning of perishable fruit, vegetables, or fish must be paid within seventy-two hours of layoff. With employee authorization, payment can be mailed to a designated mailing address. (Labor Code section 201(a).)
- Laid-off oil drilling employees must be paid within twenty-four hours of layoff (excluding Saturdays, Sundays, and holidays). With employee authorization, payment can be mailed to a designated mailing address. (Labor Code section 201.7.)
- Terminated employees engaged in the production or broadcasting of theatrical or televised motion pictures, television programs, filmed commercial advertisements, music videos, or webcasts, who had been hired for a limited period of time to provide services

Employers may not collect debts owed by employees by deducting money from earned wages.

for a particular production, need not be paid their final wages until the next regular payday. Payment may be mailed to the employee, or made available to the employee at a location specified by the employer in the county where the employee was hired or performed labor. (Labor Code section 201.5.)

- Discharged or laid-off workers employed at a venue that hosts theatrical or concert events, and who are routinely dispatched to jobs through a hiring hall established under a collective bargaining agreement with a union, are subject to the timing requirements established in the collective bargaining agreement, if those requirements differ from the time limits established under state law. (Labor Code section 201.9.)

C. PENALTY FOR LATE PAYMENT OF FINAL WAGES

If an employer willfully fails to provide a complete and on-time payment of all wages owed to an employee following a discharge, layoff, or resignation from employment, the employee is entitled to "waiting time penalties." For example, an employee who is provided with a "final paycheck" immediately upon discharge will be entitled to waiting time penalties if that final paycheck did not include overtime compensation that was earned but not paid to the employee for work performed at any time in the prior three years. A claim for waiting time penalties should always be pursued whenever any wages are owed and unpaid at the end of an employment relationship. (Labor Code section 203.)

The term "willful" means that the employer voluntarily and intentionally paid (or did not pay) whatever should have been included in the employee's final payment. It is not necessary to show an evil intent to defraud to prove that an act is willful. An employer's alleged inability to pay or ignorance of the law is not a defense. (*Davis v. Morris* (1940) 37 Cal.App.2d 269.) An employer may successfully defend a claim for waiting time penalties by proving that he had a *bona fide*, good faith, reasonable belief that the unpaid wages were not owed, particularly if the law is unclear as to the employer's obligation to pay the contested wages. But any wages that are not reasonably in dispute must be timely and unconditionally paid, or penalties will be imposed. If the employer does not have a good faith defense to payment of some portion (no matter how small) of the entire amount claimed to be due, waiting time penalties must be awarded. (Labor Code section 206(a); 8 California Code of Regulations section 13520; *Barnhill v. Robert Saunders & Co.* (1981) 125 Cal. App.3d 1.) Waiting time penalties start on the day that wages are due following separation from employment. The penalties continue to be added to the amount owed to the worker each day until full payment is made, but for no more than thirty calendar days. The daily penalty is an additional day's pay, based on the employee's daily wage rate. The employee's daily wage rate is based on all earned compensation, including both regular and overtime wages, and it must be at least the minimum wage for all daily hours worked. For example, an employee who was paid $20 an hour, with an average of ten hours of work per workday, would have a daily wage rate of $220 (non-overtime wages of $160 and overtime wages of $60), and a waiting time penalty claim of up to $6,600. (*Mamika v. Barca* (1998) 68 Cal.App.4th 487.) The wage rate used is generally the rate at the time of the separation from employment. In situations where the wage rate varied (for instance, payments based on commissions or piece rate), wages may be averaged over a longer period of time.

D. ITEMIZED WAGE STATEMENTS

Whenever wages are paid, or twice a month, an employer must provide each of its employees with an itemized wage statement, either as a detachable part of a paycheck or on a separate document if wages are paid in cash or by personal check. This itemized statement must contain all of the following information:
- Gross wages earned;
- The total number of hours worked (except for employees who are paid solely by salary and who are exempt from payment of overtime);
- For workers paid by piece-rate, the number of piece-rate units earned and all applicable rates;
- All deductions from wages, listed separately (except for deductions authorized in writing by the employee, which must be shown and totaled but need not be listed separately);
- Net wages earned;
- The starting and ending dates (with month, day, and year) of the period for which the employee is paid;
- The employee's name and either the last four digits of the employee's Social Security Number, or an employee identification number other than a Social Security Number;
- The name and address of the employer. (The name shown must be that of the actual legal entity of the employer, rather than just a fictitious business name);
- The hours worked at each applicable hourly rate of pay that was in effect during the pay period.

The statement must be properly dated and readable, in English, and be in ink or some other indelible form. The employer must keep a copy of it on file for at least three years, either at the place of employment or at some central location in California. (Labor Code section 226(a); IWC Orders section 7.)

An employee who is harmed by an employer's intentional failure to follow any of these requirements may recover either all actual damages or a penalty based on the number of pay periods during which the employer did not follow the law, whichever is greater. Penalties are set at $50 for the initial pay period, and $100 for each pay period that follows, not to exceed $4,000. The employer must also reimburse an employee who proves a violation of these laws for court costs and reasonable attorney's fees. (Labor Code section 226(e).)

An employer must allow any current or former employee to inspect or copy the employer's copies of the itemized wage statements of that employee. The employer must comply with any such request within twenty-one days of the date of the request. If the employer fails to comply within that time, the employee is entitled to recover a $750 penalty from the employer. If the employer complies by providing the employee with copies of these records, the employer may charge the employee the actual cost of making those copies. (Labor Code section 226(b), (c), (f).)

Exceptions: Public employees and certain household employees are excluded from these protections. (Labor Code section 226(d), (h).)

E. PAYMENT BY CASH OR NEGOTIABLE CHECK

It is unlawful for an employer or for anyone acting on behalf of an employer to pay an employee's wages with a check or written instrument that is not payable in cash, on demand, without discount, at any branch of the bank on which the check is written. The maker of the check (the employer, or the payroll company or other agent of the employer that issues paychecks for the employer) must have sufficient funds in the bank account (or a credit arrangement with the bank so that payment is guaranteed) at the time the paycheck is issued, and for at least thirty days thereafter. (Labor Code section 212(a)(1), (c).)

It is unlawful to pay an employee's wages by any sort of scrip, voucher, coupon, or any other instrument redeemable in merchandise or services or anything else other than cash. (Labor Code section 212(a)(2).)

If an employee presents a paycheck to the bank or other institution named on the check within thirty days of receipt, and the check cannot be immediately cashed or deposited because the employer has no account with the bank or because of insufficient funds in the account, the employee is entitled to penalty wages in addition to the unpaid wages. The penalty is based on the employee's daily wage and fringe benefit rate. Penalties begin on the date the worker tried to cash the check. Penalties continue until the amounts owed are fully paid, up to a limit of thirty days from the date of the attempt to cash the check. This penalty applies whether the non-cashable paycheck was issued for regular wages or for final wages due following separation of employment (in which case the employee will be entitled to a separate "waiting time" penalty under Labor Code section 203).

The non-cashable check penalty will not apply if the employer proves that the violation was unintentional, or the employee wins an action against the employer for the recovery of service charges under Civil Code section 1719. Generally, it is not advisable for an employee to file an action under this Civil Code statute, as it provides for a much more limited recovery than what is available under the Labor Code.

F. PAYMENT OF UNDISPUTED WAGES

In any dispute over wages, the employer is required to pay all wages the employer admits are due in a timely and unconditional manner. The employee may then pursue any available remedy for the portion of wages that have not yet been paid. The employer is prohibited from withholding payment of wages that are definitely due in order to force the employee into settling or abandoning the claim for disputed wages. (Labor Code section 206.)

G. WAGE RELEASES OR WAIVERS

It is unlawful for an employer to require an employee to sign a release or waiver of any claim for wages due or to become due. The law expressly states that any release or waiver of this sort will not be enforced. This law had been interpreted to mean that such releases or waivers cannot prevent an employee from pursuing a claim for unpaid wages, particularly when the right to the payment of the wages (such as overtime wages) cannot be set aside by private agreement. (Labor Code sections 206.5, 219(a), 1194.)

However, in a recent case, a court held that this prohibition of releases does not apply to any wage release that is signed in connection with the settlement of a "bona fide dispute" over wages. Thus, where there is a "bona fide dispute" over whether wages are due, the employer and employees may settle the claim for unpaid wages with payment of less than the full amount of wages claimed, and in connection with this settlement, the employer may obtain releases in which the employees waive their right to seek payment of any additional amounts. These releases will be enforceable and will prevent the employees from taking any further action to recover the remaining unpaid wages. (*Chindarah v. Pick Up Stix, Inc.* (2009) 171 Cal.App.4th 796.)

This is one of the few areas where federal law is more protective than state law. Under federal law, a release of a claim for wages owed under the Fair Labor Standards Act will not be enforced unless the release was obtained in connection with a settlement supervised by the U.S. Department of Labor or by a federal district court. (*Lynn's Food Stores, Inc. v. United States* (11th Cir. 1982) 679 F.2d 1350.)

As a result of the recent narrowing of state law protections regarding releases of wage claims, employees should be very careful before signing any such release. The employee may have claims that she is completely unaware of, which could be lost forever if the release is signed. It is strongly recommended that a release never be signed without first consulting an attorney with expertise in wage and hour law.

H. "PAYMENT IN FULL" CHECKS

Some employers will attempt to limit their liability for wage claims by issuing paychecks with restrictive language, for instance paychecks that state "payment in full," or "payment of all wages owed," or words of similar meaning. Where the amount owed is disputed, the employee has the right to cross out the "payment in full" language, and then cash or deposit the check. Even when the employee does not cross out the restrictive language, it will not be enforced if the employee can show that he deposited the check accidentally or without understanding the effect of the restrictive language. (Civil Code section 1526.)

If the employer includes restrictive language on a paycheck that does not cover the full amount of wages which are clearly owed to the employee, or if the employer does not have a bona fide good faith defense to payment of the unpaid wages, the restrictive language should not be enforced even if it was not crossed out by the employee. (Labor Code sections 206, 206.5; *Reid v. Overland Machined Products* (1961) 55 Cal.2d 203.)

VIII. LABOR COMMISSIONER CLAIMS

A. DECIDING WHETHER TO FILE A LAWSUIT OR A CLAIM WITH THE LABOR COMMISSIONER

Employees with wage claims can choose between having the claim decided by the labor commissioner and filing a court action. There are usually many advantages to filing a claim with the labor commissioner rather than filing an individual lawsuit. Labor commissioner proceedings are far less complicated than court proceedings, and

it is much easier for workers not represented by attorneys to present their claims to the labor commissioner. Deputy labor commissioners will provide assistance to employees in identifying potential claims, writing up the claim, serving the employer with the claim, and in attempting to resolve the claim with the employer before the case goes to hearing. If the case goes to hearing, the labor commissioner's hearing officer will probably play a more active role than a judge in court would in proactively questioning the employer and other witnesses to ensure that the facts needed to prove a claim are put into evidence. If an employee wins a lawsuit in court, the employee is responsible for "enforcing the judgment" (that is, doing what is necessary to collect the amount found due). In contrast, if an employee gets a favorable decision from a labor commissioner's hearing officer, the labor commissioner will take some actions to attempt to collect the amount found due from the employer. Finally, if an employer appeals a decision issued by a labor commissioner's hearing officer, the labor commissioner will generally provide the employee with an attorney, at no cost, to represent the employee in any follow-up proceedings.

However, there are some types of cases where it will work to an employee's advantage to file in court rather than with the labor commissioner. Some types of damages or penalties can be awarded by courts, but not by the labor commissioner. See Chapter 10, on discharge and disciplinary action, for more information on the types of damages available in lawsuits. If the employee's claim mostly consists of such damages or penalties, the employee may be forced to file a lawsuit. Claims that are of extremely high value or are very complex may be better prosecuted in court, as court proceedings typically allow the parties greater rights to obtain evidence from the other side prior to trial. Lastly, an employee whose claim is based on a widespread, systemic Labor Code violation, where other employees are similarly affected by the violation, can have a greater impact by filing a class action lawsuit instead of an individual wage claim. If successful, a class action lawsuit will result in recovery for the entire class of workers, and in the issuance of an injunction (a court order) prohibiting the employer from committing further violations.

The complexity of court proceedings (except for small claims court cases) essentially requires representation by an attorney in lawsuits filed in court. Small claims court is rarely a good option for employees, because of the low dollar limits on any claim, the prohibition on appeals by small claims plaintiffs, and the fact that judges hearing small claims cases typically lack expertise in wage and hour law.

B. THE FUNCTIONS OF THE LABOR COMMISSIONER

The California labor commissioner (also known as the chief of the Division of Labor Standards Enforcement, or DLSE) has authority to investigate employee complaints for the recovery of wages, penalties, or other compensation arising out of the employment relationship. The labor commissioner can hear and decide all types of wage claims based on California law (including IWC orders), and based on contracts between the employee and employer. However, the labor commissioner does not have authority to hear claims based on federal law. The labor commissioner has district offices throughout the state that accept and review individual claims. A complete listing of these offices can be found at http://www.dir.ca.gov/dlse/DistrictOffices.htm. Claims should be filed with the office that covers the county where the work was performed. The procedure for filing a claim is available at http://www.dir.ca.gov/dlse/Policies.htm. A claim form can be downloaded from http://www.dir.ca.gov/dlse/Form1.pdf.

After reviewing a claim, the labor commissioner can either:

- Proceed under the individual claim "Berman hearing" process (described at Labor Code section 98 and at 8 California Code of Regulations sections 13500–13508); or
- Transfer the claim to the DLSE's Bureau of Field Enforcement (BOFE), for a broader investigation of the employer's practices as to a large class of employees, with the possibility of a DLSE enforcement action (either through the issuance of a citation against the employer or through the filing of a lawsuit under Labor Code section 98.3); or
- Dismiss the claim without making any decision on the merits, leaving the claimant with the option of filing a lawsuit against the employer.

Decisions on the merits can only be made after a hearing has been held.

C. THE BERMAN HEARING PROCESS

Following the filing of the claim, the DLSE will mail a "Notice of Claim Filed and Conference Scheduled" to the claimant and the employer, summarizing the claim and scheduling a prehearing conference. This conference is held before a deputy labor commissioner. It is an informal proceeding designed to obtain general information about the claim and the employer's defenses, and to explore the possibility of a settlement. Most claims are settled during this conference. If the claim is not settled, the deputy labor commissioner will assist the claimant in filling out a complaint, which covers the issues that remain unresolved. The claimant should ask the deputy to make sure that every possible claim for wages, expenses, and penalties is included in this complaint.

Complaints are scheduled for hearing before a DLSE hearing officer who has not had prior involvement with the claim. Both sides have the right to represent themselves, or to be represented by an attorney or by a non-attorney representative at this hearing. The hearing officer has been trained to help the parties present their cases without attorneys, and to ask questions that are necessary to reach a decision. This hearing is tape recorded. Testimony is taken under oath. Both sides get to testify and present any written evidence. Both sides can question witnesses and can cross-examine witnesses called by the opposing side.

Each side also has the right to request subpoenas requiring the attendance of a witness or seeking documents for the hearing. A request for a subpoena should be directed to the hearing officer as far in advance of the hearing as possible, to give the hearing officer time to issue the subpoena and to allow sufficient time to serve the subpoena. If the claimant's case would be helped by testimony of someone who is currently employed by the defendant, the claimant may want to subpoena that witness, in order to give the witness protection to testify without interference from the employer.

Following the hearing, the DLSE hearing officer will issue an Order, Decision, or Award (ODA), summarizing the facts and applying the relevant laws and regulations to those facts, and reaching a conclusion as to the amount, if any, of the award. The ODA will contain a description of the parties' appeal rights. An appeal must be filed very quickly — within fifteen calendar days of the date the ODA was mailed, if mailed to an address in California. A late appeal cannot be considered. If an appeal is not filed on time, the ODA becomes a non-appealable court judgment. If it awarded anything to the claimant, that amount becomes enforceable like any other court judgment. (Labor Code sections 98.1, 98.2; Code of Civil Procedure section 1013(a); *Pressler v. Donald L. Bren Co.* (1982) 32 Cal.3d 831.)

D. APPEALING ORDERS, DECISIONS, OR AWARDS TO COURT

An appeal of the ODA must be filed with the California Superior Court for the county in which the work was performed. The filing of a timely appeal wipes out the ODA. The matter will be on track for a court trial in which the court will be free to make new findings of fact. But appealing an ODA can be very risky. If the party filing the appeal does not win in the court proceedings, that party will have to pay the other side's reasonable attorney's fees. If the court awards any money to the employee (even if it is less than the amount of the ODA), then the employee is considered to be the "prevailing party" (the winner). If the court awards no money to the employee, then the employer is the prevailing party. Generally, the party that files the appeal from the ODA has to pay its own attorney's fees, even if it prevails in the court proceedings. The exception to this is that if the employee appeals the ODA on a claim for unpaid minimum wages, overtime compensation, or unreimbursed business expenses, the employer must pay the employee's attorney's fees. (Labor Code sections 98.1, 98.2; *Eicher v. Advanced Business Integrators, Inc.* (2007) 151 Cal.App.4th 1363.)

Unlike DLSE hearings, court proceedings are governed by fairly complicated procedures and formal rules. It is generally unwise to proceed in court without attorney representation. If the employer appeals an ODA that awards any money to the claimant, and the claimant is unable to afford an attorney, a DLSE lawyer will represent the claimant in the court proceedings at no charge, upon the claimant's request. (Labor Code section 98.4.)

The court will allow both sides to present relevant evidence, regardless of whether that evidence had been presented in the DLSE proceedings. The issues in court are not necessarily limited to the issues that were considered by the labor commissioner. The employee can seek more money than the amount that had been awarded by the labor commissioner, even if it is the employer that filed the appeal. The court may allow the employee to present new claims for wages, other compensation, or penalties that were not requested in the DLSE proceedings. (*Murphy v. Kenneth Cole Productions, Inc.* (2007) 40 Cal.4th 1094.)

E. CLAIMS THAT MAY BE EXCLUDED FROM THE BERMAN PROCESS

Certain types of claims cannot be heard by the labor commissioner, either because the commissioner has no authority under state law to hear the claim or because the commissioner's authority to hear the claim is preempted (superseded) by federal law. Some of these types of claims must be analyzed very closely to determine whether, under the specific facts, the labor commissioner has the authority to proceed. The types of claims that are likely to present jurisdictional issues (in other words, questions about whether the labor commission has authority to hear the case) are discussed below.

1. Claims That May Be Superseded by Federal Law

a. Claims for Wages Owed Pursuant to a Collective Bargaining Agreement

If the wage claim is based on an alleged violation of a collective bargaining agreement, rather than a violation of state law, the federal Labor Management Relations Act prohibits the labor commissioner from hearing the claim. Instead, the claim must be processed and resolved through the grievance/ arbitration process contained in the collective bargaining agreement. However, claims that are based on state law (that is, claims that involve a violation of state law, rather than a violation of the collective bargaining agreement) will be heard by the labor commissioner, regardless of whether the employee is covered by a collective bargaining agreement. Claims based on state law include claims for unpaid wages where the employee was not paid (or paid less than the minimum wage) for "hours worked" under state law, wages owed as a result of the employer's violation of state law meal or rest period requirements, and penalties owed for late payment of final wages. (*Livadas v. Bradshaw* (1994) 512 U.S. 107.)

b. Claims Covered by Mandatory Arbitration Agreements

Employees who are covered by agreements that require the employee to arbitrate disputes arising out of his employment are said to be covered by a "mandatory arbitration agreement."

i. *Arbitration Provisions in Collective Bargaining Agreements*

It is quite common for collective bargaining agreements to contain a provision for binding arbitration of employment disputes. The existence of a mandatory arbitration clause in a collective bargaining agreement covering specific types of discrimination may bar a court from hearing the claim if the particular claim is clearly and unmistakably subject to binding arbitration under the agreement. (*14 Penn Plaza LLC v. Pyett* (2009) 129 S.Ct. 1456.)

ii. *Arbitration Provisions in Non-Union Employment*

In some industries, it has become common for non-union employers to require individual employees to "agree" to binding arbitration of employment disputes as a condition of obtaining or keeping a job. Non-union arbitration "agreements" often contain provisions that unfairly benefit the employer, and are often designed to prevent employees from protecting their rights.

iii. *General Principles*

Arbitration agreements will not be enforced if the arbitration procedures established under the agreement do not give the employee an effective means of protecting legal rights. (*Armendariz v. Foundation Health Psychcare Services, Inc.* (2000) 24 Cal.4th 83.)

An employee covered by an arbitration agreement should never hesitate to file with the labor commissioner. In many instances, the employer will not attempt to enforce arbitration. When it does, the labor commissioner will often actively oppose the attempt to require arbitration. In many situations, courts will deny employer efforts to compel arbitration.

c. Claims for Severance Pay

These claims are based on an agreement with an employer to provide severance pay when an employee leaves a job. In almost all cases, these claims can be heard by the labor commissioner. In a small minority of cases, an employer may have set up a severance pay plan that is regulated by ERISA, which governs pensions. In those limited situations, the labor commission may dismiss the case, because it is governed by federal law. (*California Chamber of Commerce v. Simpson* (C.D. Cal. 1985) 601 F.Supp. 104; *Velarde v. Pace Membership Warehouse, Inc.* (9th Cir. 1997) 105 F.3d 1313.)

2. Claims That Cannot Be Heard by the Labor Commissioner Under State Law

a. Claims for Damages Under the WARN Act

Under the federal Worker Adjustment and Retraining Notification (WARN) Act and California's equivalent, an employer must generally provide at least sixty days' written notice before a mass layoff or plant shutdown. The state law, which covers more employers than the federal law, applies to employers that have employed over seventy-five persons in the past twelve months. A mass layoff is defined as a layoff during any thirty-day period affecting fifty or more employees. Under this law, employees are entitled to damages for an employer's failure to provide required notice. But, these damages can only be obtained through the filing of a court action. (Labor Code sections 1400–1408.)

b. Claims for Civil Penalties Under PAGA

Under the recently enacted Labor Code Private Attorneys General Act (PAGA), individual employees can now file lawsuits against employers for civil penalties (fines that are payable to the state) for various Labor Code and IWC order violations. The law allows an individual employee to file such a lawsuit on behalf of all other employees whose rights were similarly violated. The amount of civil penalties is tied to the number of employees against whom violations were committed. As an incentive to employees to bring these sorts of actions, the law provides that 25 percent of the civil penalties that are imposed against an employer are distributed to the employees whose rights were violated, with the remaining 75 percent paid to the state. Before filing a PAGA lawsuit, an employee must give notice of the claim to the employer and to the California Labor and Workforce Development Agency (LWDA). The LWDA gets thirty-three days to decide whether or not the claim will be investigated by DLSE. If the LWDA decides not to investigate (or if after an investigation DLSE decides not to prosecute the alleged violations), the employee can proceed with a lawsuit for recovery of the civil penalties. The labor commissioner has no authority to impose PAGA penalties in a wage hearing under Labor Code section 98. The only way an employee can recover such penalties is through a court action. (Labor Code sections 2698–2699.5.)

c. Claims for Liquidated Damages for Failure to Pay the Minimum Wage

Liquidated damages (an extra award of damages beyond the unpaid minimum wages) can only be awarded by courts. The labor commissioner lacks authority to award such damages in a Berman hearing. Employees can seek these damages in court proceedings on an appeal from a Berman award, or by bypassing the labor commissioner and filing a lawsuit. Also, the labor commissioner can recover these damages for workers by filing a court action. (Labor Code section 1194.2.)

F. DEADLINES FOR FILING WAGE CLAIMS

The time limit (also known as the "statute of limitations") for filing a claim with the labor commissioner, or with a court, depends on the type of claim. The statute of limitations starts to run on the date the amount became due (also referred to as the date the claim arises). A claim is timely if, looking back from the date the claim is filed with the labor commissioner or the court, the claim arose within the applicable limitations period. These are the statutes of limitations for various claims:

- Claims for wages due under an oral contract must be filed within two years of the violation. (Code of Civil Procedure section 339.)
- Claims to enforce the right to amounts owed under a law or regulation (including minimum wages, overtime wages, pay for an employer's failure to provide required meal or rest periods, reimbursement of business expenses, reimbursement of amounts unlawfully deducted from wages, etc.) must be filed within three years of the violation. (Such claims may be brought in court, but not before the labor commissioner, under a special four-year statute of limitations under the Unfair Competition Law.) (Code of Civil Procedure section 338; Business and Professions Code section 17208; *Cortez v. Purolator Air Filtration Products Co.* (2000) 23 Cal.4th 163.)
- Claims for wages due under a written contract must be filed within four years of the violation. (Code of Civil Procedure section 337.)
- Claims for "waiting time penalties" (arising under Labor Code section 203 when an employer fails to pay all wages promptly upon separation from employment) are subject to the same time limits that apply to the claim for the unpaid wages, if the waiting time penalty claim is filed along with a claim for still unpaid wages. But if the claim for penalties stands alone, for example when the underlying wages (though late) were paid before the claim was filed, the penalty claim must be filed within one year of the violation. (*McCoy v. Superior Court* (2007) 157 Cal.App.4th 225.)

A wage claim may be partially inside and partially outside the applicable statue of limitations. In that case, the portion of the claim that was filed in time can be pursued. For example, an employee who is owed overtime going back for five years can file a claim with the labor commissioner for the most recent three years, but will be unable to claim the prior two years of wages owed.

CHAPTER 5 **BENEFITS**

BENEFITS

I. SCOPE OF THE CHAPTER

Most employers go beyond payment of wages to their workers and agree to provide benefits as well in order to attract and keep employees. State and federal laws protect employees' rights to those benefits that have been promised by an employer in a contract (such as an employer policy, employment handbook, or collective bargaining agreement). Health plan coverage (medical, hospital, dental, and vision care), vacation leave, paid or unpaid sick leave, and pension plans are among the most common benefits workers receive from their employers. Many, but not all, of these benefits are regulated by the federal Employee

Retirement Income Security Act of 1974 (ERISA). ERISA overrides state law, but when a benefit is not covered by ERISA, there may be applicable state regulations.

Workers sometimes need to take leaves of absence from work to care for family members, or themselves, if they are ill or injured. At both the federal and state levels there are "family and medical leave" laws that require many employers to grant leave for specified periods of time and for specific purposes, and to restore employees returning from such leave to the same or a substantially similar position with seniority and benefits preserved. There are important differences between the federal and the California family leave laws, particularly in the areas related to pregnancy and care for a domestic partner who is ill. In addition, the California, but not the federal, law requires that the leave be partially paid. The provisions of federal and California family and medical leave laws, their differences, rights and obligations under each, and their respective enforcement mechanisms are discussed in the sections that follow.

This chapter will also cover two additional important state benefits: State Disability Insurance, which provides partial salary replacement to most private sector and some public sector employees who are unable to work due to a temporary disability; and Unemployment Insurance, which provides benefits during periods of unemployment.

As with other areas of workers' rights, employees covered by a collective bargaining agreement may have greater rights than those set forth in this chapter. Employees should consult their collective bargaining agreement or union representative for more information on their contract rights.

II. BENEFITS UNDER ERISA

The Employee Retirement Income Security Act of 1974 (ERISA) (29 U.S. Code sections 1001 et seq.) is a federal law that governs the employment benefit plans of private employers. The law was enacted by Congress in response to employers who failed to protect the pension money of their employees. ERISA deals broadly with pension benefits and welfare benefits (for example, health benefits). It protects the interests of participants in benefit plans by requiring plans to disclose information about the plan (including important information about plan features and funding), imposing fiduciary (financial) responsibilities on those who manage and control plan assets, requiring plans to establish a grievance and appeals process for participants to get benefits from their plans, and providing participants with the right to sue for benefits and breaches of fiduciary duty.

Amendments to ERISA have expanded employees' rights. One important amendment is the Consolidated Omnibus Budget Reconciliation Act of 1986 (COBRA), which extends healthcare coverage after employment has terminated. COBRA is discussed in section III.E., p. 112. Another amendment, the Health Insurance Portability and Accountability Act of 1996 (HIPAA), is discussed in Chapter 12, section IV.B., p. 294.

ERISA regulates pension benefits and welfare benefits. A pension benefit plan provides retirement income. An employee welfare benefit plan provides medical benefits, apprenticeship or training benefits, scholarship funds, prepaid legal services, and/or other benefits.

ERISA specifically exempts from its coverage:
- Plans maintained by the federal, state, or local government for its employees;
- Plans maintained by churches for their employees;
- Plans maintained solely for the purpose of complying with Workers' Compensation, unemployment compensation, or disability laws. (29 U.S. Code section 1003(b).)

ERISA does not require employers to establish benefit plans, but rather it governs benefit plans once they have been established by the employer. ERISA overrides state law with respect to claims to recover benefits, enforce benefit rights that individuals have under ERISA, or clarify rights to future benefits.

If a benefit plan is governed by ERISA, the plan description and every claim or denial form should state that the plan is governed by ERISA. If none of the paperwork says that the plan is governed by ERISA, the plan is probably not governed by ERISA.

A. PENSION BENEFITS

ERISA divides pension benefits into two general groups:
- Defined benefit plans. With these types of plans, employees are promised a level of retirement income according to a formula that takes into account how long the employee has worked with the company.
- Defined contribution or individual account plans. With these types of plans, employees are not guaranteed a specific level of retirement benefits. Instead, each employee has a separate account, to which the employer or the employee or both may contribute. Upon retirement, and sometimes upon separation from service, the employee is entitled to the savings in his account, made up of both the contributions and any net investment income (or loss) generated by the contributions.

B. WELFARE BENEFITS

The health and welfare benefits that ERISA regulates include plans, funds, and programs established or maintained by an employer to provide medical benefits, vacation benefits, apprenticeship or training programs, daycare centers, scholarship funds, or prepaid legal services. (29 U.S. Code section 1002(1).)

Most vacation benefits are not regulated by ERISA. However, a vacation fund into which an employer makes contributions, and over which the employer forfeits control to a trustee who manages the fund, is a welfare benefit plan under ERISA. Vacation pay that comes out of an employer's general assets or payment of ordinary wages for sick leave, in contrast, are not governed by ERISA.

C. EMPLOYER'S RESPONSIBILITIES UNDER ERISA

1. Minimum Standards for Benefit Plans Under ERISA

In general, ERISA requires that an employer's benefit plan needs to be in writing and should lay out the agreed procedures for funding and providing benefits. Specifically, ERISA requires that an employer provide for the following in its pension and welfare plans:

- A summary plan description (29 U.S. Code section 1022);
- Notice to an employee if the employer denies benefits (29 U.S. Code section 1133(1));
- An appeal process that the employee or any other beneficiary may pursue if benefits are denied, either totally or partially (29 U.S. Code section 1133(2));
- Financial information (an annual report) about the plans (29 U.S. Code section 1023);
- Confidentiality about an employee's participation in the plans (29 U.S. Code section 1026(b)).

2. Employer's Duty to Fund Promised Benefits

If an employer agrees to make payments into a benefit fund when it enters into a collective bargaining agreement or other employment contract, it is required by ERISA to deliver on its promise. An employer who fails to make promised payments, willfully or with intent to defraud an employee, violates federal law. (See generally 29 U.S. Code sections 1101–1104, 1131–1132.)

Enforcement: The rules regarding ERISA rights and enforcement procedures are complex and detailed. Employees should request a copy of the summary plan description from the plan administrator, and review the rules for filing an appeal. Employees must file an administrative appeal under the plan (and attempt to pursue the appeal) before going to court. The results of any lawsuit filed later will be influenced by the facts that were raised in the administrative appeal. For this reason, it is very important to raise all potential arguments at the administrative appeal stage. Plan participants may also submit a request to the U.S. Department of Labor for help in pursuing rights under ERISA. Enforcement of rights under benefit plans governed by ERISA is by complaint to the U.S. Department of Labor. An employer who violates the reporting and disclosure requirements of ERISA may be fined and/or imprisoned. (29 U.S. Code section 1131.) Once contractual and administrative remedies have been exhausted, individuals may file civil suit in court to recover benefits due, to enforce rights, or to clarify future rights and benefits.

III. EMPLOYER HEALTHCARE PLANS

Employers are not required by law to provide health benefits. However, many choose to do so as an incentive to workers to join and remain in the employment of the employer's operation.

As noted above, in most cases such employer plans in private companies or businesses are governed by ERISA. Check the benefit or denial statements or the plan description. If the program is covered by ERISA, it should say so.

A. TRADITIONAL HEALTH BENEFITS

Traditional health plans in California cover a wide range of medical services to treat illnesses, non-job-related injuries, pregnancies, and other health conditions. (Job-related injuries and illnesses are covered by Workers' Compensation. See Chapter 8.) Plans typically cover only those services and supplies that the plan defines as medically necessary. Covered benefits may include costs of surgery, professional services for treatment of illness and injury, and inpatient and outpatient hospital care. Some employers offer dental and vision care plans as well as medical and hospital plans. Some employers also provide coverage for workers' children and spouses.

For information regarding an employee's right to continue his medical coverage after his job ends, see section III.E., p. 112. For information regarding payment for health plan coverage while an employee is on family and medical leave, see section VII.A.11., p. 137.

B. COVERAGE OF PRE-EXISTING CONDITIONS

Under California law, group health insurance plans (which include job-based plans) cannot refuse to cover an individual or charge her a different rate for the same coverage as others solely because she has a physical or mental impairment, unless the refusal or rate is based on sound actuarial principles applied to actual experience. If insufficient experience is available, the refusal or rate must be based on sound underwriting practices. (Health and Safety Code section 1367.8.) Essentially, this means that these kinds of refusals must be based on legitimate business considerations supported by statistics and studies, not on superficial prejudices or arbitrary actions.

C. PROCEDURES FOR ENFORCING TERMS OF A HEALTH INSURANCE PLAN, HEALTH MAINTENANCE ORGANIZATION (HMO)

Disputes between a covered individual and a healthcare provider that do not involve ERISA-governed plan establishment, funding, and administration issues are subject to state law regulation. Under California law, every group health insurance plan must provide enrollees with a grievance procedure to follow in the event of a dispute with the health provider. The grievance procedure must offer a resolution of the problem within thirty days. If any issue raised by a covered employee is not resolved satisfactorily by the grievance procedure, she may appeal to the California Department of Managed Healthcare

if benefits are provided through an organization (for example, an HMO such as Kaiser). (Health and Safety Code section 1368.) If benefits are provided through a regular insurance program, sometimes called an indemnity plan or a "preferred provider organization" or "PPO," this is regulated by the California Department of Insurance, which has a different procedure. The description of the plan should indicate what type of plan it is. More information on this can be found at http://www.insurance.ca.gov/contact-us/0200-file-complaint/index.cfm.

The insurance company's internal complaint procedure must be used first. After that, it is possible to bring complaints regarding denial of claims and some other matters to the Department of Insurance. California's grievance procedures do not apply to Medicare Advantage plans, where federal procedures control. (42 U.S. Code section 1395w-26(b)(3).)

D. CONVERSION OF CANCELED POLICIES

If an employer terminates group medical coverage for an entire group of employees, an affected employee has the right to convert that group policy to an individual policy that provides at least minimum benefits, regardless of any pre-existing conditions the employee may have. The employee will have to pay for the policy herself. If the group policy covered dependents, the individual employee has the right to purchase an individual policy that also covers dependents. (Health and Safety Code section 1373.6.) The individual employee also has a right to convert to an individual policy if her continuation coverage (an extension of the group coverage after termination of employment, with premiums paid by the employee) ends. (Insurance Code sections 12670–12692.5; 29 U.S. Code section 1162(5).) For a discussion of continuation coverage, see the next section. Dependents who lose their coverage for any reason also have the right to individual policies.

Exceptions: An employee and his dependents do not have the right to convert the canceled policy if any of the following occurs:

- The group policy is replaced by a group policy that gives the employee similar coverage within sixty days of the time he lost the original coverage.

- The policy was terminated because the employee failed to make a required payment when due.
- The employee was not covered during the three months before his policy was terminated.
- The employee is entitled to state or federally provided benefits, including Medicare. (29 U.S. Code section 1162.)

Enforcement: See the following section on COBRA enforcement. The California labor commissioner may enforce violations of notice requirements. File a lawsuit.

E. CONTINUATION OF COVERAGE AFTER TERMINATION OF EMPLOYMENT OR LOSS OF DEPENDENT STATUS

When an employee leaves her job, she has the right, under the federal Consolidated Omnibus Budget Reconciliation Act of 1985 (COBRA), to continue for a limited time the identical medical, dental, and vision care plans she had while employed. The employee must pay the full premium cost associated with the coverage (including any portion formerly paid by the employer) and a small administrative fee. The employee's dependents may also have independent rights to continuation of coverage under this law when the employee loses coverage, or if the dependent has lost coverage for other specified reasons. An individual (employee or dependent) is eligible under COBRA if one of the following "qualifying events" has occurred:

- The employee's employment has terminated, voluntarily or involuntarily, for a reason other than the employee's gross misconduct.
- The employee's work hours have been reduced to a level where the employer does not provide health coverage.
- The covered employee has died and the person seeking the COBRA extension was a covered dependent.
- The person seeking the COBRA extension will lose coverage because she and the covered employee have divorced or separated.
- The employee became entitled to Social Security benefits (Medicare), and the person seeking the COBRA extension was a covered dependent.
- The person seeking the COBRA extension was the employee's dependent child, and is no longer a dependent. (29 U.S. Code section 1163.)

Some employer health plans that provide coverage for an employee's dependent child who is a student in a college or other postsecondary educational institution require that the student attend school full-time to be considered a dependent. An amendment to ERISA, effective October 9, 2009, extends the dependent status (and therefore, coverage under the parent's health insurance) of a dependent child who needs a reduced course load for medical reasons. If she was considered a dependent child (and therefore covered by her parent's health insurance) under a plan based on being a full-time student at a postsecondary educational institution before the medically necessary leave is needed, this law allows her to remain a dependent for up to one year from the beginning of the medical leave, despite not being a full-time student. The leave of absence must begin while the dependent is suffering from a serious illness or injury, must be medically necessary as certified by the treating doctor, and must cause the formerly full-time student to lose student status for purposes of eligibility as a dependent under the terms of the plan or coverage. (29 U.S. Code section 1185c.) If the dependent child is unable to resume full-time attendance after one year from the beginning of the medical leave, or if she is no longer a dependent for another reason (for example, she reaches a maximum age set by the plan), the loss of dependent status would be a "qualifying event" allowing her to be eligible for COBRA.

An individual claiming the COBRA extension entitlement must pay the monthly premiums, plus any administrative fees, directly to the insurance company. Coverage ends if the individual does not pay the premiums, if she becomes covered by another group health plan, if she becomes entitled to Medicare benefits, or if her employer terminates all its health plans (in which case the affected person could convert to an individual policy under 29 U.S. Code section 1162; see section VII.A.11., p. 137).

A former employee or covered dependent can continue coverage for up to eighteen months if the reason for loss of coverage is loss of employment or reduction in hours. In some situations, coverage may continue for an additional period of time. Up to an additional eleven months of COBRA continuation coverage is available, for a total of twenty-nine months of coverage, if, prior to the sixtieth day of COBRA coverage, the former employer or other covered family member is determined by the Social Security Administration to be disabled, and timely notice is given to the plan. Also, if the family experiences another qualifying event while covered during the initial eighteen-month COBRA period, an additional coverage period of up to eighteen months may be available, for a total of thirty-six months of coverage.

During periods of high unemployment, the federal government may extend COBRA and/or provide supplemental benefits to assist unemployed workers in paying for COBRA coverage.

> *An employer must continue to pay its share of group healthcare premiums for employees on family leave.*

Family members can continue their coverage for up to thirty-six months after the covered employee's death, divorce, legal separation, the child's dependent status ends, or the covered employee becomes eligible for Medicare. (29 U.S. Code sections 1161–1168.) A program called Cal-COBRA provides similar rights to continued coverage (if the employee pays the premiums) for those employed by employers with two to nineteen employees, and, in some circumstances, may provide additional guarantees of extended insurance coverage to those getting eighteen months of coverage under federal COBRA. Additionally, if an employee's coverage has ended because of military service, she has the right to choose to extend employer-provided health coverage for herself and covered dependents for up to twenty-four months, under the Uniformed Services Employment and Reemployment Rights Act (USERRA). (38 U.S. Code section 4317; 20 Code of Federal Regulations section 1002.164.)

Under certain circumstances, if the employee is on Medi-Cal and has current private or employer-related health insurance coverage, the California Department of Health Care Services may pay his health premiums under the Health Insurance Premium Payment (HIPP) Program if it is determined to be cost-effective for the state. If the employee's health coverage covers a family member who is on Medi-Cal and has a very high-cost medical condition, the HIPP Program may pay the employee's premiums so that the family member can stay on the private policy. Eligibility for the HIPP Program is reviewed annually. If an individual is not eligible under the HIPP Program, and he is unable to work because of disability due to HIV/AIDS, the California Department of Health Care Services may pay his health premiums under the Comprehensive AIDS Resources Emergency (CARE)/HIPP Program for up to twenty-nine months. For more information on HIPP, see the California Department of Health Care Services' website on the program at http://www.dhcs.ca.gov/services/Pages/TPLRD_CAU_cont.aspx.

Also, see the following websites:

- General information: http://www.dol.gov/dol/topic/health-plans/cobra.htm
- Frequently asked questions: http://www.dol.gov/ebsa/faqs/faq_consumer_cobra.html
- Publications on COBRA: http://www.dol.gov/dol/topic/health-plans/cobra.htm#doltopics
- Information on Cal-COBRA: http://www.hmohelp.ca.gov/dmhc_consumer/hp/hp_cobra.aspx.

For information on the rights to convert to individual insurance policies and other options after COBRA coverage ends:

- http://www.dmhc.ca.gov/dmhc_consumer/hp/hp_cobra.aspx#continue
- http://www.insurance.ca.gov/ (Click on Consumers, then Information Guides, then Health Series.)

Enforcement: The California Department of Insurance handles complaints under the Cal-COBRA Program. See their website at http://www.insurance.ca.gov/contact-us/0200-file-complaint/ for information on how to file a complaint. The Federal Department of Labor (Employee Benefits Security Administration) handles issues related to federal COBRA. See their website at http://www.dol.gov/ebsa. (Click on FAQ on Cobra Health Coverage and click on Compliance Assistance.) Or file a federal lawsuit.

IV. VACATION

Although neither federal nor California law requires employers to provide paid vacation leave, most employers offer it as a part of a benefit package. An employee has no right to a paid vacation unless his employer has agreed to provide it. The employer's agreement may arise from an employment contract, a collective bargaining agreement, or the employer's policy.

In California, the courts have ruled and the Labor Code provides that a "use it or lose it" vacation policy is invalid in most instances. (*Suastez v. Plastic Dress-Up Co.* (1982) 31 Cal.3d 774, 782-784; *Boothby v. Atlas Mechanical, Inc.* (1992) 6 Cal.App.4th 1595; Labor Code section 227.3.) Vacation pay is a form of wages. It vests (meaning it is owned by the employee) as an employee earns it. Generally, earned vacation cannot be taken away once it is accrued. An exception is allowed, however, where vacation is based on a collective bargaining agreement which contains a "use it or lose it" policy. (Labor Code section 227.3.)

Employers are permitted to impose a reasonable cap on the amount of vacation that an employee can accrue. Under such a cap, no more vacation will accrue until the employee takes some of the accrued leave. Employers also can require employees to accept pay each year for accrued, unused vacation leave.

Upon termination of employment, an employer must pay the employee for all vacation that he has accrued through the final day of employment, and must do so at the employee's final rate of pay, regardless of when the vacation was earned. (Labor Code section 227.3) The rules for final payments of wages apply to final payments for earned vacation time — they must be paid within seventy-two hours. (Labor Code section 201.)

Enforcement: If the employer's vacation plan is not governed by ERISA, then employee rights are enforced through filing a complaint with the state labor commissioner through forms obtained from the Division of Labor Standards Enforcement (DLSE). DLSE forms and publications, as well as opinion letters of the labor commissioner, can be found at the DLSE website: http://www.dir.ca.gov/dlse/dlse.html. The "DLSE Enforcement Policies and Interpretations Manual" may be viewed at http://www.dir.ca.gov/dlse/DLSEManual/dlse_enfcmanual.pdf. An employer who willfully fails to pay wages owed to an employee who has been fired or quit (including payments for vacation not taken) is liable for a civil penalty equal to the employee's pay for up to thirty days. (Labor Code section 203.)

V. SICK LEAVE AND KIN CARE

Apart from requirements imposed by the family and medical leave laws, discussed below, most employers are not currently required to provide sick leave to their employees. This is, however, starting to change. San Francisco has passed a law mandating paid sick leave. (Chapter 12W of the San Francisco Administrative Code.) Legislation mandating paid sick leave has been proposed in a number of states, including California, and at the federal level. Currently, about 60 percent of employers provide a limited number of paid days off that employees can use when ill, and some others provide unpaid days off. Employers are permitted to require a doctor's note verifying the claimed illness in order to use sick days. Many require such documentation after a certain number of sick days are used in a row or if there is a pattern of sick leave use that the employer considers suspicious (such as frequently missing days before or after weekends or holidays).

In contrast to the rules applicable to vacation pay, discussed above, unused sick leave carries over into the next year only when an employer agrees to this in a contract, collective bargaining agreement, or employment policy. Some California laws provide that certain public employees — including state civil service employees and certified teachers — may carry over unused sick leave into future years. (Education Code section 44978.) Employers are not required by law to pay out unused sick leave upon termination of employment. However, some public employee pension plans and some collective bargaining agreements require that unused sick leave be added to the calculation of time worked for purposes of calculating a pension.

If an employer does provide sick leave, either paid or unpaid, employees must be allowed to use a limited amount of it for kin care, which involves caring for an ailing spouse, registered domestic partner, parent, child, or child of a registered domestic partner. (Labor Code section 233.) Employees are entitled to take up to one-half their annually earned sick leave to use for kin care. For example, an employee who is entitled to twelve days of sick leave a year can use up to six days a year to provide kin care, once the sick leave has been earned

Some non-traditional leave policies offer paid time off or "PTO" in lieu of both vacation and sick leave. It is not yet legally clear whether the requirement that employees be allowed to use a portion of sick leave for kin care applies to these leave policies. However, a good argument can be made that since the days could be used for illness, the policy cannot undermine state law providing for the use of one-half of annually accrued sick leave for kin care.

Any workplace policy that provides paid or unpaid sick leave, but that treats kin care (as defined above) time off as an absence that may lead to discharge, demotion, or suspension, or any other negative consequence, is illegal. (Labor Code sections 233, 234.)

Enforcement: File a claim with the state labor commissioner (see discussion of DLSE claims in section IV., p. 114). File a lawsuit. A finding of a violation of the law can lead to an order of reinstatement, damages (actual damages or one day's pay, whichever is greater), and other relief.

VI. STATE DISABILITY INSURANCE

A. SCOPE OF THE PROGRAM

State Disability Insurance (SDI) is a program administered by the California Employment Development Department (EDD) that provides partial wage replacement benefits to eligible workers who cannot work because of illness or injury that is not covered (or not yet found to be covered) by Workers' Compensation, is related to pregnancy or childbirth, or involves time off to care for a new child or seriously ill member of the immediate family. Prior to the illness or injury, the worker must have been either working or actively seeking employment. SDI is generally funded through payroll deductions from the paychecks of covered employees. (Unemployment Insurance Code sections 2601 et seq.; 22 California Code of Regulations sections 2601-1 et seq.)

The law covers most private employers, requiring that they provide State Disability Insurance to their employees. Employers can either withhold employee contributions and deposit them into the State Disability Insurance Program (as do the majority of private employers) or they can provide benefits under policies called Voluntary Plans (VP). Voluntary plans must offer all the benefits of SDI, must have at least one benefit that is better than SDI, and cannot cost the employee more than SDI. (Unemployment Insurance Code sections 3251–3272.)

SDI does not involve health insurance. It is strictly a partial wage replacement benefit. Benefits are based on past earnings.

The California Employment Development Department (EDD) maintains a website on SDI at http://www.edd.cahwnet.gov/Disability.

Fact sheets on State Disability Insurance in English, Spanish, Chinese, and Vietnamese can be downloaded from http://www.edd.cahwnet.gov/Disability/DI_Forms_and_Publications.htm (see heading indicating "Publications"). Phone information is available at 1-800-480-3287 (English) or 1-866-658-8846 (Spanish). To speak with a live person, call between 8 AM and 5 PM.

B. ELIGIBILITY

1. Covered Employees

It is fairly easy to determine if an employee is covered by State Disability Insurance. Payroll deductions should appear on the employee's pay stub, indicating all deductions from gross salary, including SDI deductions. It is best to check employee pay stubs for the first few months of the year and see if SDI deductions appear.

Many state agencies are exempt from the requirement to provide SDI to employees. They may provide another type of disability insurance (Non-industrial Disability Insurance, called "NDI") that tends to be inferior to SDI. (Unemployment Insurance Code section 2783.) See section VI.I.2., p. 121, on state employees for more information.

Pregnancy Disability Insurance and Paid Family Leave are administered by the State Disability Insurance Program, but some of the eligibility factors and rights may vary. For more information on these programs, see section VII., p. 121.

2. Basic Eligibility Requirements for SDI Benefits

In order to collect benefits under the SDI Program, the employee must be unable to do her regular or customary work for at least eight days. She must either be employed and have lost wages from the disability, or be actively looking for work at the time of the disability. An individual who has not been employed or who has not registered for work at a public employment office or other place approved by EDD for more than three months immediately prior to the claim is not eligible for benefits unless EDD finds that the unemployment for which benefits are being claimed is due to a disability and not due to the claimant's withdrawal from the labor market. Withdrawal from the labor market is generally interpreted as leaving work without good cause, being discharged for misconduct, or refusing to accept suitable employment. (Unemployment Insurance Code section 2676; 22 California Code of Regulations section 2601-1(u).) The employee must be under the care of a licensed healthcare provider (or accredited religious practitioner) for the medical condition.

The healthcare provider must complete a form called a medical certification. In order for the worker to be qualified to receive SDI benefits, the worker's healthcare provider must certify that the employee is unable to work at her normal, customary occupation. The forms ask the healthcare provider to indicate the diagnosis (if one is available), summarize the treatment ordered, and estimate the probable date the employee will be able to return to work. It is crucial that a healthcare provider follow the employee's condition, even if the illness or injury is one without a clear treatment option. (Unemployment Insurance Code section 2708.) Alcoholism and drug addiction generally are not considered medical conditions that would qualify an individual for benefits, unless the individual is receiving treatment for an acute condition for a limited period of time. (Unemployment Insurance Code sections 2626.1–2626.2.)

3. Earning Requirements to Qualify for Benefits

The employee must have earned at least $300 during a twelve-month base period in order to be eligible. (Unemployment Insurance Code section 2652.) The identification of the base period is important. It will affect eligibility for benefits, and the amount earned during this period of time will determine the amount of the benefits received.

The base period is a twelve-month period of employment prior to the filing of the disability claim, determined by the month in which the disability claim begins. (Unemployment Insurance Code section 2610.)

MONTH CLAIM BEGINS	BASE PERIOD
January, February, or March	12-month period ending the previous September 30
April, May, or June	12-month period ending the previous December 31
July, August, or September	12-month period ending the previous March 31
October, November, or December	12-month period ending the previous June 30

The quarter during the base period in which the employee received the highest salary determines the benefits to be paid under SDI. See the SDI benefits chart at http://www.edd.cahwnet.gov/pdf_pub_ctr/de2589.pdf to calculate benefits based on specific salaries.

A disability claim generally begins on the date that the employee's disability began. However, in some instances (such as when an individual became employed only recently, or has worked intermittently), a slight delay in filing for SDI benefits may result in higher benefits. For instance, if the earnings in the best base period quarter are higher when calculated using the most recent months of employment, starting the SDI claim slightly later could result in a higher benefit level. If an employee wants the disability claim to begin later than the date the disability began, so that there is a different base period, he may call the EDD at 1-800-480-3287. The employee should always be careful to file within the required time frame (see section VI.C.3., p. 117, for more information on time limits for filing the claim). Although eligibility requirements differ, the method for calculating base period is the same for Unemployment Insurance and SDI. To get more information on how the base year is calculated, see Item 5 under "Explanation of Items on the Notice of Unemployment Insurance Award" at http://wwwedd.cahwnet.gov/pdf_pub_ctr/de1275a.pdf.

C. APPLICATION PROCESS

1. Claim Forms

The application process for SDI is fairly straightforward. It is outlined on the EDD website at http://www.edd.ca.gov/Disability/DI_How_to_File_a_Claim.htm.

To apply for SDI, an employee needs to fill out a form called the "DE 2501." An employee can request that the DE 2501 be mailed to him by calling 1-800-480-3287, or filling out and submitting an online request form at http://www.edd.ca.gov/Disability/Disability_Request_a_Claim_Form.htm.

The DE 2501 can also be accessed on the EDD's website by going to http://www.edd.ca.gov/Disability/DI_How_to_File_a_Claim.htm. On this page, the applicant should first read the instructions for completing the claim form and then click on "DE 2501" (at the top of the page) or "Disability Insurance Claim Form" (listed several times on the right side of the page). The applicant can also access the DE 2501 directly at http://www.edd.ca.gov/pdf_pub_ctr/de2501.pdf. The applicant can print the DE 2501 form then fill it in, or type the information into the online form and then print out the filled-in form. However, the employee cannot save any information that is typed into the online form, so the applicant should print out an extra copy for his own records.

If the employee is too impaired by the disability to fill out the forms, the employee can call 1-800-480-3287 to request a form that allows him to identify a representative to fill out the form. If the employee is too impaired to call and request the form, the doctor can fill out a form indicating the person's condition, and a representative (for instance, a family member) can be identified with the authorization to fill out the application form.

2. Medical Certification

Next, the injured or ill worker should take the DE 2501 claim form to his treating healthcare provider. The healthcare provider should fill out the "Doctor's Certificate," included at the end of the form. The treating healthcare provider may be a doctor, osteopath, chiropractor, dentist, podiatrist, optometrist, or certain psychologists. In the case of a pregnancy-related disability, a nurse practitioner or licensed midwife may fill out the medical certification portion of the claim form. Accredited religious practitioners may also provide this information, but will also need to fill out a special form called a DE 2502. If the employer will coordinate payment of sick leave with payment of SDI benefits (see section VI.H., p. 119, for an explanation of integration of benefits), the applicant should get a letter from her employer indicating that sick leave will be used to supplement SDI up to her normal rate of pay. The completed application, including the medical certification and letter from the employer (if applicable), should then be mailed to the EDD nearest to the injured worker's home, as specified on the website or in the phone call with EDD.

3. Filing the Claim Form

Claims should be filed within forty-one calendar days of the first date of unemployment for which benefits can be paid. (Unemployment Insurance Code section 2706.1.) Since the first seven days are a "waiting period," the first date of unemployment for which benefits can be paid is the eighth day after the injury or illness starts. This timeline can be extended by EDD for good cause. If, for some reason, the employee cannot file the claim within forty-eight days of the start of unemployment due to disability, a letter should be attached to the application asking EDD to extend the timeline for filing for good cause and explaining what the circumstances surrounding good cause were. For instance, if the worker was in a serious accident and was hospitalized and unable to send in a claim for forty-eight days, this could be considered "good cause" to extend the timeline for filing. It is always preferable to meet the deadline.

The entire application process can be handled by mail. There is no need for the disabled worker to go to an EDD office to collect benefits.

D. DETERMINATIONS AND APPEALS

1. Determinations

When an employee files for SDI benefits, a notice is sent to the employer indicating that a claim has been filed. The employer has the opportunity to object and/or provide additional relevant information.

SDI is required by law to make a determination of eligibility for benefits within fourteen days of receipt of a properly completed application. If the application is missing important information, EDD may send it back to the employee for completion. This process will probably delay receipt of benefits. If EDD determines that the employee is eligible for SDI, benefits will be retroactive to the first date of eligibility (after the seven-day waiting period).

2. Appeals

If the application is denied, the employee has twenty days to file an appeal. The amount of benefits may also be appealed. The determination from EDD will contain detailed information about filing an appeal. These guidelines should be followed. The employee should keep a copy of any appeal filed and make sure to meet any deadlines. Deadlines may sometimes be extended for good cause, but it is always a good idea to comply with the timelines whenever possible.

Appeals are first reconsidered by the SDI administrative agency. If SDI denies the appeal, it will automatically be sent to the California Unemployment Insurance Appeals Board, which will schedule a hearing before an administrative law judge (ALJ). The claimant will receive notification of the hearing at least ten days prior to it. For more information on appeals, see http://www.edd.ca.gov/Disability/Appeals.htm. ALJ decisions may be appealed to the California Unemployment Insurance Appeals Board. (Their website may be viewed at http://www.cuiab.ca.gov/index.shtm.)

E. BENEFIT CHECKS

Benefits generally replace approximately 55 percent of lost salary, up to a maximum benefit amount. The maximum benefit amount increases annually to correspond to changes in the maximum benefit amount for Workers' Compensation Temporary Disability benefits. Beginning January 1, 2010, the highest amount of benefits any worker can receive is $987 a week for fifty-two weeks. The current amount of benefits can be found at the EDD website at http://www.edd.ca.gov/Disability/DI_Benefit_Amounts.htm (click on "DI and PFL Weekly Benefits Chart") or access the chart directly at http://www.edd.ca.gov/pdf_pub_ctr/de2589.pdf. (Unemployment Insurance Code section 2655.)

The first seven days of the claim is a waiting period. Employees receive no benefits during the waiting period.

F. DURATION OF BENEFITS

Benefits for the worker's own illness or injury may last up to fifty-two weeks, if medically justified. Benefits based on pregnancy, bonding with a new child, and family care are of shorter durations. See section VII., p. 121, for more information on these programs.

Disabled employees who are unable to work 100 percent of their previous employment (for instance, someone who must cut back to part-time as a result of the side effects of chemotherapy or who returns to work following surgery on a part-time schedule as recommended by the healthcare provider) may be eligible to collect partial disability payments. In some instances, intermittent periods of disability for the same illness or injury may be covered as part of the same claim, even though the employee is able to work at some times. In these circumstances, it is crucial that the employee report promptly and accurately to EDD regarding any change in circumstances.

G. EXCLUSIONS FROM COVERAGE

Individuals may not be excluded from coverage because of pre-existing conditions or high-risk jobs. They may be ineligible for benefits during any week that they are receiving Unemployment Insurance or Family Temporary Disability benefits (also known as Paid Family Leave), if they are receiving Workers' Compensation benefits at a rate greater than SDI, if they are in jail or prison, if they became disabled while committing a crime resulting in a felony conviction, or if they refuse to visit an independent medical examiner when they are asked to do so. They may also be disqualified from receiving benefits if they engage in fraud in an attempt to secure benefits. (Unemployment Insurance Code sections 2675–2681.) Independent contractors are not considered employees, so they are not covered by the SDI Program. They may purchase their own policies under "Elective Coverage." (Unemployment Insurance Code sections 701–713.)

The following types of employees may also be exempt from coverage:

- Interstate railroad workers;
- Domestic workers (including those who provide in-home supportive services to elderly or disabled recipients of public benefits) who

work in a private home, local college club, or local chapter of a college fraternity or sorority, in situations where the employer pays total wages (to all employees) in cash of less than $750 in any calendar quarter of the current or preceding year to individuals employed in domestic service. (Unemployment Insurance Code section 2606.5);

- Many government employees (see sections VI.I.2. and 3., p. 121);
- Some non-profit employees, if they are paid less than $50 in any calendar quarter (Unemployment Insurance Code section 641);
- Employees of organizations that claim a religious exemption.

(Unemployment Insurance Code sections 2606, 629–657.)

H. THE IMPACT OF OTHER BENEFITS

1. Workers' Compensation

If the injury is work-related, the employee should report that information to the treating healthcare provider (and the employer), indicate that fact on the SDI claim forms, and apply for Workers' Compensation (see Chapter 8). If the Workers' Compensation Insurance carrier has not started to pay any benefits yet and the case is pending, the employee may apply for and receive SDI payments until Workers' Compensation payments begin. If the Workers' Compensation payments are less than the SDI benefit amount, SDI may pay the difference. It is important to report any income from Workers' Compensation (including Workers' Compensation Temporary Disability payments) accurately to EDD. Failure to do so could lead to charges of fraud. EDD may attempt to recover benefits duplicated by Workers' Compensation benefits. (Labor Code sections 4903–4904.)

2. Sick Leave

SDI will not provide benefits to an employee receiving 100 percent salary replacement from sick leave. However, it is possible to "integrate" benefits. Integration works as follows: the employee receives SDI benefits; the employer supplements those benefits up to the level of full salary replacement. If SDI is replacing 55 percent of the disabled worker's lost income, then for each

day during which SDI benefits were received, the employee would need to use only 45 percent of a sick day. The effect of this integration of benefits is that the worker's sick leave is used up at a much slower rate.

The law does not require employers to integrate benefits, however, many employers are willing to do so. Some collective bargaining agreements and employer policies require integration of benefits. Some employers will agree to integrate benefits if an employee makes this request.

Employees who work for an employer that will integrate benefits should attach a letter to that effect from the employer to the application for SDI. If an employee has a lot of available sick leave, one simple way to handle the integration of benefits is for the employer to continue to pay full sick leave (assuming that the employee has enough sick leave accrued to cover the time he is out on leave), then, when the SDI check arrives, the employee can sign it over to the employer with a note indicating that the employer should use it to "buy back" the appropriate amount of sick leave. The employee should request confirmation that the "buy back" has taken place, and ask the employer to indicate how many days were replaced in the employee's sick leave account. The employee should not, under any circumstances, just keep the SDI check if he has received 100 percent salary from sick leave, as that could lead to charges of fraud. An alternate way of handling integration of benefits is for the employer to reduce the payment of sick leave to 45 percent of salary (or the difference between the SDI payment and full salary). However, this should not be done until the employee actually receives the SDI benefit check.

3. Long-Term Disability

If the employee is facing a long period of permanent disability, she may have rights to benefits either from a long-term disability policy (private or employment-based), or through Social Security Disability. To get more information on Social Security Disability, call 1-800-772-1213, or see http://www.ssa.gov/dibplan/index.htm. Social Security Disability benefits are available to people who have worked the required amount of time and meet the Social Security definition of disability (a medical condition that prevents the worker from doing the work she did before, prevents her from adjusting to other work, and is expected to last at least a year or result in death). This benefit is not intended to cover short-term disabilities. Benefits may also be available to low-income individuals who do not meet the earning test of Social Security Disability. Low-income individuals may be eligible for benefits under the federal Supplemental Security Income (SSI) Program, based on financial need and disability. More information can be found on SSI at http://www.ssa.gov/ssi.

Qualifying for Social Security Disability, SSI, or private long-term disability insurance can take a long time. The employee does not need to finish the SDI benefits in order to begin the process of applying for long-term disability. Private long-term disability policies tend to have very long waiting periods after claims are filed and before benefits start (frequently three to six months). If it appears that the disability is permanent or long term, the employee should begin exploring other options sooner rather than later. If there is private long-term disability insurance offered through the job (or that the employee has purchased independently), she should ask for the summary plan description, which will outline the basic requirements that must be met in order to qualify for benefits.

4. Pregnancy Disability Benefits

Pregnancy disability benefits are covered by, and administered as part of, the State Disability Insurance Program, but many of the provisions are different from those pertaining to loss of work due to injuries or medical conditions other than pregnancy. The time frame for benefits for a normal pregnancy is four weeks prior to the expected due date and six weeks after the birth. For a cesarean birth, where there are other complications (like bed rest prior to the birth), or where the nature of the job makes it impossible to continue working into late pregnancy, longer periods of leave may be approved, provided that there is medical documentation of the need for a longer leave. See section VII.C., p. 144, for more information on payments under the Pregnancy Disability Leave program.

5. Paid Family Leave Insurance Program (Also Called Family Temporary Disability Insurance Program)

Paid Family Leave benefits (also called Family Temporary Disability benefits) are covered through the State Disability Insurance Program, but many of the provisions are different from those outlined in this section. See section VII.C.2., p. 146, for more information on Paid Family Leave in California.

I. SPECIAL SITUATIONS

1. Independent Contractors

The law does not require that employers cover independent contractors under the State Disability Insurance or related programs. However, independent contractors, business owners, and other self-employed individuals may secure their own coverage under the Disability Insurance Elective Coverage Program. For more information on this program, go to http://www.edd.ca.gov/Disability/Self-Employed.htm.

To download an application form, go to http://www.edd.ca.gov/pdf_pub_ctr/de1378di.pdf.

2. State and Municipal Employees

Some unionized state and municipal employees have voted or negotiated agreements in which their members are covered by SDI. Many state employees are covered instead by programs called Non-industrial Disability Insurance (NDI). This program is generally inferior to SDI, however it is funded by the state, and the employees are not required to pay for the costs of coverage. Benefits are generally capped at $125 or $135 a week (depending on the position the employee holds) for twenty-six weeks as of 2008. (Government Code sections 19878–19885; Unemployment Insurance Code sections 2781–2783.) In order to participate in this program, a worker must be in the Public Employee Retirement System (PERS) or the State Teachers Retirement System (STRS), or be a full- or part-time state officer or employee of the legislature. The NDI program does not provide salary replacement for absences based on illnesses or injuries in the immediate family, or for bonding with a new child. See the following websites for more information:

- http://www.dpa.ca.gov/benefits/health/ndi. shtm
- http://www.dpa.ca.gov/benefits/health/ workcomp/pubs/Disability/page4.shtm

For more information on the NDI program by phone, call 209-948-3920 during regular business hours.

State and municipal employees covered by SDI (generally because their unions have negotiated inclusion in the program or, in some cases, state law allows them to vote to enter the program) can call 1-866-352-7675 for more information.

3. Federal Agencies

Federal employees are governed by federal law and should consult their human resources departments and unions for information on disability insurance programs applicable to their jobs.

VII. FAMILY LEAVE AND PREGNANCY DISABILITY LEAVE BENEFITS

In addition to the California kin-care law, discussed above, three important statutes govern leave taken because of an employee's own serious health condition, or to care for an employee's family member's serious health condition, or for pregnancy, or birth, adoption, or acceptance for foster care of a child:

- The federal Family and Medical Leave Act of 1993 (FMLA);
- The California Family Rights Act (CFRA) (part of the Fair Employment and Housing Act); and
- California's Pregnancy Disability Leave Act (PDL Act).

These laws are discussed in this section. California law cannot take away from rights that are granted under the FMLA, but it can grant additional rights. A helpful guide to family leave rights in California may found at http://www. working-families.org/learnmore/ca_paidleave. html.

A. FEDERAL FAMILY AND MEDICAL LEAVE ACT (FMLA) AND THE CALIFORNIA FAMILY RIGHTS ACT (CFRA)

The Family and Medical Leave Act (29 U.S. Code sections 2601 et seq.) and California Family Rights Act (Government Code section 12945.2.) provide up to twelve weeks a year of job-protected, unpaid leave for certain employees under certain conditions

Because of changes that went into effect in 2009 in the federal FMLA regulations, there are, as of the date that this manuscript was prepared for publication, some confusing differences between federal family leave and California's family leave laws and regulations. California is planning to make some changes in regulations to simplify the rules and make the differences less confusing, but as of press time, those changes have not taken place. Information about upcoming changes will be posted on the web at http://www.fehc.ca.gov/ act/regulation.asp.

Employees of private businesses, non-profits, and state or local public agencies in California are governed by California law. California law must provide, at a minimum, the protections guaranteed by the federal FMLA, and may go further and provide additional rights. Federal employees are governed by the FMLA, not by California law.

1. Covered Employers

The FMLA covers private employers that are engaged in interstate commerce (in other words, that deal with the movement of goods, services, or funding across state lines) and employ at least fifty workers during each of twenty or more calendar workweeks in the current or preceding calendar year. (29 U.S. Code section 2611(4)(A)(i); 29 Code of Federal Regulations sections 825.104 and 825.800.) Public employers, including state agencies, are covered by the FMLA regardless of the number of workers they employ. (29 U.S. Code section 2611(4)(A)(iii); *Nevada Dept. of Human Resources v. Hibbs* (2003) 538 U.S. 721.) Local public education agencies (public K-12 schools) and private elementary and secondary (high and junior high) schools are also covered, regardless of the number of employees on staff. (29 U.S. Code section 2618(a)(1); 29 Code of Federal Regulations section 825.600(b).)

The CFRA covers private employers that employ at least fifty workers within a seventy-five mile radius during each of twenty or more calendar workweeks in the current or preceding calendar year (Government Code section 12945.2(b).) The CFRA also covers all California public employers regardless of the number of workers they employ. The CFRA does not cover federal employees. (2 California Code of Regulations section 7297.0(d).)

2. Eligible Employees

To be eligible for leave under the FMLA and CFRA, an employee must:

- Work for a covered employer (see directly above);
- Have been employed by the employer for at least twelve months;
- Have been employed by the employer for at least 1,250 hours of service during the twelve-month period immediately preceding the start of the leave (these must be hours of actual work — not vacation or sick leave); and
- Work at a site where the employer employs at least fifty workers within a seventy-five mile radius.

(29 U.S. Code sections 2611(2)(A), 2618(a) (2)(A); 29 Code of Federal Regulations section 825.110; Government Code section 12945.2(a), (b), (c)(2); 2 California Code of Regulations section 7297.0(e).)

The twelve months that an employee must have been employed by the employer do not need to be consecutive (in a row). However, under the FMLA, the employment period before a break in service of seven or more years does not need to be counted unless the break is caused by military obligations or there is a written agreement to rehire the employee after the break in service. The employer may choose to consider the employment period prior to a seven-year break, but must do so consistently for all employees. (29 Code of Federal Regulations section 825.110(b).)

If the employee has met the 1,250 hours of service requirement, but has not worked for the employer for a total of twelve months, the employee may become eligible for family leave while he is on other leave. Since leave time counts toward length of service, the employee could meet the twelve-month length of service requirement while on other leave. The portion of leave after the employee becomes eligible for FMLA leave would be family leave, and the rights available under the FMLA could become available to the employee once the twelve-month requirement had been met. (29 Code of Federal Regulations section 825.110(d).)

3. The Impact of Service in the U.S. Armed Forces on Eligibility for Family Leave

Employees who are on leave from their jobs in order to serve in the armed forces (for instance, those serving in the National Guard who are called up for active duty) and who are reemployed by their previous employer at the end of their tours of duty are allowed to count their active duty time toward eligibility for FMLA leave. The months and hours that the employee would have worked had he not been in military service should be combined with the actual time he has worked to meet the twelve months and 1,250 hours of employment that are required to be eligible for FMLA leave. (29 Code of Federal Regulations section 825.110(b)(2)(i), (c)(2). See Department of Labor USERRA-FMLA Questions and Answers "The Effect of the Uniformed Services Employment and Reemployment Rights Act on Leave Eligibility Under the Family and Medical Leave Act" (July 25, 2002), available at http://www.dol.gov/vets/media/fmlaq-a.pdf.)

Employees who are family members of individuals serving in the armed forces have additional leave rights that are discussed in the following sections.

4. Qualified Reasons for Taking Leave

An eligible employee of a covered employer may take an FMLA/CFRA leave for any of the following reasons:

- To care for her own serious health condition;
- To care for a family member (child, parent, spouse, and, under California law only, a registered domestic partner) with a serious health condition;
- For childbirth and pregnancy-related illnesses and for prenatal care;
- To care for a newborn or child adopted by, or placed in foster care with, the employee.

(29 U.S. Code section 2612(a)(1)(A)-(D); 29 Code of Federal Regulations section 825.112; Government Code section 12945.2(c)(3).)

Employees who have family members in the armed forces, reserves, or National Guard have additional rights to take FMLA leave for the following reasons:

- Because of a "qualifying exigency" (a legal term meaning a need as outlined in the regulations, described in section VII.A.6.c., p. 126) arising from the fact that the employee's spouse, child, or parent is a covered military member on active duty or call-to-active-duty status;
- To care for a covered service member (a member or recent veteran of the armed forces) who is undergoing medical treatment, is in outpatient status, or is otherwise on the temporary disability retired list with a serious injury or illness incurred in the line of duty if the employee is the spouse, child, parent, or next of kin of the service member. The inclusion of "next of kin" (described in section VII.A.5.b., p. 124) allows an employee who is not the spouse, child, or parent of the service member, but is the nearest blood relative to the service member, to take military caregiver leave.

(29 U.S. Code section 2612(a)(1)(E), (a)(3); 29 Code of Federal Regulations section 825.112(a)(5), (6).)

5. Definition of Family Member

a. Basic Definition of Family Under the FMLA and CFRA

Under the FMLA, employees have a right to leave to care for themselves, their children, their spouses, or their parents, if any of these people are suffering from a "serious health condition." Children include biological children, adopted children, stepchildren, foster children, legal wards, and children to whom one stands "*in loco parentis*" (in the place of a parent, for instance family members raising children whose parents are not able to do so). The children must be under eighteen years of age or unable to take care of themselves because of a mental or physical disability at the time that the leave is to begin. (29 U.S. Code section 2611(12); 29 Code of Federal Regulations section 825.122(c).) However, the disability need not be permanent. The FMLA also requires that leave be granted to give birth to, adopt, or accept foster placement of a child. (29 U.S. Code section 2612(a)(1)(A), (B); 29 Code of Federal Regulations sections 825.120, 825.121.) For purposes of FMLA leave due to a family member's service in the armed forces, the definition of "child" does not include age and disability restrictions. An employee's child who is on active duty or call-to-active-duty status may be of any age. An employee who is the child of a covered service member may be of any age. (29 Code of Federal Regulations section 825.122(g), (h).)

"Parent" means a biological, adoptive, step, or foster father or mother, or any other individual who stood "*in loco parentis*" (meaning one who stood in the place of the parent, for instance a person who raised the child) to the employee when the employee was a child. "Parent" does not include parent of a spouse. (29 Code of Federal Regulations section 825.122(b).) Leaves to care for siblings with serious health conditions generally are not covered under the FMLA (unless the sibling is a covered service member of the armed forces and the employee is the sibling's next of kin).

The definition of "family" under the CFRA is similar to the FMLA definition with a few exceptions. "Child" is defined under the California law in a manner similar but not identical to that used in the FMLA: a biological, adopted, or foster child, a stepchild, a legal ward, or a child for whom the employee stands *in loco parentis* (in the place of a parent regardless of legal relationship) who is either under eighteen years of age or is an adult dependent child. "Parent" means a biological, foster, or adoptive parent, a stepparent, a legal guardian, or other individual who stood *in loco parentis* to the employee when the employee was a child. (Government Code section 12945.2(c)(1), (7).)

California's law also includes domestic partners within the definition of immediate family. (See Family Code section 297.5(a). See also 22

California Code of Regulations section 1253.12-1.) The rights of registered domestic partners with respect to a child of either of them are the same as those of spouses, so the child of a domestic partner would be treated the same as a stepchild. (Family Code section 297.5(d).)

b. Next of Kin

Under the FMLA, employees who are the spouse, child, parent, or next of kin of members of the armed forces who are injured or become ill in the line of duty have the right to take job-protected family leave to care for the covered service member. This right has now been extended to eligible family members of veterans of the armed forces, National Guard, or reserves who served within five years of starting treatment, recuperation, or therapy for an injury or illness caused by or aggravated by military service. The next of kin of a covered veteran or service member or is the nearest blood relative other than the service member's spouse, parent, or child. Blood relatives who have been granted legal custody of the service member have first priority, followed in order by siblings, grandparents, aunts and uncles, and first cousins. A service member or covered veteran may specifically designate in writing a blood relative as his next of kin for purposes of being a caregiver under the FMLA. The designated individual is then considered the only next of kin. If no designation is made, and there are several individuals who have the same family relationship with the service member, all such family members are considered the next of kin and any of them may be eligible for FMLA leave to provide care to the service member. (29 U.S. Code section 2611(18); 29 Code of Federal Regulations sections 825.127(b)(3), 825.800.)

c. Spousal Leave

The FMLA entitles an employee to take leave to provide care to a spouse with a serious health condition, but does not authorize such leave for one domestic partner to care for another. In contrast, registered domestic partners are treated substantially the same as spouses under California law. Registered domestic partners working for employers governed by the state family leave law are entitled to take CFRA leave to care for the other domestic partner who is suffering from a serious health condition. In workplaces that are only covered by federal, and not state, family leave laws (like federal agencies and military installations), leave is not available to employees needing to care for domestic partners. In addition, under the CFRA, but not the FMLA, employees with domestic partners have the same rights as employees with spouses when it comes to leave for the purposes of bearing, adopting, or fostering a child, or caring for an ill child or stepchild.

6. Definitions of Reasons for Leave

a. Serious Health Condition

i. *Generally*

Leave rights under both the FMLA and CFRA are based on a serious health condition, childbirth, or care of a newborn child. The healthcare provider should provide the information necessary to determine that a medical need is a serious health condition.

Under the FMLA, a serious health condition is an illness, injury, impairment, or physical or mental condition that involves either inpatient care in a hospital, hospice, or residential medical care facility, or continuing treatment by a healthcare provider. (29 U.S. Code section 2611(11); 29 Code of Federal Regulations section 825.113(a).) Inpatient care is an overnight stay in a hospital, hospice, or residential care facility. (29 Code of Federal Regulations sections 825.114, 825.113(b).) A serious health condition involves continuing treatment if the individual experiences one or more of the following:

- Incapacity of more than three days. A period of incapacity of more than three full days in a row that involves at least one in-person treatment by a healthcare provider within seven days of the first day of incapacity, followed by additional in-person treatments within thirty days of the first day of incapacity, or a routine of continuing treatment under the healthcare provider's supervision. The need for additional treatment visits or a routine of continuing treatment is decided by the healthcare provider, not the employer.
- Pregnancy. A period of incapacity related to pregnancy (including, for example, morning sickness, prenatal medical care, medically mandated bed rest).
- Chronic condition. A period of incapacity due to a chronic serious health condition that requires periodic visits (at least twice a year) for treatment by a healthcare provider, continues

over an extended period of time, and may cause incapacity from time to time (including, for example, asthma, diabetes, and epilepsy).

- Long-term incapacity. A period of incapacity that is permanent or long term due to a condition which may not respond to treatment (for example, Alzheimer's or a severe stroke). The individual must be under the continuing supervision of a healthcare provider even if there is no active treatment.
- Multiple treatments. Conditions requiring multiple treatments (such as restorative surgery after an injury, chemotherapy and radiation for cancer, physical therapy for severe arthritis, or dialysis for kidney disease).

(29 Code of Federal Regulations section 825.115. See *Marchisheck v. San Mateo County* (9th Cir. 1999) 199 F.3d 1068 (in which a child who was treated only once was found by a court to not have a "serious health condition").) If the leave is for the employee's own condition, the employee must be unable to perform his *actual* job in order to qualify for family leave. (*Lonicki v. Sutter Health Central* (2008) 43 Cal.4th 201.)

The term "serious health condition" in the CFRA is defined in much the same way it is under the FMLA. (Government Code section 12945.2(c)(8); 2 California Code of Regulations section

7297.0(o).) Note, however, that the definitions of "continuing treatment" may differ. While pregnancy may be a serious health condition under the FMLA if morning sickness or other pregnancy-related conditions make the employee unable to work (29 Code of Federal Regulations sections 825.113 and 825.115(b)), pregnancy is covered by the California Pregnancy Disability Leave Act, rather than the CFRA, in California. (Government Code section 12945.)

ii. *Serious Injury or Illness of a Covered Service Member or Veteran*

In order for a family member to have a right to take time off of work to care for a covered service member or veteran of the armed forces, the service member or veteran must have a "serious injury or illness" that was incurred in the line of duty or aggravated by military service. The service member must be undergoing medical treatment, recuperation, or therapy, or otherwise be in outpatient status, or otherwise be on the temporary disability list. Veterans must have been in the armed forces, National Guard, or reserves at some point within the five-year period before treatment, recuperation, or therapy. To be considered in "outpatient status," a covered service member must be assigned to either a military medical treatment facility as an outpatient or a unit established for the purpose of overseeing care for service members receiving medical care as outpatients. (29 Code of Federal Regulations section 825.127(a).)

b. Providing Care to Family Members

When an employee seeks family leave to care for a family member, the care provided is subject to certain requirements in order to qualify for family leave.

Under the FMLA and CFRA, the care that the employee provides to the individual with the serious health condition may be physical and/or psychological care. (29 Code of Federal Regulations section 825.124(a); 2 California Code of Regulations section 7297.0(a)(1)(D)(1).) For example, the employee may provide care to an individual who is unable to care for her own basic needs or safety (for example, needs such as eating, bathing, taking medication), or is unable to transport herself to the doctor. The employee may also provide psychological comfort and reassurance to an individual who is receiving inpatient or home care. Situations in which the employee needs to fill in for others who are caring for the individual, or needs to make arrangements for changes in care, such as transferring an individual to a nursing home, are also covered. (29 Code of Federal Regulations section 825.124(b).)

The employee must have some level of participation in the ongoing care of the individual with the serious health condition. In one case, it was found that taking a child to a foreign country and leaving him with relatives did not to amount to "caring for" the child, since the child was left in a place where there was no treatment available for his psychological problems. (*Marchisheck v. San Mateo County* (9th Cir. 1999) 199 F.3d 1068.) However, an employee whose sister had died, who had daily conversations with his depressed father about the sister, performed various chores around his father's house, and drove his father to counseling sessions, could have been considered to have participated in his father's treatment. (*Scamihorn v. General Truck Drivers* (9th Cir. 2002) 282 F.3d 1078.) This area of law is currently getting worked out in the courts. Providing emotional support, dealing with medical staff and decisions, and assistance with tasks all show "participation" in care.

Under California law, caring for an individual may consist of directly providing or participating in the medical care, or arranging "third party" care. (2 California Code of Regulations section 7297.0(a)(1)(D)(1).) Arranging third-party care includes moving an individual into a nursing home, but it does not cover a move to housing that does not involve medical treatment. (*Pang v. Beverly Hosp., Inc.* (2000) 79 Cal.App.4th 986.)

c. Qualifying Exigency

Under the FMLA, employees with close family members serving in the United States military may take leave based on a "qualifying exigency" resulting from the fact that a spouse, child, or parent is on, or has been called to, active duty involving possible combat or service in a national emergency. (29 U.S. Code section 2612(a)(1)(E).) Unlike military caregiver leave, qualifying exigency leave is only available to the spouse, child, or parent of a service member. Other next of kin do not have the right to take "exigency leave" for service members.

Qualifying exigencies include:
- Needs that arise because the service member is

being deployed with seven days or less of notice;
- Military events and related activities, such as official ceremonies, programs, or events;
- Certain childcare issues arising from the active-duty or call-to-active-duty status of the service member;
- Making financial and legal arrangements to address the service member's absence;
- Attending counseling provided by someone other than a healthcare provider for the employee, the service member, or a child of the service member;
- Taking up to five days of leave to spend time with a service member who is on short-term temporary rest-and-recuperation leave during deployment;
- Attending certain post-deployment activities;
- Any other event that the employee and employer agree is a qualifying exigency.

(29 Code of Federal Regulations section 825.126.)

7. Amount of Leave Allowed

a. Generally

Under both federal and California law, eligible employees must be allowed up to twelve workweeks of leave during a twelve-month "leave year" for the purposes described in the FMLA and the CFRA. (29 U.S. Code section 2612(a); Government Code section 12945.2(a).)

i. Twelve Workweeks of Leave

The amount of leave to which the employee is entitled is based on the employee's actual workweek. For example, if an employee normally works forty hours in a week, the employee is entitled to twelve weeks of forty hours per week, or 480 hours of family leave. The FMLA provides that if the employee's schedule varies from week to week, the employee's normal workweek is calculated by averaging the weekly hours worked over the twelve months before the leave period. If the employee works thirty hours a week, 360 hours of family leave (representing thirty hours a week times twelve weeks of leave) will be available, over a twelve-week period of time. (29 Code of Federal Regulations section 825.205(b).)

ii. Amount of Leave Used

Under the FMLA and CFRA, only the amount of leave actually taken may be counted toward the twelve weeks of leave to which an employee is entitled. (29 Code of Federal Regulations sections 825.202, 825.203, 825.205; 2 California Code of Regulations section 7297.3(c)(2).)

If the employee would normally be required to work overtime hours, but cannot work those hours due to an FMLA-qualifying reason, the overtime hours not worked may be counted against the employee's FMLA entitlement. However, voluntary overtime work hours that an employee does not work may not be counted against the employee's FMLA leave entitlement. (29 Code of Federal Regulations section 825.205(c).)

If an employee who is recovering from a serious health condition chooses to accept a "light duty" assignment, work hours spent performing the assignment do not count against the employee's entitlement to FMLA leave. (29 Code of Federal Regulations section 825.220(d).)

iii. *Leave Year*

Under the FMLA and CFRA, an employee's right to take a leave for the birth, foster placement, or adoption of a child expires twelve months after the child is born, placed, or adopted. (29 U.S. Code section 2612(a)(2); 29 Code of Federal Regulations section 825.120(a)(2); 2 California Code of Regulations section 7297.3(d).)

Under the FMLA, an employer can choose to compute the twelve-month "leave year" in one of four ways:
• The calendar year;
• Any fixed twelve-month leave year, such as a fiscal year, a year required by state law, or a year starting on the anniversary of an employee's employment;
• The twelve-month period measured forward from the date an employee's first FMLA leave begins; or
• A "rolling" twelve-month period measured backward from the date an employee commences a period of FMLA leave.
(29 Code of Federal Regulations section 825.200(b).) If the employer uses one of the fixed-year methods, numbers one or two above, then the employee can use the twelve weeks of leave at any time during the twelve-month period. For example, if the calendar year is used, the employee could take twelve weeks of leave at the end of one year and twelve weeks at the beginning of the following year. Under the rolling method, each

time an employee wants to take FMLA leave, the amount of time available to her is the remainder of her twelve-week allotment that she has not used in the twelve preceding months. (29 Code of Federal Regulations section 825.200(c); see *Bachelder v. America West Airlines, Inc.* (9th Cir. 2001) 259 F.3d 1112.)

CFRA leave runs at the same time as FMLA leave, subject to certain exceptions, discussed below. Under CFRA and FMLA guidelines, the employer must apply whichever method it has chosen to determine the relevant twelve-month time period consistently to *all* employees, and must notify employees as to the method chosen to determine the twelve-month time period in which family leave is calculated. (2 California Code of Regulations section 7297.3(b); 29 Code of Federal Regulations section 825.200(d).) If the employer fails to designate the computation method, then the method most advantageous to the employee is to be used. (29 Code of Federal Regulations section 825.200(e).)

b. Family Members of Those Serving in the Armed Forces
i. *Federal Law*

An employee who is the spouse, child, parent, or next of kin of a covered service member of the armed forces is entitled to up to twenty-six workweeks of FMLA leave during a single twelve-month period to care for the service member under the following conditions: the service member became injured or seriously ill in the line of duty and is medically unable to perform her duties; *and* she is currently undergoing medical treatment, recuperation, or therapy or is on the temporary disability retired list because of the injury or illness. Eligibility to take leave to care for an injured veteran was added to the law in 2009. The veteran must have an illness or injury incurred or aggravated while on active duty in the armed forces, whether or not the condition manifested itself before or after the service member became a veteran, *and* the veteran served in the military at some point during the five years before she began treatment, recuperation, or therapy.

The twelve-month period begins on the first day that the employee takes FMLA leave to care for the service member or veteran and ends twelve months from that date regardless of the method used to determine the employee's leave year for other

FMLA-qualifying reasons. An eligible employee may take more than one period of military caregiver leave if the leave is to care for a different service member or a different injury or illness to the same service member. However, the employee may take no more than twenty-six workweeks of military caregiver leave in the single twelve-month period. (29 U.S. Code sections 2611, 2612(a)(3), (4); 29 Code of Federal Regulations section 825.127(c).)

The twenty-six-week limit includes leave taken to care for the service member as well as any leave taken under the FMLA for other reasons. Leave taken for reasons other than caring for the injured or ill service member is still subject to the twelve-week limit, including leave taken for a "qualifying exigency" resulting from a family member's active duty in the armed forces. (29 U.S. Code section 2612(a)(3), (4); 29 Code of Federal Regulations section 825.127(c)(3), (4).)

ii. California Law

In addition to the rights under federal law described in the previous sections dealing with leave to care for injured or ill service members, California law provides a right to take up to ten days of unpaid leave when an employee's spouse or domestic partner, who is serving in the military, is on leave from deployment during a period of military conflict in a combat zone, or, in some cases, during a national emergency. The person serving in the military must be either a regular member of the armed forces deployed to a combat zone, or a member of the National Guard or reserves who has been ordered into active duty and deployed to a military conflict or national emergency. In order to be eligible for this leave, several conditions must be met:

- The employee requesting the leave must work an average of at least twenty hours a week as an employee. Independent contractors are not covered by this law.
- In order to be subject to this law, the employer must have at least twenty-five employees. Public, private, non-profit, and for-profit employers are covered, as long as they have the minimum number of employees. For the purpose of counting the number of employees to establish whether or not the employer is covered, the law does not distinguish between full- and part-time employees, or between employees working in California or elsewhere. All employees should count towards the minimum requirement.

- The employee requesting the leave must notify the employer about the leave within two days of receiving official notice of the military spouse's or partner's leave, and must provide written proof that the spouse or partner will be on leave from the military during the time period in question.

The employer is not permitted to refuse the request or to retaliate against the employee who makes the request. (Military and Veteran's Code section 395.10.)

c. Instructional Employees

Employees teaching for public K-12 schools and private elementary and secondary schools are subject to special rules under the FMLA. A school employee is an "instructional employee" if her main function is to teach students in a class, a small group, or individually. Teachers, athletic coaches, driving instructors, and special education assistants (for example, signers for the hearing impaired) are instructional employees. The term does not include teacher assistants or aides who do not actually teach as their principal job, counselors, curriculum specialists, cafeteria workers, maintenance workers, or bus drivers. (29 Code of Federal Regulations section 825.600(c).)

When an instructional employee takes leave that ends with the end of the academic year and begins with the start of the following academic year, the two periods of leave are considered to be consecutive, not intermittent (see section

Workers must be allowed to return from pregnancy disability leave with no change in seniority, pay, and benefits.

VII.A.8.b., p. 130). The period during a summer vacation when an employee would not otherwise be required to report to work is not counted against the FMLA leave entitlement. (29 Code of Federal Regulations section 825.601(a).)

There are special rules for instructional employees when their leave ends close to the end of the semester or academic term. If an instructional employee requests family or medical leave to begin more than five weeks before the end of a semester, and the leave will last at least three weeks, so that the employee would return to work during the last three weeks of the academic term, the employer can require the employee to take leave through the end of the term. (29 Code of Federal Regulations section 825.602(a)(1).) Similarly, if an instructional employee takes family leave beginning less than five weeks before the end of an academic term to care for a family member with a serious health condition or a newborn child and the leave will last more than two weeks, so that the employee would return to work during the final two weeks of the term, the employer may require the employee to take leave through the end of the term. (29 Code of Federal Regulations section 825.602(a)(2).) If an instructional employee takes leave during the three weeks prior to the end of an academic term for a purpose other than his own serious health condition, the employer can require that the leave extend until the end of the academic term. (29 Code of Federal Regulations section 825.602(a)(3).) However, the additional weeks (after the person is willing and able to return to work) are not counted towards the limit of twelve weeks per year of entitlement to family leave. The employer must continue to provide health insurance during the extra time after the employee is able and willing to return to work. (29 Code of Federal Regulations section 825.603(b).) These restrictions are not applicable when the leave is due to the employee's own serious health condition.

d. Couples, Married Couples, and Registered Domestic Partners Working for the Same Employer

When both partners in a relationship work for the same employer, the combined amount of family leave that they are allowed to take may be limited in certain circumstances. Since state and federal laws differ in their treatment of couples depending on marital status, there may be conflicting rights and limitations under state and federal family and medical leave laws when it comes to leave for the purposes of giving birth, adopting or fostering a child, caring for an ill parent, or caring for a spouse or domestic partner with a serious health condition.

i. *Parental Leave*

Under the FMLA, if an employee and his spouse both work for the same employer (even if they work at different facilities located more than seventy-five miles apart), the two of them may take no more than twelve weeks' total leave for the birth, adoption, or acceptance of foster placement of a child. (29 U.S. Code section 2612(f)(1)(A); 29 Code of Federal Regulations sections 825.120(a)(3), 825.201(b).) The CFRA contains a similar limitation, but applies it to both parents, regardless of their marital status. (Government Code section 12945.2(q); 2 California Code of Regulations section 7297.1(c).) Like most provisions of the leave laws, collective bargaining agreements may establish more generous leave provisions, for instance, allowing both parents to take the full leave.

ii. *Other Types of Family Leave*

Under the FMLA, the twelve-week limitation on the combined amount of FMLA leave taken by an employee and spouse who work for the same employer also applies to leave taken to care for their respective parents with serious health conditions. (29 U.S. Code section 2612(f)(1)(B); 29 Code of Federal Regulations section 825.201(b).)

If an employee and spouse work for the same employer, and they use FMLA leave to care for an injured or ill service member of the armed forces, the total combined amount of FMLA leave time that they can take is twenty-six workweeks during a single twelve-month period. The twenty-six-week limit includes leave taken to care for the service member as well as any leave taken under the FMLA for other reasons. Leave taken for reasons other than caring for a service member is still subject to the twelve-week limit. (29 U.S. Code section 2612(f)(2); 29 Code of Federal Regulations section 825.127(c)(3), (d).)

The limitation on entitlement to combined leave time for spouses who work for the same employer does not apply to family leave taken for other reasons. For example, family leave taken for the employee's own serious health condition, the serious health condition of the spouse, or the serious health condition of a child is not subject to the combined limitation. Under the CFRA, leave taken for the serious health condition of a parent is also not subject to the combined limitation. (29 Code of Federal Regulations section 825.202(c); 2 California Code of Regulations section 7297.1(c).)

8. Minimum Amounts of Leave and Intermittent Leaves

Some of the rules differ regarding intermittent leaves and the minimum amount of leave time that must be taken, depending on whether the leave is for bonding with a new child, or based on the employee's or a family member's serious health condition.

a. Minimum Amounts of Leave

The FMLA does not set a minimum amount of leave that an employee must take.

The CFRA sets no minimum amount of time that must be taken for leaves not based on bonding with a new child. Under the CFRA, the minimum time for bonding leave is two weeks (with the exception that the employee is entitled to take two separate leaves that are shorter than two weeks, but that are at least one day). (2 California Code of Regulations section 7297.3(d).)

Under the FMLA and CFRA, leave may be taken in increments as small as the shortest period of time that the employer uses to account for other absences or forms of leave. (2 California Code of Regulations section 7297.3(e); 29 Code of Federal Regulations section 825.205.) The FMLA requires that the increments used for accounting for FMLA leave be one hour or less, down to the shortest period of time the employer uses to account for other types of absences. The employer may account for FMLA leave in shorter increments than the increments used for other forms of leave. An employee's leave entitlement may not be reduced by more than the amount of leave actually taken. (29 Code of Federal Regulations section 825.205.)

b. Intermittent Leaves

"Intermittent leave" is leave taken in separate blocks of time that are all related to the same qualifying reason. (29 Code of Federal Regulations sections 825.202(a) and 825.800.) An example of an intermittent leave would be a need to take oneself or a family member to weekly physical therapy or chemotherapy appointments. Under certain circumstances, both the FMLA and CFRA allow leave to be taken intermittently or in the form of a reduced work schedule. (2 California Code of Regulations section 7297.3(a), (e); 29 Code of Federal Regulations sections 825.202, 825.203.)

i. Intermittent Leaves Based on the Serious Health Condition of the Employee or Family Member

Intermittent leave or a reduced schedule may be appropriate in a situation where the employee only needs to provide care to a family member intermittently (for example, other care is normally available, or care responsibilities are shared with others), the family member's condition only requires care on an intermittent basis, or one's own condition requires a reduced schedule. (29 Code of Federal Regulations sections 825.202, 825.203; 2 California Code of Regulations section 7297.3(e).) As long as there is a medical need for intermittent leave as determined by the healthcare provider, employer agreement is not required for leave based on a family member's serious health condition (as opposed to intermittent leave for bonding purposes; see next section). (29 Code of Federal Regulations section 825.203; 2 California Code of Regulations section 7297.3(e).) The FMLA requires that the employee make a reasonable effort to schedule planned medical treatment in the manner that disrupts the employer's operations the least. (29 Code of Federal Regulations section 825.203.)

ii. Intermittent Bonding Leaves

If an employee takes "bonding" leave because of the birth, acceptance of foster placement, or adoption of a child, the FMLA allows her to take intermittent leave or work a reduced schedule only if the employer agrees. (29 Code of Federal Regulations sections 825.120(b), 825.121(b), 825.202(c).) Under the CFRA, leave taken for the birth, adoption, or foster care placement of a child does not have to be taken in one continuous period of time. The CFRA does not require employer agreement to an intermittent leave arrangement, but it does impose a general two week minimum as discussed in subsection 8.a., above.

iii. Intermittent Leaves for Qualifying Exigencies Related to Members of the Military

Under the FMLA, employees may take intermittent leave when it is necessary because of a qualifying exigency resulting from a family member's active duty in the armed forces. (29 Code of Federal Regulations sections 825.202(d), 825.203.)

9. Notice to Employer That Employee Is Requesting Family Leave

a. Timing of Notice

When an employee's need for leave is foreseeable, he must give the employer a minimum of thirty days' notice of the need under the FMLA. (29 U.S. Code section 2612(e); 29 Code of Federal Regulations section 825.302.) If circumstances or a medical emergency do not reasonably allow an employee to provide thirty days' notice, the employee must give notice as soon as practicable, typically the same day or the next business day. If the need for leave is not foreseeable, an employer may require the employee in most circumstances to follow the employer's usual notice and procedural requirements for requesting leave. (29 Code of Federal Regulations sections 825.302(b), (d), 825.303.)

Under the CFRA, if an employee's need for leave is foreseeable, the employee must give the employer reasonable advance notice of the need for the leave, including the reason for the leave and its anticipated duration. (Government Code section 12945.2(h); 2 California Code of Regulations section 7297.4(a)(1).) An employer can require thirty days' advance notice if practicable (such as for a planned medical treatment or the birth of a child). (2 California Code of Regulations section 7297.4(a)(2).) The employee also must make a reasonable effort to schedule the treatment or medical supervision to avoid disruption to the employer's operations, as long as these arrangements are approved by the healthcare provider. (Government Code section 12945.2(i); 2 California Code of Regulations section 7297.4(a)(2).)

If thirty days' notice is not possible, notice must be given as soon as practicable. (29 Code of Federal Regulations section 825.303; 2 California Code of Regulations section 7297.4(a)(3).)

An employer cannot deny the leave because of an employee's failure to provide notice if the leave is for an emergency or was unforeseeable. (2 California Code of Regulations section 7297.4(a)(4).)

b. Information That Should Be Included in the Request for Family Leave

Though the employee is required to provide notice to the employer that she is requesting leave, she is not required to state specifically that she is requesting the leave under the CFRA or FMLA. However, the employee must give the employer enough information so that the employer can determine whether the leave qualifies as family and medical leave. The employee should state the basis for the leave request — either the employee's own serious medical condition; the birth, adoption, or placement of a foster child; or the need to care for a parent, child, spouse, or domestic partner (in California) with a serious medical condition. If the employee does not explain the reasons for the needed leave, the leave may be denied. (29 Code of Federal Regulations section 825.301(b); 2 California Code of Regulations section 7297.4.)

The employer is responsible for properly identifying leave under the FMLA or CFRA. Misidentifying FMLA leave as personal leave interferes with the employee's right to FMLA leave. (*Liu v. Amway Corp.* (9th Cir. 2003) 347 F.3d 1125.) If the employer needs more information to make a determination as to whether the leave qualifies under the law, it is the employer's responsibility to ask for it. (2 California Code of Regulations section 7297.4(a)(1); 29 Code of Federal Regulations sections 825.301(a), 825.302(c).)

If the employee asks to use accrued paid time off without mentioning any CFRA-qualifying purpose, an employer may not ask whether the employee is taking time off for a CFRA-qualifying purpose. (2 California Code of Regulations section 7297.5(b)(2)(A).) However, under both the FMLA and CFRA, if the employer denies the employee's request for leave, and the employee then provides information that the requested time off may be for a CFRA- or FMLA-qualifying purpose, the employer may ask questions about the reasons for the absence. (29 Code of Federal Regulations section 825.301(b); 2 California Code of Regulations section 7297.5(b)(2)(A)(1).)

Requests for time off to "visit" ailing parents have been found not to qualify for family leave. The employee needs to communicate the fact that he seeks to "care for" the parent. (*Stevens v. California Dept. of Corrections* (2003) 107 Cal.App.4th 285.)

The fact that an employee calls in sick or uses sick time is not enough notice that the employee seeks leave under the CFRA or FMLA for his own condition. (29 Code of Federal Regulations section 825.303(b).) CFRA leave requires the employee to have a serious health condition that makes him unable to perform the functions of his job, whereas sick time might be used for a minor illness. Forms submitted to the employer should contain sufficient information to indicate that the employee's condition qualifies him for a leave under the CFRA. (*Avila v. Continental Airlines* (2008) 165 Cal.App.4th 1237.)

If the employee has previously been granted FMLA-protected leave for a certain qualifying reason, and later seeks leave due to the same reason, the employee must specifically reference the qualifying reason again in notifying the employer. (29 Code of Federal Regulations section 825.302(c).)

c. Form of Notice That Employee Is Requesting Family Leave

There is no legal requirement that the employee's request for family leave be in writing. (See 2 California Code of Regulations section 7297.4(a); 29 Code of Federal Regulations section 825.302(c).)

d. Employer's Notice to Employees Regarding FMLA/CFRA Leaves

Employers are required to inform employees of their family and medical leave rights, including whether they are eligible for family and medical leave in specific instances and when leave has been designated as family and medical leave. If a significant portion of the employer's workforce does not speak English, the employer must translate these notices into the employees' spoken language. (29 Code of Federal Regulations section 825.300; 2 California Code of Regulations sections 7297.4(a)(6), 7297.9.)

i. *Notice of Rights*

Employers covered by the FMLA and CFRA must post a notice of employees' rights under the statutes in a conspicuous place where employees congregate and can read the guidelines. The FMLA allows the posting to be electronic as long as it satisfies all other requirements. Paper copies must be posted where employees who do not have access to company computers and applicants who apply through non-electronic means can easily see them. (29 Code of Federal Regulations section 825.300(a); 2 California Code of Regulations section 7297.9(a).) Under the FMLA, covered employers must post such a notice regardless of whether or not there are any eligible employees working at the particular worksite, and the notice must include the procedures for filing complaints. (29 Code of Federal Regulations section 825.300(a)(1), (2).) If the employer has an employee handbook or other written guidance for employees regarding benefits or leave rights, it must include an explanation of the FMLA and CFRA. (29 Code of Federal Regulations section 825.300(a)(3), (4); 2 California Code of Regulations section 7297.9(a).) If the employer does not have such written materials, it must provide a copy of the general notice to each new employee upon hiring. The copy of the general notice may be given electronically. (29 Code of Federal Regulations section 825.300(a)(3), (4).)

FMLA and/or CFRA leave cannot be considered a break in service.

ii. *Eligibility Notice and Rights and Responsibilities Notice Under the FMLA*

Within five days of when an employee requests FMLA leave or the employer learns that an employee's leave may be for an FMLA-related reason, the employer must give oral or written notice to the employee of whether the employee is eligible for FMLA leave. If the employee is not eligible, the notice must state at least one reason why the employee is not eligible (for example, the employee has not been employed by the employer the minimum number of months, the employee has not worked the minimum number of hours, or the employer does not have the minimum number of employees within a seventy-five mile radius of the worksite).

All FMLA absences for the same qualifying reason are considered a single leave, and the employee is eligible for leave for that reason throughout the leave year. (29 Code of Federal Regulations section 825.300(b).)

If an employee is found to be eligible, the employer must provide a written notice of the employee's rights and responsibilities related to taking FMLA leave. The written notice should indicate what information and documents the employer needs in order to determine if the requested leave qualifies for FMLA protection. The notice also explains the responsibilities the employee will be accepting should her requested leave qualify as FMLA leave, and the consequences if these responsibilities are not met. The following are some examples of information that the employer must include in the written notice of rights and responsibilities provided to eligible employees who are requesting FMLA leave:

- That leave may be designated and counted against the employee's FMLA leave entitlement if it qualifies as FMLA leave;
- The applicable twelve-month leave year (for example, calendar year, fiscal year, one year from start of family leave);
- Any certification requirements (for example, certification forms for healthcare providers to fill out concerning the serious health condition of the employee or his family member; see section VII.A.10., p. 134);
- The right or requirement to use paid leave (such as sick leave or vacation) during otherwise unpaid family leave;
- The right to maintain benefits during the leave;
- Applicable requirements to make premium payments to maintain health benefits during leave;
- The employee's status as either a "key employee" or not a key employee (because certain rights to return to the job may be different for key employees); and
- The right to job restoration after leave ends.

The employer may include any required certification form with the rights and responsibilities notice. If leave has already begun, the rights and responsibilities notice should be mailed to the employee's address. The notice of rights and responsibilities may be provided electronically as long as it meets all other requirements. (29 Code of Federal Regulations section 825.300(c).)

iii. Designation Notice

When an employer has enough information to determine whether or not an employee's requested leave qualifies as FMLA or CFRA leave, it must give a designation notice to the employee (within five business days under the FMLA, and within ten days under the CFRA). This designation notice informs the employee whether the leave will be considered a family and medical leave under the applicable law and the time off counted toward the twelve-week annual maximum of guaranteed leave time. The determination as to whether the leave is covered under the FMLA or CFRA is supposed to be made by the employer before the leave starts, or as soon as practicable. If the employer has enough information at the time that it issues the eligibility notice, the designation notice may be issued at the same time. The designation notice must be in writing. (29 Code of Federal Regulations section 825.300(d); 2 California Code of Regulations section 7297.4(a)(6).)

If the employee must undergo a fitness-for-duty certification before returning to work, this requirement must be included in the designation notice along with a list of the employee's essential job functions. (29 Code of Federal Regulations sections 825.300(d)(3) and 825.313(d).)

If the employer does not designate leave to be FMLA or CFRA leave within the required time, the leave may be designated as FMLA or CFRA leave after the fact as long as the employee is given proper notice and the retroactive designation does not harm the employee. The employer and employee may also mutually agree that leave qualifying for FMLA protections should be retroactively designated as FMLA leave. (29 Code of Federal Regulations section 825.301(d); 2 California Code of Regulations section 7297.4(a)(1)(B).)

The employer must notify the employee of the amount of leave that will be counted against the employee's family and medical leave entitlement. If the employer knows the amount of leave needed at the time of designation, the amount must be listed in the designation notice. If the amount of leave that will be counted against the leave entitlement cannot be determined in advance, the employer must give the employee notice of the amount of leave used upon request (at most once every thirty days if leave was taken in that period). The notice of the amount of leave that will be counted against the employee's entitlement may be written or oral, but oral notice must be confirmed in writing. (29 Code of Federal Regulations section 825.300(d)(6).)

10. Certification of the Condition Requiring Leave

a. Serious Health Condition of the Employee or the Employee's Family Member

i. *Initial Certification*

Under both the FMLA and CFRA, if an employee requests leave to care for a family member, the employer may require certification by a healthcare provider that the family member is seriously ill. A healthcare provider is defined as an individual licensed as a physician, surgeon, or osteopathic physician or surgeon who directly treats or supervises the treatment of the serious health condition, or a person capable of providing healthcare services under the FMLA. Examples of healthcare providers include doctors of medicine or osteopathy authorized to practice medicine or surgery by the state in which the doctor practices; podiatrists, dentists, clinical psychologists, optometrists, and chiropractors (limited to manual manipulation of the spine to correct a problem demonstrated by x-ray to exist) authorized to practice, and performing within the scope of their practice, under state law; and nurse practitioners and nurse-midwives authorized to practice, and performing within the scope of their practice, as defined under state law. (Government Code section 12945.2(c)(6); 2 California Code of Regulations section 7297.0(j); 29 Code of Federal Regulations section 825.800.)

The certification generally should be requested within five days after the employee gives notice of the need for leave. It may be requested later if questions arise as to the appropriateness or length of the leave. In most cases, the employee must provide the certification within fifteen calendar days of the employer's request. (29 Code of Federal Regulations section 825.305(b).) The certification must include at least the following:

- The beginning date of the health condition;
- The probable duration of the health condition;
- A statement that the serious health condition requires a family member to provide care;

- An estimate of the amount of time the employee will need to take off.

(29 U.S. Code section 2613(a), (b); 29 Code of Federal Regulations section 825.306; Government Code section 12945.2(j); 2 California Code of Regulations section 7297.4(b)(1).) Under the FMLA, the employer may also require that the employee provide contact information for the healthcare provider and the type of medical practice or specialization. (29 Code of Federal Regulations section 825.306(a)(1).)

The FMLA allows the employer to ask for a diagnosis of the serious health condition. (29 Code of Federal Regulations section 825.306(a) (3).) However, under the CFRA, the healthcare provider is not required to provide a diagnosis and may not do so without the voluntary consent of the employee. The employer cannot require the employee to provide, and cannot deny, leave based on failure to provide intimate and private information. (*Lonicki v. Sutter Health Central* (2008) 43 Cal.4th 201; Government Code section 12945.2(k)(1); 2 California Code of Regulations section 7297.0(a)(2).)

If the employee requests leave due to his own serious health condition, the employer may require a certification that includes the beginning date and probable duration of the health condition, plus a statement that the employee is unable to perform the functions of his position because of his health condition. (29 U.S. Code section 2613(b) (4)(B); 29 Code of Federal Regulations section 825.306; Government Code section 12945.2(k); 2 California Code of Regulations section 7297.4(b) (2).) The fact that the employee is able to work for a second employer during the period for which he seeks leave does not prove that he is able to do the job for the original employer. The serious health condition that prevents the employee from performing the functions of his current job may not prevent him from performing the second job even if the jobs are similar. The issue is whether a serious health condition makes him unable to do his *actual* job under the current environment. (*Lonicki v. Sutter Health Central* (2008) 43 Cal.4th 201.)

If the certification is incomplete or insufficient (for example, entries are left blank, information is vague, or information does not respond to the questions), the employer must state in writing what additional information is needed. The FMLA requires the employer to allow the employee seven calendar days to fix the certification. The employee must be given more time if he is unable to obtain the information despite good faith efforts. (29 Code of Federal Regulations section 825.305(c).)

The employer may not request additional information from the healthcare provider if the certification is complete, sufficient, and signed by the provider. However, under the federal FMLA (but not under California law), the employer may contact the healthcare provider for purposes of clarification (to decipher handwriting or to understand the meaning of a response) and authentication of the certification. The employer may not ask for information beyond what is required by the certification form. The employer must use a healthcare provider, human resources professional, leave administrator, or management official to make contact with the employee's healthcare provider. However, the employer's representative who makes contact with the provider cannot be the employee's direct supervisor. In order for a healthcare provider to discuss the individual's health condition, the healthcare provider must have a signed release from the patient or a close family member of the patient. (29 Code of Federal Regulations section 825.307.)

Sometimes an employee's serious health condition is a disability within the meaning of the Americans with Disabilities Act (ADA) or is covered under Workers' Compensation. If the employer's disability benefit plan or Workers' Compensation requires that the employee provide medical information that is not required or allowed in the FMLA certification, the employer can require that the information be provided without violating the FMLA. It must be made clear to the employee that the failure to provide such additional information affects only the employee's ability to receive applicable payments or benefits and does not affect the employee's entitlement to unpaid FMLA leave. However, the employer may consider any additional information received in determining whether the need for leave qualifies under the FMLA. (29 Code of Federal Regulations sections 825.207(a) and 825.306(c), (d).)

ii. Second and Third Medical Opinions

In some cases, if the employer doubts whether there is a serious medical condition qualifying the employee for family leave, the employer may require second and third medical opinions at its own expense. Under the CFRA, the employer may require second and third opinions only for the employee's own serious health condition. If the leave is requested for the serious health condition of a family member, the CFRA requires the employer to accept the initial certification. (2 California Code of Regulations section 7297.4(b) (1).) However, under the FMLA, the employer may require second and third opinions for the employee's own serious health condition or the serious health condition of a relative.

The healthcare provider that supplies the second opinion must not be employed on a regular basis by the employer. The employee or family member must authorize his healthcare provider to release all relevant medical information regarding the serious health condition to the healthcare provider supplying the second opinion. If the first and second opinions differ, the employer may require a third opinion (also at the employer's expense) by a healthcare provider jointly approved by the employee and employer. The third opinion is final and binding. (29 U.S. Code section 2613; 29 Code of Federal Regulations section 825.307; Government Code section 12945.2(k)(3); 2 California Code of Regulations section 7297.4(b).) However, the employer is not *required* to seek a third and binding opinion, and failure to do so does not prevent the employer from later challenging the employee's claim that a serious health condition prevents him from performing the functions of his job. (*Lonicki v. Sutter Health Central* (2008) 43 Cal.4th 201.) While the employer is waiting for the second or third opinion, the employee is entitled to the benefits of the FMLA. If the leave ultimately is not designated as FMLA leave, it may be treated as paid or unpaid leave. (29 Code of Federal Regulations section 825.307(b)(1).)

iii. Recertification

After the end of the time period the healthcare provider originally estimated in the medical certification that the employee would need, the employer may require recertification if additional leave is requested. (29 U.S. Code section 2613(e); 29 Code of Federal Regulations section 825.308(c) (1); Government Code section 12945.2(j)(2), (k)(2); 2 California Code of Regulations section 7297.4(b)(1), (2).)

Under the FMLA, an employer generally may request recertification of the reason for the employee's absence no more often than every thirty days. If the initial certification is for more than thirty days, the employer must wait until that time period has passed before requesting recertification. However, the employer may request recertification of a medical condition every six months even if the certification indicates a longer duration. The employer may request recertification of a medical condition in fewer than thirty days if circumstances described by the original certification have changed significantly or if the employer has reason to doubt the validity of the original certification. (29 U.S. Code section 2613(e); 29 Code of Federal Regulations section 825.308.)

The employer may ask for the same information in the recertification as that allowed in the original certification. However, the employer may not require second and third opinions for purposes of recertification. The employer may provide the healthcare provider with a record of the employee's absences and ask the healthcare provider if the absence pattern is consistent with the serious health condition and need for leave. (29 Code of Federal Regulations section 825.308(e), (f).)

If the serious health condition lasts more than one leave year (defined in section VII.A.7.a.iii., p. 127), the employer may require the employee to provide a new medical certification each following leave year. The new certification is treated like any other initial certification, subject to authentication and clarification, as well as to second and third opinions. (29 Code of Federal Regulations section 825.305(e).)

b. Serious Illness or Injury of a Service Member of the Armed Forces

When the employee requests leave to care for a covered member of the military with a serious injury or illness, the employer may require a certification of the circumstances that qualify the employee for military caregiver leave (for example, the service member's health condition, the service member's status in the military, and the employee's relationship to the service member). The employer may require certification from an authorized healthcare provider of the covered service member, such as:

- A United States Department of Defense (DOD) healthcare provider;
- A United States Department of Veterans Affairs (VA) healthcare provider;
- A DOD TRICARE network authorized private healthcare provider; or
- A DOD non-network TRICARE authorized private healthcare provider.

The employer may request the following information from the healthcare provider:

- The name, address, and contact information of the healthcare provider, the type of medical practice, the medical specialty, and whether the healthcare provider is a DOD healthcare provider, a VA healthcare provider, a DOD TRICARE network authorized private healthcare provider, or a DOD non-network TRICARE authorized private healthcare provider;
- Whether the covered service member's injury or illness was incurred in the line of duty on active duty;
- The approximate date on which the serious injury or illness began, and its probable duration;
- A statement or description of the medical facts about the service member's serious health condition that support the need for leave;
- Information to establish that the covered service member needs care, whether the care should be in a single continuous period of time, and an estimate of the beginning and ending dates of the need for care;
- If the employee requests intermittent leave or a reduced schedule, whether there is a medical need for periodic care, and an estimate of the treatment schedule or frequency and duration of the periodic care.

If the authorized healthcare provider is unable to

make some of the military-related determinations, the authorized healthcare provider may rely on determinations from an authorized DOD representative.

In addition, the employer may require that the employee or service member include the following information as part of the certification:

- The name and address of the employer, the name of the employee requesting leave, and the name of the covered service member;

- The relationship of the employee to the covered service member;

- Whether the covered service member is a current member of the armed forces, the National Guard, or reserves, and the service member's military branch, rank, and current unit assignment;

- Whether the covered service member or veteran is assigned as an outpatient to a military medical facility or other military medical unit established to provide service members and veterans with medical care as outpatients, and the name of the medical treatment facility or unit;

- Whether the covered service member is on the temporary disability retired list;

- A description of the care the employee will provide to the covered service member and an estimate of the leave needed.

An employer must accept an "invitational travel order" (ITO) or "invitational travel authorization" (ITA), issued to a family member to join an injured or ill service member at his bedside, as sufficient certification for the time specified in the travel order or authorization supplied by DOD.

The employer may seek authentication and clarification of the certification, ITO, or ITA, and the employer may require confirmation of the family relationship between the employee and the covered service member. However, the employer may not ask for second and third medical opinions or recertification of a service member's condition. (29 Code of Federal Regulations section 825.310.)

If the certification is incomplete, the employer must state in writing what additional information is needed. The employer must allow the employee seven calendar days to fix the certification. The employee must be given more time if he is unable to obtain the information despite good faith efforts. (29 Code of Federal Regulations section 825.305.)

c. Qualifying Exigency Resulting From the Active Duty Status of a Family Member in the Armed Forces

If the employee requests leave in relation to circumstances resulting from a family member serving on active duty or being called to active duty in the armed forces, the employer may require certification. (29 U.S. Code section 2613(f).) The employer may require the employee to provide a copy of the active duty orders or other military documentation indicating the active duty status and the dates of the active duty service of the service member. The employee must provide this information only once regarding this specific call to duty. The employer may also require the following information:

- A statement or description, signed by the employee, providing facts that support the need for leave, including information on the type of qualifying exigency and written documents that support the request for leave;

- The approximate date on which the qualifying exigency will begin;

- The dates of absence if the employee requests leave for a single, continuous period of time;

- An estimate of the frequency and duration of the qualifying exigency if the employee requests leave on an intermittent or reduced schedule basis; and

- The contact information for the individual or entity with whom the employee is meeting and a brief description of the purpose of the meeting if the qualifying exigency involves meeting with a third party.

The employer may contact the Department of Defense to verify that a covered military member is on active duty or call-to-active-duty status. The employer may also verify a meeting and the nature of the meeting with the third party if the exigency involves meeting with a third party. Other than these two instances, the employer may not request additional information if the certification is complete. (29 Code of Federal Regulations section 825.309.)

11. Medical and Other Benefits During Leave

While an employee is on FMLA and/or CFRA leave, the employer must maintain and pay its share of premiums for the employee's group healthcare coverage on the same terms as if the employee was continuously employed during the entire leave period. (29 U.S. Code section 2614(c)

(1); 29 Code of Federal Regulations section 825.209(a); Government Code section 12945.2(f)(1); 2 California Code of Regulations section 7297.5(c).) FMLA and/or CFRA leave cannot be considered a break in service. (Government Code section 12945.2(g); 2 California Code of Regulations section 7291.11(d).) The employee is entitled to any unconditional pay increases (for example, cost of living) that occur during the employee's FMLA leave. However, employees are not entitled to accrue seniority or benefits during FMLA leave, unless the employer's policy or a collective bargaining agreement provides this right for similar leaves not covered by the FMLA. (29 U.S Code section 2614(a)(3)(A); 29 Code of Federal Regulations section 825.215(c)(2).) Employees are entitled to maintain the same levels of seniority and benefits as they had when the leave started. So, if an employee's entitlement to health benefits is subject to a waiting period at the beginning of the job and the employee has not worked sufficient hours to qualify for benefits when the FMLA leave begins, the period of FMLA leave does not count toward eligibility for benefits as long as other leaves not covered by the FMLA are similarly treated. The employer is only required to provide medical benefits to which the employee was already entitled at the time he went on leave. This rule may be changed by an employment agreement, an employer policy, or a collective bargaining agreement. If a contract, policy, or labor agreement provides that other types of leave (paid or unpaid) count as hours worked for purposes of determining eligibility for health insurance, family and medical leave would need to be treated in the same manner. (29 Code of Federal Regulations section 825.215(d)(5); Department of Labor Wage and Hour Division Opinion Letter FMLA2006-4-A (February 13, 2006).)

Under the FMLA and CFRA, if the employee quits or fails to return to work at the end of her leave or notifies the employer she definitely does not intend to return to work at the end of the leave, the employer's duty to maintain health coverage ceases, and the employee may have to repay the employer's share of the group healthcare premiums contributed during the leave. (29 Code of Federal Regulations sections 825.209(f), 825.211(e)(3), 825.311(b); Government Code section 12945.2(f)(1)(A), (B); 2 California Code of Regulations sections 7297.2(c)(1)(a), 7297.5(c).) However, if the employee does not return to work because of a serious health condition or other circumstances beyond her control, the employee does not have to repay the premiums paid by the employer. (29 U.S. Code section 2614(c)(2); 29 Code of Federal Regulations section 825.213(a); Government Code section 12945.2(f)(1)(B); 2 California Code of Regulations section 7297.5(c).)

Under both the FMLA and CFRA, an employee on family and medical leave is entitled to participate in employee benefit plans other than basic health insurance (for instance, life, vision, or dental insurance) to the same extent and in the same manner as others taking unpaid leave for any other reason. If an employer covers vision and health benefits during other types of unpaid leave, it must pay such premiums for employees taking family and medical leaves. If the employer does not pay for such benefits during other unpaid leaves, it can require the employee to pay all premiums (both the employee's and the employer's share) during the family and medical leave. (29 Code of Federal Regulations section 825.209(h); Government Code section 12945.2(f)(2).)

If an individual's employment is terminated during a period of FMLA and/or CFRA leave for a reason that would have resulted in termination even if the employee were not on family and medical leave (such as a non-discretionary reduction in workforce or layoff), the employer's duty to pay group health plan premiums ceases. The employee's right to continued coverage falls under the terms for extension set forth in the Consolidated Omnibus Budget Reconciliation Act of 1986 (COBRA). (29 Code of Federal Regulations section 825.209(f).) (See section III.E., p. 112, for more information on the continuation of health benefits.)

An employer's duty to cover the employee under group health coverage also ceases if the employee fails to pay her share of the insurance premiums for thirty days while on leave, unless the employer has an established policy allowing a longer grace period. (29 Code of Federal Regulations section 825.212(a)(1).) If the employer pays the employee's contribution, the employer is entitled to recover the amount of the employee's contribution from the employee. (29 Code of Federal Regulations section 825.212(b).)

An employee may choose not to participate in a group health plan during a period of FMLA leave.

Upon return from leave, the employee is entitled to be reinstated on the same terms as prior to taking the leave without any waiting period, physical examination, or exclusion of pre-existing conditions.

12. Holidays and Closures During Leave

The FMLA and CFRA guidelines specify that if a holiday occurs within a week that an employee is on family and medical leave, the employee must count the week as a full week of FMLA or CFRA leave. However, if an employer ceases operations for a week or more while the employee is on family and medical leave, the period of non-operation does not count as part of the FMLA or CFRA leave. (29 Code of Federal Regulations section 825.200(h); 2 California Code of Regulations section 7297.3(c)(3).)

If the employee is taking family leave in increments of less than a week, a holiday occurring during the workweek will not count against the employee's family leave entitlement unless the employee was required to work on the holiday. (29 Code of Federal Regulations section 825.200(h).)

13. Rights on Returning From Leave

a. Reinstatement to the Same or Equivalent/ Comparable Position

Both the FMLA and CFRA guarantee an employee taking family leave the right to be reinstated to the same or an equivalent position upon return from leave. (29 U.S. Code section 2614(a)(1); 29 Code of Federal Regulations section 825.214; Government Code section 12945.2(a); 2 California Code of Regulations section 7297.2(a).)

An "equivalent position" (FMLA term) or "comparable position" (CFRA term) is one that is "virtually identical" to the employee's former position in terms of "pay, benefits and working conditions, including privileges, perquisites and status," and "it must involve the same or substantially similar duties and responsibilities, which must entail substantially equivalent skill, effort, responsibility, and authority." The job also must be located at the same geographic location as the employee's old job, or at a similar location. (29 Code of Federal Regulations section 825.215; 2 California Code of Regulations section 7297.0(g).)

If an employee voluntarily accepts a "light duty" assignment while recovering from a serious health condition, the employee is still entitled to be restored to the position he held before the FMLA leave once the light-duty assignment ends. However, the employee's right to restoration while on light-duty assignment ends when the twelve-month FMLA leave year ends. (29 Code of Federal Regulations section 825.220(d).)

If an employer has a consistent policy applicable to all employees of requiring a return-to-work release (under CFRA) or a fitness-for-duty certification (under FMLA) upon return from leave for the employee's own serious health condition, an employer may deny reinstatement until the employee provides such release or certification, provided that the employer gave notice to the employee about this requirement when the leave was granted. (29 Code of Federal Regulations sections 825.312 and 825.313(d); 2 California Code of Regulations section 7297.4(b)(2)(E).)

Under the FMLA, fitness-for-duty certifications must pertain to the particular health condition for which the employee took FMLA leave. The employer may require that the fitness-for-duty certification specifically address the essential functions of the employee's job. If the employee is on intermittent leave and there are reasonable safety concerns regarding the employee's ability to perform her duties, the employer may require a certification of fitness-for-duty up to once every thirty days. The employee must pay the cost of the fitness-for-duty certification. (29 Code of Federal Regulations section 825.312.)

b. Possible Employer Grounds for Refusal to Reinstate an Employee Following Family and Medical Leave

Under the CFRA and FMLA, an employer may refuse to reinstate certain highly paid key employees in order to prevent substantial and grievous economic injury to the employer's operations. (29 U.S. Code section 2614(b); 29 Code of Federal Regulations sections 825.216(b) and 825.217; Government Code section 12945.2(r); 2 California Code of Regulations section 7297.2(c)(2).) The employer may also be excused from reinstating an employee to her original position or a comparable position if the employee would not have continued in the position for reasons unrelated to her leave even if she remained working. (29 Code of Federal Regulations section 825.216(a); 2 California Code of Regulations section 7297.2(c)(1).)

Under the FMLA, the employer may be excused

from reinstating an employee if she obtained the leave through fraud or violated an employer rule against outside employment. (29 Code of Federal Regulations section 825.216(d), (e).)

The employee has no greater right to reinstatement or other conditions of employment than if she had been continuously employed during the leave period. (29 Code of Federal Regulations section 825.216(a); 2 California Code of Regulations section 7297.2(c)(1).) For example, an employee who is on family and medical leave is not shielded from being laid off as part of a workforce reduction. (*Tomlinson v. Qualcomm, Inc.* (2002) 97 Cal. App.4th 934.) However, the fact that an employer is experiencing a workforce reduction does not allow the employer to use the reduction as a pretext to violate the FMLA or CFRA by terminating an employee for unlawful reasons. (*Liu v. Amway Corp.* (9th Cir. 2003) 347 F.3d 1125.)

14. Protection Against Violations of Family Leave Laws

a. Under the FMLA

An employer must not interfere with the employee's right to take leave under the FMLA. (29 U.S. Code section 2615(a); 29 Code of Federal Regulations section 825.220.) An employer who fails to follow the notice requirements may be considered to have interfered with the employee's FMLA rights. (29 Code of Federal Regulations section 825.300(e).) Any disputes between the employer and employee as to whether leave qualifies as FMLA leave should be resolved through discussions, and the decision must be documented. (29 Code of Federal Regulations section 825.301(c).) The employer must not use the fact that an employee has taken FMLA leave as a negative factor in an employment decision. If the employer has an attendance policy, under which the employee may miss only a certain number of days regardless of the reason, FMLA leave cannot count against the employee. (29 Code of Federal Regulations section 825.220(c); *Bachelder v. America West Airlines, Inc.* (9th Cir. 2001) 259 F.3d 1112.)

It is illegal for an employer to discriminate against an employee who exercises his rights under the FMLA or gives information in a proceeding related to FMLA rights. (29 U.S. Code section 2615; 29 Code of Federal Regulations section 825.220.)

Employees cannot waive future rights under the FMLA. However, FMLA claims based on past employer conduct may be settled without the permission or approval of the Department of Labor or a court. (29 Code of Federal Regulations section 825.220(d).)

Enforcement: Employers who violate the FMLA may be liable for damages equal to the compensation and benefits lost, other actual monetary losses directly resulting from violation, and appropriate equitable and other relief (including employment, reinstatement, promotion, or any other relief tailored to the harm suffered). (29 Code of Federal Regulations sections 825.220(b), 825.400(c).) File a complaint with the U.S. Department of Labor, Wage and Hour Division. If the department finds a violation, it may pursue a lawsuit on the employee's behalf. Or, the employee can file a lawsuit herself. Suits must be filed within two years of the latest action taken that was not in compliance with the FMLA, or within three years of the latest willful violation of the act.

b. Under the CFRA

It is illegal for an employer to discriminate against an employee for exercising the right to leave under the CFRA or for giving information in a proceeding related to CFRA rights. (2 California Code of Regulations section 7297.7.)

Enforcement: File a complaint with the California Department of Fair Employment and Housing (DFEH) within one year. The DFEH can order the employer to comply with the law and can award the employee damages. (Government Code section 12970.) The employee must exhaust the administrative remedies available under the Fair Employment and Housing Act by filing a complaint to the DFEH within one year of the discriminatory act before he can file a CFRA lawsuit in state court. Lawsuits must be filed within one year of the date the DFEH issues a right-to-sue letter.

15. Differences Between California and Federal Law

The federal FMLA and California's CFRA contain very similar provisions, but there are important differences in the areas of pregnancy disability leave, leave to care for a domestic partner, and leave in connection with a relative's service in the military. The California Fair Employment and Housing Commission has a useful table comparing the laws at http://www.fehc.ca.gov/pdf/FMLA-CFRARegsTable-2.pdf.

B. PREGNANCY DISABILITY LEAVE UNDER THE CALIFORNIA PREGNANCY DISABILITY LEAVE (PDL) ACT

Even if a pregnant worker is not eligible for work-protected leave under the FMLA or CFRA, she is still entitled to job-protected, unpaid leave for pregnancy-related disabilities under the California Pregnancy Disability Leave (PDL) Act if her employer has at least five employees. (Government Code sections 12945, 12926(d) (defining employer size).) There is no minimum length of service an employee must work before being eligible to receive leave under the PDL Act. (2 California Code of Regulations section 7291.7(c).) The rights granted under this law are over and above the more general leave rights contained in the CFRA. As a result, under California law, pregnant women may have leave available to them under the PDL Act if they are actually disabled because of pregnancy, childbirth, or health problems associated with pregnancy or childbirth, in addition to leave time to care for and bond with a newborn child under the CFRA. Conditions that pose a danger to the unborn child are considered health conditions that may give rise to the right to pregnancy disability leave.

California law also requires an employer to provide reasonable accommodation, in the form of break time and a private place, for a nursing mother to express breast milk at work. (Labor Code sections 1030–1033.)

Note that regulations implementing the FMLA provide that pregnancy and related medical conditions are considered a "serious health condition" under the act. (29 Code of Federal Regulations section 825.115(b).) The CFRA does not consider pregnancy and related medical conditions to be a "serious health condition." (2 California Code of Regulations section 7297.6(b).) Under California law, pregnancy disability leave is separate from family and medical leaves under the CFRA.

1. Amount of Leave/Break Time Under the PDL Act

Under the California PDL Act, female employees who work for an employer with more than five employees are entitled to a reasonable period of leave, up to four months, if they are actually disabled due to pregnancy, childbirth, or related medical conditions. (Government Code section 12945(a).) This includes severe morning sickness or other problems due to a difficult pregnancy, and this leave may be taken intermittently. An employer may limit leave increments to the shortest period of time that the employer's payroll system uses to account for absences or use of leave. (2 California Code of Regulations section 7291.7(a)(3).)

Female state civil service employees have a special protection: the right to an unpaid leave of absence for pregnancy, childbirth, and recovery from pregnancy for a period the employee selects — up to one full year. Once the state civil service employee has selected the leave period, any change requires the employer's approval. A similar right (which may be modified by a union contract) exists for female employees of the California State University. (Education Code section 89519.)

2. Interaction Between PDL Act Leave and CFRA Leave in California

Time taken for pregnancy disability leave under the California PDL Act does not count as part of the allowable time employees may take for other types of family leave under the CFRA. If new parents work for more than a year for at least 1,250 hours for an employer with at least fifty employees, they also qualify for twelve additional weeks of job-protected, unpaid leave to bond with their new baby or newly placed adopted or foster child under the CFRA. Thus, even after a new mother is medically able to work, she must be allowed to remain on leave of absence to care for her infant, if she requests to do so, for up to twelve weeks if she qualifies for CFRA leave. (2 California Code of Regulations section 7291.13(c).)

If a female employee needs to use all four months of her pregnancy disability leave under the PDL Act before the birth of her child, in some circumstances it may be possible to use additional leave under the CFRA to cover pre-birth absences due to medical necessity. The employee should consult her healthcare provider for verification of the need for this additional leave (for eligibility standards, see section VII.A.2., p. 122). (2 California Code of Regulations section 7291.13(c)(1).) After the birth, the employer must allow her any remaining

CFRA leave to bond with the newborn child. (Government Code section 12945.2(s).) Unless her employer agrees otherwise, the maximum total leave an employee may take for pregnancy and the related birth of a child is four months of pregnancy disability leave under the PDL Act and twelve weeks of CFRA/FMLA leave. (2 California Code of Regulations section 7291.13(d).) See section VII.A., p. 121, for more information on the CFRA and the federal FMLA.

3. Notice and Medical Certification Requirements Under the PDL Act

Employees requesting PDL Act leave can do so verbally. They must notify the employer that the leave is being requested for a pregnancy disability, and inform the employer of the anticipated timing and duration of leave. (2 California Code of Regulations section 7291.10(a)(1).) An employer can also require reasonable notice of the date an employee's transfer to lighter duty (see discussion below) is expected to begin and its estimated duration.

If the need for leave is foreseeable, a pregnant employee is required to provide thirty days' notice. If it is not possible to provide thirty days' notice (for instance, when there is a lack of knowledge of approximately when leave or transfer to lighter duty will be required to begin, when there is a change in circumstances, or when there is a medical emergency), then the employee must provide notice as soon as possible. (Government Code section 12945(a); 2 California Code of Regulations section 7291.10.)

Employers may require medical certification for women taking pregnancy disability leave if they do so for other similarly situated employees. (2 California Code of Regulations section 7291.10(b).) Medical certification must be in writing by a healthcare provider and include the date on which the woman became disabled due to pregnancy, the probable duration of the disability, and a statement that due to the disability the employee is unable to work without undue risk to herself, her pregnancy, or other persons. (2 California Code of Regulations section 7291.2(d)(1).)

4. Transfer to Lighter Work or Reasonable Accommodation During Pregnancy Under the PDL Act

Employers are required to grant a pregnant employee's request to transfer to a lighter-duty position (or to a less strenuous or hazardous position), provided the need for the transfer is medically certified and it can be reasonably accommodated. Employers are not required to create additional positions, discharge another employee, promote the employee to a position for which she is not qualified, violate a collective bargaining agreement, or violate another employee's seniority. (Government Code section 12945(b)(3); 2 California Code of Regulations section 7291.6(a).)

In some cases, employees may choose to request reasonable accommodation (involving, for instance, modification of job duties, hours, etc.) rather than a transfer to lighter duty. If the request for accommodation is reasonable and documented, employers must grant such requests. (Government Code 12945(b).) (See Chapter 6 for information on reasonable accommodation requests.)

If a pregnant employee transfers to less hazardous or strenuous work, this does not eliminate her other rights. She still has the leave of absence rights previously discussed in this chapter, such as the right to take leaves, or intermittent leaves, for her own health-related conditions. (Government Code section 12945(c).)

5. Availability and Accrual of Benefits and Seniority During PDL Act Leave

Unlike the FMLA and CFRA, the employer is not required to maintain the employee's group health benefits while she is on pregnancy disability leave. However, the employee is entitled to participate in group health plans, employee benefit plans, and retirement plans to the same extent as would apply to other unpaid disability leaves of absence. Similarly, the employee is entitled to accrue seniority during a pregnancy disability leave if the employer permits such accrual during other unpaid disability leaves. At the conclusion of the pregnancy disability leave, all of the employee's benefits, including seniority, must be restored to the level they were when her leave began. (2 California Code of Regulations section 7291.11(c) and (d).)

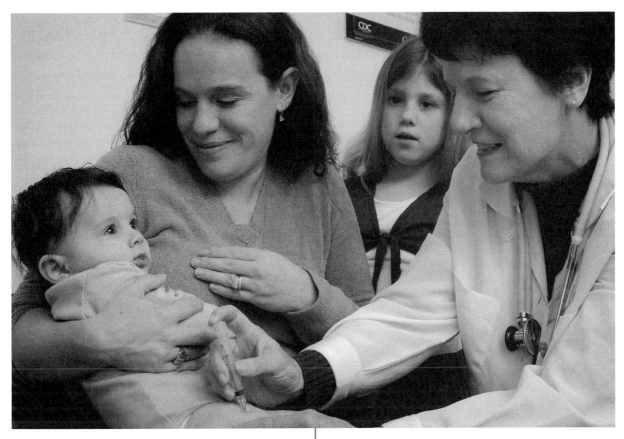

6. Rights Upon Returning From PDL Act Leave

An employee who qualifies for leave under the PDL Act leave must be allowed to return from pregnancy disability leave to her original job (or, under certain circumstances discussed below, a comparable position) when her healthcare provider certifies that there is no longer a medical need for the leave, transfer, intermittent leave, or reduced work schedule. She must be allowed to return with no change in seniority, pay, and benefits. She cannot be penalized in any way for taking pregnancy leave.

An employee on pregnancy disability leave must notify her employer when she is ready and able to return to work. The employer must then reinstate the employee to her original job or to a comparable position. If a definite date of reinstatement is agreed to at the beginning of the leave, then the employer is required to reinstate the employee to her same position on that date. (2 California Code of Regulations section 7291.9(b)(1).) If the employee's readiness to return to work does not coincide with an agreed upon date, then the employer is required to reinstate her to the same position within two days, if feasible, of the employee notifying the employer of her readiness to return. (2 California Code of Regulations section 7291.9(b)(2).)

An employer can justify a refusal to reinstate the employee to her original position if he establishes either that:

- The job was eliminated for legitimate business reasons unrelated to the leave; or
- Reinstating the employee would substantially undermine the employer's ability to operate the business safely and efficiently.

(2 California Code of Regulations section 7291.9(c)(1).)

If the employer is excused from reinstating the employee to her original position, he must reinstate her to a comparable position except in certain circumstances. (2 California Code of Regulations section 7291.9(a).) The employer can justify a refusal to reinstate the employee to a comparable position if he can prove either that:

- There is no comparable position open on the date of the employee's return or within ten days of that date, or there is no position to which the employee is entitled by company policy, contract, or collective bargaining agreement; or
- The employee took a PDL Act leave that does

not qualify for FMLA leave (for instance, it was longer than twelve weeks in duration) and, although a comparable position is available, filling it with the returning employee would substantially undermine the employer's ability to operate the business safely and efficiently. (But see the paragraph below regarding employer's treatment of other types of leaves.) (2 California Code of Regulations section 7291.9(c)(2).)

If an employee is disabled by pregnancy for longer than the guaranteed four-month period of pregnancy disability leave, her employer must offer her the same reinstatement rights as it offers other employees returning from a disability leave of similar length. (2 California Code of Regulations section 7291.9(d).)

> *Pregnant employees must be allowed to use all of their earned, paid leave time before taking unpaid pregnancy leave.*

If, at the expiration of her pregnancy disability leave, an employee takes CFRA leave for the birth of her child, her reinstatement rights are governed by the CFRA, not by the Pregnancy Disability Leave Act or the related regulations. (2 California Code of Regulations section 7291.9(e).)

Under the FMLA, an employee must be reinstated to the same or a comparable position upon returning from leave unless: she would not have continued in the position for reasons unrelated to her leave even if she remained working, she is a "key employee," she obtained the leave through fraud, or she violated an employer rule against outside employment. (See discussion of rights upon returning from FMLA leave, in section VII.A.13., p. 139, for further details.)

7. Other Forms of Prohibited Pregnancy Discrimination

Employers subject to the PDL Act cannot discharge, refuse to hire or promote, discharge

from a training program leading to employment or promotion, or harass employees on the basis of pregnancy. Pregnant women cannot be retaliated against for being pregnant or taking a pregnancy disability leave. Employers cannot refuse to accommodate a woman temporarily disabled by pregnancy to the extent that they accommodate other temporarily disabled employees. (2 California Code of Regulations section 7291.5(a).)

8. Nursing Mothers

In addition to pregnancy-related leave provisions, California law requires employers to provide reasonable accommodation to employees who wish to express breast milk during working hours. An employer must provide a reasonable amount of break time for this purpose. The employer can require the employee to use paid rest break time that it already provides. However, if that time is insufficient to meet the employee's needs, the employer must provide additional break time, although it may be unpaid. Employers are excused from this requirement only if they can show that providing such break time for the specified purpose would seriously disrupt the employer's operations. Employees are permitted to use paid lunch breaks to express milk, but such use does not excuse the employer's duty to provide a reasonable rest break for the same purpose. The employer also must provide a private place (other than a toilet stall) in close proximity to the employee's work area, for the employee to express breast milk. The employee's ordinary work area may be used if it affords her privacy. (Labor Code sections 1030–1033.)

Enforcement: File a claim for violation of the Pregnancy Disability Leave Act with the California Department of Fair Employment and Housing; then file a lawsuit if the claim is not resolved. For a violation of the rights of nursing mothers (Labor Code sections 1030-1033), file a complaint with the labor commissioner.

C. GETTING PAID DURING CFRA/FMLA/ PDL ACT LEAVES

The leave rights guaranteed under the FMLA, CFRA, and PDL Act are to unpaid leave. However, there are ways that an employee can get paid during such leave. In some situations, the use of paid leave can cover the same time as the unpaid family and medical leave defined by the statutes. In California, employees who pay into SDI can receive up to six weeks of Paid Family Leave Insurance benefits from the State Disability Insurance ("SDI") fund when they take leave for family leave purposes (including bonding with a newborn). Most private sector and some public sector employees are covered by the SDI program. See section VI., p. 115, on State Disability Insurance, for more information on this program.

1. Use of Paid Leave (Vacation, Personal Leave, Sick Leave, Other Accrued Leave)

In certain situations, an employee may choose, or may be required by the employer, to use earned paid time off during unpaid family leave.

a. Under the CFRA
i. *Paid Leaves Other Than Sick Leave and Temporary Disability Paid Family Leave*

- Under the CFRA, an employee has a right to use accrued vacation time, PTO (paid time off, where sick leave and vacation are lumped into one category), and other paid time off, other than sick leave, whenever the employee is otherwise eligible to use such leave under the policies in effect in the workplace.
- An employer may only require the employee to use paid time off (other than sick leave) if the employee has specifically requested leave for a particular event covered by the CFRA.
- If an employee asks to use paid time off (for example, vacation) without mentioning any situation that would qualify for CFRA leave, the employer may not inquire whether the employee is requesting time off for a purpose covered under the CFRA. Such a leave would not count against the twelve-week CFRA leave. So, for example, if an employee takes vacation leave to care for a member of the immediate family and does not mention the CFRA-related reason for the time off, it should not count against the employee's right to twelve weeks of leave under the CFRA.

ii. *Sick Leave*
- An employee has a right to use sick leave during a CFRA leave for the employee's own health condition.
- An employer may require the employee to use sick leave for the employee's own health condition.

- An employer may not require the employee to use sick leave for a reason other than her own health condition, over the employee's objection. Use of sick leave for a reason other than one's own health condition requires the agreement of the employer and the employee, except that employees have a right to use a limited number of sick days (one half of the days accrued during a particular year) for care of a spouse, domestic partner, parent, or child. (Labor Code section 233; see section V., p. 114, for a discussion of kin care.)

(2 California Code of Regulations Section 7297.5.)

b. Under the FMLA

The rules below apply to employees covered by federal law (primarily federal employees or military personnel). Where California laws are more protective of employees, California law will apply to employees who are subject to those laws. But state law does not govern federal or military employees.

Under the federal FMLA, an employer may require the employee to substitute paid leave for FMLA leave. In addition, an employee has the right to substitute paid leave for FMLA leave, provided she satisfies the terms, conditions, and procedural requirements of the employer's normal leave policy. If the employee does not meet the additional requirements of the paid leave policy, the employee cannot substitute paid leave, but the employee still may take unpaid FMLA leave. (29 Code of Federal Regulations section 825.207.)

If neither the employee nor the employer chooses to use paid leave during an FMLA leave, then the employee remains entitled to unused paid leave upon returning to work from the FMLA leave. (29 Code of Federal Regulations section 825.207(b).) If an employee takes leave that does not qualify for FMLA leave (for instance, for a medical need that does not qualify as a serious health condition, or to care for a family member who is not a member of the immediate family as defined by the law), then the leave does not count against the twelve-week FMLA leave entitlement. (29 Code of Federal Regulations section 825.207(c).) If the leave meets the criteria for a family and medical leave, it will generally be counted towards the employee's right to twelve weeks a year (or twenty-six weeks in the case of caring for a covered service member), even if it is covered by sick leave or disability payments, including Workers' Compensation.

If leave that is taken under an employee's disability leave plan qualifies for FMLA leave, the employer may designate the leave as FMLA leave and count it against the employee's FMLA leave entitlement. Since leave taken pursuant to a disability benefit plan is not unpaid, the substitution of paid leave does not apply. However, employers and employees may agree to have paid leave supplement the disability plan payments. (29 Code of Federal Regulations section 825.207(d).)

2. Receiving Partial Wage Replacement During Leave Through California's Paid Family Leave Insurance Program

a. Overview

California's Paid Family Leave Program is an important benefit to California workers that protects many employees who need to take time off to care for members of the immediate family or to bond with a new child from the wage loss they might otherwise suffer. It provides up to six weeks of partial wage replacement from the State Disability Insurance (SDI) fund. It is available to employees who pay into the State Disability Insurance Program (most private sector and some public sector employees) and who take a leave to provide care to a parent, spouse, registered domestic partner, or child with a serious health condition, or to bond with a new child within one year of its birth or placement for adoption or foster care. (Unemployment Insurance Code sections 3301–3306.) (See section VI., p. 115, regarding SDI.) The Paid Family Leave Program does not protect an employee's job. Leave would have to be taken under the FMLA or CFRA to guarantee job reinstatement. The two leaves can take place simultaneously.

b. Eligibility for Paid Family Leave Benefits

An employee need not be eligible for FMLA or CFRA leave in order to receive partial wage replacement under the California Paid Family Leave Act. The employee needs only to have contributed to the State Disability Insurance Program in the base period (the twelve-month period beginning seventeen months before benefits are sought; see section VI.B.3., p. 116) and have a need to take family leave for reasons covered by the program (see preceding paragraph for a list of reasons for taking Paid Family Leave). (Unemployment

Insurance Code section 2652.) For information on how the base period is calculated, see Item 5 under "Explanation of Items on the Notice of Unemployment Insurance Award" at http://www.edd.cahwnet.gov/pdf_pub_ctr/de1275a.pdf.

An employee need not have worked for an employer of a particular size or for a particular period of time to be eligible for partial wage replacement under this law. (Unemployment Insurance Code sections 2606, 675 et seq.)

c. Application for Paid Family Leave Benefits

The following rules apply to receipt of California Paid Family Leave benefits:

- The employee must make a claim for temporary disability benefits.
- The employee must complete a seven-day waiting period during which she is unable to work because she is bonding with a new child or is providing care to a parent, spouse, domestic partner, or child with a serious health condition. The seven days do not need to be consecutive. (See 22 California Code of Regulations section 3303(b)-1(a), Ex. 2.)
- The employee must file a certificate of medical eligibility with the Employment Development Department as required by Unemployment Insurance Code sections 2708, 2709. (Unemployment Insurance Code section 3303.)

Applications may be submitted by mail or over the Internet. An application form can be found by going to http://www.edd.ca.gov/Disability/PFL_Request_a_Claim_Form.htm or by calling 1-877-238-4373. Pregnant women receiving pregnancy disability benefits are automatically sent a claim form for Paid Family Leave benefits.

The EDD may require an employee to provide additional documentation regarding the medical situation of the family member requiring care and the reason why the employee's care is needed. (Unemployment Insurance Code section 3306.)

d. Paid Family Leave and Vacation

An employer may require an employee requesting Paid Family Leave benefits to first exhaust up to two weeks of earned, paid vacation leave prior to receiving Paid Family Leave benefits. One of those weeks can be counted by the employee as satisfying the seven-day waiting period before starting to collect Paid Family Leave benefits. (Unemployment Insurance Code section 3303.1(c).)

e. Duration of Paid Family Leave Benefits

No more than six weeks of Paid Family Leave benefits will be paid within a twelve-month period under the Paid Family Leave program funded through State Disability Insurance. (Unemployment Insurance Code section 3301(d).)

Since Paid Family Leave benefits for bonding with a newborn may be taken at any time during the first year of the baby's life (or placement, in the case of an adoption), some employees taking a leave longer than twelve weeks may receive higher benefits if they file on a date in which the wages during the base year will be maximized.

f. Waiting Period

The disability benefit period begins with the first day an employee establishes eligibility for Paid Family Leave benefits (after the seven-day waiting period). However, intermittent periods of leave (in other words, leaves that are not taken in one continuous period of time) to care for or bond with the same individual are considered one leave period. (Unemployment Insurance Code section 3302.1(a), (b).) Also, a leave to care for a newborn or adopted child that follows a pregnancy disability leave (see discussion in section VII.B.2., p. 141) does not require a second waiting period. (Unemployment Insurance Code section 3302.1(c).) The waiting time period of one week off work is counted as part of the twelve-week guaranteed leave under CFRA or FMLA leave to which the employee is entitled. (Unemployment Insurance Code section 3301(a)(2).) However, the employee cannot begin to collect Paid Family Leave benefits until one week after the time off work starts. The weeks during which the employee collects Paid Family Leave benefits count toward the twelve weeks of guaranteed leave under CFRA or FMLA leave. (Unemployment Insurance Code section 3303.1(b).)

g. Benefits Under Paid Family Leave

The weekly benefit amount is figured out according to the formula set forth in Unemployment Insurance Code section 2655. Benefits are based on wages earned in the "base period," which is the twelve-month period beginning seventeen months before benefits are sought (see section VII.B.3., p. 142). In other words, the base period is established according to when the claim is filed. See section VI.B.3., p. 116, for information on calculating the base period. The weekly benefits change slightly every year. See http://www.edd. ca.gov/pdf_pub_ctr/de2589.pdf for current benefits. Beginning January 1, 2010, benefits range from a minimum of $50 a week to a maximum of $987 a week. Except for salaries that are below the minimum salary levels or above the maximum levels, wage replacement is approximately 55 percent of gross (pre-tax) earnings.

h. When Paid Family Leave Benefits Are Not Available

Paid Family Leave benefits are not available during a time period when any of the following conditions exist:

- The employee has received or is eligible for unemployment compensation benefits.
- The employee has received or is entitled to receive Workers' Compensation benefits or permanent disability benefits for a work-related injury or illness.
- The employee has received or is entitled to receive California or other state disability benefits.
- Another family member is ready, willing, able, and available for the same day that the employee is providing the required care to a spouse, child, or parent with a serious health condition.

(Unemployment Insurance Code section 3303.1.)

An employee who fraudulently certifies the medical need for Paid Family Leave benefits is liable for repayment of the funds received plus a 25 percent penalty. (Unemployment Insurance Code section 3305.)

For more information on Paid Family Leave, see these websites:

- http://www.paidfamilyleave.org;
- http://www.edd.ca.gov/Disability/Paid_Family_Leave.htm;
- http://www.working-families.org/learnmore/ca_paidleave.html.

3. Getting Paid During Pregnancy Disability Leave

If the pregnant employee chooses, she must be allowed to use all of her earned, paid leave time before taking any unpaid pregnancy leave. Paid leave includes sick leave, personal leave (paid time off or "PTO"), vacation time, disability leave that is paid under an employer plan, and any other paid leave she has earned. (2 California Code of Regulations section 7291.11.)

The employee may also receive state disability pay for a pregnancy leave. (Unemployment Insurance Code section 2626(a), (b)(1).) An employee who is unable to perform her usual work because of illness or injury resulting from pregnancy, childbirth, or a related medical condition may be eligible to receive benefits through the State Disability Insurance program while she is on leave. (Unemployment Insurance Code sections 2625–2626.) For a normal pregnancy, the disability benefit period begins up to four weeks before the expected delivery date, and ends up to six weeks after the actual date of delivery. If the employee needs additional time, the doctor must indicate the need on the claim form, and the additional time for pregnancy or recovery is treated like any other medical condition. For more information on the State Disability Insurance Program, see section VI., p. 115.

Women who have recovered from their pregnancy-related disabilities and are no longer receiving SDI benefits are eligible for California Paid Family Leave for bonding with newborns, as set forth above.

VIII. UNEMPLOYMENT INSURANCE (UI) BENEFITS

A. SCOPE OF THE PROGRAM

Unemployment Insurance provides temporary, partial wage replacement to eligible workers who are unemployed through no fault of their own, available for work, physically able to work, and actively looking for work. (Unemployment Insurance Code sections 100 et seq.; regulations are found in Title 22 of the California Code of Regulations.) The program is administered by the Employment Development Department (EDD).

The program is funded by a tax on employers based on a number of factors, including how many of that employer's workers have claimed benefits in the past. Employers may be motivated to challenge the claims of former employees for Unemployment Insurance in order to keep their tax rate low.

Frequently asked questions on Unemployment Insurance are answered on the EDD website at http://www.edd.ca.gov/Unemployment/FAQs.htm. Other information (including how to file claims and appeals, location of EDD offices, determination of benefits, etc.) can be found on the EDD website at http://www.edd.ca.gov/Unemployment.

B. ELIGIBILITY

1. Overview

The wealth of a worker is not relevant to the question of eligibility for Unemployment Insurance. Eligibility is based on the following: prior employment during the "base period"; being without work for certain justifiable reasons (primarily, either leaving work for "good cause" or for a reason other than having been fired for "misconduct"); being ready, willing, and able to work; and actively seeking employment. These concepts are explained in the sections that follow.

2. Covered Employment

The first eligibility requirement is that the claimant (person filing the claim to receive unemployment compensation) has been an employee during the base period (see section VI.B.3., p. 116, for information on how to calculate the base period, and section VIII.B.3., p. 149, for more information on minimum earnings).

Independent contractors are not covered by the Unemployment Insurance Program. However, the question of who is an independent contractor and who is an employee is a complicated one. See Chapter 1, section V.A., p. 13, for more information on this distinction. Employers cannot avoid paying taxes, including unemployment taxes, simply by calling employees "independent contractors." As outlined in Chapter 1, it is the way a person works that determines whether a worker is an employee or an independent contractor.

In order to receive benefits, an applicant for Unemployment Insurance must have worked, during the base period, for an employer legally required to pay Unemployment Insurance taxes. Most types of jobs carry this requirement. There are, however, a few exceptions, including:

- Domestic workers earning less than $1,000 a quarter;
- Employees whose employer is a member of the immediate family;
- Federal employees;
- Employees of churches or other primarily religious organizations;
- Students employed by schools, colleges, and universities.

In order to collect unemployment benefits, a claimant must be legally entitled to work in the United States. Immigrants without work permits, green cards, or appropriate visas are not allowed to work legally in the United States, so they are not considered available for unemployment benefits.

3. Minimum Earnings During the Base Period

The claimant must have earned a certain minimum amount of pay during the base period (the twelve-month period of time upon which eligibility is based. See section VI.B.3., p. 116, for a description of how the base period is determined). As of 2008, the claimant must have earned either:

- At least $1,300 during any one quarter in the base period; or
- At least $900 during her highest paid quarter and a total during the entire base period of at least 125 percent of the earnings in her highest-paid quarter. (For example, a person who earned $900 during the highest-paid quarter in her base period and earned at least $1,125 — 125 percent of her highest quarterly earnings — during the entire base period, would meet the earnings eligibility requirement for Unemployment Insurance.)

The concept of base period is the same for State Disability Insurance, Paid Family Leave, and Unemployment Insurance. To get more information on how the base year is calculated, see Item 5 under "Explanation of Items on the Notice of Unemployment Insurance Award" at http://wwwedd.cahwnet.gov/pdf_pub_ctr/de1275a.pdf.

4. Employee Must Be Unemployed Through No Fault of Her Own

The EDD will investigate the reasons for which the employee left his most recent job. Generally, a claimant will be eligible for UI benefits only if he was laid off due to lack of work, terminated for reasons other than misconduct, or quit his job for good cause. It is presumed that the worker left his job through no fault of his own, unless information is provided by the worker or the former employer that shows something different.

The claimant may also be allowed to collect benefits in some cases (depending on earnings) where he is underemployed, rather than completely unemployed. For instance, a person who is let go for reasons other than misconduct from a full-time job, and secures a low-paying part-time job, may

still be eligible for some level of unemployment benefits. See section VIII.E.1., p. 153, for more information on benefits to individuals who may be employed part-time, but are still underemployed in comparison to their past work.

a. Termination for Misconduct

This is probably the most frequent grounds for employer challenge to the collection of UI benefits by former employees. The reasons for leaving the most recent job are the only relevant topics for exploration in terms of UI benefits. (Unemployment Insurance Code section 1256.) The fact that the employee was fired for misconduct or voluntarily left a previous job (before the last job held) without good cause will not make the individual ineligible for unemployment benefits.

Behavior is not considered misconduct just because the employer says it is. Poor performance based on lack of skill, inability to perform some parts of the job correctly, a single instance of good faith error in judgment or ordinary negligence, or off-duty conduct (with some exceptions) are not generally considered misconduct on the job.

In order to be considered misconduct, the following elements must all be present:
- The claimant owed a material (meaning major) duty to the employer.
- There was a substantial failure to carry out the duty. (Example: Forgetting to wish a customer "good morning" would not be a substantial breach of the duty to maintain good customer relations. Slugging the customer would be a substantial breach of the employee's duty to the employer to provide acceptable customer service.)
- The failure to carry out the duty was willful or wanton. If someone neglected to call in sick repeatedly, that could be considered willful (on purpose) or wanton (grossly negligent or recklessly unconcerned).
- The employee's failure to carry out the duty tended to harm the business interests of the employer.

The most common types of behavior leading to a finding of misconduct are generally:
- Serious insubordination. (Cursing out the employer in front of customers could be considered serious insubordination; objecting to an illegal order or politely pointing out a problem in the instructions does not rise to the

level of insubordination that would disqualify someone from receiving UI benefits.);

- Stealing from the employer;
- Repeated instances of rudeness to the public, where the employee has been warned and has the ability to control the behavior;
- Violence on the job. (However, merely raising one's voice in discussion is not considered violent behavior, nor is reasonably defending oneself against an unprovoked attack considered misconduct.);
- Use of illegal drugs or alcohol on the job;
- Sleeping on the job. (Again, the context is important. A single instance of falling asleep, perhaps due to illness or medication, is not misconduct. Regularly and deliberately sleeping on the job will most likely be considered misconduct.);
- Excessive, unexcused, unreasonable absences or tardiness. (Being out sick is not considered unreasonable in most instances, short of proven fraud. Responding to a family emergency or childcare failure is not considered unreasonable, unless an employee consistently and willfully fails to make proper plans and arrangements. Having one's car break down once would not be considered excessive. Continually missing the bus might be considered excessive tardiness, particularly if it was this employee's duty to open the door in the morning at the place of employment.).

b. Quitting for Good Cause

An employee who quits a job is presumed to have quit for good cause, unless there is evidence to overcome that presumption. Good cause is a "real, substantial, and compelling reason of such nature as would cause a reasonable person, genuinely desirous of retaining employment, to take similar action." The situation is evaluated at the time the employee left the job. An employee must take action, where possible, to resolve the problem before quitting. (22 California Code of Regulations section 1256-3.)

The following reasons are considered good cause to quit a job:

- Unsafe working conditions (greater than ordinary risks of the occupation or more hazardous for the claimant due to unique circumstances) or reasonable, good faith fear for one's health;

- Relocating to maintain a relationship with a spouse, fiancée to whom marriage is imminent, or a registered domestic partner, if the new location is not within reasonable commuting distance;
- Relocating or quitting to protect oneself from domestic violence (documentation, for instance a police report, may be required);
- Illegal discrimination or harassment based on race, color, religious creed, national origin, ancestry, disability, medical condition, marital status, sex, age, sexual orientation, or other protected characteristic;
- Illegal or unethical orders from the employer or supervisor (for instance, submitting false claims or participating in a kickback scheme or tax evasion);
- Intolerable working conditions or abusive supervisors. (These must be particularly

harsh, not just unpleasant, and of a level that would cause a reasonable person to quit. Mere disagreement or job dissatisfaction is not enough.);

- Substantial reduction in pay or job classification. A substantial salary reduction is generally considered to be at least a 20 percent pay cut;
- Definite offer of a substantially better job, which then does not materialize or ends unexpectedly, resulting in unemployment;
- The employer illegally withholds wages or commits other willful violations of the Labor Code (for instance, payment is frequently late or checks bounce).

The following situations are not generally considered to provide good cause to quit:

- The boss is unpleasant.
- The job is boring.
- The employee believes he is not doing a good job.
- The employee decides to go into business for himself.
- The employer implements a change in hours (generally this is not good cause, unless it causes extreme hardship, for instance, by making it impossible to secure childcare). What is extreme hardship is determined on a case-by-case basis. For instance, transfer of hours to the middle of the night might be considered extreme hardship if the worker was a single parent and could not secure childcare during those hours.

The following situations may be considered to provide good cause to quit in some, but not all, situations:

- A part-time job made it difficult or impossible to search for a full-time job.
- The employee was faced with a choice of resigning or being terminated. This may actually be considered a kind of discharge (known as a "constructive discharge").
- The employee quit in response to unusually harsh, unfair, excessive discipline.

In some situations, a worker may be considered to have quit a job when he did not actually state he was quitting. The following are some examples of this kind of situation, called a "constructive quit":

- An employee was convicted of, pleaded guilty to, or pleaded no contest to an offense, and was imprisoned and unable to work.
- An employee lost a license needed to maintain the job.

- An employee refused, without good cause, to work certain days.

An employee who constructively quits a job without good cause may be ineligible to receive Unemployment Insurance benefits.

5. Availability for Work

In order to receive UI benefits, the unemployed worker must be available to work. This means she must be physically and mentally capable of working in her usual job or customary occupation. A finding of ineligibility for UI benefits can result when a person is too injured or ill to work, is on vacation, or has obligations which prevent her from working during normal working hours, for example. Regarding the person who is too ill to work, see section VI., p. 115, on State Disability Insurance. The claimant's "customary occupation" is generally interpreted to mean a job similar to the last one she held, or some job held in the recent past, or some other job for which the claimant is reasonably fitted (this will depend on the claimant's prior training, experience, earnings, health, age, length of unemployment, and length of commute). If a claimant is available for work but needs a reasonable accommodation for a disability (see Chapter 6, section V.A.4., p. 168), she will be considered available for work.

6. Actively Seeking Work

In order to be eligible for UI benefits, a claimant must be actively seeking work. Contacting at least three employers a week is generally considered actively seeking work. Contacts may be made by phone, mail, email, on the Internet, in person, or by submitting an application. If the claimant is a union member and work is generally assigned through the union, contacting the union and maintaining eligibility for assignments is usually sufficient. It is a good idea to keep a detailed record of employers contacted in the course of the job search (including date of contact, person contacted, name of employer, etc.), in case any questions are raised regarding whether the claimant is actively seeking work.

There are some limited situations in which the claimant need not continue to seek work:

- The claimant is seasonally unemployed, the prospects for finding other work during the off-season are remote, and the claimant has no other customary occupation with available jobs during the off-season.

- The claimant has been laid off for a period expected to be less than thirty days (for example, an involuntary furlough for three weeks).
- The claimant has a definite promise of a job that will start within a reasonable time.

(22 California Code of Regulations section 1253(e)-1(d).)

7. Refusing Work

An applicant who refuses work must have good cause for doing so, or the refusal of a job may lead to a finding of ineligibility for UI benefits. The following reasons are examples of "good cause" for refusing work:

- The job is vacant because of a labor dispute.
- The prospective employer does not possess a legally required license for the work.
- The prospective employer does not carry Workers' Compensation Insurance.
- The cost of commuting would be more than half of gross pay.
- The job offered would not make use of the claimant's job skills and would cause her to lose proficiency in her field (depending on the length of time unemployed).
- Wages, hours, or working conditions are substantially worse than those that prevail in the occupation in the geographic area.
- The hours offered make it impossible to get childcare, and those hours are not common in the occupation. (For instance, a secretary is offered a night shift at a local law firm, but cannot accept because she is a single parent and cannot find childcare at night. However, a job offer during the day would require her to find childcare to be considered available for work, since such childcare is generally available.)

The following are examples of reasons that are not considered "good cause" for refusing work, and might result in ineligibility for UI benefits:

- The claimant does not like the commute, though it is within the reasonable range of commutes traveled by workers in the area.
- The job sounds boring or lacks prestige.
- The job is within the customary occupation, but the unemployed person wishes to change careers.

8. Part-Time Work

In certain circumstances, a claimant may seek only part-time work. To be eligible for unemployment compensation, the part-time job seeker must show *all* of the following:

- The claim is based on previous part-time work.
- She is willing to accept work with substantially similar hours as the last job.
- She is imposing no other unreasonable restrictions on the job search.
- There is a demand for part-time workers in the occupation, in the area, and for the types of hours the claimant is seeking.

A student who is attending school and wishes to work part-time is eligible to receive Unemployment Insurance under any of these conditions:

- He is attending school at night and is available for work during normal business hours.
- He is attending school during the day and is willing to abandon school to accept a job.
- He is attending school as part of a training program approved by the California Benefits Training Program.

C. APPLICATION PROCESS

The following information will be needed in order to complete an application for UI benefits:

- Name and Social Security Number;
- The unemployed worker's mailing and residence addresses;
- Name, address (mailing and physical location), and telephone number (including area code) of the worker's last employer (regardless of the length of time worked for the employer);
- Information on all employers the applicant worked for during the eighteen months prior to submitting this application, including name, period of employment, compensation earned, and how the employee was paid (for example, by check, every two weeks). Compensation includes lodging and other types of compensation (for example, commissions);
- Last date worked and the reason the applicant is no longer working;
- Gross earnings (before taxes) in the last week worked (the applicant must also report tips, lodging, and any other types of compensation received);
- Driver's license or ID card number, if available;
- Citizenship status (which may include an alien registration number).

Unemployed workers do not need to visit the EDD office to apply for benefits. Applications may be completed online, by calling a toll-free number, or by downloading the application form (the DE 1101) and faxing it or mailing it in.

To apply online, go to https://eapply4ui.edd.ca.gov and follow the directions on the screen. To apply by phone, call 1-800-300-5616.

To locate a claim form to mail in, go to https://eapply4ui.edd.ca.gov/default.htm?target=paper. The DE 1101 form can also be picked up at any EDD office. To locate an EDD office near you, go to http://www.edd.ca.gov/Office_Locator or look in the phone book under State of California, Employment Development Department.

For information on the best time to file an application, in relation to past work and wages, see https://eapply4ui.edd.ca.gov/htm/cpgInstructions.htm.

D. DETERMINATIONS AND APPEALS

1. Determinations

Once the claimant has applied for benefits, a telephone interview will be scheduled. The claimant should receive a written notice indicating initial eligibility for benefits or that benefits have been denied. If benefits are denied, the notice will provide instructions for filing an appeal.

2. Appeals

See section VI.D.2., p. 118, for more information on filing appeals. EDD handles both UI and SDI appeals. As in any legal or administrative proceeding, persons filing appeals should be sure to comply with deadlines and keep a copy of all documents related to the case and the appeal.

E. BENEFIT CHECKS

1. Determination of Amount

The EDD determines the proper amount of weekly benefit checks. Benefits are based on the wages earned during the base year. In 2010, weekly payments ranged from a minimum of $40 to a maximum of $450 (for someone who earned over $11,674 in a calendar quarter during the base year). Individual benefit levels may be changed in the future by the government. A chart showing Unemployment Insurance benefit levels tied to specific earnings during the base period is available at http://www.edd.ca.gov/pdf_pub_ctr/

de1101bt5.pdf. To challenge the calculation of the benefit amount, see the section of this chapter on Unemployment Insurance appeals, section VIII.D.2., directly above.

2. Payment Process

Checks are mailed to the unemployed worker's home every two weeks. The unemployed individual will need to fill out and return the form for continuing benefits that is enclosed with the benefit check every two weeks, or benefits will cease. It is important to report all wages received correctly. If a person receives payment for work that occurred in the past, she should report the income, and attach a note to the form clearly explaining that the amount received is not for wages earned during the current claim period, and explain the circumstances.

3. Complex Situations
a. The Impact of Earnings on UI Benefits

If the person has earnings during a particular two-week period, this should be reported on the form covering the period of time in which the money is earned (that is, when the work was done), not when the check was received. If the claimant earns under $100 in a particular week, the amount of the benefit for that week will be reduced by the amount of earnings, minus $25. If the claimant earns more than $100 in a particular week, the amount of the benefit is reduced by 75 percent of earnings. For example, if a person receiving unemployment benefits earned $600 on a temporary job one week, her benefit check for that week would be reduced by $450 (which is 75 percent of $600). If a claimant earns 1.33 times her benefit amount for the week, she would not receive a check during that week. It would not be necessary, however, to open a new claim after the temporary job is finished. The process for reactivating an existing claim is the same as filing an initial claim. The claimant could reopen the old claim by phone (calling the EDD office at 1-800-300-5616), by going online to https://eapply4ui.edd.ca.gov and filling out the form online, or by using a paper application (DE 1101) and mailing or faxing it to EDD. She would continue to receive benefits for as long as she remains eligible. Weeks when no benefits are received are not counted towards the maximum number of weeks allowed under the program.

b. The Effect on UI Benefits of Payment for Past Work, Earned Vacation, or Holidays

In some circumstances, an unemployed worker may receive payment for past work or payment for earned vacation or holiday that does not affect his eligibility for Unemployment Insurance. Payment for past work does not prevent an unemployed worker from being eligible for Unemployment Insurance, as long as the worker has completed the job and is currently unemployed. Severance pay that is paid as a *lump sum* upon the termination of employment is considered payment for past work.

Vacation and holiday pay received after an employee has been let go from the job may affect UI benefits, depending on whether the unemployed worker has been given a definite date to return to work and whether the payment is made as a lump sum or through continued regular salary payments. If an employee remains on payroll and receives regular payroll checks for a period of time that is considered vacation (with a definite date to return to the job), that may have a negative effect on eligibility for UI benefits. However, if the employer has not made a commitment to recall the worker on a specific date, holiday and vacation pay will not be deducted from UI benefits and the worker will be considered unemployed. For instance, if a university employee on a temporary contract does not have a reasonable expectation of continued employment, but is paid over the course of twelve months for work that took place during the academic year, summer wages should be considered wages for past work, not current earnings. Payment for vacation days earned in the past that is paid as a lump sum upon termination of employment is considered payment for past work.

In these complex situations, it is very important to report income accurately. EDD can check reports of income against tax records. Incorrect reports can lead to charges of fraud. The workers should explain the situation completely if the money received is not based on current earnings. If the form does not allow for a complete explanation, attach a letter explaining why income currently being received is actually payment for past work, if that is the situation.

c. Pension Payments

The full value of any pension payments made during an unemployment claim is deducted from the UI benefits.

F. DURATION OF BENEFITS

1. General Duration

Basic benefits may be paid for twenty-six weeks during a particular benefit year. The benefit year starts the week the original claim is filed. Once the unemployed worker has collected benefits for twenty-six weeks, he will not be eligible for UI benefits during the remainder of the benefit year, unless extended benefits are offered. See section F.2., directly below, for more information on extended benefits.

In order for the worker to be eligible for the entire twenty-six weeks, there are some additional prior earnings requirements. The worker must have earned, during the base year, at least the equivalent of fifty-two weeks of benefits checks.

2. Extended Benefits

Under some circumstances, the time limit (and total amount collected) may be extended by the government. Economic recessions, high unemployment rates, natural disasters, and displacement of jobs by foreign imports sometimes lead to an extension of benefits. The EDD website has current information about extensions of benefits. See http://www.edd.ca.gov/Unemployment/Extended_Benefit_Information.htm.

Also, if an individual lacks skills likely to lead to employment, she may apply to the California Training Benefit Program (CTB), which provides training and extended unemployment benefits. See section VIII.H.1., p. 155, for more information on this program.

A worker who is eligible for extended benefits will receive a weekly benefit amount equal to the amount of his regular claim.

G. THE IMPORTANCE OF DEADLINES

As in any situation involving benefits and legal procedures, it is important to pay close attention to deadlines and to respond promptly to requests for additional information. If an individual's response is late, she should write a letter (and keep a copy) to accompany the form and indicate why the response was late. If the reason was unavoidable and the individual was not at fault, the EDD may extend the deadline for good cause.

H. SPECIAL PROGRAMS

1. California Training Benefits Program

This program provides additional benefits for individuals who lack job skills and need retraining, while they attend an approved training program. In order to participate in the program, the individual must either:

- Attend a training program associated with the Workforce Investment Act or Trade Adjustment Assistance (federal programs) or the Employment Training Panel or CalWORKS (state programs);

  or

- Be out of work for at least four or more continuous weeks, be eligible for Unemployment Insurance, and apply for the Training Benefits Program no later than the sixteenth week of benefits (or sooner if the claim award is for a shorter period of time); and

- Be unemployed due to a lack of current demand for the individuals' skills in the local labor market, or have a seasonal occupation and have no other skills in current demand; and

- Require training for specific jobs for individuals who are journey-level union members, for at least twenty hours a week; and

- Attend training in a job that is in demand in the local labor market or be willing to relocate, and

- Complete a training course within one year, and be reasonably expected to complete the program successfully.

The program is only available if there have been three or more years since the beginning date of any prior participation in this program. This program provides UI benefits but does not pay for tuition, books, or other training expenses. For more information, go to http://www.edd.ca.gov/pdf_pub_ctr/de8714u.pdf

2. Work Sharing Unemployment Insurance Program

This program allows employers to sign up for a work sharing program for a group of employees when the employer reduces hours as a temporary alternative to layoff. A minimum of 10 percent of the employees (at least two people) must be affected by a reduction of at least 10 percent in wages and hours. Benefits paid are calculated based on the reduction of wages and hours. This program minimizes hardship to employees affected by temporary reductions in hours of work, and allows the employer to quickly gear up to a full workforce when the temporary period of layoff is over.

CHAPTER 6

DISCRIMINATION

I. SCOPE OF THE CHAPTER

Discrimination generally means a failure to treat all persons equally where no reasonable distinction can be found between those favored and those not favored. (*Daly v. Exxon Corp.* (1997) 55 Cal. App.4th 39.) Employees have the right to be free from unlawful discrimination in all aspects of their employment, whether the discrimination is based on:

- Race;
- Skin color;
- Sex;
- Age (if an employee is forty or older);
- Physical or mental disability;
- Medical condition (including AIDS and HIV status);
- Pregnancy;
- Religious beliefs;
- Marital status;
- National origin (country of origin and native language);
- Sexual orientation;
- Other classifications that have been legally specified.

Illegal discrimination occurs when an employer takes an adverse action with respect to hiring, firing, promotion, pay, benefits, assignment, and any other aspect of employment based on a protected classification. There are multiple legal sources for protection of the right to be free from discrimination:

- State and federal laws prohibiting discrimination;
- State and federal constitutional provisions;
- Courts decisions;
- Various administrative decisions.

In general, people are protected from discrimination based on certain characteristics, for instance race, gender, age, national origin, disability, etc. California law broadens the list of characteristics that may not be the basis of employment discrimination to include sexual orientation. The law protects people from having these factors used as a basis for discrimination.

This chapter provides an overview of the complicated area of discrimination law. It includes explanations of the specialized legal terms used to define discrimination; the types of legal claims that can be made; defenses to such claims; and the rules and procedures that govern filing, investigation, defenses against, and litigation of discrimination claims. Familiarity with the terms and rules discussed here will assist employees in protecting their rights against discrimination and will direct discussion of potential claims with employee unions, agencies investigating discrimination, and attorneys involved in the process.

In many cases, workers must bring their complaints to administrative agencies (like the California Department of Fair Employment and Housing) before they can sue in court. These procedures are discussed in section VIII., p. 180.

This chapter is organized as follows: an overview of the constitutional provisions and laws that prohibit discrimination in employment and how they are analyzed by the courts and administrative agencies; a summary of several key laws that apply to particular types of discrimination; and a discussion of the provisions prohibiting retaliation against employees for exercising their rights.

For additional information on specific types of discrimination, see Chapter 2.

II. CONSTITUTIONAL PROVISIONS PROHIBITING DISCRIMINATION

A. THE U.S. CONSTITUTION

The federal Constitution contains provisions that have been interpreted to prohibit discrimination in employment.

The Fifth and Fourteenth Amendments of the U.S. Constitution protect citizens' rights to due process and equal protection of the laws. Those clauses have been found to prohibit discrimination by federal, state, and local governments acting in the role of employer or enforcer of discriminatory laws that relate to race, sex, mental disability, birth out of wedlock, and even sexual orientation, and that affect public or private employers.

An employee can assert a claim that his federal constitutional rights have been violated by filing a lawsuit in federal court under 42 U.S. Code section 1983.

B. THE CALIFORNIA CONSTITUTION

The California Constitution contains similar provisions. Article I, section 7, protects citizens' rights to due process and equal protection of the laws. Article I, section 8, provides that a person may not be disqualified from entering or pursuing business, profession, vocation, or employment because of sex, race, creed, color, or national or ethnic origin.

In California, individuals can file suit in state court directly alleging violation of their state constitutional rights. Some provisions of the California Constitution apply only to the government or individuals acting under color of law (with apparent governmental authority). Other constitutional rights apply to public entities (like government agencies), private entities (like businesses), and individuals. An employee can file a lawsuit against either a public or private employer based on a claim of wrongful discharge.

III. DISCRIMINATION CLAIMS BASED ON CONSTITUTIONAL PROVISIONS

A. OVERVIEW

Job applicants or employees who believe they have suffered discrimination based on race, sex, color, national origin or ancestry, alien national status, mental disability, "illegitimacy," or, in some situations, sexual orientation by a public employer can file a lawsuit under 42 U.S. Code section 1983 alleging violation of their rights to equal protection and due process of law under the Fifth and Fourteenth Amendments to the U.S. Constitution. Laws and government regulations may also be challenged for being discriminatory.

B. LEVELS OF SCRUTINY

The courts use different levels of "scrutiny" (examination) when determining the constitutionality of laws that differentiate between categories of people, depending on the basis for the discrimination (such as race, sex, etc.) and whether or not the law places a burden on a fundamental right, such as the right to vote or marry.

Laws or governmental practices that discriminate based on race, immigration status, or national origin, or that categorize people in a way that burdens a fundamental right, receive "strict scrutiny." Under the "strict scrutiny" standard, a discriminatory law or practice is unconstitutional unless it is "necessary" and "narrowly tailored" in order to promote a "compelling governmental interest." (*City of Richmond v. J.A. Croson Co.* (1989) 488 U.S. 469; *Graham v. Richardson* (1971) 403 U.S. 365; *Kramer v. Union Free School District No. 15* (1969) 395 U.S. 621; *McLaughlin v. Florida* (1964) 379 U.S. 184; *Long Beach City Employees Association v. City of Long Beach* (1986) 41 Cal.3d 937.)

Laws or governmental policies or practices that discriminate based on sex or being born out of wedlock are subject to "intermediate scrutiny." Under the "intermediate scrutiny" standard, a law or practice is unconstitutional unless it is "substantially related" to an "important" governmental interest. (*Mississippi Univ. for Women v. Hogan* (1982) 458 U.S. 718; *Mills v. Habluetzel* (1982) 456 U.S. 91, 99.)

Discrimination on any other basis is given "rational basis review." Under the "rational basis" test, a law will be found constitutional as long as it is "rationally related" to a "legitimate" or "plausible" governmental interest. (See *Heller v. Doe* (1993) 509 U.S. 312, 319–320.) Traditionally, "rational basis" reviews have tended to uphold the laws being challenged. They have rarely resulted in a determination that a law unconstitutionally discriminated against the affected class of people. However, the U.S. Supreme Court has, in recent years, used more stringent (higher) standards in "rational basis" reviews when examining laws that discriminate on the basis of mental disability and sexual orientation. (See *Lawrence v. Texas* (2003) 539 U.S. 558; *Romer v. Evans* (1996) 517 U.S. 620; *City of Cleburne, Texas v. Cleburne Living Ctr.* (1985) 473 U.S. 432.)

IV. LAWS PROHIBITING DISCRIMINATION

There are several federal and California laws prohibiting discrimination in employment based on specified impermissible grounds. The laws that govern most employment discrimination claims are listed in the sections that follow. The California laws are, in most instances, more protective than the federal laws. In many cases, it is preferable to file complaints based on California discrimination law.

A. FEDERAL LAWS

The primary federal law prohibiting discrimination in employment is Title VII of the Civil Rights Act of 1964. This law and several other important laws are as follows:

1. Title VII

This law is generally referred to as "Title VII." (42 U.S. Code sections 2000e–2000e-17.) Title VII prohibits discrimination in employment on the basis of race, color, national origin, religion, and sex. Race includes physical, cultural, and linguistic characteristics. (29 Code of Federal Regulations sections 1601.1–1606.8.) Citizenship is not a protected characteristic under Title VII, and employers may distinguish between citizens and non-citizens. (*Espinoza v. Farah Manufacturing Co.* (1973) 414 U.S. 86.)

Title VII does not expressly prohibit discrimination based on sexual orientation, but the Supreme Court has found that sexual harassment of an individual based on sexual orientation is discrimination "because of sex" in violation of Title VII. (*Oncale v. Sundowner Offshore Servs., Inc.* (1998) 523 U.S. 75.) Religious discrimination is allowed in a narrow range of situations in which the individual is acting in a "ministerial capacity" or running a religious organization. (*Corp. of Presiding Bishop of Church of Jesus Christ of Latter-day Saints v. Amos* (1987) 483 U.S. 327.)

2. Age Discrimination in Employment Act (ADEA)

Discrimination in employment based on age is prohibited by the Age Discrimination in Employment Act of 1967 (ADEA). (29 U.S. Code sections 621 et seq.) The Older Workers Benefit

Protection Act (29 U.S. Code sections 623, 626, 630), an amendment to the ADEA, forbids employers from using age to target older workers in downsizing. For more information see http://www.eeoc.gov/laws/types/age.cfm. Laying off workers at the higher levels of the salary schedule to save money has been found by some federal courts to be permissible under federal law (but see below for information on California's broader protection). The U.S. Supreme Court has held that the federal ADEA protects workers over forty, but does not protect younger workers from programs that favor older workers. (*General Dynamics Land Sys., Inc. v. Cline* (2004) 540 U.S. 581.) Federal law makes mandatory retirement at a certain age illegal in most situations. The federal prohibition covers private sector employers with twenty or more employees. Under federal law, exceptions to the rule against mandatory retirement exist for a few occupations:

- Firefighters;
- Law enforcement officers;
- Employees who are employed as executives with annual pensions of at least $44,000 for two years prior to retirement.

(29 U.S. Code sections 623(j), 631(c)(1).)

3. Americans with Disabilities Act (ADA)

Discrimination based on actual or perceived disability is prohibited by provisions of the Americans with Disabilities Act of 1990 (ADA). (42 U.S. Code sections 12101 et seq.) See section V.A., p. 164, for more information on both federal and state prohibitions against disability discrimination.

4. Section 504 of the Rehabilitation Act of 1973

Discrimination based on disability is forbidden in any program or activity (for example, a college, a corporation, or an instrumentality of a state or local government) that receives federal financial assistance. (29 U.S. Code section 794.)

5. Equal Pay Act (EPA)

Discrimination in pay based on sex is prohibited by the Equal Pay Act of 1963 (EPA) (29 U.S. Code section 206(d).), which is part of the Fair Labor Standards Act. (29 U.S. Code sections 201 et seq.) The EPA is discussed in more detail in section V.C.1., p. 170. For more information see http://www.eeoc.gov/laws/types/equalcompensation.cfm.

6. Civil Rights Act of 1866/Race Discrimination

The Civil Rights Act of 1866 (42 U.S. Code section 1981.) prohibits discrimination based on race in making and enforcing contracts. This statute provides a mechanism to sue both public and private employers for intentional race discrimination. Race is interpreted broadly to mean identification of persons based on their ancestry or ethnic characteristics. (*Saint Francis College v. Al-Khazraji* (1987) 481 U.S. 604.)

7. Civil Rights Act of 1871/Other Federal Rights

Claims of employment discrimination based on alleged violations of federal rights, including constitutional rights to equal protection and due process of law, can be based on the Civil Rights Act of 1871. (42 U.S. Code section 1983.) (This provision is discussed in section IV.A.1., p. 160, concerning constitutional prohibitions against discrimination.)

8. Federal Contractors

Federal contractors and subcontractors are subject to certain prohibitions against discrimination. The contracts covered must meet certain monetary limits (see the table in section VI.A., p. 174), and may be for the purchase, sale, or use of personal property; non-personal services (for example, construction); or both. For more information on the laws and regulations covering federal contractors, see the Office of Federal Contract Compliance Programs' (OFCCP) website at http://www.dol.gov/ofccp/index.htm.

a. Executive Order 11246

Executive Orders are directives from the U.S. President. Executive Order 11246 forbids discrimination on the basis of race, color, religion, sex, and national origin. (41 Code of Federal Regulations section 60-1.1.) Federal contractors covered by this law must refrain from discrimination and take affirmative steps to ensure that applicants and employees receive equal employment opportunity. Each covered contract must have a specific equal opportunity clause included. (41 Code of Federal Regulations section 60-1.4.) Additionally, many non-construction contractors are required to have a written affirmative action program. (41 Code of Federal Regulations section

60-2.1.) Employers with contracts on or near an Indian reservation may discriminate in favor of Native Americans living on or near the reservation in question. However, these employers must not discriminate among Native Americans on the basis of religion, sex, or tribal affiliation. (41 Code of Federal Regulations section 60-1.5(a)(7).) See the law guide of the U.S. Department of Labor's Office of Federal Contract Compliance Programs (OFCCP) at http://www.dol.gov/compliance/guide/discrim.htm (supply and service contracts) and http://www.dol.gov/compliance/guide/discrcon.htm (construction contracts).

b. Section 503 of the Rehabilitation Act of 1973

Section 503 of the Rehabilitation Act of 1973 forbids discrimination against individuals with disabilities and requires employers to take affirmative steps to employ qualified individuals with disabilities. (29 U.S. Code section 793.) Federal contractors covered by this law must make reasonable accommodations for known physical or mental limitations of qualified individuals with disabilities unless it would create undue hardship for the employer. (41 Code of Federal Regulations section 60-741.21.) (See section V.A.4., p. 168, for more information on undue hardship.) Contracts must include a specific equal opportunity clause. (41 Code of Federal Regulations section 60-741.5.) Additionally, an employer with fifty or more employees and a federal contract or subcontract of $50,000 or more must have a written affirmative action program. (41 Code of Federal Regulations section 60-741.40.) See the OFCCP's law guide at http://www.dol.gov/compliance/guide/503.htm.

c. The Vietnam Era Veterans' Readjustment Assistance Act of 1974 (VEVRAA)

Under the Vietnam Era Veterans' Readjustment Assistance Act (VEVRAA), most federal contracts and subcontracts are subject to the requirements listed below regarding employment of veterans. Federal contractors covered by this law must take affirmative steps to employ and promote qualified covered veterans. Qualified covered veterans include disabled veterans, veterans who served on active duty during a war or in a campaign or expedition for which a campaign badge has been authorized, veterans who served on active duty and participated in a United States military operation for which an Armed Forces service medal was awarded under Executive Order 12985, and veterans within three years after being released from active duty. In addition, employers with fifty or more employees must have written affirmative action programs. (38 U.S. Code section 4212; 41 Code of Federal Regulations sections 60-300.1 et seq.)

9. Uniformed Services Employment and Reemployment Rights Act (USERRA)

Employers must not discriminate in employment on the basis of membership in a branch of the military, performance of service, application for service, or obligation to serve in the military. (38 U.S. Code section 4311; 20 Code of Federal Regulations section 1002.18.) The military includes the Armed Forces, the Army National Guard and the Air National Guard (when engaged in active and inactive duty training, or full-time National Guard duty), the commissioned corps of the Public Health Service, and any other category of individuals designated by the President in time of war or national emergency. (38 U.S. Code section 4303(16).) Individuals' rights under USERRA end if the person leaves the military under conditions other than an honorable discharge. (38 U.S. Code section 4304.) See the Department of Labor's website on USERRA at http://www.dol. gov/compliance/laws/comp-userra.htm and the Veterans' Employment & Training Service (VETS) information on USERRA at http://www.dol.gov/ vets/programs/userra/main.htm.

10. Resources

The U.S. Equal Employment Opportunity Commission, which enforces most federal employment discrimination laws, has a number of excellent websites on a variety of subjects.

Federal discrimination laws and prohibited actions:
• http://www.eeoc.gov/laws/statutes/index.cfm (summary of, and links to, federal employment discrimination laws);
• http://www.eeoc.gov/laws/practices/index.cfm (discriminatory practices).

Compensation discrimination under various federal laws:
• http://www.eeoc.gov/policy/docs/ compensation.html.

Race discrimination:
• http://archive.eeoc.gov/types/race.html (summary);
• http://www.eeoc.gov/policy/docs/race-color. html (compliance manual);
• http://www.eeoc.gov/policy/docs/qanda_race_ color.html ("Questions and Answers about Race and Color Discrimination in Employment").

Sex discrimination:
• http://www.eeoc.gov/laws/types/sex.cfm. Religious discrimination:
• http://www.eeoc.gov/laws/types/religion.cfm (summary).

Discrimination based on national origin:
• http://www.eeoc.gov/laws/types/nationalorigin. cfm (summary);
• http://www.eeoc.gov/policy/docs/national- origin.html (compliance manual).

Religion, ethnicity, and country of origin:
• http://www.eeoc.gov/facts/fs-relig_ethnic.html;
• http://www.eeoc.gov/facts/backlash-employee. html ("Questions and Answers about the Workplace Rights of Muslims, Arabs, South Asians, and Sikhs Under the Equal Employment Opportunity Laws").

Discrimination against workers with family caregiving responsibilities:
• http://www.eeoc.gov/policy/docs/caregiving. html.

B. CALIFORNIA LAWS

The primary California law prohibiting discrimination in employment is the Fair Employment and Housing Act (FEHA). (Government Code sections 12900–12996.) The FEHA applies to all state and municipal employers (not federal employers), and to private employers with five or more employees; to labor organizations; to employment agencies; and to apprenticeship programs. It also applies to any person or entity that aids, abets, incites, compels, or coerces illegally discriminatory conduct. (Government Code section 12940.)

The FEHA prohibits discrimination in employment based on race; color; religion; national origin or ancestry; physical disability; mental disability or medical condition; marital status; sex; sexual orientation; age (with respect to people the age forty or over); and pregnancy, childbirth, and related conditions. (Government Code sections 12940(a), 12941, 12945.) It also prohibits discrimination based on use of California's family and medical leave rights. (Government Code section 12945.2.) See Chapter 5 for more information on the California Family Rights Act.

California law makes mandatory retirement illegal for most private employers with five or more employees. Exceptions to the rule against mandatory retirement exist for a few occupations:
• Tenured university faculty;
• Physicians employed by a professional medical corporation;
• Employees who are employed as executives with annual pensions of at least $27,000 for the two years before retirement.
(Government Code section 12942.)

A recent change in the law expanded the definition of sex to include a person's gender identity (appearance and behavior, whether or not commonly associated with the sex at birth). (Government Code section 12926(p); Penal Code section 422.56(c).) Another relatively recent change is that it is an unlawful employment practice to lay off workers based on salary levels, where this action has a disparate impact on older workers. (Government Code section 12941, which provides broader protection than federal law.) The prohibition against discrimination based on marital status includes marriage, non-marriage, divorce, separation, widowhood, domestic partnership, etc. (Government Code section 12940(a); 2 California Code of Regulations section 7292.1.) Under California law, registered domestic partners have many of the same rights, protections, and benefits as spouses, although the basic civil right to marry is currently not available to same sex couples. (Family Code section 297.5.) See Chapter 2 for more information on restrictions regarding hiring spouses.

The FEHA also includes a prohibition against harassment based on race, religion, color, national origin, ancestry, physical or mental disability, medical condition, marital status, sex (including pregnancy, childbirth, and related conditions), sexual orientation, or age. This prohibition covers employers with one or more employees. (Government Code section 12940(j)(4)(A).)

Some other laws discussed in this book, such as the California Family Rights Act (CFRA), which governs family and medical leave, and the Pregnancy Disability Leave Act, which sets forth rules regarding leave for pregnancy-related medical conditions (see Chapter 5), are part of the FEHA. In addition to establishing employees' rights to take leave and the procedures to protect and promote those leave rights, those laws also prohibit discrimination against employees for exercising their rights under the statutes.

California's FEHA provides, in most cases, broader protection from discrimination than federal Title VII. California law prohibits discrimination

The U.S. Equal Employment Opportunity Commission enforces most federal employment discrimination laws.

based on marital status and sexual orientation, which are not explicitly covered under most federal laws. FEHA applies to smaller employers (with at least five employees) as opposed to Title VII, which only covers employers with at least fifteen employees. And in cases of harassment based on factors prohibited by California's discrimination law (gender, race, age, etc.), California law covers employers with one or more employees. (Government Code section 12940(j)(4)(A).) Remedies are generally better under the FEHA than under federal law.

Case law in California also permits individuals to sue employers under California's unfair competition law for discrimination that is illegal in California. (Business and Professions Code section 17200; *Herr v. Nestle U.S.A., Inc.* (2003) 109 Cal. App.4th 779.)

V. SPECIAL CONSIDERATIONS FOR DISCRIMINATION BASED ON DISABILITY, RELIGION, AND SEX, AND FOR HARASSMENT

There are specific laws prohibiting discrimination based on disability (and imposing certain employer duties regarding disabled workers), and discrimination based on religion, gender inequity in salary, discrimination based on pregnancy, and harassment based on factors prohibited by discrimination law. (See sections III., p. 159, and IV., p. 160, for a discussion of illegal bases for discrimination.) Those statutes and related rules and procedures are discussed in the sections that follow. For general information regarding discrimination, see http://www.eeoc.gov/laws/statutes/index.cfm.

A. DISABILITY DISCRIMINATION AND THE EMPLOYER'S DUTY TO PROVIDE REASONABLE ACCOMMODATION

Both the federal Americans with Disabilities Act (ADA) and California's Fair Employment and Housing Act (FEHA) prohibit unlawful discrimination based on disability. These laws apply to private employers (with fifteen or more employees under the ADA; with five or more employees under the FEHA), all state and municipal employers (under the FEHA), federal employers (under the ADA), employment agencies, labor organizations, and joint labor-management committees.

Another federal law prohibiting disability discrimination is Section 504 of the Rehabilitation Act of 1973, which covers programs and activities receiving federal financial assistance. Section 504 applies to all operations (including employment) of the covered programs. The ADA's standards are used to determine whether violations of Section 504 have occurred. (29 U.S. Code section 794.) In a recent decision (as of press time), the Ninth Circuit held that Section 504 protects independent contractors as well as employees, unlike the ADA, which protects only employees. (*Fleming v. Yuma Regional Med. Center* (2009) 587 F.3d 938.)

Employers covered by these laws are prohibited from discriminating against employees or job applicants on the basis of any actual or perceived physical or mental disability in hiring, workplace opportunities, or disciplinary action (including termination). (42 U.S. Code sections 12102–12213; Government Code section 12940.) These laws cover hidden disabilities (such as multiple sclerosis resulting in invisible impairment such as fatigue or neurological problems) as well as visible disabilities. Employers must accommodate qualified workers with disabilities who can (with accommodation if necessary and reasonable) carry out the essential functions of the job, unless implementing the accommodation would be an unreasonable hardship for the employer.

See the California Department of Fair Employment and Housing's website at http://www.dfeh.ca.gov/DFEH/Publications/PublicationDocs/DFEH-184.pdf for more information on disability discrimination.

1. Conditions Considered Disabilities

A "disability" under the federal ADA is:
- A "physical or mental impairment" that "substantially limits" a "major life activity";
- A history of such an impairment; or
- Being regarded as having such an impairment.

(42 U.S. Code section 12102(1); 29 Code of Federal Regulations section 1630.2(g).)

A recent amendment to the ADA clarified the definition of "disability" and expanded protection. As of press time, the EEOC has proposed new regulations consistent with the changes in the ADA. The definition of disability should be interpreted in favor of broad coverage. Extensive analysis should not be required to determine whether an impairment is a disability. Under the recent changes, treatments, assistive devices (except ordinary eyeglasses or contact lenses), reasonable accommodations, and learned behavioral modifications that lessen the effects of a disability are not considered in determining whether the disability substantially limits a major life activity. An impairment that is episodic or in remission (not currently causing symptoms) may still be a disability if it substantially limits a major life activity when it is active (for example, epilepsy, multiple sclerosis, and depression). (42 U.S. Code section 12102(4)(D), (E); 74 Federal Register pp. 48440–48441 (proposed Sept. 23, 2009) (to be codified at 29 Code of Federal Regulations section 1630.2(j)(3), (4)).)

Under the FEHA, the limitation need not be "substantial." (Government Code sections 12926(i)(1)(B), (k)(1)(B)(ii), 12926.1(d)(2).) Employees with disabilities that can be treated (such as diabetes) are covered by anti-discrimination laws. California law covers employees with conditions that are disabling, potentially disabling, or perceived as disabling or potentially disabling. (Government Code section 12926.1(b).) Treatments that improve the condition (like medication for mentally ill people, and insulin for diabetics) are not considered in determining whether or not a person is disabled. (Government Code section 12926.1(c).)

a. Physical Disability

A "physical disability" is any physiological condition affecting these bodily systems: neurological; musculoskeletal; special sense organs; respiratory, including speech organs; cardiovascular; reproductive; digestive; genito-urinary; hemic and lymphatic; skin; and endocrine. (29 Code of Federal Regulations section 1630.2(h)(1).) A recently passed federal law provides protection against discrimination based on genetic information. (42 U.S. Code sections 2000ff et seq.) In California, the definition of medical condition also includes any impairment related to a diagnosis or history of cancer and genetic or inherited characteristics. (Government Code section 12926(h).) Obesity can be a disability under the

FEHA if it results from a physiological condition affecting one of the basic bodily systems. (*Cassista v. Community Foods, Inc.* (1993) 5 Cal.4th 1050.) However, since the FEHA protects individuals regarded by others as having a physical condition that makes achievement of a major life activity difficult, courts may in the future find obesity to qualify as a disability. This area of the law is currently evolving.

A "mental disability" is any mental or psychological disorder, such as intellectual disability, mental retardation, organic brain syndrome, emotional or mental illness, and specific learning disabilities. (29 Code of Federal Regulations section 1630.2(h)(2); Government Code section 12926.) In California, a "mental or psychological disorder" also includes having a history of such a disorder that is known to the employer, or being regarded by the employer as having such a disorder. (Government Code section 12926(i)(3), (4).) Under California law, mental disability does not include sexual behavior disorders, compulsive gambling, kleptomania, pyromania, or illegal use of drugs. (Government Code section 12926(i).)

b. Limits on a Major Life Activity

Both federal and state regulations require that to be considered disabled the individual must be restricted in relation to performing a major life activity (defined below). A physical or mental impairment is a "disability" within the terms of the ADA if it *substantially* limits a major life activity. (42 U.S. Code section 12102(1)(A).) California law requires that the condition *limit*, rather than *substantially limit*, major life activities. (Government Code section 12926(i), (k); 2 California Code of Regulations section 7293.6.) To determine whether an individual is disabled, the question is what is the individual able to do *without* reasonable accommodation, unless the accommodation itself creates a restriction. (42 U.S. Code section 12102(4)(E); Government Code section 12926(k)(1)(B).)

Both federal and California law cover perceived disabilities (whether the individual actually has a disability or not). (42 U.S. Code section 12102(1); 29 Code of Federal Regulations section 1630.2(g); Government Code sections 12926(h), (i)(4), (5), (k)(4), (5), (m), 12926.1(b); 2 California Code of Regulations section 7293.6(e)(1)(C), (D).) If the

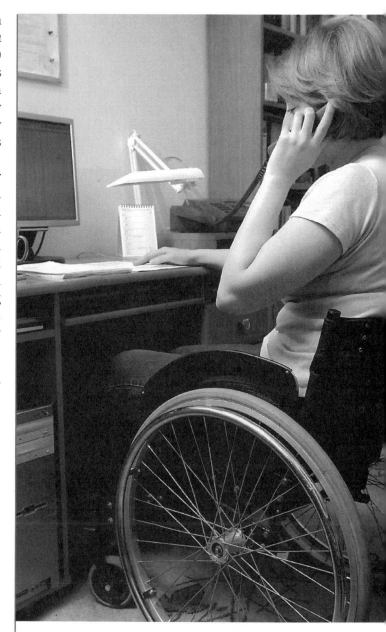

employer takes an ADA-prohibited action (for example, firing or refusing to hire an individual) based on an actual or perceived impairment that lasts or is expected to last more than six months, then the individual is "regarded as having such an impairment," whether or not the impairment limits or is perceived to limit a major life activity. (42 U.S. Code section 12102(3).) If the ADA-prohibited action is based on an individual's symptoms or treatment of the impairment, then the individual might be "regarded as" disabled even if the employer is unaware of the underlying impairment. (74 Federal Register p. 48443 (proposed Sept. 23, 2009) (to be codified at 29 Code of Federal Regulations section 1630.2(l)).)

California provides an easier standard to meet in most cases. California also explicitly covers conditions related to treatment or recovery from cancer, as well as genetic characteristics, even if they are not presently disabling. (Government Code section 12926(h).)

"Major life activities" are defined as basic functions such as working, caring for oneself, performing manual tasks, walking, seeing, hearing, eating, speaking, breathing, learning, reading, sitting, standing, lifting, bending, reaching, concentrating, thinking, reading, communicating, interacting with others, and sleeping. (42 U.S. Code section 12102(2)(A); 2 California Code of Regulations section 7293.6(e)(1)(A)(2)(a).) Under the ADA, major life activities include the operation of major bodily functions such as functions of the immune system, special sense organs, and skin; normal cell growth; and digestive, genitourinary, bowel, bladder, neurological, brain, respiratory, circulatory, cardiovascular, endocrine, hemic, lymphatic, musculoskeletal, and reproductive functions. Only one major life activity need be limited for an impairment to be considered a disability. (42 U.S. Code section 12102(2)(B), (4).)

The Equal Employment Opportunity Commision's (EEOC) proposed rules state that an impairment is a disability under the ADA if it "substantially limits" an individual's ability to perform a major life activity as compared to most people in the general population. The comparison of the individual's limited ability to the ability of most people often may be made with common sense rather than scientific or medical evidence. The impairment does not need to prevent or significantly restrict the performance of a major life activity to be a disability, but it must be more than a temporary, one-time impairment of short duration with no lasting effects. The proposed rules list some impairments that will consistently meet the definition of disability, including deafness; blindness; intellectual disability; missing limbs; mobility impairments requiring the use of a wheelchair; autism; cerebral palsy; diabetes; epilepsy; HIV or AIDS; multiple sclerosis; muscular dystrophy; major depression; bipolar disorder; post-traumatic stress disorder; obsessive compulsive disorder; and schizophrenia. Impairments that may be disabilities for some individuals (depending on the stage of the impairment, the presence of other impairments, and other factors) include asthma;

high blood pressure; learning disabilities; back or leg impairments; psychiatric impairments; carpal tunnel syndrome; and hyperthyroidism. The definition of disability is not limited to conditions on this list. The standards for determining whether an impairment is a disability should be applied in favor of broad coverage. (74 Federal Register pp. 48440–48443 (proposed Sept. 23, 2009) (to be codified at 29 Code of Federal Regulations section 1630.2(j)(2), (5), (6), (8)).)

The proposed federal rules state that the impairment substantially limits the major life activity of working if it substantially limits the individual's ability to perform or to meet the qualifications for the type of work at issue. The type of work at issue includes the job that the individual is performing or applying for and the requirements for jobs with similar qualifications or job-related requirements. An individual may obtain work elsewhere and still be substantially limited in working. In most cases, an individual with a disability will be substantially limited in another major life activity as well as in working. (74 Federal Register pp. 48442–48443 (proposed Sept. 23, 2009) (to be codified at 29 Code of Federal Regulations section 1630.2(j)(7)).)

Under California's FEHA, the inability to work the job in dispute (without accommodation) is enough to establish that an individual is substantially limited in working. (Government Code section 12926(f).)

2. Qualification for Position

To be a qualified worker entitled to protection under the ADA or California's FEHA, an individual must be able to perform the *essential functions* of the job "with or without reasonable accommodation." (42 U.S. Codes section 12111(8).)

Under California law, a function may be an essential function of a job for several reasons:

- The reason the position exists is to perform the function.
- There are a limited number of people available to perform the function.
- The function is highly specialized, and the person was hired for her expertise or ability to perform the function.

(Government Code section 12926(f).)

3. Prohibited Discriminatory Actions

Employers must not discriminate on the basis

of disability when establishing and implementing any term, condition, or privilege of employment. Terms of employment include hiring, promoting, transferring, training, laying off, terminating, granting leaves, granting raises, providing fringe benefits, etc. Other types of conduct or failure to act may also be considered discrimination. (29 Code of Federal Regulations sections 1630.4–1630.13; 2 California Code of Regulations section 7286.5(f).)

Prior to hiring, an employer is restricted in its ability to make disability-related inquiries or require medical examinations. See Chapter 2 on hiring rights for more discussion of the restrictions on pre-employment inquiries and medical examinations. For more information on this subject, see the EEOC booklet, "Enforcement Guidance: Disability-Related Inquires and Medical Examinations of Employees Under the Americans with Disabilities Act," at http://www.eeoc.gov/policy/docs/guidance-inquiries.html.

4. Reasonable Accommodation and Undue Hardship

a. Reasonable Accommodation

An employer must make a "reasonable accommodation" to an otherwise qualified applicant or employee with a disability unless doing so would impose an "undue hardship." (42 U.S. Code section 12112(b)(5); 29 Code of Federal Regulations sections 1630.9(a), 1630.15; Government Code section 12940(m); 2 California Code of Regulations section 7293.9.) A person is "otherwise qualified" if, with reasonable accommodation, he can perform the *essential functions* of the job. (29 Code of Federal Regulations section 1630.9.) The duty to reasonably accommodate extends to all services provided in connection with the job.

Employers are only required to provide reasonable accommodations regarding disabilities of which the employer is aware. (42 U.S. Code section 12112(b)(5)(A); 29 Code of Federal Regulations section 1630.9; Government Code section 12940(m); 2 California Code of Regulations section 7293.9.) Under the ADA, if an employee is "regarded as" having a disability but does not otherwise qualify as being disabled, the employer is not required to provide reasonable accommodation. (42 U.S. Code section 12201(h).) Once the employer is on notice of the disability, the employer must engage in an interactive process with the employee to explore possible accommodations. (Government Code section 12940(n).) Failure to engage in the interactive process provides the basis for legal action under the FEHA. (Government Code section 12940(n); *Wysinger v. Auto. Club of Southern California* (2007) 157 Cal.App.4th 413.)

Under California law, if the employer believes that the employee has a disability (whether or not she does), the employer must engage in an interactive process to explore reasonable accommodation. (*Gelfo v. Lockheed Martin Corp.* (2006) 140 Cal.App.4th 34.)

A reasonable accommodation is some change or modification of:

- The hiring process;
- The place or the way the work is done; and/or
- The rules regarding benefits and privileges of employment.

(29 Code of Federal Regulations section 1630.2(o).)

Reasonable accommodation may include the following types of arrangements: alternative work schedules, reassignment to a vacant position, providing equipment or other assistance, modification of office space or equipment, providing paid or unpaid leave, providing special transportation, or providing reserved parking. This is not an exclusive list. The kind of accommodation needed will vary, depending on the type of work, the conditions in the workplace, and the limitations of the disabled worker.

b. Undue Hardship

An "undue hardship" means that the accommodation would require "significant

> *To be considered disabled, an individual must be restricted in performing a major life activity.*

difficulty or expense" on the part of the employer. (42 U.S. Code section 12111(10); 29 Code of Federal Regulations section 1630.2(p); Government Code section 12926(s); 2 California Code of Regulations section 7293.9(b).)

Both the accommodation and the burden are examined in relation to a standard of reasonableness to determine whether, on balance, the employee should be protected from a negative decision based on his disability, or the employer should be excused from hiring or keeping the employee because accommodating him would defeat the business value of the employment. The size and nature of the employer are considered in determining an undue hardship.

5. Making a Request for Reasonable Accommodation

Qualified workers with disabilities should not hesitate to request reasonable accommodations. Employers should either grant them in most situations or work with the employee to determine an alternative accommodation the employer could afford.

An applicant or employee should make a request for reasonable accommodation in writing. The request should be directed to the personnel or human resources director, or to the employer's representative in charge of hiring (for applicants), or to the employee's supervisor or employer. Some employers have a special ADA accommodation request form that individuals should use.

Written accommodation requests should include all of the following:

- The date and the applicant's or employee's signature;
- A statement in simple, straightforward language that the individual is requesting a reasonable accommodation because she is an otherwise qualified person with a disability under the Americans with Disabilities Act or the California Fair Employment and Housing Act;
- The suggested accommodation, if the requesting party knows what might be helpful. For example, a change in job duties, reassignment to a vacant position, or a different work schedule;
- It is a good idea to include documentation from a medical provider. The documentation need not include a diagnosis, but it should outline the employee's functional limitations and recommend accommodation or specific limits on activities.

The applicant or employee should keep a copy of the request.

If an employer does not respond within a reasonable period of time, the applicant or employee should submit a second letter stating that she is following up on the previous request. A copy of the earlier request should be attached. If the applicant or employee does not receive an adequate response, or if she believes her employer has retaliated against her for making the request, she may file a complaint with the government. The steps to do so are outlined below.

6. Employer Response to a Request for Reasonable Accommodation

Employers must notify employees about their rights under state and federal disability laws, and engage in an "interactive process" (for instance, a discussion) with the employee. (42 U.S. Code section 12115; 29 Code of Federal Regulations section 1630.2(o)(3); Government Code section 12940(k), (m), (n).) An employer receiving a written request should realistically assess whether the accommodation would require changing an essential function of the job. If it would not, the cost should be realistically estimated. If it would be affordable given the business need satisfied by the position, the employer should provide the accommodation. If the accommodation would impose an undue hardship, then the employer should communicate with the employee or applicant and try to find a less costly accommodation.

Only in instances where no feasible accommodations can be identified may an employer legally refuse to provide accommodation to a qualified individual with a disability.

The duty to engage in the interactive process and the duty to provide the agreed-upon accommodation are separate duties. Once the employer agrees to grant a reasonable accommodation, the employer has the duty to provide that accommodation. A single instance in which the employer fails to provide the granted accommodation may violate the FEHA even though the employer has consistently provided the employee with the accommodation in the past. (*A.M. v. Albertsons, LLC* (2009) 178 Cal.App.4th 455.)

B. RELIGIOUS DISCRIMINATION AND THE EMPLOYER'S DUTY TO PROVIDE REASONABLE ACCOMMODATION

Under the FEHA, an employer is prohibited from discriminating against an individual on the basis of religion. (Government Code section 12940(a).) Religion includes all aspects of religious belief, observance, and practice. (Government Code section 12926(o).) If an employee sincerely holds a religious belief, the employer or his agent (for instance, a supervisor) is aware of that belief, and the belief conflicts with an employment requirement, the employer must make a good faith effort to explore reasonable accommodation. (*Fair Empl. & Hous. Comm'n v. Gemini Aluminum Corp.* (2004) 122 Cal.App.4th 1004.) The employer may accommodate the religious belief or observance by excusing the individual from the duties that are in conflict or by permitting the duties to be performed at another time or by another person. The employer is not required to provide an accommodation that would impose an undue hardship on the employer. (Government Code section 12940(l).)

C. SEX DISCRIMINATION

There are several laws that prohibit discrimination based on sex. Claims of discrimination in hiring or employment based on sex, including sexual harassment, under Title VII and the FEHA are discussed in this chapter. In addition to such claims, there are several specific laws against discrimination in pay based on sex and discrimination because of pregnancy. Employers are also prohibited from using sexual stereotyping, which is a form of sex discrimination under Title VII.

1. Unequal Pay

Employees have the right to receive the same compensation as a person of the opposite sex for work requiring the same skill, effort, and responsibility that is performed under similar working conditions. The federal Equal Pay Act (EPA) (29 U.S. Code sections 206–219.) specifically protects an employee's right to receive equal pay for equal work. If an employee's complaint against an employer is based solely on unequal pay for equal work because of the individual's gender,

she may want to file suit under the EPA. Potential claimants are advised to consult with their union representative or an attorney specializing in employment law to determine whether an EPA suit alone is the best option. For more information see http://www.eeoc.gov/laws/types/equalcompensation.cfm (summary, equal pay rights). California has an Equal Pay Act, located at Labor Code section 1197.5, that provides similar rights.

Enforcement: File a complaint with the EEOC or labor commissioner. File a lawsuit.

2. Discrimination Based on Pregnancy

Discrimination based on pregnancy occurs when a negative employment action is taken against an individual because she is, she is perceived to be, or she may become pregnant. For example, pregnant employees who need to take leave from work must be treated the same as disabled employees on leave. The California law against pregnancy discrimination applies to all employers with five or more employees.

As long as the employee is "able to perform the major functions necessary to the job," she cannot be refused employment or discriminated against because of pregnancy, miscarriage, abortion, or a related medical condition. (29 Code of Federal Regulations section 1604.10; Government Code section 12945; 22 California Code of Regulations section 98242.) An employer cannot refuse to hire or promote an employee just because she is pregnant or might become pregnant. (Government Code section 12940(a).)

A potential employer cannot ask an applicant any questions about birth control, family planning, abortion, or childcare. It may not ask her who will take care of her child, whether a father is in the home, or whether she is married to the father of the child. A potential employer also may not test an employee's or applicant's blood or urine for signs of pregnancy or birth control. (2 California Code of Regulations section 7290.9(b)(3).) Pregnant employees in California have the right to reasonable accommodation. (Government Code section 12945 (b)(1).)

California law is generally more protective than federal law regarding pregnancy discrimination and provides better remedies. However, federal employees are not covered by state law and will need to rely on federal law and remedies.

For information on federal prohibitions against pregnancy discrimination under the Pregnancy Discrimination Act, see http://www.eeoc.gov/laws/types/pregnancy.cfm. For more information on pregnancy discrimination in California, see http://www.dfeh.ca.gov/DFEH/Publications/CaseAnalysisManual2008Updt/Chapter%207%20Pregnancy.pdf. For more information on pregnancy disability benefits and leaves, see Chapter 5 of this book.

3. Sexual Stereotyping

Sexual stereotyping is a form of sex discrimination prohibited under Title VII and the FEHA. Employers may not evaluate employees by assuming or insisting that they match the stereotype associated with their group. (*Price Waterhouse v. Hopkins* (1989) 490 U.S. 228.) Sexual stereotyping may occur if an employer makes a negative employment decision based on preconceived notions on the basis of sex about an employee's abilities, traits, or performance. Examples of sexual stereotyping include making assumptions that a female employee with a family will have caretaking responsibilities and that those responsibilities will interfere with work performance, or making an assumption that a male is not a good employee because he has caregiving responsibilities. See the EEOC's "Enforcement Guidance: Unlawful Disparate Treatment of Workers with Caregiving Responsibilities," at http://www.eeoc.gov/policy/docs/caregiving.html for more information.

D. HARASSMENT AND HOSTILE WORK ENVIRONMENT

California law protects employees and independent contractors from harassment on the basis of all classifications protected by the FEHA. Employers covered by the FEHA may be liable for sexual harassment of employees under certain conditions. Additionally, employees (including supervisors and all other employees) may be held personally liable if they engage in harassment prohibited by the FEHA since harassment consists of conduct that is outside the scope of the employee's job. (Government Code section 12940(j); see *Jones v. Lodge at Torrey Pines Partnership* (2008) 42 Cal.4th 1158 (citing *Janken v. GM Hughes Electronics* (1996) 46 Cal.App.4th

55).) Harassment and discrimination are different violations under the FEHA. (Government Code sections 12940(a) and 12940(j)(1).) Discrimination involves changes in the terms and conditions of employment, and harassment involves messages conveyed to the employee in the social environment of the workplace. However, the evidence in both claims can overlap. For example, evidence that a supervisor took discriminatory employment actions because of an employee's disability may also support the claim that the supervisor's hostile social interaction with the employee amounts to harassment. (*Roby v. McKesson Corp.* (2009) 47 Cal.4th 686.)

1. Sexual Harassment

Sexual harassment is a form of unlawful discrimination on the basis of sex. It is one of the forms of harassment prohibited by federal law (as a form of sex discrimination) and California law. (Government Code section 12940(j).) If an employer makes a negative employment decision regarding an employee because the employee refused a supervisor's demands for sexual favors, the employer is guilty of sexual harassment. If an employer makes a positive employment decision on the employee dependent on the employee's compliance with the supervisor's sexual demands, the employer is guilty of harassment. This kind of harassment is called "*quid pro quo*" (which means "this for that" in Latin) harassment. If an employee is subjected to a severe or pervasive hostile or offensive work environment due to verbal or physical conduct of a sexual nature, the employer may be liable based on hostile work environment harassment. (42 U.S. Code section 2000e-2; 29 Code of Federal Regulations section 1604.11(a).) The conduct must be severe or pervasive (for example, more than isolated or occasional vulgar comments) to create hostile environment harassment. Isolated instances of rude, inappropriate, and offensive behavior may not amount to a hostile work environment when the acts are not sufficiently severe or pervasive to create an abusive working environment. (*Mokler v. County of Orange* (2007) 157 Cal.App.4th 121.) Whether or not there is a hostile work environment must be determined by considering all of the facts, such as the nature of the unwelcome sexual acts or words, the frequency of the acts or encounters, the total number of days over which the conduct occurred, and the context in which the conduct occurred. (*Sheffield v. Los Angeles County Dept. of Soc. Servs.* (2003) 109 Cal.App.4th 153.)

Employees are protected from sexual harassment by their employer and supervisors, but they are also protected from sexual harassment by coworkers and third parties (such as customers or clients), as long as the employer knows or should have known about the problem. (29 Code of Federal Regulations section 1604.11(d), (e); Government Code section 12940(j)(1); see also *Carter v. California Dept. of Veterans Affairs* (2006) 38 Cal.4th 914.) In some situations, employees who are not the object of any advances may still experience sexual harassment if, for instance, sexual favoritism is prevalent in the workplace and negatively affects the conditions of employment or unreasonably interferes with job performance. (*Miller v. Dept. of Corrections* (2005) 36 Cal.4th 446; see EEOC guidelines on sexual favoritism at http://www.eeoc.gov/policy/docs/sexualfavor.html.)

California law's prohibition on sexual harassment applies to employers with one or more employees. (Government Code section 12940(j)(4)(A).) At the federal level, the prohibition on sexual harassment applies to employers with fifteen or more employees. (42 U.S. Code section 2000e(b).)

Employers are required to post an information sheet from the Department of Fair Employment and Housing regarding the prohibition on sexual harassment, and to distribute these information sheets to employees. (Government Code section 12950(a), (b).) Employers with fifty or more employees are required to train supervisors every two years (and within six months of hire for new supervisors) on how to prevent and deal with sexual harassment. (Government Code section 12950.1.)

See the following for more information on sexual harassment discrimination (a form of sex discrimination):

- http://www.eeoc.gov/laws/types/sexual_harassment.cfm (summary of sexual harassment law);
- http://www.eeoc.gov/policy/docs/currentissues.html ("Policy Guidance on Current Issues of Sexual Harassment");
- http://www.eeoc.gov/policy/docs/harassment.html (employer liability for actions of supervisors).

See also section VII.A.3., p. 176, for more information on sexual harassment.

2. Harassment Based on Race, National Origin, Disability, Religion, Etc.

Title VII and California law also prohibit harassment based on other protected classifications, such as race, color, national origin, disability, pregnancy, religion, ancestry, medical condition, age, and veteran status. California law also explicitly prohibits discrimination based on sexual orientation or marital status. Racial harassment may consist of racial or ethnic slurs, "jokes," insulting comments, symbols (for instance, nooses recalling lynching of African Americans), or other verbal or physical conduct based on race or color. Derogatory racial slurs have been held not to fall within the category of free speech. (*Aguilar v. Avis Rent A Car Sys., Inc.* (1999) 21 Cal.4th 121, cert. denied 2000.) Discrimination based on factors prohibited by law can also be established by proving a severe and pervasive, unreasonably hostile and offensive work environment based on the plaintiff's membership in that protected class. If a plaintiff can show that his workplace was hostile, offensive, or intimidating based on some protected status, that such offensive hostile conduct was objectively unreasonable, and was either severe or pervasive, he may be able to prove unlawful discrimination in the form of workplace harassment, even if he has not suffered a negative employment decision. Generally, a single offensive act by another employee is not enough to establish a hostile work environment, but the result may be different if a supervisor commits the act. (*Dee v. Vintage Petroleum, Inc.* (2003) 106 Cal.App.4th 30.)

See also section VII.A.3., p. 176, for more information on harassment.

E. HATE CRIMES

1. The Definition of a Hate Crime

Some types of harassment are so severe that they are governed by criminal laws and may result in criminal and civil penalties. Hate crimes are acts of violence, threats, or intimidation based on a number of factors, including the person's actual or perceived race, color, religion, ancestry, national origin, political affiliation, sex, sexual orientation, age, or physical or mental disability. Common examples of hate crimes are gay bashing, desecration of houses of worship, cross burnings, or threatening messages.

2. California Laws That Govern Hate Crimes

The Ralph Civil Rights Act provides that all persons have a right to be free from violence against themselves or their property because of their race, color, religion, ancestry, national origin, affiliation, sex, sexual orientation, marital status, age, disability, medical condition, political affiliation, position in a labor dispute, or because another perceives them to have one or more of these characteristics. Violent acts and threats of violence are covered. (Civil Code section 51.7.) Enforcement is provided by filing complaints with the attorney general, local district attorney, or local city attorney; filing a complaint with the Department of Fair Employment and Housing; or via private lawsuit.

The Bane Civil Rights Act protects all people in California from interference with the rights guaranteed by the state or federal government. It covers only violence, intimidation, and threats of violence. For instance, it might protect someone who filed a complaint against school segregation, where the violence is based on the exercise of rights guaranteed by other laws. The civil provisions of the Bane Act may be enforced through a court order banning the behavior and awarding damages (including penalties and attorney's fees), by the attorney general or district attorney, or by a private lawsuit. This law also establishes criminal penalties enforced by the district attorney and the courts. (Civil Code section 52.1; Penal Code sections 422.6–422.93.) Penalties may include prison and revocation of parole.

VI. EMPLOYERS COVERED BY DISCRIMINATION LAWS

A. TABLE OF LAWS

The table on following pages outlines the laws prohibiting discrimination, the types of discrimination that are forbidden, and the employers who are covered by the laws. A protected characteristic is a factor that cannot legally be used as the basis for discrimination in most situations.

B. EXCEPTIONS TO COVERAGE

The following employees and employers are excluded from coverage or have limited coverage under the statutes specified above:

- Workers who are correctly classified as independent contractors are excluded from all the federal statutes (except Section 504 of the Rehabilitation Act of 1973). For more information on independent contractors, see Chapter 1.
- Title VII allows religious employers to discriminate based on religion with respect to employees with "ministerial duties" (for example, priests, pastors, rabbis, imams, or nuns) or connected with running the religious organization. (42 U.S. Code section 2000e-1(a); *Corp. of Presiding Bishop of Church of Jesus Christ of Latter-day Saints v. Amos* (1987) 483 U.S. 327.) California's FEHA also creates a narrow exemption for religious employers. It is not illegal to discriminate, based on religion, with regard to employees hired by nonprofit religious institutions primarily or exclusively for actual religious duties (generally members of the clergy or those involved in teaching or promotion of religious practices). Nonprofit religious educational institutions (that operate an educational institution as their only activity) may restrict employment to followers of the religion. Religious corporations or associations that provide healthcare to the general public may restrict employment or promotion of executives or those involved in "pastoral duties" to followers of the particular religion. However, religious corporations are prohibited from engaging in other acts of discrimination (for instance, race discrimination and sexual harassment). (Government Code sections 12926.2(d), (e), (f) and 12940(j)(4)(B).)
- American Indian tribes are not covered by Title VII, but some of their businesses may be covered. (42 U.S. Code section 2000e(b).)
- Bona fide membership clubs (other than labor unions) are not covered by Title VII. (42 U.S. Code section 2000e(b).)

It is not illegal discrimination to grant preference to veterans of military service. (Government Code section 12940(a)(4).) Congress and state legislators' top advisors, assistants, and policy experts should consult an attorney if they are involved in a situation involving discrimination, as protections and procedures for these workers may vary depending on the level of government at which they are employed and the type of discrimination they encounter.

VII. DISCRIMINATION CLAIMS UNDER TITLE VII, THE AGE DISCRIMINATION IN EMPLOYMENT ACT, AND THE FAIR EMPLOYMENT AND HOUSING ACT

To violate the law, an employer's action must involve discrimination that is legally prohibited. Most people use the words discrimination and harassment more broadly than the definitions under the law allow. For example, it is not illegal for an individual's boss to be unpleasant or to favor certain employees over others based on their personalities or whether the boss likes them. It is also not generally prohibited under these particular laws for a boss to be unpleasant or unfair to everyone. However, if it can be shown that such conduct or favoritism is based on a prohibited criterion, such as race, sex, religion, national origin, disability, etc., then the conduct based on these characteristics may be illegal.

In order to be successful in a discrimination case, the person complaining of discrimination must show a link between a protected characteristic covered by the law (for instance, gender, race, age, etc.) and the discrimination. Discrimination must involve some "adverse employment action." This term has been broadly interpreted in California to include any action that materially affects the terms and conditions of employment. While minor or trivial actions may not rise to the level of discrimination, California courts have found that any action that is reasonably likely to impair the performance or prospects for advancement of a reasonable employee may be covered if based on impermissible factors. (*Horsford v. Bd. of Trustees of California State Univ.* (2005) 132 Cal.App.4th 359; see also, *Yanowitz v. L'Oreal USA, Inc.* (2005) 36 Cal.4th 1028.) Actions like exclusion from important meetings, elimination of previously allowable flextime, and reduced workload or authority have been found to be adverse actions and may form the basis of a discrimination claim, if there is a link to a protected characteristic described above.

LAW	PROTECTED CHARACTERISTIC
Title VII (42 U.S. Code sections 2000e–2000e-17.)	Race, color, national origin, religion, sex
Age Discrimination in Employment Act (ADEA) (29 U.S. Code sections 621 et seq.)	Age
Americans with Disabilities Act (ADA) (42 U.S. Code sections 12101 et seq.)	Disabilities
Section 504 of the Rehabilitation Act of 1973 (29 U.S. Code section 794.)	Disabilities
Equal Pay Act (29 U.S. Code section 206(d).)	Sex
Civil Rights Act of 1866 (42 U.S. Code section 1981.)	Race
Civil Rights Act of 1871 (42 U.S. Code section 1983.)	Race, sex, mental disability, birth out of wedlock, and sexual orientation
Executive Order 11246	Race, color, religion, sex, and national origin
Section 503 of the Rehabilitation Act of 1973 (29 U.S. Code section 793.)	Disabilities
Vietnam Era Veterans' Readjustment Assistance Act of 1974 (VEVRAA) (38 U.S. Code sections 4211–4215.)	Being a veteran of military service
Uniformed Services Employment and Reemployment Rights Act (USERRA) (38 U.S. Code sections 4301 et seq.)	Membership in a branch of the military
California Fair Employment and Housing Act (FEHA) (Government Code sections 12900–12996.)	Race; color; religion; national origin or ancestry; physical disability; mental disability or medical condition; marital status; sex; sexual orientation; age; pregnancy, childbirth, and related conditions

EMPLOYERS COVERED

- All private employers, state, local, and federal governments, and educational institutions that employ fifteen or more workers.
- Private and public employment agencies.
- Labor organizations engaged in an industry affecting commerce.
- Joint labor-management committees controlling apprenticeship and training.

- All private employers with twenty or more employees and all state, local, and federal governments (including school districts).
- Employment agencies.
- Labor organizations.

- All private employers, state, local, and federal governments, and educational institutions that employ fifteen or more workers.
- Private and public employment agencies.
- Labor organizations engaged in an industry affecting commerce.
- Joint labor-management committees controlling apprenticeship and training.

Programs and activities receiving federal financial assistance. Programs and activities include:
- Departments, agencies, special purpose districts, or other instrumentalities of state or local government.
- Colleges, universities, postsecondary institutions, public systems of higher education, local educational agencies, systems of vocational education, or other school systems.
- Corporations, partnerships, or other private organizations.

All employees who are covered by the Federal Wage and Hour Law (the Fair Labor Standards Act). Virtually all employers are subject to the provisions of this act.

All public and private employers.

Federal, state, and local governments.

Federal contractors and subcontractors with federal contracts worth $10,000 or more in one year, except for contracts for work done outside the United States and its territories by employees recruited outside of the United States, and contracts involving work essential to national security, which are excluded.

Federal contractors and subcontractors with federal contracts worth $10,000 or more in one year, except for contracts for work done outside the United States and its territories by employees recruited outside of the United States, and contracts involving work essential to national security, which are excluded.

Federal contractors and subcontractors with federal contracts worth $100,000 or more in one year, except for contracts for work done outside the United States and its territories by employees recruited outside of the United States, and contracts involving work essential to national security, which are excluded.

All public and private employers regardless of size.

- Private employers with five or more employees. Employers with one or more employees or independent contractors are covered by the prohibition on sexual harassment.
- State and local governments (whether or not the agency has five or more employees).
- Employment agencies.
- Labor organizations.
- State licensing boards.
- Religious institutions.

A. CATEGORIES OF DISCRIMINATORY CONDUCT

1. Intentional Discrimination

Discrimination is illegal if an employer intentionally uses a protected characteristic (for instance, race, sex, age, or disability) as the basis for employment decisions, such as hiring, benefits, pay rates, raises, leaves of absence, terminations, or layoffs. The court decisions interpreting and applying Title VII (of the Civil Rights Act of 1964) and California's Fair Employment and Housing Act recognize two kinds of intentional discrimination:

- "Disparate treatment discrimination," where evidence demonstrates that an employer treats specific employees differently based on their protected characteristic;
- "Pattern and practice discrimination," where intent to discriminate is demonstrated by a pattern of discriminatory treatment of a whole group of employees based on their shared protected characteristic.

2. Disparate Impact Discrimination

Discrimination is illegal if an employer uses policies or practices that, although not discriminatory on their face (based on the words alone), have a negative effect disproportionately on members of a group sharing a protected characteristic. The discriminatory effect need not be intentional. A common example is a job application test that appears to be neutral but in practice discriminates against a group of applicants on a prohibited basis and lacks any connection to a job requirement. This type of discrimination is called "disparate impact discrimination."

3. Harassment

Discrimination is illegal if an employer harasses, intimidates, or threatens workers sexually or because of their race, national origin, gender, disability, or some other protected status. There are two types of conduct that can constitute unlawful harassment, though "quid-quo-pro harassment" is a form of sexual harassment exclusively.

- "Quid-pro-quo harassment" involves an employer offering an employment benefit to an employee in exchange for sexual favors, or an employer retaliating against an employee who refuses his or her sexual advance or request.

- "Hostile work environment harassment" involves an employer creating an unwelcome, hostile, or offensive environment for an employee based on the employee's protected status; the hostile or offensive conduct must be so severe and pervasive that a reasonable person in the employee's situation would find it intolerable. California law provides that it is an unlawful employment practice for an employer to fail to take immediate and appropriate corrective action to prevent sexual harassment of an employee by employees or non-employees (customers, clients, patients, other third parties), once the employer has notice of the harassment. (Government Code section 12940(j), (k).) In situations in which the employer may not be aware of the harassment (for example, harassment from a coworker, client, or customer), it is important to give notice to the employer (in other words, communicate clearly with them, in a way that can be proven, like in writing) that there is a problem.

(See section V.D., p. 171, for more information on harassment.)

B. EMPLOYER DEFENSES

An employer may defend discrimination claims by proving that the discrimination complained of is justified because of a bona fide occupational qualification or business necessity. These closely related concepts are narrowly construed. Intentional discrimination may be allowed if it is a bona fide occupational qualification. Disparate impact discrimination may be allowed if there is a business necessity. These concepts do not apply to harassment.

1. Bona Fide Occupation Qualification

In limited circumstances, an employer may defend intentional discrimination claims by proving that a characteristic is a "bona fide occupational qualification." This exception is very narrow. The characteristic must be reasonably necessary to the normal operation of the business, and the employer must have reason to believe that all or almost all of the people discriminated against would be unable to safely and efficiently perform the duties of the job. See Chapter 2, IV.A., p. 27, for a discussion of "bona fide occupational qualification."

2. Business Necessity

The employer may defend against charges of disparate impact discrimination by proving that the discriminatory employment practice is job-related and justified by "business necessity." The practice must measure an employee's ability to perform the job. In order to prove business necessity in California, the employer must show that there is an overriding legitimate business purpose, that the practice is necessary for the safe and efficient operation of the business, and that the challenged practice effectively fulfills the business purpose. (2 California Code of Regulations section 7286.7.) However, even if a practice is a business necessity, it may still be illegal if there is a less discriminatory practice that would serve the same purpose. See Chapter 2, IV.A., p. 27, for a discussion of "business necessity."

The employer defense under the ADEA is broader than the "business necessity" defense in other disparate impact discrimination cases. The ADEA allows disparate impact age discrimination if the employment practice is based on *reasonable factors* other than age. Under the "reasonable factors" test, an employer does not need to use less discriminatory alternatives. (29 U.S. Code section 623(f)(1); *Smith v. City of Jackson* (2005) 544 U.S. 228.)

C. HOW TO DEAL WITH EACH TYPE OF DISCRIMINATION AND HARASSMENT

1. Steps Individuals Should Take if They Are Being Harassed

The basic steps individuals should take if they are being harassed based on race, sex, or membership in other protected groups fall into three categories:
- Object;
- Document;
- Report.

a. Object

One element of harassment is that the behavior is unwelcome. An employee who is being harassed on the job should attempt to let the harasser know that the behavior is unwelcome, especially if it falls into a potentially grey area (this includes jokes, comments on appearance, and similar acts). The employee may want to write a note to the harasser, asking that the offensive behavior stop. The employee should keep a copy of the note in case it is needed in the future. Verbal statements objecting to the behavior may be effective as well, however they can result in a situation of "he said, she said," in which the harasser denies having had the conversation. A written note or a conversation held in front of a supportive witness is more useful in proving that the harasser was told that the activity was unwelcome. Some actions, like physical assault, are presumed to be unwelcome without a specific objection. Whether behavior constitutes harassment is generally judged from the perspective of a reasonable person of the worker's race, gender, or category. Sometimes objecting will stop the objectionable behavior. If not, the objection will assure that the harasser will not be able to assert the defense that the conduct was not clearly unwelcome.

b. Document

Proof of harassment can be important. Any evidence of harassment, like notes, emails, messages on answering machines, photos, etc., should be saved. If the situation is an ongoing one, the person being harassed may want to keep a diary indicating what was said or done, who said or did it, and when the act took place.

c. Report

Reporting the harassment to the employer is frequently an important step in the process. If the employer of the target of harassment also employs or does business with the harasser (for instance, the harasser is a student, vendor, customer, person who works for someone else in the same building,

As soon as someone starts to be concerned about discrimination at work, she should keep a diary of incidents.

etc.), it is critically important that the person being harassed report the situation to the employer. If this is not done, and it becomes necessary to sue, courts will not assume that the employer knew about the situation and had a corresponding duty to correct it. Employers have a duty to protect their employees from sexual harassment by third parties *if* they know about it.

Figuring out where to report harassment can be tricky, especially if the harasser is a supervisor. If the harasser is a supervisor, the target of harassment should attempt to go over the supervisor's head to the next in command or speak with someone in human resources. All public agencies and most large companies have individuals whose job it is to assist others in harassment cases.

The advice above about documenting unwelcome actions also applies to documenting reports of harassment. If harassment is reported verbally, it is a good idea to follow up with a brief note expressing thanks for the meeting to discuss the harassment. Again, the individual should keep a copy of this note, in case the employer later denies that the incidents were reported.

Enforcement: If objecting and reporting does not resolve the problem, it may be necessary to file a grievance (if the workplace is unionized), a complaint with the DFEH (or a charge with the EEOC, though DFEH complaints are preferable), and eventually a lawsuit. Employees who commit harassment prohibited by the FEHA may be held personally liable. (Government Code section 12940(j)(3).) A complaint must be filed with the DFEH within one year of the alleged discriminatory act. (Government Code section 12960(d).) A charge with the EEOC must be filed within 300 days from the date of the alleged violation. (42 U.S. Code section 2000e-5(e)(1); 29 Code of Federal Regulations section 1601.13(a)(4)(ii).)

2. Disparate Treatment Discrimination

When an employer denies an individual a position, wage, benefit, or opportunity because of the individual's protected characteristic, that

individual has suffered what the law calls disparate treatment discrimination. To establish a claim of disparate treatment, an employee must prove that the employer acted with the intent to discriminate on a prohibited basis. If there is direct evidence of discriminatory intent, such as a statement by the employer that the individual was not hired because of his race, or a written policy that discriminates on its face based on a prohibited basis, intent can be directly proved. Usually there is no such "smoking gun" and intent must be proved through circumstantial evidence (in other words, based on the circumstances surrounding the situation). (See *Ash v. Tyson Foods, Inc.* (2006) 546 U.S. 454 (evidence that a manager sometimes referred to African-American employees as "boy" could be evidence of discriminatory intent depending on factors such as context, inflection, tone of voice, local custom, and historical usage); see also *Sprint/ United Management Co. v. Mendelsohn* (2008) 552 U.S. 379 (evidence of discrimination against employees who are not part of the lawsuit by supervisors who played no role in the adverse action against the plaintiff may be relevant, depending on many factors).) With this in mind, the courts have developed the following test to establish a "prima facie" (initial) case of discrimination:

- The plaintiff is a member of a class sharing a protected characteristic.
- The plaintiff applied for, and was qualified for, an available job or other employment opportunity or benefit, or was qualified and performing satisfactorily in an existing position.
- Despite the plaintiff's qualifications, he was rejected, demoted, or his employment was terminated.
- After the plaintiff's rejection, demotion, or termination, the employer continued to seek applications from, or provide benefits to, persons with the plaintiff's qualifications, but who were not members of the class sharing the plaintiff's protected characteristic.

(*McDonnell Douglas Corp. v. Green* (1973) 411 U.S. 792; *Texas Dept. of Community Affairs v. Burdine* (1981) 450 U.S. 248.)

The plaintiff bears the burden of establishing the initial case of discrimination. The burden then shifts to the employer to show a legitimate, nondiscriminatory reason for having taken the action that harmed the plaintiff. If the employer is able to establish the fact that there were legitimate, nondiscriminatory reasons for the action, the plaintiff will need to offer evidence showing that the employer's stated reason for taking the action is actually a "pretext." A pretext is an artificial or made up rationale, used to cover up the party's real motivation.

Nonetheless, rejection of the employer's stated reasons does not automatically mean discrimination has been proven. The plaintiff still has the burden of persuasion in showing that an employer has committed illegal discrimination. (*St. Mary's Honor Ctr. v. Hicks* (1993) 509 U.S. 502.)

The four elements and burden-shifting scheme discussed above apply to federal Title VII claims, age discrimination claims under the ADEA (the plaintiff must be over 40 years of age to be a member of a protected class), and also are followed by California courts enforcing the FEHA (including provisions regarding age discrimination). (*Reeves v. Sanderson Plumbing Products, Inc.* (2000) 530 U.S. 133; *Guz v. Bechtel National, Inc.* (2000) 24 Cal.4th 317.)

If a plaintiff claims that he was discriminated against based on both race and sex, the judge or the jury must determine whether the employer discriminated based on that *combination of factors*, not just whether it discriminated on either of the individual bases. (*Lam v. Univ. of Hawai'i* (9th Cir. 1994) 40 F.3d 1551.)

A variation on the situation described above exists in so-called "mixed-motive" cases, in which the evidence indicates that the employer was motivated by both lawful and unlawful intentions. A plaintiff can win in such a case by establishing that the employer's consideration of the plaintiff's protected characteristic was a *motivating factor* in the employment decision, even though other factors also were motivating factors. Direct evidence is not required to prove employment discrimination in a mixed-motive case. Circumstantial evidence may be sufficient if it is persuasive. (*Desert Palace, Inc. v. Costa* (2003) 539 U.S. 90.)

However, a recent Supreme Court case held that the ADEA does not authorize mixed-motives age discrimination claims. A plaintiff cannot win an ADEA case by producing evidence that age was one motivating factor. In an ADEA case, the plaintiff must prove that age was the reason for the employment decision. (*Gross v. FBL Financial Servs., Inc.* (2009) 129 S.Ct. 2343.)

3. Pattern-and-Practice Discrimination

A second type of intentional discrimination, known as "pattern-and-practice discrimination," exists where an employer's hiring and employment policies cause discrimination against an entire class that shares a protected characteristic within the employer's applicant pool or workforce. (*International Brotherhood of Teamsters v. United States* (1977) 431 U.S. 324.) Pattern-and-practice claims are often pursued as class action lawsuits on behalf of the entire category of affected individuals. Often much of the same evidence is relevant to both types of discrimination claims. The following techniques are among those used to investigate and to collect evidence supporting pattern-and-practice claims.

• Developing workplace statistics (for example, comparing the percentage of applicants hired from a group sharing a protected characteristic to the percentage of qualified applicants from that group in the [geographically relevant] hiring pool);

• Taking the testimony of employees who describe discriminatory treatment;

• Presenting discriminatory statements made by management;

• Presenting examples of practices that exclude certain groups.

4. Disparate/Adverse Impact Discrimination

A third way of proving unlawful discrimination is to demonstrate that an employer's practice or policy, which at first glance appears neutral, in fact has a disproportionate (unusually high) negative impact on a group sharing a protected characteristic. Unlike the case of pattern-and-practice discrimination, it is not necessary to prove unlawful discriminatory intent to establish a disparate impact claim. (*Raytheon Co. v. Hernandez* (2003) 540 U.S. 44.) Instead, it is sufficient to produce statistical evidence demonstrating that an employer's practice has a disproportionate impact on a group sharing a protected characteristic and is not justified by business necessity. (*Griggs v. Duke Power Co.* (1971) 401 U.S. 424.) In addition, the disparate impact model can be used to challenge employer practices that are subjective (based on personal opinion), such as discretionary supervisor reviews that statistically have an adverse impact on a group of applicants or employees sharing a protected characteristic. (*Watson v. Fort Worth Bank and Trust* (1988) 487 U.S. 977.)

Under California law, the disparate impact analysis can also apply to age discrimination claims. Government Code section 12941 declares that an employer cannot make termination decisions based on salary if that basis has an adverse impact on older workers. Therefore, an employee can state a claim of age discrimination if his employer's policies have a "disparate impact" on older workers, even if it cannot be shown that the policies were intended to discriminate against older workers.

The legal standards and burden-shifting procedural rules discussed in this section apply to claims both in federal court under Title VII of the Civil Rights Act of 1964 and in state court under the Fair Employment and Housing Act. (42 U.S. Code section 2000e(m); *City & County of San Francisco v. Fair Empl. & Housing Comm'n* (1987) 191 Cal.App.3d 976.)

The scope of disparate impact cases under the ADEA is more limited. In addition to demonstrating a disproportionate impact on an age group, the plaintiff must also identify the specific practice that allegedly causes the disparate impact. (*Smith v. City of Jackson* (2005) 544 U.S. 228.)

VIII. FILING A COMPLAINT ABOUT ILLEGAL DISCRIMINATION

A. FILING COMPLAINTS AGAINST GOVERNMENT EMPLOYERS

Prior to filing some kinds of lawsuits against government employers, it is necessary to file a claim under state or federal tort claims acts. This requirement does not apply to discrimination lawsuits based on Title VII of the Civil Rights Act or California's Fair Employment and Housing Act. (*Snipes v. City of Bakersfield* (1983) 145 Cal. App.3d 861.) However, when filing other types of discrimination cases against government employers, it may be necessary to file a government tort claim within six months of the discriminatory act. This is an administrative claim against the government. Filing an administrative claim is required before filing a lawsuit in court against the government. (28 U.S. Code sections 1346, 2671–2680; Government Code sections 900 et seq.) It is a good idea to seek the assistance of an attorney promptly when filing this type of claim.

B. FILING COMPLAINTS WITH THE OFFICE OF FEDERAL CONTRACT COMPLIANCE PROGRAMS

Individuals who have been discriminated against by federal contractors or subcontractors may file a complaint with the U.S. Office of Federal Contract Compliance Programs (OFCCP), within the federal Department of Labor. A "Complaint of Discrimination in Employment Under Federal Government Contracts" may be filled out in person at an OFCCP regional office or district and area office, or it may be faxed or mailed to the appropriate regional office. See the instructions or download the form at http://www.dol.gov/ofccp/regs/compliance/pdf/pdfstart.htm. If a complaint involves discrimination against only one person, the OFCCP usually refers it to the Equal Employment Opportunity Commission.

C. FILING COMPLAINTS WITH THE DEPARTMENT OF LABOR, VETERANS' EMPLOYMENT & TRAINING SERVICE (VETS)

An individual who has been discriminated against based on service in the military may file a complaint with the U.S. Veterans' Employment & Training Service (VETS) or may file a lawsuit. (20 Code of Federal Regulations section 1002.303.) A complaint with VETS may be filed in writing, using VETS Form 1010, or electronically, using VETS Form e1010. (20 Code of Federal Regulations section 1002.288.) Instructions and forms are available at http://www.dol.gov/elaws/vets/userra/1010.asp.

D. FILING COMPLAINTS WITH THE U.S. EQUAL EMPLOYMENT OPPORTUNITY COMMISSION (EEOC) OR THE CALIFORNIA DEPARTMENT OF FAIR EMPLOYMENT AND HOUSING (DFEH)

The Equal Employment Opportunity Commission (EEOC) is the federal agency that investigates most workplace discrimination complaints (under Title VII, the ADA, and the ADEA) and enforces the laws. An individual who believes she has a discrimination case against an employer may file a charge with the nearest EEOC office in person, by mail, or by telephone. For a list of EEOC office addresses and phone numbers, see http://www.eeoc.gov/field/index.cfm.

The equivalent state agency in California is the Department of Fair Employment and Housing (DFEH). District office locations can be found at http://www.dfeh.ca.gov/DFEH/contact/locations.aspx.

By law, the EEOC and the DFEH must share information about a claim with each other, though the agency that first receives the information does the investigating.

For general information on filing a charge with the EEOC, see its website at http://www.eeoc.gov/employees/charge.cfm.

For information on filing a complaint with the DFEH, consult its website at http://www.dfeh.ca.gov/DFEH/Complaints/fileComplaint.aspx.

In most cases, it is preferable to file discrimination claims with the DFEH, rather than the EEOC. California state law provides more protections for workers in a number of areas (for instance, broader coverage for disability discrimination and sexual orientation) and has better remedies.

When a claim against an employer is based on Title VII, the ADA, the ADEA, or the FEHA, an applicant or employee will need to exhaust administrative remedies (file with the EEOC or the DFEH) before she can file a lawsuit in state or federal court.

There are some exceptions to this requirement. An employee may bring a common law claim without first exhausting administrative remedies. (*Rojo v. Kliger* (1990) 52 Cal.3d 65; *Stevenson v. Superior Court* (1997) 16 Cal.4th 880.) A common law claim is one that is not based on a particular law. Common law claims are often based on the federal or state Constitution, or earlier court cases. For more information on wrongful discharge, including discharge in violation of public policy, see Chapter 10.

The requirement to exhaust administrative remedies is subject to other exceptions, as discussed below in section VIII.F., p. 182. However, it is generally the safest course of action to exhaust administrative remedies by filing a complaint with the proper administrative agency.

Government employees may choose to pursue the internal remedies offered by the government employer *or* the administrative remedy provided by the FEHA; they are not required to exhaust both before filing a claim in court. (*Schifando v. City of Los Angeles* (2003) 31 Cal.4th 1074.) However, once the employee has chosen a remedy, the employee must exhaust the procedures of that remedy. (*Page v. Los Angeles County Probation Dept.* (2004) 123 Cal.App.4th 1135.) Adverse administrative findings must be challenged by filing a request for a writ of mandate (a court order) in Superior Court or they may become binding in later civil lawsuits. (*Johnson v. City of Loma Linda* (2000) 24 Cal.4th 61.)

E. TIME LIMITS

The following is only a general overview of the legal time allowed for filing complaints. The safest course of action is to consult an attorney with experience in employment discrimination as soon as possible after the discriminatory acts take place.

Complaints under Executive Order 11246, dealing with federal contracts, must be filed within 180 days from the date of the last discriminatory act. Complaints regarding violations of Section 503 of the Rehabilitation Act or VEVRAA, dealing with veterans of military service, must be filed within 300 days. If there is a good reason, extensions may be granted with approval of OFCCP's deputy assistant secretary. (41 Code of Federal Regulations sections 60-1.21, 60-741.61(b), 60-300.61(a).)

EEOC charges generally must be filed within 300 days of the discriminatory act(s). In California, DFEH complaints generally must be filed within one year of the last discriminatory act. (29 U.S Code section 626(d); 42 U.S. Code sections 2000e-5(b), 12117(a); Government Code section 12960.)

If the employee has been experiencing illegal discrimination over a length of time or recently became aware of discrimination in the workplace, he should file as soon as possible. Under certain circumstances, discriminatory conduct that began before the time period in which one must file can still be covered by a charge if there was a "continuing violation" of the law. California courts have found a continuing violation to occur when the employer's actions satisfy all three elements of the following test: (1) the earlier discriminatory actions were sufficiently similar to the discriminatory actions that occurred within the time period for filing the complaint; (2) the discriminatory actions occurred with reasonable frequency; and (3) the actions were not yet permanent (in other words, the employer's conduct had not yet made clear to a reasonable employee that further efforts to resolve the matter informally would be useless). The period in which complaints must be filed, called the "statute of limitations," begins to run when the employee is on notice that litigation is the only way to assert his rights. (*Richards v. CH2M Hill, Inc.* (2001) 26 Cal.4th 798.) An attorney should be consulted whenever there is any question as to whether it is still possible to file a timely complaint.

F. THE COMPLAINT PROCESS

Both the EEOC and the DFEH have a backlog of cases. This means that it can take months for a case to be investigated. If the wait becomes too long, the complainant can speak with an attorney about filing a complaint in court, or can try to resolve the issues herself, or use an in-house complaint procedure, if the employer has one. The DFEH has one year to investigate a complaint. If the agency is unable to complete an investigation within the required timeframe, they will issue a "right to sue" letter. The issuance of a "right to sue" letter shows that the complainant pursued the appropriate administrative remedies, and she may then file a lawsuit. If the EEOC has not filed a civil action or entered into a conciliation agreement within 180 days from the filing of the charge, then the EEOC will notify the charging party of the "right to sue." (42 U.S. Code section 2000e-5(f)(1); 29 Code of Federal Regulations section 1601.28.)

The best way to get and to keep the EEOC or

Many of the statutes that make discrimination illegal also have prohibitions against retaliation built into them.

DFEH investigator's attention is to be organized, polite, and persistent. Call to check on the progress of the investigation. Make the investigator's job as easy as possible by promptly supplying documents, contact information for witnesses, and anything else that supports the case.

The EEOC or one of the parties to the dispute may suggest mediation. Mediation is a voluntary process in which a neutral, trained mediator attempts to help the parties resolve the dispute. It does not take place unless both parties agree to participate. There is no cost to the parties for the mediator. The EEOC reports that in approximately two-thirds of the cases where mediation takes place, a settlement is achieved. For more information on mediation, see http://www.eeoc.gov/employees/mediation.cfm. If the mediation is not successful, the case is handled by the EEOC like any other case. The DFEH also mediates complaints.

G. FILING A LAWSUIT

If the EEOC is unable to settle the case, the agency will decide whether to bring suit against the employer in federal court. If it decides not to sue, it will issue a notice (the "right to sue" letter) closing the case and giving the complainant ninety days in which to file a lawsuit on his own behalf.

A complainant may request a "right to sue" letter from the DFEH as soon as the complaint is filed, up to one year after the complaint is filed, or after the agency has made a decision that there is no case. (Government Code section 12965.) The letter gives the individual the right to go to court on his own behalf without further delay. The DFEH will provide these letters upon request, once the complaint has been filed. A charging party may request a "right to sue" letter from the EEOC after 180 days from the filing of the charge. The EEOC may issue a "right to sue" letter prior to the 180 day limit upon request if it has determined that the EEOC probably will not be able to complete the administrative process within 180 days from the filing of the charge. (29 Code of Federal Regulations section 1601.28.) The individual must file a lawsuit within 90 days after receiving a notice of a "right to sue" from the EEOC. (42 U.S. Code section 2000e-5(f)(1).)

Note: A copy of the DFEH complaint must be served on the employer at the time of initial contact or within sixty days of the filing of the complaint,

whichever comes first. Generally DFEH serves this document on the employer (provides a copy to the employer), unless the person filing the complaint has an attorney, in which case the attorney should arrange to have the complaint served on the employer. (Government Code section 12962.)

IX. PREPARING FOR A DFEH/ EEOC INVESTIGATION

A. GATHERING EVIDENCE

As soon as an applicant or employee begins having concerns about possible illegal discrimination at work, she should keep a journal or diary of incidents. This journal should include the date, time, location, persons involved, and statements made or actions taken that the individual believes are evidence of illegal discrimination.

Applicants or employees also should keep all records that the employer gives them, along with any records that relate to their work, especially any that concern their performance, any write-ups, and any client assessments of their work or thank-you notes, if available. If an individual receives a document of any type that she believes is evidence of discrimination, such as a note or memorandum that is racially or sexually insulting or explicit, the individual should be sure to keep it. If coworkers express similar concerns, the individual applicant or employee might encourage them to do the same.

It is best to keep a file of these documents at home in a safe place, not at work.

If an employee or applicant believes he has been subjected to unlawful discriminatory treatment or harassment, that there is a pattern and practice of discrimination in his workplace, or that the employer is using a selection procedure, test, or criterion that has a disparate impact on members of a protected class that includes the employee, she should consult an attorney immediately and compile a list of potential witnesses.

B. PREPARING TO SPEAK WITH AN INVESTIGATOR

Before speaking with an EEOC or DFEH investigator, a complainant should take these steps:
- Organize evidence in support of the discrimination claim, such as statements by

others, a log of events, supporting documents, statistics showing the difference between the hiring pool and workforce of the employer in question, etc.

- Speak with coworkers who are sympathetic, who have witnessed possibly discriminatory incidents, or who have experienced what they believe is illegal discrimination themselves. The person filing the complaint may learn useful information and the support of coworkers will make the process easier. The investigator may ask for names of people who have witnessed or experienced similar incidents. However, do not pressure anyone who seems reluctant to discuss the matter.

- The claimant should jot down notes or an outline of what he wants to say before calling to file the complaint. This will increase the chance that the information given to the investigator is as complete and accurate as possible.

C. SPEAKING WITH AN INVESTIGATOR

If possible, parties should follow these practices when speaking with the EEOC or DFEH investigator:

- Choose a time when feeling calm and undistracted, and when it is possible to have a private, undisturbed conversation.

- Because the investigator is looking for evidence, a claimant should focus on the events and statements that indicate the existence of unlawful discrimination.

- No matter how justifiable a claimant's anger, it should be kept in check. While an employee or applicant may reasonably consider a supervisor to be a horrible person, the supervisor's behavior may not be illegal. Instead of venting anger at an employer, a claimant should calmly relay to the investigator information about statements and other concrete evidence of illegal practices.

X. RETALIATION

Employers may not retaliate against employees who report discrimination by the employer. Many of the statutes that make discrimination illegal also have prohibitions against retaliation built into them. Agencies like the EEOC and DFEH take retaliation claims seriously.

A. LAWS

1. Federal

It is illegal for an employer to discriminate against an employee or applicant because the individual opposed a practice that is unlawful under Title VII (42 U.S. Code section 2000e-3(a).), the ADEA (29 U.S. Code section 623(d).), the EPA (29 U.S. Code section 215(a)(3).), or the ADA (42 U.S. Code section 12203(a).). The National Labor Relations Act also prohibits retaliation under some circumstances. (29 U.S.Code section 158.)

Federal contractors and subcontractors may not harass, intimidate, threaten, coerce, or discriminate against an employee who opposes a discriminatory practice. The contractor must also ensure that the people under its control refrain from such retaliation. (41 Code of Federal Regulations sections 60-1.32, 60-250.69, 60-741.69.)

Additionally, courts may find that certain types of retaliation violate important public policy.

The employer may not discriminate against any employee or applicant because he made a charge, testified, assisted, or participated in any manner in a proceeding under these laws.

2. California

Government Code section 12940(h) prohibits employers from discriminating against any person because he has opposed any practices forbidden by the FEHA, or has filed a complaint, testified, or assisted in any proceeding under the FEHA. An employee may be held personally liable for acts of harassment prohibited by the FEHA. (Government Code section 12940(j)(3).) However, non-employers (such as supervisors) may not be held *personally* liable for their role in retaliation prohibited by the FEHA. (*Jones v. Lodge at Torrey Pines Partnership* (2008) 42 Cal.4th 1158.) The employer itself may generally be held liable for the retaliatory actions of its supervisors. (*Jones v. Lodge at Torrey Pines Partnership* (2008) 42 Cal.4th 1158; *Wysinger v. Auto. Club of Southern California* (2007) 157 Cal.App.4th 413.) An employer may also be liable for failing to prevent retaliation. (*Taylor v. Los Angeles Dept. of Water and Power* (2006) 144 Cal.App.4th 1216.)

Retaliation may also be a violation of other laws such as Labor Code section 98.6 (which prohibits discrimination, discharge, or refusal to hire because a person has enforced her rights under the

California Labor Code), or a violation of important public policies recognized by the courts.

B. ELEMENTS NEEDED TO PROVE A CASE OF RETALIATION

In order to successfully prove a retaliation case, the worker bringing the case must show that the employee was involved in "protected activity" (see definition, below); that the employer took adverse action (in other words, retaliated); and that the adverse action was taken *because of* the protected activity.

1. The Employee Must Have Engaged in Protected Activity by Opposing Discrimination

The federal provisions define "protected activity" as opposing a discriminatory practice or filing a charge, testifying, assisting, or participating in an investigation, proceeding, or hearing regarding the discriminatory practice under Title VII (42 U.S. Code section 2000e-3(a).), the ADEA (29 U.S. Code section 623(d).), or the ADA (42 U.S. Code section 12203(a).); or filing a complaint, causing any proceeding to be instituted, testifying in any proceeding, or serving on an industry committee under the EPA (29 U.S. Code section 215(a)(3).). The employee who alleges employer retaliation does not need to claim that he was the victim of the initial discriminatory practice.

Under the regulations for federal contracts, protected activities include: filing a complaint; assisting or participating in any activity related to the administration of the laws prohibiting discrimination by federal contractors and subcontractors (Executive Order 11246, Section 503 of the Rehabilitation Act of 1973, and the Vietnam Era Veterans' Readjustment Assistance Act of 1974); and exercising any other right under those laws. (41 Code of Federal Regulations sections 60-1.32, 60-250.69, 60-741.69.)

Under the Uniformed Services Employment and Reemployment Rights Act (USERRA), which protects veterans from discrimination, the following are all protected activities: taking action to enforce a protection afforded any person under USERRA, testifying or otherwise making a statement in connection with a proceeding under USERRA, assisting or participating in a USERRA

investigation, and exercising a right provided by USERRA. (38 U.S. Code section 4311(b); 20 Code of Federal Regulations section 1002.19.)

California's definition of protected activity is similar but more detailed. Opposition to practices prohibited by the Fair Employment and Housing Act (FEHA) includes:

- Seeking advice from the Department of Fair Employment and Housing (DFEH) or the Fair Employment and Housing Commission (FEHC);
- Assisting or advising someone seeking advice from the the DFEH or FEHC;
- Opposing practices reasonably believed to violate the FEHA;
- Participating in activity that is perceived as opposition to discrimination;
- Contacting or participating in proceedings of local human rights or civil rights agencies;
- Contacting or participating in proceedings of the DFEH or FEHC due to a good faith belief that the FEHA has been violated; or

- Being involved as a potential witness in a DFEH or FEHC investigation.

(2 California Code of Regulations section 7287.8.)

A retaliation claim may be brought by an employee who has complained of conduct that the employee reasonably believes in good faith to be discriminatory, even if it is later determined that the conduct is not actually prohibited by the FEHA. (*Yanowitz v. L'Oreal USA, Inc.* (2005) 36 Cal.4th 1028.)

2. The Employee Experienced an Adverse Action

Under federal law, the anti-retaliation provisions cover employer actions that are "harmful to the point that they could well dissuade a reasonable worker from making or supporting a charge of discrimination." (*Burlington Northern & Santa Fe Railway Co. v. White* (2006) 548 U.S. 53.) The action must be more than a trivial harm. The

EEOC gives examples of adverse actions including: denial of promotion, refusal to hire, denial of job benefits, demotion, suspension, discharge, threats, reprimands, negative evaluation, and harassment. (EEOC Compliance Manual section 8-II(D).) Former employees are entitled to the same protections against retaliation as current employees. (*Robinson v. Shell Oil Co.* (1997) 519 U.S. 337 (in which a negative job reference was retaliation for a terminated employee filing an EEOC charge).)

Employees are protected from a wide range of retaliatory adverse actions. Adverse actions are not limited to discriminatory actions that affect the terms and conditions of employment. For example, it could be considered retaliation if an employer filed false criminal charges against a former employee who complained about discrimination. (*Burlington Northern & Santa Fe Railway Co. v. White* (2006) 548 U.S. 53 (citing *Berry v. Stevinson Chevrolet* (1996) 74 F.3d 980).)

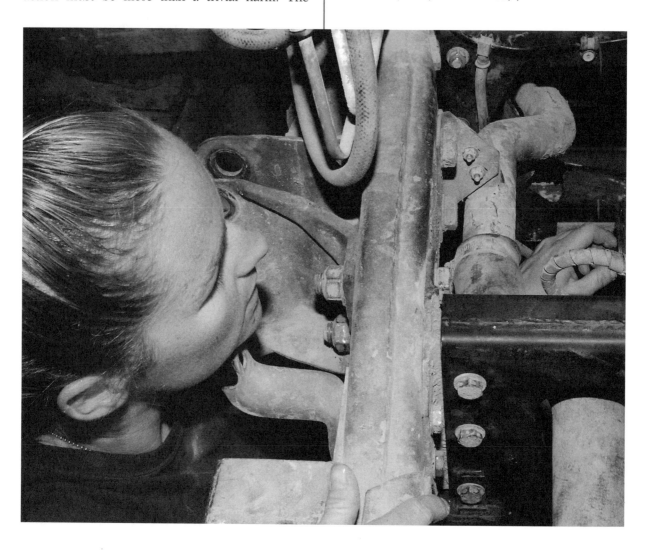

3. The Adverse Action Was Taken Because of the Protected Activity

The employee who claims that retaliation has taken place must show that the employer took adverse employment action *as a result* of the employee's opposition of the employer's discriminatory practice. This is called the "causal connection." Causal connection may be proved through direct or circumstantial evidence. Direct evidence (such as a statement by the employer that he took the adverse action because of the protected activity) is rare. The connection between the protected activity and the adverse action is often established by circumstantial evidence. An example of circumstantial evidence showing causation would be the following situation: an employee was observed by management speaking with a government investigator about a supervisor's racial harassment of a coworker. Despite a past work history in which she had received outstanding evaluations each year, she was fired the next day. The circumstances (the employee's participation in the investigation, her excellent work history, and the timing of the two events) could prove that retaliation had taken place.

The employee must show that the employer was aware of the protected activity. If the adverse action takes place soon after the employer learns of the protected activity, the timing of the two events may lead to a logical conclusion that the adverse action was taken in response to the protected activity; as a matter of law, the two events generally *must* be close in time to lead to a conclusion that retaliation occurred. (*Clark County School District v. Breeden* (2001) 532 U.S. 268 (quoting *O'Neal v. Ferguson Construction Co.* (2001) 237 F.3d 1248).) Even if the timing does not by itself *prove* that the protected act caused the retaliation, it may still provide strong evidence that the employer had a retaliatory motive for the adverse action. (*Taylor v. Los Angeles Dept. of Water and Power* (2006) 144 Cal. App.4th 1216.) If the employer's actions over time after the protected activity demonstrate a pattern of conduct that is consistent with retaliatory intent, then it may be possible to prove retaliation despite a long period between the protected activity and the adverse action. (*Wysinger v. Auto. Club of Southern California* (2007) 157 Cal.App.4th 413.) The employer may defend itself by showing that the person who made the decision on the adverse action was unaware of the employee's activity in opposing discrimination. (*Morgan v. Regents of the Univ. of California* (2000) 88 Cal.App.4th 52.) However, if others who substantially contributed to the decision had discriminatory intent, then a decision maker's ignorance does not prevent a conclusion of retaliation. (*Wysinger v. Auto. Club of Southern California* (2007) 157 Cal.App.4th 413.)

For violations of USERRA, the employee must show that the protected activity was a "motivating factor" in the employer's action. (38 U.S. Code section 4311(c)(2)(D); 20 Code of Federal Regulations section 1002.23.)

Even if an employer offers a legitimate, non-discriminatory reason for the adverse employment action, the employee can rebut it by showing that the employer's given reason is a pretext and the actual intent was retaliation. A pretext is an artificial or made up rationale, used to cover up the party's real motivation. If an employee's performance is subjected to stricter standards than other employees, or if the employer appears to search for mistakes (known as "heightened scrutiny") after the employee engages in protected activity, the situation could lead to a finding that retaliation occurred and that the stated reason for the adverse action was a pretext. (*Colarossi v. Coty U.S. Inc.* (2002) 97 Cal.App.4th 1142.)

Enforcement: File a charge with the EEOC or a complaint with the DFEH for retaliation. Violations by federal contractors and subcontractors may be reported by filing a complaint with the OFCCP. For violations of USERRA, a complaint may be filed with VETS. File a lawsuit for compensatory damages. Punitive damages may be available if the employer acted with malice or reckless indifference.

CHAPTER 7 **SAFETY, HEALTH, AND SANITATION**

SAFETY, HEALTH, AND SANITATION

I. SCOPE OF THE CHAPTER

Both California and federal laws require every employer to safeguard workers from illness, injury, and death in the workplace. To that end, the California Occupational Safety and Health Act (Labor Code sections 6300 et seq.), known as Cal-OSHA, and the federal Occupational Safety and Health Act (29 U.S. Code sections 651–678.), known as OSHA or Fed-OSHA, set forth guidelines and standards for workplace safety. Cal-OSHA's standards are stricter than those of Fed-OSHA, and in general Cal-OSHA will govern. The government agencies responsible for enforcing these laws are the California Division of Occupational Safety and Health, commonly referred to as Cal-OSHA or DOSH, and the federal Occupational Safety and Health Administration, or OSHA.

Among other obligations, employers must provide safety training, furnish protective gear and equipment, inform workers about hazardous chemicals or substances in the workplace, keep detailed safety and injury records, provide prompt medical attention when injuries occur, and notify the appropriate government agencies of serious workplace illnesses or injuries.

Employees play a key role in the safety and health of their workplaces. They are often the ones who notify regulatory agencies when unsafe practices or health violations occur. Workers have the right to make anonymous complaints to Cal-OSHA, participate in steps to ensure health and safety, and refuse to work under imminent hazardous conditions. Specific laws protect employees from retaliatory actions by their employers.

II. OBLIGATIONS OF EMPLOYERS

A. EMPLOYER'S DUTY UNDER STATE AND FEDERAL LAW TO SAFEGUARD EMPLOYEE HEALTH AND SAFETY

Both federal and state occupational safety and health laws and agencies establish employer responsibility for safeguarding employee health and safety.

1. State Law

Cal-OSHA creates practices and programs employers must follow to safeguard employee health and safety. Its requirements cover most employees in California who work for private employers and state and local government agencies. It does not cover independent contractors. (But see Chapter 1, section V.A., p. 13, for the definition of an independent contractor. Employers sometimes try to label people who are, in fact, employees as independent contractors in order to avoid employer responsibility.) The vast majority of workers in California are covered by Cal-OSHA.

Cal-OSHA requires that "every employer shall furnish and use safety devices and safeguards, and shall adopt and use practices, means, methods, operations, and processes which are reasonably adequate to render such employment and place of employment safe and healthful." The statute further requires that "Every employer shall do every other thing reasonably necessary to protect the life, safety, and health of employees." (Labor Code section 6401.)

2. Federal Law

Federal OSHA covers employees of the federal government. It requires all employers to ensure their workplaces are "free from recognized hazards" that are likely to cause death or serious physical harm to workers. (29 U.S. Code section 654(a).)

Railway, maritime, and some other workers are covered by statutes specific to their industries, either instead of or in addition to OSHA coverage.

B. RETALIATION PROHIBITED

1. General Provisions

It is unlawful to discharge or discriminate against an employee for any of the following:

- Making any oral or written occupational health or safety complaint to Cal-OSHA, or to any other governmental agency responsible for enforcing employee health and safety laws;
- Making any oral or written occupational health or safety complaint to her employer or to her own representative;
- Initiating, or causing some other person or entity to initiate, any proceeding relating to employee rights under occupational health and safety laws;
- Testifying in any proceeding relating to employee rights under occupational health and safety laws;
- Assisting Cal-OSHA in any investigation or proceeding;
- Participating in an employer-employee occupational health and safety committee established under Cal-OSHA as part of an employer's injury prevention program.
(Labor Code section 6310.)

2. Types of Complaints That Are Protected

It does not matter whether the conditions that led to the complaint actually violate an OSHA law or standard. The complaint is protected as long as it was made in good faith about working conditions or practices that the employee reasonably believes to be unsafe. (*Hentzel v. Singer Co.* (1982) 138 Cal.App.3d 290 [complaint about second-hand smoke]; *Cabesuela v. Browning-Ferris Industries* (1998) 68 Cal.App.4th 101 (complaint about truck driver's extended working hours).)

Also, there are two conditions under which it is unlawful to discharge or suspend an employee or impose a reduction in pay for refusing to perform work. The first is if the performance of that work would result in the violation of any occupational safety or health law (including the "general duty" law that requires all employers to provide a safe workplace), health or safety standard, or Cal-OSHA safety order. The second is if the performance of the work "would create a real and apparent hazard to the employee or his or her fellow employees." (Labor Code section 6311.)

Of course, an employee who refuses to perform work without adequate justification risks discipline or termination. For a worker to be protected under this law, the refusal must be because performance of the work would create a "real and apparent hazard" to the employee or to the employee's coworkers. Unfortunately, California law does not specifically define what constitutes a "real and apparent hazard." However, federal OSHA regulations contain a similar provision protecting employees who refuse to perform work that reasonably appears to pose "a real danger of death or serious injury" where there is not sufficient time to eliminate the danger through a complaint to the employer or to OSHA. (29 United States Code section 660(c)(1), 29 Code of Federal Regulations section 1977.12.) Absent these kinds of conditions (a real and apparent hazard of death or serious injury), it is not likely that Labor Code section 6311 would protect a refusal to work.

Under the federal regulation cited above, an employee is not required to prove that the perceived hazardous condition *actually* violated an occupational health or safety standard. All that must be proved is that the employee had a *reasonable and good faith belief* that performance of the work would pose imminent danger of death or serious injury. (*Marshall v. N.L. Industries, Inc.* (7th Cir. 1980) 618 F.2d 1220.)

Greater protection for refusing to work in unsafe conditions may be available through Labor Code section 1102.5(c). This law is not limited to refusals arising from workplace health and safety concerns. Under this law, an employer may not retaliate against an employee for refusing to participate in an activity that would result in a violation of a state or federal law or regulation. Applying this to the OSHA context, an employee could arguably refuse to perform work that violates an OSHA law or standard without regard to whether the performance of the work would create a "real and apparent hazard" or a "real danger of death or serious injury." However, the applicability of this less restrictive law to refusals to work motivated by occupational health and safety concerns is not fully settled.

3. Proving Unlawful Retaliation

See Chapter 11, section II.E., p. 266.

Enforcement: File a retaliation complaint with the state labor commissioner or a private lawsuit. (See Chapter 11, section II.F., p. 267.) Also, because the federal regulation concerning refusals to perform unsafe work may be more protective than state law, employees with such claims should also file a complaint with federal OSHA. Note however that there is a much shorter time frame for filing with federal OSHA (no later than thirty days following the alleged unlawful retaliation) than for filing with the state labor commissioner (six months). There is no prohibition on filing with both the state and federal enforcement agencies.

C. DUTY TO ESTABLISH AN INJURY AND ILLNESS PREVENTION PROGRAM

Each employer must establish, implement, and maintain an effective, written Injury and Illness Prevention Program (IIPP). The IIPP must include all of the following elements:

- The identity of the person responsible for implementing the IIPP program;
- The employer's system for identifying and evaluating workplace hazards, including a schedule of periodic inspections;
- The employer's procedure for correcting unsafe or unhealthy conditions in a timely manner;
- An occupational health and safety training program designed to instruct workers in general health and safety practices and specific practices regarding hazards particular to each employee's job assignment;
- The employer's system for communicating with workers about occupational health and safety matters, including provisions that encourage workers to report hazards without fear of retaliation;
- The employer's system for ensuring that workers follow safe and healthy work practices, including disciplinary actions to be taken against those who refuse to comply.

(Labor Code section 6401.7(a)(1)–(6).) Also see the California Department of Industrial Relations, Division of Occupational Safety and Health (DOSH), "Guide to Developing Your Workplace Injury and Illness Prevention Program," which outlines the requirements of these programs, at http://www.dir.ca.gov/dosh/dosh_publications/iipp.html.

D. DUTY TO CORRECT UNSAFE CONDITIONS IN A TIMELY MANNER

Each employer must correct unsafe and unhealthy work conditions and practices in a timely manner. (Labor Code section 6401.7(b).) What constitutes timely correction depends on the severity of the hazard. If the condition could cause death, correction must quickly and completely eliminate the condition. If the hazard is much less serious, such as a temporarily wet floor, a warning might be sufficient.

E. DUTY TO PROVIDE SAFETY TRAINING

Each employer must provide adequate safety and health training to the following people:
- All employees at the time the training program is first established;
- New hires after the training program is established;
- Workers reassigned to different jobs;
- All employees in a workplace where a new hazard (such as a toxic or dangerous substance, process, procedure, or equipment) is introduced;
- All employees when a previously unrecognized hazard is discovered.
(Labor Code section 6401.7(c).)
Cal-OSHA also contains the following provisions about Injury and Illness Prevention Programs (IIPPs):
- Procedures for monitoring compliance with the requirement that an employer establish an IIPP;
- Rules on keeping records about IIPPs;

Employers generally must pay for or provide safety devices and safeguards to make jobs safe and healthful.

- Special IIPP requirements for high-hazard and low-hazard industries.
For more information on IIPPs, see Labor Code section 6401.7.

F. DUTY TO KEEP RECORDS OF WORK INJURIES AND ILLNESSES

1. Log of Injuries and Illnesses

Each employer is required to maintain a detailed log of all occupational injuries and illnesses for which an employee lost time from work beyond the day of the injury or illness, or for which an employee required treatment beyond immediate first aid. This is called an OSHA 300 log. Instructions for its completion can be found at http://www.osha.gov/recordkeeping/OSHArecordkeepingforms.pdf. The employer must show the log to an employee who asks to see it. (Labor Code sections 6408, 6409.1.)

Exceptions: An employer with fewer than ten employees in a calendar year does not have to prepare a log, but is still required to submit reports to Cal-OSHA regarding incidents that result in a serious injury or death (see the following section). (Labor Code section 6410; 8 California Code of Regulations section 14300.1.) Public and private employers in certain specified retail, service, finance, insurance, or real estate industries are partially exempted from the requirement to keep a log, but they must report to Cal-OSHA incidents that result in a serious injury or death. (8 California Code of Regulations section 14300.2.)

2. Reports to the Department of Industrial Relations

Within five days after an employer learns about any injury or illness that has, or is alleged to have, "arisen out of and in the course of employment," the employer must send a report to the state Department of Industrial Relations through its Division of Labor Statistics and Research (DLSR). An employer who is insured must file the report with its insurer on the form required by the DLSR. The insurer then sends the report to the DLSR. Each report must include the name and Social Security Number of the injured worker. (Labor Code section 6409.1(a).)

Every injury that arises out of, or in the course of, employment must be included in the report, even if it did not occur at the employee's usual worksite, as long as it did occur in the course of job-related duties. For example, if an employee is hit by a car off-site while picking up work supplies as directed by a supervisor, the employee's injury is considered to have occurred "in the course of employment."

If an employee suffers a serious injury or dies as a result of a work injury or illness, the employer must contact the Division of Occupational Safety and Health by telephone or telegraph within eight hours after the employer should reasonably know of the injury or illness. Depending on the circumstances, the time frame may be extended to twenty-four hours after the employer should reasonably know of the injury or illness. The employer must file an amended report with the Department of Industrial Relations. (Labor Code section 6409.1(b); 8 California Code of Regulations sections 342, 14001.)

It is not sufficient for the employer to rely on the promise to report by a medical care provider (e.g., ambulance), other agency (fire department, etc.), or another employer (such as a controlling employer/general contractor). Each employer has an independent duty to report serious injuries or deaths on the job.

An employer must also send Cal-OSHA a summary of its log of injuries and illnesses, listing the number of each type of injury.

An employer must show its injury and illness reports and summaries to an employee who requests to see them. The logs must be kept and updated for five years. (8 California Code of Regulations section 14300.33.)

G. DUTY TO NOTIFY EMPLOYEES AND KEEP RECORDS OF HARMFUL SUBSTANCES

1. Written Records of Hazardous Substances in the Workplace

Employers (with certain exceptions noted below) must keep accurate records of hazardous substances in the workplace and of any worker exposure to potentially hazardous materials. An employer must notify each employee about the presence of hazardous substances in the workplace even if the employee has not been exposed. The employer must properly label containers holding hazardous substances and must have written procedures to inform workers of both hazardous substances in unlabeled pipes and hazards workers may encounter in performing non-routine tasks. Written procedures must also inform the employees of contractors about hazards they may encounter. (Labor Code sections 142.3(c), 6408(e), 9000–9061; 29 Code of Federal Regulations sections 1910.1200, 1990.101–1990.152.)

Employers are required to fill out Material Safety Data Sheets (MSDSs) listing all hazardous substances present in the workplace, the physical dangers and health hazards of these chemicals, safe handling procedures both in normal situations and emergencies, appropriate engineering controls, and personal protective equipment. Employers must train employees in the proper procedures for dealing with these substances and must advise employees of their rights under Cal-OSHA. The employer must make the MSDSs available to employees, unions, and physicians. (Labor Code sections 6360–6399.7.)

MSDSs are also required by federal law. (29 Code of Federal Regulations section 1910.1200(g).) Advisory guidelines for employers are set forth in Appendix E to 29 Code of Federal Regulations section 1910.1200.

2. Notification and Access to Information

An employer must notify an employee if the employee is (or has been) exposed to potentially toxic materials in concentrations higher than the limits set by occupational health and safety standards. The employee has the right to know how the employer is dealing with any problems involving exposure to hazardous substances. The employer must promptly notify the employee in writing of the problems and inform the employee of the corrective action being taken. (8 California Code of Regulations section 340.2.)

An employee and his representative have the right to see the employer's records of hazardous substances and employee exposures. The employer must make MSDSs readily accessible to the employees in the workplace during each shift. (8 California Code of Regulations section 14300.35; Labor Code sections 6398, 6408(d).)

Employers must retain records of hazardous substances for at least thirty years after the substance is no longer present at the workplace.

Enforcement: File a complaint with Cal-OSHA.

Exceptions: Certain laboratories are partially exempted. (Labor Code section 6386.)

An employer can refuse to show an employee records that would reveal trade secrets but must make the records available to medical personnel if the information is needed.

MSDS requirements do not apply to hazardous waste subject to federal Environmental Protection Agency (EPA) rules; tobacco and related products; wood and wood products; manufactured articles (formed to a specific shape or design) that do not release or cause exposure to a hazardous substance; food, drugs, or cosmetics for personal consumption; retail consumer products incidentally used by workers; retail food sale establishments; and other retail trade establishments. However, all processing and repair work areas in retail food and trade establishments are required to maintain MSDSs and make them available to workers. (29 Code of Federal Regulations section 1910.1200(b)(6).)

H. DUTY TO MONITOR EXPOSURE TO HARMFUL SUBSTANCES

Cal-OSHA standards may require an employer to monitor and measure an employee's exposure to harmful materials in the workplace. The employer must notify the employee and her union before any monitoring is carried out and allow the employee or her representative to observe the monitoring. The employee has the right to see the results of the monitoring and to obtain a copy of the report. (Labor Code section 6408(c); 8 California Code of Regulations sections 340.1, 3204.)

Employers must keep medical records about hazardous substances (like all medical records) for at least thirty years. Employees have a right to see their medical records even after they leave that place of employment. See discussion in Chapter 12.

Enforcement: File a complaint with Cal-OSHA.

I. DUTY TO PROVIDE AND ENSURE USE OF SAFETY EQUIPMENT

In general, an employer must pay for or provide adequate safety devices and safeguards to make jobs safe and healthful. In some cases, the law requires certain equipment to address specific workplace hazards. The employer must require that employees use the equipment effectively. Using protective equipment on the job is a legal requirement placed on the employer, not a matter of personal preference.

Protective devices and clothing may be interchanged among workers only if the gear has been properly cleaned before use by the next person. If protective clothing becomes wet or is washed between shifts, it must be dry before reuse. Clothing saturated with flammable liquids, corrosive substances, irritants, or oxidizing agents must be removed and not worn again until properly cleaned. (8 California Code of Regulations section 3383(c).)

Employees must wear clothing appropriate for the work. They must not wear loose sleeves, shirttails, ties, lapels, cuffs, or other loose clothing or jewelry that can become entangled in moving machinery. (8 California Code of Regulations section 3383(b).)

1. Respiratory Protective Equipment

Employers are required to implement all feasible engineering controls and administrative controls to remove harmful dust, fumes, mists, vapors, or gases at their source.

Examples of accepted engineering control measures include: enclosure or confinement of the operation, general and local ventilation, and substitution of less toxic materials. If emergency protection is needed, or if it is not practical or possible to remove all harmful dust, etc., the employer must supply employees with adequate respiratory equipment. This means that the employer must:

- Provide respirators suitable for the intended purpose;
- Develop and implement a written respiratory protection program that includes:
  o Site-specific instructions about when and how to use respirators;
  o Administration by a suitably trained administrator;
  o An outline of the procedures and schedules for respirator maintenance and inspection, employee training in proper respirator use, and respirator testing procedures.

(8 California Code of Regulations section 5144.)

2. Face and Eye Protection

An employer must provide employees with

proper face and eye protection whenever there is a risk of injuries, such as punctures, abrasions, contusions, or burns from contact with flying particles, hazardous substances, or hazardous projections. Eye protection is also required to shield employees from injurious light rays. Suitable screens or shields are considered adequate if employees are merely near, not directly exposed to, injurious rays. (8 California Code of Regulations section 3382.)

If an employee requires vision correction as well as eye protection, her employer must provide one of the following:

- Safety spectacles with lenses corrected for the individual's vision;
- Safety goggles designed to fit over the individual's eyeglasses; or
- Safety goggles with corrective lenses mounted behind the protective lenses.

(8 California Code of Regulations section 3382.)

In work environments with exposure to harmful materials or light flashes, employees are prohibited from wearing contact lenses unless medically approved precautions have been taken. (8 California Code of Regulations section 3382(c).)

For more information on the design, construction, testing, and use of eye and face protective devices, see 8 California Code of Regulations section 3382.

3. Head Protection

If the nature of an employee's work or characteristics of his worksite expose him to flying or falling objects, electric shocks, or burns, the employer must provide appropriate head protection, such as a helmet or hard hat. (8 California Code of Regulations section 3381.)

4. Body Protection

An employer must protect employees from hazardous or flying substances or objects if their work exposes parts of their bodies to these hazards. (8 California Code of Regulations section 3383(a).)

5. Hand Protection

An employer must provide protective equipment if an individual's job involves excessive exposure of hands to cuts, burns, dangerous chemicals, harmful objects, or radioactive materials. (8 California Code of Regulations section 3384(a).)

While such protection is required for work that involves the listed dangers, gloves or other hand-protection devices must not be worn where there is the risk that they will become entangled in moving machinery or materials. (8 California Code of Regulations section 3384(b).)

Exceptions: In the construction industry, hand-protection devices shall not be required where there is a danger of the devices becoming caught in moving machinery or materials. (8 California Code of Regulations section 1520.) In jobs outside the construction industry, gloves may be used with machinery or equipment provided with a "momentary contact device," meaning a device that requires constant pressure by the operator to function (for instance, the trigger on a drill). (8 California Code of Regulations sections 3384, 3941.)

6. Foot Protection

An employer must furnish appropriate protection if an employee is exposed to foot injuries on the job from the following: electrical hazards; hot, corrosive, or poisonous substances; falling objects; crushing or penetrating actions that may cause injuries; or if the employee is required to work in abnormally wet locations. (8 California Code of Regulations section 3385(a).) The employee must not wear footwear that is defective or inappropriate in a way that could lead to foot injuries. (8 California Code of Regulations section 3385(b).) Safety-toe footwear must comply with standards specified in 8 California Code of Regulations section 3385(c).

J. DUTY TO PROTECT WORKERS FROM ASBESTOS

Before any work that might disturb asbestos-containing material or release asbestos fibers, the owner, contractor, and employer must make a good faith effort to determine whether asbestos is present. The employer must notify Cal-OSHA in advance about any job containing asbestos, the potential asbestos exposure, and the practices to be followed. Any changes must also be reported to Cal-OSHA. (Labor Code sections 6501.5–6501.9; 8 California Code of Regulations section 341.6.)

For all asbestos-handling jobs, representatives of the workers, the unions, the employer, the contractor, and the property owner must hold a safety conference at which they discuss the employer's safety program and all practices and devices to be used for safety. (Labor Code section 6503.) The safety conference must be held before the actual work begins. (Labor Code section 6503.5; 8 California Code of Regulations section 341.11.)

Anyone engaging in work that might release asbestos fibers — work involving 100 square feet or more of material containing asbestos — must register with, and be certified by, Cal-OSHA. (Labor Code sections 6501.5–6508.5, 6325.5; Business and Professions Code section 7058.5; 8 California Code of Regulations section 341.6.) A copy of the registration must be posted at the worksite, along with a sign that can be read from twenty feet away, saying "Danger — Asbestos. Cancer and Lung Hazard. Keep Out." (Labor Code sections 6501.5(c), (d), 6504; 8 California Code of Regulations section 341.10.)

All employees on a job where asbestos is present must be covered by health and Workers' Compensation Insurance. The Workers' Compensation Insurance must pay for all required medical examinations and monitoring. (Labor Code section 6501.5(a)(2); 8 California Code of Regulations section 341.7(b)(2).) A qualified person must conduct air sampling and respirator-fit tests. (Labor Code section 6501.5(b)(5); 8 California Code of Regulations section 341.9(a)(5).)

Enforcement: File a complaint with Cal-OSHA. Violation of these provisions is a crime. (Labor Code section 6436; Business and Professions Code sections 7028.1, 7028.2, 7118.5.)

Exceptions: These rules do not apply to the manufacture of asbestos-containing products, the installation or repair of automotive materials containing asbestos, and certain operations involving installation, repair, maintenance, or nondestructive removal of asbestos cement pipe used outside buildings. (Labor Code section 6501.8.)

K. DUTY TO PROTECT WORKERS AGAINST LEAD HAZARDS

If any lead is used at a workplace, the employer must measure the amount of airborne lead in the work area. This measurement determines the protective actions the employer must take. (8 California Code of Regulations section 5198.)

If air levels exceed what is called the Action Level (AL) — thirty micrograms of lead per cubic meter of air, averaged over an eight-hour workday — the employer must take the following steps:

- Set up a program to monitor the air by taking a sample for several days every six months to measure the typical daily exposure level for each job classification in each work area on each shift.
- After every monitoring, give employees written notice of the resulting estimate of their exposure.
- Provide a medical evaluation for employees before assigning them to a job with exposure at or above the AL.
- If employees are exposed at or above the AL on more than thirty days a year, set up a medical surveillance program that meets the following requirements:
  ○ The medical surveillance must be performed by, or under the supervision of, a licensed physician.
  ○ The employer must give the physician a copy of the lead standard, including the appendices that outline the physician's duties.
  ○ The employer cannot charge employees for the program.

(8 California Code of Regulations section 5198.) Medical surveillance consists of medical evaluation and biological monitoring. The frequency of evaluations and monitoring depends on the exposure level in the air and the lead level in an employee's blood (BLL). If employees reach certain levels of lead in their blood, they must be removed from the job temporarily, for up to eighteen months, while still receiving full salary and benefits.

If air levels exceed what is called the Permissible Exposure Limit (PEL) — fifty micrograms per cubic meter, averaged over an eight-hour workday — the employer must take the following actions:

- Perform air monitoring every three months and inform employees of the exposure results in writing.
- Inform employees in writing about what the employer intends to do about the overexposure.
- Provide the correct respirators free of charge until the PEL is lowered by other means.
- Provide clean clothing and appropriate protective equipment.

- Provide a changing room, lunchroom, and shower facility. The employer must prohibit eating, drinking, smoking, and applying cosmetics in areas where lead levels are greater than the PEL, and must require workers to wash their hands before beginning those activities.

The employer must also furnish clean clothing and appropriate protective equipment when employees work with lead compounds that cause skin and eye irritation. (8 California Code of Regulations section 5198.)

Some requirements differ for construction work. For example, employers must provide additional protections during the assessment of exposure, and a supervisor has to make frequent and regular inspections of the job site. (8 California Code of Regulations section 1532.1.)

Enforcement: File a complaint with Cal-OSHA.

Exceptions: The lead standard does not cover agriculture. For agricultural workers, the main lead regulation is 8 California Code of Regulations section 5155, which states that the PEL is fifty micrograms per cubic meter, averaged over an eight-hour workday.

L. DUTY TO PROTECT EMPLOYEES FROM TOBACCO SMOKE

Smoking is prohibited in all enclosed places of employment in California. (Labor Code section 6404.5(a).) "Enclosed space" includes lobbies, lounges, waiting areas, elevators, stairwells, and restrooms that are a structural part of the building. (Labor Code section 6404.5(b).)

Employers are not required to provide reasonable accommodations or break rooms to smokers. (Labor Code section 6404.5(e).) If an employer does provide a break room for smokers, smoking is permissible there, provided:

- Air is moved directly to the outside (not to other parts of the building) by an exhaust fan.
- The employer complies with current ventilation or air filtration standards adopted by the Occupational Safety and Health Standards Board or the federal Environmental Protection Agency.
- The smoking room is located in a non-work area where no one, as part of his work responsibilities, is required to enter.

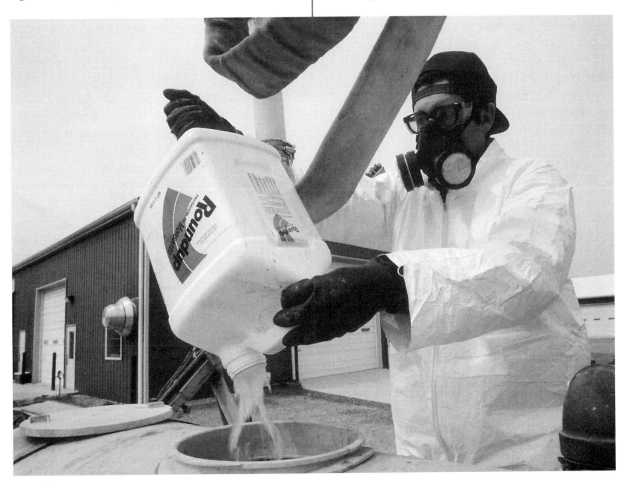

- There are sufficient nonsmoking break rooms to accommodate nonsmokers. (Labor Code section 6404.5(d)(13).)

Exceptions: It is permissible to require employees to enter smoking break rooms to perform custodial or maintenance work while the rooms are unoccupied. (Labor Code section 6404.5(d)(13)(C).)

Employers with five or fewer employees (whether full- or part-time) may permit smoking if all the following conditions are met:

- The smoking area is not accessible to minors.
- All employees who enter the smoking area consent to permit smoking.
- No employee is required or coerced to work in a smoking area.
- Air from the smoking area is exhausted to the outside, not other parts of the building.
- The employer complies with federally established ventilation and filtration standards. (Labor Code section 6404.5(d)(14).)

Limited exceptions to the ban on smoking also exist for some guest rooms and conference rooms in hotels. (Labor Code section 6404.5(d)(1)-(3).) Smoking is allowed in retail or wholesale tobacco shops and private smokers' lounges. (Labor Code section 6404.5(d)(4).) Cabs of motor trucks as defined in Vehicle Code section 410 or truck tractors as defined by Vehicle Code section 655 are also exceptions to the ban on smoking in workplaces as long as no nonsmoking employees are present. (Labor Code section 6404.5(d)(5).) Smoking is also permissible in warehouse facilities with more than 100,000 square feet of total floor space and twenty or fewer full-time employees, except for space used for offices. (Labor Code section 6404.5(d)(6).)

Exceptions also are made for theatrical production sites where smoking is an integral part of the story being produced; medical research sites where smoking is integral to the research or treatment being conducted; private residences except for ones licensed as family daycare homes during the hours of operation and in areas where children are present; and patient smoking areas in long-term healthcare facilities, as defined in Health and Safety Code section 1418. (Labor Code section 6404.5(d)(9)-(12).)

M. DUTY TO PROVIDE MEDICAL SERVICES AND FIRST AID

If an employee is injured on the job, her employer must provide access to medical services and first aid, including the following:

- Medical personnel who are readily available for advice and consultation on matters of industrial health and injury;
- If there is no infirmary, clinic, or hospital close to the workplace, someone at the workplace to provide first aid. That person must receive first-aid training equal to that provided by the American Red Cross or the Mining Enforcement and Safety Administration;
- First-aid materials approved by the consulting physician, and kept in sanitary and usable condition, readily available for workers on every job. Materials must be inspected frequently and replenished as needed;
- In any workplace where an employee's eyes or body may be exposed to a corrosive material, facilities within the work area for immediately and quickly flushing or drenching the employee's eyes and body;
- Stretchers and blankets, or other adequate warm coverings, unless ambulance service is available within thirty minutes under normal conditions;
- At isolated work locations, means of providing prompt medical attention in case of serious injuries. The employer may provide on-site medical facilities, proper equipment to promptly transport the injured person to a doctor, or a telephone system to contact a doctor, or the employer may use any combination of

Employers must provide all workers with reasonable access to clean, sanitary toilet facilities.

these methods to avoid unnecessary delay in treatment.

(8 California Code of Regulations section 3400.) Note that Labor Code section 2440 explicitly adopts the provisions about medical services and first aid enacted in fed-OSHA.

N. DUTY TO PROVIDE CLEAN TOILET FACILITIES

Employers must provide all workers with reasonable access to clean, sanitary toilet facilities. (8 California Code of Regulations sections 3364, 3365; Health and Safety Code section 5416.) To meet the requirement, the facilities must not have overflow from any toilet or drain, protruding nails, splinters, loose boards, or unnecessary holes or openings. (8 California Code of Regulations section 3362.) Refuse and garbage must be removed often enough to maintain proper sanitation. (8 California Code of Regulations section 3362.) The law also requires the following:

- Each toilet must occupy a separate compartment with a door that locks from the inside.
- The doors and walls or partitions must ensure privacy.
- Sinks or washing facilities must be equipped with running water, soap or another suitable cleansing agent, and clean individual hand towels or warm-air blowers, and each toilet stall must have an adequate supply of toilet paper.
- Toilets must be accessible at all times and, where possible, located within 200 feet of regular worksites.
- In workplaces with four or fewer workers, one toilet facility is adequate, provided it can be locked from the inside.
- In workplaces with five or more workers and workers of both sexes, there must be at least two separate toilets plainly designated by sex. (Labor Code section 2350.)
- Toilet facilities for both sexes must be comparable and adequate.
- The employer is not allowed to discriminate against a member of one sex in employment or work assignment decisions based on the need to provide separate toilet facilities.
- Drinking fountains, food and beverage storage areas, and eating and drinking facilities cannot be located in toilet rooms; no beverages or food may be consumed in toilet rooms.

- Where showers are required, the employer must provide a separate shower room for each sex unless there are fewer than five workers, in which case one shower room may be used by both sexes, if it can be locked from inside.
- Where showers are required, the showers must have hot and cold water, and the employer must provide an appropriate cleansing agent and individual clean towels.

(8 California Code of Regulations sections 3362–3366.)

O. DUTY TO PROVIDE PRIVATE CHANGING ROOMS

If a job requires that an employee change into work clothing (for example, a uniform or protective gear), the employer must provide a room or space for changing. (8 California Code of Regulations section 3367.) The changing room must meet the following standards:

- It must be reasonably private and comfortable.
- It must be separate from toilet rooms.
- It must be kept clean.
- It must provide a storage place for each employee to keep street clothes and a separate storage place for the protective clothing.

P. DUTY TO PROVIDE PURE DRINKING WATER

Employers must provide employees with free, fresh, pure drinking water that is safe for human consumption. All sources of drinking water must be maintained in a clean and sanitary condition. Employees must be given access to water at reasonable and convenient times and places. Employers cannot charge employees for water or require that they provide their own drinking water. An employer who violates this law can be fined $50 to $200 for each violation or be imprisoned for up to thirty days or both. (Labor Code section 2441.)

Additional regulations govern water used for drinking, washing, bathing, cooking, and food preparation:

- Drinking fountains and portable drinking water dispensers must not be located in toilet rooms.
- Portable drinking water dispensers must be equipped with a faucet or fountain. The

dispensers must be designed, constructed, and serviced so that they can be tightly closed and maintained in sanitary condition. The contents of the dispensers must be clearly marked.

- Drinking water must not be dipped or poured from containers, such as barrels, pails, or tanks, whether or not the container has a fitted cover.

- More than one person must not drink from or use a particular cup, glass, or other vessel. It is common at agricultural worksites to see workers sharing the same drinking glass, which is not properly washed after each use. Sharing drinking vessels in this way is a clear violation of the law.

- Water that is not safe for human consumption must not be used for drinking, washing, bathing, washing clothing, cooking, washing food, washing cooking or eating utensils, washing food-preparation or food-processing premises, or washing other personal service rooms.

- Outlets for water that is not safe to drink (for example, water for industrial or fire-fighting purposes) must be labeled in a manner understandable to all employees to indicate that the water is unsafe and cannot be used for drinking, washing, cooking, or other personal service purposes.

- Nonpotable (unsafe) water systems and systems carrying any other nonpotable substances must be installed in a manner that prevents backflow or back-siphonage into a potable (drinkable) water system.
(8 California Code of Regulations section 3363.)

Q. DUTY TO PREVENT HEAT ILLNESS

Heat illness is a serious medical condition that results from the body's inability to cope with high temperatures. It can include heat cramps, heat exhaustion, dizziness, fainting, and heat stroke, with symptoms of unconsciousness, confusion, convulsion, fast heart rate, and difficulty breathing. Employers with outdoor places of employment must take certain steps to prevent heat illness in their employees. Although "outdoor" is not defined in the Cal-OSHA standards, DOSH currently considers extended periods of time in non-air-conditioned vehicles to be outdoor work.

If no continuous supply of drinking water is available, employers must provide enough water at the beginning of the work shift for each employee to have one quart an hour for the entire shift. Employers may begin the shift with smaller quantities of water if they can replenish the water during the shift to provide one quart or more an hour to each employee. Employees should be encouraged to drink water frequently.

Employees who are suffering from heat illness, or who need a recovery period to prevent heat illness, must be allowed to spend at least five minutes in a shaded area that is either open to the air or provided with ventilation or cooling. Such access to shade must be allowed at all times. Shade means blockage of direct sunlight. Canopies, umbrellas, and other temporary structures or devices can provide shade. Shade is adequate only if it allows the body to cool. A car sitting in the sun, for example, is not adequate unless the air conditioning is running. Employers not in the agricultural industry may provide other cooling measures (such as misting machines) instead of shade if the employer can demonstrate the measure is at least as effective in allowing employees to cool.

Employers must provide training to employees on heat illness, including:

- Environmental risk factors (working conditions such as air temperature, relative humidity, heat from the sun and other sources, workload severity and duration, protective clothing, and personal protective equipment) and personal risk factors (characteristics of the employee such as age, degree of acclimatization, health, water consumption, alcohol consumption, caffeine consumption, and use of medications that affect the body's responses to heat);

- The employer's procedures for complying with the law;

- The importance of frequently drinking small quantities of water (up to one quart per hour) when the work environment is hot and employees are likely to be sweating more than usual;

- The importance of acclimatization, that is, the temporary adaptation of the body to work in the heat that occurs gradually. Acclimatization peaks in most people within four to fourteen days of regular work for at least two hours a day in the heat;

- The different types of heat illness and the common signs and symptoms;

- The importance of immediately reporting, to the employer or supervisor, symptoms or signs of heat illness in the employee or coworkers;

- The employer's procedures for responding to symptoms of heat illness, including emergency services if needed;
- The employer's procedures for contacting emergency medical services, and, if necessary, for transporting employees to a point where they can be reached by emergency medical help;
- The employer's procedures for ensuring that emergency responders will receive clear and precise directions to the worksite in case of an emergency.

Supervisors must be trained on the issues listed above. They must also be trained to implement the requirements of the law and the procedures to follow when an employee exhibits symptoms of heat illness, including emergency response procedures.

The employer's procedures must be in writing and available to employees upon request. (8 California Code of Regulations section 3395.)

Also see the DOSH website on precautions against heat illness at http://www.dir.ca.gov/ DOSH/HeatIllnessInfo.html.

R. DUTY TO ABIDE BY POSTED HAZARD AND PESTICIDE RESTRICTIONS

Cal-OSHA can prohibit ("red tag") entry into a dangerous place of employment or prohibit use of dangerous equipment as "an imminent hazard." (Labor Code sections 6323–6327.5; Food and Agricultural Code section 12978.) The employer must then post a notice of this prohibition at the work site or attach it to the equipment. It is a crime to remove this notice or to enter the place or use the equipment until the hazard is corrected and deemed safe. (Labor Code sections 6406–6407.)

It is a crime for anyone to order an employee to enter an area posted with a pesticide warning in violation of specific worker-safety regulations. (Food and Agricultural Code section 12985.)

Enforcement: File a complaint with Cal-OSHA; file a civil action. Violation may be punishable by a year in jail and a $1,000 fine.

Exceptions: Employees may enter a prohibited place in order to fix the hazard. Farm workers may enter posted fields under certain limited conditions. (3 California Code of Regulations sections 6770 – 6776.)

S. DUTY TO TAKE APPROPRIATE STEPS TO PROTECT EMPLOYEES FROM WORKPLACE VIOLENCE

As part of an employer's duty to maintain a safe and healthy workplace, the employer must take reasonable steps to deal with workplace violence. Employees have the right to expect the employer to adopt appropriate safeguards against workplace violence and to take proper steps in response to incidents or threats of violence on the job. Employees who engage in threats or violent behavior related to the workplace may face serious consequences.

1. High-Risk Situations

Although any place of employment can experience workplace violence, certain industries and types of jobs are more vulnerable to this problem.

a. Industries

Employees in the following industries are at the greatest risk of experiencing workplace violence: transportation workers (especially taxi drivers), healthcare employees (particularly those working in mental hospitals, nursing homes, and emergency rooms), security personnel (like police officers and security guards), social service workers, those employed in the retail trade (especially convenience store cashiers), and teachers.

b. Risk Factors

The following factors increase the risk of encountering violence on the job:

- Working with the public;
- Working with unstable or volatile persons;
- Handling money, valuables, or prescription drugs;
- Working where alcohol is served;
- Carrying out enforcement or inspection duties;
- Working late at night;
- Working alone, in small numbers, or in isolated or low-traffic locations;
- Working in high-crime areas;
- Having a mobile workplace (such as a taxicab or bus) or reporting to various sites during a work day.

c. Most-Common Types of Problems

Although the most common perception of

workplace violence involves violent acts by workers or former workers, in fact, these scenarios account for less that 15 percent of documented incidents of workplace violence. Seventy-five percent of documented incidents of workplace violence are related to robberies or similar crimes. Five percent of the violent incidents on the job are carried out by clients or customers. Four percent are carried out by acquaintances or other persons connected to employees (this category includes domestic violence carried out at work). Therefore, an approach to protection from workplace violence that is focused simply on "zero tolerance" for violence among employees does not address the problem.

2. Prevention Strategies

a. Workplace Violence Prevention Programs

Workplace violence prevention programs may be included within the Injury and Illness Prevention Programs required in all workplaces (see section II.B., p. 190), or they may stand alone. The most effective programs accomplish the following:

- Set clear standards for what will be considered violent behavior;
- Establish clear procedures for reporting and assessing risks or problems;
- Guarantee no retaliation for those who report such problems;
- Establish clear lines of authority and follow-up procedures during violent incidents;
- Provide employment assistance programs and worker training in defusing potentially violent situations and dealing with anger.

The DOSH website provides further guidance on workplace violence prevention: http://www.dir.ca.gov/dosh/dosh_publications/iipsecurity.html.

b. Workplace Measures to Promote Security
i. *Environmental Design Measures*

Environmental design features can be incorporated into the physical design of the workplace to promote security. Some of the most common include:

- Locked drop box safes for money;
- Signs saying personnel do not carry, or have access to, cash;
- High, wide counters or other barriers;
- Closed circuit cameras;
- Alarms or panic buttons;
- Card key access only to the workplace;
- Doors that open from the inside, even when locked from the outside.

ii. *Administrative Measures*

Administrative measures that protect against workplace violence can be established by management or by collective bargaining. These actions deal with the way work is done, and include the following examples:

- Adjust staffing levels so that employees are not on duty alone.
- Develop practices that protect workers during especially vulnerable times of day. (Common practices include using backup during closing, having guards present during cash transfers, varying the time of cash pickups, and monitoring hallways after school while teachers are working alone in their classrooms.).
- Establish "buddy systems" for workers in isolated locations (for example, regular, frequent check-in procedures).
- Create regular reporting procedures for workers traveling in the field, so that someone knows where they were last if they do not check in.
- Provide escort services to parking lots after dark.

iii. *Policies and Behavioral Measures*

Steps should be taken to ensure that workers feel comfortable reporting problems and that there is an appropriate response to incidents, risks, or threats of workplace violence. For example:

- Institute training on violence prevention.
- Develop, implement, and publicize a system by which threats will be documented, investigated, and assessed for corrective action.
- Have a clear policy regarding worker threats.
- Develop and follow a policy of non-retaliation for reporting instances or potential instances of workplace violence.
- Develop and publicize a clear policy about how threats of potential violence will be communicated to employees.
- Create a clear policy about who makes decisions regarding evacuation, lock-down, etc., in the event of an emergency, and designate a backup person or procedure.
- Provide a confidential Employee Assistance Program (EAP) for employees experiencing issues related to stress, anger management, domestic violence, etc.

iv. *Methods of Getting the Employer to Listen to Employee Concerns and Requests*

In defining effective workplace violence prevention strategies, there are steps that workers can take to ensure that employers take their concerns seriously and include workers' input in developing policies. Employees can do the following:

- Check to see if the employer has an Injury and Illness Prevention Plan, or a Workplace Violence Prevention Plan, and if it is being followed.

- If the workplace has a health and safety committee, get on the agenda and raise concerns, ask the committee to take action, or make recommendations.

- Meet with the employer in groups (or at least in a team of two) so that efforts are considered "concerted activity" and protected by labor law (see Chapter 9, section III.A., p. 228, for more information). The law protects workers represented by unions and also those who are not represented by unions when they engage in concerted action regarding workplace issues. (29 U.S. Code section 157; Labor Code section 923.)

- Request a meeting with the employer to deal with employee concerns, and come to the meeting with a list of suggested improvements.

- Document in writing any complaints, concerns, requests for meetings, and reports of incidents or threats.

Enforcement: Workers represented by a union may file grievances over violations of contract guarantees to promote a safe and healthy workplace. Workers covered by Cal-OSHA (almost all workers except those employed by the federal government) may file a complaint with the Division of Occupational Safety and Health. Federal employees may file a complaint with federal OSHA. Employees injured at work most likely are entitled to Workers' Compensation benefits (see Chapter 8).

3. Issues for Workers Accused of Workplace Violence

Incidents and threats of violent behavior in the workplace can have extremely serious repercussions. Workers should be cautious about making statements, either in anger or in jest, which could be considered threats. An employer with a "zero tolerance" workplace violence policy potentially could stretch the definition of what should be considered violent behavior and use such statements to impose discipline against employees engaged in a heated argument.

If an employee is accused of workplace violence, these are the most important steps to take:

- If there was provocation (for instance, verbal abuse, serious threats, unauthorized touching, etc.), the worker should document the situation by taking notes as soon as possible after the event, describing exactly what happened, and signing and dating the notes. The worker should describe what occurred to a trusted friend or ally.

- If there are witnesses the accused worker believes will report the facts in a helpful manner, the worker should get their names and phone numbers (home or cell phone, if possible). However, the accused should be cautious about making direct contact with witnesses, unless he is sure that this person is on his side. The worker should be careful not to do anything that could be construed as pressuring witnesses.

- The accused worker should make a list of witnesses likely to provide evidence against him. This list should be turned over to an advocate, union representative, or the accused worker's attorney if formal representation becomes necessary.

- If the accused worker is called into a meeting to discuss the event, he should ask that a union representative, attorney, coworker, or other advocate be present. (See Chapter 1, section II.A., p. 9, for more information on the right, in union settings, to have a representative present at investigatory meetings that might result in discipline.)

- The accused worker should be cautious about discussing the incident with others in the workplace. He should not make any admissions of improper behavior.

- If it appears that there will be consequences (that is, a reprimand, discipline, or termination), the accused worker should get representation. He should contact the union representative or an attorney specializing in these matters.

Employees accused of workplace violence should be extremely cautious regarding all future actions. Threats or behavior that may be construed as violent can lead to serious repercussions, including job loss.

CHAPTER 8 **WORKERS' COMPENSATION**

WORKERS' COMPENSATION

I. SCOPE OF THE CHAPTER

The Workers' Compensation system was set up to pay benefits to employees for work-related injuries or illnesses. Employers are required to carry Workers' Compensation Insurance. Employees with work-related injuries or illnesses need to file a claim for compensation, and probably should seek the advice of an attorney who specializes in Workers' Compensation. The compensation program is designed to support individuals with work-related illnesses and injuries and their dependents when they cannot work, pay for medical treatment, and, in some cases, provide limited retraining benefits. However, Workers' Compensation benefits are generally much lower than the injured worker's lost earnings.

The California Division of Workers' Compensation has an Information and Assistance Unit that provides basic information and advice, free of charge, about the rights and options of injured workers who are not represented by attorneys. Information and Assistance officers can also help injured workers fill out forms necessary to make claims and get hearings in their cases. Telephone interpretation services will be arranged where necessary for workers who do not speak English. Many offices can also provide a list of Workers' Compensation lawyers in the area, including those who speak languages other than English. Information and Assistance officers typically have a large workload, so it is important for injured workers to be persistent in making contact. There is an Information and Assistance Unit office wherever there is an office of the Workers' Compensation Appeals Board. The telephone numbers and addresses of all the Information and Assistance offices as well as other useful information can be obtained at the Information and Assistance Unit website: http://www.dir.ca.gov/dwc/IandA.html.

All employers in California are required to have Workers' Compensation Insurance, except that some large employers are allowed to be self-insured. When the term "claims administrator" is used in this chapter, it can refer either to an insurance company that has insured the employer or to the employer, if it is self-insured.

II. BASIC ELEMENTS OF THE WORKERS' COMPENSATION SYSTEM

A. PURPOSES

The Workers' Compensation laws were enacted to make sure workers who have work-related illnesses or injuries:
- Receive support payments while they are unable to work;
- Receive medical treatment;
- Are compensated for permanent disabilities;
- Receive some assistance in paying for retraining, if necessary (although recent changes in the law have greatly curtailed retraining benefits);
- Are not discriminated against by employers or employers' insurers due to the injury;
- Have some insurance coverage to provide compensation to dependents if they die as a result of a work-related illness or injury.

B. WORK-RELATED INJURIES COVERED

Injuries that arise out of, and in the course of, employment are covered by the Workers' Compensation laws. Normally, a work-related injury occurs at the job site. However, if the injury occurs elsewhere but occurs in the course of employment, the worker's injury may still be considered work-related and may still be covered. (Labor Code section 3208.)

1. Type of Work-Related Injuries

Work-related injuries are divided into three types, based on how they occur:
- Specific injuries, which occur as the result of one incident or exposure that causes a disability or need for medical treatment. (Example: A broken leg caused by a fall on the job.)
- Cumulative injuries, which occur as the result of repetitive mental or physical trauma extending over a period of time, the combined effect of which causes a disability or need for medical treatment. (Example: Carpal tunnel syndrome in the wrists, caused by repetitive motion such as typing.)
- Occupational injuries, which occur as a result of harmful workplace exposures over a period of time. (Example: Exposure to asbestos causing asbestosis and lung cancer.)
(Labor Code section 3208.1.)

When a prior injury or non-industrial medical condition is aggravated by something that occurs on the job, the worker may be eligible for Workers' Compensation. Work exposures need only be a contributing cause of symptoms or disability. Examples of situations in which conditions on the job aggravate (or "light up") prior conditions are when repetitive lifting aggravates pre-existing non-industrial arthritis, resulting in symptoms, disability, or the need for medical treatment; or when exposure to chemicals in the workplace results in the flaring up of non-industrial asthma. The employer may have to pay some medical costs and some benefits for the portion of the disability that is attributed to the job. (Labor Code sections 4663, 4664.)

2. Special Requirements in Claims for Psychiatric Injuries

A worker can be compensated for a psychiatric or emotional injury if it results in a mental disorder causing a need for medical treatment or a disability. Proving psychiatric injury is more difficult and complicated than proving physical injury. The injury must be caused by the actual events of employment, such as being harassed by a supervisor or being threatened by a customer. The injury might also be a mental disorder like depression resulting from the effects of a physical workplace injury. For example, the chronic pain and limitations and financial hardship caused by a back injury could cause depression, which is a mental disorder.

The worker must prove that the psychiatric injury (1) is a mental disorder, which was (2) caused by the actual events of the employment, and that (3) the employment is the main cause of the injury. For example, if the worker has been under great emotional stress because of job duties but also has been subject to stress at home because of family problems, the work stress has to be the predominant or main cause of the mental disorder for the disorder to be compensable. The employer can avoid having to pay any compensation for the psychiatric injury if the injury was substantially caused by a good faith, lawful, and non-discriminatory personnel action.

The worker must have at least six months of employment with the employer to succeed in a psychiatric injury claim unless the injury was caused by a sudden and extraordinary employment condition. For example, a robbery or physical attack in the workplace would be considered a sudden and extraordinary employment condition that would justify a worker with less than six months of employment claiming psychiatric injury. (Labor Code section 3208.3.)

If a worker claims a psychiatric injury, either as a result of work-caused emotional stress or because of the effects of a physical injury, the claims administrator is allowed to ask the worker questions at a deposition and at a hearing about all the other possible non-work-related causes of the mental disorder, such past and present family problems.

Enforcement: File with the Workers' Compensation Appeals Board.

C. WORKERS AND VOLUNTEERS WHO ARE NOT COVERED

The following workers and volunteers are excluded from coverage under the California Workers' Compensation Program:

- Any person employed by a parent, spouse, or child (Labor Code section 3352(a));
- Domestic workers or babysitters who were employed for fewer than fifty-two hours or who earned less than $100 in wages from their employer during the ninety days preceding a specific injury or the date of a cumulative injury or occupational disease (Labor Code section 3352(h));
- People participating in, or officiating at, amateur sporting events and people working for religious, charitable, or relief organizations who receive only aid or sustenance generally, but these people should check with an attorney or with the Information and Assistance office for advice;
- Federal employees; they are covered by the Federal Employees' Compensation Act. (5 U.S. Code sections 8101– 8122; 20 Code of Federal Regulations part 10) (see the website at http://www.doi.gov/hrm/pmanager/er11e.html);
- Civilian employees of military bases and military exchange posts; they are covered by the statutes covering federal employees;
- Employees of tribal casinos and other American Indian tribal enterprises, but tribes may have their own Workers' Compensation systems;
- Workers subject to Alternative Dispute Resolution agreements between unions and employer groups may be covered by special systems. These are called "carve outs" and operate primarily in the building trades. They require injured workers to pursue a Workers' Compensation claim through a special mediator (called an ombudsman) and arbitration, instead of filing a claim with the California Workers' Compensation system. An injured worker subject to a carve-out agreement should be able to get help through her union. (Labor Code section 3201.5.)

D. WHO QUALIFIES AS AN EMPLOYER?

The definition of employer is very broad in the Workers' Compensation system. (Labor Code section 3300.) The law makes a presumption that a person was the "employee" of anyone for whom he did work or rendered services unless he performed the services as an independent contractor. (Labor Code sections 3357, 3351.) The employer has the burden of proving that an individual who did work was not an employee, for example by showing that the worker was an independent contractor. (Labor Code section 5705.)

On a given job a worker can have more than one employer. For example, if an employee works for one person who then has him do work for another person, both may be his employer. If both of them control the work, then both are liable for any job-related injury or illness. (Labor Code section 3300.)

If an employer hires a worker to work for another person, even though the worker never knows of that other person, both the original employer and the other person may be liable for any work-related injuries or illnesses. (Labor Code section 3300.)

E. INDEPENDENT CONTRACTORS OR ALLEGED INDEPENDENT CONTRACTORS

If a person injured while working for someone else is an independent contractor, then the injured worker is not entitled to Workers' Compensation benefits. Examples of independent contractors are professionals such as lawyers and accountants who hold themselves out as having a business. Another common example is a licensed building contractor who contracts to remodel an office building. But sometimes, employers attempt to make a worker seem like an independent contractor so that the employer can avoid having to buy Workers' Compensation Insurance and pay employer taxes, such as Social Security taxes. The Workers' Compensation Appeals Board may decide, based on the facts, that an injured worker is actually an employee under the law and that the employer is liable for Workers' Compensation benefits despite the fact that the employer labeled the injured worker an independent contractor. Even if an employee signed a contract or agreement giving up employee rights to Workers' Compensation or stating that she is an "independent contractor," she still has rights guaranteed by law to injured workers if the independent contractor designation was incorrect. Whether a worker is an employee entitled to benefits or an independent contractor is a complicated legal question. An injured worker who is being called an independent contractor should get legal advice or consult with the Information and Assistance Unit. (Labor Code sections 3706–3709.5, 5001.) See Chapter 1 for more information on independent contractors. It is also worth noting that a person who is actually an independent contractor is not bound by Workers' Compensation rules and may sue for negligence in court.

III. EMPLOYEES' RIGHTS

A. RIGHT TO NOTICE OF WORKERS' COMPENSATION COVERAGE, RIGHTS, AND BENEFITS

Employers are required to post a notice in the workplace (which should also be in Spanish if there are Spanish-speaking workers) stating to whom workplace injuries should be reported, providing the name and location of the claims administrator for Workers' Compensation claims (usually an insurance company), and stating that injured workers may be entitled to medical treatment and compensation benefits. Employers are also required to provide a similar notice to new employees. Posted notices should also indicate how to get emergency treatment if needed. (8 California Code of Regulations, sections 9880, 9881.)

Enforcement: Complaints about the lack of notice to new employees or notice posted in the workplace should be made to the California labor commissioner.

B. RIGHT TO HIRE AN ATTORNEY

Workers injured on the job have the right to be represented by an attorney during the Workers' Compensation claim and appeals process. Because Workers' Compensation is a very specialized area of the law, it is important to hire an attorney who specializes in it. Consult the union or county bar association for recommendations. Also, lists of Workers' Compensation attorneys can be obtained from an Information and Assistance office.

Attorney's fees for Workers' Compensation cases are strictly regulated by the law. Any fee arrangement made with an attorney will have to be approved by a Workers' Compensation judge. (Labor Code section 4906.) Fees are generally taken from awards or settlements, and they are generally no more than 15 percent of the award or settlement. Fees from settlements must be approved by a Workers' Compensation judge. The judge will set the fee if the case is not settled and the judge issues a decision. Clients are not required to pay money in advance for attorney representation; if the client does not win the case, the attorney generally gets no fee. At the initial consultation, the attorney must give the client a "disclosure form" that explains the usual range of approved attorney's fees. The attorney must also explain the worker's right to apply for Workers' Compensation without an attorney.

It can be difficult to get representation from a Workers' Compensation attorney, in part because Workers' Compensation benefits (and attorney's fees) were greatly reduced by a law passed on 2004. Therefore, injured workers should be prepared to contact many attorneys. If an injured worker cannot get an attorney, the Information and Assistance Unit (see the information in section I, above) can usually help.

Enforcement: Complain to the Information and Assistance Unit or to a Workers' Compensation judge if it is believed that the fee arrangement with an attorney is not proper.

C. RIGHT TO MEDICAL TREATMENT

1. Right to Medical Care for Work-Related Injuries and Illnesses

Injured workers must have access to emergency medical services. (8 California Code of Regulations section 3400.) The employer must pay for all diagnosis and treatment connected with a work-related illness or injury. This right cannot be limited or waived by any agreement or union contract. (Labor Code section 4600.)

Enforcement: File an Application for Adjudication of Claim with the Workers' Compensation Appeals Board.

2. If the Employer Fails to Provide Adequate Medical Treatment

Where the employer fails or refuses to provide medical treatment or the treatment offered is clearly inadequate, the worker can try to find another doctor who will treat her. This is called self-procured medical treatment. The worker can then file a Workers' Compensation claim, if one has not previously been filed, and ask a Workers' Compensation judge to order that the employer pay the doctor's bills and reimburse the worker for out-of-pocket costs. The worker has the burden of proving that the self-procured treatment was necessary to cure or relieve the worker from the effects of the work-related injury. The medical provider who provided the self-procured treatment should also file a lien claim to obtain payment. (Labor Code 4600(a).)

If an employer or an insurance company has a medical provider network, the employer would only have to pay for the treatment if the worker got the treatment from a doctor in the network. But the worker could get treatment elsewhere at the worker's own expense or through other insurance. If the employer fails to give proper notice to the worker about the requirement that the worker pick a doctor from the network, or if the network doctors refuse to treat the worker (as they often do), then the worker can find a doctor outside the network to treat her, and a Workers' Compensation judge can be asked to order the employer to pay for the treatment. But, it is hard to find doctors who will treat a worker without advance authorization from the employer. The worker usually will have to get a Workers' Compensation judge to order the employer to pay for such self-procured treatment.

3. Right to Select One's Own Healthcare Provider

a. Designating a Personal Doctor Prior to Injury or Illness

A worker has the right to predesignate a private physician or medical group to treat the worker in the event that he suffers an industrial injury. The private physician must agree to the arrangement. Predesignation of a private physician may be a good idea where a worker has a good private physician through private insurance or a health maintenance organization because, otherwise, the worker may have to get treated for a work injury by physicians chosen by the claims administrator or the worker would be limited to picking a physician in a medical provider network. The employer must notify employees of this right and provide a form for filing the notice. The notice should state that the worker has a personal healthcare provider whom he intends to see in the event of a work-related injury. If the employer fails to provide such a notice, the worker can download the state form from the Internet (at http://www.dir.ca.gov/dwc, click on "Find a Form," scroll down to the section titled "Pre-Designation of Personal Physician" and click on form DWC 9783). Use of the form is optional. A worker can also file a letter containing the following information:

- Name of the employer;
- Statement that if the worker is hurt on the job, he wishes to receive treatment by his personal physician, and include the doctor's name, address, and phone number;

- Worker's name, signature, and date.

A worker can also obtain information as to how to predesignate a treating physician by contacting the Information and Assistance Unit.

b. Injured Workers' Right to Change Doctors After the Injury

Sometimes treating doctors do not offer treatment that injured workers believe is helping them. Furthermore, sometimes treating doctors report that a worker can go back to work when the worker believes that she cannot do so. Sometimes it is the other way around: the worker thinks she should be able to return to the job, but the treating doctor will not release the worker to return to work. In those situations, or for other reasons, a worker can ask to be treated by a new doctor, chiropractor, or acupuncturist. This request should be made in writing. The employer or insurance company must respond within five working days from the date of the request. In the case of a serious injury or illness, the employee is also entitled to a consulting doctor, chiropractor, or acupuncturist (to get, for instance, a second opinion), with the cost to be covered by the employer or the employer's Workers' Compensation insurance policy. (Labor Code section 4601(a).)

For more detailed information on changing doctors, see Chapter 3 of "Workers' Compensation in California, A Guide for Injured Workers" at http://www.lohp.org/graphics/pdf/WC06-07_engch3.pdf.

4. How to Get the Quickest Results on Treatment Decisions

To help speed up the process of getting a medical recommendation for treatment, an injured worker can do the following:

- Establish a good working relationship with the treating doctor and her office staff.
- Ask them to send the information to the claims administrator as quickly as possible.
- Ask the doctor to explain the reasons for any unusual or significant treatment, like surgery, and to reference any scientifically based medical treatment guidelines (like those of the American College of Occupational and Environmental Medicine) supporting the recommendation. If the recommended treatment does not follow standard medical guidelines, the doctor should explain why.

5. When a Claims Administrator Refuses to Authorize Treatment in Accordance With a Treating Doctor's Recommendation

Sometimes the claims administrator has authorized a treating physician to treat a worker, but refuses to authorize a particular type of treatment that the authorized treating doctor has recommended (for instance, physical therapy, an MRI, medication, or surgery). The medical treatment that an injured worker needs must be described in a medical report written by the worker's treating doctor. When the claims administrator receives the report recommending the treatment, the claims administrator can either authorize the recommended treatment (that is, agree to pay for it by notifying the doctor), or ask a "utilization review" doctor to assess whether or not the recommended treatment is medically appropriate. The utilization review doctor reviews the medical records and may communicate with the treating doctor, but the utilization review doctor does not talk to or examine the worker. The utilization review doctor will write a report, which will be sent to the treating doctor and the injured worker. If the utilization review doctor recommends against the treatment, the worker can then file a claim (if one has not been filed), object to the utilization doctor's denial of the treatment, and request an "expedited trial" before a Workers' Compensation judge on the issue of whether the claims administrator should be ordered to authorize the treatment recommended by the treating doctor. The judge would consider the treating doctor's opinion, the utilization review doctor's opinion, and the worker's testimony in deciding whether to order the treatment authorized.

In addition to medical treatment, injured workers have the right to be examined by an independent doctor called a "qualified medical evaluator" (QME). Therefore, the worker could also obtain a QME examination on the issue of whether the particular treatment recommended by the treating doctor is medically appropriate, but that would likely delay resolving the issue for several months. (For more information on a QME, see section III.C.6., p. 211.) The worker should consult with an Information and Assistance officer or an attorney as soon as possible after treatment has been denied by the utilization review doctor.

The law contains strict time limits for decision making in the utilization review process. If the situation is urgent (involving a serious threat to health) the utilization review doctor's decision regarding treatment must be made within seventy-two hours of the claims administrator's receipt of the information needed to make the decision. If the medical situation is not considered urgent, treatment decisions must be made within five working days of the claims administrator's receipt of the original doctor recommendation. If more information is needed, the time limit for the decision can be extended to fourteen days after receiving the treating doctor's request. The claims administrator must communicate the decision within twenty-four hours of the time it is made. If the claims administrator does not authorize the treatment and fails to arrange for utilization review at all, or if the utilization review report is not timely, then the Workers' Compensation judge can order the claims administrator to authorize the treatment without even considering a utilization review report. (Labor Code section 4610.)

Enforcement: File a request for an "expedited hearing" with the Workers' Compensation Appeals Board.

6. If the Employee Does Not Agree With the Doctor's Recommendations

Injured workers do not have to do what the employer's doctor tells them to do. In that doctor-patient relationship, like any other, the patient must make the final decisions about his health. In any serious case, the injured worker has the right to a second opinion, paid for by the employer. (Labor Code section 4601(a).) See section III.C.2., p. 209, on the right to change doctors.

As discussed directly above, injured workers have the right to be examined by a qualified medical evaluator (QME); employers and insurance carriers also have the right to call for such an exam. A QME examination is for the purpose of getting a medical opinion about disputed medical issues like temporary disability, extent of permanent disability, and need for medical treatment, and even the question of whether an injury, such as a cumulative injury or occupational disease, is work-related. The QME does not provide any medical treatment, but simply writes a report after examining the worker and reviewing all the records to answer the medical questions about the worker's disability and need for treatment. The QME examination is paid for by the insurance carrier. If the worker is

not represented by an attorney, then the worker picks one QME from a list of three supplied by the State of California through the Medical Unit of the Division of Workers' Compensation. If the worker is represented, then the attorney for the worker and the employer try to agree to a neutral and independent examiner, called an Agreed Medical Evaluator (AME).

Either the worker (or the worker's attorney) or the employer can start the process for having a worker examined by a neutral medical examiner (a QME or an AME) by objecting in writing, within thirty days, to a medical finding as to need for treatment or extent of disability. An unrepresented worker can choose the specialty of a QME (for instance, orthopedic surgery, chiropractic medicine, pain medicine) but must do so within ten days. Generally, a worker should try to get the

advice of an Information and Assistance officer as soon as possible after receiving a report from a treating doctor with which the worker disagrees, or consult with a lawyer. (Labor Code sections 4060–4067.)

The medical opinion of the QME or AME becomes evidence submitted to the Workers' Compensation judge, but it is not binding. A judge could decide to follow a treating doctor who has written a report instead of the QME, if the two disagree about medical issues.

To review the process, if an injured worker disagrees with the recommendations of her treating doctor about further medical treatment or disagrees with the opinions of the treating doctor about whether she is temporarily or permanently disabled, she can try to get a new treating doctor (see section III.C.2., p. 209, about changing doctors) and can get a QME evaluation. To get the QME evaluation, the worker must first object to the opinion of the treating doctor in a short letter sent to the claims administrator within thirty days of receiving the treating doctor's report. Injured workers who are not represented by attorneys

should confer with an Information and Assistance officer as soon as possible and at least before selecting a QME from the list.

IV. EMPLOYERS' OBLIGATIONS

A. DUTY TO HAVE WORKERS' COMPENSATION INSURANCE

All California employers must carry Workers' Compensation Insurance — through a private carrier or through the State Compensation Insurance Fund — or be self-insured. The cost of Workers' Compensation Insurance must be paid entirely by the employer, with no contribution from the employee. Failure to obtain Workers' Compensation Insurance or a certificate of consent to self-insure is a misdemeanor and could result in employer liability. (Labor Code sections 3700, 3700.5, 3706–3707.)

California also has an Uninsured Employers Benefit Trust Fund to make sure that benefits are paid to injured workers even if an employer violates the law by not being insured. (Labor Code sections 3710–3732.)

Enforcement: File a complaint with the state labor commissioner.

B. DUTY TO PAY FOR MEDICAL TREATMENT

Employers are responsible for paying for treatment required by employees experiencing work-related illnesses and injuries, including medical, surgical, nursing, acupuncture, and chiropractic care; hospitalization; medicines; and medical and surgical supplies (such as crutches, braces, artificial limbs, etc.). Employees with work-related injuries have a right to replacement or repair of artificial limbs, dentures, hearing aids, medical braces, and eyeglasses damaged in a work-related accident. (Eyeglasses and hearing aids are covered only if the employee is hurt in the accident that damaged them.)

While employers or their insurance carriers must pay for treatment, they tend to have lower rates than physicians commonly charge. It is important to make sure that healthcare providers understand that the case involves Workers' Compensation, and that they agree to accept the patient on those terms. (Labor Code section 5307.1.) It is illegal for a healthcare provider to charge the patient additional money when treatment takes place under the terms of Workers' Compensation. (Labor Code section 3751(b).)

Employers and insurance carriers are now required to authorize the worker's doctor to provide medical treatment for a claimed work injury within one day of a worker filing a claim form. The employer or insurance carrier must continue to pay for treatment for the injury until the worker is notified that the injury claim is being denied or until the cost of the treatment exceeds $10,000. Thus, a worker has a right to have her treatment paid for by the employer or insurance carrier during the period when the claim is being investigated, up to a maximum of $10,000, even if the claim is denied after the employer or insurance carrier completes its investigation. If the employer or insurance carrier does not authorize the treatment, then the worker should contact the Information and Assistance Office or an attorney. If the injury claim is accepted, the treatment is not limited to $10,000. (Labor Code section 5402.)

Recent changes to Workers' Compensation laws impose new caps on certain kinds of treatment. Unless the claims administrator authorizes additional visits, claimants injured after 2004 are limited to twenty-four chiropractic visits, twenty-four physical therapy visits, and twenty-four occupational therapy visits per work-related injury with a few limited exceptions. (Labor Code section 4604.5(d).)

Medical care treatment decisions are generally based on established treatment guidelines (Occupational Medicine Practice Guidelines issued by the American College of Occupational and Environmental Medicine). (Labor Code sections 4600, 4604.5.)

C. DUTY TO PAY FOR MEDICAL TESTS IN CONTESTED CLAIMS

If the employer contests a claim for Workers' Compensation, it must reimburse the employee for all reasonable and necessary expenses she incurs for laboratory fees, x-rays, medical examinations, medical records, interpreters' fees, and medical testimony to prove the claim. Those expenses are usually for diagnostic tests (for example, x-rays or MRIs) ordered by a treating doctor or a qualified medical evaluator. The employer must also pay the cost of the qualified medical evaluator's evaluation and report, and the report of a treating doctor when the report is issued to answer medical questions necessary for the worker to prove her case. (Labor Code sections 4620–4621.)

Enforcement: File with the Workers' Compensation Appeals Board.

D. DUTY TO PAY FOR MEDICAL EXAMINATIONS BY THE EMPLOYER'S PHYSICIAN

The employer may make a written demand that the employee submit to periodic examinations by a physician the employer chooses. The employer must pay for those examinations. Injured employees can choose to have their personal physician be present at these examinations, but must pay for their physician's costs. (Labor Code sections 4050–4054.)

Enforcement: File with the Workers' Compensation Appeals Board.

E. DUTY TO PAY FOR MEDICALLY RELATED TRANSPORTATION

Employers (or their insurance carriers) are responsible for the cost of transportation to and from medical treatments. If employees are required to submit to a medical examination at the request of the employer's insurance carrier or the Workers' Compensation Appeals Board, they are entitled to reimbursement for transportation, meals, and lodging (if necessary) as well. The transportation costs are usually paid at the rate of $.50 per mile, but the rate varies from year to year. (See http://www.dir.ca.gov/dwc/I&A_mileageForm.doc for information on medical transportation costs.) If the employee loses wages because of the medical examination requested by the employer, she is entitled to temporary disability benefits for the day(s) lost. (Labor Code section 4600(e).)

Enforcement: File with the Workers' Compensation Appeals Board.

V. EMPLOYEES' BENEFITS

A. TEMPORARY DISABILITY PAY

When workers are unable to work for more than three days because of a work-related injury, they are entitled to temporary disability benefits under the Workers' Compensation system. Disability entitlement begins on the fourth day after the employee leaves work. However, if the injury causes a disability for fourteen days or more or involves hospitalization, the injured worker is entitled to coverage from the first day. (Labor Code sections 4650, 4652.)

Employees should receive their first disability payment no later than fourteen days after submitting the injury claim form to the employer if the employer agrees that a work injury occurred. Subsequent payments are due every two weeks on the same weekday as the original payment, whether the disability is temporary or permanent. (Labor Code section 4650.) Injured workers who are able to work only part time may be eligible for temporary partial disability benefits. (Labor Code sections 4654, 4657.) See http://www.dir.ca.gov/dwc/WCFaqIW.html#4 for more information.

Temporary disability payments continue until the injured worker is released to return to work

Seriously injured workers have the right to a second medical opinion, paid for by the employer.

by her doctor or until the worker's condition stabilizes and becomes "permanent and stationary" (also called "maximum medical improvement"), whichever occurs first. In addition, for injuries occurring after April 19, 2004, when new laws took effect, a worker is entitled to no more than 104 weeks of temporary disability payments, with a few very limited exceptions such as cases of hepatitis, amputation, and severe burns. For injuries occurring between April 19, 2004, and December 31, 2007, the 104 weeks of temporary disability payments have to be made within two years of the date the first payment is made. For injuries after January 1, 2008, the 104 weeks of compensation must take place within five years after the date of the injury. (Labor Code section 4656.)

If a treating doctor has reported that an injured worker is temporarily disabled and the worker is not receiving temporary disability benefits and is not working, the worker can get an "expedited trial" on that issue. (Labor Code section 5502.) If the worker is not represented by an attorney, the worker should consult with the Information and Assistance Unit about requesting an expedited trial. The Workers' Compensation judge will decide if a worker is entitled to temporary disability compensation based on the reports of the treating physicians and the reports, if any, of the "qualified medical evaluator" (QME).

The weekly temporary disability compensation rate is two-thirds of a worker's average weekly earnings at the time of the injury, up to a maximum weekly compensation rate of $916.33 for injuries occurring in 2008, $958.01 for injuries occurring in 2009, and $986.69 for injuries occurring in 2010. There is also a minimum weekly compensation rate no matter how little the worker earned per week. The maximum and minimum weekly compensation rates will be adjusted upwards for inflation for injuries occurring during each year after 2010.

The worker's average weekly wages are based on her gross earnings (before taxes) including tips, food, lodging, commissions, and overtime. If the worker has more than one job at the time of injury, then the weekly earnings are based on her earnings from all jobs. (Labor Code sections 4451–4455.)

Employers may have the duty to "reasonably accommodate" an injured worker's disability. See Chapter 6, section V.A.4., p. 168, for more information on reasonable accommodation.

If the employer contests a Workers' Compensation claim and is not paying benefits, the injured worker may be entitled to receive State Disability Insurance benefits until the Workers' Compensation claim is resolved. See Chapter 5, section VI., p. 115, for more information on State Disability Insurance.

Exceptions: Employees of the University of California and the California State University are entitled to disability from the first day they leave work if the injury results from a work-related criminal act of violence against them. (Labor Code section 4650.5.)

Enforcement: File with the Employment Development Department regarding claims for State Disability Benefits (see Chapter 5, section VI., p. 115) and with the Workers Compensation Board for claims regarding Workers' Compensation.

B. PERMANENT DISABILITY BENEFITS

Once the treating doctor or a QME reports that the injured worker's condition has become permanent and stationary (also called "maximum medical improvement"), then the insurance carrier's liability for temporary disability payments ends, but the worker might be eligible for permanent disability payments. The treating doctor and the QME, if any, must write a report describing the impairments and disability caused by the injury, if any. That description is then converted into a permanent disability rating (a percentage figure) by a rater employed by the California Division of Workers' Compensation. That percentage rating is then applied to a schedule set by law that indicates the number of weeks of permanent disability

compensation to which the worker is entitled. The amount of the weekly payments is calculated as two-thirds of the worker's average weekly wages at the time of the injury, up to a maximum payment of $230 per week for most injuries. If the worker is 70 percent disabled or more, the weekly compensation rate is higher.

Permanent disability payments must begin no later than fourteen days after the last temporary disability payment is made. If the extent of permanent disability cannot be determined by that time, the employer must nevertheless begin making payments. The employer needs to make a reasonable estimate of the permanent disability compensation that will be due and continue payments until that amount has been paid. (Labor Code sections 4650, 4658–4662.)

The governor of California signed legislation in 2004 that greatly reduced the amount of permanent disability compensation (as well as other benefits) to which workers are entitled in most cases. The process for determining permanent disability is complicated. If a worker has a permanent disability, the assistance of an attorney is very helpful in assuring that the worker gets the permanent disability compensation to which he is entitled. If a worker is permanently disabled, is unable to return to his job, and will likely have to take a job that pays less money, then it is particularly important to try to get an attorney. The attorney may be able to gather evidence about the worker's loss of future earnings and increase the permanent disability rating. But workers who are unable to get an attorney can consult with the Information and Assistance Unit.

When an injured worker is being examined by a doctor, whether it is a treating doctor or a QME, it is important for the worker be sure that he lists *all* of his symptoms and complaints about *all* parts of his body. For example, the worker may be mainly concerned with his ongoing back condition, but he should be sure to tell the doctor if he is experiencing depression, or if the pain medication has caused gastrointestinal symptoms, or if he has had a weight gain because of inactivity resulting from the injury. The worker should list all of his symptoms, even if the symptoms are minor and even if he is not sure that the injury caused the symptoms. If other parts of the body are affected besides the body part first injured, the worker may be entitled to a higher permanent disability rating.

For example, injury to one arm may cause someone to use the other arm more to compensate, causing an injury to that arm too. The worker would be entitled to medical treatment for both arms and probably to a higher permanent disability rating.

The amount of a permanently disabled worker's permanent disability compensation award may be increased or reduced by 15 percent under certain circumstances. If the employer had fifty employees or more at the time of the worker's injury, and does not offer the worker her regular job, alternative work, or modified work within sixty days of the worker's condition becoming permanent and stationary, then each payment of permanent disability compensation must be increased by 15 percent. Similarly, if the employer does offer the worker regular, modified, or alternative work within the sixty days, whether or not the worker accepts the offer, the weekly payments can be reduced by 15 percent. (Labor Code section 4658.)

Enforcement: File with the Workers' Compensation Appeals Board.

C. APPLICATION FOR SOCIAL SECURITY DISABILITY INCOME FOR PERMANENTLY DISABLED WORKERS

If a permanently disabled injured worker will be unable to return to her job and may not be able to return to any job, then the worker may qualify for Social Security Disability Income (SSDI) and Medicare. Application is made through the federal Social Security Administration. The Social Security Administration's website on SSDI can be found at http://www.ssa.gov/disability.

D. COMPENSATION PAYABLE WHEN EMPLOYER OR INSURANCE CARRIER DELAYS PAYMENT OF BENEFITS

When employers or insurance carriers delay paying benefits to which the worker is entitled, additional compensation can be awarded as a penalty. For example, if the employer or insurance carrier delays paying either temporary or permanent disability, then the payments must be increased by 10 percent even if the employer or insurance carrier did not act unreasonably in delaying the benefits.

When an employer delays paying benefits, additional compensation may be awarded as a penalty.

(Labor Code section 4650.) Higher penalties of up to 25 percent of the benefits delayed (including medical treatment) may be due if the employer or insurance carrier acted unreasonably in delaying the benefits. (Labor Code section 5814.) The law regarding penalties is complicated. Workers should consult an attorney specializing in Workers' Compensation or the Information and Assistance Unit if benefits were delayed.

E. RETRAINING AND RETURNING TO WORK

Injured workers who cannot return to their original jobs because of a work-related disability may be entitled to Supplemental Job Displacement benefits. (Labor Code sections 4658.5, 4658.6; 8 California Code of Regulations sections 10133.51–10133.60.) This program replaces the previous Vocational Rehabilitation Program, which was phased out in 2004. See http://www.dir.ca.gov/dwc/SJDB/SJDB_Main.html for more information on Supplemental Job Displacement benefits, and see http://www.dir.ca.gov/dwc/rehab.html for more information on returning to work.

Supplemental Job Displacement benefits provide vouchers for $4,000 to $10,000 (depending on the degree of permanent disability) to certain injured workers who are permanently unable to do their usual job, and whose employers do not offer other work. The voucher can be used at state-approved or accredited schools (community colleges, CSU, or UC), certain accredited private schools, or programs accredited by the Federal Aviation

Administration. Vouchers can also be used to pay vocational return-to-work counselors who are authorized by the state to accept such payment.

Enforcement: File with the Workers' Compensation Appeals Board. As always, be aware of and comply with stated deadlines.

F. SURVIVORS' DEATH BENEFITS

If a worker's death was caused or hastened by the worker's injury or the effects of the injury, then the worker's dependents may be entitled to dependency benefits (also called "death benefits") and burial expenses.

The question of who qualifies as a dependent under the law can be complicated. Generally, dependents include family members and others living with and supported by an injured worker who dies as a result of the injury, and other persons who may not be living with the worker but who are supported by him. Dependency benefits are paid out at the deceased worker's temporary disability compensation rate until the total amount has been paid. Family members and other dependents of a worker who may have died as a result of a work injury or illness should consult with an attorney or the Information and Assistance Unit as soon as possible. There are strict time limits for applying for benefits. Currently, the maximum burial allowance is $5,000, and the maximum death benefit for injuries occurring after January 1, 2006 is $290,000. (Labor Code sections 4702, 4701.)

G. ACCRUED WORKERS' COMPENSATION BENEFITS WHEN A WORKER DIES

Accrued Workers' Compensation benefits are payable to a worker's dependents or heirs upon her death, whether or not the death was caused by the injury. (Labor Code section 4700.) For example, if a worker dies in a non-work-related accident and was owed temporary or permanent Workers' Compensation disability payments covering a period of time before the death, those payments should be made to the worker's dependants or, if there are no dependants, to the heirs or the personal representative of the deceased worker. (Labor Code section 4700.) However, neither temporary nor permanent disability payments are made for any period after the death of the employee.

Enforcement: The deceased worker's dependents, heirs, or representative should file with the Workers' Compensation Appeals Board.

Exceptions: Members of the Public Employees Retirement System (PERS) cannot receive death benefits under the Workers' Compensation system if they are entitled to benefits under PERS. If benefits under PERS are less than those paid under Workers' Compensation, survivors are entitled to the difference.

VI. THE CLAIM PROCESS

A. REPORTING AN INJURY AND FILING A CLAIM FORM: STEPS AND TIME LIMITS

Normally, employees are responsible for providing to their employer a written notice of work-related injuries. Notice to the employer must be provided within thirty days of the specific injury, or the date the worker became disabled from a cumulative injury or disease, or the date the worker learned the injury was work-related. The worker should report the injury to a supervisor as soon as possible.

The employer then has one working day to provide the injured worker with a claim form and notice of potential benefits, in person or by first-class mail. Even if the worker did not give written notice of the injury to the employer, the employer must provide this form if the employer learns of the injury from any source. This means that if the injured worker tells a supervisor about the injury (and does not report the injury in writing), the employer should provide the worker with a claim form to fill out.

The claim form asks for the worker's name, address, and Social Security Number, the time and address where the injury occurred, the nature of the injury, and the part of the body affected by the injury or illness. It is very important for the worker to list all parts of the body affected by the injury. For example, a worker fell and hurt her back, which is the main source of her symptoms, but she also fell on her elbow, which seems to be minor. The worker should be sure to list the elbow in the claim form in case it bothers her later.

The notice of potential benefits must include a description of the available procedures and assistance available, the procedure to use to collect compensation for the injury, the telephone number for Information and Assistance services, and a statement that the injured worker has the right to consult an attorney or an Information and Assistance officer, or both, for help with the Workers' Compensation claim. Claim forms are also available at district offices of the state Employment Development Department and the Division of Workers' Compensation, and on the Internet at http://www.dir.ca.gov/dwc/DWCForm1.pdf.

The injured worker (also known as the applicant, once a claim has been filed), or his spouse or dependent (if the worker died as a result of the injury), or an attorney needs to fill out the form and return it to the employer. If the claims administrator does not reject liability within ninety days of receiving the claim form, the injury is presumed to be work-related and qualifies for Workers' Compensation benefits. (Labor Code sections 5400–5404.) If the employer does not start compensation payments within two weeks of the claim, however, the injured worker who is unable to work because of the injury may qualify for State Disability Insurance benefits until the Workers' Compensation benefits start. See Chapter 5, section VI., p. 115, for more information on State Disability Insurance.

B. SETTLEMENTS AND WAIVERS OF RIGHTS

Any agreement by an injured worker (such as a settlement agreement) in which the worker gives up her rights to additional benefits must be approved by a Workers' Compensation judge. The judge will not approve a settlement that he does not believe is adequate or in the best interest of the injured worker. (Labor Code sections 5000–5005.) An unrepresented injured worker should talk to an Information and Assistance officer before accepting any settlement offer.

There are generally two kinds of settlements:

- "Stipulations with Request for Award," in which the worker and insurance carrier agree to the amount of temporary disability and permanent disability compensation to which the worker is entitled, but the worker's right to get further medical treatment in the future and the right to reopen the worker's claim within five years of the injury for new and further disability are both left open;

- "Compromise and Release," which is a complete settlement of future rights to all benefits, including further medical treatment and the right to reopen for new and further disability benefits. The advantage of the complete settlement is that the worker is paid a larger settlement amount because she is giving up any right to future medical treatment and the right to reopen her claim.

Enforcement: File with the Workers' Compensation Appeals Board.

If a claims administrator tries to get a worker to settle potential civil claims in addition to the Workers' Compensation claim, then the worker should get legal advice or consult the Information and Assistance Unit before agreeing to the settlement. An example of a civil claim might be a claim by a worker under either federal or state law that the employer discriminated against the worker because of race, gender, religion, or disability. An attorney specializing in Workers' Compensation can help the injured worker determine if there are any grounds for a lawsuit (for instance, negligence by a third party other than the employer).

C. FILING A CASE WITH THE WORKERS' COMPENSATION APPEALS BOARD

If the claims administrator denies liability for the claimed injury, or if the injury is admitted but the claims administrator refuses to authorize medical treatment and pay disability compensation, then the worker should file a case before the Workers' Compensation Appeals Board (WCAB). A worker files a case by filing a document entitled "Application for Adjudication of Claim." A worker should consult with an attorney or the Information and Assistance Unit, which can help the worker fill out the application.

There are strict time limits for filing the application, so the worker should not wait to file if benefits are being denied.

D. GATHERING MEDICAL REPORTS AND OTHER EVIDENCE

The next step in getting benefits is for the worker to gather the medical evidence (medical reports and records) that he will need to prove his case before a Workers' Compensation judge. At a hearing, a Workers' Compensation judge will consider medical reports and records of treating doctors, QME reports, and the testimony of witnesses, including the injured worker. A worker has the burden of proving his case under the law. The worker should make sure he has all of the reports and records of the treating doctors and QMEs. The claims administrator should supply copies of the reports and records to the worker if the worker asks for them. The Information and Assistance Unit can help the worker understand what the doctors are saying in their reports and whether what they have said is sufficient to prove the worker's case.

A claims administrator may ask questions of an injured worker at a session called a "deposition" in order to get more information about the circumstances of the injury, the worker's current symptoms, and the worker's medical history. A deposition usually occurs at the claims administrator's lawyer's office, with a court reporter who takes down all the questions and answers. A worker has to testify under oath, and if the worker does not tell the truth, he could be prosecuted for a crime. A worker should consult

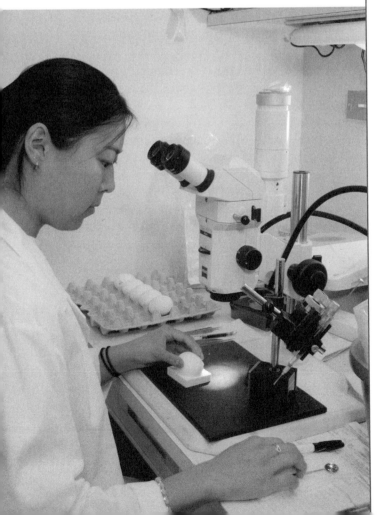

with the Information and Assistance Unit before a deposition. A worker can sometimes hire a lawyer to represent him at the deposition, even if the lawyer will not be handling the rest of the case. The claims administrator has to pay the worker's lawyer for representing the worker at the deposition.

The worker should be sure to request and keep a copy of the deposition transcript, and should review the transcript before any hearings.

E. REQUESTING A HEARING

The Workers' Compensation Appeals Board (WCAB) has Workers' Compensation judges who hear and decide cases. There are many district offices of the WCAB around the state, where hearings are held. Each district office also has Information and Assistance officers. Once an injured worker whose benefits are being denied has gathered her medical reports and other evidence, then the worker should request a hearing before a Workers' Compensation judge. The judge, after a hearing, can order the payment of benefits that are being denied. If the claims administrator is refusing to pay temporary disability compensation or to authorize medical treatment, then the worker can ask for a type of hearing known as an "expedited trial." (Labor Code section 5502.) The Information and Assistance Unit can help the worker file the form that is required to obtain a hearing. The claims administrator must provide an interpreter for the hearing in the worker's native language if the worker is not proficient in English.

F. AT THE HEARING

Many workers are not able to get lawyers to represent them. The Workers' Compensation system is set up so that a worker can appear at a hearing without a lawyer and make her own case to the judge. The hearings are more informal than in other courts. The judge will explain the procedure to the worker who does not have a lawyer and ask the worker questions to help bring out the facts. When the judge makes a decision in the worker's case, the decision will be sent to the worker. Either the worker or the claims administrator can appeal the judge's decision if she thinks the decision is wrong. An injured worker without a lawyer should meet with the Information and Assistance Unit to get ready for the hearing.

G. LAWSUITS AGAINST UNINSURED EMPLOYERS

If a worker is injured on the job and the employer does not have compensation insurance, the worker may have a choice of either filing a lawsuit in court or filing a Workers' Compensation claim against the Uninsured Employers Benefit Trust Fund. An attorney should be consulted, as these cases are more complicated than normal cases. The Information and Assistance Unit can also be of help. See the website at http://www.dir. ca.gov/dwc/claims.html for more information on the Uninsured Employers Benefit Trust Fund.

H. STOP ORDERS AGAINST EMPLOYERS

If the employer fails to pay compensation that is due to an employee or fails to obtain Workers' Compensation Insurance, the director of the Department of Industrial Relations can serve a stop order on the employer. It prohibits the employer from using any employee labor until the employer complies with Workers' Compensation regulations. (Labor Code section 3710.1.)

Enforcement: File a complaint with the state labor commissioner.

I. FILING A LAWSUIT AGAINST SOMEONE WHO CAUSED THE INJURY OTHER THAN THE EMPLOYER

When a worker has a work-related injury or illness, Workers' Compensation is almost always the worker's only available remedy against the employer or insurance carrier. That means that the worker can usually only get Workers' Compensation benefits for his injury. Even if the employer was negligent, an injured worker can only sue his employer in civil court in a few very limited situations. (Labor Code section 3602.)

However, if a person who is not the employer (or an employee of the employer) caused or contributed to a work-related injury, then the injured worker can collect his Workers' Compensation benefits and still sue the other person (called a "third party") in civil court.

For example, a worker who is driving a vehicle in the course of his employment might get rear-ended by another vehicle, injuring the worker. The worker would be entitled to Workers' Compensation benefits and could also sue the owner or driver of the vehicle that caused the accident in civil court. If the worker does obtain a recovery from the third party in civil court, however, the worker's right to further Workers' Compensation benefits might be limited. When a worker is injured by a third party in the course of his employment, the worker should seek the advice of an attorney.

J. UNLAWFUL DISCRIMINATION OR RETALIATION AGAINST A WORKER BECAUSE HE FILED A WORKERS' COMPENSATION CLAIM

If an employer punishes a worker because the worker filed a Workers' Compensation claim or made known her intention to do so, or if an employer treats a worker who has had a work-related injury worse than a worker who has a non-work-related injury or illness, then the worker can file a claim under Labor Code section 132a. Examples of unlawful discrimination would be firing a worker as punishment for filing a claim or reporting an injury or not letting a worker come back to work after an injury even though the doctors have cleared the worker to go back to work and the job is still available. If a worker proves unlawful discrimination in her claim, then the employer may have to pay a penalty to the worker of up to $10,000 and compensate the worker for lost pay. In some situations, the employer may be required to give the worker her job back. Such a claim under Labor Code section 132a is made against the employer who has to pay any benefits awarded. The insurance carrier is not involved.

Claims of discrimination under Labor Code section 132a are difficult to prove, and workers should seek advice from a lawyer or the Information and Assistance Unit. Strict time limits apply, so the worker should seek advice as soon after the act of discrimination by the employer as possible.

Enforcement: File a claim with the labor commissioner

K. WHEN THE INJURY IS CAUSED BY THE SERIOUS AND WILLFUL MISCONDUCT OF THE EMPLOYER

If a worker's injury is caused by the serious and willful misconduct of the employer, the worker could recover a penalty from the employer (not the insurance carrier) of 50 percent of all benefits paid in the case. (Labor Code sections 4553, 4553.1.) An example of serious willful misconduct by an employer that causes an injury is where a plant superintendent knows that a machine is dangerous because safety devices are not working properly, takes no action to correct the unsafe situation, and a worker is injured as a result. Such claims of serious and willful misconduct by the employer are difficult to prove, and workers should seek advice from a lawyer or the Information and Assistance Unit.

VII. ADDITIONAL SOURCES OF INFORMATION

- The Labor Occupational Health Program (LOHP), a program of the Center for Occupational and Environmental Health at UC Berkeley's School of Public Health, has several excellent publications on Workers' Compensation. See http://www.lohp.org/Projects/Workers__Compensation/workers__compensation.html.
- California's Workers' Compensation Appeals Board (part of the state Department of Industrial Relations) has a website at http://www.dir.ca.gov/dwc/dwc_home_page.htm.
- Contact information for all Workers' Compensation Appeals Board district offices (also called the Division of Workers' Compensation district offices), including Information and Assistance offices, can be found at http://www.dir.ca.gov/dwc/dir2.htm.
- The Division of Workers' Compensation has an informative list of frequently asked questions about Workers' Compensation at http://www.dir.ca.gov/dwc/WCFaqIW.html#1.
- Injured worker support groups can be very helpful. For more information on locating an appropriate group, go to http://www.worksafe.org/legal/clinics.html.
- For more information on work-related injuries and health and safety, go to http://www.worksafe.org/about/index.html.

THE RIGHT TO ORGANIZE

I. SCOPE OF THE CHAPTER

Federal and state laws protect the rights of workers to organize into unions, and to take collective action to negotiate and enforce agreements with employers regarding wages, hours, benefits, and other working conditions. These laws are the National Labor Relations Act, the Railway Labor Act, the Civil Service Reform Act of 1978, the California Agricultural Labor Relations Act, provisions of the California Labor Code, and seven public sector collective bargaining laws in California. They empower employees to form and join unions as their exclusive representatives with

their employers, bargain collectively with their employers, go on strike to gain better wages and working conditions, picket for these reasons, and engage in many other activities to improve the workplace.

The law forbids employers from engaging in many types of conduct. They cannot make employees agree not to join a union; create a company union dominated or assisted by the employer; threaten employees or offer inducements in order to thwart organizing efforts; discriminate or retaliate against employees for engaging in activities protected by the collective bargaining laws; interfere with employees' exercise of protected rights; refuse to

Federal and state laws protect the rights of workers to organize into unions.

bargain in good faith with employee unions; refuse to participate in impasse procedures designed to resolve breakdowns in collective bargaining; interfere with rights of unions to communicate with, organize, and represent employees; or refuse to provide information to the unions that is necessary and relevant to their representation of employees.

The law imposes duties on unions to bargain in good faith, participate in impasse procedures in good faith, and represent union members fairly. Other provisions are designed to ensure a fair, democratic process within unions, and to insulate unions from outside management of their internal affairs.

The law gives employers the right to respond to union activity in limited ways, such as hiring replacements for strikers. In some cases, strikes and other forms of collective action are prohibited or limited.

The rules governing the right to organize are complex. Only a general overview can be provided in this book. Readers with detailed questions regarding application of the laws discussed here are encouraged to consult the additional resources identified below, their unions, or attorneys specializing in this area of the law.

II. GOVERNING STATUTES

Most private sector workers nationwide, and public employees in California, have basic rights to organize and bargain collectively. These rights are enforced under a number of laws, and by several state and federal agencies. Most private sector workers are governed by one basic law: the federal National Labor Relations Act (NLRA). (29 U.S. Code sections 151 et seq.) It is important to note that the NLRA does *not* govern labor relations in the federal government or between state and local government employers and their employees. It also does not cover very small employers (as defined by the NLRB, based primarily on volume of business) who fall outside of the rules set by the NLRA. Separate laws govern labor relations in these other arenas, as discussed below.

A. INTRODUCTION

Understanding and exercising the rights discussed in this chapter can be complicated because an employee has to know which law governs. But determining the governing law is essential because in many cases where federal law applies to an employer, state law protections cannot be applied. This situation, in which state laws are "trumped" by federal laws, is called "preemption." Federal law generally overrules state law, but some federal laws do allow states to set higher standards. This chapter explains which laws govern many of the common issues that arise around the right to organize. However, in some cases the law is too complicated to be definitively explained here.

B. FEDERAL LABOR LAWS

1. National Labor Relations Act (NLRA)
a. Wagner Act
In 1935, Congress passed the Wagner Act, also known as the National Labor Relations Act (NLRA). (29 U.S. Code sections 151 et seq.) The NLRA authorized unions to serve as the exclusive representative of employees organized into bargaining units for purposes of collective negotiations with employers. It imposed on employers the duty to bargain in good faith with unions and prohibited discrimination against employees for engaging in conduct protected by the NLRA.

b. Taft-Hartley Act
In 1947, the NLRA was amended by the Labor Management Relations Act, known also as the Taft-Hartley Act. This law imposed many duties on unions and prohibited many union tactics and weapons, including various forms of picketing and

secondary boycotts. Secondary boycotts are efforts to pressure employers and businesses that are not directly involved in a labor dispute but that do business with the employer directly involved in the dispute.

c. Landrum-Griffin Act

In 1959, the NLRA was again amended by the Labor Management Reporting and Disclosure Act (LMRDA), also known as the Landrum-Griffin Act. The Landrum-Griffin Act imposed rules regarding internal union governance and democracy within unions, giving members rights within the union such as freedom of speech and the right to vote on officers and dues increases.

d. Overview of NLRA Provisions

Generally, the National Labor Relations Act, as amended by Congress several times, is referred to as the "National Labor Relations Act" or just NLRA. The Landrum-Griffin amendments are generally referred to separately as either the Labor Management Reporting and Disclosure Act (LMRDA) or the Landrum-Griffin Act.

Section 7 of the NLRA (29 U.S. Code section 157) states, in key part: "Employees shall have the right to self-organization, to form, join, or assist labor organizations, to bargain collectively through representatives of their own choosing, and to engage in other concerted activities for the purpose of collective bargaining or other mutual aid or protection, and shall also have the right to refrain from any or all of such activities." These rights are implemented and enforced through other provisions of the NLRA.

i. *Employer Unfair Labor Practices*

Section 8(a)(1)-(5) of the NLRA (29 U.S. Code section 158(a)(1)-(5)) prohibits the following unfair labor practices by employers:

- Interfering with, restraining, or coercing employees in the exercise of their rights under NLRA section 7;
- Dominating or interfering with the formation or administration of a labor organization or providing financial assistance to it;
- Discriminating against employees to encourage or discourage membership in a union;
- Discharging or discriminating against employees because they filed charges or provided testimony regarding an alleged violation of the NLRA;

- Refusing to bargain collectively in good faith with their employees' unions.

(29 U.S. Code section 158(a)(1)-(5).)

Related rules include prohibition of "yellow dog" contracts, agreements that compel employees to refrain from engaging in any union activity if they wish to remain employed. Union membership is a protected right, therefore "yellow dog" contracts are strictly forbidden by federal law. (29 U.S. Code section 103.)

ii. *Union Unfair Labor Practices*

Section 8(b) of the NLRA (29 U.S. Code section 158(b)) prohibits the following unfair labor practices by unions:

- Restraining or coercing (1) employees in the exercise of their rights under NLRA section 7, or (2) employers in the selection of their representatives for collective bargaining and grievance processing;
- Causing or attempting to cause an employer to discriminate against an employee because of union membership or lack of union membership, except unions may enforce a valid union security clause requiring employees to join or pay dues to a union;
- Refusing to bargain collectively in good faith with an employer;
- Some forms of picketing, boycotting, and other tactics designed to put pressure on an employer or a neutral person.

(29 U.S. Code section 158(b)(1)-(7).)

The National Labor Relations Board (NLRB) enforces the NLRA. Appeals of NLRB decisions can, in most circumstances, be taken to the federal appeals court. There is a large body of case law, both by the NLRB and the federal courts, interpreting and applying the provisions of the NLRA and the Landrum-Griffin Act. It is impossible to understand how the statutes apply to a particular situation without consulting the cases interpreting these laws. Both employers and employees are advised to consult with an attorney specializing in labor law when presented with a situation involving the provisions of the NLRA and federal labor law.

Exceptions: The following workers are not covered by the NLRA:

- Federal, state, and local government employees;
- Agricultural workers; they are covered by California's Agricultural Labor Relations Act;
- Spouses and children of employers;

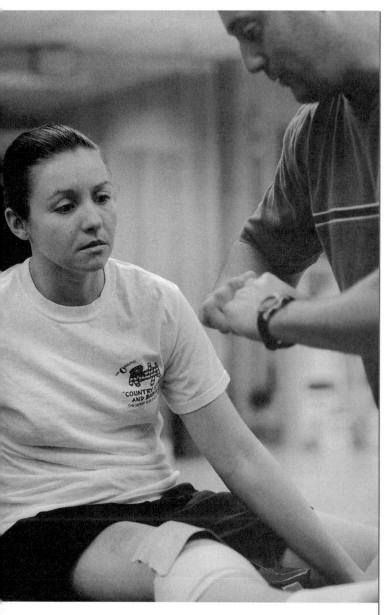

2. Railway Labor Act

The Railway Labor Act (RLA) (45 U.S. Code sections 151 et seq.) gives railroad and airline employees the right to organize and bargain collectively. The RLA was enacted in 1926, nine years before the Wagner Act. The National Mediation Board administers the portions of the RLA with respect to procedures for selecting a union and certain negotiations issues. See their website at http://www.nmb.gov. All other provisions are enforceable by lawsuit. There are important differences between the RLA and the NLRA, but many provisions are similar.

3. Civil Service Reform Act

Federal employees are covered by a separate law, the Civil Service Reform Act of 1978. (5 U.S. Code sections 7101 et seq.) This act is modeled on the NLRA but with important differences. For instance, federal employees are expressly prohibited from striking.

Enforcement: The Civil Service Reform Act is enforced by the Federal Labor Relations Authority. Their website is at http://www.flra.gov. Adverse actions (meaning discipline and discharge) are reviewed by the Merit Systems Protection Board. Their website is at http://www.mspb.gov. Many federal government workers are represented by unions. Where there is a union representing federal workers, the union's collective bargaining agreement may be the appropriate route to handle disciplinary issues. In most cases these rights must be enforced by first going to the appropriate administrative agency.

- Independent contractors;
- Employees of railroads or airlines; they are covered by the federal Railway Labor Act;
- Domestic servants working in their employer's home;
- Managers and supervisors;
- Employees of small employers; the definition of "small employer" varies according to the industry and nature of the business of the employer;
- Many employees of Indian tribes; however, employees of casinos are covered.

Note: Employees of the United State Postal Service are covered by the NLRA.

Enforcement: File a charge with the National Labor Relations Board (http://www.nlrb.gov).

C. STATE LABOR LAWS

1. State Labor Laws Covering Private Sector Employees

Since federal labor law prevails over state labor law, state laws regulating unions and employers apply only to the relatively small number of employers that are not governed by the NLRA or other federal law. It is usually necessary to show that the NLRB will not assume authority over an employer before proceeding under state law.

a. Labor Code Section 923

This law proclaims the official California state policy on labor relations and dates from the same era as the NLRA. It has been interpreted in some ways that are very similar to the NLRA. Although Labor Code section 923 can be a useful tool for employees of employers not covered by the NLRA, its application is not as broad as the NLRA.

Enforcement: File a civil suit.

b. Agricultural Labor Relations Act

California enacted the Agricultural Labor Relations Act (ALRA) (Labor Code sections 1140 et seq.) to "ensure peace in the agricultural fields by guaranteeing justice for all agricultural workers and stability in labor relations." The ALRA protects farm workers who engage in union activity. Rights afforded by the ALRA are similar to those provided by the NLRA, but the ALRA provides for some expedited election procedures to guarantee seasonal employees' rights in a timely manner.

Enforcement: File a charge with the Agricultural Labor Relations Board. Their website is at http://www.alrb.ca.gov.

2. State Labor Laws Covering Public Sector Employees

In California, public employees have the right to organize and bargain. That right is protected by seven statutes that cover the vast majority of public employees in California:

- The Meyers-Milias-Brown Act (MMBA) (Government Code sections 3500 et seq.) governs labor relations in local government, including cities, counties, and most special districts.
- The Educational Employment Relations Act (EERA) (Government Code sections 3540 et seq.) governs labor relations in the public schools (kindergarten through 12th grade) and community colleges.
- The Ralph C. Dills Act (Government Code sections 3512 et seq.), also known as the State Employer-Employee Relations Act or SEERA, governs labor relations in California state government employment.
- The Higher Education Employer-Employee Relations Act (HEERA) (Government Code sections 3560 et seq.) governs labor relations in the University of California and California State University.
- The Trial Court Employment Protection and Governance Act (TCEPGA) (Government Code sections 71600 et seq.) governs labor relations between trial court employees and trial courts.

- The Trial Court Interpreter Employment and Labor Relations Act (TCIELRA) (Government Code sections 71800 et seq.) governs labor relations between trial court interpreters and the courts.
- The Los Angeles Metropolitan Transportation Authority Transit Employer-Employee Relations Act (TEERA) (Public Utilities Code sections 99560 et seq.) governs labor relations between the Los Angeles Metropolitan Transportation Authority and its supervisory employees.

The Public Employment Relations Board (PERB) administers these acts. Their website is at http://www.perb.ca.gov. Each labor law establishes a system of exclusive representation and mandatory good faith bargaining; imposes on unions a duty of fair representation; defines the matters within the scope of bargaining; in some cases, imposes mandatory impasse resolution procedures (required steps for resolving differences in bargaining positions); and sets forth unfair practices that are prohibited for employers and employee organizations, modeled after the NLRA.

Some public employees are governed by other statutes. For instance, employees of the San Francisco Bay Area Rapid Transit District are governed by a separate law that relies on an arbitration board to settle disputes. (Public Utilities Code sections 28850 et seq.)

The unfair practice provisions of the Educational Employment Relations Act (EERA) provide a good example of a typical California public sector labor law. Government Code section 3543.5 of EERA makes it an unfair practice for a public school employer to:

- Interfere with the exercise of rights established by the act for the benefit of employees or their unions;
- Refuse to meet and negotiate in good faith with the recognized representative of the employees or knowingly furnish false information regarding a school district's financial resources;
- Interfere with, dominate, or discriminate among employee organizations; or
- Refuse to participate in legally mandated impasse procedures that are used when the parties cannot agree on a contract.

Government Code section 3543.6 of EERA makes it an unfair practice for employee organizations representing public school employees to:

- Cause or attempt to cause an employer to commit an unfair practice;

- Coerce, discriminate against, threaten reprisals, or in any way interfere with employees in the exercise of rights under the act;
- Refuse to meet and negotiate in good faith; or
- Refuse to participate in impasse procedures.

Enforcement: File a charge with the Public Employment Relations Board.

PERB decisions and orders can be researched and viewed at the agency's website at http://www.perb.ca.gov. Informative booklets ("Pocket Guides") on all of the statutes governing labor relations involving California public employees are published by California Public Employee Relations (CPER), located within the Institute for Research on Labor and Employment at the University of California, Berkeley. For an overview of California's public sector labor relations statutes and their unfair practice provisions, and related PERB and court rulings, see the *Pocket Guide to Unfair Practices, California Public Sector* (4th edition, 2006), California Public Employee Relations, UC Berkeley. For a list of Pocket Guide titles and ordering information, consult the CPER website at http://cper.berkeley.edu, or call 510-643-7093. These pocket guides are the best resource for information on the laws governing public employees in California.

III. RIGHTS OF EMPLOYEES AND THEIR UNIONS

A. RIGHT TO ENGAGE IN CONCERTED ACTION

Section 7 of the NLRA (29 U.S. Code section 157) gives employees the right to engage in concerted activity, which means the right to act with coworkers to improve wages and working conditions. An employee can engage in "concerted activity" by joining with others as an unorganized independent group in the workplace, or by joining a union. Employers are forbidden from interfering with employees who are organizing or joining labor unions. Section 7 of the NLRA also gives employees the right not to join a union or to refrain from any participation in union activities.

Basic rights conferred by NLRA sections 7 et seq. (29 U.S. Code sections 157 et seq.), Labor Code section 923, the RLA, the ALRA, and the California public employee statutes include the following:

- An employer cannot legally discipline or discharge an employee because of union membership or activities.
- An employer cannot ask an employee how he or she feels about union activities.
- An employer cannot discipline or discharge an employee because he and his fellow workers join together in an effort to improve their working conditions, pay, or benefits.
- An employer cannot ask an employee to withdraw from a union. No supervisor can ask or encourage an employee to resign from a union.
- An employer cannot attend (or send a supervisor to) union meetings. The employer cannot watch to see who attends union meetings.
- In many situations, an employer cannot forbid employees from wearing or displaying union

buttons, hats, t-shirts or other union insignia.

- An employer cannot forbid employees from soliciting support for the union during non-work time and in non-work areas.
- An employer cannot forbid employees from distributing union literature in non-work areas.
- An employer cannot discipline employees for filing complaints about working conditions with outside agencies.
- An employer cannot discipline employees for supporting legislation that benefits workers.
- An employer cannot discipline employees for walking out in protest over working conditions even though there is no union involved.

Although the NLRA and other labor laws apply when a union is involved, they also apply to what is called "protected concerted activity" even if no union is involved. Employees who act together cannot be disciplined for engaging in any form of activity that is protected, such as the actions described above. (*NLRB v. Washington Aluminum Co.* (1962) 370 U.S. 9.)

Enforcement: File a charge with the National Labor Relations Board in cases involving private employers; the Agricultural Labor Relations Board in cases involving agricultural employers; or the Public Employment Relations Board in cases involving state, municipal, educational, or local agency employees.

B. RIGHT TO BARGAIN COLLECTIVELY

These statutes also give workers the right to engage in collective bargaining through the union of their choice. Collective bargaining includes meetings between the union and the employer to discuss the terms of a collective bargaining agreement. The statutes require the union and the employer to bargain collectively in good faith by meeting at "reasonable times" and negotiating such mandatory topics as wages, hours, and other important conditions of employment. (29 U.S. Code sections 157, 158(a)(5), 158(b)(3).) Furthermore, once such an agreement is reached, it usually becomes enforceable through grievance and arbitration procedures.

Enforcement: File a charge with the appropriate agency. Enforcing the agreement can involve filing charges, grievances, or in some cases lawsuits.

C. RIGHT TO SOLICIT WORKERS TO JOIN THE UNION

Employees are allowed to engage in union organizing on company property during non-work time. This means employees can talk about the union and solicit support during non-work time. They can distribute literature during non-work time in non-work areas. If the employer does not prohibit talking generally, employees can talk about the union anytime so long as it does not involve asking employees to sign cards or pay dues. Non-work areas where employees can distribute literature include the lunchroom, break room, and parking lots. Special rules apply in healthcare institutions. Whether workers can use an email system to solicit fellow employees to support the union may depend on the company's email policy. If the employer generally allows employees to use the email system for personal communications, it cannot prohibit communications to support union activities.

The rights of non-employees are much more limited. An employer may prohibit non-employee organizers from coming onto private property and from soliciting members or distributing materials anywhere on company property. Only if there is no other reasonable means of communicating with the employees can non-employees come onto private property. (*NLRB v. Babcock & Wilcox Co.* (1956) 351 U.S. 105.)

Unions have limited access rights to private property once their members are working there. Some California trespass laws do not apply to union agents involved in labor union activity. (See California Penal Code section 602(o).) Posting a "no trespassing" sign does not eliminate these protections for union representatives. (Penal Code sections 552.1, 602.) However, these are limited exceptions. Private property owners can, in most cases, keep union organizers off their private property.

Access is also granted to organizers prior to elections under the Agricultural Labor Relations Act if a "notice to take access" is given according to the procedures adopted by the ALRB.

Enforcement: File a charge with the National Labor Relations Board or the Agricultural Labor Relations Board. File a civil suit. Defend a trespass citation. In some cases, file a federal civil rights lawsuit.

Schools, government property, and national defense property all have special rules about access.

If property generally is open to the public, union organizers cannot be excluded. California law considers shopping centers and malls to be public forums and allows access by union organizers. Because shopping centers are considered the equivalent of a public town square, expressive activity including leafleting and communication are permitted subject to reasonable rules that the shopping center may adopt. (*Robins v. Pruneyard Shopping Ctr.* (1979) 23 Cal.3d 899; *Fashion Valley Mall, LLC v. NLRB* (2007) 42 Cal.4th 850.) The extent to which these rules apply to single freestanding stores and small shopping malls is disputed.

D. WEAPONS OF INDUSTRIAL CONFLICT: PICKETING, STRIKES, LOCKOUTS, AND STRIKER REPLACEMENTS

Tactics used by workers to put pressure on employers fall into several categories.

Picketing generally involves workers, and sometimes their supporters, marching or standing near the workplace, usually holding signs. Some picketing involves a request that customers or other workers not enter the business. Informational picketing involves providing information about a dispute or workplace issue to the public.

Strikes are usually job actions in which workers refuse to work either indefinitely, until a dispute is resolved, or for a limited period of time. While most strikes involve staying away from the workplace, some strikes, called "sit-down strikes," involve workers refusing to the leave the workplace. Other types of job actions may involve various types of slowdowns.

Secondary boycotts are efforts by employees to put pressure on a business other than their own employer by discouraging or preventing customers or others from patronizing the business or entering its worksite. They involve efforts to pressure neutral parties not to do business with the employer with whom the workers have a dispute.

The level of legal protection for workers involved in these types of actions will vary, depending on the type of action and the context. It is always better, however, to engage in concerted action (action involving at least two workers, or by a worker on behalf of other workers), rather than acting alone.

The protections contained in the National Labor Relations Act are based on engaging in concerted action, not on acting alone.

1. Picketing

a. What Is Picketing?

The word "picketing" commonly evokes images of people walking in a circle in front of an establishment, carrying placards displaying a message. However, many legal decisions have produced much broader definitions of the term. What constitutes picketing and what rules apply to such activity depends on multiple considerations, particularly the *content of information* conveyed, the *nature* of the activity involved, the *purpose* of the activity, and its *effects*.

The presence or absence of placards (picket signs) does not, by itself, determine if an activity is considered picketing. For example, the presence of a large number of employees near an employer's business has been considered to be picketing even if they are carrying no placards and posting no signs. The presence of union officials at certain locations can constitute picketing. The use of inflatable rats or other disparaging symbols can constitute picketing.

b. Picketing and Free Speech Rights

Peaceful picketing for a lawful purpose falls within the free speech protections of the First Amendment to the U.S. Constitution. (*Thornhill v. Alabama* (1940) 310 U.S. 88.) The right to picket receives stronger protection when picketing is

An employer cannot legally forbid employees from distributing union literature in non-work areas.

conducted in a public place rather than a private place. (*Pittsburg Unified School District v. California School Employees Association* (1985) 166 Cal. App.3d 875.) Article I, section 2, of the California Constitution provides more protection than does the First Amendment. (*Robins v. Pruneyard Shopping Ctr.* (1979) 23 Cal. 3d 899.) Picketing can be regulated to a greater extent than pure speech because it involves an element of conduct as well. However, such regulation can be imposed only for a compelling (very important) governmental purpose and must be narrowly tailored and justified in light of the affected speech rights of employees. (*In re Berry* (1968) 68 Cal.2d 137.)

Leafleting, bannering, and other forms of communication generally are not considered picketing and are protected by the First Amendment. (*Edward J. DeBartolo Corp. v. Florida Gulf Coast Building and Construction Trades Council* (1988) 485 U.S. 568.)

c. Picketing by Government Employees

The government has greater latitude in regulating the speech of its own employees than it does in regulating the speech of members of the general public. While governmental employers may regulate employee speech that concerns matters of only personal interest (*Connick v. Myers* (1983) 461 U.S. 138), public employees retain the right to comment on "matters of public concern." (*Pickering v. Bd. of Education* (1968) 391 U.S. 563; *Perry v. Sindermann* (1972) 408 U.S. 593.) "Matters of public concern" include, among other things, statements related to unionization, union-management relationships, and loss of confidence in the management of the public entity. (*Chico Police Officers' Association v. City of Chico* (1991) 232 Cal.App.3d 635, 646.) However, when public employees make statements pursuant to their official duties, courts have held that they are not speaking as citizens with First Amendment rights, and their speech may not be protected. The key question is whether the person speaks as a citizen on a matter of public concern (in which case she is protected by the First Amendment), or as an employee within the scope of her job (in which case the employer may be able to exert more control and the employee may not be protected by the First Amendment). (*Garcetti v. Ceballos* (2006) 547 U.S. 410.)

d. Rights and Restrictions on Particular Types of Picketing

Though there is a general constitutional protection for both private and public employees to engage in picketing, rules have been crafted that protect and limit this right in particular circumstances. The NLRB and the federal courts have distinguished various kinds of picketing, and find different levels of protection for the different types of picketing categories.

The rules regarding picketing are complicated. In the union context, workers considering picketing should consult a union attorney. If there is no union contract in effect, free speech rights may protect most forms of non-violent pickets and boycotts.

i. Picketing in Public Places

Under state trespass laws, courts may restrict picketing in public places and impose limits on the number of pickets if traffic is blocked, or if the entrance or exit to the employer's place of business is obstructed.

ii. Informational Picketing

In general, employees have a protected constitutional right to engage in peaceful picketing designed to provide information to the public regarding the existence of a labor dispute. (*Thornhill v. Alabama* (1940) 310 U.S. 88.) Such "informational picketing" is used to inform the public that the employer either employs no union members or has no contract with the union; it does not seek to stop work or block the delivery of goods or services. (29 U.S. Code section 158(b)(7)(C).)

The NLRA generally does not limit picketing that is merely informational. Likewise, California's Public Employment Relations Board has upheld the right of public school employees to engage in peaceful, non-disruptive picketing. (*San Marcos Unified School District* (2003) 158 CPER 83.) Therefore, in California's public sector, non-disruptive, informational picketing is protected activity under EERA and, presumably, the other public sector statutes as well.

iii. Recognitional and Organizational Picketing

"Recognitional picketing" is designed to persuade an employer to recognize the union as the employees' representative. "Organizational picketing" is designed to persuade employees to support the union. Recognitional and organizational picketing are prohibited when another union is lawfully recognized by the employer, when a valid election was held within the previous twelve months, or when no valid petition for an election is filed within thirty days of the start of such picketing. (29 U.S. Code section 158(b)(7)(A)-(C).) Thus, if there is not a validly recognized incumbent union in the workplace (with current representation rights) and there has not been an election within the previous twelve months, employees and their unions have the right to engage in recognitional and organizational picketing for as long as thirty days. After that, the union must either seek a representation election or cease picketing. (29 U.S. Code section 158(b)(7).)

2. Strikes

a. General Protections for the Right to Strike

Private sector employees possess a limited right to engage in strikes against their own employer based on various laws and the federal and state constitutions. Strikes involve employees' constitutional rights to freedom of speech and association. Thus, police interference with a strike has been found to violate employees' rights under the First and Fourteenth Amendments to the U.S. Constitution. (*Allee v. Medrano* (1974) 416 U.S. 802.) However, the Constitution has not been interpreted to give workers an unlimited right to strike.

The Norris-LaGuardia Act of 1932 (29 U.S. Code sections 101 et seq.) removed the authority of the federal courts to issue injunctions in cases involving labor disputes. California has a similar provision, known as the "Little Norris-LaGuardia Act." (Labor Code section 1138.1.) However these statutes do not create an absolute right to strike.

The labor relations framework established by Congress through the National Labor Relations Act is designed to promote peaceful negotiations between employers and organized employees. This framework was developed with an awareness of economic weapons on both sides of the labor relationship, with employees possessing the right to strike and picket, and employers possessing the right to lock out employees and hire replacements for striking employees.

Most public sector employees in California (except firefighters and police officers) possess a common law right to strike, unless a strike is forbidden by statute or poses an imminent threat to public health and safety. (*City and County of San Francisco v. United Association of Journeymen of the Plumbing and Pipefitting Industry, Local 38* (1986) 42 Cal.3d 810.) None of California's public sector labor laws expressly forbids strikes. However, some of California's labor laws have been interpreted to place limits on public employees' right to strike.

A union or attorney should be consulted for specific strike rules in the public sector.

b. Particular Contexts, Purposes, and Effects of Strikes, and Their Effect on the Right to Strike

i. Strikes to Protest Unfair Labor Practices

Employees have the right to strike over unfair labor practices as a way to protest their employer's illegal actions. For example, if an employer commits an unfair labor practice (an act prohibited by labor law, such as refusing to bargain in good faith), employees have the right to strike, and they are entitled to return to their jobs when they end the strike and make an unconditional offer to return to work. (*NLRB v. International Van Lines* (1972) 409 U.S. 48, 50.) Whether employees are considered unfair labor practice strikers or not depends on whether the NLRB determines that the employees struck because of an unfair labor practice and whether the employer's conduct is ultimately found to be an unfair labor practice. These are uncertainties that must be evaluated in considering the decision to strike.

ii. Sympathy Strikes

Employees of one employer who refuse to cross the picket line of another employer's employees are protected by the NLRA. Such "sympathy strikes" are lawful unless forbidden by the collective bargaining agreement governing the employees who refuse to cross the line. The same rule applies in California's public sector. (*Regents of the University of California* (2004) PERB Dec. No. 1638-H.)

iii. Economic Strikes

An economic strike is an action in which employees protest the terms and conditions of their employment or their employer's position in bargaining with regard to such things. Terms and conditions of employment include (but are not limited to) wages, benefits, work rules, grievance rights, and other issues affecting the workplace and the job.

An employer cannot fire an employee for participating in such a strike. However, the employer is generally allowed to replace economic strikers permanently or temporarily. (*NLRB v. Mackay Radio & Television Co.* (1938) 304 U.S. 333.) If a permanent replacement has not been hired prior to the end of the strike, a striking employee can apply for reinstatement, and the employer is generally obligated to reinstate him.

iv. Lockouts

Employers can lock out employees to force a favorable resolution of a contract dispute. They can even hire temporary replacements if they lock out their employees. The employer can continue the lock out until it gets the union's agreement to a favorable contract.

c. Limits on the Right to Strike
i. Strikes in Violation of Collective Bargaining Agreements

A strike undertaken in violation of a no-strike clause in a collective bargaining agreement is a breach of contract. Discipline, including termination, may be administered to employees for striking or picketing in violation of no-strike agreements.

ii. Sit-Down Strikes, Slowdowns, Intermittent Work Stoppages, and "Work-to-Rule" Actions

Not all work stoppages are protected activity, regardless of their intended purpose. For example, *sit-down strikes*, in which employees remain on the employer's premises for the work stoppage and seize control of the worksite, are unlawful. (*NLRB v. Fansteel Metallurgical Corp.* (1939) 306 U.S. 240.) Employees need to use caution because the NLRB has found much conduct to be "unprotected." The NLRB has even found walkouts where the employees remain in the employer's parking lot to be unprotected by the NLRA. A *work slowdown* is also unprotected, and an employer may fire employees who participate.

Intermittent work stoppages (which stop and start multiple times) may be unprotected. However, a *one-time strike* of *short duration* (for example, for a few minutes or a single shift) is more likely to be protected.

Another tactic workers use in the workplace to apply pressure may sometimes be called an "inside game" or a "work-to-rule" campaign. It involves employees performing only those duties literally required by the employer or the collective bargaining agreement.

In California's public sector, work slowdowns or "work-to-rule" job actions have sometimes been found to be unlawful. (*El Dorado Union High School District* (1985) PERB Dec. No. 537.) Teachers' refusal to perform *required* duties as part of a job action has been found to be unlawful, but their refusal to perform *voluntary* duties may be considered lawful action. (*Poway Unified School District* (1995) PERB Dec. No. 1114.)

Intermittent strikes after the union and employer have indicated that they are at impasse and unable to reach agreement have been held to be unprotected and unlawful. (*Fremont Unified School District* (1990) PERB Dec. No. IR-54.) In the public sector in California, PERB will consider whether the strike was a "last resort" by the union and whether it was provoked by an employer's unfair practice before determining whether to seek to prevent or stop a strike.

Tactics must be carefully planned to avoid giving an employer the excuse to fire workers. Legal advice is an important part of planning such actions.

iii. Secondary Strikes or Boycotts

The NLRA prohibits strikes, picketing, and the formation of agreements that aim to prevent one employer from doing business with, or selling the goods of, another employer. (29 U.S. Code section 158(b)(4), (e).) Such actions are known as secondary strikes, secondary boycotts, or hot cargo agreements. They are an effort to take action that will affect another employer (with whom the workers do not have a labor dispute), by employees of an employer with whom the workers do have a dispute. Put another way, if the union has a dispute with employer A, it is a form of secondary boycott to pressure, by picketing or boycotting, employer B just because employer B buys goods or sells goods to employer A.

The application of rules concerning secondary boycotts is complicated. These rules do not apply to some forms of pressure (for example, most forms of leafleting) against the so-called neutral employer, but the conduct must be carefully planned. Unions are increasing their use of environmental challenges, capital strategies, lawsuits, and other "comprehensive campaigns" to resolve labor disputes. Individual workers cannot mount these kinds of tactics by themselves because of the resources needed. These tactics should be considered only after careful thought and consultation with attorneys or others who specialize in these issues.

E. DUTY TO TELL JOB SEEKERS ABOUT LABOR DISPUTES

In California, anyone advertising to fill a job must plainly and explicitly mention any labor problem at the workplace. This law applies to all forms of advertisement — newspaper, word-of-mouth, poster, letter, or other form of communication. It includes any existing or pending labor dispute — strike, lockout, trade dispute, labor disturbance, or jurisdictional dispute. (Labor Code section 973.)

Employment agencies and job listing services must give job seekers a written statement about labor conditions at any establishment to which they send an applicant. (Civil Code sections 1812.504(a)(8), 1812.516(a)(8).) The statement must notify the job seeker of the existence of any labor trouble. (Civil Code sections 1812.504(a)(8), 1812.516(a)(8), 1812.521(b), (c).)

Employment agencies and job listing services may not refer minors to workplaces with existing or pending labor disputes without notifying the job seeker of the dispute and placing a statement of the situation on the contract. (Civil Code section 1812.509(c).) Minors must be advised whether or not a union contract is in existence and whether or not union membership is required. (Civil Code section 1812.509(b).)

Enforcement: File a claim with the state labor commissioner or a complaint with the local district attorney. File a civil suit for triple and punitive damages, attorney's fees, and costs. (Civil Code section 1812.523).

F. RIGHT TO CONTROL AND DISPLAY UNION INSIGNIA

Unions control their labels, trademarks, cards, signs, and buttons. An employer must have the union's permission to use any of these identification marks. Permission must be given in writing (and must not have been revoked by the union).

Employees in the private sector are entitled to use a union card or wear a union button only if allowed to do so by the rules and regulations of that union. (Labor Code sections 1010–1018.)

Federal trademark law also may govern the use of a union's label.

Enforcement: File a claim with the state labor commissioner. File a civil suit.

G. RIGHT TO EXCHANGE SALARY INFORMATION WITH COWORKERS

Some employers tell their workers they may not discuss wage and salary information with each other. This prohibition may extend to vacation or other leave arrangements and to other information about job conditions. All such restrictions and prohibitions are illegal. Employees can exchange information, discuss what they learn, and organize to improve wages and conditions. Any action taken against them for exercising these basic rights is illegal. (29 U.S. Code section 158(a)(1).) Any restrictions imposed by employers or discrimination because of such discussion also violates California law. (Labor Code sections 232, 232.5; *Grant-Burton v. Covenant Care, Inc.* (2002) 99 Cal. App. 4th 1361.)

Enforcement: File a charge with the National Labor Relations Board. File a claim with the state labor commissioner. File a civil suit.

IV. UNION'S DUTY OF FAIR REPRESENTATION

Unions are subject to a duty to fairly represent all members of a bargaining unit, regardless of whether the bargaining unit members are also union members. In the private sector, this duty is not set forth in the NLRA, but has been stated by the courts as necessary to the union's status as the exclusive representative of the bargaining unit members. (See *Vaca v. Sipes* (1967) 386 U.S. 171.) This is called the "duty of fair representation" or DFR.

The union's first responsibility is to make decisions in the interest of the bargaining unit as a whole, even when this clashes with the interests or desires of an individual union member. As a result, some union decisions may be objectionable to individual bargaining unit members. One example would be the decision not to take an individual

member's grievance to arbitration. The union may choose not to pursue a case because winning it would result in an interpretation of the governing collective bargaining agreement that is not in the interest of the bargaining unit as a whole. Alternatively, the union may be concerned that losing the grievance could create a bad precedent, or the union may feel that its chances of winning are too small. Unions are given broad discretion when acting as the exclusive representative for the bargaining unit. Only decisions that are found to be *arbitrary*, *discriminatory*, or undertaken in *bad faith* violate the duty of fair representation. Mere negligence on the union's part does not violate the duty.

Generally, only the union can allege that the employer has violated the collective bargaining agreement. Individual employees cannot sue the employer for breach of the collective bargaining agreement without first going through all the steps outlined in the grievance arbitration procedures. Sometimes, an employee will claim an exception to the rule requiring exhaustion of administrative remedies. The employee will sue both the employer and the union, arguing that the employer violated

the collective bargaining agreement, and that the union violated its duty of fair representation and therefore use of the grievance machinery would be futile.

If an employee is claiming a violation of rights included in the collective bargaining agreement that are also found in state or federal statutes (for instance, laws against discrimination), the employee may have the right to sue without going through the steps outlined in the collective bargaining agreement. In some cases, a collective bargaining agreement can waive the rights of covered employees to file suit, but the waiver must be clear and unmistakable. In those cases, the employees are required to use the grievance and arbitration procedures with the union's help. (*14 Penn Plaza LLC v. Pyett* (2009) 129 S. Ct.1456.)

Enforcement: File a lawsuit in state or federal court under NLRA section 301. (29 U.S. Code section 185.)

Some of California's public sector labor relations statutes expressly set forth a duty of fair representation. (See EERA, Government Code section 3544.9; HEERA, Government Code section 3578; TEERA, Public Utilities Code section 99564.5.) The Dills Act applies a duty of fair representation to agency fee payers (individuals who do not wish to join the union but who are required to pay for representation-related services they receive), but the provision has been interpreted as applying to all members of the bargaining unit. (See Government Code section 3515.7(g); *California State Employees Association (Norgard)* (1984) PERB Dec. No. 451-S.) The duty of fair representation in California's public sector has been interpreted similarly to the federal duty. The duty is violated only if the union's conduct is arbitrary, discriminatory, or undertaken in bad faith (lacks a rational basis or is not based on honest judgment). (See *Rocklin Teachers Professional Association (Romero)* (1980) PERB Dec. No. 124.) The duty of fair representation applies to all public sector unions.

Enforcement: Unlike in the private sector, charges of a violation of the duty of fair representation against California's public sector unions must be filed with the Public Employment Relations Board. (*Los Angeles Council of School Nurses v. Los Angeles Unified School District* (1980) 113 Cal. App. 3d 666.)

DISCHARGE AND DISCIPLINARY ACTION

I. SCOPE OF THE CHAPTER

More than three million American workers are fired each year. Millions more are "released," "let go," or laid off. If an individual works under a contract, such as a collective bargaining agreement or a written employment agreement for a fixed period of time, that person has certain protections against being discharged. Other workers are said to work "at the will" of their employer and supposedly can be fired for any cause or no cause.

However, even "at will" workers cannot be terminated for reasons that violate their legal rights, or for reasons that violate fundamental public policies based on state and federal laws and constitutional rights. For example, an employer is not allowed to fire employees because of their race, age, religion, color, national origin, marital status, or sexual orientation; because they exercised their rights to Workers' Compensation, disability, or family leave benefits; because they refused to work under imminent hazardous conditions; because they complained to a government agency about violations of the law; because they refused to engage in illegal conduct ordered by their employers; or because they exercised their rights to vote, run for office, or act as election officials.

If an employer disciplines or discharges an

employee, the individual may have the right to know the reason or to see investigative reports that formed the basis of the action. Employers are not allowed to humiliate or harass employees, invade their privacy, or take certain other actions as a means of disciplining them or causing them to quit work. Employees should check with their union (if they have one) if disciplinary action is taken against them. Both employees and employers should become familiar with the provisions of collective bargaining contracts and employer handbooks or policies that govern the employment relationship, discipline, and discharge.

Many of the unlawful grounds for discharge (for example, discrimination, retaliation for whistleblowing, etc.) and enforcement strategies for violations of those rights are discussed in other chapters of this book.

Time limits for filing lawsuits for wrongful terminations vary depending on the type of case. See Chapter 4 for more information on wage and hour issues, and see Chapter 6 on discrimination. Grievance deadlines under collective bargaining agreements may be short. Individuals who have been wrongfully discharged should seek advice promptly.

II. WHAT IS A DISCHARGE?

A. INVOLUNTARY BREAK IN EMPLOYMENT

Discharge (sometimes called termination) means any permanent or long-term break in employment that is imposed on the employee. It includes a firing, layoff, and having one's job or position eliminated or reorganized out of existence.

If an individual is on layoff and the employer refuses to rehire him in violation of a rehire policy, the failure to rehire is considered a termination. If the employer refuses to let an employee return to work after a sick leave or any other kind of leave, the refusal is also a discharge. If an employer places an individual on an indefinite suspension, the suspension may also be a discharge.

Sometimes a resignation is actually a discharge. If an employee is told to "resign or be fired," the employee is considered to have been discharged, even if he resigns. Sometimes employers say that if employees fail to report to work for a given number of days, they have voluntarily quit. If an employee is forced to "quit" after an absence, this is considered to be a discharge. If, while an employee is out sick, his employer announces that it will consider the individual released or resigned if the employee does not return to work or get in touch, and the employee then loses his job, that termination is a discharge. Whether that discharge is allowable legally will depend on the circumstances.

B. CONSTRUCTIVE DISCHARGE

In some situations, even though an employee decides to quit a job, leaving still may be considered a discharge. These cases are called constructive discharges because they are interpreted as terminations rather than voluntary resignations. If an employee's job is made so intolerable that a "reasonable" person would leave rather than put up with it, her leaving may count as a termination. Intolerable conditions are often caused by harassment based on an individual's sex, race, ethnicity, religion, or sexual orientation; by retaliation for an individual's refusal to engage in illegal behavior or for reporting legal or safety violations; by serious safety hazards that the employer does not correct; or by extreme invasions of privacy. If a new and unreasonable condition is imposed on an individual's work, so that the individual, acting as a reasonable person, cannot keep her job, the employee's leaving may also be considered a constructive discharge. However, an employee who leaves a job when a reasonable

Even "at will" workers cannot be terminated for reasons that violate their legal rights or fundamental public policies.

person would stay is not considered to have been constructively discharged. Ultimately, judges in the higher courts decide what is "reasonable."

Some courts have ruled that to win a claim for constructive discharge the employee must show that the employer knew about the conditions and their impact on the employee, and that a reasonable employer would realize those conditions would force a reasonable person to resign. (*Turner v. Anheuser-Busch, Inc.* (1994) 7 Cal.4th 1238.) An employee who is considering leaving a job and claiming "constructive discharge" should make certain the employer has been notified about the situation and its impact on the employee. In order for a constructive discharge to be based on a single incident (rather than a series of incidents), the incident must be of a serious nature (for example, a violent assault).

III. EMPLOYMENT "AT WILL" VERSUS EMPLOYMENT THAT MAY BE TERMINATED ONLY FOR JUST CAUSE

A. "AT WILL" EMPLOYMENT

Nineteenth-century court rulings established the policy that employees worked "at the will" of their employers, unless a contract specified otherwise. Workers could be discharged for good reason, bad reason, or no reason at all.

In California, this doctrine is found in Labor Code section 2922, which states: "An employment, having no specified term, may be terminated at the will of either party on notice to the other. Employment for a specified term means an employment for a period greater than one month." (Simply working for an employer for more than one month does not mean that the employee has a contract "for a specified term." A contract "for a specified term" means that the individual must have a contract with the employer that spells out the exact time period of employment, such as four months, one year, or three years, or until the job is done.)

An "at will" employee may quit or be fired at any time. Employment in California is usually considered "at will" unless there is either an oral or written contract, or a statute or ordinance that provides that it is not "at will." However, as

discussed in the sections that follow, the exceptions carved out by court decisions and laws to the "at will" employment doctrine have placed substantial limits on the doctrine of "at will" employment in California.

The courts have developed exceptions to the assumption that employees may be discharged at will. They are (1) when the discharge violates important public policy (see section III.D., p. 243); (2) when the discharge violates a contract requiring good cause for termination; and (3) when the discharge violates the implied covenant (promise) of good faith and fair dealing (see sections that follow for more information on this).

B. JUST CAUSE OR GOOD CAUSE REQUIREMENT

Many employment relationships are not defined by the "at will" doctrine. Some include a requirement that discipline and discharge be only for just cause (sometimes called "good cause" or referred to as "for cause"). This requirement comes from multiple sources, including the state and federal constitutions and laws, employment and collective bargaining contracts, hiring letters, and employer personnel policies. (*Scott v. Pacific Gas and Electric Co.* (1995) 11 Cal.4th 454, disapproved on other grounds in *Guz v. Bechtel National, Inc.* (2000) 24 Cal.4th 317.) However, if an employment contract states that it is an "at will" contract, courts generally will not find that the employer must have cause to terminate the employee. Written contracts are considered more controlling than other evidence in interpreting the agreement between the parties. (*Guz v. Bechtel National, Inc.* (2000) 24 Cal.4th 317; *Eisenberg v. Alameda Newspapers, Inc.* (1999) 74 Cal.App.4th 1359; *Agosta v. Astor* (2004) 120 Cal.App.4th 596.)

In employment situations not covered by collective bargaining agreements, courts have defined good cause as fair and honest reasons, regulated by good faith on the part of the employer, not reasons that are trivial, arbitrary, capricious, unrelated to business needs or goals, and not pretexts, that is, false reasons given to cover up true reasons. (*Cotran v. Rollins Hudig Hall International, Inc.* (1998) 17 Cal.4th 93.)

There is a seven-part test commonly used to determine whether just cause exists when an employer disciplines or discharges an employee. It

has developed through arbitration decisions carried out under collective bargaining agreements. Some, but not all, arbitrators require that the following elements be present in order to uphold a finding of just cause for termination:

• The employee must have advance notice of what conduct is prohibited and the likely consequences of poor job performance or misconduct. However, notice may be presumed that extremely serious offenses, like violent assault and embezzlement, are prohibited.

• The employer's policies, practices, and performance standards must be reasonable and job-related.

• The employer must conduct an investigation before imposing discipline.

• The employee must be given an opportunity to respond to the issues raised by the employer as reasons for the proposed discipline, and must be allowed to direct the response to a management official who was not directly involved in making the accusations.

• There must be substantial evidence that the employee was guilty of the alleged poor performance or misconduct.

• Employees in the same or similar situations must be treated similarly.

• The degree of discipline must be reasonable in light of the seriousness of the offense, the type of employment, and the employee's record.

A lack of just cause may be found when the reasons for the employer's actions are minor, based on whims, inconsistent, or unrelated to business needs, or when the reason given is not the real reason for the discharge.

A thorough discussion of the just cause standard in employment can be found in *Just Cause: The Seven Tests*, by Adolph Koven and Susan Smith, published by the Bureau of National Affairs, Inc. See also *How Arbitration Works*, Chapter 15, by Frank Elkouri and Edna Asper Elkouori, published by the Bureau of National Affairs, Inc.

Just cause requirements can become part of an employment relationship in a variety of ways, as discussed in the following sections. The manner in which just cause requirements are applied will vary according to the fact situation.

C. SOURCES OF JUST CAUSE REQUIREMENTS

Just cause or good cause requirements are based on a number of different types of documents and situations. (*Mendoza v. Regents of the Univ. of California* (1978) 78 Cal.App.3d 168.)

1. Contractual Employment Protections
a. Collective Bargaining Agreements

If an employee is covered by a collective bargaining agreement, also known as a union contract, its provisions for discipline or discharge create an enforceable written contract that prevents the individual's employer from terminating him or her "at will."

Collective bargaining agreements often protect employees from at-will discharge by including a just cause provision stating that the employer must have a good reason to terminate or discipline a worker. Many collective bargaining agreements outline a series of disciplinary steps that an employer must follow prior to imposing discipline or discharge except in the most serious cases of employee misconduct. These steps are generally progressive. They move from less serious measures, like verbal or written warnings, through intermediate steps, such as letters to the file or perhaps a short suspension, to the most serious steps, like extended suspensions without pay and discharge.

Almost all collective bargaining agreements also provide for binding grievance arbitration of challenged disciplinary actions. Thus, if the union does not agree that the employer had good cause, followed proper disciplinary procedures, and imposed discipline that is reasonable in light of the alleged problem, an independent arbitrator may determine the fairness of the discipline or discharge.

Public employees often have appeal rights within a civil service or merit system (as discussed below), grievance rights under a union contract, or appeal rights under internal agency "grievance/ arbitration" procedures. For more information on mandatory arbitration, see Chapter 1. Grievance rights under collective bargaining agreements generally provide sufficient protections to comply with court decisions requiring due process for public employees, even if only the union (and not the employee) has the right to determine whether a grievance is taken to arbitration. (*Jones v. Omnitrans* (2004) 125 Cal.App.4th 273.)

b. Express or Implied Individual Employment Contracts With Express or Implied Just Cause Provisions

An employment relationship between an individual and an employer is often defined by a written agreement. Contracts in which all the terms are specifically outlined (either in writing or verbally) are called "express contracts." Express contracts may be written or oral (based on discussion and agreement between the parties).

Even in the absence of a written contract, some courts will find that an agreement not to terminate the employee except for good cause is *implied*. (*Cotran v. Rollins Hudig Hall International, Inc.* (1998) 17 Cal.4th 93.) Contracts may be implied by written documents (such as employee handbooks or memoranda), employer or industry practices and policies (such as providing periodic performance evaluations), job advertisements or hiring letters, or written or verbal communications from the employer that lead to the reasonable belief that the employment relationship will continue unless and until the employee's performance is substandard or she engages in some form of misconduct.

When there is an implied contract to discipline only for good cause, California courts look at the "totality of the circumstances" (in other words, the entire set of facts surrounding the situation). In some cases, the totality of the circumstances indicates that the employer and the employee agreed the employer's power to terminate the employee's job would be limited in some way. For instance, there may be assurances given that the employee will be able to stay with the employer if performance is good. In appropriate situations, the courts may restrict an employer's right to terminate at will.

i. Factors That May Indicate a Limitation on the Employer's Right to Terminate At Will

If an employee's working conditions are governed by a personnel manual or employee handbook, the procedures in that document for discipline or discharge may be considered an enforceable "implied" contract between the individual and the employer that employment will not be terminated except for just cause. The courts may find the employer does not have an unrestricted right to fire employees at will if the personnel manual provides for progressive discipline (that is, steadily increasing forms of discipline for repeated problems), sets forth an employee warning system, or guarantees employees a chance to correct a problem before being subject to discipline. But the personnel manual alone may not be sufficient to create an implied contract. It has a greater chance of being considered an implied restriction on the employer's ability to fire an employee at will when combined with other factors such as length of service, the employer's communications or assurances of continued employment, and favorable evaluations.

ii. Factors That May Indicate "At Will" Employment

A variety of factors may lead to a finding of "at will" employment rather than an implied contract requiring good cause for discipline or termination. These factors can include industry practices that reflect an "at will" employment relationship, as well as written documents which state that nothing expressed in writing, orally, or by conduct prior to the date the document is signed created a for-cause relationship (one in which the employer must have good cause to fire the employee). If an employee

If an employee is discharged, wages are due and payable immediately.

signs a contract that clearly states the job is "at will," it is most unlikely that she will be able to prove that conduct, writings, or oral representations which preceded it created a for-cause relationship. (*Halvorsen v. Aramark Uniform Servs., Inc.* (1998) 65 Cal.App.4th 1383.)

iii. Other Factors

The following factors may also be considered in determining whether a contract or promise to require just cause to terminate employment was implied:

- The existence of a probation period (implying that a just cause standard applies after the employee completes probation);
- A practice of giving job evaluations or merit increases; however, periodic assessments alone do not mean that a job is not "at will" (*Dore v. Arnold Worldwide, Inc.* (2006) 39 Cal.4th 384.);
- The fact that the worker was employed for a long period of time;
- The job announcement, pre-employment interviews, or other expressions by the employer stating or giving rise to an impression that a just cause relationship would be created;
- Any employee handbooks, posters, bulletins, training materials, affirmative action plans, or commitments stating or giving rise to the reasonable inference (impression) that a for-cause relationship would be created;
- The existence of a company complaint process or grievance procedure;
- The employer's knowledge that the worker gave up a valuable job and/or incurred substantial expense to accept the position; or
- Assurances of continued employment by the employer.

Length of service, pay raises, and promotions, standing alone, are not enough by themselves to create an implied contract in most cases.

c. Fixed-Term Employment Contracts

A fixed-term contract is one that begins and ends on specified dates. Relatively few employees have fixed-term employment contracts.

A contract for fixed-term employment may contain provisions outlining the reasons the contract may be terminated, or it may expressly state that the contract is "at will" (meaning the employee can be terminated without cause). California law provides that unless the contract itself specifies otherwise, a contract for a particular period of time may be terminated at any time by the employer in the case of an intentional violation of the duties under the contract, habitual neglect of duties, or continued inability to perform the job. (Labor Code section 2924.) California courts have held that this law provides the only reasons an employee on a fixed-term contract may be fired. (*Holtzendorff v. Housing Authority of Los Angeles* (1967) 250 Cal.App.2d 596; *Khajavi v. Feather River Anesthesia Medical Group* (2000) 84 Cal. App.4th 32.)

Although the fixed-term contract may be spoken or written, it is best to have it in writing. If the agreement is oral (spoken), then it is a good idea for the employee to write a confirming letter outlining the conversation that took place establishing the agreement.

Once a fixed-term employment contract expires, the individual's rights are the same as those of any worker. If the employee continues working past the expiration date of the fixed-term agreement, she may be considered an "at will" employee unless she negotiates a new agreement for a specified term. (Labor Code sections 2922.) If the contract expires and the employee is not retained, she is generally not considered an employee anymore. However, she may have some legal rights if the contract was not renewed for a reason that violated a specific law establishing a strong public policy on protecting workers. But a worker with an expired fixed-term contract does not have the same rights as a current or permanent employee. (*Daly v. Exxon Corp.* (1997) 55 Cal.App.4th 39; *Motevalli v. Los Angeles Unified School District* (2004) 122 Cal. App.4th 97.)

Some collective bargaining agreements establish specific rights for employees working under fixed-term contracts.

Enforcement: File a civil suit, or a grievance under the applicable collective bargaining agreement or employer complaint procedure. If the discharge involves discrimination or some other violation of a specific statute, it may be necessary to file a complaint with the administrative agency enforcing the particular law (for example, the Department of Fair Employment and Housing for violations of the state discrimination laws; see Chapter 6 for more information).

2. Public Employment

Public employees with permanent status have constitutional protections from "at will" terminations. Discharges must be justified. See section IV.F.1., p. 248, for some of the causes for which public employees may be disciplined or discharged.

Public employees have substantial rights to due process of law (notice, reasons for discharge, copies of materials on which discharge is based, and an opportunity to respond). Many temporary or probationary public workers have some rights to notice and an opportunity to respond. The great majority of government workers, including all those with permanent status, are entitled to hearing and appeal rights. The sources of these rights include court cases, state and federal laws, collective bargaining agreements, and government civil service and merit systems rules.

Permanent employees are entitled to pre-discipline notice, copies of materials on which the discharge or discipline is based, and an opportunity to respond to the charges. (*Skelly v. State Personnel Board* (1975) 15 Cal.3d 194.) The opportunity to respond need not be a full legal hearing, but it must provide the employee with a chance to clarify the situation. The right to respond must be meaningful and allow the employee sufficient time to prepare. (*Kempland v. Regents of the University of California* (1984) 155 Cal.App.3d 644.) However, if the employee who has been notified of the right to respond declines the offer to present his side of the story, his right to respond before the discipline or discharge is implemented may be considered waived. (*Mitchell v. State Personnel Board* (1979) 90 Cal.App.3d 808.) Employees are entitled to representation at this meeting. (2 California Code of Regulations section 51.5.) See section IV.A., p. 244, for more information on the right to representation at investigatory interviews that may lead to discipline.

It should be noted that an absence without leave for five consecutive working days is automatically considered a resignation for public employees. (Government Code section 19996.2.) In such a case, it is the employee who severs the employment relationship, rather than the state. Before it can consider the absence a resignation, the state must make a factual determination that the absence is for five consecutive working days and is without leave. The state must give the employee written notice of the state's impending action, including the facts supporting the action. If the employee challenges the accuracy of the facts, the state must allow her to present her version of the facts before a neutral factfinder. (*Coleman v. Department of Personnel Admin.* (1991) 52 Cal.3d 1102.)

See more discussion on the rights of public employees in section IV., p. 244.

D. WRONGFUL DISCHARGE IN VIOLATION OF FUNDAMENTAL PUBLIC POLICY

Private sector workers without union protection have some job security rights, but these are much more limited. Generally, employees have the right to do the following without fear of being discharged: refuse to violate the law, report an employer's violation of a law that protects the public, perform a legal obligation, or exercise a basic legal right.

California courts have held that workers can sue their employer for "wrongful discharge" in the following kinds of cases:

- The worker was fired for refusing to commit an illegal act or participate in an illegal conspiracy.
- The worker was fired for reporting an improper act by the employer. On whistleblowing rights, see Chapter 11.
- The worker was fired for opposing unsafe or unhealthy working conditions. On rights concerning health, safety, and sanitation, see Chapter 7.
- The worker was fired for exercising a right to free speech or another important civil right.
- The worker was fired for testifying, under subpoena, in a legal proceeding.
- The worker was fired in violation of an employment contract, a promise of a contract, or "fairness." The contract or promise may be explicit (spelled out) or implicit (implied). A judge or jury has to determine whether such a contract or promise was made.

- The worker was fired in an attempt to avoid payment of commissions and vacation.
- The worker was fired for a reason that violates fundamental public policy. This means that an employer is not acting lawfully when the termination has a tendency to injure the public or be against the public good. The policy must be found in the Constitution, the laws, or the regulations implementing the law. A claim of wrongful discharge in violation of public policy must involve a policy that benefits society at large rather than merely an individual. For example, in one California case the court held that a situation in which employees were fired for reporting the employment of undocumented workers involved fundamental public policy. (*Jie v. Liang Tai Knitwear Co.* (2001) 89 Cal. App.4th 654.) In another case, the court held that violation of the employer's internal policies or the collective bargaining agreement was an internal matter and did not involve a fundamental public policy. (*Turner v. Anheuser-Busch, Inc.* (1994) 7 Cal.4th 1238.) If an employer fired an employee after overhearing a conversation about how the employee voted in an election, that would probably violate public policy. If the rights involved may be waived, they probably do not involve a fundamental public policy. (*Lagatree v. Luce, Forward, Hamilton & Scripps* (1999) 74 Cal.App.4th 1105 (in which requiring an employee to sign an arbitration agreement did not violate public policy since the right to jury trial and a judicial forum for resolution of disputes may be waived).) The policy must be fundamental, substantial, and well established to ensure that employers have notice of prohibited conduct. (*Gantt v. Sentry Insurance* (1992) 1 Cal.4th 1083.)

Under federal law, disputes that are merely private disagreements are generally not found to be violations of fundamental public policies. However, labor laws are generally considered to be matters of fundamental public interest. Also, allowing a contract to expire is not considered a discharge for purposes of lawsuits based on violations of public policy. (*Khajavi v. Feather River Anesthesia Medical Group* (2000) 84 Cal.App.4th 32; *Motevalli v. Los Angeles Unified School District* (2004) 122 Cal.App.4th 97.)

IV. EMPLOYEE RIGHTS IN SITUATIONS INVOLVING DISCIPLINE AND DISCHARGE

Rights available to employees facing discipline or discharge vary depending on whether they are private or public sector employees, whether they are working under a collective bargaining agreement, and according to the terms of employment contracts and employer policies. However, there are a number of actions an employee should take when he fears that discipline or discharge is a possibility, and when it occurs.

A. PRIOR TO DISCHARGE OR DISCIPLINE

Before being discharged or disciplined, employees should consider the following actions:
- Employees covered by collective bargaining agreements should contact their union.
- Public employees and those working under union contracts have the right to a union representative at investigatory interviews the employee reasonably believes might result in discipline or discharge. If the employer refuses to allow a union representative to be present, the employee has the option of declining to be interviewed. However, this right is limited to situations in which discipline or termination is a possibility, not to ordinary workplace meetings with supervisors. There is no duty to bargain with the union at this meeting, but the union representative must be allowed to assist the employee and clarify the facts. (*NLRB v. J. Weingarten, Inc.* (1975) 420 U.S. 251.) Employees asked to participate in interviews with investigators hired by the employer that might result in discipline also have the right to union representation. (*NASA v. Federal Labor Relations Authority* (1999) 527 U.S. 229.)
- Employees should ask to see their personnel file and get copies of relevant documents.
- Relevant letters and memos (warnings, requests, etc.) should be saved.
- The individual would be wise to get the home telephone numbers and addresses of coworkers, especially those who might be helpful, so they can be reached later, if necessary.

B. IMMEDIATE ACTIONS TO TAKE UPON LEARNING OF DISCIPLINE OR DISCHARGE

If an employee gets fired, he should take certain steps and avoid others.

1. Seek Assistance

- If represented by a union, the individual should contact her union steward or representative right away. Most union contracts have short deadlines for filing grievances.
- If the individual is not represented by a union and thinks she may have a case for wrongful discharge, it is a good idea to immediately contact an attorney specializing in employment law.

2. Be Prepared if Meeting With the Employer

- The individual should attempt to take a union representative, friend, or trusted coworker with him to any "exit" interview or interview that might result in discipline. Employees represented by unions have a constitutional right to do this. (*NLRB v. J. Weingarten, Inc.* (1975) 420 U.S. 251.)
- Employees who are being discharged should take careful notes of anything said to them, at an exit interview or any other time, concerning the termination. Employees should be careful about what they say during the exit interview. It is okay to ask questions about the reason for the discharge, but it is not wise to give out a lot of information or to be defensive or argumentative.
- The individual should also ask the employer about the specific reason for the termination. If possible, the reasons should be obtained in writing in order to preserve a record of the employer's explanation for its action and to discourage the employer from coming up with different reasons later on. If the employer will not put the reasons in writing, but states them verbally, the employee, or someone trustworthy who accompanied the employee to the interview, should take good notes and write or type them up clearly shortly after the interview. It is a good idea to sign and date the notes as well.
- If medical reasons are given for the termination, see Chapter 6 for more information.

3. Exercise Caution if Asked to Sign Documents

- Without first consulting a union or an attorney, the individual should not sign a release, exit agreement, severance agreement, or any other form in which he promises to make no more claims against the employer.
- The employee should very carefully examine any benefits or exit forms she is given to sign. The individual should avoid signing anything if she has questions about it. It is not wise to rely solely on statements made by the person providing the forms. Particularly if the statements differ from what is on the form, employees should not take the employer's word as to what the agreement means. Employees represented by unions should consult their union representative if anything is confusing or seems out of the ordinary.
- The employee should be provided, or should demand, a copy of anything he is asked to sign.

4. Turn Over the Employer's Property

- The employee should turn over all property that belongs to the employer.
- The employee should make a list of all property turned in and have someone sign for it.

5. Examine Pension Issues, Healthcare, and Unemployment Insurance

- Employees slated for discharge should not take their contributions or shares out of a pension or profit-sharing plan or fund if they are considering contesting the termination, or if they might make a disability claim or disability retirement claim. A union, lawyer, or tax and retirement adviser should be consulted about the best steps to take with regard to pension and similar funds.
- At the exit interview or through the human resources department, the employee should ask what benefits he will receive; how long his medical and dental insurance, disability, and other fringe benefits will continue; and how he can convert them to individual coverage. The individual should also ask about all the options in his pension coverage. He should ask for any paperwork that needs to be filled out regarding pensions, health insurance, etc., and he should inquire as to the applicable deadlines.
- If the individual applies for unemployment

insurance and her employer contests her right to receive it, the individual should contact her union or an attorney, if possible. The individual should investigate how to put up the best possible fight for her unemployment benefits. If the individual thinks that she might have grounds for a lawsuit against the employer, she should obtain an attorney before the unemployment insurance benefits hearing takes place. See Chapter 5 for more information on unemployment insurance benefits.

6. Exhaust Administrative Remedies

If there are internal procedures resulting in binding arbitration that the employee can use to challenge the termination decision, or if the employee has a union and a grievance can be filed challenging the employer's action, in most instances, these complaint or grievance processes should be used. The employer's internal procedures may cover non-union workers, while union workers have access to the grievance processes in the collective bargaining agreement. Additionally, if there are government agencies charged with accepting complaints on a specific topic (for example, race or gender discrimination), the administrative remedy must be exhausted before the employee can file a lawsuit.

There are, however, some situations in which the employee might be excused from pursuing the employer's internal procedures or administrative remedies:

- The employer engages in unreasonable delay of procedures. (*Mokler v. County of Orange* (2007) 157 Cal.App.4th 121.)
- A government agency does not have the authority to decide or remedy the matter.
- Pursuing the administrative or internal remedy would result in irreparable harm to the employee (for instance, it could subject the employee to physical violence from an abusive supervisor).
- Pursuing the internal remedy clearly would be completely useless.

If the completion of a public employer's internal grievance process would not provide enough due process to create a legally binding result, the employee is not required to complete the process before pursuing a lawsuit. (*Ahmadi-Kashani v. Regents of the University of California* (2008) 159 Cal.App.4th 449 (in which the hearing did not provide for sworn testimony, cross-examination,

questioning of third-party witnesses, or the consideration of other evidence).)

Some laws specifically provide that internal administrative remedies must be used, and courts will not hear a case from a plaintiff who has not followed these rules. (*Palmer v. Regents of the University of California* (2003) 107 Cal.App.4th 899 (in which an employee of the University of California neglected to file a whistleblower's complaint with the university prior to going to court, and her case was dismissed by the court).) However, if a state law like the Fair Employment and Housing Act has its own administrative complaint procedure, public employees may choose between their agency's own internal procedure and filing a complaint with the state Department of Fair Employment and Housing. They need not file in both places. (*Schifando v. City of Los Angeles* (2003) 31 Cal.4th 1074.)

Once an employee chooses where to file a claim or complaint, she must exhaust all steps in the process and challenge any adverse findings. Exhausting all steps can include going to court to obtain a court review of any adverse administrative decisions. (*Page v. Los Angles County Probation Department* (2004) 123 Cal.App.4th 1135.) If the employee does not ask a court to review the adverse findings of an administrative agency's hearing on the matter, the findings are binding in later civil actions. (*Johnson v. City of Loma Linda* (2000) 24 Cal.4th 61.)

Decisions regarding exhaustion of administrative remedies can be tricky. If questions arise regarding the use of internal or administrative remedies, employees should consult their union or an attorney.

C. RIGHT TO PROMPT RECEIPT OF WAGES

If an employee is discharged, his wages are due and payable immediately. (Labor Code section 201.) An employee is considered discharged either when his employment is involuntarily terminated or when he is released after completion of a specific assignment or time duration. (*Smith v. Superior Court* (2006) 39 Cal.4th 77.) The employee must be paid at the place where he is discharged. (Labor Code section 208.)

When an employee quits, giving at least seventy-two hours' notice, his wages are due and payable at the end of his last shift. (Labor Code section 202.) The employee shall be paid at the office of the employer in the county where the employee has been working. (Labor Code section 208.) If the individual quits without notice, his wages are due and payable within seventy-two hours. He is entitled to receive payment by mail if he requests this method of payment and provides a mailing address. The date of the mailing is regarded as the date of payment. (Labor Code section 202.)

The individual's employer must pay his wages when due. If the employer willfully fails to pay any portion of the wages that are owed, the wages continue to add up (as if the employee were still working) until they are paid. Up to one month's worth of wages may be added to what is owed the employee as a penalty for failure to pay wages promptly. Wages will not, however, add up for more than thirty days or during any time that the individual refuses or avoids payment of his wages. (Labor Code section 203.) See Chapter 4.

Enforcement: File a claim with the state labor commissioner for "Labor Code section 203 waiting time pay."

Exceptions: Some public employees are not protected by these provisions.

For fruit, vegetable, or fish processing workers who are laid off because seasonal employment has ended, payment must be made within seventy-two hours of the layoff. An employee shall receive payment by mail if she makes the request and provides a mailing address. (Labor Code section 201(a).)

For laid-off oil drilling employees, payment must be made within twenty-four hours of termination (excluding Saturdays, Sundays, and holidays). Payment may be mailed, and the date of the mailing is the date of the payment. (Labor Code section 201.7.)

For motion picture employees whose employment ends, payment must be made by the next regular payday. (Labor Code section 201.5.) Payment may be mailed to the employee, or the employer may make the payment available at a location within the county where the employee was hired or performed the work. The payment is considered to be made on the date of mailing or the date the wages are made available. (Labor Code section 201.5(c).) See Chapter 4 for more information on remedies for non-payment or late payment of wages.

D. RIGHT TO ACCRUED VACATION

Employers are not required by law to provide paid vacation time. However, if an employer does agree to provide it, whether by a promise, policy, or collective bargaining agreement, the employer must do so. Vacation time that an individual has not used is due and payable as wages (at the individual's final rate of pay) when the employment ends, regardless of whether the individual quits, is laid off, or is fired. The employer cannot lawfully establish a policy that requires an individual to give up her right to vacation pay when she leaves employment. (Labor Code section 227.3.)

Enforcement: File a claim with the state labor commissioner. File a civil suit.

Exceptions: Vacation plans covered by collective bargaining agreements may establish different rules — for example, that employees use their vacation annually or lose it. (See Chapter 5 for more detailed discussion of vacation and other benefits.)

E. RIGHT TO KNOW REASONS FOR TERMINATION

Employees have the right to inspect and copy reports or other papers that their employers used to fire them (or to discipline them in any other way). Their employer must make these reports and papers (and the rest of their personnel files) available to them within a reasonable period after they ask to see them. (Labor Code section 1198.5.) This right continues even after they have been terminated. Employers are required to maintain personnel files of terminated employees for a minimum of two years after termination. (Government Code section 12946.) On the subject of employees' rights when an employer has an outside agency investigate them, see Chapter 3.

Employees may photocopy only those personnel papers that they have signed. They may take notes about other personnel records and papers. (See Chapter 12 for more details and citations to relevant authorities.)

Enforcement: File a claim with the state labor commissioner or a complaint with the local district attorney. File a civil suit. Violations are punishable by a fine of at least $100 or imprisonment for at least thirty days. (Labor Code section 1199.)

Exceptions: A public sector employer must make employee files available within five working days. For state government and school employees, see Chapter 12.

F. SPECIAL LAWS FOR PUBLIC EMPLOYEES

1. Reasons for Discipline or Discharge

California law contains causes for discipline (dismissal, demotion, suspension, or other forms of discipline) for some public employees. For example, any public employee may be dismissed for knowingly being a member of the Communist Party or any other organization that advocates the overthrow of the government by force or violence while the employee is a member of the organization. (Government Code section 1028.) Other California laws list specific causes for discipline for specific groups of public employees. For public employees who are not covered by statutes listing causes for discipline, reasons for discipline may be found in local ordinances, regulations, and collective bargaining agreements. Many different sources provide reasons for discipline of public employees. The statutes cover only select groups. Groups covered by special statutes are listed below.

a. State Civil Service Employees

The reasons for disciplining state civil service employees include incompetency, inefficiency, inexcusable neglect of duty, inexcusable absence without leave, willful disobedience, insubordination, fraud in securing employment, abuse of state property, incompatible outside employment, discourtesy, immoral conduct, addiction to a controlled substance, intoxication on duty, conviction of a felony or conviction of a misdemeanor involving a crime that is considered immoral, other failure of good behavior that causes discredit to the employment, improper political activity, refusal to take and follow any oath or affirmation that is required by law in connection with the employment, unlawful discrimination while acting as a state employee, and unlawful retaliation against anyone who in good faith reports information related to suspected violation of the law. (Government Code section 19572.) More information about whether specific conduct falls within the definition of an offense that may result in discipline can be obtained by consulting the precedent decisions of the State Personnel Board, which can be found at http://www.spb.ca.gov.

b. Education Employees
i. Employees of Public Schools and Community Colleges

Certain laws list causes for which public employees in education can be disciplined or discharged. Statutes in the California Education Code list reasons for discipline for teachers in elementary (K-12) schools, and employees of community colleges and the California State University. Permanent certificated employees in the elementary and secondary schools (K-12 school districts) and regular or academic employees in community colleges may be dismissed for immoral or unprofessional conduct, dishonesty, unsatisfactory performance, unfitness for service, conviction of a felony or crime that is considered immoral, and knowing membership in the

Communist Party. (Education Code sections 44932, 45303, 87732, 88122.) Permanent certificated employees of elementary and secondary schools may also be dismissed for alcoholism or other drug abuse which makes the employee unfit to associate with children. (Education Code section 44932.) Unfitness to teach is determined by considering the following factors: the likelihood that the conduct would adversely affect students or fellow teachers; the degree of the adverse effect; the timing of the conduct; the type of teaching certificate held by the party; any surrounding circumstances; the motives resulting in the conduct; the likelihood of recurrence; and the extent to which discipline might adversely impact the constitutional rights of the party or other teachers. (*Morrison v. State Bd. of Education* (1969) 1 Cal.3d. 214.)

ii. *Employees of the California State University*

Permanent and probationary employees of the California State University may be dismissed, demoted, or suspended for immoral or unprofessional conduct, dishonesty, incompetency, drunkenness on duty, failure or refusal to perform normal duties of the position, fraud in securing employment, addiction to a controlled substance, unfitness for the position, persistent refusal to obey the laws and regulations governing public schools, or conviction of a felony or conviction of a misdemeanor involving a crime that is considered immoral. (Education Code sections 89535, 89536.)

iii. *Employees of the University of California*

Employees of the University of California generally are not covered by state civil service laws, and there is no Education Code section that lists reasons for discipline for UC employees. Reasons for discipline might be found in the University's policies or in collective bargaining agreements and may be different for each campus. UC employees are covered by general laws prohibiting discrimination.

2. Constitutional Protections

Public employees who possess a "vested property interest" in continued employment generally have a constitutionally guaranteed right to procedural due process before they may be disciplined or discharged. This right is based on the Fifth and Fourteenth Amendments to the U.S. Constitution and on Article I, section 7 of the California Constitution. Both provisions prohibit the government from taking life, liberty, or property without due process of law.

In order to possess a constitutionally protected property interest in public employment, the employee must have an expectation of continued employment that is based on a statute, ordinance, personnel rule, employment agreement, collective bargaining agreement, or promise which creates a permanent employment relationship and provides that the employee can be discharged only for cause. (*Board of Regents of State Colleges v. Roth* (1972) 408 U.S. 564.)

A public employee who is discharged or significantly disciplined is entitled to a full evidentiary hearing (which includes the right to present evidence and testimony, and to cross-examine the other side's witnesses) in front of a neutral decision maker. However, the full evidentiary hearing can take place *after* the discipline is imposed, for instance, when the employee appeals the decision or requests a meeting. (*Jones v. Omnitrans* (2004) 125 Cal. App.4th 273.) The California Supreme Court has held that when public employees have a reasonable expectation of continued employment, they possess a property right in that employment and are also entitled to some due process rights (but not a full evidentiary hearing) *before* the discipline is imposed. (*Skelly v. State Personnel Board* (1975) 15 Cal.3d 194; *Civil Service Association v. City and County of San Francisco* (1978) 22 Cal.3d 552; *Ng v. State Personnel Board* (1977) 68 Cal.App.3d 600; *Mokler v. County of Orange* (2007) 157 Cal.App.4th 121 (citing *Skelly*).)

These pre-disciplinary due process rights are triggered by actions in which the employee faces loss of pay or benefits (such as demotion, a suspension of more than five days, or dismissal). Some courts have determined the amount of due process required by balancing three factors: the private interest of the employee that will be affected; the risk of mistakenly depriving the interest through procedures used, and the probable value, if any, of additional procedures; and the government interest. If the government is facing financial crisis and chooses to demote an employee instead of imposing a layoff, the government may hold a post-demotion hearing rather than a pre-demotion hearing. (*Duncan v. Department of Personnel Administration* (2000) 77 Cal.App.4th 1166.) An employee's pre-disciplinary due process rights are generally not triggered by written reprimands or reclassifications that incur no loss of pay or benefits. (*Schultz v. Regents of the University of California* (1984) 160 Cal.App.3d 768; *Stanton v. City of West Sacramento* (1991) 226 Cal.App.3d 1438; Government Code section 19576.) Federal law imposes a similar due process requirement. Federal, state, and local public employees with an expectation of continued employment are entitled to a limited pre-termination hearing and a comprehensive post-termination hearing. (*Cleveland Board of Education v. Loudermill* (1985) 470 U.S. 532.)

The *Skelly* decision provides that before a permanent public employee with a vested property interest in continued employment is discharged or significantly disciplined, he has limited pre-disciplinary due process rights. Under *Skelly*, the employer must, prior to taking action, provide the employee with:

- Written notice of the proposed action and the reasons for the action;
- A copy of the charges and materials on which the action is based;
- The right to respond orally or in writing before a final decision is made.

(*Skelly v. State Personnel Bd.* (1975) 15 Cal.3d 194.)

The employee has the right to respond; the employer must make an initial decision, based on the employee's response; discipline can then be imposed; then the employee has a right to the full hearing. The "Skelly" right to respond generally means a right to a meeting where the employee can respond to the allegations before a neutral party who will make a recommendation to the appointing authority (the public officer with the right to fire the employee). The employee has the right to representation at this meeting (for example, by a union representative). If the employee does not wish to respond to the charges in a meeting, the response can be written. Requests for "Skelly" meetings can be made verbally or in writing, but it is a good idea to make requests for "Skelly" meetings in writing and keep a copy. Employees who were notified of their rights and do not take advantage of the opportunity to respond to the charges or have a "Skelly" meeting may waive their rights. (*Flippin v. Los Angeles City Bd. of Civil Serv. Commissioners* (2007) 148 Cal.App.4th 272.)

Suspensions of fewer than five days or other less drastic disciplinary actions trigger some due process rights, but do not require *Skelly*-type procedures (notice, a copy of the charges, and a right to respond) *before* the discipline is imposed. For example, in the case of a suspension of fewer than five days, *Skelly*-type procedures which are provided *during* the suspension or within a reasonable time *after* the suspension may provide sufficient due process. The due process to which the employee is entitled may vary with the degree of punishment involved. (*Civil Serv. Association v. City and County of San Francisco* (1978) 22 Cal.3d 552; *Bostean v. Los Angeles Unified School District* (1998) 63 Cal.App.4th 95.)

Employees who are absent without leave because they are participating in a strike are still entitled to a pre-discharge "Skelly" notice and hearing. (*International Brotherhood of Elec. Workers v. City of Gridley* (1983) 34 Cal.3d 191.)

Due process protections also may arise where termination of a public employee has a serious impact on a person's reputation for honesty or involves another serious stigma. These protections may extend to probationary employees who do not otherwise have the same level of rights to continued employment as permanent employees. An example of such a termination would be termination for serious misconduct, or other accusations which seriously impair the employee's chances of future employment and damage the employee's reputation in the community. Where this damage to reputation is likely, an employee, even a probationary employee, is entitled to a pre-termination hearing to clear his name. (*Paul v. Davis* (1976) 424 U.S. 693; *Lubey v. City and County of San Francisco* (1979) 98 Cal.App.3d 340.) The termination must involve something more serious than mere incompetency or inability to get along with coworkers in order to generate the increased requirements for due process. (*Murden v. County of Sacramento* (1984) 160 Cal.App.3d 302.)

3. Collective Bargaining-Related Rights

Public employees in California have rights protected by seven collective bargaining statutes. (See Chapter 9 for an overview of California's collective bargaining statutes.) Among the rights provided by those laws and by the cases that

The laws that prohibit discrimination in the workplace generally prohibit retaliation for reporting discrimination.

have interpreted them is the right to have a union representative present during any meeting with the employer that is reasonably likely to result in discipline or which takes place under "highly unusual circumstances." (See *Redwoods Community College Dist. v. Pub. Employment Relations Bd.* (1984) 159 Cal.App.3d 617; *NLRB v. J. Weingarten, Inc.* (1975) 420 U.S. 251.)

4. Civil Service Protections

Many public employees are also protected by civil service or merit system provisions that prescribe grounds for discipline, pre-disciplinary procedures, and appeal rights and procedures. For example, employees of the State of California generally can appeal disciplinary matters to the State Personnel Board. (See Government Code sections 19570 et seq.) See their website at http://www.spb.ca.gov. Local governments often have civil service systems and procedures. Public school districts often have merit system procedures governing discipline and appeal rights.

Public employees should be certain that they obtain copies of the personnel rules and disciplinary procedures applicable to their employment. The employee's union should be contacted immediately in case of disciplinary action, whether it is about to happen or has already occurred.

Informative booklets ("Pocket Guides") on all of the statutes governing labor relations involving California public employees are published by California Public Employee Relations (CPER), located within the Institute for Research on Labor and Employment at the University of California,

Berkeley. For an overview of the due process rights of public employees in California, see Emi Uyehara, *Pocket Guide to Due Process in Public Employment*, 2005, Regents of the University of California. More generally, see Bonnie G. Bogue, Carol Vendrillo, and Liz Joffe, *Pocket Guide to Workplace Rights of Public Employees*, second edition, 2005, Regents of the University of California. For an overview of California's public sector labor relations statutes and their unfair practice provisions (regarding rights related to union activity and concerted action with or on behalf of other workers) and related Public Employment Relations Board (PERB) and court rulings, see Carol Vendrillo and Eric Borgerson, *Pocket Guide To Unfair Practices, California Public Sector*, fourth edition, 2006, Regents of the University of California. For a list of all Pocket Guide titles and ordering information, consult the CPER website at http://cper.berkeley.edu, or call 510-643-7093.

Decisions and orders of the Public Employment Relations Board can be researched and viewed at the agency's website: http://www.perb.ca.gov. PERB is the agency charged with administering the collective bargaining laws covering the state, city, county, and special district employees in California. It also covers public school, state college, state university, and trial court employees.

5. Protections for Specific Groups of Public Employees

Specific laws govern certain groups of public employees. Probationary state employees have rights with respect to rejection during the probationary period. (Government Code sections 19173 and 19175.) Police employees have special rights regarding discipline and discharge. (Government Code section 3508.1.) These provisions establish the timing of discipline, the notice required, the employee's opportunity to respond, and other due process protections. For an overview of the due process rights of peace officers in California, see Cecil Marr and Diane Marchant, *Pocket Guide to the Public Safety Officers Procedural Bill of Rights Act*, thirteenth edition, 2009, Regents of the University of California. State civil service managers are also subject to special disciplinary procedures. (Government Code sections 19590–19593.)

6. Federal Civil Service Employees

Non-probationary employees working in federal civil service positions are subject to rules and procedures governing "adverse action" for misconduct, referred to as "Chapter A75." (5 U.S. Code sections 7501 et seq.) An employee who is disciplined through this procedure can appeal to the Merit Systems Protection Board. See their website at http://www.mspb.gov.

Enforcement: File a civil service appeal with the Merit Systems Protection Board. File discrimination complaints (see Chapter 6 for types of discrimination covered by federal law) with the EEOC. See their website at http://www.eeoc.gov. If represented by a union, the employee should contact the union. An attorney with public sector expertise should be consulted.

G. SPECIAL EMPLOYEE RIGHTS IF TERMINATION IS BASED ON AN INVESTIGATION

Certain rules must be followed if the employer seeks a report on an employee from a consumer reporting agency (an organization that regularly collects or evaluates information about consumers for a fee or on a cooperative nonprofit basis for the purpose of providing consumer reports to third parties). Consumer reports are communications about a consumer and may include information on the consumer's credit worthiness, credit standing, credit capacity, character, general reputation, personal characteristics, or mode of living. See Chapter 3 for a more detailed discussion.

1. Right to Notice of the Investigation

The employer must notify the employee in writing of an investigation by a consumer reporting agency for purposes other than an employer's suspicion of wrongdoing or misconduct. The notice must include the contact information of the agency, the purposes of the report, the scope of the investigation, and a summary of the employee's right to inspect the agency's files. The employer also must provide a box to check on a written form for the employee to indicate a desire to receive a copy of the report. (Civil Code sections 1785.20.5(a) and 1786.16(a)(2), (b); 15 U.S. Code section 1681b(b)(2)(A)(ii).) If the investigation is in connection with an employer's suspicion of wrongdoing or misconduct, the employer does not need to notify the employee. (Civil Code section 1786.16(c); 15 U.S. Code section 1681a(x)(1)(B).) Also, if an employer has an employee investigated without using an outside agency, it does not need to provide detailed notice. (Civil Code section 1786.53(b)(2).)

Once the employee is notified about the investigation, the employer may obtain the report only with the employee's written consent. (Civil Code section 1786.16(a)(2)(C); 15 U.S. Code section 1681a(o)(5)(A).) However, the employer may be able to take an adverse employment action against an employee who does not give consent. (*Kelchner v. Sycamore Manor Health Center* (M.D. Pa. 2004) 305 F.Supp.2d 429.)

Enforcement: If the violation was negligent, file a civil suit to recover actual damages, court costs, and attorney's fees. If the violation was grossly negligent or willful, punitive damages may be available. (Civil Code section 1786.50; 15 U.S. Code sections 1681o, 1681n.) Reckless disregard of the notice obligation is a willful violation. (*Safeco Insurance Co. of America v. Burr* (2007) 551 U.S. 47.) Damages for invasion of privacy or defamation may also be available. (Civil Code section 1786.52.)

2. Rights when Negative Outcome Results from Investigation

The employer must notify an employee of a negative decision based on an investigation. Before any adverse action is taken based on a report by a consumer reporting agency, the employee must be provided with a copy of the report and a description of his rights. (15 U.S. Code section 1681b(b)(3).)

After the adverse employment action is taken, the employer must notify the employee that he is denied the job, promotion, or transfer, or is discharged based on a consumer report. The employer must tell the employee the name, address, and telephone number of the agency that produced the report. The employee must be notified in writing of his rights (such as the right to obtain a free copy of the report within sixty days from the agency that provided the report, the right to obtain a copy of the report from any other consumer reporting agency, and the right to dispute the accuracy or completeness of the information within). (Civil Code sections 1785.20, 1785.20.5,

1786.40(a); 15 U.S. Code section 1681m(a).) If the employer conducted the investigation itself, the employer must notify the employee of the right to receive a disclosure of the nature of the report. (15 U.S. Code section 1681m(b)(2).) Public records relied on must be disclosed regardless of whether the employee waived the right to see them. (Civil Code sections 1786.53(b)(4) and 1786.53(a)(3).)

Enforcement: File a civil suit for damages, punitive damages, and attorney's fees. (Civil Code sections 1785.31 and 1786.50.) File a civil suit for invasion of privacy or defamation (Civil Code section 1786.52.) and/or a civil suit for penalties and punitive damages for violation of the Fair Credit Reporting Act. (15 U.S. Code sections 1681n and 1681o.)

Exceptions: The employee's rights are limited when investigations result in negative outcomes concerning the employer's suspicion of misconduct or wrongdoing. Federal law requires that the employer disclose a summary of the report, not a copy of the report itself. The employer does not need to disclose the sources used to prepare the report. (Civil Code section 1786.16(c); 15 U.S. Code section 1681a(x)(2).)

3. Right to Inspect Personnel Record

The employee has the right to inspect any investigation report that the employer has used as the basis for discharging or disciplining him. Also, the employee is entitled to inspect any personnel record maintained by the employer that relates to the employee's performance or to any grievance concerning the employee. (Labor Code section 1198.5) This right continues even after the individual is terminated until the statute of limitations (time limit for legal action) on any claims has run out. Relevant records must be made available to the employee within a reasonable period of time after the employee asks to see them. (Labor Code section 1198.5.) The records must be made available at the employee's workplace or at the place where the employer stores the records, with no loss of compensation to the employee. However, these requirements do not apply to records relating to the investigation of criminal offenses or to letters of reference. A public employer must make the report available within five working days. For state government and school employees, see Chapter 12. On public employees' rights to receive copies of reports, see the next section.

Enforcement: File a claim with the state labor commissioner. File a civil suit. Violation of this law is a misdemeanor. (Labor Code section 1199.)

See Chapter 3 for information related to investigations by the employer.

H. RIGHTS WHEN THE EMPLOYER USES A DETECTIVE

1. Public Utility Employees

Employees who work for any public utility or public service corporation have special rights if a detective, special agent, or "spotter" is used to report on their integrity or honesty or on a breach of any company rules. Before the employer can discipline or discharge an employee based on a report by a special agent, detective, or "spotter," the employer must give the employee notice and, if the employee requests, a hearing. At the hearing, the company must disclose the specifics of any alleged misconduct and allow the employee to present testimony in his or her defense. (Public Utilities Code section 8251.) Under the statutes protecting public employees' bargaining rights (see Chapter 9), all workers represented by a union have the right to the assistance of a union representative at any hearing.

California courts have held that where a public utility (or other private entity) is extensively regulated by the state and enjoys a virtual monopoly, it is prohibited, just as public agencies are prohibited, from using its power in an unconstitutional fashion. (*Gay Law Students Association v. Pacific Tel. & Tel. Co.* (1979) 24 Cal.3d 458.)

Enforcement: File a complaint with the local district attorney. File a civil suit. An employer who violates these provisions is guilty of a misdemeanor punishable by one year in jail or a fine of $100 to $600 or both. (Public Utilities Code section 8252.)

2. Commercial, Retail, and Service Employees

A shopping investigator is a person who is not employed exclusively by the employee's own company, that is, a person who is not an in-house employee. Such an investigator has been defined as a person who shops "to test integrity of sales, warehouse, stockroom, and service personnel, and evaluates sales techniques and services rendered to customers"; or who "reviews an establishment's policies and standards to ascertain employee performance requirements"; or who "buys merchandise, orders food, or utilizes services to evaluate sales technique and courtesy of employees, carries merchandise to check stand or sales counter and observes employees during sales transaction to detect irregularities in listing or calling prices, itemizing merchandise, or handling cash"; or who "delivers purchases to an agency conducting shopping investigation service" and who writes a report of these investigations. (Labor Code section 2930(b).) Such a person must be licensed as a private investigator or be employed by a licensed private investigator (in which case only the licensed investigator may report to the employer). (Business and Professions Code sections 7521, 7522, 7523.)

Employees who work in a service, retail, or commercial establishment have two closely related rights concerning the use of "shopping investigators":

- If the employer intends to discipline or discharge the employee as a result of the report of a shopping investigator, then the employee must be given a copy of the report before she is disciplined or discharged.
- If an employer wants to see an employee for an interview that might result in a discharge for dishonesty, and the interview will be based wholly or partially on the report of a shopping investigator, then the employee must be given a copy of the report before the end of the interview. (Labor Code section 2930(a).)

Enforcement: File a civil suit.

Exceptions: This law applies only to reports by investigators meeting the definition of shopping investigators.

V. UNLAWFUL GROUNDS FOR DISCHARGE OR DISCIPLINARY ACTION

Specific statutes impose restrictions on employers seeking to discharge or discipline workers in violation of the workers' rights. Many of these rights are described in other chapters of this book and cross-references to those discussions are included below. Other legal protections are outlined in sections of this chapter. If an employee is disciplined or discharged in violation of any of these laws, she may sue the offending employer.

A. DISCRIMINATION

1. General Information
See Chapters 2 and 6.

2. Duty to Accommodate Physical Disabilities and Religious Beliefs
See Chapter 6.

3. Duty to Accommodate Alcoholic Rehabilitation Programs
See Chapter 6.

B. EXERCISE OF RIGHTS DURING THE HIRING PROCESS
See Chapter 2.

C. EXERCISE OF RIGHTS CONCERNING INVESTIGATIONS AND POLICE REPORTS
See Chapter 3.

D. EXERCISE OF WAGE AND HOUR RIGHTS
See Chapter 4.

E. EXERCISE OF BENEFIT PROTECTIONS
See Chapter 5.

F. EXERCISE OF SAFETY AND HEALTH PROTECTIONS
See Chapter 7.

G. EXERCISE OF WORKERS' COMPENSATION RIGHTS
See Chapter 8.

H. EXERCISE OF THE RIGHT TO ORGANIZE
See Chapter 9.

I. EXERCISE OF WHISTLEBLOWER PROTECTIONS
See Chapter 11.

J. MILITARY SERVICE

Employees may not be disciplined or discharged for the following reasons related to military service:
- Past military service;
- Present or future military, reserve, or national guard duties;
- Absences due to military service.

(Military and Veterans Code sections 394 and 394.5; 38 U.S. Code section 4311.)

K. EXERCISE OF LEGAL OR CONSTITUTIONAL RIGHTS

There are a wide variety of rights that are considered "protected rights," meaning that employees cannot be disciplined or discharged for exercising them.

1. General Rights

Employees may not be disciplined or discharged for exercising the following legal rights:
- Refusing to give the employer the rights to an invention that the employee developed during non-work hours without the employer's equipment, supplies, facilities, or trade secret information. (See Labor Code sections 2870 and 2871.);
- Asserting the special rights of seamen, fishermen, and divers (consult the union or an attorney) (33 U.S. Code section 948; 46 U.S. Code section 2114; 46 U.S. Code app. section 1506.);
- Asserting the special rights of farm workers, migrant workers, and seasonal workers (consult the union or an attorney) (29 U.S. Code sections 1801 et seq.);
- Asserting any rights under the state Labor Code or enforced by the labor commissioner, including filing or preparing to file a complaint, opposing violations of the law, assisting others in filing a complaint, or providing information to any enforcement agency. (Labor Code sections 98.6, 6310, 6312, 6399.7; Government Code section 12940(h); 29 U.S. Code sections 158(a)(4), 623(d), 1140, 1141; 42 U.S. Code section 2000e-3(a).) The federal Sarbanes-Oxley Act of 2002 protects employees of publicly traded companies (and in some instances private companies) who report corporate fraud and/or violations of securities law. (15 U.S. Code sections 7201 et seq.) For more information on protections against termination for disclosing corporate fraud, see Chapter 11, section IV.J., p. 277;

- Lawful conduct that occurs in non-work hours, away from the workplace. (Labor Code sections 96(k), 98.6.) Two court decisions from the Fourth District Court of Appeals of California have narrowed the scope of activities that are protected under this law, ruling that conduct is not protected under Labor Code sections 96(k) and 98.6 unless it is protected by the Constitution or some other law. (*Barbee v. Household Auto. Finance Corp.* (2003) 113 Cal. App.4th 525, citing 83 *Opinion of the California Attorney General* 226 (2000); *Grinzi v. San Diego Hospice Corp.* (2004) 120 Cal.App.4th 72.) However, since other appellate courts and the California Supreme Court have not addressed the issue, whether Labor Code section 96(k) bars an employer from taking adverse action against an employee for all lawful conduct off the job is not legally clear at the present time;
- Disclosing or refusing to disclose wages (Labor Code section 232.);
- Disclosing working conditions, other than proprietary, trade secret, or legally privileged information (Labor Code section 232.5.);
- Being subject to garnishment or assignment of wages (a court order diverting wages) (Labor Code section 2929(b); Family Code section 5290.);
- Refusing to patronize an employer (for instance, purchase clothing from the employer) (Labor Code section 450.);
- Refusing to authorize disclosure of medical information under certain circumstances. See Chapter 12 for more information (Civil Code section 56.20(b).);
- Opposing discriminatory acts of others that the employee reasonably believes are prohibited under the Fair Employment and Housing Act (FEHA). (Government Code section 12940(h); 2 California Code of Regulations section 7287.8.) For more information on opposing discrimination, see Chapter 6, section X., p. 184;
- Reporting patient abuse (Government Code section 12940(g).);
- Serving in the military (Military and Veterans Code section 394.);
- Voluntarily participating in an in-patient or out-

patient alcohol or drug rehabilitation program, provided that it does not cause undue hardship for the employer (Labor Code section 1025.);

- Participating in jury duty (Labor Code section 230(a).);
- Taking time off work to appear in court as a witness when compelled by subpoena or other court order;
- Serving as a volunteer firefighter, reserve police officer, or emergency rescue worker (Labor Code section 230.3.);
- Refusing to commit an illegal act (Labor Code section 1102.5.);
- Taking time off to appear in a child's school regarding a suspension. Prior notice to the employer is required (Labor Code section 230.7.);
- Taking time off (up to forty hours a year, not to exceed eight hours in any month) to participate in a child's school or daycare activities. This protection only covers employees working for employers that have twenty-five or more employees working at the same location. Prior notice to the employer is required (Labor Code section 230.8.);

- Using sick leave to attend to the illness of a child, parent, spouse, domestic partner, or child of the domestic partner (Labor Code section 233.). See Chapter 5 for more information on family leave;
- Taking time off as a victim of domestic violence or sexual assault to obtain a restraining order, seek care/counseling, or relocate (Labor Code sections 230(c), 230.1.);
- Taking time off as a victim of a crime, an immediate family member of a victim, a registered domestic partner of a victim, or the child of a registered domestic partner of the victim in order to attend judicial proceedings related to the crime (Labor Code section 230.2(b).);
- Enrolling in an adult literacy program as long as there is no undue hardship on the employer (Labor Code sections 1041, 1044.);
- Giving or advocating for medically appropriate healthcare if the employee is a physician (Business and Professions Code section 2056.).

For more information on retaliation for filing or assisting in complaints about illegal activities, see Chapter 11, section II.E., p. 266.

Employees may claim that they were discharged in violation of constitutional rights. However, constitutionally guaranteed rights (such as the right to privacy) are not absolute.

The right to privacy, which is explicitly guaranteed to all employees by the California Constitution (California Constitution, Article I, section 1), is affected by a person's reasonable expectation of privacy. Courts generally have found, for instance, that employees do not have a reasonable expectation of privacy on an employer's computer equipment, even if the computer is taken and used in the employee's home. If a person is on notice that something is not considered private, that may affect whether an expectation of privacy is reasonable. (*TBG Insurance Servs. Corp. v. Superior Court* (2002) 96 Cal.App.4th 443.) In a recent case, it was decided that an employee could not reasonably expect that his workplace computer was free from the control of his employer, since the computer was accessible by the employer's technology department and the employees were informed of a program that was installed to allow the employer to monitor Internet traffic. (*United States v. Ziegler* (9th Cir. 2007) 474 F.3d 1184.)

2. General Rights for Public Employees

Public employees have more protection in regard to claims that they were discharged in violation of constitutionally guaranteed rights, since their employer is the government, and government action is more closely regulated than private action in terms of the Constitution. Even probationary or temporary public employees have the right to a court determination of the reason for the dismissal if they claim that their constitutional rights were violated. (*Ofsevit v. Trustees of the California State Univ.* (1978) 21 Cal.3d 763.)

Some courts have interpreted constitutional guarantees very broadly, finding that certain rights surround basic protections. For instance, a court held that the First Amendment guarantee of freedom of expression protects the constitutional right of a public employee to wear a beard (absent any serious public safety issues to the contrary). (*Finot v. Pasadena City Bd. of Education* (1967) 250 Cal.App.2d 189.)

Public employers may not condition employment on giving up constitutional rights unless there is a "compelling" public interest. Before depriving public employees of constitutional rights, the employer must show: that the restriction related to constitutional rights rationally relates to the enhancement of public service; that the public benefits to be gained by the restriction outweigh the impairment of constitutional rights; and that there are no alternatives less damaging to the employee's constitutional rights. (*Bagley v. Washington Township Hosp. Dist.* (1966) 65 Cal.2d 499.) A probationary public employee or one who serves at the pleasure of the appointing authority may not be dismissed for exercising his constitutional rights, unless there is a compelling state interest supporting the dismissal. However, if the exercise of constitutional rights is not involved, good cause is not constitutionally required before the probationary employee may be dismissed. The employee bears the burden of proving that he was dismissed for exercising constitutional rights. (*Bogacki v. Bd. of Supervisors of Riverside County* (1971) 5 Cal.3d 771.)

3. Public Employees and Free Speech

The rights of public employees to free speech, and to be free of discipline or discharge for actions involving speech, have been somewhat limited by court cases. Several factors must be considered in analyzing the free speech rights of public employees:

- Is the employee acting as a private citizen or in her role as a public employee?
- Does the speech deal with a matter of public concern, or just with a personal or internal office matter?
- Was the speech the predominant motive for the discipline or discharge?

In general, individuals speaking in their roles as public employees have fewer free speech rights than those speaking as private citizens, and public employers may exercise some reasonable control on statements made by public employees. Speech dealing with matters of public concern (for instance, illegal acts by public officials or illegal misuse of public funds) carries greater protection than speech dealing with personal matters or other matters not of general public concern. (*Garcetti v. Ceballos* (2006) 547 U.S. 410; *Connick v. Myers* (1983) 461 U.S. 138; *Perry v. Sindermann* (1972) 408 U.S. 593.) (For example, see *Chico Police Officers' Association v. City of Chico* (1991) 232 Cal.App.3d 635, in which speech related to the desire for the benefits of unionization, employer-

CHAPTER 10

employee relationships, and the loss of confidence in management of the public agency was considered a matter of public concern.) Once it is established that the employee spoke on a matter of public concern, the government has the burden of proving that it had adequate justification for treating the employee differently from any other member of the general public. If other legitimate reasons existed for the discipline or discharge, the employee's right to free speech may not be found to bar the action of the public agency. (*Mt. Healthy City School Dist. Bd. of Education v. Doyle* (1977) 429 U.S. 274.) The government has a greater burden when it tries to regulate speech in advance. (*United States v. National Treasury Employees Union* (1995) 513 U.S. 454.)

See Chapter 11 for more information on the rights of whistleblowers.

4. Right to Oppose or Report Violations of the Law — Retaliation Prohibited

No employer may make or enforce a policy preventing an employee from disclosing information to a government agency where the employee has reasonable cause to believe the information discloses a violation of the law. The laws that prohibit discrimination in the workplace generally prohibit retaliation for reporting discrimination. See Chapter 6 for discussions of various federal and California laws that prohibit discrimination.

Employers may generally be held liable for the retaliatory acts of supervisors. (*Wysinger v. Auto. Club of Southern California* (2007) 157 Cal.App.4th 413.)

For more information on protection of employees who reasonably report suspected misconduct, see Chapter 11.

5. Political Rights

a. Rights Related to Voting

An employee may not be threatened, disciplined, or discharged for the following political reasons:
- The fact that the employee voted or did not vote;
- How the employee voted;
- The fact that the employee registered or did not register to vote;
- The fact that the employee signed or did not sign petitions;
- Political party membership or other affiliation;

- Membership in a political or interest group;
- Political opinions; or
- Political activities.

(Labor Code sections 1101, 1102; Elections Code sections 18520–18522, 18540; Education Code sections 7050–7057; California Constitution, Article II, section 4; Article VII, section 8(b).)

Political activity includes participation in lawsuits, wearing symbols, and associating with others to advance beliefs and ideas. (*Gay Law Students Association v. Pacific Tel. & Tel. Co.* (1979) 24 Cal.3d 458.) Representing a political party by appearing before a governing body, expressing political opinions in letters to the editor of a newspaper, and active participation in labor union activities are also political activity. (*Ofsevit v. Trustees of the California State Univ.* (1978) 21 Cal.3d 763.)

An employer is responsible for the acts of its supervisors, managers, officers, and agents in protecting employees' political rights. No one may ask (or keep records) about an employee's political opinions or activities. (Government Code section 19703.) No political materials may be attached to an employee's pay envelope or paycheck. (Elections Code section 18542.)

Enforcement: File a complaint with the state attorney general or the local district attorney. File an appeal with the State Personnel Board. File a civil suit for damages and other relief if the employee is subjected to political pressure. Violation of these laws is a crime. In some cases, it may be a felony. Violators are subject to at least one year in jail and a fine. (Elections Code section 18502.)

Exceptions: Police and other public safety officers may not engage in political activity while on duty or in uniform. (Government Code section 3302.) School districts may establish some restrictions on political activity during working hours on school premises. (Education Code section 7055.) Some recent court cases have upheld restrictions on public officials making unauthorized statements as public officials.

As discussed above, only a "compelling" public interest justifies restraints on constitutional rights, including restraints on the political activities of public employees. (*Bagley v. Washington Township Hosp. Dist.* (1966) 65 Cal.2d 499.)

b. Right to Run for or Hold Office

Employers cannot harass, discipline, suspend,

discharge, or discriminate against workers who run for or hold a public office. A company rule against this kind of political activity by employees is unlawful. (Labor Code sections 1101, 1102; California Constitution, Article I, section 3; Article II, section 1.)

Enforcement: File a complaint with the state attorney general or local district attorney. File a civil suit. Violation of these laws is a crime.

Exceptions: This protection does not necessarily mean that workers will be granted time off from work to run for or hold office. However, an employer cannot refuse to grant leave for political activities if leave is granted for educational or other personal activities.

State and local government employees involved in activities funded by the federal government may not be candidates for election to a partisan public office. They can, however, be candidates for any California local, county, or judicial office (since all these offices are nonpartisan in California). They can be candidates for positions on a political party central committee, or convention delegates, or other party officials. (5 U.S. Code sections 1501–1508; 5 Code of Federal Regulations sections 151.111, 151.122.)

No restrictions apply to employees of schools, colleges, universities, or research institutions, or to county superintendents of schools. Such employees can run for any office. (Education Code section 7052.)

c. Right to Serve as an Election Officer

Workers cannot be discriminated against because they serve as election officers on election day. They cannot be disciplined, suspended, or discharged for absence from work to fulfill this civic duty. (Elections Code section 12312.) They should, however, give the employer advance notice that they will be absent and serving as an election officer. Employers are not obligated by law to compensate employees for days they are absent due to service as an election officer, unless this provision is contained in a collective bargaining agreement or handbook, or the employee is able to use paid vacation or other paid leave days.

Enforcement: File a complaint with the state attorney general or local district attorney. File a civil suit. In some cases, violation is a felony.

L. DISPLACEMENT BY A WORKFARE WORKER

1. General Rules Prohibiting Displacement

The term "Workfare" refers to jobs and training established or conducted for welfare recipients. It covers employment, pre-employment preparation, on-the-job training, transitional employment, supported work, training grants (whether paid in full or diverted into wages), and training program positions. (Welfare and Institutions Code sections 11320 et seq.)

Workers cannot lose jobs because employers are providing a Workfare job or training. They cannot be displaced wholly or partially by a Workfare participant. They cannot be denied currently available overtime opportunities because the employer hires a Workfare participant. An employer cannot use Workfare participants to fill any positions to which current employees might be promoted.

An employer cannot fill a position with a Workfare participant until the employer has complied with all provisions of the union contract or merit system.

No Workfare participant is permitted to do work that is available as a result of a strike or other labor dispute. No Workfare activity is legal that results in a strike or other labor dispute.

All Workfare participants are "employees" and are covered by all the rights described in this book. People engaged in Workfare and on-the-job training must be paid at comparable wage rates to non-Workfare employees and trainees. No discrimination is allowed on the basis of age, race, disability, physical or mental handicap, sex, religion, sexual preference, or national origin.

No Workfare participant can fill any position that was created by a termination, layoff, or reduction in the workforce if the employer intended to obtain Workfare participants as replacements.

Workfare participants cannot be penalized in any way for refusing to accept an employment or training assignment that:
- Violates any of these rules;
- Involves more than the daily or weekly hours of work customary to the occupation;
- Involves conditions that violate health and safety standards;
- Involves employment not covered by Workers' Compensation Insurance; or

- Violates the terms of the participant's union membership.

2. Rules for Pre-Employment Positions

The Workfare program establishes "pre-employment preparation positions" that involve short-term work (maximum one year) and limited hours (maximum thirty-two a week), working for public employers and nonprofit agencies.

Pre-employment preparation positions may not:

- Result in the total or partial displacement of current employees;
- Replace work that had been done by an employee who was terminated or laid off or whose position was eliminated by a reduction in workforce (the intent of the employer is irrelevant);
- Replace work that would have provided opportunities for current employees to be promoted;
- Provide work that does not comply with applicable personnel procedures or collective bargaining agreements;
- Provide work customarily performed by a worker in a job classification within a recognized bargaining unit;
- Replace work in a bargaining unit in which funded positions are vacant (a pre-employment preparation position may fill an established vacant position if that position is unfunded in a public agency budget);
- Provide work in a bargaining unit in which any employee is on layoff; or
- Provide work that results in a strike, lockout, or other bona fide labor dispute, or that violates a collective bargaining agreement.

(Welfare and Institutions Code sections 11320, 11322.8, 11324.6, 11324.7, 11328.2.)

Enforcement: File a complaint with the state Department of Social Services or county welfare department. See the Department of Social Services' website at http://www.dss.cahwnet.gov/cdssweb/PG22.htm for information on filing a complaint. File a civil suit.

VI. MITIGATION OF DAMAGES

Individuals who have been wrongfully fired from a job have a duty to mitigate their damages. Generally this means that the individual must search for a comparable job. He need not accept a job that is substantially lower paying, inferior, or requiring relocation.

If the employer offers to rehire the individual, refusal to accept the offer of reemployment may cut off damages as of the date of the offer, absent special circumstances. Circumstances that could justify refusing an offer of reemployment include situations where returning to the job presents a risk to the individual's physical or mental health.

The employer has the burden of proving that a discharged employee failed to mitigate damages.

VII. UNLAWFUL EMPLOYER DISCHARGE AND DISCIPLINARY ACTIONS

A. HUMILIATION, VIOLENCE, FRAUD, OR DEFAMATION

In some circumstances, workers may sue employers for wrongful disciplinary actions, even if they fall short of termination. The following are examples, not a complete list, of such unlawful actions by an employer:

- Humiliating an employee;
- Directing outrageous slurs and insults at an employee;
- Defaming, libeling, or slandering an employee or maliciously publishing or communicating injurious falsehoods about him, about the reasons for discharge, about the quality of his work, or similar statements;
- Physically assaulting an employee or subjecting her to assault or battery by a supervisor or coworker;
- Raping, attempting to rape, or otherwise sexually assaulting an employee;
- Refusing to allow an employee to recover his personal property, tools, or papers from his desk or locker; stealing or "converting" his property;
- Invading a worker's privacy or spying on private matters;
- Revealing private information about an employee to others; or
- Violating laws related to privacy (for example, eavesdropping, misusing photos or fingerprints, releasing medical or psychological information). (See Chapter 3.)

It is also a misdemeanor to use misrepresentations to prevent a past employee from securing future employment. (Labor Code section 1050.)

The law in this area, created by court rulings, changes rapidly. Employees should consult their union or an attorney before assuming that any of the listed actions are grounds for a lawsuit in their situation.

B. HARASSMENT BASED ON PERSONAL CHARACTERISTICS

It is against the law for an employer to harass an employee or to allow other employees, supervisors, customers, clients, or patients to harass an employee because of age, sex, race, national origin, marital status, physical disability, or other personal characteristics. See Chapter 6. Sexual harassment is illegal. Harassment of gays is illegal. Embarrassing or making life difficult for a worker who has a disability or who practices a particular religion is illegal.

Harassment includes but is not limited to:

- Verbal harassment (for example, epithets, derogatory comments, or slurs);
- Physical harassment (for example, assault, impeding or blocking any movement, or any physical interference with normal work or movement);
- Visual forms of harassment (for example, derogatory posters, cartoons, or drawings);
- Requests for sexual favors (unwanted sexual advances that condition an employment benefit on an exchange of sexual favors).

(2 California Code of Regulations section 7287.6(b); 22 California Code of Regulations section 98244; 29 Code of Federal Regulations sections 1604.11, 1606.8.)

Employers must take action to prevent harassment by anyone. (Government Code section 12940(h)–(j).)

Enforcement: File a complaint with the Department of Fair Employment and Housing. File a civil suit.

Exceptions: Most religious nonprofit corporations are exempted from these provisions, but an employee of a religious nonprofit who suffers harassment may file a civil suit under different laws. Employees of religious nonprofits may file claims of harassment under Title VII, the federal law prohibiting discrimination, as long as the claims do not involve religious principles or the religious employer's authority to hire ministers. (*Bollard v. California Province of the*

Society of Jesus (9th Cir. 1999) 196 F.3d 940; *Elvig v. Calvin Presbyterian Church* (9th Cir. 2004) 375 F.3d 951.) Employees of religious nonprofits may also file claims for harassment based on common law or other state laws prohibiting harassment (for example, the Civil Rights Act). See Chapter 6.

C. VIOLATION OF ABORTION-RELATED RIGHTS OF HEALTHCARE WORKERS

The abortion-related rights of medical workers are fully protected. Registered nurses, licensed vocational nurses, physicians, or other employees of a hospital, health facility, or clinic cannot be required to participate in inducing or performing an abortion if they file a written statement in advance with their employer or the facility. The statement need only indicate that they have an ethical, moral, or religious basis for refusing to participate in abortions. They cannot be penalized in any way for filing this statement or for refusing to participate in abortions.

Employees who work at a hospital, health facility, or clinic that does not perform abortions are also protected from negative actions related to abortions. They cannot be penalized in any way because they participate in abortions performed elsewhere. (Health and Safety Code section 123420.)

Enforcement: File a civil suit. File a complaint with the local district attorney. Violation is a misdemeanor.

Exceptions: The right to refuse to participate in abortion care does not apply to either medical emergency situations or jobs where the employee's normal assignment is in a part of the facility that cares for abortion patients.

CHAPTER 11 **WHISTLEBLOWING AND REFUSING TO PARTICIPATE IN AN ACTIVITY THAT VIOLATES THE LAW**

WHISTLEBLOWING AND REFUSING TO PARTICIPATE IN AN ACTIVITY THAT VIOLATES THE LAW

I. SCOPE OF THE CHAPTER

Reporting an employer's suspected violation of a state or federal law or regulation is called "whistleblowing." Some types of employees have a duty to report certain violations such as suspected child abuse or environmental hazards that they encounter in their work. Most employees, while not required to report violations, are protected from retaliation for bringing a violation or suspected violation to the attention of the appropriate authorities. Protected activities include reporting the suspected violation to a government or law enforcement agency, testifying before a governmental committee, or cooperating with government investigators who are looking into the suspected violation. It is illegal for an employer to use threats or coercion to keep an employee from engaging in any of these protected activities, or to force an employee to give false information to government investigators or to destroy or alter evidence. It is also illegal for an employer to retaliate against an employee for having engaged in any of these protected whistleblowing activities.

California law goes beyond the protection of whistleblowing and also protects employees who refuse to participate in activities that violate a state or federal law or regulation. It is unlawful for an employer to retaliate against an employee because of that employee's refusal to participate in unlawful activity, or because an employee exercised this right or reported illegal activity in a former job.

The laws that prohibit discrimination in the workplace also prohibit retaliation for reporting discrimination. See Chapter 6 for discussion of the various federal and California provisions that prohibit retaliation for engaging in protected activity under the anti-discrimination laws.

Unlawful retaliation may consist of any sort of adverse employment action, such as discharge, demotion, reduction in pay, denial of a promotion, failure to hire or rehire, transfer to a less desirable location or shift, change in job duties, or harassment.

Employees subject to unlawful retaliation are entitled to be "made whole" for the damages suffered. The remedy will vary based on the nature of the unlawful retaliation. The object of the remedy is to restore the employee to the job and to the economic position he would be in had there been no unlawful retaliation. Typically, an employee who was unlawfully discharged for whistleblowing or for refusing to participate in unlawful activity is entitled to reinstatement and back pay for lost wages.

II. GENERAL WHISTLEBLOWING PROVISIONS

A. RIGHT TO REPORT VIOLATIONS

Whistleblowing protections are found in many federal and state laws. Under California law, Labor Code section 1102.5 provides comprehensive whistleblowing protection. This law protects all private and public employees who work in California, except for federal employees. (Labor Code section 1106.) There are other laws that offer additional, more specific protections to public employee whistleblowers, discussed below.

Labor Code section 1102.5 makes it unlawful for an employer to:

- Adopt or enforce any rule or policy preventing an employee from disclosing information to a government or law enforcement agency, if the employee reasonably believes that the information discloses a violation of a federal or state law or regulation.

- Retaliate against an employee for disclosing information to a government or law enforcement agency, if the employee reasonably believes that the information discloses a violation of a federal or state law or regulation.

To be protected as a whistleblower under this law, the employee must disclose the suspected violation to a government or law enforcement agency. There is no requirement that the employee make the disclosure to the specific agency that has jurisdiction to investigate or enforce the law or regulation allegedly violated. Disclosure to any government or law enforcement agency is sufficient.

Whistleblowing is obviously more effective when the disclosure is directed to the proper agency. The state attorney general is required to maintain a whistleblower hotline to receive calls from persons who have information regarding possible violations of state or federal laws or regulations. The telephone number to reach this hotline is 800-952-5225. The attorney general is required to refer all calls received on this hotline to the appropriate governmental agency for review and possible investigation. (Labor Code section 1102.7.)

Reporting suspected violations to a private employee's own employer is not a protected activity under this law. (*Green v. Ralee Engineering Co.* (1998) 19 Cal.4th 66.) However, private employees who report suspected occupational safety or health violations to their own employers are protected under a different law, Labor Code section 6310, which prohibits retaliation for making any bona fide complaint to an employer about unsafe working conditions or work practices. Unlike private employees, employees of public agencies are protected for disclosures of any suspected violations (not just occupational safety and health violations), where the disclosures are made to their own employers. (Labor Code section 1102.5(e).)

The employee is protected whether or not the information disclosed reveals a violation of federal or state law or regulation, as long as the employee had a reasonable basis for suspecting illegal activity. (Labor Code section 1102.5(b).) Conversely, the employee is not protected if the disclosure was made in bad faith without any reasonable basis. The disclosure is protected whether it relates to suspected illegal activity by an employer, coworkers, supervisors or managers, clients or customers, suppliers, contractors, or anyone else. (*Gardenhire v. Housing Authority* (2000) 85 Cal. App.4th 236.)

There are certain exceptions to this protection against retaliation for disclosing suspected illegal activity. (Labor Code section 1102.5(g).) Under these exceptions, employers are permitted to maintain policies that prohibit disclosures that would violate any of the following:

- Confidential communications between an attorney and the attorney's client;
- Confidential communications between a physician and the physician's patient;
- Trade secret information.

However, trade secret confidentiality is not absolute. It cannot be asserted to conceal fraud or otherwise foster injustice. (Evidence Code section 1060.) For example, if a grower fraudulently labels its produce as organic, an employee would be protected from retaliation for disclosing to a government agency that the grower is actually spraying the produce with pesticides, notwithstanding the grower's claim that its use of pesticides is a trade secret.

It is illegal to fire an employee because the employer fears she might file a complaint with a government or law enforcement agency. (*Lujan v. Minagar* (2004) 124 Cal.App.4th 1040.) It is also illegal for an employer to retaliate against an employee for having previously engaged in protected whistleblowing with regard to a prior employer (Labor Code section 1102.5(d).) or to refuse to hire a job applicant for having engaged in protected whistleblowing with regard to a prior employer. (Labor Code section 98.6(a).)

B. RIGHT TO REFUSE TO PARTICIPATE IN ILLEGAL ACTIVITY

In 2003, the California Legislature amended Labor Code section 1102.5 to add a new category of protected conduct. With this amendment, the law now prohibits employers from retaliating against an employee for refusing to participate in an activity that would result in a violation of a federal or state law or regulation. (Labor Code section 1102.5(c).) The refusal to participate in an illegal activity will not be protected unless the activity would actually violate a federal or state law or regulation.

Prior to the enactment of this amendment, there was no explicit right under the Labor Code to refuse to participate in an unlawful activity, except under Labor Code section 6311, which protects employees who refuse to perform work that violates an occupational safety or health law and where the violation "would create a real and apparent hazard to the employee or his or her fellow employees." Also, a series of court cases held that an employee could win a lawsuit against an employer for wrongful termination in violation of public policy if the employee had been discharged for refusing to participate in an illegal activity, but only if the refusal implicated a "fundamental or substantial" public policy. (*Stevenson v. Superior Court* (1997) 16 Cal.4th 880.) For example, a court ruled against a truck driver who was fired for refusing to drive an unregistered truck, because the registration violation did not implicate "fundamental public policy concerns," such as health, safety, or crime prevention. (*DeSoto v. Yellow Freight Systems, Inc.* (9th Cir. 1992) 957 F.2d 655.)

In contrast, Labor Code section 1102.5(c) does not contain any distinction between unlawful activities that implicate "fundamental or substantial public policy concerns" and those that do not. Under the plain language of this statute, a refusal to participate in an activity that would violate any federal or state law or regulation is protected. Under this law, the refusal to drive a truck with an expired registration would be protected, as it is a violation of state law to drive a vehicle without current valid registration.

Every employee who refuses to perform work that she has been ordered, or is expected, to perform as part of her job requirements risks discharge or lesser discipline for what the employer will undoubtedly describe as insubordination. Employees should be as certain as possible that any such refusal to perform work will be protected under the law. Whenever circumstances permit, an employee considering whether to refuse to perform work because the performance of that work would amount to participation in an illegal activity should first confirm, with an employment attorney or a union representative, that the activity in question would actually violate a federal or state law or regulation.

C. RIGHT TO APPEAR BEFORE GOVERNMENT COMMITTEES AND IN JUDICIAL PROCEEDINGS

Employees have the right to testify as a witness before any committee (or subcommittee) of the state legislature or either house of Congress. (Government Code sections 9400, 9414, 19251.5; 18 U.S. Code sections 1505, 1512–1515.) It is a crime to attempt to coerce any person not to appear before a legislative committee, or to retaliate against an employee because he appeared before a committee. It is a crime for anyone even to ask an employer to prevent an employee from testifying. Employees cannot be prevented from communicating with a government agency if the communication may lead to an appearance before a committee.

An employer may not discharge or in any manner retaliate against an employee for taking time off to appear in court as a witness in any judicial proceeding, as long as the appearance was required by a subpoena or any other court order. (Labor Code section 230(b).) Employees are entitled to use any available vacation time, personal time off, or compensatory time off for any such required court appearance. (Labor Code section 230(g).)

D. FALSE EMPLOYER REPORTS PROHIBITED

It is a crime for an employer to make any false reports to government agencies (either routine reports or responses to investigations by a government agency). It is also a crime to threaten an employee in an attempt to force him to make false reports or destroy information requested by a government agency. If an employee gives in to an employer's request to make a false statement or alter documents, he may also be subject to criminal prosecution. (Penal Code sections 115, 118, 126–137, 153; 18 U.S. Code sections 1505, 1512–1515.)

E. PROVING UNLAWFUL RETALIATION

To initially establish a claim for unlawful retaliation for any protected activity (such as whistleblowing or refusal to perform work that would violate a state or federal law or regulation), an employee must show that (1) she engaged in the type of activity that is protected by law, and following that, (2) the employer took some adverse employment action against her, and (3) that there was some "nexus" or "causal connection" between the exercise of the protected activity and the adverse action.

1. Adverse Employment Actions

An "adverse employment action" is defined as one that "materially affects the terms and conditions of employment." It encompasses not only ultimate employment decisions, such as discharge, suspension, demotion, failure to hire, or the denial of a promotion, but also the entire spectrum of employment actions that are reasonably likely to adversely and materially affect an employee's job performance or opportunity for advancement in her career. (*Yanowitz v. L'Oreal, Inc.* (2005) 36 Cal.4th 1028; *Patten v. Grant Joint Union High School District* (2005) 134 Cal.App.4th 1378.) Under this standard, transfers, changes in work shift or job duties or work location, or written reprimands that could adversely affect promotional opportunities may constitute an "adverse employment action." (*Akers v. County of San Diego* (2002) 95 Cal.App.4th 1441.)

2. Establishing a Connection Between Protected Activity and Adverse Employment Action

The "nexus" or "causal connection" between the exercise of the protected activity and the adverse employment action may be established by direct evidence or by circumstantial evidence. An example of direct evidence would be an admission by the employer that the adverse action was imposed because the employee engaged in some legally protected activity. The most typical circumstantial evidence that tends to prove a "causal connection" is the closeness in timing between the protected activity and the adverse action, coupled with evidence that the employer knew or reasonably would be expected to have known that the employee engaged in this protected activity prior to the imposition of the adverse employment action. This circumstantial evidence establishes an inference that the adverse action was taken in retaliation for the protected activity.

3. The Burden of Proof

Once the employee establishes this initial or "prima facie" claim, the burden shifts to the employer to justify the adverse action, that is, to show that there was a legitimate, non-retaliatory reason for the adverse action. In defending itself against a retaliation claim, an employer will typically try to prove that there was a "business justification" for the adverse action; that it was imposed for non-discriminatory disciplinary reasons because of problems with the employee's job performance; or that action was taken because of legitimate economic reasons such as the need to reduce staff.

The burden then shifts back to the employee to prove that reasons asserted by the employer for its action are not the true reasons, but merely a pretext designed to conceal the retaliatory motive. The employee may do this either by showing that the employer's asserted justification is not believable, or that the employer was more likely motivated by a retaliatory reason than by its asserted lawful reason. (*Mokler v. County of Orange* (2007) 157 Cal.App.4th 121.) The employee may rebut the employer's defense by showing the employer simply is not telling the truth about the employee's job performance. Even if there were job performance issues, the employee can rebut the employer's defense by showing "disparate treatment," that is, that despite the employer's claim that the adverse action was imposed for disciplinary reasons, other employees (who did not engage in the protected activity) were not similarly disciplined for similar job performance issues or infractions. Or the employee may establish a retaliatory motive by showing that the employer knew about the alleged job performance issue for a significant amount of time before the employee engaged in the protected activity, and only took action against the employee after she engaged in the protected activity. An employer's claim that the employee was "let go" for economic reasons can be rebutted by showing that the employer then hired someone else to fill that position.

4. Retaliation as the Motivating Factor

When all of the evidence is weighed, the employee will prevail if retaliation was the motivating factor for the adverse action. Retaliation will be considered as the motivating factor if the adverse employment action would not have happened but for the employee's protected activity. (Labor Code section 1102.6.)

F. PURSUING AN UNLAWFUL RETALIATION CLAIM

Employees in the private sector generally have two options for pursuing an unlawful retaliation claim — either through the labor commissioner's office or through the courts. Some types of retaliation claims may also need to be filed with a state or federal administrative agency before going to court. Also, unionized employees covered by collective bargaining agreements may have the right to challenge the retaliation by filing a grievance.

1. Enforcement Through Administrative Remedies

Administrative remedies are actions (sometimes referred to as charges, complaints, or grievances) that take place outside of the court system. They fall into several categories.

- Employees may have grievance and arbitration rights under union collective bargaining agreements.
- Public employees may have administrative appeal rights under public agencies (for instance, the State Personnel Board for state employees).
- Some employers (for instance, the University of California and the California State University) may have internal appeal mechanisms.
- Employees may have the right to file complaints with state enforcement agencies (for instance, the Department of Fair Employment and Housing, or the labor commissioner) or federal agencies such as OSHA or the Wage and Hour Division of the Department of Labor, to seek remedies for violations of laws enforced by those agencies.

a. The Labor Commissioner (California Division of Labor Standards Enforcement)

The labor commissioner has investigatory and prosecutorial authority over a wide range of unlawful retaliation claims based on laws contained in the California Labor Code, including claims of retaliation arising under Labor Code section 1102.5 for whistleblowing or for refusing to engage in unlawful activities. The labor commissioner also enforces claims for unlawful retaliation for exercising rights that are protected by more than thirty other laws, including the right to file a wage claim and to testify before the labor commissioner (protected under Labor Code section 98.6), the right to disclose information about wages or working conditions (Labor Code sections 232, 232.5), the right to engage in political activity (Labor Code sections 1101, 1102), the right to complain about suspected workplace safety or health violations (Labor Code section 6310), and the right to refuse to perform unsafe work that is likely to result in death or serious injury (Labor Code section 6311).

The procedures for filing the retaliation claim with the labor commissioner, and for the investigation of the claim, are set out at Labor Code section 98.7. The claim must be filed within six months of the retaliation giving rise to the claim. This six-month deadline may be extended for good cause, but the standards for such an extension are quite strict. For example, an extension will not be granted if the reason for the late filing was because the employee was not aware of the right to file a claim.

The labor commissioner will assign the claim to a retaliation complaint investigator who is responsible for interviewing the claimant, the employer, and any witnesses, and for examining any relevant documents. The investigator prepares a report that sets out the facts, and that reaches a conclusion as to whether the employer unlawfully retaliated against the employee. If the labor commissioner concludes that the employer engaged in unlawful retaliation, the determination will contain an order directing the employer to take specific remedial actions, including, where appropriate, reinstatement or rehiring, and reimbursement of lost wages and interest. If the employer does not comply with this order within ten work days, the labor commissioner is required to file a lawsuit against the employer to obtain the appropriate relief. An attorney for the labor commissioner will prosecute the lawsuit, at no charge to the claimant.

If the labor commissioner determines that the employer did not engage in unlawful retaliation, the claim is dismissed. Notwithstanding this dismissal, the claimant has the right to proceed on the claim by filing a lawsuit against the employer. The labor commissioner will not participate in that lawsuit. Of course, the employer will undoubtedly use the labor commissioner's determination against the employee to try to convince the court that the claim lacks merit. But the court is not bound by the labor commissioner's determination, and it may be possible for the claimant to prevail in the lawsuit, in which case the court may order reinstatement, back pay, and any other appropriate relief.

b. Other Administrative Agencies

While the labor commissioner (Division of Labor Standards Enforcement, Department of Industrial Relations) provides remedies for whistleblowers based on protections guaranteed through the California Labor Code, a number of other agencies (for example, the Department of Fair Employment and Housing for issues involving certain anti-discrimination laws; and federal agencies like the Department of Labor and the Equal Opportunity Employment Commission for violations of federal laws) provide administrative remedies and processes for laws they enforce. See section II.F., p. 267, and also directly below, for more information.

c. Exhausting Administrative Remedies

The term "exhausting administrative remedies" generally means filing appropriate administrative appeals and seeing them through to their conclusion.

It is important that whistleblowers exhaust their administrative remedies before filing a lawsuit. This means that whistleblowers should report the misconduct as appropriate, given the situation, and should take advantage of any appeal rights (including union grievance rights, state personnel board proceedings, employer appeal systems) they have. Failure to exhaust administrative remedies can mean that the employee loses a lawsuit down the road. (*Campbell v. Regents of the University of California* (2005) 35 Cal.4th 311.) Administrative remedies that should be exhausted may include internal remedies (for example, employer grievance procedures) or external administrative remedies (for instance, complaints filed with the Department of Fair Employment and Housing or the labor commissioner), depending on the right violated.

The California Whistleblower Protection Act requires University of California employees who have been subjected to retaliation to exhaust the administrative remedies provided by statute before filing a lawsuit. (Government Code section

8547.10.) The employee may sue for damages only after he has first filed a complaint with the appropriate university officer and exhausted his administrative remedies, or if the university has failed to reach a decision within the required time limits. (Government Code section 8547.10(c).) California State University employees are similarly required to exhaust administrative remedies. (Government Code section 8547.12.) Exhausting administrative remedies may, in some cases, involve filing a court action (called a "writ of mandamus") after the agency in charge of enforcing the law has made a decision. (*Ohton v. Board of Trustees of the California State Univ.* (2007) 148 Cal.App.4th 749.)

There are some exceptions to the rule that whistleblowers must exhaust their available administrative remedies. These exceptions include situations in which the administrative agency cannot provide an adequate, meaningful remedy; when the subject of the dispute is not within the agency's power to decide; or when filing an administrative claim would clearly be useless. There is also an exception to the requirement that whistleblowers utilize their administrative remedies before filing a lawsuit if the administrative agency indulges in unreasonable delay. (*Mokler v. County of Orange* (2007) 157 Cal.App.4th 121.) However, in most cases the safest route for a whistleblower is to exhaust internal and external remedies. (*Campbell v. Regents of the University of California* (2005) 35 Cal.4th 311; *Palmer v. Regents of the University of California* (2003) 107 Cal.App.4th 899.)

With regard to exhausting remedies under collective bargaining agreements, the first question is what kind of right is the whistleblower seeking to enforce? If it is a right which only exists in the collective bargaining agreement, then the worker must seek enforcement through the contract's grievance and arbitration procedure. (*Livadas v. Bradshaw* (1994) 512 U.S. 107). In some cases, where the collective bargaining agreement requires enforcement of discrimination rights or other rights covered by state or federal laws through the grievance and arbitration process, it may be necessary to pursue that process, rather than filing a lawsuit. (*14 Penn Plaza LCC v. Pyett* (2009) 129 S.Ct. 1456.) However, waivers of the right to use judicial remedies must be clear and unmistakable in order to be effective. (*Wright v. Universal Maritime Service Corp.* (1998) 525 U.S. 70.)

2. Enforcement Through the Courts

There is a great deal of controversy over whether an employee can bypass the labor commissioner or another administrative agency entirely, and file a court action alleging a violation of the particular statute that prohibited employer retaliation. Although the issue is far from resolved, a number of courts have held that employees are required to "exhaust their administrative remedies" before filing a retaliation lawsuit in court, subject to some of the requirements outlined in the previous section.

Once the administrative remedy is "exhausted," or where the facts create an exception to the requirement that the whistleblower pursue the administrative remedy, the person may file in court. If it looks as if this will be necessary, it is important to consult an attorney promptly.

In some cases an employee can file a lawsuit based on the "tort" of wrongful termination in violation of public policy without first filing a claim with an administrative agency, or in addition to other claims. Cases alleging a violation of public policy generally involve employer actions that are not in the public interest, but where there may not be specific laws on the books dealing with enforcement of a right. For instance, if a transportation system employee complains about improper activities that could lead to problems with public safety, but the regulations involved do not contain a specific statement prohibiting retaliation for whistleblowing, an employee might be able to file a lawsuit claiming that the employer's retaliation "violates public policy." An attorney with experience in the area should be consulted regarding what type of lawsuit should be filed.

Enforcement: File a claim with the state labor commissioner (for retaliation prohibited by the Labor Code). File a complaint with the Department of Fair Employment and Housing (for violation of laws administered by that agency, such as the Fair Employment and Housing Act, the California Family Rights Act, the Unruh Civil Rights Act, and the Ralph Civil Rights Act). File a charge with the federal Equal Employment Opportunity Commission (for retaliation for reporting or objecting to violations of Title VII or other federal anti-discrimination laws). File a complaint with the Department of Labor regarding retaliation for whistleblowing related to laws administered by the Department of Labor, including:

> *A whistleblower who has experienced retaliation should immediately seek assistance from his union or an attorney.*

- The Fair Labor Standards Act. Retaliation complaints are made to the Wage and Hour Division.
- The Employee Retirement Income Security Act. Retaliation complaints are made to the Employee Benefits Security Administration.
- The Occupational Safety and Health Act. Retaliation complaints are made to the Occupational Safety and Health Administration (OSHA).
- The Consumer Credit Protection Act. Retaliation complaints are made to the Wage and Hour Division.
- The Employee Polygraph Protection Act. Retaliation complaints are made to the Wage and Hour Division.
- The Federal Employees' Compensation Act. Retaliation complaints are made to the Office of Workers' Compensation Programs.
- The Family and Medical Leave Act. Retaliation complaints are made to the Wage and Hour Division.
- The Uniformed Services Employment and Reemployment Rights Act. Retaliation complaints are made to the Veterans' Employment and Training Service (VETS).

For a summary of many of the Department of Labor's principal laws, see http://www.dol.gov/compliance/laws/main.htm.

File a complaint with the local district attorney for violation of state criminal laws, or with the U.S. attorney for violation of federal criminal laws. File a civil suit. Criminal punishment under the federal statutes may include up to ten years in prison and a fine. (18 U.S. Code sections 1505, 1512–1515.) State punishments for retaliation against whistleblowers may range up to one year in prison and a fine of $5,000. If the employer is a corporation or a limited liability company, it may also be fined up to $10,000. (Labor Code sections 1102.5(e), (f), 1103; Penal Code sections 136.1, 137.)

Several laws permit the filing of private lawsuits when employees or others discover illegal or wrongful actions by their employers or other entities.

Under the federal False Claims Act, those who submit false claims for payment of government funds are subject to damages and penalties. Individuals, on behalf of the government, are allowed to bring civil actions under this law and may be awarded a portion of the recovered funds if the case is successful. (31 U.S. Code sections 3729 et seq.)

The California False Claims Act encourages employees who discover fraudulent claims of amounts over $500 to, or by, state and local entities to file private lawsuits to protect public funds. If they prevail, they may recover attorney's fees, costs, and damages. (Government Code sections 12650–12656.) The Private Attorneys General Act permits employees (and others) to file a lawsuit on behalf of the government in the event of suspected violations of the California Labor Code (for violations of workers' rights). Those who win can collect attorney's fees, costs, and up to 25 percent of the penalties imposed on the employer. (Labor Code section 2699.)

Whistleblower laws do not protect employees who engage in illegal activities.

III. SPECIAL PROTECTIONS FOR SPECIFIC WORKERS

A. STATE EMPLOYEES

State employees have the right to report possible violations of the law in confidence to the state attorney general, to the Joint Legislative Audit Committee, to the state auditor, or to any other appropriate authority. The employee's identity will be kept confidential. State employees are permitted to report all information related to an actual or suspected violation of state or federal law

occurring on the job or directly related to the job. They also are permitted to report governmental activities that are economically wasteful or involve gross misconduct, incompetence, or inefficiency. (Government Code sections 8547–8547.12.)

It is unlawful for anyone to pressure state employees not to report possible violations of the law. It is unlawful to discharge, discipline, discriminate against, or coerce state employees for reporting or intending to report violations of the law. A state employee who reports improper or illegal government activities to his employer is considered to have reported these acts to a government agency.

The U.S. Supreme Court has recently held that a public employee's legal rights as a whistleblower are not based on the constitutional right to free speech, but are instead based on specific laws that prohibit retaliation against employees who report suspected violations of the law. (*Garcetti v. Ceballos* (2006) 547 U.S. 410.) Thus, public employees do not have unlimited rights of free speech, and their First Amendment rights (constitutional rights guaranteeing free speech) relate to their right as private citizens, not to their statements related to their public duties.

Enforcement: File an appeal with the State Personnel Board. File a civil suit. Retaliation against whistleblowers is punishable by a fine of up to $10,000 and jail for up to one year. In addition, the person who retaliates may be subject to civil damages, including punitive damages and reasonable attorney's fees. (Government Code section 19683.)

B. SCHOOL AND COLLEGE EMPLOYEES

It is a crime for anyone to discipline, or attempt to discipline, an employee of a school district, community college district, or the office of the county superintendent of schools for appearing before a government body. This protection covers appearances before the district's governing board, a board of education, a legislative committee, or any other government board, commission, or council. (Education Code sections 44040, 87039.)

Enforcement: File a complaint with the local district attorney. Violation of these provisions is a misdemeanor.

C. HOSPITAL WORKERS

A special law protects hospital workers who report abuse of a child, elder, or dependent adult patient transferred into their hospital. This law protects physicians, registered nurses, licensed vocational nurses, clinical social workers, and persons in charge of a ward or part of a hospital who report abuse or neglect. It covers patients transferred from hospitals, intermediate-care facilities, skilled nursing facilities, foster homes, daycare centers, "small family homes" for handicapped children, home-finding agencies, care facilities for the elderly, and residential facilities providing twenty-four-hour non-medical care.

If someone transferred into the hospital appears to have suffered neglect or abuse, hospital workers must report this to both the police and the county health department, stating the extent and nature of the injury or condition. Hospital workers cannot be harassed, disciplined, suspended, or discharged for making this report. (Penal Code section 11161.8; Labor Code sections 1102.5–1105.) See section IV., below, on the duty and right to report specific violations.

Enforcement: File a complaint with the state Department of Fair Employment and Housing or the local district attorney. File a claim with the state labor commissioner. File a civil suit. A supervisor or employer who violates this law is punishable by six months in jail or a fine of $1,000 or both. (Penal Code section 11162.)

D. CHILD DAYCARE WORKERS

A special state whistleblowing rule applies to employees of child daycare facilities (with certain exceptions noted below). They are protected against retaliation if they do any of the following:

- Report a possible violation of the daycare licensing laws or regulations, or laws concerning staff-child ratios, transportation of children, or child abuse;
- Refuse to perform work in violation of a licensing law or regulation, provided they notify the employer of the violation before refusing to violate the licensing law or regulation;
- Testify or plan to testify at hearings, assist others in complaining, or provide information to enforcement agencies.

An employer cannot discharge, demote, or suspend an employee for taking any of the actions outlined above. It is illegal to attempt to prevent a witness from testifying in any trial or proceeding authorized by law. (Penal Code section 136.1.) It is illegal to threaten, discipline, or discriminate against them in any way. (Health and Safety Code sections 1596.881, 1596.882.)

Enforcement: File a claim with the employer within forty-five days and with the state labor commissioner within ninety days of violation of these rights. (Health and Safety Code sections 1596.882, 1596.883.) File a civil suit or criminal action. (18 U.S. Code sections 1505, 1512–1515 or Penal Code sections 136–137.)

Exceptions: This child daycare law does not apply to clinics, healthcare facilities, state-licensed community care facilities (providing twenty-four-hour non-medical residential care), public recreation programs, cooperative childcare where no payment is involved, family daycare homes where only the operator's own children and one other child are cared for, extended daycare programs operated by public or private schools, some school-based parenting programs, child daycare programs that operate only one day a week for no more than four hours, some temporary childcare services where parents and guardians are on the same premises as the daycare service; or some programs that provide classroom instruction for a limited period when school is not in session.

IV. DUTY AND RIGHT TO REPORT SPECIFIC VIOLATIONS

A. VIOLATIONS OF THE LABOR CODE AND UNEMPLOYMENT INSURANCE CODE

Employees have the right to file claims, testify in proceedings, or otherwise exercise any rights under the Labor Code or Orders of the Industrial Welfare Commission without being discriminated against by their employer. (Labor Code section 98.6.)

An employee may complain about safety or health conditions or practices in the workplace. The employer may not discriminate against an employee for making a complaint, causing proceedings to be instituted, testifying in such proceedings, or participating in an occupational health and safety commission. (Labor Code section

6310.) Also, an employee may not be discharged because she refuses to perform an activity that would create a real and apparent hazard to the employee or her coworkers in violation of the Labor Code or any occupational safety or health standard or order. (Labor Code section 6311.)

An employee may also complain, cause a proceeding to be instituted, or testify regarding non-compliance with the Hazardous Substances Information and Training Act. (Labor Code section 6399.7.)

An employee may seek information from the Employment Development Department (EDD) concerning rights under the Unemployment Insurance Code or the Labor Code, cooperate with any investigation by the EDD, or testify in any proceeding regarding the Unemployment Insurance Code or Labor Code. (Unemployment Insurance Code section 1237.)

Enforcement: File a claim with the state labor commissioner. File a civil suit.

B. VIOLATIONS BY EMPLOYERS WITH STATE CONTRACTS

If an employer has a construction or service contract (or subcontract) with the state government, employees are obligated to report contract violations to the contracting department of the state or the project inspector or resident engineer. If they fail to report a violation, employees can be subject to criminal felony prosecution and be held liable for double the losses that the state suffers. (Public Contract Code sections 10281–10284.)

C. ASSAULTS OR MENACING ACTS BY STUDENTS

School employees are required to report any assaults or menacing acts by a student. This obligation applies to all employees and supervisors of school districts, community college districts, and the office of the county superintendent of schools. It is a crime for any school employer or district official to attempt to prevent a school employee from making the report. Assaults or menacing acts must be reported by school employees to the appropriate law enforcement authorities of the county or city where the incident occurred. (Education Code sections 44014, 87014; Labor Code sections 1102.5–1105.)

Enforcement: File a complaint with the local district attorney. File a civil suit.

D. ABUSE OR NEGLECT OF A CHILD, ELDER, OR DEPENDENT ADULT

All people have the right to report the illegal abuse of themselves or abuse or neglect of another person. An employee is specifically protected by law from harassment, discipline, or discharge for reporting the abuse or suspected abuse of a child, senior citizen, or dependent adult. If an employee reports abuse to a protective agency, his identity remains confidential. The employer cannot be informed except with the employee's consent or by a court order.

For the whistleblower laws that protect people who report child abuse, see Penal Code sections 11165–11174; Labor Code sections 1102.5-1105. For the laws on elder or dependant adult abuse, see Welfare and Institutions Code sections 15600–15637; Labor Code sections 1102.5–1105.

Certain workers (for example, teachers, health practitioners, firefighters) who are in contact with children, and trained in identifying and reporting child abuse, have a legal duty to report child abuse. Health practitioners, care custodians, clergy, and employees of adult protective service agencies and local law enforcement agencies are legally required to report elder abuse. Agencies that find placements for disabled individuals of any age are required to report abuse, neglect, and health and safety problems. (Welfare and Institutions Code section 15630.)

Enforcement: File a complaint with the local district attorney or state attorney general. File a claim with the state labor commissioner. File a civil action.

E. VIOLATIONS OF CHILDCARE LICENSING REGULATIONS

Employees have the right to complain about violations of licensing or other laws relating to child daycare facilities without experiencing retaliatory threats of discharge or discipline. Employers may not discriminate against an employee for causing a proceeding to be instituted, testifying in such a proceeding, or refusing to perform work in violation of a licensing law after notifying the employer of the violation. Written notification of

facilities, group homes, social facilities, home-finding agencies, intermediate-care facilities, and foster family homes.

Individuals who help a patient, resident, or other employee to report violations, or who provide information or testimony to an investigating agency, are also protected from retaliation on the job. An employer cannot discharge or discipline them or in any way retaliate against or harass them, nor can the employer expel or retaliate against a patient or resident who lodges a complaint or cooperates with an investigation. (Health and Safety Code sections 1417–1439, 1538, 1539, 1599; Labor Code sections 1102.5–1105; Welfare and Institutions Code sections 9701, 9715.)

Enforcement: File a complaint with the state Licensing and Certification Division of the Department of Public Health, the Office of the State Long-Term Care Ombudsman, or the local district attorney. File a claim with the state labor commissioner. File a civil suit. Violation may be a misdemeanor. Civil penalties of up to $10,000 for each violation plus attorney's fees may be available.

their rights shall be provided to employees at the time of their employment. (Health and Safety Code Section 1596.881.)

Enforcement: File a complaint with the labor commissioner.

F. VIOLATIONS OF PATIENTS' RIGHTS IN LONG-TERM CARE FACILITIES

Workers at long-term healthcare or residential facilities have the right to report violations of patients' rights (for example, the right to privacy and dignity, the right to leave the facility). They also have the right to ask for an inspection. They are protected against retaliation for this whistleblowing. If they are disciplined or terminated within 120 days of complaining about violations of patients' right, it is presumed that the discipline or termination is in retaliation for the whistleblowing. The employer then has the burden of proving that the discipline or termination was not retaliatory.

For the types of facilities covered, see Health and Safety Code sections 1250, 1502, 1569.2. They include the following: nursing homes, hospitals, residential care facilities, skilled nursing facilities, adult daycare facilities, extended-care

G. VIOLATIONS OF PATIENTS' AND PRISONERS' RIGHTS IN INSTITUTIONS

Employees have the right to report suspected violations of the rights of institutionalized people, including prisoners, resident juveniles, patients, developmentally disabled or handicapped clients, and recipients of custodial or residential care. Employees cannot be discharged, disciplined, threatened, harassed, blacklisted, or discriminated against for making such a report to the proper authorities. (42 U.S. Code section 1997d; Labor Code sections 1102.5–1105.) Employees can report any denial of basic rights of patients or prisoners. These rights are detailed in 42 U.S. Code section 9501.

Some of these rights, such as the right to leave and the right to private telephone calls, may be restricted in certain cases. These rights are restricted for inmates in a jail, prison, or detention facility, under Penal Code section 2600. The rights of those involuntarily committed to mental institutions as a danger to self or others are restricted under Welfare and Institutions Code sections 5000–5337. Additionally, persons under a court order of guardianship or conservatorship may lose some of these rights. (42 U.S. Code sections 1997–1997j,

9501; Health and Safety Code section 1599.1; Welfare and Institutions Code sections 5325, 5325.1; Penal Code sections 3400–3409, 3500–3524, 4011, 4019.5–4023.6, 4027– 4030.)

A very few of these rights may be restricted for medical or legal reasons. In each case, the restriction must be recorded in the patient's or client's records, along with an explanation and the name of the person ordering the restriction.

Enforcement: File a report with the appropriate state agency for the particular institution (Health and Safety Code section 1424(e).), with a copy to the Office of Civil Rights of the federal Justice Department, to ensure that the whistleblower is protected. File a complaint with the local district attorney or state attorney general. File a claim with the state labor commissioner. File a civil suit.

Exceptions: The special federal protection regarding civil rights of the institutionalized person (42 U.S. Code section 1997) is limited to facilities that are run by, or that provide services to, or that receive funding from, a state or local government agency (Medi-Cal, Medicare, and Social Security funding does not qualify for this purpose).

H. ENVIRONMENTAL SAFETY VIOLATIONS

1. Environmental and Nuclear Hazards

Federal laws protect workers who report possible violations of environmental protection or nuclear safety laws. It is illegal for an employer to discharge, discipline, harass, blacklist, discriminate against, or retaliate against environmental or nuclear whistleblowers in any way. Whistleblowers are protected if they report (or are about to report) a violation or if they provide (or are about to provide) information or testimony to an investigating agency. (15 U.S. Code section 2622; 33 U.S. Code section 1367; 42 U.S. Code sections 300j-9(i), 5851, 6971, 7622, 9610; Labor Code sections 1102.5–1105.) On safety, health, and sanitation violations in general, see Chapter 7.

State law makes it a crime to conceal, alter, or destroy records about hazardous materials or to lie about such materials. Anyone found guilty of violating the law is punishable by fines of up to $50,000 per day and two years in prison. (Health and Safety Code section 25191; Labor Code sections 1102.5–1105.)

Enforcement: File a written complaint with the U.S. Department of Labor, Wage and Hour Division (must be filed within thirty days of most violations, within 180 days of nuclear safety violations). File a complaint with the local district attorney. File a civil suit. File a claim with the state labor commissioner.

2. Asbestos Violations in Schools

Employees have the right to notify the public about any asbestos problem in school buildings. No state or local educational agency receiving federal funds can retaliate against employees in any way for doing so. (20 U.S. Code section 3608.)

Enforcement: File a civil suit.

3. Strip-Mining Violations

Federal law protects workers who report possible violations of the strip-mining, surface-mining, and land-reclamation laws. It is illegal for an employer to discharge, discipline, harass, blacklist, retaliate against, or discriminate against whistleblowers in any way. Whistleblowers are protected if they report (or are about to report) a violation or if they provide (or are about to provide) information or testimony to an investigating agency. (30 U.S. Code section 1293; Labor Code sections 1102.5–1105.)

Enforcement: File a written complaint with the secretary of the interior, U.S. Department of the Interior, with a copy to the employer and to the U.S. Department of Labor, Wage and Hour Division, within thirty days of the violation. File a complaint to the local district attorney. File a civil suit. File a claim with the state labor commissioner.

I. LAND AND SEA TRANSPORTATION VIOLATIONS

1. Commercial Vehicle Unsafe Conditions

Employees' rights to report, complain about, and testify about unsafe commercial motor vehicles are fully protected. Employers are not allowed to discipline, discharge, or in any way discriminate against workers who complain about possible violations of a commercial motor vehicle safety rule or regulation. These protections extend to independent contractor drivers as well as employees. (49 U.S. Code section 31105; Labor Code sections 1102.5–1105, 6310–6312.)

For the definition of commercial motor vehicle, see 49 U.S. Code section 31101.

Enforcement: File a written complaint with the federal Occupational Safety and Health Administration, in the Department of Labor, which must be filed within 180 days of the violation. File a complaint with the local district attorney. File a civil suit. File a claim with the state labor commissioner.

2. Railroad Accidents, Injuries, or Unsafe Conditions

Employees' rights to report, complain about, and testify about railroad accidents, unsafe railroad conditions, and violations of railroad safety laws are protected by federal law. An employer cannot discipline, discharge, or in any way discriminate against employees for a safety-related report, complaint, or testimony. It is illegal for an employer to try to keep employees from voluntarily telling people what they have witnessed in connection with a job-related injury or death. (45 U.S. Code section 60; 49 U.S. Code section 20109.)

Enforcement: File a complaint with the U.S. attorney. File a civil suit. Some violations are crimes punishable by imprisonment and fines.

3. Illegal Conditions for Workers at Sea

A complex and unique set of protections apply to workers at sea.

a. Inadequate Vessel or Provisions

The right to complain about an unseaworthy vessel or unfit food or quarters is protected in a number of ways. Employees with questions about this should consult their union.

Enforcement: File a lawsuit with the U.S. District Court, the Coast Guard shipping commissioner, U.S. consular officials, Customs Service officials, or the commanding officer of a U.S. Navy vessel.

b. Unsafe Boating Conditions

It is a crime for an employer to retaliate against workers for enforcing boat safety rules. This applies to charter or "for hire" boats, including whale-watching boats. It is illegal for anyone to threaten employees with loss of work or charter earnings for enforcing boat safety rules. Safety rules include life preserver requirements, bad-weather cancellations, and Coast Guard licensing. Employees cannot be discharged or disciplined for reporting unsafe boating conditions. (Harbors and

Navigation Code sections 773–774.4; Labor Code sections 1102.5–1105.)

Enforcement: File a complaint with the local district attorney. File a civil suit. Violators are punishable by six months in jail or a $1,000 fine or both. The person who operates, owns, controls, or manages a charter is liable for a civil penalty of up to $50,000 for each violation.

c. Marine Accidents and Injuries

The right to report and testify about marine casualties is protected. A marine casualty is any of the following events, if it happens at sea or on board a maritime vessel: the death of a person, serious injury to a person, material loss of property, material damage affecting the seaworthiness or efficiency of the vessel, and significant harm to the environment.

It is a crime for anyone to threaten, discharge, harass, discipline, blacklist, discriminate against, or coerce workers at sea in order to prevent them from reporting or testifying about a marine casualty, make them give a false report or testimony, make them leave the country, or make them change a report or their testimony. (46 U.S. Code sections 6101, 6306; Labor Code sections 1102.5–1105.)

Enforcement: File a complaint with the U.S. secretary of transportation or the U.S. attorney. File a civil suit. Violations are punishable by one year in jail and a $5,000 fine.

d. Unsafe Cargo

Federal law specifies safety requirements for cargo containers that can be transferred to and carried by ship, train, and truck without unloading and reloading the contents. A safe container will not break or spill cargo, can be hoisted safely, can support other containers stacked on top, is properly labeled, and is periodically inspected. Workers cannot be discharged, disciplined, or discriminated against in any way for reporting an unsafe container or any related violation. (46 U.S. Code app. sections 1501, 1506; Labor Code sections 1102.5–1105.)

Special rules on container safety protect longshore and related harbor workers. (See 29 Code of Federal Regulations sections 1918.85, 1918.86; 8 California Code of Regulations sections 3466, 3460.)

Enforcement: File a report with the U.S. Department of Labor within sixty days of the violation, with a copy to the U.S. secretary of transportation. File a civil suit.

J. CORPORATE FRAUD AND CORRUPTION

The federal Sarbanes-Oxley Act of 2002 protects employees of publicly traded companies (and in some instances private companies) who report corporate fraud and/or violations of securities law. Employees, attorneys, auditors, or contractors who report such problems in publicly traded companies to the head of the company, and, if no action is taken, to the company's audit committee or board of directors, or who assist in an investigation into activities reasonably believed to violate such laws, are protected from retaliation from the company and its executives, officers, employees, contractors, subcontractors, or agents. Employees in private companies who report fraud or illegal activities to law enforcement are protected. Reports to the news media are not protected by this law. (15 U.S. Code sections 7201 et seq.)

Enforcement: File a complaint within ninety days of the retaliation with the Department of Labor. Within the Department of Labor, the Occupational Safety and Health Administration deals with complaints regarding retaliation in violation of the Sarbanes-Oxley Act. (29 Code of Federal Regulations sections 1980.100 et seq.) Remedies may include reinstatement, back pay, interest, and other damages to make the employee whole. Violations involving publicly traded companies may result in criminal penalties.

V. WHAT TO REMEMBER WHEN PLANNING TO BECOME A WHISTLEBLOWER

- In most cases employees will be protected only if they actually report a suspected violation of the law to a state or federal agency, or if they can prove that the employer thinks they are about to make such a report.
- The suspected violation reported must have some relationship to the public (for instance, the public's interest in having the law enforced), more than minor, private personnel matters.
- Reporting a reasonable suspicion of an employer's illegal activity qualifies the reporting employee for whistleblower protection, as long as the suspicion is reasonable, even if it is eventually found that the act was not illegal.
- Good faith reports regarding suspected violations are protected, but bad faith reports (for example, one made strictly for harassment purposes, where there is no reasonable suspicion of wrongdoing) are not protected.
- For their own protection, whistleblowers should keep a paper trail in a secure location, indicating the reasons they believe that a violation of the law has occurred, the report to state or federal agencies, and any negative actions taken against them by their employer (including discussions related to their report of illegal activities).
- In general, when whistleblowers experience retaliation for whistleblowing activities, they should utilize available administrative remedies, including internal complaint procedures, procedures provided by government agencies charged with enforcing the law, union grievances, etc.
- Whistleblowers should keep their own copies of previous evaluations, letters of commendation, and similar materials, in case the employer attempts to retaliate by alleging poor performance on the job.
- Whistleblowing laws do not protect employees who commit illegal acts (for instance, theft of confidential material). Whistleblowers should remember that their focus should be on reporting the suspected violation; they are not required to conduct a full investigation, especially if documents are not legally available to them.
- A whistleblower who has experienced retaliation on the job should immediately seek legal assistance. Letting a long period of time go by after the retaliation occurs can sometimes damage the whistleblower's case.

CHAPTER 12 **PERSONNEL FILES AND HEALTH RECORDS**

PERSONNEL FILES AND HEALTH RECORDS

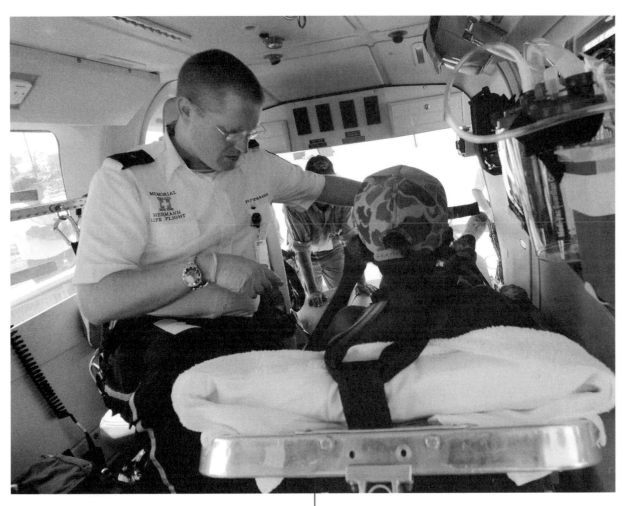

I. SCOPE OF THE CHAPTER

Employees have a right to privacy in their personal information, protected by the state and federal constitutions, state and federal statutes, and court cases applying them. Employees whose personal information is unlawfully gathered, disclosed, or misrepresented have available to them both statutory and common law claims for invasion of privacy through which they can seek a remedy.

Employees also have the right to see and comment on their own personnel files. An employer has the responsibility to maintain various records about an individual's employment (for example, records about job duties, pay, hours worked, industrial injuries, and pension benefits), and to keep them for specific periods of time, sometimes continuing after the employment relationship has ended. The law protects the confidentiality of employees' personal records and data: third parties (for example, public schools, police departments, and drug rehabilitation programs) cannot give certain information about an individual to that individual's employer. As well, an employer cannot give third parties (like prospective employers) certain information about their employees. The Privacy Act prohibits federal agencies from disclosing personal information maintained by them to third parties.

The privacy of individuals' health records also is protected by the law. Individuals have the right to inspect most of their health records and to have health providers of their choice examine those that are not available to the individuals personally. Other people or groups, including employers, generally cannot see individuals' health records without their consent, and special protections apply to sensitive records, such as those about mental health, HIV/AIDS, developmental disabilities, and drug or alcohol addiction and treatment. An employer who does gain access to an individual's medical information has an obligation to protect the employee's privacy.

II. CONSTITUTIONAL PRIVACY PROTECTIONS

A right to privacy has been found to be implicit in the Bill of Rights, set forth in Amendments 1 through 10 of the federal Constitution. (See *Griswold v. Connecticut* (1965) 381 U.S. 479.) Federal constitutional restrictions constrain the government's power as the employer. California is one of seven states that have enacted a constitutional right to privacy, set forth in Article I, section 1, of the California Constitution. That provision applies to both public and private entities. (*Hill v. NCAA* (1994) 7 Cal.4th 1.) The California Supreme Court has interpreted that provision as serving to prevent and remedy the overly broad gathering and retention of unnecessary personal information by the government and businesses, the improper use of information obtained for a particular purpose, and the absence of a reasonable check on the accuracy of existing records. (*White v. Davis* (1975) 13 Cal.3d 757.) The right to privacy found in the California Constitution also prohibits improper disclosure of employee personnel files to third parties. (*Board of Trustees, Stanford Univ. v. Superior Court* (1981) 119 Cal.App.3d 516.)

III. PERSONNEL FILES

A personnel file is a record kept by an employer documenting an individual's employment status and history. Labor Code section 1198.5(a) defines "personnel file" as any file relating to the employee's performance or any grievance concerning the employee. All such records kept by an employer constitute an individual's personnel "file," whether kept in a single file or multiple files.

A. AN INDIVIDUAL'S RIGHT TO SEE THE EMPLOYMENT FILE

1. In General

An individual has the right to inspect his personnel records at his worksite or wherever the records are stored. The employee must not lose compensation if he has to travel to a location other than the workplace to see his records. (Labor Code 1198.5.)

If an individual's employment is covered by a collective bargaining agreement, he should check with his union to determine if special rules about personnel files apply to the covered workplace. If an individual is a public employee, he should check the civil service or personnel rules concerning his file. Public employees also have the right to copy information in their files and request corrections in their personnel files. If the request is denied, the public employee may submit a memo of reasonable length to the file. (Civil Code sections 1798.30–1798.37.) School district, community college, and state university employees have added protections. See the sections that follow for more information.

Employees may find it worthwhile to check their personnel files for accuracy. If there is incorrect or missing information, the employee should request that it be corrected. If that is not effective, the employee should write a memo to the file, have a third party review it for appropriateness, and ask that it be added to the personnel file. Public employees have a legal right to have such information added. Even where there is no specific legal right to add material, many employers permit their employees to add letters to their personnel files.

Public and private employers are subject to strict laws requiring the employer to keep copies of payroll records and make those records available for inspection and copying. Payroll records must be made available within twenty-one days of the request for inspection and copying. (Labor Code section 226; Civil Code sections 1798.30 et seq.)

Similarly, employers are required to maintain

accurate payroll records and to allow state officers access to such records at a reasonable time upon request. (Labor Code section 1174.) Upon request, an employee is entitled to a copy of any personnel documents she has signed as a condition of employment. (Labor Code section 432.) The Industrial Welfare Commission is charged with regulating wages, hours, and working conditions for employees in specified occupations and trades in California (including professional, technical, clerical, service, food preparation, certain housekeeping and laundry services, sales, transportation, recreation, broadcast, film, agricultural, construction, drilling, logging, and mining jobs). These wage orders require that the employer make the employee's records available for inspection upon reasonable request. (See http://www.dir.ca.gov/IWC/wageorderindustries.htm.)

Although private sector employees are not legally guaranteed the right to receive a copy of personnel records (other than records she has signed), some employers will provide copies. If the employer will not provide a copy, the employee should take detailed notes when she inspects the file.

Enforcement: Regarding rights violations related to payroll records, file a claim with the state labor commissioner through forms obtained from the Division of Labor Standards Enforcement (DLSE forms and publications, as well as opinion letters of the labor commissioner, can be found at the DLSE website: http://www.dir.ca.gov/dlse/dlse.html). File a complaint with the local district attorney. File a civil suit. In case of a violation of an employer's duty to maintain and make available payroll records, an employee or the labor commissioner can recover a penalty of $750. (Labor Code section 226(f).) An employee who suffers injury as a result of an employer's failure to comply with its payroll recordkeeping obligation or with the employee's request to review or copy the records is entitled to recover actual damages or $50 for the first violation and actual damages or $100 for each additional violation, whichever is greater, plus costs and attorney's fees. (Labor Code section 226(e).)

In addition, an employer who fails to keep payroll records as required by Labor Code section 226(a) or to provide a wage deduction statement to an employee is subject to a $250 civil penalty for the first violation and a $1,000 civil penalty for each additional violation. (Labor Code section 226.3.) An employee who brings a civil court action to require compliance with a request to view payroll records is entitled to an award of costs and attorney's fees. (Labor Code section 226(g).) An employer who knowingly and intentionally violates the law regarding payroll records is guilty of a misdemeanor and subject to a fine of up to $1,000 and imprisonment of up to one year in jail, or both. (Labor Code section 226.6.) An employer who violates the law regarding an employee's access to personnel records is guilty of a misdemeanor punishable by a fine of at least $100 or imprisonment for at least thirty days. (Labor Code section 1199.)

Exceptions: Labor Code section 226 does not, for the most part, apply to public employers. (Labor Code section 226(h).) An employee does not have the right to see or copy employee records relating to the investigation of possible criminal activity, letters of reference (unless these records have been used to discipline or discharge the employee), or records related to pre-hire matters including those related to promotional exams or exams prepared by identifiable exam committee members. (Labor Code section 1198.5(d)(1)-(3).)

Special rules apply to public employees. See section III.A.3.a., below.

2. Union Rights

Unions have the right to obtain information about employees they represent, subject to some basic limitations. The National Labor Relations Act imposes an obligation on the employer to provide relevant information needed by the union to perform its duties as the employees' representative, including information needed to enable the union to evaluate grievances intelligently. (*NLRB v. Acme Indus. Co.* (1967) 385 U.S. 432; *Detroit Edison Co. v. NLRB* (1979) 440 U.S. 301.) The specific information that must be supplied to the union will depend on the circumstances of a particular case.

3. Special Rules for Public Employees

a. Privacy Act Protections

The Privacy Act of 1974 (5 U.S. Code section 552a) protects individuals by restricting the disclosure of personally identifiable records maintained by federal agencies and granting individuals access to agency records pertaining to them. The records may include information about education, financial transactions, medical history, and criminal or employment history of an individual. (5 U.S. Code section 552a(a)(4), (5).) Federal agencies covered by the Privacy Act are any executive department, military department, government corporation, government controlled corporation, or other establishment in the executive branch of the government, or any independent regulatory agency. (5 U.S. Code section 552(f).) Federal entities that are not part of the executive branch are generally not covered by the Privacy Act, nor are state and local government agencies. The act only protects individuals who are United States citizens or aliens lawfully admitted for permanent residence. (5 U.S. Code section 552a(a)(2).) The individual who is the subject of the record must be the one to assert her rights under the act. If an individual asks for access to any information about herself in the system, the agency must allow her (and if she wishes a person of her choosing) to review the record and have a copy made. (5 U.S. Code section 552a(d).)

Enforcement: File a civil suit.

b. Public Employees' Rights to Inspect Their Personnel Files

i. Rights Shared With Private Sector Employees

The right to inspect one's personnel files applies to public sector, as well as private sector, employees in California. (Labor Code section 1198.5; Civil Code section 1798.34; Government Code section 31011.)

ii. Rights of Public School and Community College Employees

Employees of public schools and community colleges are also entitled to inspect their personnel files in accordance with Labor Code section 1198.5. (Education Code sections 44031(a), 87031(a).) The following additional provisions apply to public school and community college employees' inspection of personnel files:

- Derogatory information cannot be entered into an employee's file unless and until the employee is given notice and has an opportunity to examine and comment on the information.
- The employee must be allowed to review the derogatory information during normal business hours and must be released from normal duties without loss of pay in order to do so.

- The employee does not have a right to review the records at a time when he is required to render actual services to the employing school district (such as during a class the employee is required to teach).
- Non-credentialed public school employees are entitled to review their numerical scores on written examinations.
- Beyond the entitlement of non-credentialed public school employees listed above, no public school employee is entitled to review ratings, reports, or records that were obtained prior to the employment of the person involved, prepared by identifiable examination committee members, or obtained in connection with a promotional examination.
(Education Code sections 44031(b), 87031(b).)

iii. Rights of Employees of the California State University and the University of California

Employees of the California State University have the right to inspect all "reports, documents, correspondence, and other material which pertain to the employee which are kept by the university or college." (Education Code section 89546(a).)

CSU employees also have the following additional rights:

- To have personnel decisions about them, such as promotion, retention, or termination decisions, be based primarily on information in their personnel files. If a decision or recommendation is based on other reasons, those reasons must be given in writing and put into the employee's personnel file, so that the employee has access to them.
- To have another person of their choice (for example, a union representative) accompany them to inspect the records.
- To request an exact copy of their entire personnel files or any portion of them. Employees must make the request in writing and pay the copying costs. The CSU employer must provide the copy within ten calendar days of an employee's request.
- To request correction or deletion of items that, after examining their records, they believe are not accurate, relevant, timely, or complete. They must make the request in writing, explain exactly which portions they want to correct or delete, and give their reasons. The

employee's written statement becomes part of the permanent file. The president of the university must respond to the employee's statement within twenty-one calendar days. If the president refuses the employee's request, the reasons for the refusal must be stated in writing. The president's written refusal also becomes part of the employee's permanent record. (Education Code section 89546.)

University of California employees are entitled to access "all personal information, as defined in subdivision (a) of Section 1798.3 of the Civil Code, contained in any employee record that is maintained by the University of California that pertains to the individual." (Education Code section 92612(a).) Civil Code section 1798.3(a) defines "personal information" as follows:

...any information that is maintained by an agency that identifies or describes an individual, including, but not limited to, his or her name, Social Security Number, physical description, home address, home telephone number, education, financial matters, and medical or employment

history. It includes statements made by, or attributed to, the individual.

The term "agency" in that definition means "every state office, officer, department, division, bureau, board, commission, or other state agency," but does not include the legislature, the courts, or the State Compensation Insurance Fund. (Civil Code section 1798.3(b).)

Enforcement: File a claim with the state labor commissioner or file a complaint with the local district attorney. File a civil suit.

iv. Rights of Peace Officers

Peace officers have specific rights with regard to their personnel files. A negative comment cannot be entered into a peace officer's personnel file without the officer first reading and signing the document to indicate that he is aware of the comment. If the officer refuses to sign the document, a notation indicating the officer's refusal to sign must be made on the document, and it must be signed by another officer. An officer has the right to file a written response within thirty days to any adverse comments entered in his personnel file. The response must be attached to the adverse comments. (Government Code sections 3305, 3306.)

A peace officer has the right to inspect personnel files used to determine the officer's qualifications for employment and promotion, or the basis for disciplinary action. The officer must be allowed to inspect the file within a reasonable period of time after the request was made, and to see it at reasonable times and intervals, during usual business hours, with no loss of compensation. (Government Code section 3306.5(a), (b).)

The officer may make a written request that material mistakenly or unlawfully placed in the personnel file be corrected or deleted. The request must include a statement, which will become part of the personnel file, describing the changes requested and the reasons supporting the changes. Within thirty days, the employer must either grant the request or notify the officer of the decision to deny the request. If the request is denied, a written statement of the employer's reasons for denying the request must be added to the personnel file. (Government Code section 3306.5(c), (d).)

Enforcement: File a civil suit. Court orders or other relief may be granted to remedy the violation and prevent similar violations in the future. If the employer is found to have acted maliciously, additional penalties may be awarded. (Government Code section 3309.5.)

B. EMPLOYER'S DUTY TO MAINTAIN RECORDS

Employers are required by law to maintain certain payroll records, such as sufficiently detailed information about the hours an employee works, the employee's pay rate, and any other information the employer needs to correctly calculate the wages and benefits owed to the employee. (Labor Code section 226.) If an employer does not keep adequate records and there is a dispute, the court will generally accept the employee's testimony as to hours worked.

Personnel files generally must be kept for two years, although other periods apply to some items. Personnel files of employees who were terminated still must be kept for two years, and, if a former employee, current employee, or job applicant pursues an administrative complaint, lawsuit, or other similar action against an employer, the employer must retain all records relating to that employee and incident for the duration of the proceedings, until all appeals have been resolved. (Government Code section 12946.)

The chart on pages 286 and 287 lists the records that an employer must maintain, the longest duration specific records must be kept, and the statutory sources for the retention requirements.

Enforcement: File a claim with the state labor commissioner. File a civil suit. Enforcement of the laws that apply to employer record keeping varies greatly. Some violations are misdemeanors punishable by jail time, fines, or both. (Labor Code sections 226, 226.6, 1199; Government Code section 12946.)

See Chapter 7 for more information on workplace safety and health. See Chapter 8 for information on work injuries covered by Workers' Compensation. See Chapter 3 for information regarding employer investigations, police records, and other records-related issues.

C. PERSONNEL FILE PRIVACY PROTECTIONS

The law limits both the information an employer may release to prospective employers or other third parties and the information an employer may obtain from third parties about an individual. Wrongful disclosure may occur in many circumstances. Under California law, an employer must take reasonable steps to protect the confidentiality of an employee's personal information, including the contents of the employee's personnel file. (See generally, California Constitution, Article I, section 1 (guaranteeing the right to privacy); *Hill v. NCAA* (1994) 7 Cal.4th 1; *Board of Trustees, Stanford Univ. v. Superior Court* (1981) 119 Cal.App.3d 516.)

Some statutes also address particular kinds of information that employers must try to safeguard, such as the knowledge that an employee is illiterate (Labor Code section 1042); is participating in a drug or alcohol rehabilitation program (Labor Code section 1026; Health and Safety Code section 123125); an employee's personal financial information (unless the agency seeking it presents a written authorization for specific information) (Civil Code section 1785.20.5); medical information (Civil Code sections 56.20, 56.35) (medical records are discussed in detail in section IV., p. 289); public school or college transcripts or files (20 U.S. Code section 1232g; Education Code sections 49076, 76240–76246); and home addresses of law enforcement employees and their families (Penal Code section 146e).

There are restrictions on the release of information concerning an individual's employment termination. Regardless of whether an individual left employment voluntarily or was terminated, the former employer cannot misrepresent what happened to prevent the individual from obtaining employment. An employer who does so is guilty of a misdemeanor. (Labor Code sections 1050, 1052.) An employer is permitted to answer truthfully if asked why an individual's employment was terminated. (Labor Code section 1053.) An employer is permitted to respond in good faith to questions from current, former, or prospective employers as to whether or not the employer would rehire or retain a current or former employee, unless the reason the employer would not retain the employee is related to exercise of constitutional rights, a labor dispute, or any other activity protected by law. (Civil Code section 47(c); Code of Civil Procedure section 527.3.) Also, California public schools are required to report certain facts (termination of employment, misconduct, sexual misconduct) to the Commission on Teacher Credentialing. (5 California Code of Regulations sections 80303–80304; Education Code section 44242.5(b)(4).)

There are federal and state laws that entitle members of the public to obtain copies of government documents, but these laws do not require disclosure of confidential personnel or payroll records. (5 U.S. Code section 552(b)(6); Government Code section 6254(c).) However, passport information and police disciplinary records are considered personnel records. They need not be disclosed to the public. (*United States Department of State v. Washington Post* (1982) 456 U.S. 595; *Copley Press v. Superior Court* (2006) 39 Cal.4th 1272.) In addition, under California law, disclosure of public employees' salary figures is permitted, on the theory that this information relates to expenditures of government funds, not personnel records. (*International Federation of Professional and Technical Engineers, Local 21 v. Superior Court* (2007) 42 Cal.4th 319.)

An employee also has the right to sue her employer, supervisor, or anyone else who puts into her personnel file false statements of fact that might hurt the employee's reputation (defamatory/libelous statements). (*Manguso v. Oceanside Unified School District* (1979) 88 Cal. App.3d 725.) However, to provide a basis for a defamation lawsuit, the statements in question must be intentionally false representations of *fact*. Opinions, even if they are unfair and unsupported by fact, cannot provide a basis for a defamation claim. (*Jensen v. Hewlett-Packard Co.* (1993) 14 Cal. App.4th 958, 969-970.) Such unfounded opinions placed into a personnel file could, however, give rise to a claim for violation of the implied covenant of good faith and fair dealing that is implicit in every contract. (*Jensen v. Hewlett-Packard Co.* (1993) 14 Cal.App.4th 958, 969-970.)

In some cases, conduct that conveys a factual representation may be defamatory, such as if an employee has been terminated and his employer has security personnel remove him from the building in a manner that falsely suggests that the individual has committed a crime. (*Shaw v. Hughes Aircraft Co.* (2000) 83 Cal.App.4th 1336.) Whether the information has been distributed to others is generally an important factor in privacy, defamation, and libel cases. Employers may successfully defend actions against them for violation of privacy by showing that the information was not disseminated. The law governing defamation is quite technical and complex. Legal advice should be sought before asserting that defamation has occurred.

Unless an employee provides written authorization, the employer cannot obtain confidential information about the individual from any of the following:

- Public schools or colleges (20 U.S. Code section 1232g(b); 34 Code of Federal Regulations section 99.30);
- Addiction treatment programs (42 U.S. Code section 290dd-2);
- Mental health service providers (Civil Code section 56.104; Welfare and Institutions Code sections 5328, 5540);
- Anyone with information about the individual's HIV (human immunodeficiency virus) status (Health and Safety Code sections 120975–121125).

(45 Code of Federal Regulations section 164.508; Civil Code section 56.20.)

An employer cannot obtain information or records, from an employee or anyone else, about an arrest that did not result in the individual's conviction. (Labor Code section 432.7.) This

DURATION RECORDS MUST BE RETAINED	TYPE OF RECORDS	SOURCE OF LEGAL REQUIREMENT
1 YEAR (Or duration of claims or litigation involving such records, whichever is longer)	PROMOTION, DEMOTION, LAYOFF • Promotion applications • Records of every promotion, demotion, transfer, layoff, or training selection decision • Records of every failure or refusal to hire or promote • All test papers • All disciplinary and discharge records	• 29 Code of Federal Regulations sections 1620.32, 1627.3
2 YEARS (Or duration of claims or litigation involving such records, whichever is longer)	HIRING AND JOB DUTIES • Job applications • Resumes • Other job inquiries sent to employer • Employment referral records • Applicant identification records • Help wanted ads • Opportunities for training, promotion, or overtime • Job opening notices sent to employment agencies or labor unions • Employment testing results • Terms and conditions of employee's employment	• Title VII of the Civil Rights Act of 1964 • Americans with Disabilities Act • Age Discrimination in Employment Act • California Fair Employment and Housing Act
3 YEARS	EMPLOYEE WAGES • Time cards • Wage rate calculation tables for straight time and overtime • Shift schedules • Individual employee's hours and days • Employee's occupation and job assignments • Records explaining wage differentials between sexes • Explanation of additions to, and deductions from, paychecks • A copy of each collective bargaining agreement, trust agreement (for example, health, pension), benefit plan, or individual employment contract that affects the employee's job • A written memo summarizing each unwritten employment understanding or agreement that affects an employee's wages and hours • All tips received by employer on employee's behalf • All hours worked by employees when tips were received; all hours worked without tips, amount paid during each type of work • Time records documenting each meal period, each split-shift interval, and the total daily hours worked • All incentive plans and accurate production records when used in any incentive plan • All retroactive wage payments and periods covered • The value of all board, lodging, and other non-cash compensation furnished to employee, and whether or not the employee actually received it	• Fair Labor Standards Act • California Labor Code • 29 Code of Federal Regulations sections 516.2, 516.5, 516.24
3 YEARS from hire date or 1 year after cessation of employment, whichever is later.	EMPLOYMENT ELIGIBILITY FORMS (Federal I-9 Forms)	• Immigration Reform and Control Act

DURATION RECORDS MUST BE RETAINED	TYPE OF RECORDS	SOURCE OF LEGAL REQUIREMENT
4 YEARS	PAYROLL/EMPLOYMENT • Name, Social Security Number, address, age, sex, occupation • The dates the employee was hired, rehired, recalled, and terminated • Individual wage records • Time and day workweek begins • Places of employee's work for employer • Regular hourly rate • Hours worked (daily and weekly) • Weekly overtime earnings • Daily or weekly straight time earnings • Deductions from or additions to wages • Wages paid each pay period • Payment dates, gross amounts, and periods • Cash value of all remunerations other than cash that were given to employee • All special payments, gifts, bonuses, prizes, and the like, given to an employee and the periods of service for which the special payments were made • Tax records of all remuneration and other compensation paid to the employee • All of an employee's W-2, W-3, W-4, and W-4E forms • The amounts and dates of state and federal income taxes withheld from an employee's pay • The amount of all unemployment insurance taxes paid on an employee's behalf and the periods of work covered • Copies of all tax returns, tax schedules, and statements concerning income tax, FICA deductions, and unemployment insurance taxes • Every report an employee gave to the employer concerning tips and gratuities	• Fair Labor Standards Act • California Unemployment Insurance Code • California Labor Code • Social Security Act
5 YEARS	OCCUPATIONAL HEALTH AND SAFETY/INJURY • Employer's log of occupational injuries and illnesses for each workplace and reports on them to OSHA, as required by law (for the information that must be reported, see Chapter 7)	• Occupational Safety and Health Act (OSHA)
5 YEARS after the last date of treatment	WORKERS' COMPENSATION • Case file for each claim or case about a work-related injury or illness, whether the claim was granted or denied • Employer's Report of Occupational Injury and Illness • All medical reports • All Workers' Compensation Appeals Board orders and reports • A copy of every letter of denial or notice of termination of benefits sent to an employee or employer • All reports to the Division of Industrial Accidents • A record of all benefits paid to an employee and the periods covered • An estimate of future liability	8 Code of Calif. Regulations section 10102
6 YEARS	PENSION AND BENEFIT PLANS • All records used in administering any pension or employee benefit plan, including all vouchers, worksheets, and receipts • All statements indicating whether payments have been made to any benefit fund on an employee's behalf as well as the amount paid and the period covered by the payments	• Employee Retirement Income Security Act of 1974
DURATION OF EMPLOYMENT PLUS 30 YEARS (If an employer goes out of business, employees may still be able to get health and toxic exposure records from the U.S. National Institute of Occupational Safety and Health or a related agency. A union or attorney should be contacted for assistance.)	MEDICAL • Medical and employment questionnaires • Medical histories • Results of medical exams • Lab test reports and x-ray films • Medical opinions, diagnoses, progress notes, and recommendations • Descriptions of medical treatments and prescriptions • Employees' medical complaints • Doctors' reports regarding industrial injuries • Any log of an occupational injury or illness for which treatment exceeded first aid or the employee lost days away from work • Records of hazardous substances at the workplace and any worker exposure to potentially hazardous materials (must be kept for thirty years after the substance is no longer present at the workplace)	• Occupational Safety and Health Act (OSHA)

CHAPTER 12

prohibition does not cover arrests for which the individual is out on bail or on his own recognizance. An arrest that did not result in conviction is one in which the case ended in a dismissal, a verdict of not-guilty, or decision by the district attorney to drop the case. (Labor Code section 432.7(a). See also 11 California Code of Regulations section 721(e).) For more detailed information, see Chapter 3.

Enforcement: File a complaint with the employer. If the employer refuses to take action, initiate an administrative appeal process or grievance procedure, if any. If no appeal process exists, or if the appeal is unsuccessful, file a claim with the state labor commissioner. (Labor Code sections 95(a), 96, 98–98.7.) File a civil suit asking for a court order to remove or correct misinformation or prevent inappropriate disclosure, plus damages suffered as a result of the employer's actions, and punitive damages, if the violation was willful. Violations of certain statutes constitute criminal offenses, usually misdemeanors, punishable by fine or imprisonment. (For instance, Labor Code section 1199(c) makes it a misdemeanor to fail to comply with Labor Code section 1198.5.)

Exceptions: In certain circumstances, an employer may be compelled by a court or administrative body to provide access to personnel information. For example, an employer must provide income and benefits information if an employee is involved in a child, family, or spousal support payment proceeding. (Family Code section 3664.) Generally, employers also must disclose information when requested to do so by the police pursuant to an investigation of suspected criminal conduct. When an employee's confidential personnel information is subpoenaed, the employer must provide notice and an opportunity to object to the release of records to the employee. (Code of Civil Procedure sections 1985.3(b), 1985.4, 1985.6(b).)

Employers must keep employees' personal identification information secure.

D. SOCIAL SECURITY NUMBER PRIVACY

California law restricts the ways in which an employer can use or disclose an individual's Social Security Number (SSN). All persons or entities, including employers, are prohibited from doing any of the following:

- Publicly posting or displaying, or otherwise communicating or making available to the public, an individual's SSN;
- Printing an individual's SSN on any card required for the individual to access products or services provided by the person or entity;
- Requiring an individual to transmit her SSN over the Internet, unless the connection is secure or the SSN is encrypted;
- Requiring an individual to use her SSN to access an Internet website, unless a password or unique identification number or other authentication device is also required to access the website;
- Printing an individual's SSN on any materials that are mailed to the individual, unless state or federal law requires the SSN to be on the document; exceptions are allowed for application or enrollment forms sent by mail, or to establish, amend, or terminate an account, contract, or policy, or to confirm the accuracy of the SSN; however, when mailing the SSN is permitted, it must be in a sealed envelope, not a postcard where the SSN is visible;
- Encoding or embedding a SSN in or on a card or document, including using a barcode, chip, magnetic strip, or other technology, in place of removing the SSN as required by law.
(Civil Code section 1798.85.)

Additionally, when the employer gives an employee an itemized earnings statement, it must contain only the last four digits of the Social Security Number. (Labor Code section 226(a).)

Exceptions: If federal law establishes a unique patient identification system, then medical entities, providers, and contractors who comply with the federal law will be deemed to be in compliance with the California statutory protections of SSN privacy. (Civil Code section 1798.85(e).)

For more information on safeguards employers must use with regard to employees' personal information, see section V.B.3., p. 300.

IV. HEALTHCARE RECORDS

Because of the privacy issues at stake, California and federal law provide numerous protections regarding healthcare records. California law has longstanding statutory provisions governing how, by whom, to whom, under what circumstances, for what purposes, and under what procedures medical information may be released. In 2003, a new federal rule protecting privacy in medical records went into effect, the Health Insurance Portability and Accountability Act ("HIPAA"). HIPAA is a broad statute that applies primarily to the transfer of medical records and information between and among insurance carriers and healthcare providers (doctors, dentists, psychiatrists, chiropractors, clinics, hospitals, and health maintenance organizations). It has certain implications in the employment context, as discussed below.

A. CALIFORNIA LAW

California state law safeguards include the following:

- The right to inspect and copy one's own medical care records;
- Limits on how, when, and from whom an employer may obtain medical information and on when and to whom that information may be released by an employer or by an individual's healthcare providers;
- Procedures that healthcare providers must follow when releasing medical information to a third party.

In California, the Confidentiality of Medical Information Act (Civil Code sections 56–56.37, 56.245.) generally prohibits healthcare providers from releasing detailed medical information about an individual without the individual's written authorization (certain exceptions, noted in the sections that follow, do apply). To protect people's privacy, the law strictly limits the release of psychiatric, developmental disability, genetic disease, AIDS/HIV status, and drug or alcohol addiction/treatment information. Additionally, both an individual's employer and any health service provider that receives public funds are required to protect the confidentiality of patient records, and penalties may be imposed on them if they fail to do so. (Welfare and Institutions Code section 5328.)

1. Right to Inspect Health Records

Individuals have the right to inspect their healthcare records (with some exceptions detailed later in this section) and to receive copies of them from their healthcare providers (for example, their physicians, dentists, psychiatrists, chiropractors, clinics, and hospitals). (Health and Safety Code section 123110. For a complete list of the providers and entities covered, see Health and Safety Code section 123105.) A healthcare provider must allow an individual or his representative to inspect the records within five days of the individual's written request. The individual may have one person of his choice accompany him. (Health and Safety Code section 123110(a).) If the individual requests copies of all or some of his records, the provider must furnish those copies to him within fifteen days. The individual has to pay reasonable copying costs (not to exceed 25 cents a page for photocopying or 50 cents a page for copying from microfilm) and administrative costs associated with providing the copies. (Health and Safety Code section 123110(b).)

Enforcement: Complaint to the appropriate state licensing board for the healthcare provider (for information on the complaint process, visit the Medical Board of California's website at http://www.medbd.ca.gov/consumer/complaint_info.html). Complaint to the local district attorney. Civil suit for an order to enforce, or remedy the violation of, privacy/non-disclosure rights and for attorney's fees. A willful violation by a provider may constitute an infraction, punishable by a fine of up to $100 as well as disciplinary action, including license suspension or termination of the offender's employment. (Health and Safety Code section 123110(i).) A provider who refuses to allow an individual to inspect or copy her records because she has an outstanding bill may also be subject to a fine or disciplinary action. (Health and Safety Code section 123110(j).)

Exceptions: Instead of giving an individual access to the entire record, a healthcare provider is allowed to give the individual a summary within ten working days of his request. If the record is very large or if the individual was released from the healthcare facility within the past ten days, the provider is allowed up to thirty days to provide the summary. (Health and Safety Code section 123130(a).) If the individual does not want a summary, his attorney may obtain copies of the

complete medical records by submitting a signed authorization on the individual's behalf. The individual will have to pay reasonable copying and administrative costs. (Evidence Code section 1158.)

Providers may deny an individual direct access to mental health, drug treatment, or alcohol addiction treatment records. At the time they deny access, they must make an entry in the individual's records about the refusal, and they must inform the individual of his right to have copies of all his mental health, drug treatment, or alcohol addiction treatment records given to any physician, psychiatrist, licensed psychologist, or licensed clinical social worker whom the individual names. (Health and Safety Code sections 123125, 123115(b).)

Providers may deny direct access to x-rays, EKGs, EEGs, and electromyography tracings. An individual may obtain those records by naming a health provider to whom the records should be released. The records must then be given to that healthcare professional within fifteen days of the written request. (Health and Safety Code section 123110(c).)

2. Release of Records Without Consent Prohibited

Under the Confidential Medical Information Act, with a few notable exceptions specified later in this section, a healthcare provider cannot release detailed medical information about an individual to an employer unless the individual has signed a written authorization. (Civil Code section 56.20(c).) This requirement prevents healthcare providers from giving an employer detailed information about an individual. The provider may, however, provide general information about an individual's treatment and general condition, unless the individual has explicitly prohibited the provider from releasing this information.

If an individual wants to allow release of detailed medical information, the individual must provide an authorization that meets all of the following requirements:

- It is written in the individual's own handwriting or typed in fourteen-point type or larger.
- It is clearly separate from any other statements the individual may have signed.
- It is signed and dated by the individual (or the individual's representative, if the individual is incompetent).

- It states the limitations, if any, on what information may be revealed and how the information may be used.
- It specifies who may release the information and to whom the information may be released.
- It states the date after which the authorization will no longer be valid.
- It advises the individual who signs the authorization of the right to receive a copy of the authorization.

(Civil Code section 56.21.)

Employers should use forms that have been drafted to comply with these requirements. If the individual requests a copy of the authorization, the employer must provide it. (Civil Code section 56.22.)

The individual may cancel or modify the authorization in writing at any time, but the change will take effect only when the provider actually knows that the individual has withdrawn or changed the authorization. (Civil Code sections 56.21, 56.24.)

An applicant or employee cannot be discharged, disciplined, or discriminated against in any way by an employer for refusing to sign or for canceling an authorization. However, in certain circumstances (for example, to support a claim for disability or sick leave), an individual may be required to provide relevant medical information. (Civil Code section 56.20(b).)

Exceptions: A healthcare provider may disclose medical information if the disclosure is compelled or authorized by any of the following: a subpoena issued by a court or in an administrative proceeding; as part of discovery in litigation; or pursuant to a search warrant, coroner's inquiry, other specific legal requirements.

A healthcare provider may disclose medical information to the following people or entities in the following situations: other healthcare professionals, for the purpose of diagnosis or treatment; the person or entity paying for the healthcare services, to the extent necessary to allow responsibility for payment to be determined; a governmental agency, to determine eligibility for government payment-assistance programs when the individual (the patient) is comatose or otherwise medically unable to consent to disclosure and no other arrangements for healthcare payment have been made; a person or entity that provides billing, claims management, medical data processing, or other administrative services; organized committees, agents of professional societies or of medical staffs of licensed hospitals, licensed healthcare service plans, professional standards review organizations, peer review organizations, or professional liability insurers, who are engaged in reviewing healthcare services with regard to medical necessity, level and quality of care, or justification of charges; an entity responsible for licensing or accrediting the healthcare provider; or public health researchers and others, for bona fide research, but with all identifying information about individual patients removed. (Civil Code section 56.10(c).)

If an employer has paid for employment-related health services and requested notification of results in advance, the provider may release information to the employer if it is relevant to a lawsuit, arbitration, grievance, or other claim to which the individual and the employer are parties, and if the employee has raised issues regarding medical history and treatment. However, the information may be used only in that particular proceeding. If the employer has paid for a medical exam to determine whether a functional limitation based on the individual's medical condition would entitle her to a leave from work or would limit her ability to perform her present job (for example, an exam to determine the employee's fitness for duty), the provider may disclose information on work restrictions but cannot, without the employee's consent, state the medical cause for the limitation. (Civil Code section 56.10(c)(8).)

3. Employer's Duty to Protect Confidentiality of Records

Just as healthcare providers may not release medical records without an individual's authorization under most circumstances, an employer also generally cannot release any medical information about an individual without his authorization. In this context, medical information includes any facts about the individual's medical history, mental or physical condition, or treatment. Specific safeguards apply to sensitive kinds of medical information.

An employer's authority to use medical information in ways that affect an individual's employment (for example, termination or disciplinary decisions, promotions, or other job opportunities) is limited. See Chapters 6 and 10 for more information on discrimination based on health issues.

Exceptions: An employer can disclose and use an individual's medical information without his prior authorization in the following instances:

- The employer may give medical information to an individual's treating doctor or hospital when the individual is unconscious or otherwise unable to sign an authorization. (Civil Code section 56.20(c)(4).)

- The employer can use properly obtained medical information to determine an individual's eligibility for paid and unpaid leave from work for medical reasons. (Civil Code section 56.20(c)(3).)

- The employer can use properly obtained medical information in administering employee benefit plans, including health plans, disability income plans, and Workers' Compensation plans. (Civil Code section 56.20(c)(3).)

- If an individual raises an issue concerning her own medical history, mental or physical condition, or treatment in a lawsuit, arbitration, grievance procedure, or other claim or challenge, the employer can use properly obtained medical information in responding to that issue. (Civil Code section 56.20(c)(2).) The information may be used or disclosed only in connection with that proceeding. (Civil Code section 56.10(c)(8)(A).)

- When medical information is required by governmental entities such as the state insurance commissioner, the Department of Insurance, the Department of Managed Care, the Division of Industrial Accidents, or the Workers' Compensation Appeals Board, those entities may obtain an individual's medical information. (For a more complete list, see Civil Code section 56.30.)

4. Special Protections for Mental Health and Other Sensitive Records

To protect an individual's privacy, an employer is permitted only limited access to information in records about the individual's psychiatric or mental health treatment, developmental disability, participation in drug or alcohol treatment programs, genetic disease, and AIDS or HIV status. These rules apply to providers of psychiatric care, treatment for a developmental disability or genetic disease, and drug or alcohol addiction treatment, as well as to halfway houses, crisis lines, free clinics, mental disability services, suicide prevention services, detoxification clinics, methadone programs, drug-screening labs and clinics, counseling centers, rehabilitation programs, and other programs. (Health and Safety Code sections 123125, 123135.)

Because information of this type could likely be used to deny an individual employment, it is prudent not to sign an authorization for its release without consulting with a union or lawyer. If an individual has already signed an authorization, the individual may cancel it by immediately giving a written, signed note requesting cancellation of the authorization to any provider with records of this nature. A copy of the cancellation should be retained for the individual's own records. As soon as the healthcare provider receives the cancellation, no information can lawfully be released.

Discrimination in employment based on disability is prohibited; for discussion of this and related issues, see Chapter 6. See also discussion of employer investigations, Chapter 3.

a. Psychiatric and Mental Health Records

Both federal and California laws protect an individual's privacy regarding psychiatric and mental health records. (42 U.S. Code section 9501(1)(H); Welfare and Institutions Code sections 5328–5330.) Information from these records cannot be disclosed except in very limited, specific situations (for example, communications between two mental health professionals or disclosure of information to a court). Under California law, mental health and psychiatric records cannot be released to an employer without the employee's prior written authorization.

Enforcement: File a civil suit for damages and attorney's fees. If the release of information is found to be willful and knowing, an individual may recover as much as $10,000 or three times the actual amount of damage suffered because of the release, whichever is greater. (Welfare and Institutions Code section 5330(a)(1), (2).)

If the individual was fired or demoted, or suffered some other loss because someone illegally released the individual's records to the employer, the individual may sue based on these issues. If the individual has not signed an authorization allowing the employer access to the individual's mental health records, and the individual discovers that the records have been obtained anyway, an attorney should be consulted to determine whether there are grounds for a suit.

b. Developmental Disability Records

Release of information and records obtained in the course of providing intake, assessment, and disability-related services to persons with developmental disabilities requires prior written authorization. If the developmentally disabled person lacks the capacity to provide consent, that person's legal guardian or conservator may authorize release of the records. (Welfare and Institutions Code section 4514.)

c. Drug and Alcohol Addiction Treatment Records

Under federal law, the identity of a person participating in a drug or alcohol addiction treatment program and all records of diagnosis or treatment must generally be kept confidential. An employer can obtain these records only if an employee provides specific prior written authorization. The authorization cannot be a general one — the individual must authorize release of information about and from the addiction-treatment program itself for the employer to obtain those records. (42 U.S. Code section 290dd-2.)

If an employer has information about an individual's participation in an alcohol or drug rehabilitation program, the employer must make reasonable efforts to safeguard the individual's privacy about this matter. (Labor Code sections 1025, 1026.)

d. Genetic Testing Results

If an individual has been tested or received treatment for a genetic disorder (for example, sickle-cell anemia or Tay-Sachs disease), all test results and personal information about the disorder must be kept confidential. Information may be released to a third party only if the individual provides prior written informed consent. This means that an employer cannot obtain these records unless the individual specifically consents in writing. (Health and Safety Code section 124980(j).)

Enforcement: File a civil suit for damages of up to $10,000 plus reasonable attorney's fees and costs. (Health and Safety Code section 124980(l).)

e. AIDS/HIV Testing Results

California law includes numerous protections to ensure the confidentiality of AIDS and HIV test results. (For legal definitions of AIDS and HIV, see Health and Safety Code section 120775.) No one, including an employer, may disclose or use medical information about whether an individual is infected with, or has been exposed to, HIV without the individual's prior authorization, unless the individual is an injured worker claiming that she was infected or exposed due to an incident in the course of her employment. (Civil Code section 56.31.)

Disclosure of HIV test results without an individual's authorization will result in imposition of penalties. (Health and Safety Code sections 120980, 120990, 121015, 121025.) If the individual is incapacitated medically and unable to consent, however, the law does allow a legal guardian or similar individual to consent to release of the information.

Without an individual's written authorization, no person may test the individual's blood for evidence of HIV antibodies or of the virus itself. If a treating physician wants to obtain an individual's blood for testing, the individual's agreement to allow release of the test results to a third party must be informed. This means that the individual must understand the consequences of giving consent and agree to do so voluntarily. (Health and Safety Code section 120990(a).) No one, including an employer, can force an individual to take an AIDS or HIV test against his will.

An employer cannot use any AIDS-research-related information or any personally identifying information about an individual from public health records to decide whether or not to hire that individual. (Health and Safety Code sections 121025(f), 121115.) This prohibition means that an employer cannot screen applicants and employees for AIDS or HIV infection and cannot make employment decisions such as whether to hire, promote, or terminate based on HIV test results.

Enforcement: File a civil suit against the party that disclosed the records without the individual's authorization. (Health and Safety Code section 120980(a)–(d).) The law provides for civil penalties and actual damages.

An employee who is discharged based on HIV test results or refusal to take an HIV test, in addition to having a claim of discrimination under the Americans with Disabilities Act, may have a cause of action (grounds for a lawsuit) for wrongful discharge. See Chapter 6 on discrimination and Chapter 10 on discharge and disciplinary action for details.

B. FEDERAL HEALTH INSURANCE PORTABILITY AND ACCOUNTABILITY ACT (HIPAA)

HIPAA places restrictions on access to, and disclosure of, "protected health information" by "covered entities." The law also gives individuals certain rights to access their health records and correct misinformation contained in them.

1. Organizations Covered by HIPAA Requirements

These organizations include health plans (including HMOs) and healthcare providers (both are sometimes referred to as "covered entities" by HIPAA) who transmit health information in electronic form; most doctors, nurses, pharmacies, hospitals, clinics, and nursing homes; employers who self-insure employee medical benefits or provide on-site health clinics; and government health benefit programs like Medicare and Medicaid. (45 Code of Federal Regulations sections 160.103, 164.105.) See http://www.hhs.gov/ocr/hipaa for fact sheets, regulations, and other HIPAA-related resources.

2. Protected Information

"Protected health information" includes the following individually identifiable medical information and must remain confidential: information that an individual's doctors, nurses, and other healthcare providers put in his medical record; conversations an individual's doctor has with nurses and others about the individual's care or treatment; information about an individual in his health insurer's computer system; medical billing information; and most other health information about an individual maintained by covered entities. (45 Code of Federal Regulations section 160.103.)

Exceptions: "Protected health information" for purposes of HIPAA does not include employment information maintained solely for employment purposes. (45 Code of Federal Regulations section 160.103.) Also excluded from HIPAA protection are medical records from which all personal identifiers have been removed. (45 Code of Federal Regulations section 164.514.)

3. Individual Rights

HIPAA gives individuals certain rights.

a. Right to Receive a Notice of Rights

Healthcare providers are obligated to provide notice to individuals, telling them how their health information may be used and shared, what their rights are, what the healthcare provider's duties are, and where to file a complaint if they believe their rights under HIPAA have been violated. (45 Code of Federal Regulations section 164.520.)

b. Right to Inspect and Obtain a Copy of One's Own Health Records

Access to requested health records should be provided within thirty days of the request, at a reasonable time and place, for a reasonable copying and mailing cost, unless the plan or provider has a permissible reason to deny access. (45 Code of Federal Regulations section 164.524.) The deadline can be extended once for another thirty days if the entity provides a written statement of its reason(s) for the delay and the anticipated date by which the entity will grant or deny the request. (45 Code of Federal Regulations section 164.524(b).)

Exceptions: Certain records may be withheld, including: psychotherapy notes; information compiled for use in civil, criminal or administrative proceedings; information compiled for the purposes of ongoing research; records that are subject to the federal Privacy Act (5 U.S. Code section 552a.); information obtained from a third party under a promise of confidentiality (45 Code of Federal Regulations section 164.524(a)(2)(v).); and in situations in which a licensed healthcare professional has determined that the access requested is likely to endanger the life or physical safety of the individual or another person, or place the individual or another person in danger of substantial harm. (45 Code of Federal Regulations section 164.524(a)(3), (4).)

Employees have the right to see and comment on their own personnel files.

c. Right to Appeal Denial of Access to Health Records

If the plan or provider denies the request in whole or in part, it must give the individual access to any remaining health information not considered legally withheld, and must provide written notice of the reason for the denial, a statement explaining the individual's right to have the decision reviewed, information regarding how to file a complaint, and information about who possesses the records if the covered entity does not have them. (45 Code of Federal Regulations section 164.524(d)(2), (3).)

If the individual requests review of the denial, the covered entity must designate a licensed healthcare professional who was not directly involved in the denial to review the decision. That person must determine, within a reasonable period of time, whether or not to grant access, and she must provide a written notice of her determination to the individual. The healthcare plan or provider must comply with the decision of the reviewer. (45 Code of Federal Regulations section 164.524(d)(4).)

d. Right to Make Corrections to Health Information

A covered entity must permit an individual to submit a request to amend his medical record. (45 Code of Federal Regulations section 164.526.) The procedure for a request to amend medical records is similar to appeals of denials of access to health records, described directly above. The covered entity's procedure may require that the request be in writing and include a reason for the proposed change to the medical record, as long as the procedure gives advance notice of this requirement. (45 Code of Federal Regulations section 164.526(b)(1).)

e. Right to Receive an Accounting of Disclosures

An individual is entitled to request and receive from covered entities a report that lists most disclosures of his protected health information (other than the exceptions listed below), for a period of up to six years prior to the request. The report must include, for each disclosure, the date of the disclosure, name (and, if known, the address) of the person or organization that received the protected health information, the purpose of the disclosure, and a brief description of the information disclosed. (45 Code of Federal Regulations section 164.528(b)(1)-(3).)

Individuals are not entitled to receive a report on disclosures made under the following circumstances:
- To carry out treatment, payment, and healthcare operations;
- To the individuals themselves;
- Pursuant to a written authorization by the individual;
- For the covered entity's telephone directory (for instance a hospital's log of in-patients);
- For national security or intelligence purposes;
- To corrections institutions or law enforcement officials;
- As part of a "limited data set" (partially de-identified) used for research, public health, or healthcare operations purposes (45 Code of Federal Regulations section 164.514(e)).

(45 Code of Federal Regulations section 164.528(a)(1).)

4. Permissible Purposes and Recipients of Protected Health Information

Generally, protected health information can be shared for the following purposes or with the following recipients: for an individual's treatment and care coordination; to pay doctors and hospitals for an individual's healthcare and help with the internal operations of the healthcare provider's business; with an individual's family, relatives, friends or others he identifies as involved with his healthcare or healthcare bills, unless the he objects; to oversee the quality and level of medical and nursing home care; to protect the public's health, such as by reporting when a particular illness has affected an individual's geographic area; or to make required reports to the police, such as reporting gunshot wounds. (45 Code of Federal Regulations sections 164.502(a)(1), 164.506.)

5. Information That Can Be Used Unless the Individual Objects

Unless the individual objects (an opportunity to object must be given), a covered entity (for example, a hospital) can maintain a directory including information such as the individual's name; location in the facility (for example, hospital room number); condition described in general terms that do not communicate specific medical information about the individual; and religious affiliation (which may be given to members of the clergy). (45 Code of Federal Regulations section 164.510(a)(1).)

An exception to the requirement that an individual be given an opportunity to object to the release of protected health information exists when the information is needed for emergency medical treatment. Such emergency disclosure is permitted where it is consistent with any prior authorization by the individual and where it is in the individual's best interest as determined by the covered healthcare provider's professional judgment. (45 Code of Federal Regulations section 164.510(a)(3).)

Permitted disclosure (after an opportunity to object or if lack of objection can reasonably be inferred from the circumstances) includes the release of protected health information to a family member, other close relative, close personal friend, or other person identified by the individual, when the information is directly relevant to the friend or family member's care of the individual, or their payment for the individual's treatment; and for the purpose of notifying or locating individuals responsible for the care, payment for treatment, or disposition upon death of the individual. (45 Code of Federal Regulations section 164.510(b)(1), (2).)

6. Information That Cannot Be Used Without Written Authorization

Generally, without an individual's written authorization, covered entities may not:

- Give an individual's health information to her employer for employment-related actions or decisions, or in connection with any other benefit or employee benefit plan (45 Code of Federal Regulations section 164.504(f)(3)(iv).);
- Use or share an individual's information for marketing or advertising purposes (45 Code of Federal Regulations section 164.508(a)(3).); or
- Use or disclose private notes about an individual's mental health counseling sessions, except in the following instances: use is required by the therapist in order to provide the psychological counseling, disclosure is for the purpose of training other mental health practitioners, use is necessary for the entity providing mental healthcare to defend itself legally in a lawsuit by the individual, or use is required as part of professional/administrative oversight of the counseling service. (45 Code of Federal Regulations section 164.508(a)(1), (2).)

7. Content, Requirement, and Use of Written Authorizations

A covered entity may not require an individual to provide an authorization for release of protected health information as a condition of the following: receiving treatment, payment of incurred costs, enrollment in a health plan, or eligibility for benefits. However, a covered entity may require the release of protected health information as a condition of the individual's participation in a research project such as a clinical trial, for purposes of authorization of, or payment for, treatment, or if the care is sought exclusively for the purpose of creating a medical record or report. (45 Code of Federal Regulations section 164.508(b)(4).)

To be effective, an authorization must be written in plain language. A copy must be given to the individual. (45 Code of Federal Regulations section 164.508.)

An individual may cancel an authorization (provided that the cancellation is in writing), but this will not affect any action the plan or provider has already taken as a result of the authorization. An individual may cancel an authorization for release of medical records except in situations where the authorization was a condition of obtaining insurance coverage and the law or the insurance policy itself provides the insurer with the right to contest a claim for coverage. (45 Code of Federal Regulations section 164.508(b)(5).)

8. Health Information That Can Be Used by, or Disclosed to, Covered Entities/ Employers Without an Individual's Written Authorization or Opportunity to Object

Certain protected health information, for certain purposes and to certain recipients, can be used or released without an individual's written authorization or without affording the individual an opportunity to object, as summarized in the following sections.

a. Workers' Compensation

Covered entities, including employers covered by HIPAA, are permitted to disclose protected health information when authorized by laws relating to Workers' Compensation or other similar programs that provide benefits for work-related injuries without regard to fault. (45 Code of Federal Regulations section 164.512(l).)

b. Public Health

Entities covered by HIPAA are permitted to disclose protected health information to government and public health authorities for public health purposes and activities, such as:

- Reporting of diseases, injuries, and vital statistics to public health authorities or other government authorities for the purposes of monitoring, preventing, or controlling diseases, injuries, or disabilities;
- Reporting child abuse or neglect to appropriate governmental entities;
- Reporting other abuse, neglect, or domestic violence;
- Reporting and responding to problems related to the safety, quality, or effectiveness of products or activities regulated by the federal Food and Drug Administration;
- Notifying a person that he has been exposed to a communicable disease.

(45 Code of Federal Regulations section 164.512(b), (c).)

Disclosure is also permitted to employers if the covered entity provides healthcare on behalf of the employer and if the information will be used to evaluate a medical situation at the workplace or to determine whether the individual has a work-related injury. The information must consist of findings regarding the evaluation of the medical situation or work-related injury that the employer needs in order to comply with statutory record-keeping requirements. The employee must be given written notice that the protected health information will be disclosed to the employer by either posting a notice or providing a copy of the notice to the employee. (45 Code of Federal Regulations section 164.512(b)(1)(v).)

c. Healthcare Oversight

Covered entities are also permitted to disclose and use protected health information for purposes of "oversight activities authorized by law." These activities include audits; civil, administrative, and criminal investigations, proceedings, or actions; inspections, licensure, or disciplinary actions; other activities necessary for oversight of the healthcare system; government benefits programs for which health information is relevant to beneficiary eligibility; or government regulatory programs or civil rights laws for which health information is necessary for determining compliance with program standards or legal standards. (45 Code of Federal Regulations section 164.512(d)(1).)

Exceptions: The permission for disclosure of protected health information described above does not apply to investigations of an individual that are not directly related to her receipt of healthcare, or to her claim of qualification for public benefits. (45 Code of Federal Regulations section 164.512(d)(2).)

d. Court or Administrative Order

Covered entities are permitted to release protected health information in response to an order from a court or administrative tribunal as long as only the information expressly authorized by the order is released. (45 Code of Federal Regulations section 164.512(e)(1)(i); Civil Code section 56.10(b).)

e. Subpoena

Covered entities are also permitted to release protected health information in response to a subpoena, discovery request, or other lawful process, without an order from a court or administrative tribunal. (45 Code of Federal Regulations section 164.512(e)(1)(ii)-(vi); Civil Code section 56.10(b); Code of Civil Procedure section 1985.3(c).)

The person whose records are being sought must be notified when a subpoena is issued to produce the personal records. If the person objects, she may file a written objection to the release of information, and a decision will be made by the court or administrative officer who issued the subpoena as to whether the information should be released. (Code of Civil Procedure section 1985.3.)

f. Law Enforcement

Covered entities are also permitted to disclose protected health information for law enforcement purposes when legally required. Some laws require the reporting of certain types of wounds or other physical injuries. Covered entities may also be required to comply with the terms of a court order, warrant, or subpoena. (45 Code of Federal Regulations section 164.512(f)(1).)

In addition, covered entities may disclose limited information (name, address, Social Security Number, blood type, type of injury, date and time of treatment, distinguishing physical characteristics) to assist law enforcement personnel in locating a criminal suspect, material witness, or missing person. (45 Code of Federal Regulations section 164.512(f)(2)(i).)

Other than those particular pieces of information, covered entities are prohibited from disclosing to law enforcement personnel (for purposes of identifying a criminal suspect, material witness, or missing person) any protected health information related to an individual's DNA; dental records; or type, samples, or analysis of body fluids or tissue. (45 Code of Federal Regulations section 164.512(f)(2)(ii).)

Covered entities are also permitted to disclose protected health information to law enforcement personnel in order to identify a victim of a crime. Disclosure is permitted in any of the following circumstances:

- The individual agrees to the disclosure;
- The healthcare provider is unable to obtain the person's agreement because of incapacity or other emergency circumstance. However, the information must be necessary to determine if a crime has been committed by someone other than the victim, and the information must not be used against the victim;
- The immediate law enforcement activity would be materially and adversely affected by waiting until the individual is able to agree to the disclosure and the disclosure is in the best interest of the individual as determined by the healthcare provider.

(45 Code of Federal Regulations section 164.512(f)(3).)

A covered entity, including an employer who is covered by HIPAA, may also disclose protected health information that it believes in good faith reveals the commission of a crime on the premises of that covered entity. (45 Code of Federal Regulations section 164.512(f)(5).) Emergency medical staff may disclose information that reasonably informs law enforcement personnel of the commission of a crime and the identities of the victim(s) and perpetrator(s). (45 Code of Federal Regulations section 164.512(f)(6).)

A covered entity is permitted to use or disclose protected health information if it believes in good faith that the information is necessary to prevent or lessen a serious and imminent threat to the health or safety of a person or the public, and that the disclosure is to a person or persons reasonably able to prevent or lessen the threat. Disclosure is also permitted to identify or apprehend an individual who admitted participation in a violent crime that the covered entity reasonably believes may have caused serious physical harm. (45 Code of Federal Regulations section 164.512(j)(1).)

Exception: Such information cannot be disclosed if it is obtained through psychological counseling or a request for a referral to counseling designed to treat or prevent the activity that the disclosure would report. (45 Code of Federal Regulations section 164.512(j)(2).) An employer covered by HIPAA cannot disclose an employee's protected health information in order to assist identifying or apprehending a criminal suspect, if the employer obtained that information through the employee's request for a counseling referral to prevent the behavior at issue.

g. Other Miscellaneous Rules

Other special rules govern disclosure of protected health information related to decedents; receipt of public benefits; medical research; organ donation; military or veteran's activities; federal security personnel; protective services for the President; and custody of inmates. (45 Code of Federal Regulations section 164.512(f)(4), (g), (h), (i), (k).)

9. Employer's/Covered Entity's Duties to Protect Individuals' Privacy

Healthcare providers and health insurers who are covered by HIPAA must keep individuals' information private by training their employees how healthcare information may and may not be used and shared, and by taking appropriate and reasonable steps — organizationally, administratively, physically, and technically — to keep health information secure. (45 Code of Federal Regulations sections 164.306, 164.308, 164.310.)

Enforcement: If an individual believes her rights are being denied or health information is not being protected, she can:

- File a complaint with her healthcare provider, health insurer, or employer (if the employer is a covered entity under HIPAA); or
- File a complaint with the federal Secretary of Health and Human Services, Office for Civil Rights. (See the Office for Civil Rights' website at http://www.hhs.gov/ocr/index.html.)

The complaint must be filed within 180 days of the claimed violation; be in writing; provide the name, address, and telephone number of the person or entity that is the subject of the complaint; describe the acts or omissions believed to be in violation of HIPAA; and present any other relevant information. (45 Code of Federal Regulations section 160.306.) (For additional details or to obtain a complaint form, call 1-800-368-1019 or see http://www.hhs.gov/ocr/privacy/hipaa/complaints/index.html.)

If the complaint cannot be resolved through informal means mediated by the Office for Civil Rights, then an investigation will be initiated. If violations are found, civil monetary penalties up to $100 per violation and $25,000 per calendar year may be imposed. If either party requests a hearing after a formal determination has been made, then formal discovery and a formal evidentiary hearing before an administrative law judge will be conducted. (45 Code of Federal Regulations sections 160.312–160.552.)

V. IDENTITY THEFT

One of the fastest growing crimes in the United States, identity theft is a concern in the workplace, where employers commonly require applicants and employees to provide personal data. The law continues to evolve with respect to privacy. California has been active in passing legislation to ensure that employers keep the personal information in their possession secure. When a breach of security takes place, employers have a duty to inform employees whose personal information has been compromised. Victims of identity theft should quickly take certain steps to limit the damage.

A. WHAT IS IDENTITY THEFT?

Identity theft is defined as the unauthorized use of personal identifying information to commit fraud or other crimes. (Penal Code section 530.5; 18 U.S. Code section 1028; 16 Code of Federal Regulations section 603.2.) The personal identifying information is often used to obtain credit, goods, or services.

Personal identifying information is any name or number that may be used to identify a specific person. (Penal Code section 530.55; 16 Code of Federal Regulations section 603.2.) Items that

are considered personal identifying information include:

- Name;
- Social Security Number;
- Date of birth;
- Home address;
- Driver's license number;
- Account number;
- Biometric data (such as fingerprints or other unique physical representations);
- Medical information.

Enforcement: Identity theft is a misdemeanor, punishable by a fine, imprisonment less than one year, or both. (Penal Code section 530.5.) File a complaint with the district attorney. File a civil suit. Victims are also protected against claimants attempting to collect on debts created by identity thieves. (Civil Code section 1798.93.)

CHAPTER 12

B. EMPLOYER OBLIGATIONS

Employees provide various forms of personal identification when they are hired, making it important for employers to practice responsible maintenance of the information in their possession. Employers' duties are discussed below.

1. Duty of Reasonable Security

California law requires businesses to use reasonable security measures to protect personal information from unauthorized access. (Civil Code section 1798.81.5.)

Personal information means first name or initial and last name, in combination with one or more of the following data elements when either the name or data element is not encrypted or redacted:
- Social Security Number;
- Driver's license number or California Identification Card number;
- Account number or credit or debit card number, in combination with any required security code, access code, or password that would permit access to an individual's financial account;
- Medical information (any individually identifiable information, in electronic or physical form, regarding medical history, mental or physical condition, or medical treatment or diagnosis);
- Health insurance information (policy number or subscriber identification number, any unique identifier used by a health insurer to identify the individual, or any information in an individual's application and claims history, including any appeals records).

(Civil Code section 1798.81.5(d).)

As discussed earlier in the chapter, specific provisions govern the way Social Security Numbers are handled. Employers are prohibited from using or displaying SSNs in certain ways that might lead to exposure. (Civil Code section 1798.85.) See section II.D., p. 288.

Employers are required to properly dispose of information about employees that has been obtained through consumer reports. (15 U.S. Code section 1681w.) See Chapter 3 regarding consumer reports.

Reasonable measures must be taken to prevent unauthorized access to employees' personal identifying information. Examples of such measures include:

- Implementing and monitoring compliance with policies and procedures that require destruction of papers (by burning, pulverizing, or shredding), so consumer information cannot be read or reconstructed;
- Implementing and monitoring compliance with policies and procedures that require the destruction of electronic media so consumer information cannot be read or reconstructed;
- Exercising due diligence in hiring and monitoring third parties who engage in the business of record destruction, to assure proper disposal of consumer information.

(16 Code of Federal Regulations section 682.3.)

2. Duty When Breach Occurs

California law requires any business that owns computerized data containing personal information to disclose any improper release of the data. When an employer has reason to believe that an unauthorized person has acquired unencrypted personal information about an employee, that employee must be notified. (Civil Code section 1798.82.)

A breach occurs when there is an unauthorized acquisition of computerized data that compromises the security, confidentiality, or integrity of personal information. (Civil Code section 1798.82(d).)

Notification is required when there is a breach of personal information (see definition of "personal information" in section B.1., directly above). (Civil Code section 1798.82(e).)

The notification should be made as soon as possible. (Civil Code section 1798.82(a).) Notification may be delayed if a law enforcement agency determines that it would impede a criminal investigation. (Civil Code section 1798.82(c).)

Enforcement: File a lawsuit requesting a court order and seeking to recover losses caused by failure to provide required notifications. (Civil Code section 1798.84.)

3. Safeguards

There are a number of policies and procedures that employers can implement to protect against the unauthorized disclosure of personal information in their possession.

- Employers should only collect the personal information about their employees that is necessary, depending on the nature of the business and the requirements of the position.

- Sensitive personal information should be stored securely with limited access.
- Measures should be in place to identify anyone who has accessed files.
- Training should be offered to employees on identity theft and prevention measures.

For advice from the Federal Trade Commission, see "Protecting Personal Information: A Guide for Business" at http://www.ftc.gov/infosecurity.

C. RECOMMENDED EMPLOYEE ACTIONS SHOULD IDENTITY OR PERSONAL DATA THEFT OCCUR

When personal information has been compromised, there are certain steps an employee should take, as well as specific rights he should exercise.

1. Report Identity Theft to Credit Bureaus

When an individual has a reasonable belief that he has been or is about to become a victim of identity theft, he should contact one of the three major credit bureaus.
- Equifax Credit Information Services, Inc.
  1-888-766-0008
  http://www.equifax.com
- TransUnion Fraud Victim Assistance Department
  1-800-680-7289
  http://www.transunion.com
- Experian
  1-888-397-3742
  https://www.experian.com

Requesting a fraud alert from one of these bureaus will cause all three to be notified. The fraud alert will be placed in the victim's file, requiring potential creditors to verify the identity of a person before issuing credit in the victim's name. (Civil Code section 1785.11.1; 15 U.S. Code section 1681c-1.) People should monitor activity on their credit reports when they believe they have been victims of identity theft.

2. File a Report With Law Enforcement Agency

A victim of identity theft should make a report to the local police, who can issue an identity theft report. Additionally, the victim might want to make a complaint to the Federal Trade Commission.

(The Federal Trade Commission's Identity Theft Hotline may be reached at 1-877-438-4338, and their complaint form is available online at https://www.ftccomplaintassistant.gov/.) The information from the complaint is made available to other law enforcement agencies and may be incorporated into the identity theft report.

More information on fraud alerts and security freezes can be found in Chapter 3, section III., p. 44.

3. Contact Creditors

If the identity thief has opened new accounts or accessed existing accounts, the victim should contact the creditors immediately to notify them of the identity theft. The individual should communicate with the creditor's security or fraud department. A victim should ask that accounts that have been used fraudulently be "closed at the consumer's request," and he should ask creditors not to hold him responsible for new accounts opened fraudulently.

4. Additional Measures

These steps and more are outlined on the following websites:
- California Office of Privacy Protection's "Identity Theft Victims Checklist" at http://www.privacy.ca.gov/res/docs/pdf/cis3english.pdf
- California Attorney General's Tips for Victims at http://ag.ca.gov/idtheft/tips.php
- Privacy Rights Clearinghouse's "Fact Sheet 17(a): Identity Theft: What to Do if It Happens to You" at http://www.privacyrights.org/fs/fs17a.htm
- Federal Trade Commission's Identity Theft Site at http://www.ftc.gov/bcp/edu/microsites/idtheft.

CHAPTER 12

FINDING STATE AND FEDERAL LAWS AND REGULATIONS

Laws and regulations can be found online or at local law libraries. All major cities and most county seats have law libraries. To find the nearest public law library, visit http://www.publilawlibrary.org/find.html. You can also check the phone book under "Libraries" or call the local courthouse. Law librarians are often very helpful to non-lawyers seeking information.

The following websites provide online access to state and federal laws and regulations:

California Laws: http://www.leginfo.ca.gov/calaw.html

California Regulations: http://ccr.oal.ca.gov

California Industrial Welfare Commission Orders: http://www.dir.ca.gov/iwc/wageorderindustries.htm

U.S. Laws: http://www.law.cornell.edu/uscode/ (Note: this resource is free, but you will be asked to register before using it)

U.S. Regulations: http://ecfr.gpoaccess.gov

FEDERAL AND STATE GOVERNMENT AGENCIES

FEDERAL GOVERNMENT AGENCIES

DEPARTMENT OF LABOR
200 Constitution Avenue, NW
Washington, DC 20210
Tel: 1-866-4-USA-DOL
(1-866-487-2365)
TTY: 1-877-889-5627
http://www.dol.gov/

Employee Benefits Security Administration (ERISA enforcement)
http://www.dol.gov/ebsa/
http://www.dol.gov/ebsa/erisa_
enforcement.html

LOS ANGELES REGIONAL OFFICE
1055 East Colorado Blvd., Suite 200
Pasadena, CA 91106-2357
Tel: 626-229-1000
Fax: 626-229-1098

SAN FRANCISCO REGIONAL
OFFICE
90 Seventh Street, Suite 11-300
San Francisco, CA 94103
Tel: 415-625-2481
Fax: 415-625-2450

Employment & Training Administration, Federal Bonding Program
California State Bonding
Coordinator
CA Employment Development
Department
800 Capitol Mall, MIC-37
Sacramento, CA 95814
Tel: 916-657-5190
Fax: 916-657-0055
http://www.bonds4jobs.com/state-coordinators.html

Occupational Safety and Health Administration (Fed-OSHA)
Regional Office, Region 9
90 Seventh Street, Suite 18-100
San Francisco, CA 94103
Tel: 415-625-2547;
1-800-475-4020 (Complaints)
Fax: 415-625-2534
http://www.osha.gov/

Office of Federal Contract Compliance Programs
Pacific Regional Office
90 Seventh Street, Suite 18-300
San Francisco, CA 94103
Tel: 415-625-7800
Fax: 415-625-7799
Email: OFCCP-PA-PreAward@dol.
gov
http://www.dol.gov/ofccp/contacts/
ofnation2.htm

LOS ANGELES DISTRICT OFFICE
11000 Wilshire Blvd., Suite 8103
Los Angeles, CA 90024
Tel: 310-235-6800
Fax: 310- 235-6833

ORANGE AREA OFFICE
770 The City Drive, Suite 5700
Orange, CA 92868
Tel: 714-621-1631
Fax: 714-621-1640

SAN DIEGO DISTRICT OFFICE
5675 Ruffin Road, Suite 320
San Diego, CA 92123-1362
Tel: 858-467-7002
Fax: 619-557-6609

SAN FRANCISCO DISTRICT
OFFICE
90 Seventh Street, Suite 11-100
San Francisco, CA 94103
Tel: 415-625-7828
Fax: 415-625-7844

SAN JOSE DISTRICT OFFICE
60 South Market Street, Suite 410
San Jose, CA 95113
Tel: 408-291-7384
Fax: 408-291-7559

Office of Workers' Compensation Programs
Pacific Region
90 Seventh Street, Suite 15-100
San Francisco, CA 94103
Tel: 415-625-7575
http://www.dol.gov/owcp/

Veterans' Employment and Training Service
Office of the Assistant Secretary
U.S. Department of Labor
200 Constitution Avenue, NW,
Room S-1325
Washington, DC 20210
Tel: 202-693-4701
http://www.dol.gov/vets/

Wage and Hour Division
Tel: 1-866-4-USWAGE
(1-866-487-9243)
http://www.dol.gov/whd/

EAST LOS ANGELES DISTRICT
OFFICE
100 N. Barranca Street, Suite 850
West Covina, CA 91791
Tel: 626-966-0478;
1-866-4-USWAGE
(1-866-487-9243)
Serving San Bernardino County
and portions of Los Angeles and
Riverside Counties

LOS ANGELES DISTRICT OFFICE
915 Wilshire Blvd., Suite 960
Los Angeles, CA 90017-3446
Tel: 213-894-6375;
1-866-4-USWAGE
(1-866-487-9243)
Serving Kern, Santa Barbara, San
Luis, Obispo, and Ventura Counties
and portions of Los Angeles County

ORANGE AREA OFFICE
770 The City Drive South,
Suite 5710
Orange, CA 92868-4954
Tel: 714-621-1650;
1-866-4-USWAGE
(1-866-487-9243)
Serving Orange County

SACRAMENTO DISTRICT OFFICE
2800 Cottage Way, Room W-1836
Sacramento, CA 95825-1886
Tel: 916-978-6123;
1-866-4-USWAGE
(1-866-487-9243)

SAN DIEGO DISTRICT OFFICE
5675 Ruffin Road, Suite 310
San Diego, CA 92123-1362
Tel: 858-467-7015;
1-866-4-USWAGE
(1-866-487-9243)
Serving Imperial and San Diego
Counties and portions of Riverside
County

SAN FRANCISCO DISTRICT
OFFICE
90 Seventh Street, Suite 18-300
San Francisco, CA 94103-6719
Tel: 415-625-7720;
1-866-4-USWAGE
(1-866-487-9243)

SAN JOSE AREA OFFICE
60 South Market Street, Suite 420
San Jose, CA 95113-2354
Tel: 408-291-7730;
1-866-4-USWAGE
(1-866-487-9243)

DEPARTMENT OF HEALTH AND HUMAN SERVICES, OFFICE FOR CIVIL RIGHTS

200 Independence Avenue, SW
Room 509F HHH Bldg.
Washington, DC 20201
http://www.hhs.gov/ocr/

REGION IX - SAN FRANCISCO
90 Seventh Street, Suite 4-100
San Francisco, CA 94103
Tel: 415-437-8310
TDD: 415-437-8311
Fax: 415-437-8329

DEPARTMENT OF THE INTERIOR

1849 C Street, NW
Washington, DC 20240
Tel: 202-208-3100
Email: feedback@ios.doi.gov
http://www.doi.gov/

DEPARTMENT OF JUSTICE

Civil Rights Division

950 Pennsylvania Avenue, NW
Office of the Assistant Attorney
General, Main
Washington, DC 20530
Tel: 202-514-4609
TDD: 202-514-0716
Fax: 202-514-0293; 202-307-2572;
202-307-2839
Division Directory: http://www.
justice.gov/crt/mgmtndx.php
http://www.justice.gov/crt/

Office of Special Counsel for Immigration-Related Unfair Employment Practices

950 Pennsylvania Avenue, NW
Washington, DC 20530
Tel: 202-616-5594
Worker Hotline: 1-800-255-7688
TDD: 202-616-5525;
1-800-237-2515
Employer Hotline: 1-800-255-8155
Fax: 202-616-5509
Email: osccrt@usdoj.gov
http://www.justice.gov/crt/osc/index.
php

United States Attorneys

http://www.justice.gov/usao/offices/
index.html#c

CENTRAL DISTRICT OF
CALIFORNIA
http://www.justice.gov/usao/cac/

1200 U.S. Courthouse
312 North Spring Street
Los Angeles, CA 90012
Tel: 213-894-2434
Fax: 213-894-0141

411 West Fourth Street, Suite 8000
Santa Ana, CA 92701-4599
Tel: 714-338-3500
Fax: 714-338-3708

3880 Lemon Street, Suite 210
Riverside, CA 92501
Tel: 951-276-6210
Fax: 951-276-6202

EASTERN DISTRICT OF
CALIFORNIA
http://www.justice.gov/usao/cae/

501 I Street, Suite 10-100
Sacramento, CA 95814
Tel: 916-554-2700
Fax: 916-554-2900

2500 Tulare Street, Suite 4401
Fresno, CA 93721
Tel: 559-497-4000
Fax: 559-497-4099

NORTHERN DISTRICT OF
CALIFORNIA
http://www.justice.gov/usao/can/

450 Golden Gate Avenue,
Box 36055
San Francisco, CA 94102
Tel: 415-436-7200
Fax: 415-436-7234

1301 Clay Street, Suite 340S
Oakland, CA 94612
Tel: 510-637-3680
Fax: 510-637-3724

150 Almaden Boulevard, Suite 900
San Jose, CA 95113
Tel: 408-535-5061
Fax: 408-535-5066

SOUTHERN DISTRICT OF
CALIFORNIA
http://www.justice.gov/usao/cas/

880 Front Street, Room 6293
San Diego, CA 92101
Tel: 619-557-5610
Fax: 619-557-5782

516 Industry Way, Suite C
El Centro, CA 92251
Tel: 760-370-0893
Fax: 760-370-0894

A P P E N D I X   B

EQUAL EMPLOYMENT OPPORTUNITY COMMISSION (EEOC)

131 M Street, NE
Washington, DC 20507
Tel: 202-663-4900
TTY: 202-663-4494
http://www.eeoc.gov/

LOS ANGELES DISTRICT OFFICE
255 E. Temple, 4th Floor
Los Angeles, CA 90012
Tel: 1-800-669-4000
TTY: 1-800-669-6820
Fax: 213-894-1118

SAN FRANCISCO DISTRICT OFFICE
350 The Embarcadero, Suite 500
San Francisco, CA 94105
Tel: 1-800-669-4000
TTY: 1-800-669-6820
Fax: 415-625-5609

FRESNO LOCAL OFFICE
2300 Tulare Street, Suite 215
Fresno, CA 93721
Tel: 1-800-669-4000
TTY: 1-800-669-6820
Fax: 559-487-5053

OAKLAND LOCAL OFFICE
1301 Clay Street, Suite 1170-N
Oakland, CA 94612
Tel: 1-800-669-4000
TTY: 1-800-669-6820
Fax: 510-637-3235

SAN DIEGO LOCAL OFFICE
555 W. Beech Street, Suite 504
San Diego, CA 92101
Tel: 1-800-669-4000
TTY: 1-800-669-6820
Fax: 619-557-7274

SAN JOSE LOCAL OFFICE
96 N. Third Street, Room 250
San Jose, CA 95112
Tel: 1-800-669-4000
TTY: 1-800-669-6820
Fax: 408-291-4539

FEDERAL TRADE COMMISSION (FTC)

Consumer Response Center
600 Pennsylvania Avenue, NW
Washington, DC 20580
Toll-free helpline: 1-877-FTC-HELP
(1-877-382-4357)
TTY: 1-866- 653-4261
Toll-free identity theft helpline:
1-877-ID-THEFT (1-877-438-4338)
TTY: 1-866-653-4261
http://www.ftc.gov/

11877 Wilshire Blvd., Suite 700
Los Angeles, CA 90024
Tel: 1-877-382-4357
TTY: 1-866-653-4261

901 Market Street, Suite 570
San Francisco, CA 94103
Tel: 1-877-382-4357
TTY: 1-866-653-4261

MERIT SYSTEMS PROTECTION BOARD

1615 M Street, NW
Washington, DC 20419
Tel: 202-653-7200
V/TDD: 1-800-877-8339
Toll Free Message Line:
1-800-209-8960
Fax: 202-653-7130
http://www.mspb.gov/

Western Regional Office
201 Mission Street, Suite 2310
San Francisco, CA 94105-1831
Tel: 415-904-6772
Fax: 415-904-0580
Email: sanfrancisco@mspb.gov

NATIONAL LABOR RELATIONS BOARD (NLRB)

1099 Fourteenth Street, NW
Washington, DC 20570-0001
Tel: 202-273-1000
Spanish: 1-866-667-NLRB
(1-866-667-6572)
TTY: 1-866-315-NLRB
(1-866-315-6572)
http://www.nlrb.gov/

LOS ANGELES REGIONAL OFFICES
888 South Figueroa Street, 9th Floor
Los Angeles, CA 90017-5449
Tel: 213-894-5200
Fax: 213-894-2778

11150 West Olympic Blvd.,
Suite 700
Los Angeles, CA 90064-1824
Tel: 310-235-7352
Fax: 310-235-7420

OAKLAND REGIONAL OFFICE
Oakland Federal Building
1301 Clay Street, Room 300-N
Oakland, CA 94612-5211
Tel: 510-637-3300
Fax: 510-637-3315

SAN FRANCISCO REGIONAL OFFICE
901 Market Street, Suite 400
San Francisco, CA 94103-1735
Tel: 415-356-5130
Fax: 415-356-5156

SAN DIEGO REGIONAL OFFICE
555 West Beech Street, Suite 418
San Diego, CA 92101-2939
Tel: 619-557-6184
Fax: 619-557-6358

SOCIAL SECURITY ADMINISTRATION

Find your local office: https://secure.
ssa.gov/apps6z/FOLO/fo001.jsp
Tel: 1-800-772-1213
TTY: 1-800-325-0778
http://www.ssa.gov
http://www.ssa.gov/pgm/links_
disability.htm (Disability Insurance
Program)
http://www.ssa.gov/pgm/links_ssi.
htm (Supplemental Security Income
Program, SSI)

If you have a problem, first contact
your local office or call the 800
number. If you still need help, write
to either of these offices (include
SSN or claim number).

Office of Public Inquiries
Windsor Park Building
6401 Security Blvd.
Baltimore, MD 21235

Regional Public Affairs Office
PO Box 4201
Richmond, CA 94804
http://www.ssa.gov/sf/

STATE GOVERNMENT AGENCIES

AGRICULTURAL LABOR RELATIONS BOARD

915 Capitol Mall, 3rd Floor
Sacramento, CA 95814
Tel: 916-653-3699;
1-800-449-3699
http://www.alrb.ca.gov/

EL CENTRO SUBREGIONAL OFFICE
1699 West Main Street, Suite L
El Centro, CA 92243
Tel: 760-353-2130
Fax: 760-353-2443

SALINAS REGIONAL OFFICE
342 Pajar Street
Salinas, CA 93901-3423
Tel: 831-769-8031
Fax: 831-769-8039

VISALIA REGIONAL OFFICE
1462 W. Walnut Avenue
Visalia, CA 93277-5348
Tel: 559-627-0995
Fax: 559-627-0985

CALIFORNIA STATE AUDITOR

Bureau of State Audits
555 Capitol Mall, Suite 300
Sacramento, CA 95814
Tel: 916-445-0255
TTY: 916-445-0033
Fax: 916-327-0913
Whistleblower's Hotline:
Tel: 1-800-952-5665
TTY: 1-866-293-8729
Fax: 916-322-2603
http://www.bsa.ca.gov/

DEPARTMENT OF CONSUMER AFFAIRS

Consumer Information Division
1625 North Market Blvd.,
Suite N-112
Sacramento, CA 95834
Tel: 1-800-952-5210
TDD: 1-800-326-2297
Email: dca@dca.ca.gov

DEPARTMENT OF CORPORATIONS

1515 K Street, Suite 200
Sacramento, CA 95814
Tel: 916-445-7205;
1-866-ASK CORP
(1-866-275-2677); 916-324-9011
http://www.corp.ca.gov

REGIONAL OFFICE, NORTHERN CALIFORNIA
1390 Market Street, Suite 810
San Francisco, CA 94102
Tel: 415-557-3787

REGIONAL OFFICE, SOUTHERN CALIFORNIA
320 W. Fourth Street, Suite 750
Los Angeles, CA 90013
Tel: 213-576-7500

DEPARTMENT OF FAIR EMPLOYMENT AND HOUSING

Tel: 1-800-884-1684
TTY: 1-800-700-2320
Fax: 916-478-7320
http://www.dfeh.ca.gov/DFEH/
default/

BAKERSFIELD DISTRICT
4800 Stockdale Hwy., Suite 215
Bakersfield, CA 93309
Tel: 661-395-2729;
1-800-884-1684
TTY: 1-800-700-2320
Fax: 661-395-2972

FRESNO DISTRICT
1320 E. Shaw Avenue, Suite 150
Fresno, CA 93710
Tel: 559-244-4760;
1-800-884-1684
TTY: 1-800-700-2320
Fax: 559-244-4819

LOS ANGELES CENTRAL DISTRICT
1055 W. Seventh Street, Suite 1400
Los Angeles, CA 90017
Tel: 213-439-6799;
1-800-884-1684
TTY: 1-800-700-2320
Fax: 213-439-6715

OAKLAND DISTRICT
1515 Clay Street, Suite 701
Oakland, CA 94612
Tel: 510-622-2941;
1-800-884-1684
TTY: 1-800-700-2320
Fax: 510-622-2951

SACRAMENTO DISTRICT
2218 Kausen Drive, Suite 100
Elk Grove, CA 95788
Tel: 916-478-7230;
1-800-884-1684
TTY: 1-800-700-2320
Fax: 916-478-7338

SAN DIEGO DISTRICT
1350 Front Street, Suite 1063
San Diego, CA 92101
Tel: 619-645-2681;
1-800-884-1684
TTY: 1-800-700-2320
Fax: 619-645-2683

SAN FRANCISCO DISTRICT
1515 Clay Street, Suite 701
Oakland, CA 94612
Tel: 510-622-2941;
1-800-884-1684
TTY: 1-800-700-2320
Fax: 510-622-2951

SAN JOSE DISTRICT
2570 N. First Street, Suite 480
San Jose, CA 95131
Tel: 408-325-0344;
1-800-884-1684
TTY: 1-800-700-2320
Fax: 408-325-0339

SANTA ANA DISTRICT
2101 E. Fourth Street, Suite 255-B
Santa Ana, CA 92705
Tel: 714-558-4266;
1-800-884-1684
TTY: 1-800-700-2320
Fax: 714-558-6461

DEPARTMENT OF INDUSTRIAL RELATIONS

Office of the Director
455 Golden Gate Avenue
San Francisco, CA 94102
Worker hotline: 1-866-924-9757
Public Information Office:
415-703-5070
http://www.dir.ca.gov/

APPENDIX B

Division of Apprenticeship Standards

Email: DAS@dir.ca.gov
http://www.dir.ca.gov/DAS/

FRESNO DISTRICT OFFICE
2550 Mariposa Mall, Room 3080
Fresno, CA 93721
Tel: 559-445-5431
Fax: 559-445-6294

LOS ANGELES DISTRICT OFFICE
320 W. Fourth Street, Suite 830
Los Angeles, CA 90013
Tel: 213-576-7750
Fax: 213-576-7758

SACRAMENTO DISTRICT OFFICE
2424 Arden Way, Suite 160
Sacramento, CA 95825
Tel: 916-263-2877
Fax: 916-263-0981

SAN DIEGO DISTRICT OFFICE
7575 Metropolitan Drive, Suite 209
San Diego, CA 92108
Tel: 619-767-2045
Fax: 619-767-2047

SAN FRANCISCO DISTRICT
OFFICE
455 Golden Gate Avenue, 10th floor
San Francisco, CA 94102
Tel: 415-703-1128
Fax: 415-703-5427

SAN JOSE DISTRICT OFFICE
100 Paseo de San Antonio,
Room 125
San Jose, CA 95113
Tel: 408-277-1273
Fax: 408-277-9612

Division of Labor Standards Enforcement/Office of the Labor Commissioner

455 Golden Gate Avenue, 9th Floor
San Francisco, CA 94102
Tel: 415-703-4810
Minimum wage hotline:
1-888-ASK-WAGE
(1-888-275-9243)
Fax: 415-703-4807
http://www.dir.ca.gov/dlse/dlse.html

BAKERSFIELD DISTRICT OFFICE
5555 California Avenue, Suite 200
Bakersfield, CA 93309
Tel: 661-395-2710
Recorded information:
661-859-2462

EL CENTRO DISTRICT OFFICE
1550 W. Main Street
El Centro, CA 92243
Tel: 760-353-0607
Recorded information:
760-353-2544

FRESNO DISTRICT OFFICE
770 E. Shaw Avenue, Suite 222
Fresno, CA 93710
Tel: 559-244-5340
Recorded information:
559-248-8398

LONG BEACH DISTRICT OFFICE
300 Oceangate Street, Suite 302
Long Beach, CA 90802
Tel: 562-590-5048
Recorded information:
562-491-0160

LOS ANGELES DISTRICT OFFICE
320 W. Fourth Street, Suite 450
Los Angeles, CA 90013
Tel: 213-620-6330
Recorded information:
213-576-6227

OAKLAND DISTRICT OFFICE
1515 Clay Street, Suite 801
Oakland, CA 94612
Tel: 510-622-3273
Recorded information:
510-622-2660

REDDING DISTRICT OFFICE
2115 Civic Center Drive, Room 17
Redding, CA 96001
Tel: 530-225-2655
Recorded information:
530-229-0565

SACRAMENTO DISTRICT OFFICE
2031 Howe Avenue, Suite 100
Sacramento, CA 95825
Tel: 916-263-1811
Recorded information:
916-263-5378

SALINAS DISTRICT OFFICE
1870 N. Main Street, Suite 150
Salinas, CA 93906
Tel: 831-443-3041
Recorded information:
831-443-3029

SAN BERNARDINO DISTRICT
OFFICE
464 W. Fourth Street, Room 348
San Bernardino, CA 92401
Tel: 909-383-4334
Recorded information:
909-889-8120

SAN DIEGO DISTRICT OFFICE
7575 Metropolitan Drive, Room 210
San Diego, CA 92108
Tel: 619-220-5451
Recorded information:
619-682-7221

SAN FRANCISCO DISTRICT
OFFICE
455 Golden Gate Avenue,
10th Floor
San Francisco, CA 94102
Tel: 415-703-5300
Recorded information:
415-703-5444

SAN JOSE DISTRICT OFFICE
100 Paseo de San Antonio,
Room 120
San Jose, CA 95113
Tel: 408-277-1266
Recorded information:
408-277-3711

SANTA ANA DISTRICT OFFICE
605 West Santa Ana Blvd., Bldg. 28,
Room 625
Santa Ana, CA 92701
Tel: 714-558-4910
Recorded information:
714-558-4574

SANTA BARBARA DISTRICT
OFFICE
411 E. Canon Perdido, Room 3
Santa Barbara, CA 93101
Tel: 805-568-1222
Recorded information:
805-965-7214

SANTA ROSA DISTRICT OFFICE
50 D Street, Suite 360
Santa Rosa, CA 95404
Tel: 707-576-2362
Recorded information:
707-576-2459

STOCKTON DISTRICT OFFICE
31 E. Channel Street, Room 317
Stockton, CA 95202
Tel: 209-948-7771
Recorded information:
209-941-1906

VAN NUYS DISTRICT OFFICE
6150 Van Nuys Blvd., Room 206
Van Nuys, CA 91401
Tel: 818-901-5315
Recorded information:
818-908-4556

VAN NUYS DISTRICT OFFICE
– ENTERTAINMENT WORK
PERMITS
6150 Van Nuys Blvd., Room 100
Van Nuys, CA 91401
Tel: 818-901-5484

Division of Occupational Safety and Health (Cal-OSHA or DOSH)

Tel: 510-286-7000
Consultation service for employers:
1-800-963-9424
http://www.dir.ca.gov/dosh/

CONCORD DISTRICT OFFICE
1450 Enea Circle, Suite 525
Concord, CA 94520
Tel: 925-602-6517
Fax: 925-676-0227

FOSTER CITY DISTRICT OFFICE
1065 East Hillsdale Blvd., Suite 110
Foster City, CA 94404
Tel: 650-573-3812
Fax: 650-573-3817

FREMONT DISTRICT OFFICE
39141 Civic Center Drive, Suite 310
Fremont, CA 94538-5818
Tel: 510-794-2521
Fax: 510-794-3889

FRESNO DISTRICT OFFICE
2550 Mariposa Street, Suite 4000
Fresno, CA 93721
Tel: 559-445-5302
Fax: 559-445-5786

LOS ANGELES DISTRICT OFFICE
320 W. Fourth Street, Suite 850
Los Angeles, CA 90013
Tel: 213-576-7451
Fax: 213-576-7461

MODESTO DISTRICT OFFICE
4206 Technology Drive, Suite 3
Modesto, CA 95356
Tel: 209-545-7310
Fax: 209-545-7313

MONROVIA DISTRICT OFFICE
750 Royal Oaks Drive, Suite 104
Monrovia, CA 91016
Tel: 626-256-7913
Fax: 626-359-4291

OAKLAND DISTRICT OFFICE
1515 Clay Street, Suite 1301
Oakland, CA 94612
Tel: 510-622-2916
Fax: 510-622-2908

REDDING FIELD OFFICE
381 Hemsted Drive
Redding, CA 96002
Tel: 530-224-4743
Fax: 530-224-4747

SACRAMENTO DISTRICT OFFICE
2424 Arden Way, Suite 165
Sacramento, CA 95825
Tel: 916-263-2800
Fax: 916-263-2798

SAN BERNARDINO DISTRICT
OFFICE
464 W. Fourth Street, Suite 332
San Bernardino, CA 92401
Tel: 909-383-4321
Fax: 909-383-6789

SAN DIEGO DISTRICT OFFICE
7575 Metropolitan Drive, Suite 207
San Diego, CA 92108
Tel: 619-767-2280
Fax: 619-767-2299

SAN FRANCISCO DISTRICT
OFFICE
121 Spear Street, Suite 430
San Francisco, CA 94105
Tel: 415-972-8670
Fax: 415-972-8686

SANTA ANA DISTRICT OFFICE
2000 E. McFadden Avenue,
Suite 122
Santa Ana, CA 92705
Tel: 714-558-4451
Fax: 714-558-2035

SANTA ROSA DISTRICT OFFICE
1221 Farmers Lane, Suite 300
Santa Rosa, CA 95405
Tel: 707-576-2388
Fax: 707-576-2598

TORRANCE DISTRICT OFFICE
680 Knox Street, Suite 100
Torrance, CA 90502
Tel: 310-516-3734
Fax: 310-516-4253

VAN NUYS DISTRICT OFFICE
6150 Van Nuys Blvd., Suite 405
Van Nuys, CA 91401
Tel: 818-901-5403
Fax: 818-901-5578

VENTURA FIELD OFFICE
1000 Hill Road, Suite 110
Ventura, CA 93003
Tel: 805-654-4581
Fax: 805-654-4852

WEST COVINA DISTRICT OFFICE
1906 W. Garvey Avenue S.,
Suite 200
West Covina, CA 91790
Tel: 626-472-0046
Fax: 626-472-7708

Division of Workers' Compensation

1515 Clay Street, 17th floor
Oakland, CA 94612-1402
Tel: 510-286-7100
Recorded information:
1-800-736-7401
http://www.dir.ca.gov/DWC/dwc_
home_page.htm

Workers' Compensation Appeals Board Offices

ANAHEIM
1065 N. PacifiCenter Drive,
Suite 170
Anaheim, CA 92806
Tel: 714-414-1800
Information and Assistance Unit:
714-414-1801

BAKERSFIELD
1800 30th Street, Suite 100
Bakersfield, CA 93301-1929
Tel: 661-395-2723
Information and Assistance Unit:
661-395-2514

EUREKA
100 H Street, Suite 202
Eureka, CA 95501-0481
Tel: 707-445-6518
Information and Assistance Unit:
707-441-5723

FRESNO
2550 Mariposa Mall, Suite 4078
Fresno, CA 93721-2219
Tel: 559-445-5051
Information and Assistance Unit:
559-445-5355

GOLETA
6755 Hollister Avenue, Suite 100
Goleta, CA 93117-5551
Tel: 805-968-0258
Information and Assistance Unit:
805-968-4158

LONG BEACH
300 Oceangate Street, Suite 200
Long Beach, CA 90802-4304
Tel: 562-590-5001
Information and Assistance Unit:
562-590-5240

LOS ANGELES
320 W. Fourth Street, 9th floor
Los Angeles, CA 90013-2329
Tel: 213-576-7335
Information and Assistance Unit:
213-576-7389

MARINA DEL REY
4720 Lincoln Blvd.,
2nd & 3rd floors
Marina del Rey, CA 90292-6902
Tel: 310-482-3820
Information and Assistance Unit:
310-482-3820

OAKLAND
1515 Clay Street, 6th floor
Oakland, CA 94612-1402
Tel: 510-622-2866
Information and Assistance Unit:
510-622-2861

OXNARD
1901 N. Rice Avenue, Suite 200
Oxnard, CA 93030-7912
Tel: 805-485-2533
Information and Assistance Unit:
805-485-3528

POMONA
732 Corporate Center Drive
Pomona, CA 91768-2653
Tel: 909-623-4301
Information and Assistance Unit:
909-623-8568

REDDING
2115 Civic Center Drive, Suite 15
Redding, CA 96001-2796
Tel: 530-225-2845
Information and Assistance Unit:
530-225-2047

RIVERSIDE
3737 Main Street, Suite 300
Riverside, CA 92501-3337
Tel: 951-782-4269
Information and Assistance Unit:
951-782-4347

SACRAMENTO
160 Promenade Circle, Suite 300
Sacramento, CA 95834-2962
Tel: 916-928-3101
Information and Assistance Unit:
916-928-3158

SALINAS
1880 North Main Street,
Suites 100 & 200
Salinas, CA 93906-2037
Tel: 831-443-3060
Information and Assistance Unit:
831-443-3058

SAN BERNARDINO
464 W. Fourth Street, Suite 239
San Bernardino, CA 92401-1411
Tel: 909-383-4341
Information and Assistance Unit:
909-383-4522

SAN DIEGO
7575 Metropolitan Drive, Suite 202
San Diego, CA 92108-4424
Tel: 619-767-2083
Information and Assistance Unit:
619-767-2082

SAN FRANCISCO
455 Golden Gate Avenue, 2nd floor
San Francisco, CA 94102-7014
Tel: 415-703-5011
Information and Assistance Unit:
415-703-5020

SAN JOSE
100 Paseo de San Antonio,
Room 241
San Jose, CA 95113-1402
Tel: 408-277-1246
Information and Assistance Unit:
408-277-1292

SAN LUIS OBISPO
4740 Allene Way, Suite 100
San Luis Obispo, CA 93401
Tel: 805-596-4153
Information and Assistance Unit:
805-596-4159

SANTA ANA
605 W. Santa Ana Blvd., Bldg. 28,
Room 451
Santa Ana, CA 92701
Tel: 714-558-4121
Information and Assistance Unit:
714-558-4597

SANTA ROSA
50 D Street, Room 420
Santa Rosa, CA 95404-4771
Tel: 707-576-2391
Information and Assistance Unit:
707-576-2452

STOCKTON
31 E. Channel Street, Room 344
Stockton, CA 95202-2314
Tel: 209-948-7759
Information and Assistance Unit:
209-948-7980

VAN NUYS
6150 Van Nuys Blvd., Room 105
Van Nuys, CA 91401-3370
Tel: 818-901-5367
Information and Assistance Unit:
818-901-5367

**Industrial Welfare
Commission (IWC)**
801 K Street, Suite 2100
Sacramento, CA 95814
Email: IWC@dir.ca.gov
http://www.dir.ca.gov/IWC/
Wage Orders: http://www.dir.
ca.gov/iwc/wageorderindustries.htm

**Occupational Safety & Health
Appeals Board (OSHAB)**
2520 Venture Oaks Way, Suite 300
Sacramento, CA 95833
Tel: 916-274-5751
Prehearings: 916-274-5791
Fax: 916-274-5785
Email: oshappeals@dir.ca.gov
http://www.dir.ca.gov/oshab/oshab.
html

SOUTHERN CALIFORNIA OFFICE
100 N. Barranca Street, Suite 410
West Covina, CA 91791
Tel: 626-332-1145
Fax: 626-966-4490

**Occupational Safety & Health
Standards Board (OSHSB)**
2520 Ventura Oaks Way, Suite 350
Sacramento, CA 95833
Tel: 916-274-5721
Email: oshsb@dir.ca.gov
http://www.dir.ca.gov/oshsb/oshsb.
html

Office of the Labor Commissioner
See Department of Industrial Relations, Division of Labor Standards Enforcement

DEPARTMENT OF INSURANCE
Consumer Communications Bureau
300 S. Spring Street, South Tower
Los Angeles, CA 90013
Tel: 1-800-927-HELP (4357);
213-897-8921
TDD: 1-800-482-4TDD (4833)
http://www.insurance.ca.gov/

DEPARTMENT OF JUSTICE/ OFFICE OF THE ATTORNEY GENERAL
Public Inquiry Unit
PO Box 944255
Sacramento, CA 94244-2550
Tel: 916-322-3360;
1-800-952-5225
Fax: 916-323-5341
TTY/TDD: Dial 711
English TTY/TDD: 1-800-735-2929
Spanish TTY/TDD: 1-800-855-3000
Voice: 1-800-735-2922
http://ag.ca.gov/

FRESNO
2550 Mariposa Mall, Room 5090
Fresno, CA 93721
Tel: 559-445-6590

LOS ANGELES
300 S. Spring Street
Los Angeles, CA 90013-1230
Phone: 213-897-2000

OAKLAND
1515 Clay Street
PO Box 70550
Oakland, CA 94612-0550
Tel: 510-622-2100

SACRAMENTO
1300 "I" Street
PO Box 944255
Sacramento, CA 94244-2550
Tel: 916-445-9555

SAN DIEGO
110 West A Street, Suite 1100
PO Box 85266-5299
San Diego, CA 92186-5266
Tel: 619-645-2001

SAN FRANCISCO
455 Golden Gate Avenue,
Suite 11000
San Francisco, CA 94102-7004
Tel: 415-703-5500

District Attorneys
http://www.cdaa.org/daroster.htm

ALAMEDA COUNTY
1225 Fallon Street, Room 900
Oakland, CA 94612
Tel: 510-272-6222
Fax: 510-217-5157
Email: alcoda@co.alameda.ca.us
http://www.alcoda.org/

ALPINE COUNTY
PO Box 248
Markleeville, CA 96120
Tel: 530-694-2971
Fax: 530-694-2980
http://www.alpinecountyca.gov/district_attorney

AMADOR COUNTY
708 Court Street, Room 202
Jackson, CA 95642
Tel: 209-223-6444
Fax: 209-223-6304
http://www.co.amador.ca.us/index.aspx?page=64

BUTTE COUNTY
25 County Center Drive,
Administration Building
Oroville, CA 95965
Tel: 530-538-7411
Fax: 530-538-7071
http://www.buttecounty.net/da/

CALAVERAS COUNTY
891 Mountain Ranch Road
San Andreas, CA 95249
Tel: 209-754-6330
Fax: 297-754-6645
http://www.co.calaveras.ca.us/cc/Departments/DistrictAttorney.aspx

COLUSA COUNTY
547 Market Street, Suite 102
Colusa, CA 95932
Tel: 530-458-0545
Fax: 530-458-8265
http://www.colusada.net/

CONTRA COSTA COUNTY
725 Court Street, 4th Floor
Martinez, CA 94553
Tel: 925-957-2200
Fax: 925-957-2240
http://www.co.contra-costa.ca.us/index.aspx?NID=203

DEL NORTE COUNTY
450 H Street, Room 171
Crescent City, CA 95531
Tel: 707-464-7210
Fax: 707-465-6609

EL DORADO COUNTY
515 Main Street
Placerville, CA 95667
Tel: 530-621-6472
Fax: 530-621-1280
Email: eldoda@co.el-dorado.ca.us
http://www.co.el-dorado.ca.us/eldoda/

FRESNO COUNTY
2220 Tulare Street, Suite 1000
Fresno, CA 93721
Tel: 559-488-3141
Fax: 559-488-2800
Email: districtattorneyfsd@fresno.ca.gov
http://www.co.fresno.ca.us/Departments.aspx?id=156

GLENN COUNTY
PO Box 430
Willows, CA 95988
Tel: 916-934-6525
Fax: 916-934-6529
Email: gcda@jps.net
http://www.countyofglenn.net/govt/departments/district_attorney/

HUMBOLDT COUNTY
825 Fifth Street
Eureka, CA 95501
Tel: 707-445-7411
Fax: 707-445-7416
Email: districtattorney@co.humboldt.ca.us
http://co.humboldt.ca.us/distatty/

IMPERIAL COUNTY
940 West Main Street, Suite 102
El Centro, CA 92243
Tel: 760-482-4331
Fax: 760-353-2707

INYO COUNTY
PO Drawer D
Independence, CA 93526
Tel: 760-878-0282
Fax: 760-878-2383

KERN COUNTY
1215 Truxtun Avenue
Bakersfield, CA 93301
Tel: 661-868-2340
Fax: 661-868-2700
Email: da@co.kern.ca.us
http://www.co.kern.ca.us/da/

KINGS COUNTY
1400 West Lacey Blvd.
Hanford, CA 93230
Tel: 559-582-0326
Fax: 559-584-4127
http://www.countyofkings.com/da/
index.html

LAKE COUNTY
255 N. Forbes Street
Lakeport, CA 95453
Tel: 707-263-2251
Fax: 707-263-2328
http://www.co.lake.ca.us/
Government/Directory/District_
Attorney.htm

LASSEN COUNTY
220 S. Lassen Street, Suite 8
Susanville, CA 96130
Tel: 530-251-8283
Fax: 530-251-2692
http://www.co.lassen.ca.us/govt/
dept/district_attorney/default.asp

MADERA COUNTY
209 West Yosemite Avenue
Madera, CA 93637
Tel: 559-675-7726
Fax: 559-673-0430
http://www.madera-county.com/
district-attorney/

MARIN COUNTY
3501 Civic Center Drive, Room 130
San Rafael, CA 94903
Tel: 415-499-6450
Fax: 415-499-6734
http://www.co.marin.ca.us/depts/
DA/main/index.cfm

MARIPOSA COUNTY
PO Box 730
Mariposa, CA 95338
Tel: 209-966-3626
Fax: 209-966-5681
http://www.mariposacounty.org/
index.aspx?nid=74

MENDOCINO COUNTY
PO Box 1000
Ukiah, CA 95482
Tel: 707-463-4211
Fax: 707-463-4687
Email: da@co.mendocino.ca.us
http://www.co.mendocino.ca.us/da/

MERCED COUNTY
2222 M Street
Merced, CA 95340
Tel: 209-385-7381
Fax: 209-725-3669
Email: dainfo@data.co.merced.ca.us
http://www.co.merced.ca.us/index.
aspx?nid=67

MODOC COUNTY
204 S. Court Street, Room 202
Alturas, CA 96101
Tel: 530-233-6212
Fax: 530-233-4067

MONO COUNTY
PO Box 617
Bridgeport, CA 93546
Tel: 760-932-5550
Fax: 760-932-5551
Email: monoda@qnet.com
http://www.monocounty.ca.gov/
departments/district_attorney/
district_attorney.html

MONTEREY COUNTY
PO Box 1131
Salinas, CA 93902
Tel: 831-755-5470
Fax: 831-796-3389
http://www.co.monterey.ca.us/da/

NAPA COUNTY
PO Box 720
Napa, CA 94559
Tel: 707-253-4211
Fax: 707-253-4041
Email: district_attorney_office@
co.napa.ca.us
http://www.countyofnapa.org/pages/
department.aspx?id=4294967341

NEVADA COUNTY
110 Union Street
Nevada City, CA 95959
Tel: 530-265-1301
Fax: 530-478-1871
http://www.mynevadacounty.com/da/

ORANGE COUNTY
401 Civic Center Drive West
Santa Ana, CA 92701
Tel: 714-834-3600
Fax: 714-834-5880
http://www.orangecountyda.com/
home/index.asp

PLACER COUNTY
10810 Justice Center Drive
Roseville, CA 95678
Tel: 530-889-7000
Fax: 530-889-7129
http://www.placer.ca.gov/
Departments/DA.aspx

PLUMAS COUNTY
520 Main Street, Room 404
Quincy, CA 95971
Tel: 530-283-6303
Fax: 530-283-6340
http://www.plumascountyda.org/

RIVERSIDE COUNTY
4075 Main Street
Riverside, CA 92501
Tel: 951-955-5400
Fax: 951-955-5682
http://www.rivcoda.org/

SACRAMENTO COUNTY
PO Box 749
Sacramento, CA 95812
Tel: 916-874-6218
Fax: 916-874-5340
Email: da@saccounty.net
http://www.sacda.org/

SAN BENITO COUNTY
419 Fourth Street
Hollister, CA 95023-3801
Tel: 831-636-4120
Fax: 831-636-4126

SAN BERNARDINO COUNTY
316 N. Mountain View Avenue
San Bernardino, CA 92415
Tel: 909-387-8309
Fax: 909-387-6444
Email: da@da.co.san-bernardino.
ca.us
http://www.co.san-bernardino.ca.us/
da/

SAN DIEGO COUNTY
330 W. Broadway, Suite 1300
San Diego, CA 92101
Tel: 619-531-4040
Fax: 619-237-1351
Email: publicaffairs@sdcda.org
http://www.sdcda.org/

SAN FRANCISCO COUNTY
880 Bryant Street, 3rd Floor
San Francisco, CA 94103
Tel: 415-553-1752
Fax: 415-553-8815
Email: districtattorney@sfgov.org
http://www.sfgov.org/site/frame.
asp?u=http://www.sfdistrictattorney.
org/

SAN JOAQUIN COUNTY
PO Box 990
Stockton, CA 95202
Tel: 209-468-2400
Fax: 209-465-0371
Email: info@sjcda.org
http://www.co.san-joaquin.ca.us/da/

SAN LUIS OBISPO COUNTY
1035 Palm Street
San Luis Obispo, CA 93408
Tel: 805-781-5800
Fax: 805-781-4307
http://www.slocounty.ca.gov/da.htm

SAN MATEO COUNTY
400 County Center, 3rd Floor
Redwood City, CA 94063
Tel: 650-363-4636
Fax: 650-363-4873
http://www.co.sanmateo.ca.us/
portal/site/districtattorney

SANTA BARBARA COUNTY
1112 Santa Barbara Street
Santa Barbara, CA 93101
Tel: 805-568-2300
Fax: 805-568-2398
http://www.countyofsb.org/da/
index.asp

SANTA CLARA COUNTY
70 West Hedding Street, West Wing
San Jose, CA 95110
Tel: 408-792-2855
Fax: 408-286-5437
Email: sccda@solis.sbay.com
http://www.santaclara-da.org/portal/
site/da/

SANTA CRUZ COUNTY
701 Ocean Street, Room 200
Santa Cruz, CA 95060
Tel: 831-454-2400
Fax: 831-454-2227
Email: dao@co.santa-cruz.ca.us
http://datinternet.co.santa-cruz.
ca.us/

SHASTA COUNTY
1525 Court Street, 3rd Floor
Redding, CA 96001-1632
Tel: 530-245-6300
Fax: 530-245-6334
http://www.da.co.shasta.ca.us/

SIERRA COUNTY
100 Courthouse Square
Downieville, CA 95936
Tel: 530-289-3269
Fax: 530-289-2822

SISKIYOU COUNTY
PO Box 986
Yreka, CA 96097
Tel: 530-842-8125
Fax: 530-842-8137
Email: da@co.siskiyou.ca.us
http://www.co.siskiyou.ca.us/da/
index.htm

SOLANO COUNTY
675 Texas Street, Suite 4500
Fairfield, CA 94533
Tel: 707-784-6800
Fax: 707-784-7986
Email: solanoda@solanocounty.com
http://www.solanocounty.com/
depts/da/default.asp

SONOMA COUNTY
600 Administration Drive,
Room 212J
Santa Rosa, CA 95403
Tel: 707-565-2311
Fax: 707-565-2762
http://www.sonoma-county.org/da/
index.htm

STANISLAUS COUNTY
832 Twelfth Street, Suite 300
Modesto, CA 95353
Tel: 209-525-5550
Fax: 209-525-5545
http://www.stanislaus-da.org/

SUTTER COUNTY
PO Box 1555
Yuba City, CA 95992
Tel: 530-822-7330
Fax: 530-822-7337
http://www.co.sutter.ca.us/doc/
government/depts/da/da_home

TEHAMA COUNTY
PO Box 519
Red Bluff, CA 96080
Tel: 530-527-3053
Fax: 530-527-4735

TRINITY COUNTY
PO Box 310
Weaverville, CA 96093
Tel: 530-623-1304
Fax: 530-623-2865
http://www.trinitycounty.org/
departments/DA-Coroner/
dacoroner.htm

TULARE COUNTY
221 South Mooney Blvd., Suite 224
Visalia, CA 93291
Tel: 559-733-6411
Fax: 559-733-6982
http://www.da-tulareco.org/

TUOLUMNE COUNTY
423 N. Washington Street
Sonora, CA 95370
Tel: 209-588-5450
Fax: 209-588-5445
Email: da@tuolumnecounty.ca.gov

VENTURA COUNTY
800 South Victoria Avenue
Ventura, CA 93009
Tel: 805-654-2501
Fax: 805-654-3046
Email: da.criminal@mail.co.ventura.
ca.us
http://da.countyofventura.org/index.
htm

YOLO COUNTY
301 Second Street
Woodland, CA 95695
Tel: 530-666-8180
Fax: 530-666-8185
Email: yoloda@yoloda.org
http://www.yolocounty.org/index.
aspx?page=510

YUBA COUNTY
215 Fifth Street, Suite 152
Marysville, CA 95901
Tel: 530-749-7770
Fax: 530-749-7363
http://www.co.yuba.ca.us/
Departments/DA/

DEPARTMENT OF MANAGED HEALTH CARE
980 Ninth Street, Suite 500
Sacramento, CA 95814-2725
Tel: 1-888-466-2219
Fax: 916-255-5241
http://www.hmohelp.ca.gov/

EMPLOYMENT DEVELOPMENT DEPARTMENT (EDD)

PO Box 826880, MIC 83
Sacramento, CA 94280-0001
http://www.edd.ca.gov/default.htm

Paid Family Leave

855 M Street, Suite 810
Fresno, CA 93721
Mailing Address: PO Box 997017
Sacramento, CA 95799-7017
English: 1-877-238-4373
Spanish: 1-877-379-3819
Cantonese: 1-866-692-5595
Vietnamese: 1-866-692-5596
Armenian: 1-866-627-1567
Punjabi: 1-866-627-1568
Tagalog: 1-866-627-1569
TTY: 1-800-445-1312
California State Government
Employees covered by Paid Family
Leave for State Employees (PFL-SE):
1-877-945-4747
http://www.edd.ca.gov/Disability/
Paid_Family_Leave.htm

State Disability Insurance (SDI)

PO Box 826880 - DICO, MIC 29
Sacramento, CA 94280-0001
English: 1-800-480-3287
Spanish: 1-866-658-8846
State Government Employees
covered by State Disability Insurance
for State Employees
(SDI-SE): 1-866-352-7675
State Government Employees
covered by Nonindustrial Disability
Insurance (NDI):
1-866-758-9768
http://www.edd.ca.gov/Disability/
Disability_Insurance.htm

CHICO
645 Salem Street
Chico, CA 95928-5576
Mailing Address: PO Box 8190
Chico, CA 95927-8190

CHINO HILLS
15315 Fairfield Ranch Road,
Suite 100
Chino Hills, CA 91709
Mailing Address: PO Box 60006
City of Industry, CA 91716-0006

EUREKA
409 K Street, Suite 201
Eureka, CA 95501-0529
Mailing Address: PO Box 201006
Stockton, CA 95201-9006

FRESNO
2550 Mariposa, Room 1080A
Fresno, CA 93721-2270
Mailing Address: PO Box 32
Fresno, CA 93707-0032

LONG BEACH
4300 Long Beach, Suite 600
Long Beach, CA 90807-2011
Mailing Address: PO Box 469
Long Beach, CA 90801-0469

LOS ANGELES
888 South Figueroa Street, Suite 200
Los Angeles, CA 90017-5449
Mailing Address: PO Box 513096
Los Angeles, CA 90051-1096

NORTH LOS ANGELES
15400 Sherman Way, Room 500
Van Nuys, CA 91406
Mailing Address: PO Box 10402
Van Nuys, CA 91410-0402

OAKLAND
1600 Harbor Bay Pkwy., Suite 120
Alameda, CA 94502
Mailing Address: PO Box 1857
Oakland, CA 94604-1857

REDDING
1325 Pine Street
Redding, CA 96001-0603
Mailing Address: PO Box 8190
Chico, CA 95927-8190

RIVERSIDE
PO Box 469
Long Beach, CA 90801-0469

SACRAMENTO
PO Box 201006
Stockton, CA 95201-9006

SAN BERNARDINO
371 W. Third Street
San Bernardino, CA 92401
Mailing Address: PO Box 781
San Bernardino, CA 92402-0781

SAN DIEGO
9246 Lightwave Avenue, Building A,
Suite 300
San Diego, CA 92123-6404
Mailing Address: PO Box 120831
San Diego, CA 92112-0831

SAN FRANCISCO
745 Franklin Street, Suite 300
San Francisco, CA 94102
Mailing Address: PO Box 193534
San Francisco, CA 94119-3534

SAN JOSE
297 West Hedding Street
San Jose, CA 95110-1628
Mailing Address: PO Box 637
San Jose, CA 95106-0637

SANTA ANA
605 West Santa Ana Blvd.,
Building 28
Santa Ana, CA 92701-4024
Mailing Address: PO Box 1466
Santa Ana, CA 92702-1466

SANTA BARBARA
128 East Ortega Street
Santa Barbara, CA 93101-1631
Mailing Address: PO Box 1529
Santa Barbara, CA 93102-1529

SANTA ROSA
606 Healdsburg Avenue
Santa Rosa, CA 95401
Mailing Address: PO Box 700
Santa Rosa, CA 95402-0700

STOCKTON
528 North Madison Street
Stockton, CA 95202-1917
Mailing Address: PO Box 201006
Stockton, CA 95201-9006
Mailing Address for State
Government Employees:
PO Box 2168
Stockton, CA 95201-2168

Unemployment Insurance (UI)

PO Box 826880 - UIPCD, MIC 40
Sacramento, CA 94280-0001
English: 1-800-300-5616
Spanish: 1-800-326-8937
Chinese: 1-800-547-3506;
1-866-303-0706
Vietnamese: 1-800-547-2058
TTY: 1-800-815-9387
http://www.edd.ca.gov/
Unemployment/default.htm

HEALTH AND HUMAN SERVICES AGENCY

1600 Ninth Street, Room 460
Sacramento, CA 95814
TEL: 916-654-3454
http://www.chhs.ca.gov/Pages/
default.aspx

Department of Aging

1300 National Drive, Suite 200
Sacramento, CA 95834-1992
Tel: 916-419-7500
Fax: 916-928-2268
TDD: 1-800-735-2929
Long-Term Care Ombudsman
Program: 1-800-231-4024
Email: webmaster@aging.ca.gov
http://www.aging.ca.gov/

Department of Public Health, Licensing and Certification

PO Box 997377, MS 3000
Sacramento, CA 95899-7377
Tel: 916-552-8700,
1-800-236-9747
http://www.cdph.ca.gov/programs/
LnC/Pages/LnC.aspx

Department of Social Services, Community Care Licensing Division

Email: cclwebmaster@dss.ca.gov
http://www.ccld.ca.gov/

Adult Care Program Offices

Statewide Adult Program Office
744 P Street, MS 8-3-90
Sacramento, CA 95814
Tel: 916-657-2592
Fax: 916-653-9335

Statewide Adult Program Office
5900 Pasteur Court, Suite 125,
MS 29-19
Carlsbad, CA 92008
Tel: 760-929-2121
Fax: 760-929-2133

Los Angeles Tri-County Adult Care
Regional Office
1000 Corporate Center Drive,
Suite 500, MS 31-11
Monterey Park, CA 91754
Tel: 323-980-4934
Fax: 323-980-4912
Counties: Los Angeles, Santa
Barbara, Ventura, and San Luis
Obispo

Central Coast Local Unit
360 South Hope Avenue,
Suite C-105, MS 29-09
Santa Barbara, CA 93105
Tel: 805-682-7647
Fax: 805-682-8361
Counties: Santa Barbara, Ventura,
and San Luis Obispo

Woodland Hills Local Unit
21731 Ventura Blvd., Suite 250,
MS 29-14
Woodland Hills, CA 91364
Tel: 818-596-4334
Fax: 818-596-4376
Counties: Los Angeles and Ventura

Sierra-Cascade Adult Care Regional
Office
770 E. Shaw Avenue, Suite 330,
MS 29-02
Fresno, CA 93710
Tel: 559-243-8080
Fax: 559-243-8088
Counties: Fresno, Inyo, Kern, Kings,
Madera, Mariposa, Mono, and
Tulare

Sacramento Local Unit
2525 Natomas Park Drive,
Suite 270, MS 19-35
Tel: 916-263-4700
Fax: 916-263-4744
Counties: Alpine, Amador,
Calaveras, El Dorado, Merced,
Nevada, Placer, Sacramento, San
Joaquin, Stanislaus,
Tuolumne, and Yolo

Chico Local Unit
520 Cohasset Road, Suite 6,
MS 29-05
Chico, CA 95926
Tel: 530-895-5033
Fax: 530-895-5934
Counties: Butte, Colusa, Del Norte,
Glenn, Humboldt,
Lassen, Modoc, Plumas, Shasta,
Sierra, Siskiyou, Sutter,
Tehema, Trinity, and Yuba

Southern Adult Care Regional Office
770 The City Drive, Suite 7100,
MS 29-28
Orange, CA 92868
Tel: 714-703-2840
Fax: 714-703-2868
Counties: Orange and part of Los
Angeles

Riverside Local Unit
3737 Main Street, Suite 600,
MS 29-26
Riverside, CA 92501
Tel: 951-782-4207
Fax: 951-782-4967
Counties: Riverside and San
Bernardino

San Diego Local Unit
7575 Metropolitan Drive, Suite 109,
MS 29-06
San Diego, CA 92108
Tel: 619-767-2300
Fax: 619-767-2252
Counties: San Diego and Imperial

Greater Bay Area Adult Care
Regional Office
1515 Clay Street, Suite 310,
MS 29-21
Oakland, CA 94612
Tel: 510-286-4201
Fax: 510-286-4204
Counties: Alameda, Contra Costa,
San Francisco, and San Mateo

San Jose Local Unit
2580 N. First Street, Suite 350,
MS 29-07
San Jose, CA 95131
Tel: 408-324-2112
Fax: 408-324-2133
Counties: Monterey, San Benito,
Santa Clara, and Santa Cruz

Rohnert Park Local Unit
101 Golf Course Drive, Suite A-230,
MS 29-11
Rohnert Park, CA 94928
Tel: 707-588-5026
Fax: 707-588-5080
Counties: Lake, Marin, Mendocino,
Napa, Solano, and Sonoma

Senior Care Program Offices

Statewide Senior Care Program
Office
744 P Street, MS 10-90
Sacramento, CA 95814
Tel: 916-657-2592
Fax: 916-653-9335

Statewide Senior Care Program
Office
5900 Pasteur Court, Suite 125,
MS 29-19
Carlsbad, CA 92008
Tel: 760-929-2121
Fax: 760-929-2133

Northern California Senior Care
Licensing Office
101 Golf Course Drive, Suite A-230,
MS 29-11
Rohnert Park, CA 94928
Tel: 707-588-5026
Fax: 707-588-5080
Counties: Humboldt, Del Norte,
Lake, Marin, Mendocino, Napa,
Solano, and Sonoma

Sacramento Senior Care Local Unit
2525 Natomas Park Drive,
Suite 270, MS 19-35
Sacramento, CA 95833
Tel: 916-263-4700
Fax: 916-263-4744
Counties: Amador, Calaveras,
El Dorado, Sacramento, San
Joaquin, Stanislaus, and Tuolumne

Chico Senior Care Local Unit
520 Cohasset Road, Suite 170,
MS 29-05
Chico, CA 95926
Tel: 530-895-5033
Fax: 530-895-5934
Counties: Butte, Colusa, Glenn,
Lassen, Modoc, Nevada,
Placer, Plumas, Shasta, Sierra,
Siskiyou, Sutter, Tehama,
Trinity, Yolo, and Yuba

Central California Senior Care
Licensing Office
851 Traeger Avenue, Suite 360,
MS 29-16
San Bruno, CA 94066
Tel: 650-266-8800
Fax: 650-266-8841
Counties: Alameda, Contra Costa,
San Francisco, and San Mateo

Fresno Senior Care Local Unit
770 E. Shaw Avenue, Suite 330,
MS 29-02
Fresno, CA 93710
Tel: 559-243-8080
Fax: 559-243-8088
Counties: Alpine, Fresno, Inyo,
Kern, Kings, Madera, Mariposa,
Merced, Mono, and Tulare

San Jose Senior Care Local Unit
2580 N. First Street, Suite 350,
MS 29-07
San Jose, CA 95131
Tel: 408-324-2112
Fax: 408-324-2133
Counties: Monterey, San Benito,
Santa Clara, and Santa Cruz

Greater Los Angeles Senior Care
Licensing Office
21731 Ventura Boulevard,
Suite 250, MS 29-14
Woodland Hills, CA 91364
Tel: 818-596-4334
Fax: 818-596-4376
Counties: Los Angeles, Santa
Barbara, Ventura, and San Luis
Obispo

Santa Barbara Senior Care Local Unit
360 South Hope Avenue,
Suite C-105, MS 29-09
Santa Barbara, CA 93105
Tel: 805-682-7647
Fax: 805-563-5549
Counties: Santa Barbara, Ventura,
and San Luis Obispo

Southern California Senior Care
Licensing Office
7575 Metropolitan Drive, Suite 109,
MS 29-06
San Diego, CA 92108
Tel: 619-767-2300
Fax: 619-767-2252
Counties: Imperial, Orange,
San Diego, Riverside, and San
Bernardino

Orange Senior Care Local Unit
770 The City Drive, Suite 7100,
MS 29-28
Orange, CA 92868
Tel: 714-703-2840
Fax: 714-703-2868
County: Orange

Riverside Senior Care Local Unit
3737 Main Street, Suite 600,
MS 29-26
Riverside, CA 92501
Tel: 951-782-4207
Fax: 951-782-4967
Counties: Riverside and San
Bernardino

Children's Residential Program Offices

Statewide Children's Residential
Program Office
744 P Street, MS 19-50
Sacramento, CA 95814
Tel: 916-445-4351
Fax: 916-323-8352

Statewide Children's Residential
Program Office
1000 Corporate Center Drive,
Suite 300, MS 29-17
Monterey Park, CA 91754
Tel: 323-981-3850
Fax: 323-981-3875

Northern California Regional Office
2525 Natomas Park Drive,
Suite 270, MS 19-35
Sacramento, CA 95833
Tel: 916-263-4700
Fax: 916-263-4744
Counties: Amador, El Dorado,
Sacramento, San Joaquin
Solano, Stanislaus, and Yolo

Chico Local Unit
520 Cohasset Road, Suite 170,
MS 29-05
Chico, CA 95926
Tel: 530-895-5033
Fax: 530-895-5934
Counties: Butte, Calaveras, Colusa,
Del Norte, Glenn, Humboldt, Lake,
Lassen, Modoc, Nevada, Placer,
Plumas, Shasta, Sierra, Siskiyou,
Sutter, Tehama, Trinity, Tuolumne,
and Yuba

Central California Regional Office
2580 N. First Street, Suite 350,
MS 29-07
San Jose, CA 95131
Tel: 408-324-2112
Fax: 408-324-2133
Counties: Monterey, San Benito,
Santa Clara, and Santa Cruz

Fresno Local Unit
770 E. Shaw Avenue, Suite 330,
MS 29-02
Fresno, CA 93710
Tel: 559-243-8080
Fax: 559-243-8088
Counties: Alpine, Fresno, Inyo,
Kings, Madera, Mariposa, Merced,
Mono, and Tulare

Rohnert Park Local Unit
101 Golf Course Drive, Suite A-230,
MS 29-11
Rohnert Park, CA 94928
Tel: 707-588-5026
Fax: 707-588-5080
Counties: Marin, Mendocino, Napa,
and Sonoma

San Bruno Local Unit
851 Traeger Avenue, Suite 360,
MS 29-16
San Bruno, CA 94066
Tel: 650-266-8800
Fax: 650-266-8841
Counties: Alameda, Contra Costa,
San Francisco, and San Mateo

Pacific Inland Regional Office
3737 Main Street, Suite 600,
MS 29-26
Riverside, CA 92501
Tel: 951-782-4207
Fax: 951-782-4967
Counties: Riverside, Imperial, and
San Bernardino

Orange County Local Unit
770 The City Drive, Suite 7100,
MS 29-28
Orange, CA 92668
Tel: 714-703-2840
Fax: 714-703-2868
County: Orange

San Diego Local Unit
7575 Metropolitan Drive, Suite 109,
MS 29-06
San Diego, CA 92108-4402
Tel: 619-767-2300
Fax: 619-767-2252
County: San Diego

Los Angeles and Tri-Coastal
Counties Regional Office
1000 Corporate Center Drive,
Suite 200A, MS 31-08
Monterey Park, CA 91754
Tel: 323-981-3300
Fax: 323-981-3425
Counties: Los Angeles, Kern,
Ventura, Santa Barbara, and San
Luis Obispo

Los Angeles Metro and Valley
Regional Office
6167 Bristol Parkway, Suite 210,
MS 31-09
Culver City, CA 90230
Tel: 310-568-1807
Fax: 310-417-3680
County: Los Angeles

Woodland Hills Local Unit
21731 Ventura Boulevard,
Suite 250, MS 29-14
Woodland Hills, CA 91364
Tel: 818-596-4334
Fax: 818-596-4376
County: Los Angeles

Santa Barbara Local Unit
360 South Hope Avenue,
Suite C-105, MS 29-09
Santa Barbara, CA 93105
Tel: 805-682-7647
Fax: 805-563-5549
Counties: San Luis Obispo, Santa
Barbara, and Ventura

JOINT LEGISLATIVE AUDIT COMMITTEE

1020 N Street, Room 107
Sacramento, CA 95814
Tel: 916-319-3300
Fax: 916-319-2352

LABOR AND WORKFORCE DEVELOPMENT AGENCY

801 K Street, Suite 2101
Sacramento, CA 95814
Tel: 916-327-9064
http://www.labor.ca.gov/

PUBLIC EMPLOYMENT RELATIONS BOARD (PERB)

1031 Eighteenth Street
Sacramento, CA 95814
Tel: 916-322-3198
Fax: 916-327-7955 (administration)
Fax: 916-327-7960 (board
members, Appeals Office)

LOS ANGELES REGIONAL OFFICE
700 N. Central Avenue, Suite 200
Glendale, CA 91203
Tel: 818-51-2822
Fax: 818-551-2820

SAN FRANCISCO REGIONAL
OFFICE
1330 Broadway, Suite 1532
Oakland, CA 94612
Tel: 510-622-1016
Fax: 510-622-1027

STATE BAR OF CALIFORNIA

180 Howard Street
San Francisco, CA 94105
Tel: 415-538-2000
http://www.calbar.ca.gov/state/
calbar/calbar_home.jsp

LOS ANGELES OFFICE
1149 S. Hill Street
Los Angeles, CA 90015
Tel: 213-765-1000

STATE PERSONNEL BOARD

801 Capitol Mall
Sacramento, CA 95814
Tel: 866-844-8671
Tel: 916-653-0799
(appeals information)
Email: appeals@spb.ca.gov (general
appeals information)
http://www.spb.ca.gov

LABOR ORGANIZATIONS

California Labor Federation,
AFL-CIO
600 Grand Avenue, Suite 410
Oakland, CA 94610
Tel: 510-663-4000
Fax: 510-663-4099
www.calaborfed.org

The Alameda Labor Council,
AFL-CIO
100 Hegenberger Road, Suite 150
Oakland, CA 94621
Tel: 510-632-4242
Fax: 510-632-3993
www.alamedalabor.org

Butte and Glenn Counties AFL-CIO
Central Labor Council
PO Box 840
Magalia, CA 95954
Tel: 530-873-3680
Fax: 530-873-3680
www.ca.aflcio.org/35

Central Labor Council of Contra
Costa County AFL-CIO
1333 Pine Street, Suite E
Martinez, CA 94553
Tel: 925-228-0161
Fax: 925-228-0224
www.cclabor.net

Five Counties Central Labor
Council, AFL-CIO
900 Locust Street, Room 7
Redding, CA 96001
Tel: 530-241-0319
Fax: 530-241-0319
ca.aflcio.org/516

Fresno-Madera-Tulare-Kings Central
Labor Council
3485 W. Shaw Avenue, Suite 101
Fresno, CA 93711
Tel: 559-275-1151
Fax: 559-276-2150
ca.aflcio.org/fmtkclc

Central Labor Council of Humboldt
and Del Norte Counties AFL-CIO
840 E Street, Suite 9
Eureka, CA 95501
Tel: 707-443-7371
Fax: 707-443-0819
ca.aflcio.org/38

Kern, Inyo and Mono Counties
Central Labor Council, AFL-CIO
200 W. Jeffrey Street
Bakersfield, CA 93305
Tel: 661-324-6451
Fax: 661-324-0799
ca.aflcio.org/42

Los Angeles County Federation of
Labor, AFL-CIO
2130 W. James M. Wood Blvd.
Los Angeles, CA 90006
Tel: 213-381-5611 x120
Fax: 213-383-0772
www.launionaflcio.org

Marysville Central Labor Council,
AFL-CIO
468 Century Park Drive
Yuba City, CA 95991
Tel: 530-743-7321
Fax: 530-743-1613
ca.aflcio.org/40

Merced-Mariposa County Central
Labor Council, AFL-CIO
625 W. Olive Avenue, Suite 103
Merced, CA 95348
Tel: 209-722-3636
Fax: 209-722-9640
ca.aflcio.org/41

Monterey Bay Central Labor
Council, AFL-CIO
931 E. Market Street
Salinas, CA 93905
Tel: 831-422-4626 x11
Fax: 831-422-4676
www.montereybaylabor.org

Central Labor Council of Napa and
Solano Counties AFL-CIO
2540 N. Watney Way
Fairfield, CA 94533
Tel: 707-428-1055
Fax: 707-728-1393
ca.aflcio.org/44

North Bay Labor Council, AFL-CIO
2525 Cleveland Avenue, Suite A
Santa Rosa, CA 95403
Tel: 707-545-6970
Fax: 707-544-6336
www.ca.aflcio.org/nblc

Orange County Labor Federation,
AFL-CIO
309 N. Rampart Street, Suite A
Orange, CA 92868
Tel: 714-385-1534
Fax: 714-385-1544
www.oclabor.org

Sacramento Central Labor Council,
AFL-CIO
2840 El Centro Road, Suite 111
Sacramento, CA 95833
Tel: 916-927-9772
Fax: 916-927-1643
www.ca.aflcio.org/sacramentolabor

Central Labor Council of San
Bernardino and Riverside Counties
1074 E. La Cadena Drive, Suite 1
Riverside, CA 92507
Tel: 909-825-7871
Fax: 909-825-0110
ca.aflcio.org/48

San Diego and Imperial Counties
Labor Council, AFL-CIO
3737 Camino del Rio S., Suite 403
San Diego, CA 92108
Tel: 619-228-8101
Fax: 619-281-1296
www.unionyes.org

San Francisco Labor Council,
AFL-CIO
1188 Franklin Street, Suite 203
San Francisco, CA 94109
Tel: 415-440-4809
Fax: 415-440-9297
www.sflaborcouncil.org

Central Labor Council of San
Joaquin and Calaveras Counties
235 N. San Joaquin Street
Stockton, CA 95202
Tel: 209-948-5526
Fax: 209-948-2652
ca.aflcio.org/51

San Mateo County Central Labor
Council, AFL-CIO
1153 Chess Drive, Suite 200
Foster City, CA 94404
Tel: 650-572-8848
Fax: 650-572-2481
www.sanmateolaborcouncil.org

Labor Council of South Bay
AFL-CIO
2102 Almaden Road, Suite 107
San Jose, CA 95125
Tel: 408-266-3790
Fax: 408-266-2653
ca.aflcio.org/53

Central Labor Council of Stanislaus
and Tuolumne Counties
1125 Kansas Avenue
Modesto, CA 95351
Tel: 209-523-8079
Fax: 209-523-2619
ca.aflcio.org/496

Tri-Counties Central Labor Council
816 Camarillo Springs Road, Suite G
Camarillo, CA 93012
Tel: 805-641-3712
Fax: 805-643-9426
ca.aflcio.org/517

ACRONYMS

ADA	Americans with Disabilities Act
ADEA	Age Discrimination in Employment Act
AL	Action level
ALJ	Administrative law judge
ALRA	Agricultural Labor Relations Act
ALRB	Agricultural Labor Relations Board
AME	Agreed Medical Evaluator
BFOQ	Bona fide occupational qualification
BLL	Blood lead level
BOFE	Bureau of Field Enforcement
Cal-OSHA	California Occupational Safety and Health Agency
CFRA	California Family Rights Act
COBRA	Consolidated Omnibus Budget Reconciliation Act of 1986
CPER	California Public Employee Relations (Program)
CTB	California Training Benefits (Program)
CTO	Compensatory time off
DFEH	Department of Fair Employment and Housing
DLSE	Division of Labor Standards Enforcement
DLSR	Division of Labor Statistics and Research
DMV	Department of Motor Vehicles
DOD	Department of Defense
DOSH	Division of Occupational Safety and Health
EDD	Employment Development Department
EEOC	Equal Employment Opportunity Commission
EERA	Educational Employment Relations Act
EPA	Equal Pay Act
ERISA	Employee Retirement Income Security Act of 1974
FBP	Federal Bonding Program
FCRA	Fair Credit Reporting Act
FEHA	Fair Employment and Housing Act
FMLA	Family and Medical Leave Act
FTC	Federal Trade Commission
HEERA	Higher Education Employer-Employee Relations Act
HIPAA	Health Insurance Portability and Accountability Act
HMO	Health maintenance organization
IIPP	Injury and Illness Prevention Program
IRS	Internal Revenue Service
ITA	Invitational travel authorization

ITO	Invitational travel order
IWC	Industrial Welfare Commission
LMRDA	Labor Management Reporting and Disclosure Act (Landrum-Griffin Act)
LWDA	Labor and Workforce Development Agency
MMBA	Meyers-Milias-Brown Act
MOU	Memorandum of understanding
MSDS	Material Safety Data Sheet
NDI	Non-industrial Disability Insurance
NLRA	National Labor Relations Act
NLRB	National Labor Relations Board
ODA	Order, Decision or Award
OFCCP	Office of Federal Contract Compliance Programs
OSHA	Occupational Safety and Health Administration (federal)
PAGA	Private Attorneys General Act
PDL	Pregnancy Disability Leave (Act)
PEL	Permissible exposure limit
PERB	Public Employment Relations Board
PERS	Public Employee Retirement System
PPO	Preferred provider organization
PTO	Paid time off
QME	Qualified Medical Evaluator
RLA	Railway Labor Act
SDI	State Disability Insurance
SEERA	State Employer-Employee Relations Act
SSDI	Social Security Disability Income
SSI	Supplemental Security Income
SSN	Social Security Number
STRS	State Teachers Retirement System
TCEPG	Trial Court Employment Protection and Governance Act
TCIELRA	Trial Court Interpreter Employment and Labor Relations Act
TEERA	(Los Angeles Metropolitan Transportation Authority) Transit Employer-Employee Relations Act
UI	Unemployment Insurance
USERRA	Uniformed Services Employment and Reemployment Rights Act
VA	Veterans Affairs (Department of)
VEBA	Voluntary Employees' Beneficiary Association
VETS	Veterans' Employment & Training Service
VEVRAA	Vietnam Era Veterans' Readjustment Assistance Act
WCAB	Workers' Compensation Appeals Board

INDEX

S

Safety, health, and sanitation
  asbestos exposure, 195–196
  body protection, 195
  changing rooms, 199
  correction of unsafe conditions, 192
  drinking water, 199–200
  face and eye protection, 194–195
  federal law, 190
  first aid, duty to provide, 198–199
  foot protection, 195
  generally, 189–190
  hand protection, 195
  hazardous substances (*See* Hazardous substances)
  head protection, 195
  heat illness, duty to prevent, 200–201
  Injury and Illness Prevention Programs (IIPP), 191
  lead exposure, 196–197
  medical services, duty to provide, 198–199
  obligations of employers, 190–203
  Permissible Exposure Limit (PEL), 196–197
  pesticide restrictions, 201
  records of injuries and illnesses
    log, 193
    reports to DLSR, 193–194
  respiratory care equipment, 194
  retaliation
    generally, 190
    proof of, 191
    protected complaints, 190–191
  state law, 190
  tobacco smoke exposure, 197–198
  toilet facilities, 199
  training, 192
  violence in workplace (*See* Violence in workplace)
Salaried employees, paycheck regulations, 97
Salary basis requirement, 70
Salespersons
  IWC orders, exemption from, 70
  paycheck regulations, 97
San Francisco
  "living wage" ordinances, 78
  sick leave in, 114
San Francisco Bay Area Rapid Transit District, 227
Sanitation. *See* Safety, health, and sanitation
Sarbanes–Oxley Act of 2002, 277
Schools. *See* Educational employees; Public schools
Scrip, payment of wages by, 100
SDI. *See* State Disability Insurance (SDI)
Searches and seizures, drug testing as, 42–43
Secondary boycotts, 230, 233–234
Security alerts, 46
Security freezes, 46–47
Seniority, effect of pregnancy disability leave on, 142
Serious health condition, family leave for. *See* Family leave
Service charges, 80–81
Service employees, use of detectives in discharge or discipline, 253–254
Seventh workday of week, wages for, 87
Severance pay, wage claims excluded from Labor Commissioner jurisdiction, 104
Sex discrimination. *See* Gender discrimination
Sexual harassment, 23, 171–172
Sexual orientation, prohibited questions of applicants, 23
Sexual stereotyping, 23, 171
Ships and vessels, whistleblowers and, 276–277

Sick leave
  complaints for violations, 115
  family leave, use for, 145
  right to, 114–115
  SDI, effect on, 119

Significant risk of injury or disease, discrimination based on, 28
"Sit-down strikes," 230, 233
Sleep time, 77
Slowdowns, 233
Small claims courts, complaints in, 12
Social Security
  disability benefits, 119–120
  independent contractors
    employees wrongfully treated as, 14–15
    exemption from coverage, 13
  numbers
    identity theft and, 300
    privacy of, 288–289
  Social Security Disability Income (SSDI), 216
  Supplemental Security Income (SSI), 120
Social Security Administration, United States, claims with, 15
Social Services Department
  Community Care Licensing Division, 62
  residential elder care facilities and, 61
  workfare workers, complaints regarding replacement by, 260
Solicitation of union members, right of, 229–230
Special Counsel for Immigration-Related Unfair Employment Practices, complaints with, 22
Split-shift pay, 87
Spousal leave, 124
"Stand-by" time
  away from employer's premises, 75–76
  at employer's premises, 76
State Compensation Insurance Fund, 212
State contracts, whistleblowers and, 273
State Disability Insurance (SDI)
  amount of benefits, 118
  appeals, 118
  applications, 117
  claim forms, 117
  covered employees, 115–116
  determinations, 117–118
  Disability Insurance Elective Coverage Program, 120
  domestic employees, coverage of, 118–119
  duration of benefits, 118
  earning requirements, 116
  eligibility for, 115–116
  exclusions from coverage, 118–119
  federal employees, 121
  independent contractors
    employees wrongfully treated as, 14
    exclusion from coverage, 13, 120
  long-term disability, effect of, 119–120
  medical certifications, 116–117
  Non-industrial Disability Insurance (NDI), 115, 121
  nonprofit organizations, coverage of, 119
  Paid Family Leave Insurance Program (*See* Paid Family Leave Insurance Program)
  pregnancy disability, effect of, 115, 120, 148
  public employees, 121
  railroad employees, coverage of, 118
  religious organizations, coverage of, 119
  scope of, 115

Y

ABOUT THE AUTHORS

DAVID A. ROSENFELD

David Rosenfeld, of Weinberg, Roger and Rosenfeld in Alameda, California, has practiced union-side labor law since his graduation from the University of California, Berkeley, Boalt Hall School of Law, in 1973. Mr. Rosenfeld has argued many important cases before the United States Supreme Court, the California Supreme Court, various federal and state courts of appeal, and the National Labor Relations Board. He had primary responsibility for an important wage and hour case before the California Supreme Court that broadened an employer's obligation to pay for all hours worked to include travel time in company vehicles.

Mr. Rosenfeld's creative and unusual strategies, both inside and outside the courts, have been used effectively by unions throughout the country. His booklet, *Offensive Use of the California Labor Code*, has taught California unions and worker advocates to best use wage and hour issues to their advantage. He teaches at UC Berkeley's Boalt Hall School of Law, and has recently designed and taught the course, "Representing Low Wage Workers."

MILES E. LOCKER

Miles Locker is well known for his sixteen years of service as an attorney for the California State Division of Labor Standards Enforcement (DLSE), including three years as chief counsel for the State Labor Commissioner. While at the DLSE, he played a major role in the development of the division's enforcement policies and legal interpretations. Before working for the DLSE, Mr. Locker represented public safety employees and unions as an attorney with the San Francisco law firm of Carroll, Burdick & McDonough, and prosecuted unfair labor practice complaints for the Agricultural Labor Relations Board. He is now a partner in the San Francisco employment law firm of Locker Folberg LLP. His practice consists of consulting and expert witness services in connection with wage and hour issues, litigating wage and hour class actions and individual cases, and litigating unlawful retaliation and wrongful termination cases.

Mr. Locker has practiced before federal courts, including the United States Supreme Court, state courts at every level including the California Supreme Court, and various administrative agencies. His recent article, "A Riddle Wrapped in a Mystery: State Wage and Hour Provisions," dealing with the applicability of state wage and hour laws to public employees, was published in the December 2008 issue of *California Public Employee Relations (CPER)*.

NINA G. FENDEL

Nina Fendel is of counsel at Weinberg, Roger and Rosenfeld, and editor of the Public Works Compliance Website. She graduated in 1982 from New College School of Law. She is an attorney and legal educator specializing in helping non-lawyers to understand the law, and in creating legal resources that provide practical, comprehensive, and up-to-date information to attorneys and others in a wide variety of legal areas. She has worked for the California Department of Industrial Relations, the Painting and Drywall Work Preservation Fund, the Legal Services Foundation, the National Paralegal Institute, and with many unions and labor/management groups. In 1984, Ms. Fendel, along with Patricia Gates, authored the *Public Works Manual*, the first practice-oriented national publication on union efforts to promote compliance with public works laws. From 1988 to 2006, she worked for the California Faculty Association (NEA/SEIU 1983).

ABOUT THE UC BERKELEY CENTER FOR LABOR RESEARCH AND EDUCATION

The Center for Labor Research and Education (Labor Center) is a public service and outreach program of the UC Berkeley Institute for Research on Labor and Employment. Founded in 1964, the Labor Center conducts research and education on issues related to labor and employment. Its curricula and leadership trainings serve to educate a diverse new generation of labor leaders. The Labor Center carries out research on topics such as job quality and workforce development issues, and works with unions, government, and employers to develop innovative policy perspectives and programs. The Center provides an important source of research and information on unions and the changing workforce for students, scholars, policymakers, and the public.